INSIDER'S GUIDE TO GRADUATE PROGRAMS IN CLINICAL AND COUNSELING PSYCHOLOGY

Seldin

INSIDER'S GUIDE

to Graduate Programs in Clinical and Counseling Psychology

2002/2003 Edition

John C. Norcross
Michael A. Sayette
Tracy J. Mayne

THE GUILFORD PRESS
New York London

© 2002 The Guilford Press
A Division of Guilford Publications, Inc.
72 Spring Street, New York, NY 10012
www.guilford.com

All rights reserved

No part of this book may be reproduced, translated, stored in a retrieval system, or transmitted, in any form or by any means, electronic, mechanical, photocopying, microfilming, recording, or otherwise, without written permission from the publisher.

Printed in the United States of America

This book is printed on acid-free paper.

Last digit is print number: 9 8 7 6 5 4 3 2 1

ISBN 1-57230-721-8

ISSN 1086-2099

CONTENTS

TABLES AND FIGURES

Tables

Figures

ABOUT THE AUTHORS

John C. Norcross received his baccalaureate *summa cum laude* from Rutgers University. He earned his master's and doctorate in clinical psychology from the University of Rhode Island and completed his internship at the Brown University School of Medicine. He is Professor and former Chair of Psychology at the University of Scranton, a clinical psychologist in independent practice, and past-president of the APA Division of Psychotherapy. Dr. Norcross has published more than 150 articles and has authored or edited 12 books, the most recent being the *Authoritative Guide to Self-Help Resources in Mental Health, Therapy Relationships That Work, Psychologists' Desk Reference,* and *Systems of Psychotherapy: A Transtheoretical Analysis.* He has served on the editorial boards of a dozen journals. Among his awards are the Pennsylvania Professor of the Year from the Carnegie Foundation and Distinguished Practitioner from the National Academies of Practice. Dr. Norcross has conducted workshops and research on graduate study in psychology for many years.

Michael A. Sayette received his baccalaureate *cum laude* from Dartmouth College. He earned his master's and doctorate in clinical psychology from Rutgers University and completed his internship at the Brown University School of Medicine. He is Associate Professor of Psychology at the University of Pittsburgh, with a secondary appointment as Associate Professor of Psychiatry at the University of Pittsburgh School of Medicine. Dr. Sayette has published primarily in the area of substance abuse. His research, which is supported by the National Institute on Alcohol Abuse and Alcoholism and by the National Institute on Drug Abuse, concerns the development of psychological theories of drinking and drug use. He currently serves as a reviewer on a National Institutes of Health grant review study section, and is a member of the editorial boards of the *Journal of Abnormal Psychology* and the *Journal of Studies on Alcohol.* Dr. Sayette has presented seminars on applying to graduate school at several universities in North America and Europe.

Tracy J. Mayne received his baccalaureate from the State University of New York at Buffalo, where he graduated *magna cum laude* and *Phi Beta Kappa.* He received his Ph.D. as an Honors Fellow from Rutgers University and completed his internship and postdoctoral fellowship at the University of California at San Francisco Medical School and the Center for AIDS Prevention Studies. He spent 2 years as an international scholar at the Institut Nationale de la Santé et de la Recherche Médicale in France and 3 years as the Director of HIV Epidemiology and Surveillance at the New York City Department of Health. Dr. Mayne currently directs Outcomes Research for Pfizer Pharmaceuticals, and is an Adjunct Associate Professor at New York and Columbia Universities. Dr. Mayne has published numerous articles and chapters in the area of health psychology and emotion, with a special focus on HIV/AIDS. He is the coeditor of *Emotions: Current Issues and Future Directions,* published by The Guilford Press.

ACKNOWLEDGMENTS

To paraphrase John Donne, no book is an island, entire of itself. This sentiment is particularly true of a collaborative venture such as ours: a coauthored volume in its seventh edition comprising the contributions of hundreds of psychologists and of reports on individual doctoral programs provided by training directors throughout North America. We are grateful to them all.

We are also indebted to the many friends, colleagues, and workshop participants for their assistance in improving this book over the years. Special thanks to Ms. Patricia Castle, who spent countless hours collecting and organizing data on individual program reports, and to Ms. Melissa Hedges for her ongoing assistance with various aspects of this project. Seymour Weingarten and his associates at The Guilford Press have continued to provide interpersonal support and technical assistance on all aspects of the project. Special thanks to our families for their unflagging support and patience with late night work!

Finally, our efforts have been aided immeasurably by our students, graduate and undergraduate alike, who courageously shared their experiences with us about the application and admission process.

PREFACE

One of the benefits of applying to clinical and counseling psychology programs is that you earn the right to commiserate about the process afterwards. It was a night of anecdotes and complaints (while doing laundry) that led us to review our travails and compare notes on the difficulties we each experienced during the admission process. We emerged from three diverse backgrounds: one of us (T.J.M.) graduated from a large state university, took time off, and then entered a doctoral program; one of us (M.A.S.) graduated from a private liberal arts college and immediately pursued a doctorate; and another one of us (J.C.N.) graduated from a liberal arts college within a major state university after 5 years and then pursued doctoral studies.

Although we approached graduate school in different ways, the process was much the same. We each attempted to locate specific information on clinical and counseling psychology admissions, looked to people around us for advice, took that which seemed to be sound, and worked with it. Not all the advice was good (one professor went so far as to suggest a career in the theater instead!), and it was difficult to decide what was best when advice conflicted.

All in all, there was too little factual information available and too much unnecessary anxiety involved. No clearly defined or organized system was available to guide us through this process. So we decided to write an insider's guide to graduate programs in clinical and counseling psychology.

The last 10 years have seen the entire process of choosing schools and applying become progressively more difficult. Approximately 65,000 bachelor's degrees are awarded every year in psychology, and about 20% of the recipients go on to earn a master's or doctoral degree in psychology (Jalbert, 1996). Clinical and counseling psychology programs continue to grow in number and to diversify in mission: 202 APA-accredited doctoral programs in clinical psychology, 65 APA-accredited doctoral programs in counseling psychology, 10 APA-accredited programs in combined professional–scientific psychology, dozens of non-APA-accredited doctoral programs, and hundreds of master's programs. Which should you apply to? And which type of program is best for you—counseling or clinical, practice-oriented Psy.D. or research-oriented Ph.D.?

We shall take you step by step through this confusing morass and help you make informed decisions best suited to your needs and interests. In this new edition, we provide separate information on the number of students applying to each program, the number of applicants that program accepted, and the number of accepted students who elected to attend that program. These detailed numbers will help you avoid the rampant confusion among the terms *applicants*, *acceptances*, and *enrollments*. In addition, we describe how you can capitalize on the Internet revolution to ease the graduate school admissions process—locating compatible programs, securing school information, communicating with potential faculty mentors, and downloading application forms. Throughout the book, we provide Web sites to access for additional information and direction. We also explore crucial issues regarding admission criteria, acceptance rates, financial aid, and theoretical orientations to help you decide which program best fits your needs.

What we would most like to do, in clear and concise language, is to help *you* through this process, from the initial decision to apply through your final acceptance. In Chapter 1, we describe the predominant training models in clinical and counseling psychology and alternatives to these disciplines. In the next chapter, we discuss the essential preparation for graduate school—the course work, clinical experiences, research skills, entrance examinations, and extracurricular activities. From there, in Chapter 3, we get you started on the application process and assist you in understanding admission requirements. In Chapter 4, we show you how to systematically select schools on the basis of multiple considerations, especially research interests, clinical opportunities, theoretical orientations, financial assistance, and quality of life. Then in Chapter 5, we take you through the application procedure itself—forms, curricula vitae, personal statements, letters of recommendation, academic transcripts, and the like. Last, in Chapters 6 and 7, we take you through the perils of the interview and the complexities of the final decision. With multiple worksheets and concrete examples, we will help you feel less overwhelmed, better informed, and, in the end, more aware that *you* are the consumer of a program that best suits *your* needs.

We have conducted original studies on graduate psychology programs for this book in an effort to inform your decision making. These results provide information on the differences between clinical and counseling psychology programs (Chapter 1), programs' research areas (Appendix E), clinical and practica sites (Appendix F), admissions criteria, application odds, financial assistance, and more. Indeed, we have extensively surveyed all APA-accredited programs in clinical, counseling, and professional–scientific psychology and present detailed information on each in the Reports on Individual Programs. A detailed Time Line (Appendix A) and multiple worksheets (Appendices B, C, and D) also provide information and guidance on the heretofore treacherous journey of applying to graduate programs in clinical and counseling psychology.

This volume will assist anyone seeking admission to graduate school in clinical and counseling psychology, both master's and doctoral degrees. However, the primary focus is on Ph.D. and Psy.D. applicants, as the doctorate is the entry-level qualification for professional psychology. Just as a master's degree in biology does not make one a physician, a master's in psychology does not, by state licensure and APA regulation, typically qualify one as a psychologist. Forty-eight states require the doctorate for licensure or certification as a psychologist; almost half the states grant legal recognition of psychological associates, assistants, or examiners with a master's degree (APA Practice Directorate, 1991). But the material presented here is relevant for master's (M.A. or M.S.) applicants as well.

With this practical manual, we wish you an application process less hectic and confusing than ours, but equally rewarding in the end result. Good luck!

INSIDER'S GUIDE TO GRADUATE PROGRAMS IN CLINICAL AND COUNSELING PSYCHOLOGY

CHAPTER 1

INTRODUCING CLINICAL AND COUNSELING PSYCHOLOGY

If you are reading this book for the first time, we are assuming you are either considering applying to graduate programs in clinical and counseling psychology or are in the process of doing so. For even the best prepared applicant, this can precipitate a great deal of stress and confusion. The mythology surrounding this process is foreboding, and you may have heard some "horror" stories similar to these: "It's the hardest graduate program to get into in the country"; "You need a 3.8 grade point average and 700s on your GREs or they won't even look at you"; "If you haven't taken time off after your bachelor's and worked in a clinic, you don't have enough experience to apply."

Having endured the application process ourselves, we know how overwhelming the task appears at first glance. However, we have found that much of the anxiety is unwarranted. It does not take astronomical test scores or years of practical experience to get into clinical and counseling psychology programs. Although these qualifications certainly help, they are not sufficient. Equally important are a knowledge of how the system works and a willingness to put in extra effort during the application process.

Clinical and Counseling Psychology

Before dealing with the question of "how to apply," we would like to address "why" to apply and what clinical and counseling psychology are about. Reading through the next section may be useful by making you aware of other programs of study that may be more suitable to your needs.

Let us begin with clinical psychology, the largest specialty and the fastest growing sector in psychology. Two-thirds of the doctoral-level health service providers in the American Psychological Association (APA) identify with the specialty area of clinical psychology (VandenBos, Stapp, & Kilburg, 1981). A census of all psychological personnel residing in the United States likewise has revealed that the majority reported clinical psychology as their major field (Stapp, Tucker, & VandenBos, 1985).

A definition of clinical psychology was adopted jointly by the APA Division of Clinical Psychology and the Council of University Directors of Clinical Psychology (see Resnick, 1991). That definition states that the field of clinical psychology involves research, teaching, and services relevant to the applications of principles, methods, and procedures for understanding, predicting, and alleviating intellectual, emotional, biological, psychological, social, and behavioral maladjustment, disability, and discomfort, applied to a wide range of client populations. The major skill areas in psychology essential for the field of clinical psychology are assessment; intervention; consultation; program development, supervision, administration, and evaluation of these services; conduct of research; and application of ethical standards. Perhaps the safest observation about clinical psychology is that both the field and its practitioners continue to outgrow the classic definitions.

Indeed, the discipline has experienced a veritable explosion since World War II in numbers, activities, and knowledge (Barron, 1986; Strickland, 1985). Since 1949, the year of the Boulder Conference (see below), there has been a nearly 1,300% increase in psychology doctoral graduates. Approximately 2,200 doctoral degrees are now awarded annually in clinical psychology—1,400 Ph.D. degrees and 700 to 900 Psy.D. degrees (Belar, 1998). All told, doctoral degrees in clinical psychology account for about 40% of all psychology doctorates. As

TABLE 1-1. Popularity and Doctorate Production of Psychology Subfields

Subfield	Percentage of doctoral-level psychologists[a]	Number of Ph.D.s awarded[b]		
		1976	1994	1998
Clinical	44%	883	1329	1350[c]
Cognitive	1%	—	76	113
Counseling	11%	267	464	448
Developmental/child	4%	190	158	267
Educational	6%	124	98	61
Experimental	3%	357	143	149
Industrial/organizational	6%	73	124	189
Personality	1%	62	20	24
Physiological	1%	133	46	92
Psychometric/quantitative	2%	27	23	106
School	5%	143	81	186
Social	3%	209	145	673
Other or general	12%	387	560	673
Total	100%	2883	3287	3681

[a]From "Census of psychological personnel: 1983" by J. Stapp, A. M. Tucker, & G. R. VandenBos, 1985, *American Psychologist, 40,* 1317–1351. © 1985 American Psychological Association. Reprinted by permission.

[b]National Research Council, *Summary Report of Doctoral Recipients from United States Universities* (selected years), Washington, DC: Author.

[c]Plus 700–900 Psy.D. degrees awarded annually.

a consequence, the Division of Clinical Psychology is regularly the first or second largest division within the APA. Table 1-1 demonstrates the continuing popularity of clinical psychology and the growing number of clinical doctorates awarded annually.

These trends should continue well into the new millennium. After a drop in the early 1980s, the percentage of psychology majors among college freshmen has continued to increase nationally to over 3%. In fact, the proportion of college freshmen who explicitly express an intention of becoming clinical psychologists has steadily risen to 1.3% (Astin, Green, & Korn, 1987). A recent nationwide survey of almost 2 million high school juniors, reported in the *Occupational Outlook Quarterly,* found that psychology was the sixth most frequent career choice. Indeed, according to recent data from the U.S. Department of Education, interest in psychology as a major has never been higher (Murray, 1996). So, if you are seriously considering clinical or counseling psychology for a career, you belong to a large, vibrant, and growing population.

Counseling psychology is the second largest specialty in psychology and another rapidly growing sector. As also shown in Table 1-1, counseling psychology has experienced dramatic and sustained growth over the past three decades. We are referring here, of course, to counseling *psychology*, the doctoral-level specialization in psychology, not to the master's-level profession of counseling. This is a critical distinction: our book and research studies pertain specifically and solely to counseling psychology programs, not counseling programs.

The distinctions between clinical psychology and counseling psychology have steadily faded. Graduates of counseling psychology programs are eligible for the same professional benefits as clinical psychology graduates, such as psychology licensure, independent practice, and insurance reimbursement. The APA ceased distinguishing many years ago between clinical and counseling psychology internships: there is one list of accredited internships for both clinical and counseling psychology students. Both types of programs prepare doctoral-level psychologists who provide health care services.

At the same time, five robust differences between clinical psychology and counseling psychology are still visible. First, clinical psychology is larger than counseling psychology: in 2001, there were 202 APA-accredited doctoral programs in clinical psychology and 65 APA-accredited doctoral programs in counseling psychology (APA, 2001) currently accepting students. Table 1-1 reveals that these counseling psychology programs—in addition to some unaccredited programs—produce about 500 doctoral degrees per year. By contrast, clinical psychology programs produce approximately 2,200 doctoral degrees (1,400 Ph.D. and 700 to 900 Psy.D.) per year. Second, clinical psychology graduate programs are almost exclusively housed in departments or schools of psychology, whereas counseling psychology graduate programs are located in a variety of departments and divisions. Our research (Turkson & Norcross, 1996) shows that, in rough figures, approximately one-quarter of doctoral programs in counseling psychology are located in psychology departments, one-quarter in departments of counseling or counseling psychology, one-quarter in departments or colleges of education, and one-quarter in assorted other departments. The historical placement of counseling psychology programs in education departments explains the occasional awarding of the Ed.D. (doctor of education) by counseling psychology programs.

A third difference is that clinical psychology graduates tend to work with more seriously disturbed populations and are more likely trained in projective assessment, whereas counseling graduates work with healthier, less pathological populations and conduct more career and vocational assessment. Fourth, counseling psychologists more frequently endorse a client-centered/Rogerian approach to psychotherapy, whereas clinical psychologists are more likely to embrace behavioral or psychodynamic orientations. And fifth, both APA figures (APA Research Office, 1997) and our data (Bechtoldt, Norcross, Wyckoff, Pokrywa, & Campbell, 2001) consistently reveal that 15% more clinical psychologists are employed in full-time private practice than are counseling psychologists, whereas 10% more counseling psychologists are employed in college counseling centers than are clinical psychologists. Studies on the roles and functions of clinical and counseling psychologists do in fact substantiate these differences, but the similarities are far more numerous (Brems & Johnson, 1997; Fitzgerald & Osipow, 1986; Tipton, 1983; Watkins, Lopez, Campbell, & Himmel, 1986a, 1986b).

In order to extend this previous research, we recently completed a study of APA-accredited doctoral programs in counseling psychology (95% response rate) and clinical psychology (99% response rate) regarding their number of applications, characteristics of incoming students, and research areas of the faculty (Norcross, Sayette, Mayne, Karg, & Turkson, 1998). We found

- The average acceptance rates of Ph.D. clinical (6%) and Ph.D. counseling (8%) psychology programs were quite similar despite the higher number of applications to clinical programs (270 vs. 130).
- The average grade point averages (GPAs) for incoming doctoral students were identical in Ph.D. clinical and Ph.D. counseling psychology programs (3.5 for both).
- The average GRE scores of accepted students were similar, with Ph.D. clinical students having slightly higher scores as a group.
- The counseling psychology programs accepted more ethnic minority students (25% vs. 18%) and master's students (67% vs. 21%) than the clinical psychology programs.
- The counseling psychology faculty were far more interested than clinical psychology faculty in research pertaining to minority/cross-cultural issues (69% vs. 32% of programs) and vocational testing (62% vs. 1% of programs).
- The clinical psychology faculty, in turn, were far more interested than the counseling psychology faculty in research pertaining to psychopathological populations (e.g., attention deficit disorders, depression, personality disorders) and activities traditionally associated with medical settings (e.g., neuropsychology, pain management, pediatric psychology).

Please bear in mind that these systematic comparisons reflect broad differences in the APA-accredited Ph.D. programs; they say nothing about Psy.D. programs (which we discuss later in this chapter) or non-accredited programs. Also bear in mind that these data can be used as a rough guide in matching your interests and characteristics to clinical or counseling psychology programs. The notion of discovering the best match between you and a graduate program is a recurrent theme of this *Insider's Guide*.

As shown in Table 1-2, clinical and counseling psychologists devote similar percentages of their day to the same professional activities. About one-half of their time is dedicated to psychotherapy and diagnosis/assessment and a quarter of their time to research and administration. A stunning finding was that over half of clinical and counseling psychologists were routinely involved in all seven activities—psychotherapy, assessment, teaching, research, supervision, consultation, and administration. Flexible career indeed!

The scope of clinical and counseling psychology is continually widening, as are the employment settings. Many people mistakenly view psychologists solely as practitioners who spend most of their time seeing patients. But in truth, clinical and counseling psychology are wonderfully diverse and pluralistic professions.

TABLE 1-2. Professional Activities of Clinical and Counseling Psychologists

	Clinical psychologists		Counseling psychologists	
Activity	% involved in	Average % of time	% involved in	Average % of time
Psychotherapy	84	37	74	28
Diagnosis/assessment	74	15	62	12
Teaching	50	9	60	18
Clinical supervision	62	7	54	6
Research/writing	47	10	50	8
Consultation	54	7	61	7
Administration	52	11	56	15

Note. Adapted from "Clinical psychologists in the 1990s: II" by J. C. Norcross, R. S. Karg, & J. O. Prochaska, 1997b, *The Clinical Psychologist, 50*(3), 4–11; and from "Contemporary counseling psychology: Results of a national survey" by C. E. Watkins, F. G. Lopez, V. L. Campbell, & C. D. Himmell, 1986a, *Journal of Counseling Psychology, 33*(3), 301–309.

Consider the employment settings of American clinical psychologists: 40% in private practices, 19% in universities or colleges, 5% in psychiatric hospitals, 9% in medical schools, 4% in general hospitals, another 5% in community mental health centers, 4% in outpatient clinics, and 11% in "other" placements (Norcross, Karg, & Prochaska, 1997a, 1997b). This last category included, just to name a few, child and family services, correctional facilities, rehabilitation centers, school systems, health maintenance organizations, psychoanalytic institutes, and the federal government.

Although many psychologists choose careers as clinicians in private practice, hospitals, and clinics, a large number also pursue careers in research (Crowe, Grogan, Jacobs, Lindsay, & Mack, 1985). For some, this translates into an academic position. Uncertainties in the health care system are increasing the allure of an academic position, where salary is less tied to client fees than in a clinical position. Academics teach courses and conduct research, usually with a clinical population. They hope to find a "tenure-track" position, which means they start out as an assistant professor. After a certain amount of time (typically 5 or 6 years), a university committee reviews their research, teaching, and service, and decides whether they will be hired as a permanent faculty member and promoted to associate professor. Even though the tenure process can be a pressured one, the atmosphere surrounding assistant professors is very conducive to research activity. They are often given "seed" money to set up facilities and attract graduate students eager to share in the publication process. (For additional information on the career paths of psychology faculty, consult *The Psychologist's Guide to an Academic Career*, Rheingold, 1994, or *Career Paths in Psychology*, Sternberg, 1997.)

But even this range of primary employment settings does not accurately capture the opportunities in the field. About half of all clinical and counseling psychologists hold more than one professional position (Norcross et al., 1997a; Watkins et al., 1986a). By and large, psychologists incorporate several pursuits into their work, often simultaneously. They combine activities in ways that can change over time to accommodate their evolving interests. Of those psychologists not in full-time private practice, over half engage in some part-time independent work (Norcross et al., 1997b). Without question, this flexibility is an asset.

As a university professor, for example, you might run a research group studying aspects of alcoholism, treat alcoholics and their families in private practice, and teach a course on alcohol abuse. Or, you could work for a company supervising marketing research, do private testing for a school system, and provide monthly seminars on relaxation. The possibilities are almost limitless.

This flexibility is also evident in clinical and counseling psychologists' "self-views." About 60% respond that they are primarily clinical practitioners, 20% are academicians, 7% administrators, 5% researchers, 5% consultants, and 2% supervisors (Norcross et al., 1997b; Watkins et al., 1986a).

Also comforting is the consistent finding of relatively high and stable satisfaction with graduate training and career choice. Over two-thirds of former and current graduate students in clinical and counseling psychology express satisfaction with their post-baccalaureate preparation. Moreover, 87 to 91% are satisfied with their career choice (Norcross et al., 1997b; Tibbits-Kleber & Howell, 1987; Watkins et al., 1986a). The conclusion we draw is that clinical and counseling psychologists appreciate the diverse pursuits and take advantage of their professional flexibility, which plays a significant role in their high level of career satisfaction.

The diversity in professional choice has produced a diversity of training models in professional psychology. Without a firm understanding of the differences in these training models, many applicants will waste valuable time and needlessly experience disappointment. Let us now distinguish between the two prevalent training models in clinical psychology—the Boulder model and the Vail model. Counseling psychology has parallel differences in training emphases; however, it does not typically employ the same terms as clinical psychology and only one APA-accredited counseling psychology program offers the Psy.D. degree.

The Boulder Model (Ph.D.)

The first national training conference on clinical psychology was held during 1949 in Boulder, Colorado (hence, the "Boulder model"). At this conference, equal weight was accorded to the development of both research competencies and clinical skills. This dual emphasis resulted in the notion of the clinical psychologist as a *scientist–practitioner*. Clinical psychologists were considered first and foremost as psychologists and were to have a rigorous, broad-based education in psychology. Their training would encompass statistics, history and systems, and research, with core courses in development, biopsychology, learning, and the like. The emphasis was on psychology; clinical was the adjective.

The Boulder conference was a milestone for several reasons. First, it established the Ph.D. as the required degree, as in other academic research fields. To this day, all Boulder model, scientist–practitioner programs in clinical psychology award the Ph.D. degree. Second, the conference reinforced the idea that the appropriate location for training was within university departments, not separate schools or institutes as in medicine and dentistry. And third, clinical psychologists were trained for simultaneous existence in two worlds: academic/scientific and clinical/professional.

The important implication for you, as an applicant, is to know that Boulder model programs provide rigorous education as a researcher along with training as a clinician. Consider this dual thrust carefully before applying to Boulder model programs. Some first-year graduate students undergo undue misery because they dislike research-oriented courses and the research projects that are part of the degree requirements. These, in turn, are preludes to the formal dissertation required by Boulder model programs. Many applicants are specifically seeking this sort of training.

A recent movement toward a "bolder" Boulder model has been crystalized by the 1995 creation of the Academy of Psychological Clinical Science (APCS). According to its official Web site, APCS is "an alliance of leading, scientifically oriented, doctoral training programs in clinical and health psychology, committed to empirical approaches to advancing knowledge," which was established in response to rapid changes taking place in the field of clinical psychology. "The Academy seeks as members those programs that are strongly committed to research training and to the integration of such training with clinical training." APCS includes 38 clinical psychology Ph.D. programs. These programs are listed in Table 1-3. More information on APCS can be found on their Web site: http://w3.arizona.edu/~psych/apcs/apcs.html.

Based on the data from our previous editions of the *Insider's Guide* we found that, compared to non-member programs, APCS programs admitted a marginally lower percentage of applicants (who had higher GRE scores) and were more likely to provide full financial support. APCS programs also subscribed more frequently to a cognitive-behavioral orientation, reported a stronger research emphasis, and engaged more frequently in research supported by extramural funding agencies than did non-APCS programs (Sayette, Mayne, Norcross, & Giuffre, 1999). Students interested in a Boulder-model clinical Ph.D program may find these programs to be especially attractive in that they represent empirically based, research-focused training.

Other applicants are seeking training more focused on the practice of psychology than on research. For these applicants, there is an alternative to the Boulder model: the Vail model of training psychologists.

The Vail Model (Psy.D.)

Some dissension with the recommendations of the Boulder conference emerged at later meetings; however, there was a strong consensus that the scientist–practitioner prototype, Ph.D. degree, and university training should be retained. But in the late 1960s and early 1970s, change was in the wind. Training alternatives were entertained, and diversification was encouraged. This sentiment culminated in a 1973 national

TABLE 1-3. APA-Accredited Clinical Psychology Ph.D. Programs That Are Members of the Academy of Psychological Clinical Science (APCS)

University of Arizona
Arizona State University
Boston University
University of California–Berkeley
University of California–Los Angeles
University of California–San Diego
University of Delaware
University of Denver (Department of Psychology)
Emory University
University of Illinois at Chicago
University of Illinois at Urbana–Champaign
Indiana University
University of Iowa
University of Kentucky
McGill University
University of Memphis
University of Minnesota
University of Missouri
University of Nevada–Reno
Ohio State University
University of Oregon
University of Pennsylvania
Pennsylvania State University
University of Pittsburgh
Purdue University
Rutgers University
San Diego State University and University of California–San Diego Medical School (joint program)
University of Southern California
University of South Florida
State University of New York–Binghamton
State University of New York–Stony Brook
Vanderbilt University
University of Virginia (Department of Psychology)
University of Washington
University of Wisconsin–Madison
Yale University

training conference held in Vail, Colorado (hence, the "Vail model").

The Vail conferees endorsed different principles, leading to a diversity of training programs (Peterson, 1976, 1982). Psychological knowledge, it was argued, had matured enough to warrant creation of explicitly professional programs along the lines of professional programs in medicine, dentistry, and law. These "professional programs" were to be added to, not replace, Boulder-model programs. Further, it was proposed that different degrees should be used to designate the scientist role (Ph.D.—Doctor of Philosophy) from the practitioner role (Psy.D.—Doctor of Psychology). Graduates of Vail model professional programs would be *scholar/professionals*: the focus would be primarily on clinical service provision and less on research.

This revolutionary conference led to the emergence of two distinct training models typically housed in different settings. Boulder model programs are almost universally located in graduate departments of universities. However, Vail model programs can be housed in three organizational settings: within a psychology department; within a university-affiliated psychology school (for instance, Rutgers and Adelphi); and within an independent, "freestanding" psychology school (e.g., California School of Professional Psychology). These latter programs are not affiliated with universities but are independently developed and staffed. Table 1-4 lists APA-accredited clinical Psy.D. programs.

Clinical psychology now has two established and complementary training models with Ph.D. programs producing approximately twice as many doctoral-level psychologists per year as Psy.D. programs. Although Boulder model programs still outnumber Vail model programs, Vail model programs enroll, as a rule, three to four times the number of incoming doctoral candidates (Mayne, Norcross, & Sayette, 1994). This creates a numerical parity in terms of psychologists produced.

The differences between Boulder model and Vail model programs are quantitative, not qualitative. The primary disparity is in the relative emphasis on research: Boulder programs aspire to train producers of research; Vail programs train consumers of research. Even Vail programs require some research and statistics courses; you simply cannot avoid research sophistication in any accredited psychology program. The clinical opportunities are very similar for students in both types of programs.

As we discuss in subsequent chapters, there are trade-offs between Vail and Boulder model programs. Vail model professional programs provide slightly more clinical experience and courses but less research experience and fewer courses than Boulder model programs

TABLE 1-4. APA-Accredited Psy.D. Programs in Clinical Psychology

Adler School of Professional Psychology
American School of Professional Psychology–Hawaii Campus
American School of Professional Psychology–Virginia Campus
Antioch New England Graduate School
Baylor University
Biola University[a]
California School of Professional Psychology–Alameda[a]
California School of Professional Psychology–Fresno[a]
California School of Professional Psychology–Los Angeles[a]
California School of Professional Psychology–San Diego[a]
Carlos Albizu University–Miami Campus
Carlos Albizu University–San Juan Campus[a]
Central Michigan University
Chicago School of Professional Psychology
University of Denver[a]
Florida Institute of Technology
Forest Institute of Professional Psychology
Fuller Theological Seminary[a]
George Fox University
Georgia School of Professional Psychology
University of Hartford
Illinois School of Professional Psychology–Chicago
Illinois School of Professional Psychology–Meadows
Immaculata College
Indiana State University
Indiana University of Pennsylvania
University of Indianapolis
James Madison University (clinical/counseling/school)
Loma Linda University
Long Island University/C.W. Post Campus
Loyola University in Maryland
Massachusetts School of Professional Psychology
Minnesota School of Professional Psychology
Nova Southeastern University[a]
Pace University (school/clinical)
Pacific University
Pepperdine University
Rutgers University[a]
Spalding University
Virginia Consortium in Clinical Psychology
Wheaton College
Widener University
The Wright Institute
Wright State University
Yeshiva University
Yeshiva University (school/clinical)

[a] These institutions also have APA-accredited Ph.D. programs in clinical psychology.

(Tibbits-Kleber & Howell, 1987). Vail model programs afford easier (but not easy) admission but less financial assistance than Boulder model programs. As a rule, students in professional programs tend to be older, are more likely to have master's degrees already, and possess more experience in clinical activities than their Boulder model counterparts (Farry, Norcross, Mayne, & Sayette, 1995; Mayne et al., 1994). Both Vail and Boulder programs have similar admission criteria which favor grade point average, entrance examination scores, letters of recommendation, and so on. (All these topics are covered in detail in later chapters.)

Several studies have demonstrated that initial worries about stigmatization, employment difficulties, licensure uncertainty, and second-class citizenship for Psy.D.s have not materialized (see Hershey, Kopplin, & Cornell, 1991; Peterson, Eaton, Levine, & Snepp, 1982). There do not appear to be strong disparities in the pre-internship clinical skills of Ph.D. and Psy.D. students as evaluated by internship supervisors (Snepp & Peterson, 1988). Nor are there discernible differences of late in employment except, of course, that the more research-oriented, Boulder model graduates are far more likely to be employed in academic positions and medical schools (Gaddy, Charlot-Swilley, Nelson, & Reich, 1995). While Vail model graduates may be seen as second-class citizens by Boulder model traditionalists, this is not the case among health care organizations or individual consumers.

One disconcerting trend is that Vail model graduates do not perform as well as Ph.D. graduates on the national licensing examination for psychologists ("How

Do Professional . . . ," 1997; McGaha & Minder, 1993; Yu et al., 1997). That is, doctoral students who graduate with a professional degree (the Psy.D.) score lower, on average, than doctoral students who graduate from a traditional clinical psychology Ph.D. program on the Examination for Professional Practice in Psychology (EPPP), the national licensing test. Higher EPPP scores have been reliably associated with smaller-sized clinical programs and larger faculty-to-student ratios, in addition to traditional Ph.D. curricula.

Vail model graduates are typically less rigorously trained than Boulder model graduates in research, evaluation, and statistical skills. These skills are likely to be particularly valued in the future as master's-level psychotherapists increasingly become first-line providers of psychotherapy, whereas doctoral-level psychologists perform more supervision, research, and teaching functions. The Psy.D. degree is explicit in providing training for practice, and to the extent that doctoral-level psychologists may do less psychotherapy in the new health care systems, a broad training may prove advantageous. Regardless of whether training occurs in the context of a Psy.D. or Ph.D. program, it is wise to seek training and competence in a variety of professional activities, not solely psychotherapy.

A final difference between Ph.D. and Psy.D. programs concerns the length of training. Students in Ph.D. programs take significantly longer, approximately 1.5 years longer, to complete their degrees than do Psy.D. students (Gaddy et al., 1995). Various interpretations are given to this robust difference, from "Psy.D. training is more focused and efficient" on one pole, to "Ph.D. training is more comprehensive and rigorous" on the other.

Which model do clinical psychologists themselves prefer? In one of our studies (Norcross, Gallagher, & Prochaska, 1989), we found that 50% favored the Boulder model, 14% the Vail model, and the remaining 36% both models equally. However, as expected, preferences varied as a function of one's own doctoral program: 93% of the psychologists trained in a strong Boulder tradition preferred the Boulder model or both equally, and 90% of the psychologists trained in a strong Vail tradition preferred the Vail model or both equally.

The key task for you as a potential applicant is to recognize the diversity in training emphases. We describe this as the practice–research continuum. On one end of the continuum are the Psy.D. programs and a few Ph.D. programs that are practice oriented. These account for roughly 30% of APA-accredited clinical doctoral programs. In the middle of the continuum are the equal-emphasis Ph.D. programs that, as the name implies, emphasize both research and practice. These programs account for about 40% of APA-accredited clinical programs. On the other end of the continuum are the research-oriented Ph.D. programs that account for approximately 30% of the accredited programs (Mayne et al., 1994). Since the practice-oriented programs accept and graduate far larger numbers of students than research-oriented programs, the proportion of new doctorates in clinical psychology is almost equally divided among the practice, equal emphasis, and research programs.

The bottom line for applicants to clinical psychology programs is one of choice, matching, and parity. You have the choice of two training models (and all the programs in between the two extremes). The choice should be matched to your strengths and interests. Parity has been achieved in that at least half of all doctorates in clinical psychology are awarded by professional Vail model programs (Turkington, 1986). The choices are yours, but make informed decisions.

A Word on Accreditation

Accreditation comes in many guises, but the two primary types are institutional accreditation and program accreditation. Institutional applies to an entire institution. Seven regional accreditation bodies, such as the Commission on Higher Education of the Middle States Association of Colleges and Schools, oversee accreditation for the university or college itself. A school receives accreditation when it has been judged to have met minimum standards of quality for postsecondary education.

Beware of any institution that is not accredited by its regional accreditation body. A degree from this institution may not be recognized by licensing boards, certifying organizations, or insurance companies (Dattilio, 1992). It is necessary to be particularly careful about nontraditional or external degree programs that offer the option of obtaining a degree based on independent study, typically away from the institution itself. Some of these are reputable programs, but many are "diploma mills" (Stewart & Spille, 1988). If you have any doubt, inquire thoroughly into whether or not the degree program, as well as the institution as a whole, is recognized by professional associations. This can be accomplished by referring to the booklet, *Doctoral Psychology Programs Meeting Designation Criteria*, jointly published by the Association of State and Provincial Psychology Boards (ASPPB) and the National Register of Health Service Providers in Psychology (1999).

The second type of accreditation important to applicants to a doctoral program pertains to the clinical or counseling psychology program itself. Specialized accreditation of the discipline is performed by the American Psychological Association (APA). This accreditation is a voluntary procedure for the program itself, not the entire institution. Most programs that are capable of meeting the requirements of APA accreditation will choose to apply for accreditation. Accreditation of a clinical or counseling psychology program by APA presumes regional accreditation of the entire institution.

The APA only accredits doctoral programs in the four specialty areas of clinical psychology, counseling psychology, school psychology, and combined professional–scientific psychology. The last category is for those programs that afford doctoral training in two or more of the specialties of clinical, counseling, and school psychology. The "combined" doctoral programs represent a relatively new development in graduate psychology training, and thus are relatively small in number, about 3% of APA-accredited programs. In emphasizing the core research and practice competencies among the specialities, combined programs try to enlist their respective strengths and to capitalize on their overarching competencies. In doing so, the hope is that a combined program will be "greater than the sum of its parts" (Salzinger, 1998). For students undecided about a particular speciality in professional psychology and seeking broad clinical training, these accredited combined programs warrant a close look.

As of 2001, APA had accredited 202 clinical psychology programs (43 of these awarding the Psy.D. degree), 65 counseling psychology programs (1 of these awarding the Psy.D. degree), and 10 combined professional–scientific psychology programs (including 3 Psy.D. programs) that are currently accepting students (APA, 2001). The "Reports on Individual Programs" in this book provide detailed descriptions of these 277 clinical psychology, counseling psychology, and combined programs, respectively.

Take note that APA does not accredit master's programs. Accordingly, references to "accredited" master's psychology programs are to regional or state, not APA, accreditation.

The program accreditation criteria can be obtained from the APA Office of Accreditation (www.apa.org/ed/accred.html). The general areas assessed include institutional support, sensitivity to cultural and individual differences, training models and curricula, faculty, students, facilities, and practicum and internship training. These criteria are designed to insure at least a minimal level of clinical and research quality.

The APA (1990) recognizes three categories of accreditation. Accreditation is granted to programs that meet the criteria in a satisfactory manner. "Accredited, inactive" is the designation for programs that have not accepted students for 2 years. This indicates that the program is taking a hiatus, usually as part of a restructuring process. "Accredited, probation" is the designation for programs that were previously accredited but are not currently in satisfactory compliance with the criteria.

Our reports on individual programs, located in the back of this book, provide crucial descriptive and application information on each APA-accredited doctoral program in clinical and counseling psychology. The APA Education Directorate updates the listing of accredited programs annually in the December issue of the *American Psychologist* and bimonthly on their Web site, www.apa.org/ed.

How important is it to attend an APA-accredited program? The consensus ranges from slightly important to absolutely essential. APA accreditation ensures a modicum of program stability, quality, and integrity. Graduates of APA-accredited programs are practically guaranteed to meet the educational requirements for state licensure. Students are in a more advantageous and competitive position coming from an APA-approved program in terms of their internship choices (Drummond, Rodolfa, & Smith, 1981) and their eventual employment prospects (Walfish & Sumprer, 1984). The federal government, the Veterans Administration, and most universities now insist on a doctorate and internship from APA-accredited programs. Graduates of APA programs also score significantly higher, on average, than do students of non-APA-accredited programs on the licensure exam (Kupfersmid & Fiola, 1991). Licensure and employment as a psychologist are not precluded by attending a non-APA-accredited program, but the situation is tightening. All other things being equal, an accredited clinical or counseling psychology program is a definite asset over a nonaccredited program.

Clinical Alternatives

In addition to doctoral programs in clinical and counseling psychology, we would like to describe several alternative programs of study that should be considered. We have classified these programs along a clinical–research continuum. The clinically oriented programs are outlined first. Portions are abstracted from APA's (1986) *Careers in Psychology*. (To obtain a free copy, write to: Order Department, APA, 750 First Street NE, Washington, DC 20002-4242.) Additional details on 15 helping professions can be accessed online at www.lemoyne.edu/OTRP/. *A Student Guide to Careers in the Helping Professions* by Melissa Himelein provides information on typical job duties, potential earnings, required degrees, and the like.

You are restricted neither to clinical/counseling psychology nor even to psychology in selecting a career in mental health. School psychology, as discussed below, is a viable alternative. Also note that psychology is only one of four nationally recognized mental health disciplines, the others being psychiatry (medicine), clinical social work, and psychiatric nursing.

We do not wish to dissuade you from considering clinical or counseling psychology, but a mature career choice should be predicated on sound information and contemplation of the alternatives. A primary consideration is what you want to do clinically—your desired activities. Conducting psychotherapy is possible in any of the following fields. Prescribing medication is currently restricted to physicians and some nurses, although psychologists are making a strong push for prescription privileges around the country. Psychological testing and empirical research are conducted by psychologists. As discussed previously, psychologists also enjoy a wide range and pleasurable integration of professional activities. Following is a sampling of alternatives to a doctorate in clinical and counseling-psychology.

1. School Psychology. Some undergraduates have a particular interest in working clinically with children, adolescents, and their families. Admission into the few Boulder model programs with a child clinical specialty is particularly competitive. A doctorate in school psychology is much more accessible, with two or three times the acceptance rate of clinical psychology programs. The APA (2001) has accredited 52 of these programs, which provide doctoral-level training in clinical work with children in school settings.

One disadvantage of pursuing a career as a master's-level school psychologist lies in the fact that, unlike the other alternatives, one's professional work may be limited to the school. If this limitation is not a concern, then training as a school psychologist can be an excellent option for those interested in clinical work with children and families (Halgin, 1986).

At the doctoral level, school psychologists are credentialed to function in both school and nonschool settings. Research finds substantial overlap in the coursework and requirements of child clinical programs and school psychology programs (Minke & Brown, 1996). Some differences remain, of course—such as more courses in consultation and education in school programs and more courses in psychopathology in child clinical programs—but the core curricula are quite similar. School psychology training at the doctoral level is broadening to include experience outside of the school setting and with adolescents and families as well (Tryon, 2000).

2. Community Psychology. This field shares with clinical and counseling psychology a concern with individual well-being and healthy psychological development. However, community psychology places considerable emphasis on preventing behavioral problems (as opposed to only treating existing problems), adopting a broader ecological or community perspective, and focusing on changing social policies and systemic concerns.

Graduate training in community psychology occurs within clinical or clinical community psychology programs or within explicitly community psychology programs. The former are clinical psychology programs with an emphasis on or a specialization in community; these doctoral programs are listed in Appendix E (Research Areas) under "community psychology." Eighteen explicitly community doctoral programs are described in a Spring 1996 special supplement of *The Community Psychologist* (copies of the publication can be obtained from Dr. Jean Ann Linney, Editor, *TCP*, 251 Gambrell Hall, University of South Carolina, Columbia, SC 29208 for $3.00 made payable to "Society for Community Research and Action"). If your clinical interests lean toward prevention and community-based interventions, then by all means check out a specialization or a program in community psychology. The Web sites at www.apa.org/divisions/div27 and www.communitypsychology.net provide further information about the field and training programs.

3. Clinical Social Work. A master's degree in social work (M.S.W.) is a popular clinical alternative these days. Several advantages of this option are a much higher rate of admission to M.S.W. programs, GREs less often required for admission, fewer research requirements, an emphasis on professional training, and completion of the M.S.W. in less than half the time necessary to obtain a psychology Ph.D. With legal regulation in all 50 states and third-party vendor status (insurance reimbursement) in 46 states, social workers are increasingly achieving autonomy and respect, including increased opportunities for independent practice. The major disadvantages lie in the less comprehensive nature of the training, which is reflected in a lower pay scale as compared to clinical psychologists. Not becoming a "doctor" and not being able to conduct psychological testing also prove troublesome for some.

Students interested in clinical social work as a career should peruse an introductory text on the profession and should probably also contact the National Association of Social Workers (NASW). This organization provides detailed information on the emerging field, student membership, and accredited programs in clinical social work. NASW resources can be accessed via the Web (socialworkers.org), the telephone (1-800-742-4089), or good old-fashioned mail (750 First Street, NE, Suite 7000, Washington, DC 20002-4241). Peterson's Web site on social work programs is also handy—Petersons.com/graduate/select/socw.html.

4. Psychiatry (Medicine). Students often dismiss the possibility of applying to medical schools, believing that medical school admission is so difficult that it is out of the question (Halgin, 1986). However, the student interested in the biological aspects of psychology and the more severe forms of psychopathology may find this an attractive choice. Although the application process necessitates a more rigorous undergraduate training in the "hard" sciences than most psychology programs, the admission rate may also be higher than the most competitive doctoral programs in clinical and counseling psychology. Of the 40,000 people applying to medical school annually, about 40% are admitted, and almost half of them are women. The average GPA of applicants accepted to medical school is between 3.4 and 3.5 (*New York Times*, October 15, 1995). Medical school thus remains an attractive option for many students headed toward a career in the mental health professions. For further information and demystification of this subject, refer to *Medical School Admissions: The Insider's Guide* (Zebala, Jones, & Jones, 1999) or *The Complete Medical School Preparation and Admissions Guide* (Goliszek, 2000).

The advantages of a medical degree should be recognized. First, an M.D. (allopath) or D.O. (osteopath) allows one to prescribe medication. Second, the average income for psychiatrists is higher than for psychologists. Third, a medical degree permits more work in inpatient (hospital) facilities. Applicants should not dismiss this possibility out of hand, and should explore medicine as a viable alternative, especially if their interests lie on a more biological level.

5. Psychiatric Nursing. Although sometimes regarded as the handmaiden of psychiatry, master's-level psychiatric nursing is an autonomous profession. The employment opportunities for nursing are excellent at this time, especially for psychiatric nurses who have the flexibility of working in hospitals, clinics, health centers, or private practice. Of course, psychiatric nurses are nurses first and are required to obtain a bachelors degree (B.S.N.) and to become registered (R.N.) prior to obtaining their master of science in nursing (M.S.N.). They do not conduct psychological testing and rarely perform research, but psychiatric nurses practice psychotherapy in both inpatient and outpatient settings. Further, certified nurse practitioners now have the authority to write medication prescriptions in 47 states.

6. Psychology and the Law. There is a great deal of interest in the burgeoning amalgam of psychology and law, as evidenced by an APA division, two energetic professional societies, and at least four scholarly journals (Bersoff et al., 1997). Doctoral students must be trained in both fields, of course, increasing the length of graduate training. At least five programs now award law degrees and psychology doctorates together—joint J.D. and Ph.D./Psy.D. programs. Graduates pursue both clinical and research careers—practicing law in mental health arenas, specializing in forensic psychology, working in public policy, and pursuing scholarship on the interface of law and psychology, for example. This is an exciting career, albeit one requiring extra commitment in terms of effort and knowledge during doctoral studies. Peruse the Web sites and links at www.unl.edu/uslap-ls and flash.lakeheadu.ca/~pals/forensics/ for additional information on psychology and the law and its graduate programs.

7. Other. Counselor education, music and art therapy, student guidance, occupational or recreational therapy, rehabilitation counseling, and a plethora of other human service programs can be attractive alternatives to clinical and counseling psychology. They are typically less competitive master's-level programs in which admission rates are quite high and in which the training is quite practical. Relative disadvantages of these programs, in addition to lack of a doctorate, include less prestige, lower salaries, diminished probability of an independent practice, and variable licensure status across the United States.

If one or more of these options seem more suited to your needs, discuss it with a psychology advisor, interview a professional in that field, or write to APA for additional information.

Research Alternatives

Some graduate students enter clinical or counseling psychology to become researchers. They are less interested in working with clinical populations than researching clinical phenomena. If you are most interested in research, here are some nonclinical alternatives that may appeal to you.

1. Social Psychology. Social psychology is concerned with the influence of social and environmental factors on behavior. Issues such as personality, attitude change, group processes, interpersonal attraction, and self-constructs are some of the research interests. Social psychologists are found in a wide variety of academic settings and, increasingly, in many nonacademic settings. These include positions in advertising agencies, personnel offices, corporations, and other business settings.

2. Industrial/Organizational Psychology. This branch of psychology focuses on the individual in the workplace. Industrial/organizational psychologists frequently select and place employees, design jobs, train people, and help groups of workers to function more effectively. A Ph.D. in this area often leads to a job in industry or self-employment as a consultant. Industrial/organizational psychologists earn among the highest median salaries compared to other areas of psychology (Kohout & Wicherski, 1992). Academics find positions in both psychology departments and business schools. The Society for Industrial and Organizational Psychology (1998) produces a useful book entitled *Graduate Training Programs in Industrial/Organizational Psychology and Related Fields*, which describes 178 graduate programs in "I/O" psychology and how to contact each. It is available free from the society's Web site (www. siop.org) or in hard copy for $5.00 from the SIOP Administrative Office, P.O. Box 87, Bowling Green, OH 43402-0087. Students interested in pursuing a career in I/O psychology should obtain, beyond psychology classes, courses in management, marketing, and organizational behavior as well as research experience.

3. Behavioral Neuroscience. For the student more interested in biological research, the workings of the brain and hormonal systems, and the influence of the brain on behavior, programs in neuroscience may be appropriate. By employing animal subjects, researchers can control the conditions of their studies to a level often elusive when using human subjects. Research areas include learning, psychopharmacology, memory, and motivation. For example, recent investigations on memory have provided valuable insight into the etiology and course of Alzheimer's disease. Go to www.andp.org/training/usindex.htm for a splendid list of graduate programs in neuroscience.

Recent research demonstrates that neuroscience graduate programs expect entering students to possess course work and lab work beyond the standard psychology curriculum (Boitano, 1999). Essential courses would include biology, chemistry, calculus, and introduction to neuroscience, and desirable courses would sample from cell biology, biochemistry, and anatomy and physiology. These are all possible, with adequate planning, to incorporate into the psychology major, should you decide on this path relatively early in your undergraduate career. The Web site (www.undergraduateneuroscience.org/) of Faculty for Neuroscience (FUN) provides a bounty of useful information on preparing for a career in neuroscience.

4. Developmental Psychology. The developmental psychologist studies behavior change beginning at the prenatal stages and extending through the lifespan. Areas such as aging, identity, and development of problem-solving abilities are popular areas within developmental psychology. The characteristics of individuals at different age ranges, such as the work of Piaget on child cognition, are of particular interest to developmental psychologists. Geropsychology, or the psychology of aging, has become a popular specialty of this area as the increasing elderly population in this country presents special needs that currently are being insufficiently addressed. Employment opportunities in geropsychology are sure to grow over the next several decades.

5. Cognitive Psychology. Cognitive psychology may be an attractive option for students whose interests lie in the exploration of human thought processes. Major areas include language structure, memory, perception, attention, and problem solving. Research in cognitive psychology has gained insight into what in the past was considered inexplicable behavior and has led to significant gains in the understanding of clinical disorders. For example, research into how moods affect the interpretation of ambiguous events has implications for the study of depression. Much research on the accuracy of eyewitness testimony has been conducted by cognitive psychologists. Recently cognitive programs have emphasized artificial intelligence and cognitive neuroscience.

6. Experimental Psychology. Often a student is interested in research but has not yet defined an area of interest. Or a student has a very specific area of interest in a certain psychopathology but does not desire to do clinical work. In either case, there are programs that offer degrees in experimental psychology. Programs exist that allow a student to explore various research areas, such as animal learning or memory. Other programs focus on experimental psychopathology, which is geared more specifically for the researcher interested in clinical populations. Experimental programs offer excellent training in research methods, statistical analysis, and a great deal of hands-on research experience.

7. Sport Psychology. This emerging specialization typically entails both research and applied activities. Research focuses on all aspects of sports, whereas clinical services include psychological assessment, individual psychotherapy, and group consultation. Research and training encompass stress management, self-confidence, mental rehearsal, competitive strategies, and sensory-kinetic awareness. Consult the *Directory of Graduate Programs in Applied Sport Psychology* (Sachs, Burke, & Schrader, 2001) for information on specific psychology programs. Consult, too, the Web site of APA's Division of Exercise and Sport Psychology at www.psyc.unt.edu/apadiv47/ for information on career possibilities in this area.

8. Medicine. A medical degree (M.D., D.O.) earned concurrently or sequentially with a psychology doctorate (Ph.D., Psy.D.) may allow the greatest flexibility of all the aforementioned programs of study. This option allows one to practice medicine and psychology while also affording a basic education in research and statistics. For an extremely bright and motivated student, this can be a real possibility, but it is certainly the most challenging of all the alternatives. Earning two doctoral degrees will take almost twice as long as earning either alone. This choice is for someone interested in the biological aspects of behavior in addition to gaining a rigorous education in the scientific study of human behavior.

Once again, if your interest lies in research, there are many options available besides clinical and counseling psychology. Talking to a professional in the relevant discipline and consulting textbooks about the discipline will help you to explore that option more fully. An increasing number of websites also offer valuable career advice. Four of our favorites are:

- www.psychwww.com/careers/index.htm
- www.lemoyne.edu/~hevern/PsychSTAC/career.html
- www.apa.org/students/
- www.socialpsychology.org/career/htm

A Word on "Backdoor" Clinicians

The APA ethical guidelines outline two pathways to becoming a clinical or counseling psychologist. The first is to complete a doctoral program and formal internship in clinical or counseling psychology. The second is to obtain a nonclinical psychology doctorate and then to complete a formal respecialization program in clinical or counseling psychology, which includes the internship. Formal training and supervised experience, not simply the desire to become a clinical or counseling psychologist, are required according to the APA ethical code.

In the past some psychologists obtained doctorates in developmental, experimental, social, or educational psychology or in a psychology-related discipline and managed to practice as "clinical psychologists" or "counseling psychologists." This was possible because of the paucity of clinical and counseling psychology doctoral programs and because of "generic" state licensure laws, which recognize only one broad (generic) type of psychologist. However, this educational and licensure process circumvents the established pathway, increases the prospects of inadequate training, and in some cases results in unethical representation. Hence the term "backdoor"—unable to enter through the front door, they sneak in through the back entrance. Major universities, the federal government, the Veterans Administration, and practically all universities now insist on the doctorate (or respecialization) in clinical or counseling psychology for employment as a clinical or counseling psychologist. Although individuals with nonclinical psychology doctorates may be eligible for state licensure, they will be increasingly unable to identify themselves as clinical or counseling psychologists.

Circuitous routes to becoming a clinical or counseling psychologist may still exist, but they have become far less common and ethical. We emphatically recommend against these "backdoor" practices on both clinical and ethical grounds.

To Reiterate Our Purpose

The purpose of this book is to help you navigate the heretofore unknown and frightening process of applying to clinical and counseling psychology graduate programs. But nothing can eradicate the fact that gaining admission to such competitive programs requires a good deal of time and energy. There are the matters of taking the appropriate undergraduate courses, gaining clinical experience, acquiring some research competencies, requesting letters of recommendation, locating the appropriate schools to which to apply, succeeding on entrance examinations, completing the application, creating personal statements, traveling to interviews, and deciding which program actually to attend. We have known people who have quit jobs or taken months off just to invest all their time applying. However, with this book and a fair degree of organization, we hope to make such extremes unnecessary.

Emotional strain is an inherent part of the application process. This is unlike many job interviews, where you are marketing yourself merely as a provider of services. Here you are marketing yourself as a human being. This is a personal process. The application forms and interviews require self-exploration and even a certain amount of justification. Why do you like clinical work? What do you like about spending time with people who are disturbed? Do you really enjoy research? You may end up questioning your answers and may feel compelled to examine the beliefs that have led you to this point in your life.

With the help of this book, you ultimately become the consumer for a program best fitted to you. And 86% of students say that their sense of fit with a program is the single most important factor in choosing a graduate program (Kyle, 2000). By negotiating this process in an informed and systematic manner, you can develop a self-perception as a consumer of clinical and counseling psychology graduate programs. Many interviewers recommend that the final interview should be approached by the applicant in this way. With this approach to the admission process, much of the stress can be allayed.

Although the application process itself can appear intimidating, or the prospect of being rejected upsetting, we urge you *not* to allow fear to cause you to abandon the process altogether or to dismiss the option prematurely. Do not allow yourself to be one of the students who gets rejected unnecessarily. If you apply to the appropriate programs and present yourself with a certain amount of savvy, your chances of getting in are vastly improved.

Our Approach

Having now counseled hundreds of clinical and counseling psychology aspirants and conducted scores of workshops on applying to graduate school, the three of us have gravitated toward a particular approach to the topic. It might be called *realistically encouraging*.

It is realistic in that we present the hard facts about the competition for entrance into doctoral psychology programs. We will not resort to the disservice of feeding you illusions ("Anyone can become a psychologist!"), even though the reality may leave you feeling discouraged at times.

Still, our approach is unabashedly encouraging in that we support people seeking their goals. With knowledge and perseverance, most of our students have made it. Consider the real-life story of Justin, a success story in the quest for a doctorate in clinical psychology.

Justin almost flunked out of college during his first 2 years, before discovering his abiding interest in clinical and counseling psychology. He took his GREs late in his senior year without adequate preparation but obtained combined verbal and quantitative scores of 1100. His applications to doctoral programs that year were hastily and poorly prepared. Justin was, to complicate matters, grossly unaware of typical admission requirements, acceptance rates, and application guidelines. He had no clinical experience whatsoever and had never engaged in research beyond course requirements. Not surprisingly, letters of recommendation about him were mildly positive but without detail or conviction (the deadly, two-paragraph "He/ she's nice, but we haven't had much contact" letters). He received dismal rejections, not even a hint of a possible interview or finalist pool.

Well, as people are apt to do, Justin was about to give up and throw in the towel. But he then attended one of our workshops and began to understand that he had neglected virtually every guideline for sophisticated application to graduate school. The next year was devoted to preparing himself for the hunt: He took extra courses after receiving his degree in order to increase his GPA and to improve his GRE psychology score; he volunteered 10 hours a week at two supervised clinical placements; he worked 20 hours a week for a small stipend as a research assistant; and he copublished three articles. Not surprisingly, his letters of recommendation were now enthusiastic and detailed. That year, Justin obtained six acceptances into clinical doctoral programs with full financial support at three of them.

There *are* concrete steps you can take to improve your application. It is as much knowing how to apply as it is your actual credentials. And if you do get rejected once, many steps can enhance the probability of acceptance the next time around, as in Justin's case. Knowledge of the process can make a tremendous difference. The following chapters provide suggestions and strategies that will increase your attractiveness as an applicant.

CHAPTER 2

PREPARING FOR GRADUATE SCHOOL

People begin the graduate school application process at different stages in their lives. You may be a first- or second-year undergraduate or a junior or a senior. Maybe you have a bachelor's degree in psychology and have worked for a year or two. Perhaps you are a master's-level counselor or social worker who has decided to return for a doctorate. Or maybe you were not a psychology major but have decided you want to make a career change. Depending on your perspective, your needs will be somewhat different. Therefore, each perspective is addressed separately throughout this chapter.

But whatever your current status, recognize this about becoming a clinical or counseling psychologist: *Do not wait until the year of your application to begin the preparation.* Securing admission into competitive doctoral programs necessitates preparation throughout your undergraduate career and any intervening years. Good grades, adequate test scores, clinical work, and research experience cannot be instantaneously acquired simply because you have made a decision to pursue clinical or counseling psychology as your career.

Plan ahead of time using the knowledge and strategies presented in this chapter. Preparing for graduate study is *not* for seniors only (Fretz & Stang, 1980). Timeliness is everything, or, in the vernacular, "you snooze you lose" (Mitchell, 1996).

Much of the "advice" bandied about by fellow students and even some faculty is hopelessly general. Their well-intentioned comments are meant to be universal—one size fits all. However, this advice is akin to the bed of the legendary Greek innkeeper, Procrustes, who insisted on one size bed and who stretched or shortened his unfortunate guests to fit that bed! Do not fall prey to these Procrustean maneuvers; different applicants have different needs. Understanding your particular circumstances and needs will produce an individualized plan for applying to graduate school.

Different Status, Different Needs

Underclassmen

Some of you will be undergraduates, not yet in your senior year. By getting a head start, you can take the appropriate courses and attain the optimal clinical and research training possible at your institution. The more time invested in preparation, the better able you will be to meet the requirements of the application process with confidence, which puts you in a very desirable position. This book will provide you with information that can help guide your undergraduate experiences, academic as well as clinical. The "Time Line" presented in Appendix A outlines important steps to be taken during your freshman, sophomore, and junior years.

Seniors

Some of you are seniors, deciding whether or not to go directly on to graduate school. This is a difficult time, and you are likely to be given advice ranging from "everyone *must* take time off" to "if you take a year, you'll lose the momentum and study skills and never go back." Obviously, this decision is based on the needs and experiences of each individual. There are two guidelines, however, that can help you muddle through these decisions.

1. Are you primarily interested in becoming a practitioner and wish to have only a minimal amount of research training? If so, a practice-oriented psychology program will probably best suit your needs. These

programs tend to put a dual emphasis on clinical experience and research experience (Piotrowski & Keller, 1996). They favor applicants who have a master's degree or have been involved in a clinical setting and who will come into a program with some clinical skills already in their repertoire. The average age of students admitted into these programs is slightly higher than that in research-oriented programs, reflecting time spent out of school in a work environment. Consequently, if you are interested in a practice-oriented program, you could take time off to gain relevant experience in clinical work and research.

2. Are you interested in a program that is primarily research oriented? If you have a solid grounding in research as an undergraduate, such a program is less likely to emphasize the need for postgraduation work experience. The necessary and sufficient research experience can certainly be attained during an undergraduate education without taking time off. Adding work experiences and clinical skills to an application, however, can only improve your chances of getting accepted to a research-oriented program.

The decision to postpone graduate school for a year or more can be influenced by the time constraints of the application process. Applications for doctoral programs in clinical and counseling psychology are typically due between early January and mid-February of the year before you plan to attend school. First-semester seniors just beginning an honors or research project may not be in a position to showcase their talents effectively by application time. The additional preparation for the Graduate Record Examination (GRE) (see Entrance Examinations) may lead a potential applicant to elect to wait a year before applying.

For all these reasons, first-semester seniors may not easily meet the requirements of the recommended Time Line presented in Appendix A. This is a frequent predicament, the solution to which is to wait another year to apply or to do what you can in the remaining time available. In either case, do not give up! Rather, review the Time Line carefully and check off what you have and have not accomplished before making the momentous decision to go for it this year, or to wait until next year. Some shortcuts may well be necessary to apply this year; the ideal time line will need to be modified to fit your reality (Keith-Spiegel, 1991). Some of the items will have to be sacrificed, some accomplished later or more hastily, and others with great energy.

Should you elect to wait a year after receiving your baccalaureate degree, you will begin the application process almost immediately after graduation. In addition to gaining research and clinical experience, the year away from school is spent applying to graduate school. This is *not* a year to relax or "goof off"; rather, it should be an intense year of preparation for graduate admission.

Our research on the admission statistics of APA-accredited clinical psychology programs demonstrates that, on average, approximately three-quarters of incoming doctoral students held bachelor's degrees only and one-quarter possessed a master's degree (Mayne et al., 1994; Norcross et al., 1998). However, this generalization is limited by significant differences among the types of programs: research-oriented Ph.D. programs enrolled a significantly higher percentage of baccalaureate-level students (85% on average; 15% master's), while Psy.D. programs enrolled more master's-level students (47% on average).

In summary, the advantages of taking time off depend on the type of psychology program you desire and the strength of your current credentials. If you desire to focus exclusively on clinical work and a Psy.D. degree, it may be advisable to take time off to gain some practical experience and to save some money. If you are more research oriented and already possess skills in this area, you may be in a position to apply at present. If your current credentials—grades, GRE scores, research—are marginal, then another year may also be required.

In using this book, you will be introduced to the admission criteria for graduate school. And by using the worksheets, you can determine how well-prepared you are to apply to schools at this point. Following the steps in this book will help you assess how prepared you are to apply to graduate school successfully and whether some time out in the "real world" would be advised.

Previous College Graduates

Some of you are college graduates and have already taken time off, or you are a member of the working world contemplating a career change. A solid work record and a mature perspective on psychology are certainly advantageous. However, these alone will not compensate for a lack of course work or experience more germane to clinical or counseling psychology. By reviewing the admissions criteria for graduate programs and using the worksheets provided, you will be able to evaluate the degree of your preparation in order to decide whether it is prudent to begin the application process immediately or to bolster some of your weaker areas before beginning. Pay particular attention to the steps listed under "application year" in the Time Line (Appendix A).

Returning Master's-Level Clinicians

Some of you will be master's-level clinicians interested in obtaining the doctorate in clinical or counseling psychology. Although your wealth of clinical experience gives you an immediate edge over undergraduates in the admissions race to practitioner-oriented programs, you cannot ignore the importance assigned to standardized test scores and research experience.

In clinical psychology, Psy.D. programs and practice-oriented Ph.D. programs tend to accept proportionally more incoming students with master's degrees than with baccalaureate degrees only. Interestingly, counseling psychology programs also seem to prefer master's-level students: Two-thirds of incoming students in APA-accredited counseling psychology programs already held their master's. Of course, these are merely averages that mask the huge differences between, for example, the one-third of counseling psychology programs which *only* accept master's recipients and the one-tenth of programs which primarily accept baccalaureate recipients (Turkson & Norcross, 1996).

Hines (1985) conducted a survey of clinical psychology doctoral programs regarding their policies and experiences in accepting students with master's degrees in psychology. Following are several of the salient findings.

The first question was "What effect (if any) will having a master's degree have on an applicant's chances for admission to your program?" Most responses indicated that having a master's per se made little or no difference, with some respondents suggesting that it was the student's performance in the master's program that was more important. However, 10% answered that having a master's degree had a definite positive effect. Only 3% indicated that having a master's would have a definite negative bias.

The second question requested that respondents rate the importance of seven criteria for admission to their programs. Each criterion was rated on a five-point, Likert-type scale ranging from least important to most important. The three highest ratings were for GRE scores, letters of recommendation, and research experience. The rest, in descending order of importance, were undergraduate grades, graduate grades, quality of the master's program, and clinical practicum experience.

As you can see, GRE scores and research experience definitely do count in admissions decisions for master's-level applicants. The lower ratings given to graduate grades and to undergraduate grades reflect a difference among schools in whether graduate or undergraduate grades are considered more important. The standard deviation for graduate grades was particularly high, indicating wide variability in the importance placed on graduate grades among different programs. Comments suggested that some schools tended to downplay graduate grades "because they are universally high"; another suggested that "high grades don't help, but poor grades hurt."

Having a master's degree in and of itself, then, neither helps nor hinders your chances in most admission decisions. It is not possessing the graduate degree per se that matters, but the quality of performance in academic courses, clinical practica, and research experiences during master's training and thereafter that give a definite edge in the admission process. This is particularly true for Psy.D. and practice-oriented Ph.D. programs, which enroll a much higher percentage of master's-level students (Mayne et al., 1994).

Master's degree recipients with combined Verbal and Quantitative GRE scores below 1,000 can take hope from a study of similar students admitted to Ph.D. programs (Holmes & Beishline, 1996). Ten such applicants were admitted by virtue of "compensatory virtues" such as presentations or publications that helped mitigate the effect of low GRE scores. If you find yourself in this position, emphasize the other, positive elements of your application and, again, seriously consider Psy.D. clinical and Ph.D. counseling psychology programs that enroll a higher percentage of master's-level students (Norcross et al., 1998). Assuming other parts of your credentials are acceptable, master's recipients should not be discouraged from applying to doctoral programs on the basis of GRE scores alone.

While clinical experience is valued, for most doctoral programs this factor is a secondary consideration to research. The vast majority of clinical and counseling doctoral programs prefer a thesis or a journal article over a graduate internship or post-master's clinical experience (Keller, Beam, Maier, & Pietrowski, 1995). All programs expect evidence of conducting empirical research: Ph.D. programs favor it over clinical experience and Psy.D. programs weigh it equally with clinical experience.

A Master's Degree First?

A common question during our graduate school workshops is whether students should secure a master's degree before seeking the doctorate. Fortunately, our workshop participants and you realize that no simple answer is possible for such a complex question. Nonetheless, the following are some broad reasons for seeking a master's degree first.

- *Low grade-point average.* The vast majority of doctoral programs will not consider applicants with a GPA below 3.0.
- *Weak GRE scores.* Similarly, doctoral programs rarely accept bachelor-level applicants whose combined Verbal and Quantitative scores fall below 1,000.
- *Scarce research or clinical experiences.* Doctoral admission committees understandably desire that you have had some direct experience with those activities you intend to pursue for a lifetime.
- *Uncertain career goal.* Indecision about your subfield in psychology, or outside of psychology, is a strong indicator for a master's program initially.
- *Late application.* Doctoral programs hold to earlier deadlines than do master's programs, so those students waiting too late to apply will be redirected to master's programs.
- *Terse letters of recommendation.* By virtue of late transfer into a university or into psychology, some students simply lack sufficient contact with faculty for them to write positive and detailed letters of recommendation expected by doctoral programs.
- *Inadequate coursework in psychology.* Doctoral programs require a minimum level of education in the discipline prior to acceptance, typically at least 16 credits of psychology course work.

Completing a rigorous master's program in psychology can correct many of the foregoing impediments to acceptance into a doctoral program. As we describe in Chapter 7, students typically strengthen their grade-point average, acquire clinical and research experience, sharpen their career goals, and establish close relationships with faculty during the 2 years of a master's program. For these and other reasons, many students opt for a master's degree at one institution before seeking the doctorate at another.

Various types of doctoral psychology programs were recently surveyed in detail regarding the value of a clinical master's degree for gaining admission to their doctoral programs (Bonifzi, Crespy, & Rieker, 1997). Assuming a *good* undergraduate GPA and *good* GREs, the effect of having a master's degree on the applicant's chances for admission was negative for 7% of the programs, neutral for 48% of the programs, and positive for 45% of programs. However, assuming *mediocre* GPA and *mediocre* GREs, the effect of having a master's was more neutral than positive overall. Put another way, it is clearly the applicant's overall credentials—rather than possession of a master's degree—that carries the day.

This same study (Bonifzi et al., 1997) and our own research (Mayne et al., 1994; Norcross et al., 1998) consistently demonstrate that Ph.D. clinical programs hold a positive bias toward baccalaureate-level applicants. By contrast, Psy.D. clinical, Ph.D. counseling, and Ph.D. school psychology programs view master's degree recipients more favorably and accept higher proportions of master's-level applicants. Keep these biases in mind as you consider the selection criteria of graduate schools.

Graduate School Selection Criteria

As an applicant, your perceptions of graduate admissions criteria probably differ from those of the admissions committee. Some of the things you may think are important are actually not so important (Collins, 2001). For two examples, your GRE Advanced Psychology score is less important than your GRE Verbal and Quantitative scores, and your extracurricular accomplishments do not count as much as you might like (Cashin & Landrum, 1991). On the other hand, you probably underestimate the importance of other admissions criteria; two examples are letters of recommendation and research experience, which students routinely underestimate compared to admissions committees (Nauta, 2000).

In this section we acquaint you with the data-based practices of graduate admissions committees. Learn what they value in graduate applicants and then tailor your application to those criteria in order to maximize your success.

Research and experience have consistently indicated that the two most important *objective* criteria for graduate school admission are GPA and GRE performance. The implications for enhancing your application are thus clear: maintain your GPA and prepare thoroughly for the GREs.

A number of studies have been conducted to determine the relative importance of *nonobjective* selection criteria in psychology graduate programs. The findings of one of four studies (Norcross, Hanych, & Terranova, 1996) are reproduced in Table 2-1. This table presents the average ratings of various criteria for admission into doctoral programs and master's programs in psychology. A rating of 3 denotes high importance, 2 moderate importance, and 1 low importance. The top two rated variables for doctoral programs were letters of recommendation and research experience. Compared to doctoral programs, master's programs deemphasize research experience in their admissions decisions. Note, too, that extracur-

TABLE 2-1. Importance of Nonobjective Criteria in Psychology Admissions Decisions

	Graduate programs	
Criteria	Doctoral programs	Master's programs
Letters of recommendation	2.77	2.66
Research experience	2.55	2.06[a]
Work experience	2.01	2.04
Clinically related service	2.00	2.03
Extracurricular activity	1.35	1.42

Note. From "Graduate study in psychology: 1992–1993" by J. C. Norcross, J. M. Hanych, & R. D. Terranova, 1996, *American Psychologist, 51,* 631–643. © 1996 American Psychological Association. Reprinted by permission.

[a]Significant differences between doctoral and master's programs.

ricular activity is valued significantly lower than the other four variables; in other words, being heavily involved in student organizations and campus activities does not carry nearly as much weight as these other considerations.

Another study (Eddy, Lloyd, & Lubin, 1987) investigated the selection criteria of APA-accredited doctoral programs in clinical psychology. Program directors rated the importance of each type of undergraduate preparation on a scale ranging from very low importance, 1, to very high importance, 5. Table 2-2 presents the mean ratings and standard deviations for clinical psychology programs.

Research experience emerged as the top-rated variable. The authors of the study concluded that there is simply no better way to increase one's chances for acceptance than research. Personal visit to a department (on your own or on an invited interview), computer proficiency, and human service experience were also highly valued. However, as in the previous study, extracurricular activities, such as Psi Chi membership, were rated relatively unimportant.

To sum up, the results of these and other studies (e.g., Mayne et al., 1994; Munoz-Dunbar & Stanton, 1999; Purdy, Reinehr, & Swartz, 1989) indicate that the ideal doctoral applicant has high GRE scores, strong letters of recommendation, some research experience, clinical exposure, and high overall GPA, with particularly high grades in the final 2 years. The results also consistently indicate that the admission requirements for doctoral programs are more stringent than for master's programs.

TABLE 2-2. Importance Assigned by Clinical Psychology Doctoral Programs to Various Types of Undergraduate Preparation

Preparation	Mean	*SD*
Research experience	4.28	0.91
Personal visit to department	3.14	1.41
Computer knowledge and skills	3.00	0.85
Paid human service experience	2.90	1.07
Volunteer human service	2.85	1.13
Double major with basic science	2.78	1.10
Master's degree	2.16	0.99
Double major with social science	2.08	0.84
Psi Chi membership	2.00	0.94

Note. From "Enhancing the application to doctoral professional programs: Suggestions from a national survey" by B. Eddy, P. J. Lloyd, & B. Lubin, 1987, *Teaching of Psychology, 14,* 160–163. © 1987 Lawrence Erlbaum Associates. Reprinted by permission.

TABLE 2-3. Undergraduate Courses Required or Recommended by APA-Accredited Clinical Psychology Programs

	Percentage of programs		
Psychology course	Required	Recommended	Either
Statistics	65	29	94
Experimental methods/research design	48	19	68
Abnormal/psychopathology	29	22	51
Physiological/biopsychology	10	23	33
Learning/cognition	10	19	30
Personality	15	13	28
Child/developmental	11	13	24
Social psychology	7	16	23
History and systems	6	9	16
Tests and measures/psych testing	6	8	15
Laboratory course	6	5	11
Sensation and perception	3	2	5
Computers	1	3	4
Clinical/psychotherapy	1	1	2
Comparative	1	1	2
Motivation and emotion	1	1	2
Neuropsychology	1	0	1

Note. Adapted from "Admission requirements, acceptance rates, and financial assistance in clinical psychology programs: Diversity across the practice–research continuum" by T. J. Mayne, J. C. Norcross, & M. A. Sayette, 1994, *American Psychologist, 49,* 605–611.

The remainder of this chapter highlights these pivotal criteria used by graduate admissions committees in selecting their students. We consider, in order, course work, clinical experience, research skills, entrance examinations, and extracurricular activities.

Course Work

Although graduate programs differ in the courses they prefer you to have taken prior to admission, there are some "core" courses that nearly all require (Smith, 1985). These include Introduction to Psychology, Statistics, Experimental Design/Research Methods, Abnormal Psychology, Physiological Psychology/Biopsychology, and Learning/Cognition.

A survey of 161 clinical doctoral programs in the United States and Canada revealed that both Vail and Boulder model programs hold similar expectations on desirable undergraduate course preparation (Mayne et al., 1994). Approximately 75% of the programs require or recommend specific undergraduate courses, 15% require an undergraduate psychology major, and the remainder have no set policy on the matter.

Table 2-3 presents the percentage of psychology courses required (first column), recommended (second column), and either required or recommended (third column) for entry into APA-accredited clinical programs. Bear in mind that these figures systematically *underestimate* the actual percentage of programs requiring these courses since they do not include those graduate programs requiring a psychology major as a prerequisite and thus probably requiring most of the courses listed in Table 2-3. Introduction to Psychology was presumed to be a prerequisite for these advanced psychology courses and was therefore omitted from the table. Courses you should complete, according to these results, are Statistics, Experimental Design/Research Methods, Abnormal Psychology, Physiological Psychology, Learning/Cognition, Personality, and Child/Developmental Psychology.

Doctoral programs require more courses on average than do master's programs (Smith, 1985). Accordingly, both to meet admissions criteria and to improve your GRE psychology test score, we heartily recommend that you complete Social Psychology, History and Systems, Psychological Testing (or Tests and Measures), and at least one laboratory course. The safest plan, of course, is to complete a rigorous undergraduate major in psychology to satisfy all these courses, but a well-planned minor in psychology may suffice. The rule of thumb: the more competitive the graduate program, the more stringent the required undergraduate course work.

If you were not a psychology major, it is still important that you take the minimum of six core courses mentioned. In addition, you may have to invest additional time studying for the Psychology Subject test of the Graduate Record Examination (more about this later).

If you have been out of college for several years and feel deficient in this course work, you might consider taking a course or two as a part-time student at a local college or university. This will shore up your record and prepare you more fully for admission and the GRE. Those of you who are not psychology majors but have studied extensively for this test and have done well will often be considered favorably by admissions committees.

Beyond these classes, we recommend an introductory computer science course, particularly if you are interested in research-oriented programs. Not only will it accustom you to the workings of computers, which are standard research fare, but it will also serve as a springboard for learning the statistical software used for data analysis. Recall that computer proficiency is rated a moderately important admission variable by doctoral programs.

Graduate selection committees prefer a broad undergraduate background in a variety of arts and sciences (Fretz & Stang, 1980). Exposure to biological sciences, math competency, and verbal skills are generally valued. If you are anxious or phobic regarding oral presentations, then by all means complete a public speaking course. Composition and writing courses are also vital; you may well face three or four major papers each semester in graduate school.

At this point, you may want to glance at the reports on individual programs following Chapter 7 to get a better idea of which courses particular programs recommend or require of applicants. You will find the specific courses that each accredited clinical and counseling psychology program recommends as well as requires applicants to have taken.

For students who have gotten an early start or who are seniors, we would like to suggest considering advanced course work. To allay any anxieties, we would emphasize that the vast majority of applicants do *not* take these courses as undergraduates. Your application can be very strong without taking the courses we are about to mention. However, those fortunate enough to be in a position to add these to their academic transcripts should seriously consider taking advantage of the opportunity.

Consider an advanced or graduate statistics course. Statistical acumen is highly regarded, especially in research-oriented programs, and advanced knowledge may pave the way for funding as a graduate assistant or research assistant. Another suggestion would be to take a course specifically focused on one of the data analysis programs. Learning one of the major statistical packages—Statistical Analysis System (SAS) or Statistical Package for the Social Sciences (SPSS) — is a definite advantage. Such knowledge increases your employability and may catch the eye of a professor in need of a data analyst. Lastly, we suggest an advanced course in physiological psychology or biopsychology. This is certainly helpful in increasing your understanding of the biological aspects of behavior, an increasingly important focus in psychology today. If you have the time and abilities, these courses can help distinguish a very good application from an outstanding one.

Learning about psychology and achieving good grades are important components of academic work. But classes are also important in that they provide you with the opportunity to become acquainted and form relationships with faculty. It is natural to feel shy around faculty, especially if you are part of a 300-person lecture class. Substantial courage may be required to muster the nerve to ask a question or to stay after class and introduce yourself. Equally anxiety provoking is a visit alone to a professor's office during office hours. In the one case, you expose yourself in front of your peers; in the other, you are individually vulnerable and do not have a crowd of faces to blend into. *But find a way to become comfortable in approaching faculty members.*

The irony of student reticence to approach faculty is that professors generally would like more students to approach them. Many faculty sit alone during office hours wondering why students never come to see them. They love to have students come after class or during office hours with questions. Ideas for questions can include something mentioned in the lecture or something you encountered in the readings. You do not have to be a star pupil or ask brilliant questions to begin a conversation with a professor. If you want to continue developing a relationship, ask professors about their research or other courses they are teaching.

What is the importance of meeting faculty? Three compelling reasons come to mind. First, having a mentor to advise you in your growth as a future psychologist is invaluable. There is no better way to learn about psychology than in a one-on-one, mentoring relationship.

When you apply to graduate school, having a professor to guide you through the process is one of the biggest advantages you can have. Second, eventually you will need faculty to write letters of recommendation on your behalf. Whether you are applying to graduate school or for employment, everyone wants a few references regarding your performance and responsibility. Occasionally faculty members are asked to write a letter for a pupil who has taken a lecture course with 100 or more students—the professor may not even know the student until he or she requests a letter! It makes a huge difference if you have spent some office hours or time after class with a faculty member, and he or she knows you more personally. And third, once you get to know professors, you may have the opportunity to work for them on a research project or as part of their clinical activities. You will be working closely with your major professor in graduate school, and you might as well begin as soon as possible as a colleague-in-training. Though more will be said about this later, we cannot overemphasize the need to cultivate such a relationship and the rewards that can ensue.

Beyond meeting professors, read your textbooks with an eye toward graduate school. If you come across an interesting study, note the author and check in the back of the text for the reference. When you have time, you may want to go to the library and read the original article. If it is recent, note the author's university. You will be surprised at how much you can learn about the field just by doing your typical class work.

As mentioned earlier, your GPA is a very important criterion for admission. Three types of GPA may be considered by graduate programs: overall GPA, psychology GPA, and GPA during your junior and senior years. Schools vary in the importance they place on these different scores, with some programs only considering one or two of them. When receiving information from schools, determine which GPAs they evaluate and also how much importance they place on them. For example, if you have an overall GPA of 3.2 (on a 4-point scale where $A = 4$, $B = 3$, $C = 2$, and $D = 1$), a psychology GPA of 3.6, and a junior/senior GPA of 3.5, you might concentrate on schools that emphasize the latter two averages.

Our research has shed light on the average GPAs among incoming doctoral and master's students in psychology (Norcross et al., 1996). For doctoral programs, the mean and median GPA is 3.5 for all undergraduate courses, 3.6 for psychology courses, and 3.6 for the last 2 years of course work. For master's programs, the mean and median GPA is 3.3 for all undergraduate courses, 3.4 for psychology courses, and 3.4 for the last 2 years of course work. Please employ your statistical sagacity in interpreting these figures: half of the incoming students will possess GPAs above these medians, and half of the students will possess GPAs below these medians.

Although we do not want to discourage anyone, a GPA below 3.0 is considered by most APA-accredited programs as unsatisfactory. Regardless of the prestige of the institution, admissions committees view a GPA under 3.0 as below the acceptable limits of quality course work. If this applies to you, consider: taking additional courses to bolster your GPA; retaking courses to increase it; and completing a master's program first to show doctoral admissions committees you can perform academically at a higher level. Try to speak with an academic advisor about how best to improve your standing within the workings of your own institution.

Academic performance in your junior and senior psychology courses is particularly vital. Regardless of the type of GPAs emphasized by a graduate program, these courses affect your overall, final 2 years, and psychology GPAs.

Your "academic" performance is not limited to exam grades in the classroom. Faculty members—several of whom will render a letter of recommendation on your behalf—also assess your interpersonal skills, verbal ability, and professional commitment in the classroom, outside formal course work, and in everyday interactions. The direct implication is to avoid undesirable interpersonal behaviors—say, for instance, silliness, arrogance, and hostility—in any interactions with your professors (Keith-Spiegel, 1991).

Although such undesirable behaviors may be obvious, students are frequently unaware of the importance faculty attach to good questions, genuine attentiveness, respectful disagreements, office visits, mature disposition, interpersonal responsibility, and so forth. These are the characteristics a student heading for graduate studies should manifest in and outside of the classroom.

Finally, there is a corpus of general knowledge regarding clinical and counseling psychology that may not have been covered in your courses. This body of information includes at least a cursory understanding of diagnosis, for example, the *Diagnostic and Statistical Manual*, 4th ed. (DSM-IV); various assessment devices, such as the Minnesota Multiphasic Personality Inventory-2 (MMPI-2) and the Wechsler intelligence scales (WAIS-III, WISC-III); and ordinary therapy practices, such as individual, group, and family therapy. You must have a passing familiarity with theoretical orientations, for example, cognitive-behavioral, psychodynamic, family systems, and eclectic, in order to understand program materials. If you are not already familiar with these concepts, it would be wise to review an introductory textbook. You should also be gaining knowledge specifically about clinical psychology as a field and about the current issues within this field. Toward this end, we suggest you begin reading the *APA Monitor*, a publication sent to all APA members and student affiliates, or the *APS Observer*, the newsletter distributed to all members of the American Psychological Society (APS). Both publications feature articles dealing with psychology in general and clinical/counseling psychology in particular. You can become an APA or APS affiliate and receive a subscription, peruse your library's copy, or ask to borrow a professor's old issues.

Clinical Experience

What is clinical experience? In its loosest sense, it involves spending time working in any number of human service programs. Graduate programs in clinical and counseling psychology expect that you will have some experience working with emotionally, intellectually, or behaviorally disadvantaged people. Many students volunteer some time during their undergraduate years, whereas other people get paid as part of a summer job or during their time off. In research-oriented Ph.D. programs, you will be expected to have some clinical experience as a prelude to your clinical training and as an aid to researching clinically relevant problems. Experience of this nature will be considered essential.

What kinds of clinical experience count? Largely two types—paid and volunteer—under individual supervision. Paid part-time work in a clinical setting may be available in your community (but your involvement should not be at the expense of your academic performance). Returning master's-level clinicians will obviously have a multitude of employment possibilities, whereas undergraduates will have to search vigilantly for part-time employment.

For college students, a prime opportunity is to complete an undergraduate clinical practicum (or field experience) for academic credit. This is a great way to "kill two birds with one stone." One study (VandeCreek & Fleisher, 1984) found that over two-thirds of colleges and universities provided undergraduate practica in psychology. Further, students consistently rate fieldwork as one of the most rewarding experiences and relevant courses in their college career. The advantages in terms of your application credentials are many: clinical experience, academic credit, familiarity with human service agencies, professional supervision, and exposure to potential sources for research pursuits and letters of recommendation.

Check with your undergraduate advisor and the college catalogue to determine whether such an opportunity exists for you. To learn more about the specific placements, you should consult the Psychology Department or the faculty member responsible for fieldwork placements.

In selecting a place to work or volunteer, please consider several factors. Although it may be difficult to accomplish, it is ideal to gain clinical experience in an area that complements a research interest. For example, if your research is in the area of alcohol abuse, you might seek experience in a college counseling center or a substance abuse prevention program. Find out exactly what your responsibilities will entail.

The optimal program is one that will train you in clinical skills (such as crisis counseling on a hot line), will allow you to deal directly with clients, and will provide regular supervision by an experienced clinician. Supervision is probably the most important consideration in choosing a clinical setting. It is important that you be supervised by a professional, one with at least a master's degree, though preferably a doctorate. Determine the qualifications of the person who will be supervising your work. Aside from the valuable insight supervisors can offer, they may also be familiar with faculty at different graduate programs and assist you in selecting schools. In addition, you may eventually decide to request letters of recommendation from them. Letters from a clinical supervisor are particularly important for practice-oriented graduate programs. In a later section we offer suggestions regarding approaching professors for letters of recommendation. The same strategies apply here.

If you are volunteering, you should insist on receiving supervision. Learn not only who will supervise you, but also how often and for what length of time. You will need to be assertive when searching out and interviewing possible agencies. If this seems difficult for you, try to remember that you are a volunteer—giving your time and energy, without financial compensation, to an agency that is in need of people like yourself. You seek only experience and supervision. You are a valuable commodity, so do not sell yourself short!

Numerous settings are available to people seeking clinical experience. Here are several excellent sources of hands-on experience that can be found in most communities:

- *Crisis hot lines.* These typically provide training in counseling skills, suicide prevention, and outreach services. The clientele range from sexual assault victims to suicidal teens to lonely elderly who need to talk with someone. Volunteers usually provide telephone counseling, although opportunities to work with an emergency outreach team may also be available. This can be a great way to gain exposure to a multitude of psychopathologies and to acquire fundamental helping skills. One word of caution: New members of most crisis hot lines are expected to take a large share of the midnight to 8 A.M. shifts. Be prepared to pay your dues.

- *Centers for homeless or runaway adolescents.* Much of what is done in these settings is similar to case management, in that these teenagers need to be put in contact with the appropriate social service agencies. However, in-house counseling may also be provided to these youths, who frequently come from disadvantaged families. Be particularly careful about specifying the supervision arrangement before starting. The facilities are often understaffed and financially strapped, meaning you may have to be assertive to get the training you desire.
- *Schools for emotionally disturbed children and adolescents.* These placements offer exposure to both educational and clinical services. Educational activities might include tutoring, classroom management, and one-on-one homework supervision. Clinical activities typically entail recreational supervision, art therapy, and perhaps individual, group, and family therapy.
- *Supervised homes for the developmentally disabled or chronically mentally ill.* These are unlocked transitional facilities where clients live and work in a therapeutic milieu (an environment consisting of peers). Depending on your prior experience, you might be expected to conduct skills training, recreational counseling, and work/school supervision. The programs are often behavioral, affording you experience with reinforcement schedules, shaping techniques, and token economies. Often the goal is to graduate clients into the outside world.
- *Summer camps for the physically challenged, developmentally disabled, or emotionally disturbed.* These can be either day or overnight camps, where counselors are expected to supervise recreation or train campers in skills and vocational activities. The positions are usually paid, ideal for college students who want to gain field experience while working for the summer. They also tend to be full-time positions, while they last. They offer short-term but rather intensive training.
- *Community mental health centers.* These provide experience with a population of patients suffering from serious mental disabilities such as schizophrenia, biploar affective disorders, substance abuse, and anxiety disorders. The programs vary but are likely to include an outpatient department, partial (day) hospitalization, and an education/outreach wing. Duties may include helping out during recreational activities or actual therapy work with individuals or groups. Though supervising recreational activities allows contact with patients, you might not be observing any clinical techniques. Do not be shy about asking for greater responsibilities!
- *College peer programs.* These provide students with peer education and assistance on specific disorders, such as bulimia or substance abuse. Less common but still available is peer counseling on more general concerns, for example, "Need to Talk? Call Us." Both peer education and peer counseling programs are typically flexible in the number of hours you must work and usually provide training in listening and counseling skills. They may also provide an opportunity to begin learning about a specific clinical disorder.
- *Women's resource centers.* These are typically multiservice centers that offer or coordinate a plethora of human services for women—rape crisis counseling, domestic violence education, "safe homes" for victims of abuse, and so on. Possible activities likewise vary, but the training and *esprit de corps* are highly regarded. Students with abiding interest in women's issues and feminist therapy will find these placements particularly satisfying.
- *Drug and alcohol treatment facilities.* These offer a variety of detoxification and rehabilitation interventions designed to help patients cope with the physical and psychological components of addictions. Although not all "D & A" programs will afford undergraduate field placements, substance abuse is one of the most popular research areas in clinical and counseling psychology (see Appendix E). Students can gain exposure to several models of addiction, interact with a multidisciplinary treatment team, and observe clinical services with substance abusers across gender, racial, and socioeconomic lines.

A word of caution about initial clinical encounters. Be careful not to generalize from one experience. One of the authors worked with runaways at a crisis center for adolescents in the Times Square area of New York City. The rate of employee turnover at this facility was exceptionally high. The "success" rate for clients was low, and the population was difficult indeed. Although it was a rich experience, some of the volunteers became disillusioned with psychology as a result of working there. Settings vary considerably, depending on the populations they serve and the resources available. An unpleasant experience may only mean that the specific population you were working with was not ideally suited to you. Try something else, and you may feel quite differently.

Though clinical work is important (and often rewarding), remember it is only one of several experiences you must acquire for admission to graduate school. Some Ph.D. applicants make the mistake of accumulating a wealth of clinical experiences at the expense of gaining an adequate research background. By doing so, you may be inadvertently presenting yourself as being uninterested in research or perhaps better suited to the Psy.D. than the Ph.D. program. Clinical experience must be balanced with research competencies. This balance will be weighted toward clinical work or research depending on your desire to gain either a Psy.D. or Ph.D. or whether the Ph.D. program is practice or research oriented.

Research Skills

Research experience, as discussed earlier in this chapter, is one of the most important admission criteria to nearly all Ph.D. programs in clinical and counseling psychology. To a lesser but still significant degree, Psy.D. programs also value your research experience for what it communicates about your intellectual ability and professional commitment. Recall the conclusion of one study on graduate school admission: there is simply no single better way to enhance an application than by obtaining research experience (Eddy et al., 1987). The desired skills—to critique the literature, to apply methodological reasoning, to write in scientific language, among others—are essential. Even though all psychologists need not produce original research, all must intelligibly consume and apply research.

Gaining research experience is largely dependent on your own initiative. It can be an intimidating process, and a knowledge of the potential opportunities can be beneficial in helping you to maximize your gains during the course of your research.

Let us begin by outlining six common avenues for students engaging in scholarly research. The first is probably the most frequent—volunteering to work with a faculty member on one of his or her research projects. A second avenue is to complete a student research program for a notation on your transcript but not academic credit. Students identify potential professors to work with from a faculty directory of research interests, jointly complete a learning contract, and then devote a minimum number of hours (say, 75) throughout a semester working directly with the faculty sponsor. A third option is to enroll in independent psychology research for academic credit. This entails individual study and research under the supervision of a faculty member and is ordinarily limited to junior and senior psychology majors.

A fourth and increasingly common approach is to work or volunteer for a researcher outside of your university—in a hospital, medical center, research institute, or industry, for example. Especially in large cities, researchers with major grants depend upon individuals (both pre- and post-baccalaureate) for many elements of study management, data collection, and statistical analyses. If you have taken a statistics or research methods course that included SPSS or SAS, you may find that you have sufficient skills for an entry-level position on an active research team outside of a university.

A fifth alternative, restricted to matriculated undergraduates, is to complete an honors thesis in either a departmental or a university-wide honors program. As with additional courses and postcollege work, an honors thesis is a "feather in your cap." For students desiring to move straight into a Ph.D. program, it is one means of presenting evidence to graduate admissions committees that you are capable of performing graduate-level work. Many schools allow motivated students to complete an honors thesis, an original study that the student conceptualizes, conducts, analyzes, and has some hope of presenting at a regional conference or even publishing. An honors thesis shows a genuine commitment to psychology and is a palpable sign of ability in the applicant.

A sixth and final avenue toward acquiring research competencies is restricted to master's students. A comprehensive paper or a formal master's thesis, requiring original research, practically guarantees additional experience with research. For this reason, undergraduates denied admission directly into doctoral programs frequently enter master's programs to gain valuable research (and clinical) competencies. And remember: The majority of clinical psychology doctoral programs prefer masters-level applicants to have completed a thesis (Piotrowski & Keller, 1996).

Whatever avenue you eventually pursue, the procedures are quite similar. Following is a step-by-step guide to help you make the most of your research experience.

Determining Your Interests

The first step is finding a research area that interests you. If you are not interested in the work, it will diminish your energy and enthusiasm and probably your decision to apply to a graduate program. A good place to begin is to read through your department brochure or website describing faculty interests and current research. If you are out of school, check with a local university. If the program has a graduate psychology faculty, so much the better—look to those professors first.

Once you have a list of faculty interests, you may find someone interesting but not be sure exactly what the research is all about ("I've heard about autism and think I'd like to study it, but I don't really know much about it. . . ."). If specific publications are not provided in the website or brochure, or if reprints are not posted in the department, then you can go to *PsycLIT* or *PsycINFO* (found in most university libraries; ask at the reference desk) and read what that professor has published in the area over the last 3 to 5 years. This should make it easier to decide which professor you would like to approach to volunteer to do research with. *Do not narrow your choices too quickly!* Find at least two or three professors whose work initially interests you.

Selecting Professors

Next, find out more about that professor as a person. Do you know people who have taken a class with him or her? What did they think? Are there other undergraduate or graduate students working with this professor now? What do they do exactly, and what is it like working under this person? Is the professor easy to get along with? Is the professor helpful to students? Do not be afraid to approach people and ask questions.

Having narrowed the choice to two or three professors whose work interests you and with whom you think you might get along, you might consider the rank of the professor. There are tenured faculty (a *full* or *associate* professor) and untenured (an *assistant* professor), both with respective advantages and disadvantages.

Full or associate professors have usually been in the field longer and will probably have colleagues at other universities. If the person you work with is well known, it gives your letter of recommendation that much more weight. If your professor's reputation in the field is strong, with a long list of publications, you are also likely to learn a bit more and increase your own attractiveness as a candidate. However, once a faculty member becomes tenured, he or she is no longer under the same pressure to produce research as when he or she was pursuing tenure. Thus, you should establish that tenured faculty are actively engaged in research and are currently publishing their work.

Assistant professors are newer to the field, probably 1 to 6 years postdoctorate. They are often in more need of undergraduate help and will likely involve you to your full potential. The possibility of being included on a presentation or publication as a coauthor may also be increased. What they lack in terms of a reputation built on years of publications may be balanced by their energy and their motivation to produce.

One word of caution: Some professors have large research facilities and employ vast numbers of undergraduates to help them with their data management. If there are 10 or 15 undergraduates working in a lab, the attention given to each individual tends to decrease, as well as the value of the research experience. This is not to say you should not work in a large research group—simply consider this as one factor to be used in making the decision.

An optimal research context, then, is one in which there is a faculty member or research mentor who has an established reputation in his or her field of inquiry, a record of producing publishable research, similar interests to your own, a history of working successfully with students, a propensity to share authorship credit with students, and the ability to construct discrete research projects. Be guided by these general principles in selecting professors to approach, but do not expect all these qualities to be available to you.

Making Initial Contact

Having chosen a professor you would like to work with, it is now time to make yourself known to him or her. You need to schedule an appointment or approach the professor during posted office hours. It is natural for you to be nervous! However, the more familiar with his or her work you are, the more secure you are likely to feel. Once again, read what the professor has written. Additionally, it helps to remember that you are coming to the professor to offer your services. A good opening line might be, "Hello, Dr. Jones, my name is Chris Smith. I've been doing some reading on autism and came across several articles you've written. I'm pretty interested and was wondering if I could help out in some way with the project you're working on now." As the conversation progresses, let the professor know your long-term goals as well as your immediate desire both to contribute as a member of the research team and to acquire research skills. Let him or her know you are seriously considering clinical or counseling psychology—it will increase your appeal.

Negotiating Research Responsibilities

"Well Mr./Ms. Smith, I'd be very interested in speaking with you about helping out with my research. . . ." You have made the contact. If the professor does not need help, you have lost nothing and gained the experience. Ask if he or she knows of someone with similar interests who is looking for help, or simply approach the next person on your list.

After the initial contact, your next move is dictated by your professor's needs and your abilities. Regardless of all your wonderful qualities, be prepared to run some of the grunt work! Photocopying needs to be done, literature searches need to be conducted, and at times you might well be expected to do some lab cleanup. You are "low person on the totem pole," so approach this with humility. But if you have experience with test administration or statistical analysis, let the professor know, being aware that ultimately your activities will be dictated first by his or her needs. However, if grunt work is the full extent of your duties, your needs are not being addressed properly. Spending 2 years doing nothing but photocopying would be a waste of time.

Research experience is, above all, an opportunity to learn. Volunteer to be trained to be of more use. For example, learn the computer skills to input data or word process. Learn to score and, more importantly, to *understand* a Minnesota Multiphasic Personality Inventory-2 (MMPI-2) or a Beck Depression Inventory (BDI). Learn how to calibrate and run psychophysiological equipment. Whatever equipment or tests there are in the lab, find out about them and their use. And always ask questions about what you do not understand. When it comes time to put your research on your curriculum vitae, these are the responsibilities you will want to list.

Some researchers have a weekly lab group or research meeting with graduate students, undergraduates, or both. These might entail a discussion of the project at hand, or a presentation on another area within the field, or a training session for new people. In any of these cases, it is an opportunity to learn more about your area of interest. If you have not been invited to these meetings, go ahead and ask about them. Optimize your contact with your professor! Convey your willingness and enthusiasm. Give your professor reason to write an outstanding letter of recommendation.

Finally, there are some instances where undergraduates are solely supervised by graduate students and have no contact with the professor in charge of the project. This can happen if faculty members have a large number of students working with them or if they are well known and are continually approached by masses of students. Being supervised exclusively by a graduate student is an undesirable situation for a potential applicant. Although there is much to be learned from graduate students—and they are fresh from the application process themselves—a letter of recommendation from a graduate student does not carry the same weight as one from a professor. Moreover, a lack of interaction with the professor means that he or she must depend solely on graduate students for feedback as to your work, thus detracting from the value of his or her assessment.

This is *not* to say that you must avoid research opportunities that are primarily supervised by graduate students. Personal access to the faculty member is, however, one of several important factors to be considered in your decision on where to volunteer for research experience.

Arranging Credit and Semesters

Most schools allow students to take a certain amount of research for academic credit. If the opportunity is available, take advantage of it. Some professors may even demand that you sign up for credit, because it institutes a contract between them and you as to the number of hours per week required and how long they can count on you to work with them. Generally speaking, multiply the number of course credits by 3, and this will give you the number of weekly hours that you should anticipate spending doing research.

Expect to spend at least two semesters on a project. This demonstrates your commitment and allows ample contact between you and your professor. Thus, it is a good idea to work with someone at least 1 year before you plan to apply to graduate school. For instance, begin research in fall 2002 if you are applying in fall 2003 for a fall 2004 entrance to graduate school.

In terms of research, there is no such thing as too much for a Ph.D. applicant. The longer you have worked on a project and the greater your responsibilities, the more attractive you are as an applicant. Ideally, you would work with two professors over the course of your undergraduate education. This is not necessary, but when schools expect three letters of recommendation, having two letters reporting on two different research experiences is particularly strong. Although they will allocate less attention to research than Ph.D. applicants, Psy.D. applicants are reminded that research is still an important admission criterion.

One word of caution: Do not overextend yourself. Be realistic about the amount of time you can commit. Some students try to juggle two or three research projects at once and end up performing poorly on them all. It is far more important to concentrate your energies and perform solidly on one project than it is to spread yourself too thin. Do as much research as your studies and other commitments allow.

An ideal time to begin research is during the summer, when you can balance it with a part- or full-time job. Since most undergraduates and some graduate students leave during the summer, professors may be short-staffed during this period. It is a good opportunity to optimize your usefulness at the outset and increase your chances of picking up desirable skills.

The net result of your research experiences will be skill enhancement and professional identification. Depending on the nature of your project, you will probably have engaged in a literature search, hypothesis generation, experimental design, data collection, statistical analyses, and the write-up.

Presenting and Publishing Research

Presenting or publishing your research is a definite asset. Opportunities for presentation are numerous: a department or university colloquium, a local or regional undergraduate psychology conference, a state or national psychology convention. Participation in student research conferences is viewed favorably as an index of your professional identification and commitment. Check with your advisor about these opportunities and other possibilities for your work to be seen by colleagues.

Publication of your research in a scholarly journal is held in very high regard by graduate admissions committees. As we discuss in Chapter 6, research experience leading to a coauthored publication is the most highly rated final selection criterion for Ph.D. (though not necessarily Psy.D.) admission decisions following the interview. The peer-review process by which journals accept papers for publication gives a seal of collegial affirmation that the research contributes to the scientific understanding of behavior. Although not common, undergraduate publication is slowly becoming more frequent.

If your research project is not quite up to the standards of a competitive, peer-reviewed journal, then by all means consider sending the paper to a journal publishing student research in psychology. One such publication is the *Psi Chi Journal of Undergraduate Research*, which has the twofold purpose of fostering the scholarly efforts of undergraduate psychology students and of providing them with a valuable learning experience. Other publications of student research in psychology are *Modern Psychological Studies*, *Journal of Psychology and Behavioral Sciences*, *Journal of Psychological Inquiry*, and the electronic journal *Der Zeitgeist: The Student Journal of Psychology*. All these journals publish research in psychology conducted and written by students. Look for their instructions to authors on the Web (www. Lemoyne.edu/OTRP/otpresources), on departmental bulletin boards, or in *Eye on Psi Chi* (the national newsletter of Psi Chi).

Of course, though submission to these journals can be instructive, publishing in them does not carry as much weight as publication in established peer-reviewed journals. In fact, recent research suggests that a student publication in an undergraduate journal may be judged neutral or even unfavorably by research-oriented professors in a doctoral programs (Ferrari & Davis, 2001). So, always aim to publish your research in peer-reviewed, scholarly journals.

Still impressive is a paper presentation at a state, regional, or national meeting. Only between 10% and 20% of undergraduate psychology majors present their research at some type of research conference, whether local, regional, or national (Terry, 1996; Titus & Buxman, 1999).

Most regional and national meetings are listed in each issue of the *American Psychologist*, *APS Observer*, and *Eye on Psi Chi*. These meetings are also listed on the Psi Chi Web site. Psi Chi members who present papers can receive a certificate recognizing their excellence in research. This award should be duly noted on your curriculum vitae and application. Refer to *Eye on Psi Chi,* ask your local Psi Chi moderator, write to the Psi Chi National Office (825 Vine Street, P.O. Box 709, Chattanooga, TN 37403) or consult their Web site at www.psichi.org to receive the form entitled "Certificate Recognition Program for Paper Presentations by Psi Chi Members."

Different graduate programs will assess your research experience in different ways, of course. Nonetheless, as an aid to applicants, we reproduce below (with permission) two rating scales employed at different times by one clinical program (University of Rhode Island) over the past 10 years. The first rating scale emphasizes research activity. Examples of relevant activities might include producing honors theses, serving as a research assistant, conducting independent research, coauthoring scientific publications, and developing significant skills relevant to research, such as data analysis and interviewing.

Rating	Criteria
5	Senior author of one or more articles in significant journals in addition to experience that provided a basis for extensive mastery of one or more directly related research skills.
4	Coauthor of one or more articles in significant journals in addition to experiences providing considerable familiarity with one or more directly relevant research skills.
3	Project leadership or significant participation in research activity (beyond activities connected with course work) serving to provide for considerable development of

mastery of one or more relevant research skills.

2	Experience that provides a basis for some familiarity with relevant research skills.
1	Little if any experience according to these criteria.

The second rating scale, now in use at the University of Rhode Island, favors four criteria in evaluating research experience.

1. *Demonstrated research productivity*: sole or coauthorship of research publications, presentation of papers at scientific meetings, other tangible indications of research achievement.
2. *Breadth and quality of experience*: development of one or more research skills, data collection with different populations, work on more than one project.
3. *Research interest*: the strength of interest in research can be inferred from research activity over a sustained period of time and recommendations from research supervisors documenting skills, motivation, participation, and accomplishments.
4. *Individual autonomy*: responsibility for planning, implementing and carrying out research tasks as a member of a research team or evidence of independent work.

Rankings are based on the aforementioned criteria and assigned as follows:

Rating	Criteria
5	Satisfies all four criteria
4	Satisfies three criteria
3	Satisfies two criteria
2	Satisfies one criterion
1	Evidence of some prior research involvement or interest

Research is an area of your application that will be considered important and, at most Ph.D. programs, weighted heavily. Balance is the key. On the one hand, an absence of research experience is usually seen as a serious drawback to an application. On the other hand, over committing yourself to multiple projects at one time can lead to poor performance and a neglect of clinical experience and GRE preparation. And do not forget, research also provides you with the opportunity to make professional contacts. The professors or graduate students with whom you collaborate are excellent sources of information about the field and about applying to graduate schools.

Entrance Examinations

About 90% of doctoral clinical psychology programs (Mayne et al., 1994; Steinpreis, Queen, & Tennen, 1992) and 80% of doctoral counseling psychology programs (Turkson & Norcross, 1996) require you to complete two exams: the Graduate Record Examination (GRE) General Test and the GRE Psychology Subject Test. The two GRE tests are often used to complement each other in admission decisions because the General Test is a measure of developed abilities and the Subject Test is an index of achievement in a specific field of study. The Miller Analogies Test (MAT) is required by fewer programs, about 3% of doctoral programs and 12% of master's programs in psychology (Murray & Williams, 1999).

Blanket statements about testing are difficult because not all schools require all tests, and some schools require additional testing (e.g., in the past the University of Minnesota required clinical psychology applicants to take the MMPI—a personality inventory!). Moreover, not all schools weigh these tests equally among the application criteria. Some schools clearly state a minimum score that all applicants must obtain, whereas others state that they have no such criteria. Interestingly, a study at Boston University (Rem, Oren, & Childrey, 1987) showed that even without an imposed cutoff, applicants admitted into its program had GRE scores of 600 or better. This suggests that even if a school does not emphasize standardized test scores, (1) scores can still play a major role in the selection of candidates, or (2) applicants with high exam scores are also the applicants considered most desirable on the other admissions criteria.

Consequently, the best assistance that can be offered is a brief description of each test, an overview of minimum preferred and actual GRE scores of incoming graduate students, guidelines for deciding how much preparation will be needed, and some suggestions as to the available study aids for each test.

GRE General Test

Use of GRE scores for admission to clinical and counseling psychology programs continues to be the norm and continues to be controversial (Dollinger, 1989; Ingram, 1983; Sternberg, 1997). The traditional rationale—buttressed by some evidence—is that the GRE is ordinarily more valid than undergraduate GPA in predicting graduate school success (Boudreau et al., 1983; Goldberg & Alliger, 1992). Another rationale is that GRE performance is an "equalizer" among the diverse curriculum requirements and grading practices in thousands of undergraduate institutions. The entrance exam is probably the only standardized measure of all applicants that an admissions committee has. Does a 3.7 GPA and stellar letters of recommendation from Backward College reflect more, the same, or less knowledge and skill than a 3.3 GPA and strong letters of recommendation from Ivy League University? Since all students take the identical GRE test, the playing field is somewhat leveled.

The empirical research indicates that the GRE Genderal Test has modest predictive validity for graduate school performance. In a meta-analysis of studies conducted in psychology and counseling departments, Goldberg and Alliger (1992) found that GRE scores predicted about 8% of the variance in graduate school GPA. In a later meta-analysis of two dozen studies encompassing more than 5,000 test takers over the past 30 years, Morrison and Morrison (1995) similarly found that 6% of the variance in graduate-level academic achievement, as represented by graduate GPA, was accounted for by GRE scores. These and other studies (e.g., Chernyshenko & Ones, 1999; Kuncel, Hezlett, & Ones, 2001) indicate that GRE General Test scores are generalizably valid in a modest way for all sorts of measures of graduate performance, especially when selection/admission ratios are taken into account. At the same time, Subject Test scores tend to be better predictors than the General Test scores (Kuncel et al., 2001).

The Educational Testing Service (ETS), located in Princeton, New Jersey, provides a free booklet entitled *GRE Information & Registration Bulletin* (Graduate Record Examinations, 2001) which describes the test and offers examples of the types of questions you can expect to encounter on each section. You can obtain the same information and register for the test by visiting GRE online at http://www.gre.org. In addition, at this Web site you can order (with a credit card) ETS test preparation books and download preparation software directly onto your home computer.

The test is very similar in format to the Scholastic Aptitude Test (SAT) that most of you took prior to college. The three subscales on the GRE General (or aptitude) Test are Verbal, Quantitative, and Analytical. Each scale yields a separate score with a mean of 500 and a standard deviation of 100, with an 800 maximum. All items are multiple-choice in format, and scores on the test are based on the number of correct answer choices selected. Of the three reported subscores, most graduate schools use the Verbal and Quantitative scores in evaluating candidates.

The GRE General Test is now available only on computer; the traditional paper-and-pencil version was phased out in 1999. This computer-based test contains one 30-minute Verbal section, one 45-minute Quantitative section, and one 60-minute Analytical section. In addition, a pretest section or research section may be included, but answers to these sections do not count toward your score. All told, you will probably spend about 4 hours at the testing center.

The GRE registration booklet and the free tutorial software (POWER PREP, available at www.ets/org/cbtdemo.html) will familiarize you with the computer-based adaptive format of the test. Briefly put, adaptive testing means that your responses to the early items determine the difficulty level of subsequent items and your range of possible scores. As you answer each question, the computer immediately scores that question and your preceding answers to determine which question is presented next. Correct answers lead to increasingly difficult items (and eventually higher test scores); incorrect answers lead to less difficult items (and lower test scores). As a consequence, you may not skip any questions and you may not go back and change a previous answer. An equally important consequence is that you should be very familiar with the test format and computer functions before test day!

In deciding how much and what type of preparation you will need for this test, ask yourself several questions you should ask yourself:

1. What were my SAT scores? These two tests are highly correlated in a positive direction, so this may be your first clue as to how much work is ahead of you.
2. How well have I done on multiple-choice tests in college? There is a certain savvy to taking standardized tests, and this is one way to assess yours.
3. How anxious do I become in a testing situation? A moderate amount of test anxiety is optimal: Too little anxiety can breed indifference, but too much begets interference. If you tend to approach tests with more than moderate discomfort, you might benefit from additional preparation aimed at relaxing yourself and building your confidence.
4. Can I discipline myself to do the necessary studying? If you are in need of additional preparation, this question is important in deciding what the most appropriate form of preparation will be for you. Be honest with yourself. If you cannot imagine sitting down regularly and studying independently for the GREs, you might be better off taking a preparatory course offered privately in most cities.

Students typically spend an inordinate amount of time worrying about the GREs. The myth exists that clinical applicants need 650 on each of their subtests to be considered seriously. This is simply not the case.

TABLE 2-4. Minimum GRE Scores Preferred by APA-Accredited Clinical Psychology Programs

	Psy.D. programs		Practice-oriented Ph.D.		Equal-emphasis Ph.D.		Research-oriented Ph.D.		All programs	
Preferred minimum score	*M*	*SD*	*M*	*SD*	*M*	*SD*	*M*	*SD*	*M*	*SD*
Quantitative scale	544	46	566	58	580	44	598	36	581	46
Verbal scale	533	50	566	58	583	46	598	36	580	48
Analytical scale	520	27	567	58	583	32	606	44	579	46
Psychology subject test	542	49	601	17	581	48	605	43	587	47

Note. Adapted from "Admission requirements, acceptance rates, and financial assistance in clinical psychology programs: Diversity across the practice–research continuum" by T. J. Mayne, J. C. Norcross, & M. A. Sayette, 1994, *American Psychologist, 49,* 605–611.

Some practice-oriented programs do not even require the GREs. On the other hand, many APA-approved programs prefer GREs of 600 or above. The average GRE score (combined Verbal and Quantitative) of first-year graduate students in psychology master's programs is 1033; in doctoral psychology programs, 1206 (Norcross et al., 1996).

However, even these averages mask considerable variation in preferred minimum GRE scores. In our study of the admission statistics of APA-accredited clinical doctoral programs (Mayne et al., 1994), we found that the preferred minimum scores differed consistently according to the type of program. As shown in Table 2-4, research-oriented clinical Ph.D. programs preferred the highest GRE minimum scores—about 600 each for the Quantitative, Verbal, and Analytical scales. Psy.D. programs were willing to accept lower (but still not low) minimum GRE scores—about 520 to 540 each on the three scales. In between these two poles is the remainder of clinical and counseling psychology doctoral programs, which expect a minimum score of 550 to 560 on each of the scales, on average (Turkson & Norcross, 1996).

Even if your scores are lower than 550, you can bolster other areas of your application to overcome low scores. But if your GREs are below 500, then most doctoral programs in clinical and counseling psychology will not seriously consider your application. In this case, it will probably be necessary to take them again after taking a preparatory course or after spending time with a study guide.

But here overconfidence can be disastrous. Even if you obtained 700 SATs, aced every multiple-choice exam in college, and are cool-headed in testing situations, you should still familiarize yourself with the test format and complete the practice test offered in the application booklet. It certainly would not hurt to prepare more, but this should be considered the bare minimum. However, most people are likely to fall somewhat short of this ideal and will need some sort of study aid to realize their full GRE potential.

There are many self-study manuals and software packages available at major book stores that may be sufficient for a disciplined applicant to ready him- or herself for the test. The books provide helpful test-taking hints, vocabulary and math reviews, and sample tests that the student can self-administer. Many even include actual questions given on past GREs that can provide a real flavor for the material likely to be seen on testing day. The software packages administer sample tests and give helpful hints. Sample questions, practice manuals, and downloadable practice software packages can also be found and ordered on the GRE Web site at http://www.gre.org. If you study using a manual, marking the answers you miss on the practice tests and readministering those questions until you can do them quickly can also be a good drill for bolstering your weak points. Lastly, give yourself *at least* 6 weeks of study time if you decide to use a manual or 8 weeks if you do not have a lot of time to devote solely to studying.

Students feeling less confident, more anxious, or "out of the exam business" should contemplate private courses designed to help you prepare for the GRE. They offer a number of benefits beyond those of study guides:

- A structured time one or more times a week when the material is taught by an impartial instructor who can assess the student's strengths and weaknesses.
- An abundance of study materials and the possibility of individual tutoring.
- The chance to take tests under actual test-taking conditions (especially helpful for those with test anxiety).

TABLE 2-5. Comparison of the GRE General Test and the GRE Psychology Subject Test

	General test	Subject test
Content assessed	Broad knowledge	Specific knowledge in psychology
Test format	Computer	Paper-and-pencil
Administration schedule	Throughout the year	Three times per year (Nov., Dec., & Apr.)
Recommended test date	Summer of junior year Early Fall of senior year	November (Ph.D./Psy.D.) Fall of senior year December (master's)
Administration format	Individual	Group
Test cost (2001–2002)	$105	$130
Repeat policy	May repeat test once per calendar month	May repeat test as often as it is offered up to 5 times per year
Testing time	2 hours, 45 minutes (includes a 10-minute break)	2 hours, 50 minutes (no break)
Scoring procedure	Adaptive: your early responses determine difficulty level of subsequent questions	Total items answered correctly minus one-fourth the the number answered incorrectly
Skipping questions	Not permitted; computer administers one question at a time	Permitted
Scores provided	3 scores (Verbal, Quantitative, & Analytical)	1 total score, 2 subscores
Scores range	200–800	200–990
Score mean (*SD*)	500 (100)	540 (100)
Recommended preparation	Intense	Moderate

- Specific work on test-taking skills and the short-cuts that can make problems easier.
- Brief introduction to relaxation exercises to counter test anxiety.

The imposed structure on studying and the conscious use of test-taking skills can be very useful. Although these classes cannot guarantee that they will improve your scores, they are undoubtedly the best course of action for some students. Having worked for one of these agencies, we have seen the benefits of this system for many students.

Many students attempt to strengthen their vocabulary for the GRE Verbal section by preparing flashcards or memorizing a vocabulary word each day. The early research on the word-a-day method suggests it can slightly enrich your vocabulary (Prevoznak & Bubka, 1999), but more importantly, it gets you into the swing of GRE preparation and the admissions process. If you are inclined to try this method, consider receiving a word a day from the Web site, www.wordsmith.org, which presents a word with its pronunciation and examples. It requires only a couple of minutes per day.

Scheduling *when* to take your general GRE should be carefully considered. If you do poorly on the test, you can retake it. Consequently, it is precautionary to take it at least 6 months before the application deadline, which gives you time to study and prepare for a second administration. For undergraduates planning to apply to graduate school during their senior year, this means taking it during the summer following your junior year or early fall of the senior year. For graduates, this means taking it the spring before you plan to apply. Even if you improve your scores, the current ETS policy is to send to each institution scores from *all* your tests taken during the last 5 years.

We are frequently asked by students in our graduate school workshops if they should retake the GRE General Test if they are dissatisfied with their original scores. Our immediate answer is: it depends. If you studied diligently for the test and if you performed on the test similar to the practice tests, then no—do not retake the test. But if any of the following 5 factors apply to you, then retaking the test once seems like a good idea (Keith-Spiegel & Wiederman, 2000): (1) You were ill the day you took the GRE; (2) you were immobilized by test anxiety; (3) you did not prepare for the test content; (4) you were unfamiliar with the computer-based format and the adaptive design; (5) your SAT scores were much higher than your GRE scores.

Your GRE score can partially determine where to apply. Low scores suggest applying only to institutions whose cutoffs you meet. In this way, your GREs can help you make realistic decisions as to your chances of being accepted at a given school and ultimately whether or not to apply there.

GRE Psychology Subject Test

The General Test measures knowledge acquired over a long period of time and not indigenous to any specific field of study. By contrast, the Subject Tests—like the Psychology Subject Test—assume an undergraduate major or extensive background in the specific subject. Consequently, the test may be relatively difficult if you were not an undergraduate psychology major.

Another difference between the General Test and the Subject Test lies in the mode of administration. The General Test is a computer-based test available year-round at over 400 test centers. The Subject Test, by contrast, continues to be a paper-based test offered three times during the academic year.

Table 2-5 summarizes the differences between the GRE General Test and the GRE Subject Test. These profound test differences will lead to different preparation and test-taking strategies on your part.

The GRE Psychology Test consists of about 215 multiple-choice questions. Each item has five options, from which you select the correct or best response. The total time allotted for the test is 2 hours and 50 minutes.

The GRE Psychology Test yields a total score and two subscores. Virtually all programs, however, concentrate on the total score, not on the subscores. The preferred minimum score is 587 for clinical psychology doctoral programs and 541 for counseling psychology doctoral programs (Mayne et al., 1994; Turkson & Norcross, 1996). That is, most programs will be expecting you to secure a score at or above this number. But here again, as shown in Table 2-4, the preferred minimum ranges from a low of 542 in Psy.D. programs to a high of 605 in research-oriented Ph.D. programs.

The two subscales are an Experimental or natural science orientation and a Social or social science orientation. The Experimental subscore covers questions in learning, cognition, perception, comparative psychology, sensation, and physiological psychology. The Social subscore includes an equal number of questions in personality, clinical, abnormal, developmental, and social psychology. The questions assess knowledge of theory and the ability to identify the psychologists associated with those theories, the ability to draw conclusions from experimental data, and the capacity to evaluate research designs.

Percentages of questions devoted to a subject area will vary somewhat from one test administration to another. Nonetheless, one set of investigators (Waters, Drew, & Ayers, 1988) found these approximate percentages on past tests:

Physiological/comparative psychology	14%
Developmental psychology	12%
Learning and motivation	12%
Sensation and perception	12%
Clinical/abnormal psychology	11%
Personality and social psychology	11%
Cognition and complex human learning	10%
Applied psychology	9%
Research methodology	9%

Scores on the GRE Psychology (or Advanced) Test are best predicted by your GRE General Test scores and the number of basic psychology courses completed. The irony is that students can obtain excellent grades in all their psychology courses but still not perform adequately on the Psychology Test if they have not taken the critical courses. A narrow focus on—and many courses in—clinical psychology will probably detract from your score since this one area only accounts for 10 to 12% of the test items. The questions are drawn from courses most commonly offered at the undergraduate level within psychology (ETS, 1995).

A maximum number of "traditional" courses in psychology, as represented in the foregoing list, and a minimum of special topics and "pop" psychology will prepare you best for the GRE Psychology Subject Test. Choose your elective courses for breadth and rigor, not merely your specialized interest.

The GRE Psychology Subject Test is designed to be challenging. Students accustomed to getting 90% correct on in-class exams often worry about the large number of items they miss. The average student answers about half the items correctly, misses about 30%, and omits 20% (Kalat & Matlin, 2000). Because your score is based on the number of questions answered correctly minus one-fourth of the questions answered incorrectly, guessing does *not* lower your score. You are not penalized for guessing; but you are rewarded for eliminating one or two possible answers.

Adequate preparation is essential for this test. We—and others—suggest three steps: (1) obtain the free ETS booklet *A Description of the Advanced Psychology Test;* (2) read a good introductory psychology textbook; and (3) purchase one of the study guides with practice tests. Our favorite study guides are *Practicing to Take the GRE Psychology Test* (published by the GRE board, which can be ordered at the ETS Web site), *Graduate Record Examination—Psychology* (Raphael & Halpert, 1999; published by Prentice-Hall), *Best Preparation for the GRE in Psychology* (Kellogg, 2000; published by Research & Education Association), and *Cracking the GRE Psychology* (Jay, 1999; published by Princeton Review). If these three steps do not suffice, then private courses in preparing for the psychology test are available.

The standard error of measurement for the GRE is quite small, and retaking the General Test in the absence of any *intense* remediation is unlikely to result in a significant change in your score. Your Psychology Test scores, however, may be significantly different if intervening study or additional courses occur between the test sessions.

A graduate school may adopt one or more policies in handling cases in which a candidate reports two sets of GRE scores: Consider only the most recent one; consider the higher of the two scores; or average the scores. The latter is probably the best alternative, since it creates the least bias and is the most reliable.

GRE Writing Assessment

A new GRE Writing Assessment was introduced in October 1999. It is offered independently of the GRE General Test and the GRE Subject Tests. The assessment consists of two analytical writing essays: a 45-minute "Present Your Perspective on an Issue" essay and a 30-minute "Analyze an Argument" essay. Each essay is scored on a 6-point holistic scale by two college faculty members. Your score represents the average of your scores for the two essays. The scores are not available at the test center; rather, they are mailed to you within 15 days of the test.

Since the Writing Assessment has just recently become available, it is too early to know how many graduate programs will eventually require it. At this time, carefully check the application requirements for each program.

Miller Analogies Test

A few clinical and counseling psychology doctoral programs request the MAT, a 50-minute test consisting of 100 word analogies. Your score is the total number correct; the mean for students intending to study psychology in graduate school is 50 to 51 (The Psychological Corporation, 1994). As with the GREs, booklets are available to help improve your scores on the test, and it is useful to take practice tests to familiarize and prepare yourself for the actual event. There are states in which the MAT cannot be administered (e.g., New York) because of test disclosure laws enacted in those states, so be sure to locate the testing center nearest you.

The MATs are less frequently required by graduate schools than either of the GRE tests. Because the tests can be scheduled at any time, through a network of over 600 testing centers nationwide, you might consider taking this test after you have received your GRE scores and after you have selected the schools you would like to apply to. You may save yourself some time and money if none of the schools that interest you require the test.

Part of the expense of applying to graduate school is the cost of sending test scores. One possible way to reduce costs is to make copies of the test results sent to you and mail them with your application. Any school that is interested in you will request that you have the scores "officially" sent to them. Any school not interested will not need your official scores, and you will have saved the expense of having them forwarded.

Two words of caution must accompany this possibility. First, only do this if you send in your application early. Unless you check with a school before the application deadline to make sure that this procedure will not exclude you as an applicant, you should not send copies. Second, some students send copies of test scores after altering the original document, for example, whiting out poor scores or past scores, putting scores in different columns, and even falsifying scores. *You must never resort to these practices!* These should immediately invalidate your application, and any school that accepts you will need official copies sent anyway. Saving money should not interfere with the processing of your application.

Finally, low scores on entrance exams do not automatically preclude you from applying to clinical or counseling psychology graduate programs. Rather, low scores mean you must select and apply to programs that do not emphasize test scores or that accept scores in your range. You can partially compensate in other areas to help offset weak tests. As with each admission criterion, standardized test scores are only one part of the overall picture of a candidate. The best anyone can do is to make his or her overall application as attractive as possible.

Extracurricular Activities

Empirical research and personal experience alike indicate that an applicant's extracurricular pursuits are accorded less weight than GPAs, GRE scores, research competency, and clinical experience. The research reviewed earlier in this chapter clearly bears this point out. However, extracurricular activities, such as Psi Chi membership and campus involvement, are still considered in evaluating the "total person" of the applicant.

The admission implications are thus proscriptive and prescriptive. Strictly in terms of enhancing your candidacy (not in terms of other goals, such as life satisfaction), you should favor good grades and research experience over extracurricular activities. Involvement in dozens of student organizations will not compensate for meager grades and research. When confronted with time conflicts, recall that admissions committees place a premium on variables other than intense campus commitments.

Having stated the obvious but unpleasant facts, we would also urge you to routinely engage in *some* campus and community pursuits. The reasoning here is that clinical and counseling psychology programs seek well-rounded individuals with diverse interests. The "egghead" or "Mr. Peabody" image is to be avoided in the practice of psychology, where your interpersonal skills are as critical as your scientific preparation. Moderate involvement can also better acquaint you with faculty members, who may serve as sources of recommendations, and with the discipline of psychology itself. You can create professional opportunities by simply being involved in departmental activities. "Familiar faces" are frequently given first shots at clinical or research opportunities.

Applicants frequently learn too late that active involvement outside of the classroom is an indispensable education in and of itself. Consider the following student qualities contained in many standard letter of recommendation forms:

- Academic performance
- Organizational skills
- Interest/enthusiasm
- Interpersonal skills
- Emotional stability
- Communication skills
- Originality/resourcefulness
- Social judgment
- Responsibility/dependability
- Stress tolerance

Most of these dimensions refer to faculty–student interactions *outside* of the classroom, not to your course grades. Many a bright student has sabotaged his or her educational experience, recommendation letters, and career goal by not becoming involved outside of the classroom.

In your extracurricular activities, try to exhibit the chief personality trait which, interacting with intelligence, relates most to vocational success—namely, conscientiousness (Jensen, 1998). Be responsible, dependable, organized, and persistent. This trait applies to every kind of educational and job success; what's more, you want colleagues and friends to document in their letters of recommendation that you are extraordinarily conscientious.

Four specific suggestions come to mind regarding the type of extracurricular activities to pursue. First, join departmental student organizations, such as the Psychology Club, Psi Chi, and the American Psychological Society's Student Caucus. Second, we heartily recommend that you join the American Psychological Association (APA) and/or the American Psychological Society (APS) as a student affiliate. Your APA affiliation brings with it monthly issues of the *American Psychologist*, the flagship journal, and the *APA Monitor*, the association's newspaper. Similarly, APS membership includes subscriptions to the monthly journal *Psychological Science* and the *APS Observer*. Student membership in professional associations reflects favorably on your commitment to the discipline, and this affiliation should be recorded on your curriculum vitae. Your psychology advisor will probably have applications for student affiliation in his or her office; if not, write directly for them (APA Membership Department, 750 First Street, NE, Washington, DC, 20002-4242; APS, 1010 Vermont Avenue, NW, Suite 1100, Washington, DC 20005-4907).

Third, additional campus and community commitments should be guided by your interests. But those associated with human services, social causes, and artistic endeavors seem to be differentially rewarded. These will obviously vary with the locale; examples include Hand-in-Hand, campus ministries, course tutoring, peer advising, homeless shelters, women's centers, BACHUSS, SADD, theater productions, creative writing, Amnesty International, and the like.

A fourth and invaluable extracurricular experience is to attend a regional or national psychology convention. The benefits are many: socializing you into the profession; learning about current research; discovering how students and professors present research; meeting and hearing nationally known psychologists; adding to your growing professional network; attending and perhaps participating in sessions designed for prospective graduate students (e.g., the Psi Chi sessions and workshops); experiencing the intellectual stimulation; and enjoying the interpersonal camaraderie of fellow students and psychologists (Lubin, 1993; Tryon, 1985). For all these reasons, we have never—and we mean *never*—heard a single graduate school applicant express disappointment about attending his or her first psychology convention.

The challenge for most prospective psychologists is to locate and afford travel to one of the regional or national psychology conferences. To locate upcoming conferences in your area, ask your psychology professors, consult the lists regularly published in *Eye on Psi Chi* and *American Psychologist*, and keep an eye open for announcements and posters on departmental bulletin boards. "Convention season" in psychology is from March to May, when the regional psychological associations hold their annual conventions. These include the Eastern Psychological Association, Midwestern Psychological Association, Rocky Mountain Psychological Association, Western Psychological Association, and Southeastern Psychological Association. To afford the travel and lodging, consider organizing a convention trip with your fellow students, requesting information on special hotel and registration rates for students, volunteering as a convention assistant, and holding fund-raisers with psychology student organizations to offset your expenses. By hook or crook, definitely plan on expanding your extracurricular horizons by attending a psychology convention.

Finally, extracurricular activities should reflect your active and passionate pursuit of excellence. This is, after all, your chosen profession, your career, your future. Join honor societies, compete for awards, pursue honors, and consider applications for Truman, Rhodes, and Fulbright scholarships. You should be actively investigating undergraduate grants for your research, such as those administered nationally by Psi Chi or those awarded locally in your university. Passivity doesn't cut it in graduate school (or life).

In this chapter, we described five admission criteria—course work, clinical experience, research skills, entrance examinations, and extracurricular activities—and suggested ways to improve in these areas. The material covered in this chapter is concerned with how you as the applicant can improve your credentials or marketability. But the application process goes both ways. In addition to selling yourself, you are also a consumer, evaluating the programs and deciding which ones are for you. The next two chapters help you evaluate characteristics of graduate programs.

CHAPTER 3

GETTING STARTED

Up to this point, we have focused on what can be done to enhance your credentials before beginning the application process. At some point, you must take realistic stock and evaluate where you stand as an applicant. Maybe you have taken your GREs. Perhaps you have signed up for some advanced psychology courses and have a satisfactory GPA. You are or have been supervised in a clinical setting and have begun research. You have reviewed your credentials and found that you have many strengths but also some weaknesses. You either shore up the deficient areas or make a decision to go ahead with what you have and hope to sell it well. In other words, you are ready to get started with the application process.

Process is an appropriate word to describe the endeavor that you are about to begin. The way you approach this task will greatly influence your chances of gaining admission. Sure, you can simply complete an application and passively wait for an interview. And this may work if your credentials are extremely strong. But for most individuals, an informed approach to the process can make all the difference!

Prospective graduate students frequently become nervous about the application process for several reasons. Perhaps the following remarks sound familiar: "Well, I have good recommendations and a 3.2 GPA, but my GREs are low"; "I have good GREs and spent a year working on a suicide hot line, but I don't have a lot of research experience"; "Although my credentials are excellent, all the schools that I applied to only accept eight out of 300 applicants." Whichever of these situations applies, simply submitting an application minimizes your chances of acceptance. There is a great deal you can do to increase your admission probabilities and to decrease your anxiety as you compare yourself to exaggerated standards.

Common Misconceptions

We would like to begin by dispelling four common misconceptions about clinical and counseling psychology programs. The first misconception: There is a direct correlation between a university's undergraduate reputation and the status of its psychology graduate programs. In fact, there is no such correlation. Many of the best undergraduate institutions—Harvard, Princeton, and the elite liberal arts colleges, for example—do not even have graduate studies in clinical or counseling psychology.

A second misconception is that you should apply to a graduate psychology program on the basis of that institution's sports performance. We have met a number of students who have used this selection criterion with unfortunate consequences. Please do not allow your application decisions to rest on whether a school has an excellent football team or whether their basketball team made it to the Final Four of the NCAA tournament! Do not scoff at the reality of this practice; careful research has demonstrated that winning a national championship in a visible college sport consistently translates into increased applications to the winning institution (Toma & Cross, 1998).

A third and pervasive myth about graduate psychology programs is that "hardly anyone gets in—only 10% of all the people who apply." Like most stereotypes, this one does have a grain of truth. The average acceptance rate for *all* APA-accredited doctoral programs in clinical and counseling psychology is, in fact, 10% (Mayne et al., 1994; Turkson & Norcross, 1996).

TABLE 3-1. Average Acceptance Rates for APA-Accredited Clinical Psychology Programs

	Psy.D. programs		Practice-oriented Ph.D.		Equal-emphasis Ph.D.		Research-oriented Ph.D.		All programs	
All programs	*M*	*SD*	*M*	*SD*	*M*	*SD*	*M*	*SD*	*M*	*SD*
Number of applications	192	112	204	111	240	114	244	93	233	107
Number of acceptances	42	36	20	13	21	22	13	7	20	21
% of applicants accepted	23	16	10	4	10	9	6	5	10	10

Note. Adapted from "Admission requirements, acceptance rates, and financial assistance in clinical psychology programs: Diversity across the practice–research continuum" by T. J. Mayne, J. C. Norcross, & M. A. Sayette, 1994, *American Psychologist, 49,* 605–611.

However, this single number is very misleading on several counts. First, the 10% figure applies only to APA-accredited doctoral programs in clinical and counseling psychology. The average acceptance rates are substantially higher for master's programs in clinical psychology (41%) and counseling psychology (53%; Kohout & Wicherski, 1993). Second, the percentage of applicants accepted varies tremendously from doctoral program to doctoral program. As noted in the reports on individual programs following Chapter 7, acceptance rates at freestanding professional schools can be as high as 50% and at research-oriented programs, such as Yale and Pennsylvania State, as low as 2%. This is not simply a matter of individual differences between programs. As summarized in Table 3-1, the percentage of applicants accepted tends to be a function of the type of program. Research-oriented Ph.D. programs accept only 6% of their applicants, on average, while the corresponding figure is 10% for programs that emphasize research and practice equally and for programs that emphasize practice. Psy.D. programs accept an average of 23% of their applicants. Third, the 10% average refers to acceptance rates for individual graduate programs, *not* the acceptance rate for the entire applicant pool in any given year. Although only 10% of applicants to a single doctoral program might be accepted to that *particular* program, about 35% to 45% of the entire applicant pool will be accepted to *some* clinical doctoral program (Korn, 1984). And half a chance isn't that bad.

A fourth common misconception is that there is an authoritative list of the finest graduate programs in clinical psychology. In reality, unlike business or law schools, there is no definitive ranking of the "best" psychology graduate programs. The quality of a program depends on what *you* are looking to get out of it. The best school for someone seeking to become a psychologist conducting psychoanalytic psychotherapy in private practice is probably not going to be the program of choice for someone who has set his or her heart on becoming a psychophysiological researcher at a medical school. Each person could attend the "best" school for psychology in his or her area.

What we want to do is to shift the burden from you trying to meet a school's admissions demands to you finding a school that meets *your* needs. Graduate schools are looking for students with direction and passion. This does not mean you have made an irrevocable commitment to an area of research or type of clinical work. It means that you have an idea of what type of professional work you would like to do and toward which theoretical orientation(s) you seem to be leaning. You are selecting an institution based on your belief that it will mold you in the direction *you* have chosen. Schools will look for this attitude in your statement of purpose. During your interviews, you will be asked about which professors you want to work with and what thoughts you have about their research projects. Even more likely, you will be directly asked, "Why are you applying here instead of someplace else?" By identifying your graduate training goals, you will impress interviewers at your selected programs with your direction and passion.

Costs of Applying

Applying to graduate school is an expensive proposition—not only in terms of your valuable time but also in terms of hard money. Application fees average $30 per doctoral program and $25 per master's program. Only 7% of graduate schools let you apply for free (Norcross et al., 1996). The fee (in 2001) for the GRE General Test is $105, with a $40 rescheduling fee, and the Psychology Subject Test costs another $130. ETS will send your GRE scores free of charge to five graduate schools that you designate in advance; however, each additional score report costs $13. Throw in the costs of transcripts, photocopying, postage, and the innumerable telephone calls, and the investment can become quite costly. All told, we estimate that applying to 12 schools will run about $1,000 (and that number can increase depending on the cost of traveling to multiple interviews).

The good news is that graduate schools are sensitive to financial hardship and that, for many students, the burdensome short-term cost is an excellent long-term investment. Schools build into the application process allowances for students who cannot afford the expense. Even the GRE has a fee waiver for students in dire financial circumstances. One of us was supporting himself on a meager social service salary and was able to keep the cost down to a few hundred dollars.

Moreover, think of the application cost as an investment in yourself and in your career. If you gain acceptance into a doctoral program with tuition remission and a stipend for 4 years, your $1,000 can be converted into a $60,000 to $100,000 payback over the course of your graduate school career.

The bottom line in getting started is this: anticipate the costs of applying to graduate school and plan to have the funds (or waivers) available before you begin completing the application forms.

Starting Early

Let's discuss timing up front. Applications are typically due from the last week in December to the second week in February. The sooner you begin preparing, the more advantage you can take of an aggressive, early start to the admission process. As mentioned in earlier chapters and in the Time Line (Appendix A), for undergraduates, ideally this would take place the summer of your junior year. For others, this would best occur the summer of the year before you actually plan to attend graduate school. If it is past that point, you are not too late. You can follow the steps we will describe as late as October of your application year.

Applying to graduate school is like planning a political campaign or a military operation. It is impossible to begin too soon or to be too thorough (Megargee, 1990). Recognize this about the application process and *start almost a year before you expect to begin graduate school.* Completing the application materials in the Fall semester alone will consume as much time as a 3-credit course!

Virtually all APA-accredited clinical and counseling psychology programs only accept matriculating students for their fall semesters. As mentioned earlier, in order to be accepted for the fall of 2003, most doctoral programs have application deadlines anywhere from late December 2002 to February 2003. The typical deadline for doctoral programs in clinical and counseling psychology is January 15 (Norcross et al., 1996). Accordingly, you will need college transcripts, test scores, and letters of recommendation, not to mention time to prepare yourself before the application deadline. You should expect to begin no later than the fall of the year before you intend to attend graduate school. If you are willing to put in the maximum effort to get into a program, expect to begin the spring before that.

The APA has accredited 202 doctoral programs in clinical psychology, 65 doctoral programs in counseling psychology, and 10 doctoral programs in combined professional-scientific psychology throughout the United States and Canada. Toss in non-accredited doctoral programs and the mass of master's programs in clinical and counseling psychology and you wind up with roughly 500 graduate programs (Norcross et al., 1996). How does one proceed in whittling this list to a manageable number?

To begin the selection process, ask yourself, "What kind of research or clinical work do I like? Is there some article I've read or presentation I've heard that really interests me?" There is a certain advantage if you have already conducted research or had some clinical experience as an undergraduate and know something about a field. And if you have completed an honors project or thesis, you may even have a certain amount of expertise. Or you may decide you would like to try something different now.

For example, suppose you have an interest in suicidology, but you are not exactly sure that you want to do research in that area or exactly what that research would entail. Or you think you'd like to specialize in suicide prevention, but you're not sure how psychologists deal with that issue clinically. There are several approaches you can take to familiarize yourself with this area. Ask one of your professors for some readings. Check out a current textbook in the area. Go to a suicide or crisis center and read through their literature. Then decide whether or not you like the questions being asked and the methods people are currently using to answer them.

In summary, have an idea of the field(s) in which you would like to work, either the ones with which you are already familiar or those you are willing to research. Familiarize yourself with the questions being asked and the techniques being used to answer them. Use as many sources as possible to gain information to help you narrow down your interests and educate yourself about them.

In addition to the resources in this book, a number of Internet resources will help you at this stage of the process. You can familiarize yourself with psychology graduate programs in the United States and Canada by accessing a large number of Web sites. Our favorites are:

- www.apa.org/students/ (APA's site for students includes a list of accredited programs, relevant articles, and other useful materials)
- www.wesleyan.edu/psyc/psyc260/ranking.htm (useful page features hyperlinks to 185 departments in the USA offering a Ph.D. in psychology)
- www.clas.ufl.edu/CLAS/american-universities.html#A (links for a a plethora of American universities)
- www.psychwww.com/resource/deptlist.htm (an impressive listing of over 1,000 psychology department Web sites)
- www.petersons.com/graduate/select/224010se.html (brief descriptions of programs offering graduate training in clinical psychology)
- www.petersons.com/graduate/select/224020se.html (as above, but for counseling psychology)
- www.gradschools.com/listings/menus/psych_clinic_menu.html and www.gradschools.com/listings/menus/psych_cmt_menu.html (for searching clinical and counseling psychology programs, respectively, with the added ability to search by geographic region)
- www.jobweb.org/catapult/gguides.htm (links to sites about applying to and financing graduate school, and about making the transition to grad school)

All these—and other—sites enable you to take a virtual tour of graduate programs in professional psychology. Develop an early feel for various departments and begin to sharpen your interests.

Next is the task of putting this knowledge to use. You have ideas that interest you, and you now need to learn which programs can provide these research or clinical opportunities. Though knowing how much you enjoy research or clinical work may not take a lot of reflection, deciding whether to select a research-oriented, a practice-oriented, or an equal-emphasis program is a question with far-reaching ramifications. This question tends to divide people into three groups: the research oriented (scientists); the clinically oriented (practitioners); and the dually committed (scientist–practitioners). The following sections are designed to lead each group in its appropriate direction. These groups tend to follow three rather distinctive career paths in the profession of clinical and counseling psychology (Bernstein & Kerr, 1993; Conway, 1988).

We have repeatedly surveyed the APA-accredited clinical and counseling psychology programs in the United States and Canada over the past 16 years. Their responses to our questionnaires (e.g., Farry et al., 1995; Mayne et al., 1994; Norcross et al., 1998; Turkson & Norcross, 1996; Sayette & Mayne, 1990; Sayette et al. 1999) can serve as the basis for your initial selection of schools. By using their responses, we will lead you through an exercise that will provide you with a list that ranks schools by how closely they meet your expectations and interests.

As you peruse the Reports on Individual Programs, bear in mind that the listings are alphabetical, not geographical. We list the programs alphabetically as they are on the APA (2000) materials, but sometimes the order is counterintuitive. For example, the University of Arkansas is not listed under "U," but between Arizona State University and Auburn University. Thus, you might need to look under two letters to identify specific programs of interest.

For the Research Oriented and Dually Committed

This section gives guidance to those applicants who are more centrally focused on research and those with equal clinical and research interest. We group these two sorts of applicants together because their initial selection of schools will place a bit more emphasis on the research available at each school and secondarily on the clinical work available. Given the materials provided, this will allow people with an equal emphasis to cast their nets as widely and as efficiently as possible.

The first question we asked of each program in our studies was "In which areas of research are your faculty presently working? Do they presently have a grant in that area?" Appendix E offers a list of all the research areas provided by these schools along with the number of faculty presently interested in these areas and an indication of whether they have a grant. This information provides you with an index of how intensively each program is pursuing this area of research. Thus, a program with three faculty members researching autism that has a grant supporting some of their work indicates serious involvement on the part of that faculty.

Find your areas of interest in the appendix; underneath them you will see a list of programs doing that type of research. In addition, you will know the number of professors with whom you could potentially work and whether there is any grant money supporting this research.

A few words of caution in interpreting this appendix: Not all schools were equally comprehensive in completing the survey. Some schools only included core faculty, whereas others included all adjunct faculty. This accounts for what seems to be an overrepresentation of some institutions in the list. Also, some schools had research interests combining two different areas and listed a single grant under both.

Appendix B, entitled "Worksheet for Choosing Schools," is used in the selection of the schools you will eventually apply to. Begin by writing your research interest in the far left-hand column. In the next column, marked "Schools," write the list of schools under that heading in Appendix B. In columns 3 and 4, write down the number of faculty in that area at each school and whether they are grant funded. In addition, some schools merely indicated the presence of grant funding and not the total number of grants. Thus, a "1" in the "Grants" column indicated *at least* one grant. A "0" indicates no grants, and numbers greater than 1 indicate multiple grants.

There are two worksheets provided in Appendix B, allowing you to explore different areas of interest. If you have more than two main areas of interest, unless they are closely related, you may find the list becoming exceptionally long. In this case, you may wish either to narrow your areas of interest or to complete this worksheet with the aid of a trusted professor who can help you pare down the list of schools to a more manageable number. If you have more than one area of interest, put stars next to the schools that have faculty doing research in both of them.

If your interests lean toward research, then you want to pick a school highly rated in the area of research you would like to pursue. How do you evaluate the clinical and counseling psychology programs on your list in terms of research? Refer to Table 3-2, which is adapted from the results of the *Social Sciences Citation Index* (SSCI) and *Science Citation Index* (SCI) databases. More than 225 psychology journals from 1986 through 1990 were analyzed to determine the institutions with the highest citation impact. The goal was to identify the institutions employing faculty members who authored the most frequently referenced articles in psychology journals. The table lists, in rank order, the highest citation impact institutions for psychology research. Citation impact is determined by the frequency with which articles written by members of a particular institution are cited, taking into account the total number of articles published by faculty from that institution. Only those institutions with an APA-accredited clinical or counseling program are included on this list. It should also be noted that the list only includes those institutions that produced at least 100 papers over the 5-year span; as a result, several smaller institutions with clinical or counseling psychology programs did not make the list. The University of New Hampshire and the University of Toledo, for instance, had high impact ratings but did not produce sufficient numbers of articles to be considered. This organization recently published an updated list covering the years 1990–1994 (Pendlebury, 1996). Because that listing only included the top 25 programs, we have retained the previous listing, which included 50 programs. Of note, the University of Denver (#2), the University of Rhode Island (#7), and the University of Waterloo (#21) were all included in this updated list. See Pendlebury (1996) for additional rankings of research productivity.

Using Table 3-2, write the citation impact ranking for each school in column 5, labeled "Citation Rank." Be advised that this ranking reflects the psychology department in general, not just the clinical or counseling program. In fact, about 25% of the institutions on the original list of 50 were deleted because they do not have clinical or counseling psychology programs. Inclusion of these nonclinical influences will affect the ranking of the schools you have selected. Still, this will provide you with a rough idea of where each school stands in terms of its research. Our position is that a school that makes it onto this list is probably a strong research-oriented institution. If the school fails to appear on the table, then it may or may not emphasize psychological research. Recognize that only about 20% of APA-accredited programs appear on this list.

Table 3-2 also contains a column headed "Faculty Production Rank." This number represents the rank ordering of APA-accredited clinical psychology programs on the basis of the total number of clinical faculty members trained by that program (Ilardi, Rodriguez-Hanley, Roberts, & Seigel, 2000). Any program that received a ranking of 60 or above has an established track record of producing clinical psychologists who, themselves, later assumed clinical psychology faculty positions. Remember that these lists heavily favor older programs and that no single measure can ever capture the excellence of graduate education. And, again, only about 20% of APA-accredited clinical programs appear on the list. Still, the list does direct students interested in academic careers to programs that have historically excelled in this domain.

As mentioned, any APA-accredited program must provide both clinical and research training. Thus, it is important also to evaluate the clinical opportunities available. As already mentioned, Psy.D. programs by definition emphasize practice and train students to be professional psychologists. Although it is possible to obtain excellent research training at a Psy.D. program, this is not the primary emphasis of such programs.

TABLE 3-2. Institutions with the Highest Citation Impact and Clinical Faculty Production in Psychology

Citation rank	Institution[a]	Citation impact	Faculty production rank
2	University of Vermont	5.16	—
6	University of Pennsylvania	4.70	29
8	Stanford University	4.62	—
9	University of Illinois	4.51	1
10	University of Pittsburgh	4.47	10
11	University of Oregon	4.43	26
13	Temple University	4.29	—
14	New York University	4.28	34.5
15	Northwestern University	4.27	48.5
16	University of California–Berkeley	4.22	34.5
17	Vanderbilt University	4.10	13.5
18	University of Michigan	4.09	3
21	University of Rochester	3.88	15.5
23	University of California–Los Angeles	3.84	9
24	Indiana University	3.83	7.5
25	University of Washington	3.70	13.5
29	Yale University	3.65	18.5
30	State University of New York at Stony Brook	3.58	2
32	University of Connecticut	3.44	29
33	University of Western Ontario	3.43	—
34	University of California–Santa Barbara	3.41	—
35	University of Kentucky	3.38	—
36	University of British Columbia	3.24	58
38	University of Virginia	3.23	—
39	Duke University	3.19	18.5
40	Columbia University	3.16	29
41	University of Minnesota	3.16	3
43	University of Massachusetts	3.13	42.5
44	Michigan State University	3.10	31.5
45	University of Utah	3.09	38
46	University of Colorado	3.07	53.5
47	University of Miami	3.06	58
48	Rutgers University	3.02	18.5
49	State University of New York at Buffalo	3.02	38
50	Texas A & M University	3.00	—

Note. Adapted from 1986–1990 *Social Sciences Citation Index* (SSCI) and *Science Citation Index* (SCI) databases. © 1992 Institute for Scientific Information. Also adapted from S. S. Ilardi, A. Rodriguez-Hanley, M. Roberts, & J. Siegel (2000), "On the origins of clinical psychology faculty: Who is training the trainers?," *Clinical Psychology: Science and Practice, 1,* 346–354. Adapted by permission.

[a]Institutions without APA-accredited programs in clinical or counseling psychology have been omitted from this table.

Consequently, a student with a clear research orientation should probably choose a Ph.D. program. For the research oriented, this column will be used to cross schools off their application list. Look up each school on your list in the reports on individual programs. If any of these schools offer only Psy.D. programs (see Table 1-4), you can delete that program.

The first column under the "Clinical" section of Appendix B is marked "Orientation." Under each program listed in the reports on individual programs, you will see a list of five theoretical orientations:

- Psychodynamic/psychoanalytic
- Radical behavioral/applied behavioral analysis

- Systems/family systems
- Humanistic/existential
- Cognitive/cognitive-behavioral

If you are clearly committed to (or strongly leaning toward) one of these particular orientations, then it is important that some portion of the faculty share that orientation with you. Check each program on your list and see if a suitable percentage of the faculty shares your orientation. If so, mark the "Orientation" column with a "+" sign. If not, mark it with a "–" sign.

If you are unsure of an orientation, or see yourself as eclectic, then be sure there is a wide variety of faculty orientations. If there is representation among the faculty in four or more of these orientations, that's a good sign. If the total you get when adding up all the percentages in the different orientations is greater than 100%, this is also a plus. It means some (or most) of the faculty bridge orientations and are integrative themselves. In other words, professors are listed under more than one category. In either case, mark the "Orientation" column with a "+" sign. If the faculty are of one or two orientations and without overlap, then mark this column with a "–" sign.

The second column under "Clinical" is "Res/Clin." Turn to Appendix F, "Specialty Clinics and Practica Sites." This is a list of several types of specialty clinics or practica areas available at different schools. Specialty clinics focus on and have available to them a specific clientele, such as depressed or eating-disordered clients. Practica are placements where students will conduct clinical work in their second, third, and/or fourth years of study. Some practica also specialize in a certain clientele. If you have a research interest in a particular population, it is important that the population be available for you to study and that you have the chance to work with that population clinically in order to broaden your understanding of them. For this reason, it may be important for a researcher to have a specialty clinic or practicum in his or her area.

Look up your research area in Appendix F. If any of the schools on your list in Appendix B has a clinic or practicum in that area, mark the "Res/Clin" column with a plus.

Once again, this is just one indicator and must be kept in perspective. Most programs will have their own psychological training clinic, where a wide range of clinical populations may be seen or made available for research. Additionally, a faculty member may have a research population readily available in the community. And last, a few programs did not include practica placements off campus in the community, thus underrepresenting their practica opportunities. Still, being informed about a clinic or practicum specializing in your population of interest is certainly an advantage in selecting potential graduate programs.

The third column under the "Clinical" section is marked "Rank." Here, we can refer to a program's production of students who go on to distinguished careers as clinicians, as measured by becoming ABPP Diplomates and by election as Fellows in APA's Division of Clinical Psychology or Division of Counseling Psychology. The "ABPP" refers to diplomate status awarded by the American Board of Professional Psychology, which certifies excellence in 11 fields of psychology, including clinical psychology and counseling psychology. Applicants for ABPP must have at least 5 years of postdoctoral experience, submit examples of their clinical work, and pass an oral examination. The entrance requirements and performance standards are more rigorous than those involved in licensure and represent excellence in applied psychology. Fellowship in APA is based on evidence of unusual and outstanding performance in psychology.

One study (Robyak & Goodyear, 1984) investigated the graduate school origins of ABPP Diplomates and APA Fellows in clinical and counseling psychology. Although older and larger doctoral programs are obviously favored in such a historical study, the results nonetheless give some indication of institutional reputation and their graduates' accomplishments. Table 3-3 presents the top 25 institutional origins of clinical psychology diplomates and fellows as well as the top 12 institutional origins of counseling psychology diplomates and fellows. Clinical psychology diplomates graduated from 153 different universities; fellows from 92. Counseling psychology diplomates graduated from 55 universities; fellows from 46.

If a school is listed in Table 3-3, place a "+" in the "Rank" column in the "Clinical" section. Though many schools not listed on this table provide fine clinical training, this listing indicates that the program is outstanding in terms of its track record for producing excellent professional psychologists.

Finally, there is a column in Appendix B marked "Self-Rating." The first question we asked each school to answer was, "On a 7-point scale, how research or clinically oriented would you rate your program?" (1 = clinical emphasis; 4 = equal emphasis; and 7 = research emphasis). You will find the school's rating of itself under each individual listing in the reports on individual programs sections. Mark this number under the "Self-Rating" column.

What you now have before you is a list of programs that offer research in your area of interest. You also have the number of faculty in the area that you might work

TABLE 3-3. Institutional Origins of Clinical and Counseling Psychology Diplomates and Fellows

University	Rank order	
	Diplomates	Fellows
Clinical psychology		
New York University	1	2
Columbia University	2	1
University of Chicago	3	3
University of California–Los Angeles	4	14
University of Michigan	5.5	9
University of Iowa	5.5	5
University of Minnesota	7	6
Northwestern University	8	7.5
University of California–Berkeley	9	15.5
Harvard University	10	7.5
Pennsylvania State University	11	17.5
Purdue University	12.5	—
Boston University	12.5	17.5
Ohio State University	14	4
University of Washington	15	5.5
University of Southern California	16	11.5
Duke University	18	—
Stanford University	18	10
University of Texas	18	—
University of Pittsburgh	20	11.5
University of Kansas	21	—
Case Western Reserve University	23.5	—
University of Illinois at Urbana–Champaign	23.5	—
Yale University	23.5	13
University of Pennsylvania	23.5	—
Counseling psychology		
Columbia University	1	2
Ohio State University	2	3
University of Minnesota	3	1
New York University	4	4.5
University of Michigan	5	—
University of Chicago	6	8
Stanford University	7	7
University of Iowa	8	7
University of Texas	9.5	—
University of Wisconsin	9.5	—
Catholic University	11.5	—
Harvard University	11.5	4.5

Note. From "Graduate school origins of diplomates and fellows in professional psychology" by J. E. Robyak & R. K. Goodyear, 1984, *Professional Psychology: Research and Practice, 15,* 379–387. © 1984 American Psychological Association. Reprinted by permission.

with and whether they presently have, or are presently applying for, funding. Finally, you have an approximate rank of that school's research standing.

In clinical terms, you have some sense of whether that school will conform to your theoretical orientation, whether it has special clinical training in your area of interest, how it ranks in terms of producing outstanding clinicians, and whether it rates itself as emphasizing clinical work or research.

Given the information before you, you may already want to begin crossing programs off your list. If you're research oriented, and the program is a Psy.D. program or rates itself a 1, 2, or 3 (meaning it is practice oriented), you may choose to delete that school. Alternatively, if your interests reflect equal research and clinical emphasis and you lean toward a psychodynamic orientation, you may want to cross off a school that rates itself as a 7 (very research oriented) and/or whose faculty is 100% behavioral.

Your revised list of schools can probably satisfy your research and clinical interests. In addition, you have the start of a ranking system, which at this point gives you a rough idea of how well each school conforms to your interests and needs. Unfortunately, this provides you with only half of the information you need to begin writing to schools. The second part of this process asks, "How close do you come to the standards they specify?" This is covered in a later section entitled "Assessing School Criteria."

For the Clinically Oriented

This section gives guidance to those applicants who are more centrally focused on clinical work. These applicants will want to begin to choose their schools based on their theoretical orientation and the availability of clinical opportunities.

The first thing that you will want to do is turn to Table 1-4, which lists all the APA-accredited Psy.D. programs. With this list, turn to Appendix B, "Worksheet for Choosing Schools." Under the column marked "School," write the names of the programs found in Table 1-4. In addition to these programs, you may have a specific population in mind that you are especially eager to work with. Perhaps you already have a sense that you want to work specifically with patients suffering from anxiety disorders. In this case, turn to Appendix F. This appendix, "Specialty Clinics and Practica Sites," lists several sorts of specialty clinics or practica areas available at different schools. Specialty clinics focus on and have available to them a specific clientele, such as depressed or eating-disordered clients. As mentioned in the previous section, practica are placements where a student will conduct clinical work in his or her second, third, and/or fourth year of study, and some practica also specialize in treating a certain clientele. For a clinically oriented student, it would be especially desirable to be in a program with a specialty clinic in his or her particular area of treatment interest. Therefore, write down the names of programs with specialty clinics or practica in your area of interest on your list in Appendix B.

A word of caution is in order. Most programs will have their own psychology training clinic where a wide range of clinical populations may be seen or made available for research. Practica may also be available in a wide range of settings in the community, providing fertile ground for a rich clinical experience. Still, a clinic or practicum specializing in a population that is of special interest to you is a definite plus and an additional piece of information on which to base your decision. If a program both offers a Psy.D. and has a specialty clinic in your area, put a star next to it.

The next important column for the clinically oriented applicant is marked "Orientation." In the reports on individual programs, you will find each school listed, along with information pertaining to its program. Among that information, you will see a list of five basic theoretical orientations, followed by the percentage of the faculty that subscribes to that orientation:

- Psychodynamic/psychoanalytic
- Radical behavioral/applied behavioral analysis
- Systems/family systems
- Humanistic/existential
- Cognitive/cognitive-behavioral

If you are clearly committed to (or strongly leaning toward) one of these particular orientations, then it is important that some portion of the faculty share that orientation with you. Check each program on your list and determine if a suitable percentage of the faculty shares your orientation. If so, mark the "Orientation" column with a "+" sign; if not, mark it with a "–" sign.

If you are unsure of your orientation or see yourself as eclectic, then be sure there is a wide variety of faculty orientations. If there is representation among the faculty in four of these orientations, that's a good sign. If the total you obtain after adding up all the percentages in the different areas is greater than 100%, this is also advantageous. It means some (or most) of the faculty bridge orientations and are eclectic themselves. In either case, mark the "Orientation" column with a "+" sign. If you're eclectic and the faculty are of one or two orientations and do not overlap, then mark this column with a "–" sign.

The next column is marked "Res/Clin." As we mentioned previously, even if you are looking for a clinically oriented program, you still will have to do research: a lengthy professional paper or dissertation at the very least! Consequently, it is important that someone in your program is doing research in an area that interests you. With this in mind, look through Appendix E and find the area(s) of research that you find interesting. Under each area, you will find a list of schools that have researchers in that field. If any of the schools on your list in Appendix B is listed here, place a "+" in the column marked "Res/Clin."

The third column under "Clinical" is marked "Rank." Here, we can refer to a program's production of students who go on to distinguished careers as clinicians, as imperfectly measured by their becoming ABPP Diplomates and by election as Fellows in APA's Division of Clinical Psychology and Division of Counseling Psychology. The "ABPP" refers to diplomate status awarded by the American Board of Professional Psychology, which certifies excellence in 11 fields of psychology, including clinical psychology and counseling psychology. Applicants for ABPP must have at least 5 years of postdoctoral experience, submit examples of their clinical work, and pass an oral examination. The entrance requirements and performance standards are more rigorous than those involved in licensing and represent excellence in applied psychology. The APA Fellowship is based on evidence of unusual and outstanding performance.

One study (Robyak & Goodyear, 1984) investigated the graduate school origins of ABPP Diplomates and APA Fellows in clinical and counseling psychology. Although older and larger doctoral programs are obviously favored in such a historical study, the results nonetheless give some indication of institutional reputation and their graduates' accomplishments. Table 3-3 presents the top 25 institutional origins of these diplomates and fellows as well as the top 12 institutional origins of counseling psychology diplomates and fellows. Because this list indicates programs that have historically produced outstanding clinicians, place a "+" in this column for any program included in Table 3-3. Though many schools not listed in this table offer fine clinical training, the list provides an indication of the Ph.D. programs (Psy.D. programs are too new to be listed) that are likely to offer the sort of clinical training you seek.

Finally, there is a column in Appendix B marked "Self-Rating." In the reports on individual programs you will find each school's rating of itself (1 = clinical emphasis; 4 = equal emphasis; and 7 = research emphasis). Mark this number under the "Self-Rating" column. Though Psy.D. programs are practice oriented by definition, they vary on how much research they expect their students to conduct. Thus, their ratings will allow you to guide your expectations of what each program will expect of you. This self-rating will also help you avoid a Ph.D. program with a specialty clinic in your area that is clearly research oriented.

What you now have before you is a list of programs that are clinically oriented and/or that offer a specialty clinic or practica in your area of interest. You have some sense of whether these schools will conform to your theoretical orientation and whether they have ongoing research in your area of clinical interest. You also have their self-rating of the program's emphasis on clinical work or research.

Given the information on your worksheet, you may already want to begin crossing programs off your list. If you're clearly practice oriented and a Ph.D. program offers a specialty clinic in your area but rates itself with a 6 or 7 (very research oriented), you may choose to delete that school. Alternatively, if you're very behaviorally oriented, you may want to cross off a school where 100% of the faculty is psychodynamic/psychoanalytic.

Your revised list of schools can provide you with clinically oriented training and possibly special clinical training in your population of choice. In addition, you have the start of a ranking system that at this point gives you a rough idea of how well each school conforms to your interests and needs. Unfortunately, this only provides you with half the information you need to begin writing to schools. The second half of this process is related to how closely you come to the specified standards of these programs. This is covered in the "Assessing School Criteria" section.

For the Minority Applicant

Before continuing to the assessment of program criteria, it is important to discuss the special case of minority applications. "Minority" in this context primarily refers to racial or ethnic background, although with women comprising 67% of all doctoral students in psychology, a few graduate student programs are starting to treat men as minority applicants. Ethnic minority applications account for 17% of all applications to doctoral programs in psychology (APA Research Office, 2000).

Nearly every APA-accredited program makes special efforts to recruit minority applicants (Munoz-Dunbar & Stanton, 1999), recognizing the need in our society for well-trained minority professionals. Typical methods for recruiting underrepresented groups to clinical and counseling psychology programs are offers of financial aid, the use of personal contacts, visits to other schools, use of APA's Minority Undergraduate Students of Excellence (MUSE) program, special events, reimbursements of application fees, and preferential screening (Steinpreis et al., 1992). Programs often make an extra effort to review minority applications to ensure that qualified candidates are given appropriate consideration.

In fact, a recent study of Vail-model professional psychology programs revealed that 82% of them implemented formal minority admissions policies designed to improve racial representation (Young & VandeCreek, 1996). The study found that

- 94% of the programs gave extra points on ratings of application materials to minority applicants;
- 69% of the programs waived or lowered GRE scores for minority applicants;
- 41% of the programs waived or lowered GPA cutoffs for minority applicants; and
- 21% of the programs interviewed all minority applicants, regardless of the quality of their application materials.

As a consequence, ethnic minorities in the applicant pool are significantly more likely than whites to receive offers of admission (Munoz-Dunbar & Stanton, 1999). The generic guidelines and the following worksheets in this *Insider's Guide* may thus not accurately reflect a minority applicant's enhanced chances of acceptance. We recommend that you carefully read program descriptions regarding their minority selection procedures and encourage you to apply to programs at all levels of competitiveness and admissions criteria.

Both the American Psychological Association and the American Psychological Society are committed to ensuring that the practice of psychology—and the production of psychologists—is in the vanguard of addressing the needs of culturally diverse populations. The APA's Commission on Ethnic Minority Recruitment, Retention, and Training in Psychology produces several valuable publications in this regard. Contact APA to obtain copies of these informative publications, notably *For College Students of Color Applying to Graduate & Professional Programs*.

Although the special consideration given minority applicants may appear to be advantageous, it also represents a special challenge. One well-qualified minority student we knew was advised by a university career services counselor that he would have no problem getting into the school of his choice. He applied to several very competitive programs, and received acceptances and offers of financial aid across the board. Unfortunately, he skipped the process of matching his interests with the strengths of the program, given the strength of his application and the special consideration he anticipated receiving. After one year, he was actually looking to transfer into another program that had more faculty conducting research and therapy in his areas of interest. The moral of the story is: Don't let the potential advantage of being a minority candidate become a disadvantage. Just because you can get into a program doesn't mean that it is the best program for you. A rigorous approach to the application process is the best approach for everyone.

Assessing School Criteria

Assessing the particular criteria used by each clinical or counseling psychology program to evaluate applicants is an important step in the process of applying to graduate school. To illuminate this point, we would like to relate the story of one applicant we knew several years ago. She was an Ivy League graduate, a 3.8 psychology major, who had conducted research with a prominent psychologist. She had fine letters of recommendation and some clinical experience with developmentally disabled children, but her GREs were in the low 500s. Thinking that her credentials were excellent, she applied to the most competitive research programs and one clinically oriented program. She was rejected across the board at these top research schools and just barely made it into what she had mistakenly considered her clinically oriented "safety school." Her mistake was to ignore the fact that all the research oriented schools to which she applied specified minimum GRE scores of 600 or more. Her application was unsuccessful because she ignored one piece of information each school had indicated to be essential. She was nearly rejected in the more clinically oriented program she had felt was a "sure thing" because she did not have the clinical experience they were looking for. And she was lucky that that particular doctoral program did not have GRE requirements beyond her range!

The moral of the story is twofold: (1) Attend closely to the admission standards of each program. If a school sets standards you cannot realistically meet, you need to work very, very hard to get them to make an exception. In other words, think twice about applying there. (2) Apply to schools with a range of admission criteria, and do *not* consider a clinically oriented school a "safety school." A real safety school is one that announces admission requirements that you exceed by a wide margin. This does not guarantee acceptance, but does dramatically increase the probability of making it into their finalist pool.

Now, turn your attention to Appendix C, "Worksheet for Assessing Program Criteria." In Appendix C, you will rate yourself as to how well you conform to each school's admission requirements. The aim is that you not waste time and money applying to schools that indicate in no uncertain terms that you do not fall within the limits of their criteria. There is no reason to feel inadequate because you fall short of these specifications. There may be schools on your list with requirements you do meet or exceed. If you are unable to meet the minimum requirements of any schools on your list, you should seriously consider taking time off to better prepare yourself or applying to less competitive master's programs.

Begin by transferring the name of each school from Appendix B to the "School" column of Appendix C. Simply copy the list from one table to the other. Also copy the number in the "Self-Rating" column from one worksheet to the other. Next, look up the first school on your list in the reports on individual programs. Read through all the information provided just to start familiarizing yourself with that program.

As you begin filling out Appendix C and listing each school's admission criteria, remember that these are simply indications of your strength as an applicant to each school. These scales are not set in stone and do not guarantee that you will be accepted. You may not readily fall into any of the categories listed and will have to make some rough approximations for yourself. Or you may find that you fall between categories and have to add 0.5 point here or subtract 0.5 point there. If you think it is appropriate to modify the categories or scoring systems, by all means do so. *The most important result is not an absolute number but a relative sense of how well you meet each program's admission criteria.*

You may also find that a school does not require certain test scores, or gives no minimum or mean GRE scores, or doesn't have preferred or mandatory courses. In this case, simply score a "0" in the appropriate column. When it comes time to total each school's score, this will neither detract from nor add to your ability to meet their requirements.

Now, go to the respective reports on individual programs and look at the prerequisite courses. You will see two questions pertaining to course preparation prior to applying: "What courses are required for incoming students to have completed *prior* to enrolling?" and "Are there courses you recommend that are not mandatory?" Underneath each question you will find a list of courses that the particular school assigned to each category. On your list in Appendix C, under the column marked "Courses," score yourself as follows (in this table, "M" indicates "mandatory" and "R" indicates "recommended"):

+2 You have taken all the M and R courses and earned B+ or better in them all.

+1 You have taken all the M courses and/or several of the R courses and earned B+ or better.

0 You have taken all the M courses, but none of the Rs, or earned B– or lower in some M courses.

–1 You have not taken one or two of the M courses, or have earned B– or lower in several of them.

–2 You have not taken several or any of the M courses or have received D or less in some of the M or R courses.

The next section on each "Program" page is marked GREs and GPA. This section gives mean scores, cutoff scores, or preferred scores for the GREs and GPAs for each program listed. As you might expect, if a program indicates that they utilize a cutoff score, they will typically not even consider an applicant whose scores fall below that minimum (though, once again, minority applications may receive special consideration). A preferred score indicates that they would like you to have at least that score but may consider applicants whose scores are below that level. In this section and on the "Program" page, "M" indicates a mean score, "C" indicates and cutoff score, and "P" indicates a preferred score. Realize that accepted applicants will often have scores well above a cutoff. Eventually, when you secure information materials from the different programs, check to see what the average scores were for those accepted into each program. This information will be important to use to modify your evaluation of how you compare to those being accepted into the program.

On your list, under the columns marked "GRE-V" (verbal), "GRE-Q" (quantitative), and "GRE-S" (psychology subject test), score yourself as follows:

+2 You exceed the school's M or P score by at least 100 points.

+1 You exceed the school's M or P score by more than 50 but less than 100 points.

0 You meet the school's M or P minimum or exceed it by less than 50 points.

- **−1** You do not meet the school's P score, but are less than 100 points below it.
- **−2** You are below the school's C score or are below the P score by 100 points or more.

For GPA, we asked programs if they had a cutoff or preferred score and asked if that applied to more than one type of GPA. It is not uncommon for programs to look at full GPA (all undergraduate courses taken), psychology GPA (only psychology courses), and junior/senior GPA (all courses taken in the last 2 years of college). Similar to GRE scores, students entering programs often have GPAs significantly higher than these preferred scores. A few schools are also interested in graduate psychology GPA, if applicable. Again, it is wise to review the average GPA of incoming students when you receive the information packets from the various schools. Under the column marked "GPA," score yourself as follows (M is for mean GPAs; P is for preferred GPAs):

- **+2** You exceed the school's M or P GPA by 0.5 points or more.
- **+1** You exceed the school's M or P GPA by less than 0.5 points.
- **0** You meet the school's M or P GPA.
- **−1** You do not meet the school's P GPA, but are less than 0.2 below it.
- **−2** You are below the school's C GPA or are below the P by more than 0.5 points.

Next, look back to the second column of Appendix C, "Self-Rating." This is how the school rates itself on the practice–research continuum. If a school emphasizes one more than the other, this gives some indication of what it would consider important in an applicant. A school that stresses research will probably desire an applicant to have some amount of research experience. Under the "Research" column in Appendix C, rate yourself as follows:

- **+2** The school rates itself as a 6 or a 7 and you will have completed an honors thesis or will have at least 2 years of experience in psychology research.
- **+1** The school rates itself as a 4, 5, 6, or 7 and you will have at least 1 year of experience in psychology research.
- **0** The school rates itself as a 1, 2, or 3.
- **−1** The school rates itself as a 4 or 5, and you have no research experience.
- **−2** The school rates itself as a 6 or 7, and you have no research experience.

Similarly, a program emphasizing clinical work will prefer that an applicant enter with some practical experience in human services or health care. Under the "Clinical" column, rate yourself as follows:

- **+2** The school rates itself as a 1 or a 2, and you will have worked in a full-time (35+ hr./week) clinical position for at least 1 year.
- **+1** The school rates itself as a 1, 2, 3, or 4 and you will have volunteered part-time (8+ hr./week) at a clinical facility for at least 1 year.
- **0** The school rates itself as a 5, 6, or 7.
- **−1** The school rates itself as a 3 or 4, and you have no clinical experience.
- **−2** The school rates itself as a 1 or 2, and you have no clinical experience.

At this point, you should have completed the first nine columns of Appendix C from "School" to "Clinical."

Additional information provided for each program in the reports on individual programs are "How many applications were received in 2001?," "How many applicants were accepted in 2001?," and "How many accepted students will enter?" These give a rough estimate of the competitiveness of a program. You may be amazed at how high this ratio can become. In applying to schools, be realistic and reasonable. You may have a sterling application, but when Yale accepts roughly 1 in 50 applicants, you had best be applying to other places as well. On the other hand, some APA-accredited Psy.D. programs accept more than 1 in 3.

Bear in mind: Programs accept more applicants than actually end up attending. This makes programs appear more restrictive than they actually are. This is why we recently added the third item regarding the number of students who will enter the program—a number invariably smaller than the number of accepted students. For example, an applicant gaining acceptance to five places will ultimately reject four schools. A program planning on an incoming class of six students will accept more than six before gaining their new class. Nonetheless, apply to several schools with a range of competitiveness simply as a precautionary measure.

In the column marked "Compete" in Appendix C, record the ratio of applications to acceptances. It should be noted that competitiveness is difficult to quantify. Although we have selected the ratio of applicants to acceptances as our measure, other relevant criteria include test scores and GPA. Since we have already discussed these criteria, we are using this opportunity to highlight yet another area related to competitiveness.

The last column is marked "Total." Add the numbers under the "Courses," "GRE-V," "GRE-Q," "GRE-S," "GPA," "Research," and "Clinical" columns. This will provide you with a total somewhere between -14 and +14, which is a rough indication of how well you meet each school's admission requirements and expectations.

Now you have a grand list of programs that are performing research or clinical work in the areas you have specified. In addition, you have several indications of how well each school will address your needs and expectations as a graduate student. Finally, you have a rating of yourself as an applicant to each program.

The best way to begin your decision-making process is to select the programs that have admission requirements within your reach. As you look through the "school requirements" part of your list, note any –2s. Unless you can reasonably expect to change these to zeros or better before you start to complete your applications, you may be better off dropping these schools from your list. After that, you will then have to decide for yourself what are reasonable places to apply.

Below is a rating system based on your "Total" column for each school. Although this system may help you decide where to write for information, it is by no means definitive. *These are rough approximations*, and ultimately you will have to decide where to apply based on this and any other information to which you may be privy. From the "Total" column of Appendix C, judge each program as follows:

10 to 14 Your chances are very good. Apply to many of these schools, since your application may be especially strong here.

6 to 9 Your chances are good. These schools are within your reach, as you exceed in several of the qualities they value.

4 to 5 Your chances are moderately good here, but be sure to apply to some schools where you rank more highly.

0 to 3 These schools are within your range of abilities. Your application may not be outstanding, but it is somewhere between "adequate" and "more than adequate." Be sure also to apply to several schools in a higher range.

–1 to –4 These schools are a stretch for you. Go ahead and apply to a few, but the bulk of your applications should go to schools on which you achieved a higher score.

< –4 These schools are looking for something different from your experience or performance at this time. If you really wish to attend a school in this range, take time off or attend a master's program to bolster your research, clinical, and academic performance.

Although this worksheet embodies many of the relevant criteria used by admissions committees, it of course cannot integrate all possible criteria. If a professor has expressed interest in working with you, for example, the worksheet total may underestimate your chances for acceptance. Other useful resources when selecting your list of schools include specific professors, undergraduate psychology advisors, and bulletin boards in the psychology building that display postgraduate brochures. Graduate students at your local university can also be helpful, and a few large universities have even created notebooks on clinical and counseling psychology graduate programs (Todd & Farinato, 1992). Take advantage of all the information available to you to augment the data provided in the reports on individual programs.

Using the system in Appendix C, delete some of the schools that have admission criteria outside of your present range. This will enable you to begin the next phase: selecting schools that match your expectations in terms of the training you desire.

For the research-oriented applicant, these decisions may be easiest. Look at the schools left on your worksheet. Note the number of faculty interested in your research area(s) and whether any of them are funded. Grant funding is a rough indicator of the intensity of the program's commitment to this particular research area. The assumption is that a grant-funded area may offer more opportunities to study the issue and may be more likely to be actively generating the most current research. In addition, grant funding has the potential of making assistantship money available. This by no means suggests that a program that does not have a grant in your area is not conducting current research or will not have money available to you. Additionally, a program with several faculty in an area may simply be "between" grants. Thus, the number of faculty alone also can indicate a school's commitment to this area of research.

Next, check the school's productivity ranking and their self-rating as being more practice or research oriented. Again, if you are more research oriented, you may well find yourself crossing those schools off your list that are low on productivity and that are clearly clinically oriented. You are going to find that this shortens your list but that you still have a number of

678 Wilmington Drive
Derby, NY 14047

September 3, 2002

Director of Admissions
Department of Psychology
Bogus University
1234 Monument Square
Upstate, NY 14000

Dear Sir or Madam:

I am interested in applying to your Ph.D. (Psy.D.) program in clinical (counseling) psychology for the fall of 2003. Please send me an application and any information you have available concerning your program. Kindly include financial aid information as well.

Thank you for your time and consideration.

Sincerely yours,

Chris Smith

FIGURE 3-1. Sample letter (or e-mail) requesting application and information.

schools that cover a wide range of desirability. This is exactly where you want to be at this point! What you desire is a list of 15 to 30 schools for which you will secure additional information. Then, you can begin fine-tuning and selecting the 10 to 20 schools to which you will actually apply.

If you are more strongly oriented toward clinical work, you will find yourself crossing schools off your list that are clearly research oriented, favor theoretical orientations different from your own, or are too restricted for your needs. The schools highlighting clinical work, and especially those sharing your orientation or providing a specialty clinic or practicum in your area, will be the most desirable.

Those of you who are not certain what you want may decide to take time off or to attend a master's program before applying to doctoral programs in clinical or counseling psychology. These steps will probably help you formulate a clearer picture of your professional interests and career trajectories.

The applicant who equally emphasizes clinical and research training is the most challenged. You want a program that is research oriented, but not at the cost of clinical work. But you also want a program that will offer high-quality clinical experience without sacrificing high standards in research. Using your list, find the schools that are moderate or high in productivity and that have a number of people interested in your area. Check to see that they rate themselves as a 4 or 5, indicating that they emphasize clinical and research work nearly equally. Then, check to see if their theoretical orientation conforms to your own and whether they have a specialty clinic or practicum in your area. Again, you are going to find a range of schools, some conforming to your needs better than others. This is exactly what you want at this point in the process.

You are now ready to gather the detailed information necessary to choose among the 15 to 30 schools you will use for your selection pool. If your number of schools does not fall within these parameters, you should consider modifying your list. The Web site, mailing address, and e-mail address of each program are listed with each entry in the reports on individual programs. At this point, all you need is to spend a few hours on the Web, or to send a brief letter requesting information and an application. If you are requesting information by post or e-mail, the message or letter should be neat, typed, and focused. Figure 3-1 shows a sample letter or e-mail.

Congratulations! You have taken the first steps in your application process.

CHAPTER 4

SELECTING SCHOOLS

Between late summer and late fall you will need to spend time on the World Wide Web, or e-mail or "snail mail" a letter similar to the one displayed in Figure 3-1 to a number of schools for information. You will scan Web sites, download files, or receive large envelopes stuffed with packets and guides describing each program. You are ahead of the game if you begin during late summer, because most applicants will not be starting this process for another three to four months. This is an opportunity for you to take advantage of an early start to set yourself apart as an organized and optimal candidate.

In order to select schools that best suit your needs and interests, we again return to the questions: What is it I want for myself? What is it I'm interested in doing? And where do I want to do it? A firm commitment to a single clinical interest, research area, geographic location, or theoretical orientation is not required at this time; however, the more specific your interests, the more intelligent a choice you are going to make.

In the last chapter we helped you to get started in narrowing down your choices of potential graduate programs. We did so by considering your credentials and interests and by searching for potential matches with the requirements and offerings of various graduate programs. In this chapter we will continue to help you by reviewing five critical variables to take into account in narrowing your choices: research interests, clinical opportunities, theoretical orientations, financial aid, and quality of life.

A Multitude of Considerations

Each graduate school applicant is undeniably unique in his or her reasons for applying to particular programs in clinical or counseling psychology. As we advise students and conduct workshops on graduate school admission, we hear a litany of specific restrictions: "I have to stay close to my spouse in Los Angeles," "It must be a Catholic school," "I can only attend if I receive full financial aid," "I am interested solely in cognitive-behavioral programs," "I would really like to be near the mountains," "The program must have lots of women faculty," and so on. There is obviously no single, definitive list of factors to consider in selecting potential schools. Although we will examine in some detail the five most common variables, we will be unable to canvass the almost infinite range of reasons for selecting programs to which to apply.

In an idyllic world, graduate student aspirants would have sufficient funds and freedom to consider any clinical or counseling psychology program in the country. In the real world, however, you may be limited in your choice by financial, family, and geographic considerations. While we appreciate these very real constraints, we encourage you not to be prematurely limited by your own vision. Try to think broadly and boldly. It is, quite simply, your career at stake.

Geographic location will be a determining factor for some applicants. By this we mean both the area of the country and proximity to significant others in your life, such as parents, spouses/partners, siblings, or lovers. If you do not possess the mobility to relocate to another area of the country, then you might delay applying until your situation changes or apply only to regional schools, even if they are less desirable in some ways. Don't spend time, money, and energy on futile missions, in this case applying to programs you will be unable to attend.

At the same time, we heartily encourage you to "get out of town." Far too often students restrict themselves unnecessarily to schools close to their homes or to their undergraduate institution. Yet, graduate programs that better match their needs may be located across the country or four states south. Your future demands that you "look around" the entire country and Canada.

The gender, ethnicity, or sexual orientation of the professional psychology communities of schools may be an influential factor for other applicants. If this is the case for you, obtain updated resource directories from the American Psychological Association and apply accordingly. Three examples are APA's *Graduate Faculty Interested in the Psychology of Women*, *The Directory of Ethnic Minority Professionals in Psychology*, and *Graduate Faculty Interested in Gay and Lesbian Issues in Psychology* (available online at www.apa.org/pi/wpo/gradfac/html). The reports on individual programs also present the percentage of ethnic minority and women students in each clinical and counseling psychology program; these can be a useful source of direction in your choice.

Our general point is this: Think through your personal criteria for applying to certain programs and then be proactive in securing information about those criteria. Even if your choice of schools is limited, make it an informed choice. Accept as you must the restrictions in the range of potential graduate schools, but do not leave your future to chance.

Research Interests

The Web site for most programs, or the materials contained in their information packets, should include a list of psychology faculty in that department and their current research. You are looking to learn something from these faculty, so our advice is to find the ones who are experts in the areas of interest to you. If you are interested in family therapy, locate those psychologists active in training and research in that field. If you are interested in alcohol studies, find the alcohol researchers or clinicians. Download the faculty member's Web page, or the description provided by the department. Read their descriptions carefully *with a highlighter.* What kind of questions are they asking? Have you asked yourself those same questions? Is this the sort of thing you can envision yourself exploring? Have you read a sample of what they have written?

In selecting professors whose interests parallel your own, you are searching for a good *match.* You are looking for mentors—psychologists who will take you on as an apprentice and teach you about your chosen field. The more similar your views are, the better the match. For example, if you are clinically oriented, psychodynamically disposed, and interested in private practice, you might choose to cross off your list a program with professors who operate exclusively from behavioral and research perspectives. This does not mean your interest has to be pinpoint focused. Knowing you would rather investigate or treat an area psychodynamically may be enough to narrow your list of schools down to a sufficient range. But it is our experience that the more focused you are, the better fit you can find.

As you peruse the faculty list and other materials, you should begin to get a sense of whom you would like to work with, who is going to have the facilities to allow you to research or treat the population in which you are interested. You should eventually have a list of 10 to 20 programs that have faculty with whom you would like to work and a general idea of what each of them does.

Having created such a list of programs, we suggest that you review some of the articles or books that these professors have written. Many Web sites include a list of each faculty member's recent publications. So examine their bibliographies on the Web, inspect the program brochure, or search the *Psychological Abstracts* on *PsycLIT* for the last 3 to 5 years to locate some recent publications; then go to the library and look them up. What methods do they use? What are the specifics of their psychotherapy or research that really hold your attention? If you find yourself quickly getting bored or saying, "So what? OK, so alcoholics tend to smoke more? Who cares?", then you have a very important piece of information. If you are finding these articles interesting, you are on the right track. This is a time to get excited about your field and where you want to work!

Here are some additional bits of information you can gather that can help whittle down the number of applications to be sent. The resources you can use to answer these questions are (1) the data provided by the director of training in the "Reports on Individual Programs" in this book, (2) the program's Web page, (3) the information packet provided by the school, (4) a visit to the campus or correspondence with faculty, and (5) interviews with professors and/or graduate students at your own school about the programs in question. The important thing is to get the information and corroborate it, if possible.

When it comes to your research interests, discover if there is a medical school library or science facilities at your disposal. Library facilities in general should be a prime consideration, but we have found that medical libraries in particular contain journals and books not usually available elsewhere. An associated medical school or hospital may also have facilities and populations available for your research. Find out if they are present, and then find out what their relationship is to the Psychology Department. In addition, learn more about the research space specific to your area. For example, does someone have the equipment you need, actual lab or research space, funding? If you desire to conduct research in cardiovascular psychophysiology and you have found a professor who has published several articles, determine if he or she has equipment to monitor cardiac responses. If not, there should be equipment available somewhere in the department.

We realize that this process requires a great deal of time and energy. It may also provoke anxiety in an already exhausting application process. This is one reason why we advocate an early start. Again, we would like to emphasize that it is very possible to get into a program without doing this extra work. This preparation, however, will give you the edge you may need to get into the program of your choice or to overcome any weaknesses that exist in your application.

Clinical Opportunities

Having read articles by the professors with whom you would like to work, you know better which ones you find interesting. However, if your interest is primarily clinical, it is possible you might find that the person you're most interested in working with does not have recent publications in your area(s) of interest. Or you know a program has an alcohol clinic, but you can't figure out which professors treat clients there. Your first recourse should be to search the university's Web site to try to locate this information. If it is not on the clinical or counseling program's Web page, it may exist somewhere else within the university's Web site. If all else fails, call the department and ask to speak with the director of training. Simply ask this person for materials specific to the clinic you would like to work in, or ask to speak with the director of that clinic or practicum site to determine which faculty are practicing there.

Now, we are going to suggest something that we have found to be a powerful way of making some final decisions about where to apply and increasing your chances of being accepted there. During the late summer or early fall of the year you apply, contact a few of the professors you have been investigating. Write the ones whose interests seem most closely aligned to your own. Though we suggest sending an actual letter, those who find this daunting can send an e-mail. Most program Web sites include faculty e-mail addresses.

There are many reasons to directly contact a faculty member. First, it gives you an opportunity to gain information you probably could not gather in any other way—information about the program, its facilities, its faculty, and students. Second, these letters give you a chance to get to know someone you are genuinely interested in working with. It gives you a chance to evaluate how happy you would be in a mentorship with this faculty member. Of course, there must be aspects of this person's research or clinical work that attract you. If you do not know his or her interests or the literature well enough to be able to demonstrate a working knowledge of the individual's contributions within the field, do *not* write to him or her. Professors routinely receive letters from people looking to make contact, and unless you can pique their interest and demonstrate familiarity with their work, you are unlikely to receive a response.

Whether your interests are oriented toward research, clinical work, or both, you are not looking to take this person or his or her field by storm. You are looking to make a contribution in this particular area, a contribution made *after* you have taken the time to learn and gain experience in the field under their mentorship. Or, you are looking to gain experience and clinical training with an experienced practitioner.

Take a moment to look at this relationship from the professor's perspective. If she is a researcher, then she is looking for students to help with that research, for students with the knowledge and drive to run studies. If she is a clinician, then she is looking for individuals eager for supervision who will be able to carry a client load. And that is what you have to offer. You are looking for the best fit of a program and faculty to your interests.

Contacting a professor is not an absolute necessity. Many students are admitted to very good programs and then take 1 or 2 years to explore, to figure out what they want and where they fit in. In fact, some programs require students to work with a variety of professors during their initial year before selecting an adviser. Nonetheless, it is to your advantage to spend sufficient time deciding which professors would be best suited for you. Take the time and energy to explore in yourself what you want, to locate programs and professors who seem appropriate; then go ahead and make the contacts with them to test the waters.

Figures 4-1 and 4-2 show sample letters/e-mails of introduction, the former for research oriented applicants and the latter for those who are clinically oriented. *These are not forms to copy in which you simply insert your own words where appropriate!* You may want to show your letter to a professor to preview how well it is likely to be received.

What if the person does not respond within a month? You could try once more, though only once, and if you tried e-mail first, try a written letter the second

246 Wood Street
Babylon, NY 14000

September 3, 2002

Roger Morris, Ph.D.
Department of Psychology
University of Southern States
13 Peachtree Drive
Wilkesville, VA 15000

Dear Dr. Morris:

I am a student at Babylon University, where I have been working with Dr. Frances Murrow, studying the effects of self-esteem on math performance anxiety. As I was searching the literature, I read several articles you had written concerning the use of relaxation techniques to improve self-esteem and test anxiety.

After reading your paper "The Uses of Relaxation in Schools" (December issue of *School Psychology*), I had some questions I hoped you could answer. We used several of the questionnaires that you used in that study. In looking at our data, we have found that subjects respond quite differently to the Test Anxiety Questionnaire at various times in the semester. We found that the further into the semester students progressed, the more their anxiety affected their scores. Have you also found this to be true in your research? Secondly, I have begun to wonder if self-efficacy might not be a factor affecting both test anxiety and self-esteem. I noticed that you had done some early work involving self-efficacy and was wondering what ideas you might have on this subject.

On a related matter, I will soon be applying to clinical psychology doctoral programs that offer research training in performance anxiety. I would be very interested in learning whether you routinely supervise the research of doctoral students at the University of Southern States on this topic and, if so, whether you will be taking any new students in the next academic year.

Thank you for your time and consideration. I look forward to hearing from you.

Sincerely yours,

Chris Smith

FIGURE 4-1. Sample letter of introduction—research oriented.

time. If that does not succeed, this person has probably given you a message that he or she does not want to make the contact. This does not mean that you will not be able to work with that individual if you get accepted. He or she may simply be busy or on sabbatical.

If the selected professor does write back, then it may be the beginning of a working relationship. Even if you are not accepted to his or her program or ultimately decide not to attend, you are making professional contacts in your field. There is no guideline as to exactly how to act from here, since each professor is different. But you should begin getting a sense of whether this is the right person (and program) for you.

If the task of introducing yourself to a professor "cold" seems overly daunting, consider alternatives. Local and regional conferences present prime opportunities for meeting potential mentors and gathering information about graduate programs. Numerous societies hold yearly conferences in which research is presented in specialty areas of psychology. For example, if one of your interests lies in health psychology or behavioral medicine, there is the Society for Behavioral

246 Wood Street
Babylon, NY 14000

September 3, 2002

Pat Morris, Ph.D.
Department of Psychology
University of Southern States
13 Peachtree Drive
Wilkesville, VA 15000

Dear Dr. Morris:

I am a student at Babylon University, where I recently completed an upper-level course in clinical/counseling psychology. My professor, Dr. Frances Ellis, discussed your social problem-solving program targeted to elementary school children. Dr. Ellis spoke highly about the manner in which you use your clinical findings to derive theoretical models of problem solving and use these models to guide your interventions.

I am interested in learning more about school-based social problem-solving programs. I have been involved in such a project with Dr. Ellis and wish to continue my education in this area. I am preparing applications for Psy.D. programs and would like to learn more about your particular program. Specifically, what opportunities exist for clinical Psy.D. students to work on your social problem-solving program? My interests are based primarily in the clinical and applied aspects of your school-based program. I would like to help train teachers in imparting social problem-solving skills to students.

I would appreciate any materials that you could send me describing your problem-solving program in greater detail. I am especially interested in the role for Psy.D. students. Thank you for your time and consideration.

Sincerely yours,

Chris Smith

FIGURE 4-2. Sample letter of introduction—clinically oriented.

Medicine, the American Psychosomatic Society, the Society for Psychophysiological Research, and many others. If, for another example, your interests lie in psychotherapy, there are the annual conferences of the Society for Psychotherapy Research, the APA Division of Psychotherapy, and the Society for the Exploration of Psychotherapy Integration. Your psychology advisor can probably suggest several societies in each area of psychology.

Student membership in a scientific society brings a number of benefits. For beginners, it will probably provide you with a directory of members, their addresses, and often their areas of research. Such a directory is an easy way of quickly ascertaining who is doing research in your area, and where. Most scientific organizations will invite you to join their electronic listserve. With membership also typically comes a newsletter or a journal, which can give you a sense of the leaders in the field.

Attending a conference can provide a great deal more information, as we have already emphasized in Chapter 2. If you are interested in particular professors, you may have a chance to see them "in action" if they are presenting a poster or a paper. In this way, you can get acquainted with the person and the research without taking the risk of formally introducing yourself. Alternatively, you may approach the professor directly and express your interest in the research or ask your psy-

TABLE 4-1. Questions to Ask about Psy.D. Programs

Is the program freestanding or part of a university? (If freestanding:) Is it a for-profit school?
If the program also has a clinical Ph.D. program, are the "best" practicum opportunities available to Psy.D. students or Ph.D. students? Is it possible to take the Ph.D. courses as well? What is the relationship between the Psy.D. and Ph.D. students?
Will the internship be in the third or fourth year (i.e., do you complete an internship before or after your dissertation)?
What percentage of Psy.D. students receive financial support? What is the annual tuition?
Are practicum opportunities available outside the institution or only in the institution?
Are there opportunities for live supervision? Do the full-time faculty perform the clinical supervision?
Does the school offer exposure to a variety of theoretical orientations, or is it dominated by one orientation?
Is it possible to gain experience working with . . . ? With families? With groups?
What types of clinical populations are available?
How interested are the faculty in the students?
Do the faculty have independent practices? What percentage of the faculty are full-time?
What percentage of first-year students complete the program? How many years does it typically require to complete the program?
What is the size of the incoming class? How many students are in a typical graduate course?

chology advisor to make the introduction. Many graduate students first met their mentors in these ways.

After you have communicated with a professor, it may be appropriate to ask to tour this person's research lab or clinical facilities. This is a very important time, in that you will get a chance to gather all sorts of information if you visit a school ahead of time. Meeting this person face to face, getting a sense of his or her personal, clinical, and research style, and seeing how you might fit into an ongoing team can be indispensable information. If you do find yourself in the position of visiting a professor before interviews, use the advice in Chapter 6 to help guide you in gathering information during this phase.

During your visit try to determine if this department's psychological clinic serves the surrounding community or just the college community. College students are fine clients with whom to begin, but you will probably desire a greater diversity of populations and disorders. Learn more about the school's affiliated or specialized departmental clinics. Who can work there and when? Who does the supervision? Do you have to be affiliated with a specific professor, or is there a competitive process toward earning that placement? If you're choosing a school in part based on the availability of this clinic, how available will this clinic really be to you?

Table 4-1, "Questions to Ask about Psy.D. Programs," contains questions more specific to Psy.D. and clinically oriented Ph.D. applicants. This list was compiled, in part, by surveying the clinical Psy.D. students at the Graduate School of Applied and Professional Psychology at Rutgers University and asking them what questions they had (or wish they had) asked when applying to Psy.D. programs.

Theoretical Orientations

A question related to clinical and research opportunities is whether the graduate program will provide you with training in the desired theoretical orientations. We are not recommending that you prematurely affiliate with any theoretical camp; rather, we suggest that you identify those orientations you are interested in learning more about and those you are not. Several programs in the Northeast are strongly committed to a psychoanalytic approach and offer few, if any, training opportunities beyond that. The obvious implication is to avoid

TABLE 4-2. Theoretical Orientations of Faculty in APA-Accredited Clinical and Counseling Psychology Programs

Orientations	% of clinical faculty (*n* = 177 programs)	% of counseling faculty (*n* = 56 programs)
Psychodynamic/Psychoanalytic	26	21
Applied behavioral analysis/Radical behavioral	9	5
Family systems/Systems	18	21
Existential/Phenomenological/Humanistic	10	28
Cognitive/Cognitive-behavioral	46	44

Note. Adapted from *Doctoral training in counseling psychology: Admission statistics, student characteristics, and financial assistance* by M. A. Turkson & J. C. Norcross, 1996. Paper presented at the annual conference of the Eastern Psychological Association, Philadelphia, PA.

applying to programs that will not offer supervised experience in your approach(es). By the same token, you may scratch programs from your preliminary list that rigidly adhere to a behavioral persuasion if you are disinclined toward behaviorism.

The "Reports on Individual Programs" provide the approximate percentage of faculty in each program who subscribe to the five most popular theoretical orientations—psychodynamic/psychoanalytic, behavioral analysis/radical behavioral, family systems/systems, existential/phenomenological/humanistic, and cognitive/cognitive-behavioral. Let these figures guide you in ruling out a few programs that fail to address your theoretical predilections or, if you are uncommitted, that neglect exposure to multiple or integrative approaches to clinical work.

Table 4-2 presents the average percentage of faculty endorsing these five theoretical orientations in APA-accredited clinical and counseling programs. In general, the cognitive and cognitive-behavioral tradition predominates, accounting for almost half of the faculty members. Radical behaviorism is relatively infrequent, with psychodynamic, systems, and humanistic theories falling in between these two extremes. These global figures do not specifically include the integrative/eclectic orientation, which is the most popular approach of contemporary mental health professionals (Norcross & Goldfried, 1992), although the fact that the percentages add up to more than 100% indicates that faculty practice across orientations. Note too that the counseling psychology faculty endorse the humanistic/existential orientations much more frequently than do the clinical psychology faculty (28% versus 10%).

These average percentages also mask significant differences among programs as a function of their placement along the practice–research continuum. Research-oriented programs, as a rule, have a higher percentage of cognitive-behavioral faculty, while practice-oriented programs have a higher percentage of psychodynamic faculty (Mayne et al., 1994). The upshot is to investigate thoroughly the area of psychology (clinical, counseling) and the type of program (practice-oriented to research-oriented) that regularly provide training in your preferred theoretical orientation(s).

In addition to reviewing the listing of theoretical orientations in the reports on individual programs, those of you with an intense hankering for training in a particular theoretical orientation may want to peruse specialty directories. A number of professional societies maintain or publish lists of graduate programs that offer training in their theory of choice. The Association for Advancement of Behavior Therapy (AABT), for example, publishes a directory of graduate programs in behavior therapy and experimental clinical psychology (send for information from AABT, 305 Seventh Avenue, New York, NY 10001, or fax 212-647-1865). The Society for the Exploration of Psychotherapy Integration (SEPI), for another example, has pulled together a list of integrative and eclectic training programs throughout North America (see Norcross & Kaplan, 1995). Consult your advisors regarding the existence of speciality directories in your field of interest.

The popularity of theories, as with other professional fads, undergoes transformation over time. Extrapolating from historical trends and expert predictions (Norcross, Alford, & DeMichele, 1992), eclectic/integrative, systems, and cognitive persuasions will be in the ascendancy in the future. By contrast, classical psychoanalysis and existentialism are expected to decline. In an era of managed care, theoretical orientations that emphasize problem-focused treatments and document their effectiveness (e.g., behavioral and cognitive-

TABLE 4-3. Percentage of Students Recieving Financial Aid in APA-Accredited Clinical Psychology Programs

	Psy.D. programs	Practice-oriented Ph.D.	Equal-emphasis Ph.D.	Research-oriented Ph.D.
Tuition waiver only	9	15	10	1
Assistantship only	16	26	10	13
Waiver and assistantship	13	46	63	81
Any financial aid	37	87	83	95

Note. Adapted from "Admission requirements, acceptance rates, and financial assistance in clinical psychology programs: Diversity across the practice–research continuum" by T. J. Mayne, J. C. Norcross, & M. A. Sayette, 1994, *American Psychologist, 49,* 605–611.

behavioral therapy) will thrive in a health care climate that increasingly demands accountability.

Financial Aid

The next question, and it is by no means premature, is the availability of financial aid. Unless you can afford to pay for graduate school on your own or you are prepared to take out substantial loans, you need to have some idea of the probability of support. This is not a suggestion to avoid schools with scarce financial aid. It is a suggestion not to apply only to schools with scarce financial aid.

Figuring the total cost of full-time graduate study must include both academic expenses and living expenses. The academic side includes tuition, fees, supplies, books, and journals. The living side includes rent, transportation, food, clothing, insurance, and entertainment. Not surprisingly, most graduate students are relatively poor; at least you will have company in your financial misery (Fretz & Stang, 1980). Find out what fellowships, teaching assistantships, and research assistantships are available. In particular, find out the percentage of first-year students who receive assistantships. Is it 100%, 50%, or 0%?

On average, 57% of full-time doctoral students in psychology receive some support from the program; the remaining 43% do not. The picture is less encouraging for full-time master's students in psychology: only 23% receive any support (Gehlman, Wicherski, & Kohout, 1995). As you can see, the probability of financial support from the program itself is a very salient issue in narrowing down choices.

The reports on individual programs sections provide the approximate percentages of incoming doctoral students who receive tuition waiver only, assistantship/fellowship only, and both tuition waiver *and* assistantship/ fellowship for responding doctoral programs. Table 4-3 summarizes these data by type of clinical psychology program and indicates that the probability of securing financial aid from the school varies according to the research–practice orientation of the program (Mayne et al., 1994). About 95% of students in research-oriented Ph.D. programs receive some financial assistance while only 37% of Psy.D. students receive any aid. In between these poles are the practice-oriented and equal-emphasis Ph.D. programs.

In other words, higher acceptance rates come at a (tuition and living) cost to the incoming student. More rigorous admission standards and acceptance odds translate into increased probability of substantial financial aid (Kohout, Wicherski, & Pion, 1991; Mayne et al., 1994). In the most extreme case (Psy.D. vs. research-oriented Ph.D. programs), students are four times more likely to gain acceptance but six times less likely to receive full funding (stipend plus tuition waiver). An awareness of these probable trade-offs among the different types of programs will better enable you to make informed choices regarding your applications and career trajectories.

There *is* financial aid available from graduate schools to students possessing sterling credentials, and we wish to reaffirm its existence. Nevertheless, the increasing number of acceptances into clinical and counseling psychology doctoral programs during a period of economic "downsizing" raises difficult questions about internal funding opportunities and federal financial assistance. Our findings (Mayne et al., 1994) on financial aid portend a "pay as you go" expectation for up to half of all doctoral candidates in clinical and counseling psychology. This is particularly true, as we have seen, in Psy.D. and practice-oriented Ph.D. programs. The explicit expectation, as is true in such other practice disciplines as medicine and law, is that graduates will be able to repay their debt after they are engaged in full-time practice. We should note, however, that uncertainties regarding health care—specifically changes in insurance coverage for mental health—in the United States make this expectation difficult to evaluate at the present time.

The debt may be substantial. Research demonstrates that 74% of recent graduates in clinical psychology and 60% in counseling psychology reported debt related to graduate studies. Graduates of Vail-model Psy.D. and Ph.D. programs reported a median debt of $53,000 to $60,000. Recipients of Boulder-model clinical Ph.D.s, by contrast, reported a median level of debt of $22,000 (Kohout & Wicherski, 1999). With a median starting salary of approximately $45,000 for new psychology doctorates (APA, 2000), this debt represents a significant financial burden for many years. In large part, this difference in debt between Psy.D.s and Ph.D.s is attributable to the huge differences in financial aid between Vail-model and Boulder-model programs as pictured in Table 4-3. The APA researchers who compiled these data conclude, "It is important to disseminate this information to students who may be considering a career in psychology—so that their decisions can be fully informed" (Kohout & Wicherski, 1999, p. 10). We wholeheartedly agree.

Many schools include specific Web pages on financial aid. In addition to general information, they often list school- or program-specific scholarships and fellowships available to incoming students. It is worth the added effort to examine the financial aid pages at each school to search for special scholarship programs that you may be eligible for.

In addition to aid provided by the school itself, financial assistance is available from external private and public organizations. This funding comes under various names—self-sought, external, independent—to distinguish it from financial aid provided internally by the university. A variety of scholarships and fellowships is offered annually, but you will need to research those that pertain to your circumstances.

Your local Office of Career Services and Office of Financial Assistance should be able to direct you to potential sources of external support for graduate studies. One very useful resource is *Financing Graduate School*, a compact paperback authored by Patricia McWade (1996). The subtitle captures the importance of the topic—*How to Get the Money for your Master's or Ph.D.* The book transverses the entire geography of financial aid—grant applications, loan possibilities, federal and state support, and other sources of money for graduate study. A companion volume from the same publisher is *Peterson's Grants for Graduate and Postdoctoral Study*, which details over 1,400 potential fellowships, scholarships, grants, and awards. Peterson also offers a free online cram course in financial aid at www.petersons.com/ resources/finance.html. Be sure to check out the loads of advice and searchable databases on line at www.finaid.com and at www.ed.gov/ prog_info/SFA/ StudentGuide.

Federal funding is also available for pyschology graduate students, either in the form of training and research grants to institutions, which then fund graduate assistantships, or in the form of fellowships and dissertation grants awarded directly to students (Bullock, 1997). The National Science Foundation (NSF) funds separate competitions for Graduate Fellowships and for Minority Graduate Fellowships. Note that NSF does not support clinical or counseling research per se, only research directed at elucidating basic functioning, not focused on disease-related processes. The National Insitutes of Health (NIH) also funds psychology student awards through the National Institute of Mental Health, the National Institute on Drug Abuse, the National Institute on Alcohol Abuse and Alcoholism, and the Office of AIDS Research. Check out these programs through their Web pages: www.nsf.gov and www.nih.gov.

A number of specialty directories is also available free of charge from philanthropic and professional organizations. Among the more prestigious (and therefore, more competitive) are the predoctoral fellowships sponsored by the Danforth Foundation, Ford Foundation, and Armed Forces Health Professions Scholarship. The American Psychological Association (1995) publishes *A Directory of Selected Scholarship, Fellowship, and Other Financial Aid Opportunities for Women and Ethnic Minorities in Psychology and Related Fields*, which we highly recommend. APA also offers an online list of resources for financial assistance at www.apa.org/ ppo/fineduc.html. Explore all these and other possibilities early and actively.

Guaranteed student loans are also available for graduate students, but these are loans that must be repaid. The Federal Family Education Loan Program includes the subsidized Federal Stafford Loan, formerly known as the Guaranteed Student Loan, and the Federally Insured Student Loan. Students may borrow up to $8,500 per academic year. These loans are subsidized at reasonable interest rates, and repayment does not begin until 6 months after graduation, or following withdrawal from the program. In addition to this $8,500, another unsubsidized $10,000 per year can be borrowed, for which interest is due quarterly while the principal is deferred. The total amount that can be borrowed, including both subsidized and unsubsidized portions, and including undergraduate years, is currently $138,500. Some institutions also award Federal

Perkins Loans, a long-term loan program with a 5% interest rate available to graduate students demonstrating financial need. Other state loan programs exist; check these out as well. The bottom line is that every full-time graduate student is eligible for loans to finance his or her education, if necessary.

Quality of Life

A fifth and final variable concerns the quality of student life. It may be difficult to imagine, but occasionally you will want a break from graduate studies, to relax or engage in some nonpsychological pursuit! You should have a handle on the specifics of your own needs. Can they be met by the university and surrounding community? Do you want museums, fine dining, and professional theater? Then you probably want to live in or near a large city. If not, do you have a car capable of regularly getting you to one? Or do you get away to the mountains, enjoy rock climbing and camping, or find the city distracting? Or do you prefer to work late at night and need a campus that's safe after dark? Then be sure to apply to some more rural places. Also, consider whether you have friends or family nearby. Having a place to escape to can be important, especially if you do not have the funds to *really* escape. You are not going to base your decisions exclusively on any of these factors. But you can increase the probability of having everything you want by applying to schools you know can provide it all.

The Web is an excellent resource for investigating locations, towns, and cities that are far away and that you may not have the time or finances to visit at this time. Most cities have their own Web pages, which include pictures, maps, lists of attractions, and so on, for potential visitors and residents. Take the time to "virtually" explore the towns and cities of programs on your list. You may find that it is far more (or less) desirable than you had imagined.

The weight accorded to the quality of life in application decisions varies considerably among people. At one extreme are those applicants who give little thought to program location and heavily value the research and clinical opportunities. In the words of one colleague, "I'd live in hell for 4 or 5 years [the time it ordinarily takes to complete a doctorate] to be trained by the best people in my field." At the other extreme are those who will only apply to programs situated near family, friends, or an attractive metropolitan community. "Five years," they say, "is too long to be away from what I need as a person." We will not be so presumptuous as to advise which position you should adopt for yourself, except to remark that you should carefully weigh personal (location, fit) and professional (reputation, opportunities) considerations.

Putting It All Together

Having seriously reflected on your own interests and having carefully examined the clinical opportunities, research training, theoretical orientations, financial aid, and quality of life of various programs, you are very close to beginning to complete applications. Now is the time to put together all the information you have obtained about yourself and graduate programs in the form of a final list of schools—anywhere from 10 to 20, depending on the specificity of your interests and needs. As you make a neat pile of the applications you are about to complete, make one last check to insure that you are applying to the programs that best fit your needs. You may do this informally by mentally reviewing the program information you have obtained from various sources or you may do this systematically by completing Appendix D.

To complete Appendix D, write the name of each school in the first column. In column 2, "School Criteria," write the total you computed for each school in Appendix C. This is an index of your strength as an applicant and should range from about 5 to 15. For each of the next five columns, you can rate your impressions about each school on a 5-point scale. It is important that you create these scales yourself in ways that are personally relevant to you. The important thing is to know where each school rates in these areas in terms of your needs and desires. Below are some examples of rating systems you might model your own after.

In the column marked "Research," rate how strongly you feel toward the professors you have singled out as wanting most to work with:

1 I do not know enough about them, but their research is in my area.

3 I like the specifics of their research but do not know enough about their lab or their personalities.

5 I have been in contact with these professors and am impressed by their facilities and by them personally. I would like to work with them.

In the column marked "Clinical," rate each school according to how its opportunities suit your needs.

1 The school has only a psychological training center that treats students and I want more experience.

3 The school has a good psychological training center, but it has no practica in the community, and getting various populations may be difficult.

5 The school has many excellent clinical opportunities, including a specialty (e.g., eating disorders) clinic in the area that most interests me.

Or, possibly:

1 The school requires students to find their own clinical placements in the community, and I don't think I like that system.

3 The school has a college counseling center, but I'm not interested in working only with college students.

5 The school has a good psychological services center, and that's all I need.

"Theoretical Orientation" is the following column:

1 The program avers strict adherence to, and training in, a theoretical orientation that is in contrast to mine.

3 The program offers some courses and supervision in my preferred theoretical orientation.

5 The program provides considerable training in my preferred theoretical orientation plus other opportunities.

Next, consider "Financial Aid":

1 There is no funding for first-year students and no mention of outside means of support, and I need it.

3 I am likely to get at least tuition remission and have the possibility of working part-time for the university. It is especially likely that I could be a resident advisor and get free housing.

5 For the last 5 years, all first-year students have gotten full support from grants or fellowships and full tuition remission.

Or, possibly:

1 There is no funding for first-year students and no mention of outside means of support.

3 I am likely to get at least tuition remission, though only for the first 2 years.

5 The school guarantees tuition remission for 4 years, and that's all I need.

And last, rate the "Quality of Life":

1 This program is located in an unattractive area and seems bereft of culture.

3 I am indifferent to the location, and there is culture within the college community.

5 The area is ideal for me, and there are museums, concert halls, and theaters nearby.

Or, possibly:

1 This university is located in an unsafe section of a large city where I don't know anyone.

3 This university is located in a small city, and a friend of mine also attends.

5 This university is located in a small college town, and I have several close relatives and friends there.

Now look at this list. Are you applying to schools within a realistic range of admission criteria? Are you applying to at least some programs where you like the faculty, where the clinical facilities are suitable, where the theoretical orientation is compatible, where financial aid is available, and where you will feel comfortable living? If the answer to all of these is "No," then go back a step. Find at least a few schools where these qualities are present, possibly in abundance, and add them to your list of applications.

CHAPTER 5

APPLYING TO PROGRAMS

You are ready to start completing the applications. You have assessed your interests and have located programs that can provide the training and mentorship you desire. You have evaluated your own credentials and have chosen programs that will consider you seriously. You have received information on and applications from these programs either by mail or by perusing and downloading materials from the 90% of clinical programs with Web pages (Corcoran, Michels, & Ahina, 1999). You have carefully looked at their research offerings, clinical opportunities, theoretical orientations, financial aid, quality of life, and other variables of importance to you. Your task now is to actually apply to these schools.

You should attack this application process with all the drive and commitment you can muster. Try to emulate the manic zeal of successful medical school applicants. As they will readily inform you, the application itself reflects directly on your potential as a graduate student. In a real sense, your professional future is at stake.

A completed application will typically consist of the following elements: application form, curriculum vitae, personal statement, letters of recommendation, transcripts, entrance examination scores, and an application fee. This chapter traces the requisite steps of compiling, completing, and transmitting these materials in a coordinated fashion. But before we address the nuts and bolts of doing so, let us touch upon the crucial question of how many programs to apply to.

How Many?

The average number of applications made by students to clinical and counseling psychology programs is about 13. The precise number to which you should apply depends on the strength of your credentials and the competitiveness of the programs to which you are applying; more applications are indicated for weaker credentials and more competitive programs. Our rule of thumb is to apply to *at least* 10 to 12 programs: five "safe" or "insurance" programs (you clearly meet or exceed their standards); five "target" or "ambitious" programs (your credentials just make or miss their requirements); and perhaps one or two "reach" or "stretch" programs (where you do not approximate their standards but you have a particular hunch, research compatibility, or personal relationship that has a chance of sweeping you into the finalist pool). We have met industrious students who have applied to over 40 programs and confident students who have applied to just five or six.

But "don't pull a Missar," as we say at the University of Scranton. David Missar was an exceptional undergraduate and good-humored fellow (who gave us permission to use his story as a lesson for others to learn). He had a sky-high GPA, impressive GREs, a practicum to his credit, and even a coauthored publication. He was feeling a bit too confident in applying to only four doctoral programs, all located around his home town of Washington, DC, which happens to have some of the most competitive programs in the country. Despite his stellar academic credentials, Dave did not receive any acceptances his first year simply because his research interests and strengths did not "match" those of the clinical faculty and institutions to which he applied. Had he applied to a greater number or larger variety of programs, he surely would have been accepted somewhere, as he was easily the next year when he corrected his miscalculations.

Application Form

You have 10 to 20 applications in front of you. The deadlines range from mid-December to mid-February. You have used the fall to investigate potential programs—the faculty, the professors, the orientations, the location, and the cost. It is now time to actually start writing.

One of the easiest parts is filling out the application itself. It must be neat and typed, so make sure you think ahead of time before you type in an answer and have to white it out. If you download an application from the Web, be sure it is on clean, white, high-quality paper. Some students have found it useful to make a copy of the application and complete a first draft on the photocopy. The completed application reflects on you; keep it as professional and neat as possible.

Some programs allow you to submit an application through e-mail or the World Wide Web. We *strongly* advise against this. Taking the time to carefully consider (and often change) portions of your application is an important part of the process. Your personal statement requires a great deal of thought and will go through many revisions. By completing the application and reading it over several times before mailing it, you are likely to catch and have the opportunity to revise errors or poor choices. This is one of the places where we suggest against taking full advantage of technological advances!

Online applications can be an Internet nightmare. You don't know what your completed application will look like. You don't know where it goes—or where it does not go. You can easily fail to indicate essential information, such as faculty members you desire to work with. On the other hand, online applications are quick, potentially less expensive, and the software improving rapidly. So, if you elect to submit an application online (against our advice), please be careful. Proofread the document several times and try to cut and paste a fully formed personal statement from a word processing file.

Begin the applications at least 1 month before the earliest deadline. Some applicants, particularly undergraduates in their senior year, wait until the end of the fall semester on the holiday break. *This is too late*—do not wait, lest you be rushed, unprepared, and working on too tight a deadline.

Unlike the medical school process, which uses an identical application form for each school, practically every graduate program in psychology has its own, unique application. Providing the same information over and over again in slightly different formats can become frustrating and time consuming. Several years ago a committee recommended a standardized graduate application form to reduce the paperwork, but comparatively few programs have instituted it. Nonetheless, it provides a good idea of the information that will be requested of you:

- Full name
- Previous and maiden names
- Citizenship status
- Semester of entrance
- Current mailing address
- Permanent home address
- Educational history
- Degree sought
- Field of study
- Relevant courses taken
- Grade point averages
- Academic honors
- Clinical experience
- Special qualifications
- Employment history
- Teaching/research experience
- Career objectives
- References

Submitting applications is worse than filling out income tax returns (Fretz & Stang, 1980). Allow yourself enough uninterrupted time to do it carefully and completely. Illegible handwriting, incorrect spelling, and poor grammar will hurt your chances.

Some additional tips (Fretz & Stang, 1980):

- Keep the application forms for each school separated. Individual file folders might help. Since the forms are often poorly marked, you may not otherwise know which forms belong to what school.
- Enclose with each application a self-addressed, stamped postcard that the school can return to verify receipt of your application. On the back of the card simply type: "Please send to verify receipt of application to ____________________ University."
- Make a photocopy of each application before mailing it. Graduate schools and the postal service have been known to lose—or misplace—entire forms. A photocopy will enable you to quickly resubmit if necessary.
- Submit the application materials in a new legal size envelope on which you have typed the correct designation and your return address.

On a side note, completing application forms for graduate school marks a good time to critically examine the impression that your voice- and e-mail are communicating to others. A Dave Matthews tune on your answering machine may entertain fellow students, but probably not the director of clinical training. Cute e-mail addresses, such as studmuffin@phonyemail.com, may delight romantic partners, but certainly not the dean of the graduate school. So now may be the time to alter those messages and convey a more professional demeanor.

Curriculum Vitae

Curriculum vitae means, literally, "the course of your life." The vitae or CV summarizes your academic and employment history in a structured form, similar to a resume. Figures 5-1 and 5-2 present two possible formats for a CV; you will need to adapt these samples to your individual needs. Although the samples are single-spaced and occupy only one page, CVs are double spaced between entries and occupy several pages.

As a general comment, keep the CV honest, terse, and positive. Never fabricate, but perhaps "embellish" appropriately. The line to be drawn here is demarcated by whether or not you can look an interviewer directly in the eye and factually defend an entry that could subsequently be corroborated by a supervisor, professor, or another person. Structured brevity is the key; lengthy expositions of experiences are best left to personal statements or job descriptions. And this "academic resume" should be positive, upbeat in tone. Avoid any negative features that might red-flag your application. Save confessions and excruciating honesty for the clergy and psychotherapist. Omit sections that do not apply to you, such as "Presentations" or "Publications" if you have had none at this point in your career.

Let's proceed through the different sections of a CV and offer some additional hints. Distinguish between a current address and a permanent home address, if this applies to your living circumstances. Include telephone numbers and e-mail addresses at which program directors or professors can easily reach you. Information on your marital status and dependents is definitely optional. Regarding education, list degrees as "anticipated" if they have not yet been awarded. Impressive grade point averages may also be listed here. Honors are listed in chronological order, usually excluding those obtained in high school. Clinical experiences and research experiences can be listed together or separately, depending on what will strengthen your CV, but in either case indicate position title, relevant dates, number of hours, duties performed, and the supervisor. Include any presentations or publications in APA style, thereby demonstrating your familiarity with the psychologist's publication manual. The names of references should be listed only after you have obtained their permission to do so. *Never list a reference on a CV or application form unless you have secured that person's agreement to write a letter in support of your application.*

Here is an idea to enhance the CV for students who have developed specific research or computer competencies. List them on your vitae as a separate section. Computer skills might include proficiency with SPSS, SAS, Pascal, Harvard Graphics, Chartmaster, SigmaScan, SigmaPlot, CricketGraph, and Aldus Pagemaker. Research skills might include performing computerized library searching on *PsycLIT* or *Medline*, administering the Wisconsin Card Sorting Test (or another psychological test), or operating an electroencephalograph (EEG). Also include here any special skills, such as fluency in foreign languages or proficiency in American Sign Language. A faculty member screening applications may realize that these competencies are exactly what he or she is looking for in a new graduate assistant or research assistant. So use your CV to highlight your abilities! Omit this optional section if you have none or only one specific competency; in the latter case, describe the special qualification in your personal statement.

What should *not* be put on the CV? Hayes and Hayes (1989) recommend eliminating listings of religion, hobbies, pets, favorite books, and items of that kind. They are unnecessary; save them for a resume. Nor is a photograph customary.

Padding of all varieties must be avoided. Padding occurs when a reader reacts to the CV as more form than substance ("Who are they trying to fool?!"). Potentially risky is listing professional projects under way—one or two legitimate research projects may pass but any more will probably be considered suspect. Other signs of padding, and therefore sections to exclude, are conventions attended, journals read, and projects you worked on in a nonprofessional capacity.

Although much of the information contained in the CV is requested on the application form itself, we believe the inclusion of a CV enhances your application—providing it is properly prepared. A CV denotes a scholarly demeanor, highlights your accomplishments, and communicates familiarity with the workings of academia.

Specific comments on the form and style of the CV might prove useful. Place the date (month and year) on the upper right-hand corner of the CV. In this way, you can submit an addendum if your credentials significantly improve by, say, having a paper accepted for

November 2002

CURRICULUM VITAE

Name:	Ted E. Bear
Address:	15 Easy Street Babylon, NY 12345
Telephone:	(516) 555-1212
E-mail:	bear@babu.edu
Date of Birth:	March 15, 1980
Place of Birth:	Scranton, Pennsylvania
Social Security #:	123-45-6789
Citizenship:	United States of America

Education:

H.S. Diploma: Cherry Hill High School, City, State, June 1998
B.S. (anticipated): Psychology (Clinical Track), Babylon University, May 2002

Honors and Awards:

New York State Regents Scholarship, 1998–2000
Dean's List, Babylon University, 2001–2002
Psi Chi, 2002
Babylon University Honors Program, 2000–2002
Who's Who Among Students in American Colleges & Universities, 2002

Clinical Experience:

Mental Health Technician, Friendship House, Jackson, Wyoming, June 2000–August 2001. Duties: recreational counseling and supervision of 20 behaviorally and emotionally disturbed children. Supervisor: Doris Day, M.S. 40 hours weekly.

Telephone Counselor, Mesopotamia County Community Crisis Center, Babylon, New York, 1999–2000. Duties: used a crisis intervention model to counsel a wide range of callers. Supervisor: Randal Kaplan, M.A. 4 hours weekly.

Research Experience:

Research Assistant, Babylon University, Department of Psychology, September 2000–June 2002. Duties: word processing, manuscript preparation, and data analyses for Chris Demanding, Ph.D. 15 hours weekly.

Honors Research, Babylon University with Rita Murrow, Ph.D., 2001–2002. Duties: proposed and conducted an original project; data input and analysis using SPSSx; write-up and oral defense.

Professional and Honor Societies:

Psi Chi, National Honor Society in Psychology
American Psychological Association (student affiliate)
Alpha Gamma Epsilon Omega (National Honor Society in Ergonomics)

Presentations and Publications:

Bear, T. E., & Murrow, F. A. (2001, April). *Self-esteem and math performance: Another look.* Paper presented at the meeting of the Babylon Psychological Association, New York.

Murrow, F. A., & Bear, T. E. (2001). The effects of self-esteem on math test performance. *Journal of Psychology, 46,* 113–117.

References:

Frances Murrow, Ph.D., Associate Professor, Department of Psychology, Babylon University, Babylon, NY 12345. Voice: 516-555-1212; e-mail: murrow@babu.edu

Chris Demanding, Ph.D., Professor and Chair, Department of Psychology, Babylon University, Babylon, NY 12345. Voice: 516-555-1212; e-mail: les@babu.edu

Doris Day, M.S., Senior Therapist, Horror House, 78 Oak Street, Jackson, WY 12345. Voice: 307-555-1212

FIGURE 5-1. One format for curriculum vitae.

Ted E. Bear November 2002

A. Personal History:

Business Address:	Department of Psychology Babylon University Babylon, New York 12345
Phone:	(516) 555-1212
Home Address:	1017 Jefferson Avenue Cherry Hill, NJ 08002
Phone:	(609) 555-1212
E-mail:	bear@babu.edu
Birthdate:	March 15, 1980
Citizenship:	United States of America

B. Educational History:

Babylon University, Babylon, New York
Major: Psychology (Clinical Track)
Degree: B.S. (anticipated), May 2002
Dean's List, 2001–2002
Who's Who Among Students in American Colleges & Universities, 2002
Honors Thesis: Investigation of the relationship between self-esteem and math performance (Chairperson: Rita Murrow, Ph.D.)

C. Professional Positions:

1. Telephone Counselor, Mesopotamia County Community Crisis Center, Babylon, New York. Part-time position, 1999–2000. Duties: used a crisis intervention model to counsel a wide range of callers. Supervisor: Randal Kaplan, M.A.
2. Mental Health Technician, Friendship House, Jackson, Wyoming. Full-time summer position, 2000. Duties: recreational counseling and supervision of 20 behaviorally and emotionally disturbed children. Supervisor: Doris Day, M.S.
3. Research Assistant, Babylon University. Half-time position, 2001–2002. Duties: word processing, manuscript preparation, and data analysis. Supervisor: Chris Demanding, Ph.D.

D. Membership in Professional Associations:

Psi Chi (National Honor Society in Psychology)
American Psychological Association (student affiliate)
Alpha Gamma Epsilon Omega (National Honor Society in Ergonomics)

E. Professional Activities:

President, Babylon University Chapter of Psi Chi, 1999–2000
Member of Program Committee, Babylon University Psychology Conference, 2000

F. Papers Presented:

Bear, T. E., & Murrow, F. A. (2001, April). *Self-esteem and math performance: Another look.* Paper presented at the meeting of the Babylon Psychological Association, New York.

G. Publications:

Murrow, F. A., & Bear, T. E. (2001). The effects of self-esteem on math test performance. *Journal of Psychology, 46,* 113–117.

H. References:

Frances Murrow, Ph.D., Associate Professor, Department of Psychology, Babylon University, Babylon, NY 12345. Voice: 516-555-1212; e-mail: murrow@babu.edu

Chris Demanding, Ph.D., Professor and Chair, Department of Psychology, Babylon University, Babylon, NY 12345. Voice: 516-555-1212; e-mail: les@babu.edu

Doris Day, M.S., Senior Therapist, Horror House, 78 Oak Street, Jackson, WY 12345. Voice: 307-555-1212

Note. Adapted from Hayes & Hayes (1989) with the permission of the authors.

FIGURE 5-2. Another format for curriculum vitae.

publication or receiving your department's "student of the year" award. Lay out the information in an attractive and organized manner. Use a consistent format both within each section and between sections. For example, if you opt to list your clinical experiences from the most recent to the past, then maintain this format in all the other sections. Proofread the document carefully; review it with an advisor before you print it. It ideally would be produced on a laser printer with a few fonts, but any letter-quality printer will suffice. Staple the pages together when finished (Hayes & Hayes, 1989).

The CV, like personal statements (below), should be printed on standard-sized white or cream stock. Purchase good quality bond paper for these documents. Avoid onionskin paper, goldenrod color, odd-sized papers, memo pads, green or red ink, and other unconventional or "cheap" materials.

Personal Statements

Another bridge you must cross is writing the statement of purpose. Every school will want to know why you chose clinical or counseling psychology and the area within it that you plan to study. Admissions committees will also want to know how you came to this decision and what sorts of goals you have in mind. Each application will ask this question in a slightly different way because each school has slightly different expectations and approaches to training. *Read the instructions carefully.* Do not just word process one statement and submit it to everyone.

Do not misinterpret the meaning of *personal* in *personal statement.* This essay is not the place to espouse your philosophy of life, to describe your first romance, or to tell the story about your being bitten by the neighbor's dog and subsequently developing an anxiety disorder. Instead, think of the essay as a *professional statement.* Write about your activities and experiences as an aspiring psychologist (Bottoms & Nysse, 1999).

An analysis of 360 essays required as part of the graduate application process demonstrated wide variability in the content requested (Keith-Spiegel, 1991). The most frequent requests were to articulate

- Career plans
- Clinical experiences
- Interest areas
- Specific faculty of interest
- Research experiences
- Autobiographical statement
- Academic objectives
- Reasons for applying to that particular program
- Educational background

To reiterate: Carefully read the question, individualize your response to each program, and respond to all parts of the question posed to you.

Be attentive to what the program requests. If they stress research, highlight your research interests and experience. If they stress clinical work, highlight the development of these interests and your training experiences to date. Show how you started with a question or a clinical observation, how you pursued that question, and how it developed into a greater understanding of the issues at hand and a need to know more. Then demonstrate how this led you to pursue psychology and how this program meets your needs and is ideal to your continuing to pursue knowledge in this area. State the goals you wish to attain with this knowledge, the sort of career path you hope to work toward. If you are committed to the Boulder model, indicate how research is useful and how it is clinically applicable.

If you can make this connection in your own work, you will impress on the admission committee the sort of integration APA sets forth as its ideal.

Graduate selection committees value clarity, focus, and "passion" in personal statements (Keith-Spiegel, 1991). Clarity and focus are typically construed as indicators of lucid thought, realistic planning, and self-direction, all valuable assets in a graduate student. At the same time, try to communicate a heartfelt commitment to your chosen career. "Passion" is not too strong a term—even relentless, obsessed, committed, fascinated; in short, what we call "catching the fever!"

The personal statement is a prime opportunity to induce a match with the research and clinical interests of a faculty member. Many programs, as we have said, attempt to match faculty with incoming graduate students on the basis of mutual interest, for example, family therapy, women's issues, or neuropsychological assessment. This matching strategy is more often employed by research-oriented than practice-oriented programs, but attempt it in all of your statements.

To illustrate, consider the clinical admissions process of the University of Ottawa, a program with an equal emphasis between research training and clinical training. Like many programs, they create a finalist pool by eliminating applications with inadequate GPAs and GRE scores. Then each of the clinical faculty members reviews all the finalist applications in order to locate several possible matches. These applicants then receive interviews. As you can see, and as we have repeated throughout this book, gaining admission into competitive doctoral programs is not limited simply to one's credentials but also includes a match in research and clinical interests.

Here, then, are a few general guidelines for writing personal statements that increase the probability of a match:

- Mention at least two and perhaps up to four of your interests. This obviously covers a wider range than a single interest.
- Cast your interests in fairly broad terms. Not administering the Wisconsin Card Sorting Test, but neuropsychological assessment. Not a mail survey of counseling psychologists, but the characteristics and practices of psychotherapists.
- Nominate at least two professors with whom you would like to work at that particular graduate program. This, too, enhances the chance of a successful match.

A commonly asked question is, "How personal should I get in my personal statement?" Although there is no universally correct answer, some suggestions can be offered. A personal detail, such as describing how growing up with a handicapped or disturbed sibling has affected your life and decision to enter psychology, is appropriate. However, depicting the situation in intimate detail without relating it to its contribution to your own growth may lead an admissions committee to question your judgment. A rule of thumb is to be introspective and self-revealing without sounding exhibitionistic. For example, it is appropriate for an applicant to state how personal life experiences have contributed to better self-understanding, but it sounds peculiar when the applicant goes into great detail about particular relationships or early life events (Halgin, 1986). Although allusions to a history of psychotherapy in personal statements does not appear to overly stigmatize candidates or lead disproportionately to their rejections (Schaefer, 1995), we recommend against including your personal therapy in written materials. Better to save such intimate disclosures for the personal interview, if appropriate.

Many personal statements are ineffective because, first, the student fails to spend time preparing them and, second, the student fails to be "personal" (Osborne, 1996). Therefore, as an applicant you should devote a substantial amount of time thinking, writing, rethinking, and rewriting the personal statement. Your statement should include personal details that relate to your ability to be a successful graduate student and that demonstrate maturity, adaptation, and motivation—the very characteristics sought be admissions committees.

A good idea is to show some humility. Even if you have golden research and clinical experiences and 1600 GRE scores, you are still entering as a student. You are coming to learn. Show some awareness of the areas you hope to develop during your graduate school experience.

Be prepared to back up the claims you make in your personal statements. If you profess a working knowledge of, say, experiential psychotherapy, then be prepared for questions on the work of Carl Whitaker, Leslie Greenberg, and Alvin Mahrer. Similarly, if you claim fluency in Spanish, then expect one of the interviews to be conducted entirely in Spanish (Megargee, 1990).

The "to do's" of personal statements are process suggestions and thus difficult to pinpoint, but the "not to do's" are content oriented and easier to delineate (Whitbourne, 1999). We characterize three such "nots" as the three H's: Humor, Hyperbole, and Hard luck stories. Humor rarely works in a formal written statement; so unless you are an unusually gifted satirist, we recommend you avoid jokes and funny stories about your life. Similarly, hyperbole rarely impresses the admissions committee. References to your "overwhelming childhood trauma" and "triumph over undiagnosed learning disabilities" cast doubt on the veracity and accuracy of your judgment. And hard luck stories typically come off feebly. Many students financed their undergraduate educations, many survived disastrous relationship choices, and many muddled through three academic majors before finding their niche in psychology. Avoid making adversity the theme of your statement.

One way to make your personal statement sparkle is to describe any teaching assistantships or experiences. Talk about how you learned leadership skills and teamwork in this role. Specific examples of how you responsibly handled challenging course or teaching activities will lead the reader to infer you possess the "right stuff."

Your personal statement should tell a compelling, integrative story of a reflective individual who explicates accomplishments without joking or bragging or sobbing. As our colleague Sue Krauss Whitbourne (1999) puts it: Don't say it softly or loudly, just say it clearly!

You will be asked in practically every personal statement and personal interview why you chose to apply to *this* particular graduate program in clinical or counseling psychology. Table 5-1 presents a *portion* of a sample statement, addressing this ubiquitous question, written by one of our undergraduate students in his successful bid for entry into a clinical psychology doctoral program committed to the scientist–practitioner model. His reasons for applying to "Bogus University" are presented only as a single example; your

TABLE 5-1. Sample Autobiographical Statement

It is my strong desire to attend a doctoral program in clinical psychology. I am seeking a program committed to the Boulder model, training scientist–practitioners able to serve society in a variety of capacities. The program I attend should stress the importance of understanding and integrating the broad field of psychology, as well as providing the knowledge and training specific to clinical psychology.

After a thorough review of more than 50 programs in clinical psychology, I have chosen to apply to Bogus University for a number of reasons. First, your program is known for producing stellar graduates, and has been repeatedly recommended to me by several psychology faculty. Second, Bogus University allows students to immerse themselves in research relatively early in their graduate careers. Third, I am drawn toward several of your faculty members, including Dr. Babe Ruth for her work in substance abuse and cognitive therapy, and Dr. Ty Cobb for his work in sexual health, stress, and coping. I would be pleased to have either of these faculty members as my mentor. Fourth, the available clinical experiences would allow me to work with a population I find of particular interest, such as adults and families at the Psychological Services Center. And fifth, I am looking to attend school in a scenic area of the country where both my fiance and I think we would be comfortable.

statements will need to be tailored to your interests and credentials as well as the application instructions. You should also note that this is just one part of an entire autobiographical statement.

Nonetheless, his why-I-applied-to-your-program statement illustrates several important points. First, he advances multiple reasons for applying to that particular program. Five reasons sound much more convincing than just one or two. Second, his reasons for applying to Bogus U. primarily address his professional match with the program (their reputation, faculty members, clinical opportunities) but nicely concludes with a personal touch (geographic location). Third, he mentions two specific faculty and several potential research interests in an attempt to maximize the chances of a "match." Fourth, the statement reflects his careful reading and incorporation of the program's self-description; for example, he cites the opportunity to immerse himself early into research and names the Psychological Services Center. Fifth, the statement is systematically organized and clearly written—indicators of an organized and clear-thinking graduate student!

Compose your personal statement as carefully as you would an important term paper. Write several rough drafts and then set it aside for a few days. Avoid slang words on the one hand, and overly technical or elaborate words on the other. Stick to the information requested; avoid too many "ruffles" and lengthy expositions of your own philosophy (Fretz & Stang, 1980). Write as many drafts as necessary until the statement sounds right to you. Before you finish your personal statement, have friends read it for grammar, spelling, and typos. Regardless of the content, technical accuracy really makes a difference. Once it is error free, have one or more faculty members read it and make suggestions. Let them know where the statement is going, and they should be able to guide you on form and appropriateness.

We hope that the suggestions in this section are helpful in guiding you in writing your personal statement. It is also our hope that they are not too constraining. This is the part of the application where a committee gets to see you in a more personal light, an area where "you can be you."

Letters of Recommendation

What does an admission committee gain from letters of recommendation? The answer is a personal but objective evaluation of your work from someone experienced in the field. They desire a more objective sense of your abilities and experience than what you provide about yourself. Consequently, it is best to have at least two of the people writing your letters be at the doctoral level in psychology or psychology-related disciplines. One fine letter from a master's-level clinician is usually acceptable, but he or she will not be in a position to attest to your ability to complete doctoral studies. By the same token, bachelor degree recipients, friends, and relatives should never write letters of recommendation to doctoral programs—they simply do not have the experience or knowledge of what it takes to earn a doctorate. Letters from politicians and your psychotherapists typically are inappropriate as well—they tend to write personal and psychological testimonies instead of academic letters of reference.

Choose people with whom you have worked for a long enough period, preferably for a year or more. That

TABLE 5-2. Professors' Pet Peeves: Avoiding Neutral Letters of Recommendation

Students sometimes are unaware of how some of the seemingly innocuous things they do and say can annoy their professors. In turn, the professors provide students with less than enthusiastic letters of recommendation. Here are some examples suggested by William W. Nish of Georgia College, reprinted with his kind permission.
Be quick to apply such concise labels as "busy work," "irrelevant," and "boring" to anything you do not like or understand. Not only is this a convenient way of putting the professor down, but also you will not be bothered with the inconvenience of understanding something before you judge it.
Always be ready with reasons why you are an exception to the rules established for the class, such as the dates for submitting written assignments.
Avoid taking examinations at the same time as the rest of the class. Be certain to take it for granted that the professor will give you a make-up exam at your convenience, regardless of your reason for missing the exam.
Be very casual about class attendance. When you see your professor be sure to ask, "Did I miss anything important in class today?" This will do wonders for his or her ego. By all means expect the professor to give a recital of all of the things you missed instead of taking the responsibility for getting the information from another member of the class.
Be consistently late to class and other appointments. This shows other people how much busier you are than they are.
Do not read your assignments in advance of class lecture and discussion. This actually allows you to study more efficiently, for you can take up class time asking about things that are explained in the reading.
Avoid using the professor's office hours or making an appointment. Instead, show up when he or she is frantically trying to finish a lecture before the next class hour and explain that you must see him or her right that minute.
Do not participate in such mundane activities as departmental advising appointments. Instead, wait until the last minute for approval of your schedule, and then expect the professor to be available at your convenience.

Note. Adapted with the permission of William W. Nish.

does not include a professor you have taken a single class with, even if you did get an A. If you wrote a particularly strong paper in the class and the professor knows you a bit better, then he or she could serve as a reference, but this reference is still not the most desirable. At best this person can say, "This student was always on time, attended every class, participated in discussions, attended office hours, and tested very well. On this basis I consider him/her an intelligent student and a good candidate for graduate school."

By contrast, the admissions committee wants to hear something like: "This student has worked with me for 1 year. During that time she scored MMPIs, ran subjects using a Grass Model 7 polygraph, analyzed data, and conducted her own honors thesis. She was dependable and worked beyond what was required by the department. Given this student's intelligence, motivation, and responsibility, I think she would make an outstanding graduate student." Though the above is a strong example, the point is that you want someone to attest to your ability and responsibility.

Table 5-2 lists some of the self-sabotaging things students do to receive neutral letters of recommendation. Although presented for its humorous nature, it also provides sage warnings about interpersonal behaviors that annoy professors.

Most graduate programs request three or four letters of recommendation. Try to secure letters that will give the admissions committee the information it desires. At a practice-oriented program, two letters from clinical supervisors and one from a research advisor might be prudent. At a research-oriented school, two letters from research advisors and one from a clinical supervisor would probably be more appropriate. All things being equal, it is preferable to have your "research" letters come from faculty. However, if you believe that a letter from an employer would be significantly more helpful than that of a professor with whom you were not well acquainted, then it is probably a good idea to use the employer.

Our general advice was recently confirmed in an interesting study (Keith-Spiegel & Wiederman, 2000) that asked members of admissions committees to rank sources of recommendation letters. Raters were asked to assume that the letters from these different sources were equally positive so that rating variations were due solely to the referee's characteristics. The most valuable sources of letters of recommendation were (in order): (1) A mentor with whom the applicant has done considerable work; (2) The applicant's professor, who is also a well-known and highly respected psychologist; (3) An employer in a job related to the applicant's professional goals; (4) The chair of the academic department in which the applicant is majoring; (5) A professor from another department from whom the applicant has taken a relevant upper-division course. By contrast, a letter from a graduate teaching assistant was rated, essentially, as no help. And a letter from one's personal therapist was actually rated negatively!

Very important: First ask the person writing the letters whether he or she *can* write you a good one. Ask this direct and specific question: "Can you write a good letter of recommendation for me?" If the person is hesitant or gives any indication of having reservations, *ask someone else!* A bad letter of recommendation is deadly. Better to have one letter from a professor who gave you an "A" than from someone who might express reservations about your abilities. "I don't know" is better than "I know, but I have reservations."

The way you approach professors for a recommendation is an underappreciated topic. You will ask specifically, "Can you write a good recommendation for me?" If the person responds unhesitantly in the affirmative, we strongly recommend that you provide that person with a letter similar to that shown in Figure 5-3. The person writing a letter of recommendation needs adequate information in order to produce a credible and informative letter. You can be powerful in shaping a professor's letter of recommendation!

This letter—and the attendant course listing and CV—will promote accuracy and detail. These are essential characteristics of strong letters of recommendation in that the admissions committee looks for positive tone *and* detail. A two-paragraph laudatory letter on the order of "Great student, fine person" simply doesn't make the detailed case for your admission into competitive doctoral programs.

What admissions committees also find useless in letters are duplicate and irrelevant information. One set of researchers (Elam et al., 1998) queried members of admissions committees and discovered the five least helpful aspects of letters of recommendation:

- Repetition of information from the application (e.g., repeating grades, honors, and scores available elsewhere on the application)
- Unsubstantiated superlatives or vague generalities
- Detailed descriptions of grades in one particular course
- Lack of strong relationship between applicant and letter writer
- Inclusion of irrelevant information, such as religious beliefs or hearsay

Put another way, give your referees sufficient data to render informed and positive letters about your personal characteristics, academic strengths, and interpersonal skills so that they do not resort to filling your recommendations with irrelevant content.

Here's how one doctoral program (University of Rhode Island) attempts to translate the content of recommendation letters into numerical categories.

1 Summary recommendations in all three letters are neutral or negative. Positive and negative assessments are listed. Overall evaluation in all three is neutral.

2 Letters meet criteria between anchor points 1 and 3.

3 Summary recommendations in all three letters are positive and general. Positive statements from all three letters. Statements are general in nature.

4 Letters meet criteria between anchor points 3 and 5.

5 Summary recommendations in all three letters are excellent and detailed. Positive statements from all three letters are very favorable and very detailed in their support.

Note, again, that the emphasis is on positive tone *and* supportive detail. This is the desired result of your extra work in providing references with factual information and assertive requests for letters of recommendation. A "liability letter" is one that communicates limited knowledge of the applicant, leading an admissions committee to conclude that the person was only minimally connected to professors in his or her undergraduate or master's department (Halgin, 1986).

Many universities provide their own form for recommendations as part of the application package. Your institution will probably have one of two ways of

246 Wood Street
Babylon, NY 14000

November 2002

Leslie Jones, Ph.D.
Department of Psychology
East Coast University
1200 Faculty Building
Hausman, MD 43707

Dear Dr. Jones:

Thank you for agreeing to write a letter of recommendation on my behalf. I hereby waive (or do not waive) my right to inspect the letter of recommendation written for me and sent to the designated schools of my choice. I am applying to (master's, doctoral) programs in clinical (counseling) psychology. My earliest deadline is ____ ___________.

Here are the courses I have taken from you.

Fall 2000	Abnormal Psychology	A–
Spring 2001	Clinical Psychology	B+
Fall 2002	Undergraduate Research	

Here are other activities in which I have participated.

September 2001–January 2002	Research Assistant
2000–2001	Vice President of Psi Chi

My latest GRE scores were 600 Verbal, 590 Quantitative, and 580 Analytical. My Psychology Subject Test score was 610.

Finally, I attach a copy of my current vitae and a list of psychology courses for any additional information that might prove useful. Please feel free to call me at 555-1212 or to e-mail me at Chris_smith@phonyemail.com. Thanks again.

Sincerely yours,

Chris Smith

Encls.

FIGURE 5-3. Sample letter to request a letter of recommendation.

handling these forms. One way is to provide your professor with these forms and stamped envelopes addressed to the schools to which the forms are to be sent. This is a small but crucial precaution—do not take the chance that postage will delay return of the letter. It is also courteous: Your professor is doing you a favor taking considerable time and contemplation to write a good letter. Another way is to provide your professor with these forms; he or she will then complete them and return them to the Office of Career Services/Planning for processing and mailing. Ask your reference which method he or she prefers.

These recommendation forms from the individual schools may appear to be quite different at first glance; however, closer inspection will reveal that they request essentially the same information. The forms typically ask the people writing the letters to note the length of time they have known you and in what capacities. Then the referees are asked to rate your research ability, originality, writing skills, organizational ability, maturity, interpersonal skills, persistence, and similar qualities on a structured grid. Typical forms request an appraisal of the applicant in terms of ten qualities in comparison with others applying for graduate study whom the referees have known in the applicant's proposed field of study. The rating grid offers responses of top 3%, next 10%, next 20%, middle third, lowest third, and unable to judge. On most forms, an open space is then presented for a narrative description of your strengths and weaknesses. The forms usually conclude with a request for a summary rating: a check mark on a continuum from "not recommended" to "highly recommended" or a numerical value representing an overall ranking of this student to others taught in the past or some similar estimate.

A recent study identified and categorized the most frequent characteristics of applicants that recommenders were requested to rate on the forms (Appleby, Keenan, & Mauer, 1999). The resulting list—based on the analysis of 143 recommendation forms—describes the characteristics that psychology graduate programs value in their applicants. In descending order of frequency, the top dozen are

- Motivated and hardworking
- High intellectual/scholarly ability
- Research skills
- Emotionally stable and mature
- Writing skills
- Speaking skills
- Teaching skills/potential
- Works well with others
- Creative and original
- Strong knowledge of area of study
- Character or integrity
- Special skills, such as computer or lab

One important lesson to be learned from the results of this study is that graduate school aspirants should make a concerted effort to behave in ways that allow them to acquire relevant skills (research, writing, speaking, computer) and to be perceived by at least three of their professors as motivated, bright, emotionally stable, capable of working well with others, and possessing integrity (Appleby et al., 1999).

These forms, by law, will contain a waiver statement asking whether you do or do not waive your right to inspect the completed letter of reference. The Family Education Rights and Privacy Act of 1974 (the so-called Buckley Amendment) mandated that students over age 18 be given access to school records unless they waive this right. This is a complicated topic, but we advise applicants to waive their right of access *providing*, as previously discussed, the person writing the letter knows the student well and has unhesitantly agreed to serve as a reference. Do not waive access—or better yet, do not request letters—from persons you do not trust or do not know.

A confidential letter carries more weight. By waiving your right to access, you communicate a confidence that the letters will be supportive, and you express trust in your reference. In fact, over 90% of health professional schools prefer letters of recommendation that are waived by the student (Chapman & Lane, 1997). Our experiences and naturalistic studies (e.g., Ceci & Peters, 1984; Shaffer & Tomarelli, 1981) suggest that professors' honest evaluations will be compromised when you have access to what they have written. By waiving the right, you are communicating an intent to have the "truth" told. Otherwise, an admissions committee may lump the letter with all the other polite and positive testimonials (Halgin, 1986).

In making your choice of whether to waive or not to waive, be clear about the law. Most students correctly know that if they waive their rights they may never see the letter. However, many students erroneously think that choosing not to waive their rights means that they can see their letter if they do not get accepted or that they have a right to preview the letter before it is sent (Ault, 1993). These are common fallacies, but fallacies nonetheless.

The relevant laws do not dictate that professors must show students the completed letter. One study (Keith-Spiegel, 1991) of college faculty found that 17% never show students their letters of recommendation, 46% usually do not, 8% only to students they know well, 15% only if students ask, and 14% routinely show students their letters. Nor does the law guarantee a student access to letters if the student is rejected from a graduate program; in fact, students may inspect their files at a graduate school only after they have been accepted at and enrolled in that graduate school (Ault, 1993).

Going one step further, contrary to some students' beliefs, faculty do *not* have to write letters of recommendation for students.

Letters are a common and voluntary courtesy, not a job requirement. Why might faculty members decline to write a letter for a student? The single most common reason is that they don't know the student well enough (Keith-Spiegel, 1991). Other frequent reasons given by faculty are that they question the student's motivation level, emotional stability, academic credentials, or professional standards. If faculty defer on your request for a letter, politely inquire about their reasoning and graciously thank them for their candor.

Play it safe and provide the reference form at least 6 weeks before the deadline. Completing your recommendation may not be the top priority of the person you have asked to write it, or he or she may be out of town prior to the deadline. Do not take any chances that a letter will be late. Allow 2 weeks and ask if the letter has been sent. Call the school after 4 weeks to see that it has been received. Be politic: Do not pester, but do follow up.

Transcripts and GRE Scores

An application file will not be complete—and probably not even considered by the admissions committee—unless the required academic transcripts and entrance examination scores have been received. Your task here consists of requesting the appropriate agencies to transmit official copies of these materials to the graduate schools of your choice and then ensuring that the schools have received them.

With respect to transcripts, you must request that the Registrar's Office of all attended colleges and universities mail an *official* copy of your transcript directly to the graduate school. An official copy will contain the seal, stamp, and authorized signature of the institution. The cost of transcripts varies from place to place, but it averages $3 to $5 per copy. Submit transcript requests at least 1 month before the application deadline. Many universities take 2 weeks during the semester to process these requests. The form requesting a transcript or the cover address will most likely accompany the transcript itself and thereby enter your graduate application file. Accordingly, this request form or mailing address should be typed or printed neatly.

A reminder: Request an unofficial copy of your own transcript in September or October prior to applying. Inspect it closely for errors and omissions. Horror stories abound regarding erroneous transcript entries misleading admissions committees—an initial grade of I (incomplete) becoming an F (failure), honors credits not registered, unpaid term bills delaying transcripts, and so on. Don't leave it to chance; check it out yourself.

With respect to GREs, score reports will automatically be mailed to you and to the four graduate schools you listed on your GRE registration form. The mailing date for the score reports is approximately 6 weeks after the test date for paper-based testing (Psychology Subject Test) and 2 weeks for computer-based testing (General Test). Your copy of the score report is intended only for your information; official reports are sent directly by ETS to the score recipients you designate. This procedure—as with the Registrar transmitting an official transcript—"is intended to ensure that no questions are raised about the authenticity of a score report" (GRE, 2001, 16).

You will probably be applying to more than the four schools you initially designated for score reports. Toward this end, you can use the "Phone Service for Additional Score Reports" by dialing 1-888-GRE-SCORE. The charge is $6.00 per call plus $13.00 for each report requested, and your scores will be mailed out within five working days. Or, you can submit an "Additional Score Report Request Form," published by ETS and obtainable at your Career Services Office, and remit your payment of $13.00 for *each* score recipient listed. The ETS pledges in writing to "make every effort to send your score reports within ten working days after receipt of your request" (GRE, 2001), but you should allow for at least 1 month. You may have your GRE scores transmitted at any time during the 5-year period after they are initially reported. Remember: Only send unofficial copies of your GRE scores if you are applying well before the deadline, and telephone to be sure that this does not impede your application.

Unsolicited Documents

A frequently asked question is, "What if a program doesn't ask for something that I'd like to send?" Some examples are the curriculum vitae, a research paper, and job descriptions. If a school does not want additional documents, they will state it clearly on the application. In that case, do as they request. But even then, you may be able to make it a part of your application if you have come to know a professor at the school and have shared any of these documents with him or her. In general, it is a good idea to send a curriculum vitae, research paper, and/or job descriptions if they are applicable.

If you have relevant work and clinical experiences but can only use one for a letter of reference, then include a curriculum vitae or job description. One benefit is that these allow you to spend less time focusing on the details of these work experiences in your personal statement. You can refer to how the experiences influenced you without having to waste space explaining exactly what you did.

As a professional, you will need a CV eventually, and we recommend you begin one even if you do not use it in every application. Start a vitae file and toss notes and memos into it regarding assistantship duties, noteworthy activities, committee assignments, professional associations—in short, everything you need to update your vitae (Hayes & Hayes, 1989).

A job description details your specific duties and responsibilities. When asking a supervisor to write a job description, ask him or her to focus on your specific tasks and how well you performed them rather than asserting how well suited to graduate school you are. This allows you to spend less time describing what you did and how well you did it when writing your personal statement. For example, one of us worked with a psychotherapist conducting a social skills group for preadolescents. In his personal statement he was simply able to speak about how that experience had affected him. By referring to the "enclosed job description," the personal statement did not get bogged down in the details of this experience. Further, if you performed well at this job, having a supervisor's positive assessment allows you to be more modest in your personal statement.

If you have a large number of work experiences, be careful not to overwhelm an admissions committee with paperwork. Choose two, or at the most three, experiences that showcase your diversity and that will highlight characteristics not likely tapped by those writing your official letters of recommendation. If you send more job descriptions than this, you may weaken their impact and increase the chances that the most laudatory ones will not be read (or at least not carefully).

If you have written a thesis or a research paper and have received feedback that it is well written, then include it. If there is someone whose research corresponds with your own, this may open a door for you. However, if there is a question as to your paper's quality, then do not to send it. A questionable paper may do more harm than good.

Application Fees

Last but unfortunately not least, most schools require application fees. These fees range from $0 to $100 per school, and average $30 for doctoral programs and $25 for master's programs (Norcross et al., 1996). Send a personal check or a cashier's check (never cash). Attach the check securely and prominently on the front of the application with a paper clip.

If you are in financial need or are experiencing trouble meeting application expenses, read the application instructions carefully. There is usually a statement allowing fees to be waived because of financial hardship. You may consider calling a school to ask how to go about having the application fee waived. That some students cannot afford the fees is the reason schools make the allowance in the first place. Graduate schools are sensitive to the impoverished status of many applicants, so please feel no compunction about requesting a fee waiver if it might apply to you.

Check and Recheck

At this point, you have typed the applications, requested letters of recommendation (and seen to it they were sent), written your personal statement, asked to have transcripts and GREs transmitted, and copied the unsolicited documents you plan to include in your applications. Once again, before you actually submit the material, have one of your professors check that it is accurate and well written. Have friends review it for typos and spelling. All material should be typed or word processed: it should look neat, error-free, and professional. It represents you in a very real way. Anything handwritten or tattered can convey the message that you are careless, unprofessional, and insensitive to the issues at hand when applying. Submission of materials should reflect a meticulous attention to detail.

After all this effort, make certain your application is received on time. We suggest (if you can afford the extra expense) that you send your application via FedEx, UPS, Express, or certified mail. Each of these systems will allow you to track your materials to ensure they have arrived and to have the name of the person to whom they were delivered. This may come in handy if your application is accidentally delivered to the administrative assistant for the social psychology program! However, our suggestion does not imply that you should wait until the last minute to express mail your application, implying procrastination (not a positive quality in a graduate student). Do express mail, but do it well ahead of the deadline.

Regardless of how you send your application, check to see that it has been received and processed. It is not inconceivable that in a large university an application can be misfiled (it happened to one of us!). Call the admissions office and verify that the material has been received. Some students prefer to include a self-addressed postcard to verify receipt, as discussed earlier, whereas others prefer the telephone. In either case, you have invested too much sweat, time, and money to leave the application to chance. Do not rely on graduate schools to keep you apprised; take personal responsibility.

CHAPTER 6

MASTERING THE INTERVIEW

The application is in the mail and out of your hands. Following the short-lived relief of finishing the applications, this period can be a nerve-racking time. You have sold yourself on paper, and now it is up to the program to decide which applicants it will choose to contact.

The doctoral admissions process has been characterized as "multiple hurdles," with some of the hurdles applied sequentially (King, Beehr, & King, 1986). The initial hurdle in most programs is the GRE and GPA score minimums. The second hurdle is rating of applications on such criteria as clinical experience, research skills, letters of recommendation, and the like. Being invited for an interview means you have successfully leaped these early hurdles, and this is a great compliment in and of itself. The final and determining hurdle for many, but not all, programs is the personal interview.

Not all schools have interviews, and they will state in the application if they do not. Make a note of this so that you do not become distressed when you are not invited. We wonder which is worse: the disappointment of not being asked to interview or the stress of being asked!

Periodic surveys of graduate departments of psychology (Kohout et al., 1991) have found that approximately one-half of doctoral programs in clinical and counseling psychology require a formal face-to-face interview before a decision to accept. Another one-quarter of these programs interview applicants by telephone before acceptance. The remaining one-quarter encourage (but do not require) applicants to visit programs, arrange formal interviews for applicants who plan to visit the department, or request accepted candidates to visit before making their final decision.

Three-quarters of clinical and counseling psychology programs, then, require some type of personal interview, be it by phone or in person, prior to acceptance. Since some programs absolutely insist on interviews in person, do *not* apply to distant programs requiring an in-person interview unless you can afford it. Only in very rare instances will programs reimburse the applicant for all interview costs, and only 10% of the programs reimburse for some of the costs (Kohout et al., 1991). In other words, 90% of the programs expect you to absorb all the interview expenses personally.

Expect to hear from interested doctoral programs that require interviews from mid-February through late March. Programs rarely contact students in the finalist pool after March 30 because the first round of offers usually goes out on April 1. It is still possible to be contacted, however, if you are on the alternate or waiting list.

If you have not received an interview request or a rejection letter by the third week of March, then calmly e-mail or telephone the doctoral program and inquire about the status of your application. If you have been rejected, politely thank the person. You never know, you may apply there again or have professional contact with the people from that program in the future. If your application is still being considered, it is permissible to ask when you might expect a decision. Just be careful not to be rigid or demanding.

The Dual Purpose

The interview is a critical opportunity for information gathering, not only for the program but also for you. That is, the dual purpose of an interview is for the program to check you out and for you to check the program out. Perhaps right now it seems outrageous to contemplate evaluating a doctoral program—you're probably delighted just to be asked! But a few interviews and an acceptance or two will reorient your perspective.

If you go on more than one interview, these interactions will give you information that will be the deciding factor in choosing which school to attend. You will find out about clinical training, student life, program fit, research facilities, and the like. They will be looking at your social skills, your emotional stability, your professional maturity, your focus, and your goals. The interviewers may want to see the development of your pursuits, the connection between your research and clinical work, or perhaps your adherence to the Boulder or Vail model. You may be asked pointed questions and will be expected to ask probing questions about the program.

Although the interview is often one of the most anxious periods for an applicant, it need not be. As with anything else in the application process, the more you prepare, the more confident and less nervous you will feel.

A few basic observations about the interview process will contribute to your preparation. The interview is highly charged for the applicants and programs alike. *Both* wish to be evaluated positively and to achieve the best match. You are not alone in trying to put your best foot forward! Interview styles, moreover, vary tremendously—from a conversational tone to grueling questions, from casual to formal, from mundane content to intrusively personal content. Be prepared for all styles, and remember that all count equally in the final analysis.

That final analysis is the program's unenviable task of deciding which of the interviewees they will eventually select for admission. Programs ordinarily interview two to three times as many students as they can admit. The pool must be whittled down from, say, 200 applicants, from which 25 are selected for interviews, and from which 10 to 15 will be tendered an offer to obtain 7 confirmed acceptances.

Rehearsal and Mock Interviews

Rehearse the interview beforehand with a professor, a fellow student, or a knowledgeable friend. Although the research-oriented schools are usually less personal and invasive in their interviews, it may behoove you to get accustomed to being asked personal questions without being thrown, and answering appropriately. Such practice is invaluable, especially for preparing you to think on your feet. Rehearsing also will desensitize you to some degree, take some of the edge off of your anxiety, and add to your comfort with the process. During the interview you are on stage, selling yourself, and knowing what the interview is all about can only help you.

Moreover, in keeping with the dual purpose of the interview, rehearsing will afford you practice in the interview style you seek to convey. A respectful and curious tone—"I am wondering about the chances of receiving an assistantship if I am fortunate enough to be accepted?"—is preferable to a blunt and forceful disposition—"How much will you pay me if I come?" How you phrase a question is important. The interviewer will be more impressed with your eagerness to learn if you ask how many courses in an area are *offered* as opposed to how many are *required* (Megargee, 1990).

Your interview preparation should direct attention to your physical appearance. Appearance, which includes both attire and grooming, will be an influential factor in attributions made about you. We recommend a two-piece suit or jacket and tie for men and a dress, pant suit, or skirt and blouse for women. Three-piece suits and "funeral outfits" are out. Plan your interview clothes, try them on, and lay them out well before the interview to assure that they fit, are clean, and are in good repair (Keith-Spiegel, 1991). Clothing should err on the side of conservative and formal; better to be overdressed and loosen a tie or remove a scarf than to be underdressed for the occasion. Avoid flashy colors and loud fashions. Wear shoes that are well maintained; as your parents have probably told you, the way you take care of your shoes communicates a lot about you. Jewelry should be conservative and understated. Questions about the program and other written material should be held in a professional attache or briefcase (leather if you can afford it). The location and weather will influence your choice of clothing, and reliable answers about expected attire can be provided by graduate students with whom you are staying prior to the interview itself.

Rehearsing should also entail preparation for frequently asked questions of applicants. Table 6-1 presents common interview questions to anticipate and prepare for. *We strongly recommend that you have a concise and thoughtful response ready for each of these.* An "I haven't really given that question much thought" answer hurts. Role-play these questions with a professor or, better yet, undergo a "mock interview" at your career services center. During this pretend experience, request that the interviewer ask several of the questions in Table 6-1 and videotape the encounter.

Of course, you cannot anticipate all possible questions. Some interviewers pride themselves on avoiding these stock questions and instead asking novel ques-

TABLE 6-1. Common Interview Questions to Anticipate

1. Why do you want to be a psychologist?
2. What qualifications do you have that will make you a successful psychologist?
3. What attracts you to *our* program?
4. Will you tell me a little about yourself as a person?
5. What are your future plans and goals as a psychologist?
6. What do you see as your strengths and weaknesses?
7. What do you bring into the program? What are your special attributes?
8. Have you ever had personal therapy? If yes, what sort of issues did you work on? If no, why not?
9. What are your research interests? Tell me about your research project/honors thesis.
10. What is your theoretical orientation?
11. Which of our faculty members do you think you would work with?
12. Where else have you applied or interviewed?
13. Can you tell me about a recent clinical encounter? How did you conceptualize or treat your last client?
14. What are your hobbies, avocations, favorite books, and interests outside of psychology?
15. What questions do you have for me?

tions, thus precluding rehearsed and polished replies. The rationale behind these queries, such as "Who are your heroes?", is that they give a glimpse into your natural response style and tap into some spontaneous information processing. One method to handle novel queries is to delay thoughtfully, remark that it is one you have not heard before, request a moment of contemplation, and then respond forthrightly.

Interview Style

The objective of your interview style is to present yourself as a confident, knowledgeable, and genuine person—an imperfect human, to be sure, but one without major interpersonal deficits or gross psychopathology. Even if you are anxious, try to appear relaxed, calm, confident. Any anxiety you may be experiencing is understandable and should be dealt with maturely. Strive to be as genuine, mature, and natural as possible.

The interview is designed for the interviewer to get to know you as a person—your interpersonal skills, career goals, and clinical acumen. One of the few empirical studies on the role of the personal interview in the admission process in doctoral psychology programs found that the rating of an applicant's clinical potential was the most highly weighted measure among all the interview data. Ratings of verbal skills and research skills also contributed to the prediction equation, but ratings of clinical potential contributed most to discriminating among groups of accepted applicants, alternates, and rejected applicants beyond that which could be accounted for by such objective measures as GRE scores and GPAs (Nevid & Gildea, 1984). In one way or another, you must impress the interviewers as someone they would be comfortable sending a member of their own family to for professional treatment.

The following factors, according to Fretz (1976), have been found to lead to rejection of an applicant during interviews:

- Poor personal appearance
- Overbearing, overaggressive, know-it-all style
- Inability to express yourself clearly—poor voice, diction, grammar
- Inadequate interest and enthusiasm—passive, indifferent
- Lack of confidence and poise—nervousness, appearing ill at ease
- Making excuses, evasiveness, hedging on unfavorable factors in record
- Lack of tact and maturity
- Condemnation of past professors

- Little sense of humor
- Emphasis on whom you know
- Inability to take criticism
- Failure to ask questions about the program

The last point is worth emphasizing. Each interviewer will want to get to know you as a person and will expect you to ask questions. Nothing is tougher on an interviewer than the person who does not ask questions or simply responds "Yes" or "No."

So even if it has been a long day, when the fifth interviewer asks you if you have any questions, don't reply, "No, all my questions have already been answered." And respond to the questions of the fifth interviewer with the same enthusiasm as you showed to the first interviewer (Megargee, 1990).

At the same time that you are conveying clinical potential and a mature interpersonal presence, you want to acquire the factual program information necessary to make informed decisions. Table 6-2 is a list of questions that you can have answered when you interview (or if you correspond with a professor and have an earlier chance to tour the facilities). You should ask some of these questions during the interview, others before, and others after. Some should be asked of professors, because they are best suited to answer them and asking can make you look prepared and informed. Some should be asked of first-year students because they have most recently been through the process and are closest to your situation. Some questions are better asked of fourth-year students because they are about to leave and may have less investment in hiding the program's shortcomings.

The best questions to ask are those that indicate initiative, curiosity, and responsibility (Hersh & Poey, 1984). Try to communicate motivation to learn and eagerness to participate in many activities; avoid questions that promote a speculation that you are demanding, complaining, or single-minded.

A caveat: Never ask for information that is available in the program description or the graduate catalog. These questions make you appear unprepared for the interview and uninterested in the program.

Alternatively, link your specific question to general information sent to you. Examples might include: "I read that all of your first-year students receive an assistantship and tuition remission. Is this also true of second-year students?" "Your graduate catalogue lists a Marital Therapy course, a special interest of mine, but it does not indicate if clinical supervision in that area is available." "While reading about your impressive Psychological Services Clinic, I wondered how many of the full-time clinical faculty provided supervision there." And so on.

The intent is to get beyond the gloss and formality of the published program descriptions to the lived and personal experiences of the program participants. Virtually all descriptions of clinical and counseling psychology programs, for example, will allude to ample opportunities for practical experience in off-campus placements. But when you directly ask students, "What is your clinical placement like?" their answers may diverge substantially from the published information. Their responses may indeed be positive, but it is not uncommon to learn that some of the placements are 50 miles away, do not offer a stipend at all, and are very competitive. To be sure, be tactful in your questioning, but also be assertive in securing crucial data.

Program directors (e.g., Hersh & Poey, 1984) have nominated certain questions to *avoid* asking. These unwittingly annoy interviewers or communicate an undesirable impression: questions regarding the typical length of a graduate-student week, which may indicate fear of hard work or a long week; persistent inquiries regarding an area of interest that the graduate program only minimally provides; questions reflecting resistance to learning the major theoretical orientation presented by that program; and antagonistic questions concentrating on the perceived limitations of the program, be they financial, faculty, or geographical.

Bring your list of questions with you to the interview, but do not constantly have it in plain sight to check off. Your task is to ask the questions of the most appropriate individuals in a respectful manner. On a similar note, many people have "palm pilots" to help organize personal information. Though you might use one to make an important note at the *end* of an interview, keep them put away during the interview itself. And on that note, cell phones and beepers should be left at home, or turned off during the interview. Having one beep or buzz will be disruptive, and actually checking a pager or taking a call would be seen as *extremely* unprofessional and rude.

Extreme ideologies—religious, sociopolitical, or clinical—also do not bode well in interviews. One interesting study (Gartner, 1986) mailed mock graduate school applications to professors of clinical psychology. The results showed that professors were more likely to admit an applicant who made no mention of religion than they were to admit an otherwise identical applicant who was identified as a fundamentalist Christian. Do not deny your beliefs, of course, but try to avoid expressions of rigid extremes. Academics favor informed pluralism and critical open-mindedness.

TABLE 6-2. Interview Questions an Applicant Might Ask

Clinical

Is training available in different theories?
Is the supervision individual or group?
Do the full-time faculty conduct the supervision?
What type of supervision will I receive?
When do I actually begin clinical work?
How much clinical training occurs before I start practica?
How many practica are offered?
What are your off-campus clinical practica like? Where are they located?
What types of patient populations are available?
Are specialty clinics available?
Do the faculty have active private practices?
Do faculty serve as clinicians or consultants at local mental health facilities?

Research

What is the student–faculty ratio?
About how many dissertations and master's theses are chaired by each faculty member?
When and how am I assigned an advisor?
Does this person have weekly research meetings?
Could I sit in on a lab meeting?
How many of the core faculty are currently actively involved in research projects (e.g., regularly publishing)?
Do any research grants finance graduate students?
If I wanted to change my mentor or advisor, is that allowed?
How many lab computers are available to graduate students?
Is mainframe computer time free? Is photocopying?
Is SAS or SPSS available?
What is the relationship with the medical school?

Finances

What percentage of students receive full financial support (assistantship plus tuition waiver)?
What types of fellowships are available?
What types of research and teaching assistantships are available?
What is the average amount of a 9-month assistantship?
Who gets tuition remission? What are my chances?
Do the stipends cover the costs of living in this area? How are the rents?
What percentage of students receive funding during the summer?
Do any of the assistantships include health insurance?

Quality of Life

What is it like to live around campus? Is it safe? Expensive?
Is housing available? Do most students live on campus?
What is the off-campus housing situation like? The neighborhoods?
Where can I go to get a housing application today?
Are there theaters, movies, decent restaurants nearby?
Is there public transportation, or do I need a car?
What are some of the campus events, clubs, etc.?
Is the Graduate Student Association active?
Do the students socialize frequently?
Do people tend to associate only with other research team members, or is there a sense of student cohesion?
Do students and faculty attend the colloquia?

Department and Politics

Are there regular department meetings?
What is the standing of the psychology department within the university?
How do the different branches of psychology interact?
What are the professional goals of the current students?
How many fifth-, sixth-, seventh- . . . year students are there?
Is there a sense of competition or cooperation among the students?
How much emphasis is put on course work and grades?
How common are Cs?
Do professors tend to collaborate on projects?
Do I actually get a master's degree along the way? When is this usually done?
Can the program be undertaken on a part-time basis? What percentage of the student body is part-time?
When do I take the qualifying exams? What are they like? How many people fail? Can they be retaken?
Could I see a course schedule for next (or last) semester?
Are teaching opportunities available for graduate students?
For applicants who already have a master's: Once accepted, how are transcripts evaluated regarding credits?

Outcomes

Where do your students complete their internships?
What percentage of your students obtains an APA-accredited internship?
What is the average length of the program (including internship)?
What percentage of your incoming students eventually earn their doctorates here?
Do dissertations usually get published?
In what type of settings do most of your graduates eventually find employment—academic, private practice, clinics?

Bernard Lubin (1993), a former national president of Psi Chi and a veteran of conducting admission interviews, enjoins applicants to present themselves as *knowledgeable* and *collaborative* during the interview. Being familiar with the research interests and productivity of the program faculty can go a long way. Carefully reading the program's guide and identifying faculty publications through PsycLIT are direct evidence of a mature and scholarly attitude. This leads to presenting yourself as a potential collaborator: welcoming opportunities to work with faculty members and fellow students, displaying an affirming and positive attitude toward interdependent activities.

A final piece of advice on interview style concerns your nonverbal behavior. Some applicants are so preoccupied with asking questions and trying to impress the interviewer that they neglect the way they present themselves nonverbally. But interviewer impressions of candidate personality are heavily dependent upon nonverbal behaviors (Anderson & Shackleton, 1990). Maintaining eye contact, making changes in posture, and varying facial expressions strongly contribute to an image as an active, mature, and enthusiastic person. The research consistently advises interviewees to keep high levels of eye contact with the interviewer and to display frequent positive facial expressions to maximize their chances of success. Your mock and actual interviews should strive for an interpersonally engaging style that creates personal liking and that cultivates an impression of interpersonal and intellectual skill.

Stressful Questions

This brings us to consider a prominent fear, namely, being placed on the spot with intensely personal questions. You may have heard stories about applicants being asked intimate questions about their families of origin, romantic relationships, and personal history they would prefer not to share. You should be prepared to answer personal questions about such relationships and self-perceptions. Answering these questions in a straightforward manner contributes greatly to the interviewer's evaluation of the applicant.

The nature of these questions varies with the interviewer's style as well as the program's theoretical orientation. Applying to a research-oriented behavioral program, however, is no guarantee that you will not be interviewed by a psychodynamic member of their faculty. Questions pertaining to family conflict or to your personal therapy could arise. Anticipating such questions can help you to determine how to handle them most comfortably and to decide how much information you are willing to disclose. Knowing where to set your professional boundaries can lead to a smoother interview.

One stressful but popular question concerns your personal weaknesses. Applicants naturally wonder how honest to be about their deficits and try to balance the need for honesty with the need to leave a favorable impression of themselves. We have found three strategies useful in approaching this question. One is to minimize an existing limitation: showing your awareness of it but not articulating the full severity or manifestation. If being taken advantage of frequently is your perceived weakness, for example, you might reply on the order of "Occasionally I find myself being taken advantage of by others in small but consistent ways." A second response strategy is to turn the weakness into a possible strength. Following the same example, you might remark that "I give to a fault on occasion and find some people will take advantage of my tendency to find the best in people." A third possible strategy is to express your awareness of the weakness and your efforts to remediate it; this reply demonstrates both introspective and corrective attitudes. "I've been working to become more conscious of how people, especially personality-disordered clients, can take advantage of me. My overtrusting nature is slowly giving way as I attend more closely to this relationship pattern." Whatever strategy—or combination of strategies—you elect, the response must be consistent with who you are. A phony or inauthentic response can immediately strike an applicant from further consideration.

One stressful situation necessitates your careful preparation. A few programs and faculty use what is called a "stress interview." In this interview, the faculty member intentionally acts inappropriately and tries to intimidate applicants, simply to see how they handle the stress of the situation. This can come in many forms: long silences after you answer questions; asking overly intimate questions; disagreeing violently with your position or answer; feigning disinterest in you as an applicant; or even giving you coffee in one hand, a powdered donut without a napkin in the other, and then handing you an article to browse! Knowing ahead of time that this can happen is crucial, because you can remind yourself that it is not personal but simply part of the process. In a few programs, the professors place all the applicants in an empty room and suggest they speak with each other while the professors observe the interpersonal process: no other directions, no other structure. This all serves to compound the students' anxiety.

Stress interviews are designed to assess how comfortable you appear under such interpersonally challenging conditions. The interviewers deliberately arrange situations or ask questions that you cannot predict, for examples, "How would you redesign a giraffe?" or "Where is Oregon?" The particular answer you give is not as important as the manner in which you answer. Here your interpersonal savvy and presence can triumph. The interviewer is testing your reaction to stress: Do you react to stress with humor, anxiety, self-denigration, anger? The stress interview is an ambiguous, semiprojective device.

The advice is to remain calm and polite, yet assertive. Generally, it is not wise to become entangled in a verbal battle or retreat into an apologetic or defensive stance. In the face of an inappropriately personal question, a "I wonder how that question relates to my admission here?" will demonstrate both your personal boundaries and your willingness to broach a difficult topic. In the face of continuing conflict, a polite "we respectfully disagree" can suffice, and leave it at that (Heppner & Downing, 1982).

Practicing stress interviews with professors or peers may sufficiently desensitize you to enable you to keep your head and field the situation without too much ego bruising. Another way to prepare yourself is to stay overnight before the interview and take the opportunity to ask graduate students which professors might conduct such an interview, allowing you to know ahead of time that this person is likely to intentionally try to stress you. Foreknowledge and preparation are the best defenses.

Group Interviews

Admission interviews in clinical and counseling psychology differ markedly from one program to another. At one extreme, a few programs invite you for a single, 2-hour interview with a senior faculty member. That's it—no tour, no group interview, no program orientation, and no interaction with current graduate students. At the other extreme, several programs employ extensive and innovative interviews lasting up to 6 hours. At Fordham University's counseling psychology program (Kopala et al., 1995), for example, the interview process entails a brief orientation to the program, individual interviews with a faculty member and a graduate student, a videotaped group experience, a 30-minute writing sample, an open session with current graduate students, and then a closing session with the director of training. A long and intimidating day!

Most doctoral programs in clinical and counseling psychology fall somewhere between these two extremes. Virtually all programs will arrange for at least one individual interview with a faculty member and for some interactions with current doctoral students. A healthy proportion of programs will also include admission interviews featuring multiple candidates in the same room at the same time. This group interview may be conducted in the interest of sheer efficiency, of observing your interpersonal style, or both.

Our advice on your interview style and objectives in these group interviews remains essentially the same as for the individual interviews, but there are a couple of twists. First of all, strive to be pleasant and honest with the other interviewees. Share your experiences, never denigrate their credentials, and treat them like future colleagues (which they may very well be). A negativistic or superior attitude is likely to be held against you in the final deliberations of the admission committee.

Second of all, since it is a group situation, try to present yourself as an admirable facilitator. Don't be a group psychotherapist or a control maniac, but a pleasant and respectful cofacilitator of the interview process. If you have already asked a few questions about the program, for instance, you might say that you have additional questions but would first like other people to have an opportunity to have their questions answered. As they say in the social psychology literature, try to manifest both a high task orientation and a high social orientation.

Whether it is an individual interview or a group interview, here are a few additional tips regarding the interview.

- Always bring extra copies of your CV. Every interviewer may have not received a copy or may have not yet reviewed it, so bring along copies to present and leave with people (Megargee, 1990).
- Take cash along in case you are invited to lunch or dinner with graduate students.
- Most places will give you a chance to room with a student the night before the interview. If possible, take advantage of this opportunity. It will allow you to acquire a great deal of information ahead of time. You will get a sense of student life and campus community from people in a position to know.
- It is also a good idea to ask for a tour the day or night before the interview. Ask to see the library, some of the labs, and the computer facilities. Get comfortable with the psychology building and, if possible, the rooms where the interviews will be held.
- Be sociable and friendly the night before the interview but do not drink heavily or party hearty (though you may be invited!). Get a solid night's sleep, and eat a sensible meal that morning.

TABLE 6-3. Sample Telephone Card

University of Alexandria

Reasons for my interest: Great reputation in child psychopathology and psychotherapy; specific professors (Smith, Adams); geographic location; has speciality clinic in behavioral medicine.

Key professors:

Dr. Smith: child psychopathology; substance abuse

I read your May [2001] article in *Journal of Bogus Psychology*, in which you found offspring of alcoholics to be more receptive to the anxiety-reducing effects of alcohol than control subjects. Do you expect to continue this line of research next year? Is an assistantship available?

Dr. Adams: behavioral medicine; psychotherapy

I was impressed that you have a separate clinic in behavioral medicine at your school. What type of clients do you most often treat? What opportunities are there for clinical experience for students?

Other professors with potential interest:

Dr. Jones: prevention

Dr. Watson: forensic psychology

Program questions: [Refer to Table 6-2 for representative listing]

When do I begin seeing clients in the training clinic?

What percentage of incoming students are financially supported?

What are the research opportunities in child psychopathology?

- Be compulsive and double-check your interview schedule. Being late or missing an interview (even when it is not your fault) can reflect poorly on you.

If you follow these steps, you will find it easier to relax during the interview. The more prepared you are, the more confident and at ease you will feel.

Telephone Interviews

Two situations may dictate a telephone interview. In the first, you are asked to visit the school for an interview, but you cannot afford to do so. This is no reason to be embarrassed, and the more straightforward you are about it the better. You can request a phone interview in advance if you do not have the resources for an actual visit. In the second situation, you receive the dreaded, unannounced phone interview. At least one of the programs you apply to will probably call without prior notice and ask to speak with you on the spot.

Luckily, if you anticipate telephone interviews, you really have nothing to worry about. One strategy is to rarely or never take a phone interview "cold." Consider telling the caller, "I'm sorry, but I was just leaving for an appointment. Could you leave a number and arrange for me to call you back?" This buys you time to review your information on that program and to prepare for the interview. However, you do not want to communicate disinterest in the program.

Another strategy is to prepare phone cards, palm pilot notes, or computer files. These are 3 × 5 index cards or short files that you make for each program to which you applied. On it, record a few specific reasons for your interest in that school and the name(s) of the professor(s) you are interested in working with, a little about their research areas, and questions you may have about clinical training or facilities (many of the questions in Table 6-2). Table 6-3 is an example of such a card. Keep a stack of these by the phone, or on a computer by the phone and in moments you will find the card for a particular school and not be caught unaware! This little extra effort can prevent a serious detraction from your application. If you receive one of these calls and cannot remember which professors are at that school, their areas of research, or the kind of facilities they have, it tells the interviewer that you are not as serious about his or her program as you are about others. This could place you lower than someone who has this information "off the top of his or her head."

A Note of Thanks

Once you have completed an interview, whether by telephone or in person, a brief note of thanks to the interviewer is in order. This gesture serves multiple purposes: It demonstrates your social skills, communicates your gratitude to the faculty and students involved, reaffirms your interest in the program, and keeps your name alive in the admission process. Seldom will such a brief note do so much for you.

The "who" and "what" of these thank-you letters are almost entirely dependent on your interview experiences. The "who" should certainly include anyone who has shown you special attention, such as a graduate student you roomed with the night before or after the interview, a professor who personally escorted you around a lab or clinic, or a faculty member who offered an unscheduled interview. Letters to several people are often called for. If the interview was less personal, then at a minimum send the Director of Training a letter of appreciation. A sample letter is displayed in Figure 6-1. An e-mail note of appreciation may suffice, but we definitely prefer an ordinary letter by mail, because it will probably be placed in your application file for all to see and appreciate.

The "what" of the letter must be individualized to your particular experiences, but will probably contain at least three components: an expression of gratitude for the interview, an enumeration of your favorable impressions of the program, and a reiteration of your interest in attending that program. Try to personalize each letter by referring to specific topics or experiences; for instance, recall your discussion of potential research studies or mention the friendliness of the graduate students. There is no definitive list of do's and don't's, but don't send a generic, impersonal letter and don't promote your candidacy. Do sound appreciative and personal. As with all written materials, insure that your

246 Wood Street
Babylon, NY 14000

March 16, 2002

Barry Bonds, Ph.D.
Director of Clinical Training
Department of Psychology
University of Western States
13 Orangegrove Drive
Wilksville, CA 98765

Dear Dr. Bonds:

I want to thank you for interviewing me for a position in your clinical psychology doctoral program. I enjoyed meeting with your faculty and staff and learning more about the program. My enthusiasm for the program was particularly strengthened as a result of my interactions with Drs. Timothy Hogan, Elizabeth Cannon, and Carole Buchanan.

I want to reiterate my strong interest in attending your program; the University of Western States offers a great deal that appeals to me. Please feel free to call me at (123) 456-7890 or e-mail me at csmith@uofs.edu if I can provide you with any additional information.

Again, thank you for the interview and your consideration.

Sincerely yours,

Chris Smith

FIGURE 6-1. Sample letter of appreciation to an interviewer.

letter communicates an image of sincerity and professionalism. Most of the letters should probably be word-processed, but a neat, handwritten note is appropriate if an interview was relatively informal and personal.

The Wait

Once you have finished the interviews and mailed the thank-you letters, it is a waiting game. But not for the programs, which still have a finalist pool of students much larger than they are able to accept! The interview process has probably weeded out a few, but the faculty are left with too many finalists, all of whom have very acceptable GPAs, GREs, and letters of recommendation.

What, then, are the *final* selection criteria? This pivotal question was addressed in a study by Keith-Spiegel, Tabachnick, & Spiegel (1994), who had 113 faculty members actively involved in selecting psychology Ph.D. students rate criteria used in making the last cuts in admission decisions. (Results of this study should *not* be generalized to Psy.D. or Vail-model programs.) The faculty members were asked to imagine that they were left with a pool of finalists, three times the size of the number they can accept, all of whom had strong undergraduate GPAs, GRE scores, and letters of recommendation. They then rated 31 final variables in terms of importance on a five-point Likert scale (5 = very important; 3 = somewhat important; 1 = not important).

Congruent with this book's advice and earlier studies, the top-rated criteria in clinical programs pertained to student match with the program and its faculty, research experience resulting in a journal article or a paper presentation, and the clarity and focus of the applicant's statement of purpose. Considered to be somewhat to generally important on average in assisting selection committees with the final admission decisions were research assistant experience; reputation of the student's referees; relevant field or clinical experience; membership in an underrepresented ethnic minority group; knowledge and interest in the program; number of statistics, methodology, and hard science courses completed; prestige of the psychology faculty in the student's undergraduate department; reputation of the undergraduate institution itself; and honors bestowed on the student by that undergraduate institution. Rated as not important or minimally important were such variables as the student's geographic residence, Psi Chi membership, and a close relationship between the student and former graduates of that program.

Demand always exceeds supply in competitive clinical and counseling psychology programs. The three primary criteria used to evaluate applicants by doctoral selection committees—grade point averages, GREs, and letters of recommendation—typically fail to narrow the applicant pool to the small number of slots available. At that point, research skills, clinical experiences, "good match" factors, and writing skills come to the fore (Keith-Spiegel et al., 1994). Bear these considerations in mind as you approach your interview—just as we have in preparing this book.

And now you wait until contacted with the final decision of the admissions committee. Until the week before April 1, it is probably not a good idea to telephone a program and ask where you stand. Applicants who make repeated calls may appear overly anxious and can be a source of irritation to the staff (Mitchell, 1996). The one exception is if you have received other offers, and the program you would most like to attend has not contacted you—a situation covered in Chapter 7.

This brings us to the last step in the application process and the final chapter of the *Insider's Guide*.

CHAPTER 7

MAKING FINAL DECISIONS

As with any realm of human affairs, good decisions regarding graduate school require time, preparation, and knowledge (Scott & Silka, 1974).

By April 1, all APA-accredited clinical and counseling psychology programs will make their first round of acceptance offers. At this point you will have two weeks to make your final decision as to where you want to go to school. By APA regulations, you have the right to consider offers until April 15, at which time an offer may be withdrawn. So you must be thoughtful but decisive in these 2 weeks.

To protect applicants from making hasty, premature decisions, all APA-accredited programs and most others have agreed to allow candidates until April 15 for a final decision (or the first Monday after April 15, if April 15 falls on a weekend). This is in accordance with a resolution adopted by the Council of Graduate Schools in the United States in 1965, approved by 317 universities and colleges, and further modified by the Council of Graduate Departments of Psychology (COGDOP) in 1981. As presented in the *Graduate Study in Psychology,* this resolution reads as follows:

> Acceptance of an offer of financial aid (such as graduate scholarship, fellowship, traineeship, or assistantship) for the next academic year by an actual or prospective graduate student completes an agreement which both student and graduate school expect to honor. In those instances in which the student accepts the offer before April 15, and subsequently desires to withdraw, the student may submit in writing a resignation of the appointment at any time through April 15. However, an acceptance given or left in force after April 15 commits the student not to accept another offer without first obtaining a written release from the institution to which the commitment has been made. Similarly, an offer by an institution after April 15 is conditional on presentation by the student of the written release from any previously accepted offer. It is further agreed by the institutions and organizations subscribing to the above Resolution that a copy of this Resolution should accompany every scholarship, fellowship, traineeship, and assistantship offer.

Acceptances and Rejections

What do you do when one program makes you an offer and you are still waiting to hear from another program you would prefer to accept? To begin with, *don't say yes to any school until you are certain that this is where you want to go!* Once you say "yes," that is it. You are committed. Saying yes to another school can endanger your acceptance at both places. If you have any reservations, do not feel pressured to say yes. Thank the person and say that you have been made other offers and you need a few days to consider this crucial decision.

As previously mentioned, if you have received offers but have not heard from the programs that most interest you, telephone them. Explain that you are considering offers but that you do not want to act on them until you know what your status is there. It's OK to say, "I've been accepted at University X and Y, but I am most interested in your program. Can you give me any indication where my application stands, or at least whether it is still being considered?"

The "Guidelines for Graduate School Offers and Acceptances," adopted by the Council of University Directors of Clinical Psychology (1993), specifically

TABLE 7-1. Student Reasons for Choosing a Clinical Psychology Doctoral Program

Reason	Mean rating	Rank
Reputation of the program	4.29	1
Amount of clinical supervision	4.27	2
Training facilities available	4.21	3
Appropriate mentors available	4.19	4.5
Emotional atmosphere of the program	4.19	4.5
Tuition waiver available	4.10	6
Amount of stipend offered	4.07	7
Theoretical orientation	4.04	8
Diversity of program	4.00	9
Specific specialty training available	3.89	10
Research experience available	3.85	11
Expected length of program	3.82	12
Amount of research supervision	3.80	13
Success of previous graduates	3.79	14
Specificity of the training program	3.66	15
Geographic location	3.60	16
Specific professor to work with	3.57	17
Family/significant others in area	3.00	18
Recreational activities available	2.69	19
Number of minority members in program	2.48	20
Break required during program	2.30	21

Note. From "Reasons why applicants select clinical psychology graduate programs" by S. Walfish, D. E. Stenmark, J. S. Shealy, & S. E. Shealy, 1989, *Professional Psychology: Research and Practice, 20,* 350–354. © 1989 American Psychological Association. Reprinted by permission.

encourage directors of training (or admissions) to apprise students of their position on the alternate list. Typically this entails a placement of high, middle, or low on the alternate list. If such a designation is used, the operational definition of "high on the alternate list" is that, in a normal year, the student would receive an offer of admission (but not necessarily funding) prior to the April 15 decision date.

Earlier, we emphasized the point that you should not accept an offer until you are certain that is the place you want to attend. On the other hand, if you have been accepted at three programs, and one of them is obviously less suited to your needs, be considerate of other applicants and decline that offer. The program can then make their offer to someone else who may very much want to attend that school. *Only keep two offers alive at any one time.* Otherwise, a huge "logjam" or "bottleneck effect" will occur across the country, with each program waiting for a few students to decide.

As long as there is a possibility that you may attend a certain program, be careful not to decline prematurely. As other students decline at these schools, you may be offered a better financial package if you have not yet made a formal commitment.

When all is said and done, how will you decide on which offer to accept? This is an extremely difficult question to answer because of the multiple factors involved and because the final determinant will be how you, as an individual, weigh these various factors.

One study (Walfish, Stenmark, Shealy, & Shealy, 1989) had 201 first-year graduate students rate the reasons for their final selection of a doctoral clinical program. Their average ratings are shown in Table 7-1, where a rating of 1 was "very unimportant" and 5 was "very important." As seen there, the most important factors were the reputation of the program, the amount of clinical supervision, the training facilities, availability of mentors, and the emotional atmosphere of the program. We have emphasized throughout the preceding chapters the importance of the first four factors, but not the last.

The emotional and interpersonal ambience of a program should not be underestimated. A very significant influence on you will be interactions with faculty and other students. The faculty–student relationship may be the single most important factor in your intellectual and professional development, and this relationship may be formal or informal, distant or close. Concurrently, the vast majority of graduate student time is spent with other students rather than with faculty members. You are likely to retain these personal contacts and professional relationships with them over the years. Moreover, fellow students are essential sources of encouragement, companionship, and inspiration. You want a good, lasting "fit" with the program (Scott & Silka, 1974).

In choosing a graduate program to attend, both white and ethnic group students place a premium on general factors such as program quality, training opportunities, emotional atmosphere, and financial aid. At the same time, however, ethnic minority applicants rate the relevance of multicultural factors higher than do white students (Bernal et al., 1999; Toia, Herron, Primavera, & Javier, 1997). These considerations include minority students in the program, presence of minority faculty, research on minority topics, and opportunity to work with multicultural clients. Be particularly attentive to the program's diversity as it relates to your interests and goals.

The reasons for choosing a clinical psychology program, as shown in Table 7-1, are largely self-evident, but two reasons *not* listed in that table deserve some consideration. *Attrition rates* refers to the percentage of students not completing the program. Attrition has been characterized as a "hidden crisis in graduate education" (Lovitts & Nelson, 2000). Between 13% and 17% of full-time psychology students, on average, formally leave programs without completing their doctorates (Kohout et al., 1991). Attrition in graduate programs is not solely related to academic ability; life problems, financial difficulties, interpersonal conflicts, and program dissatisfaction enter into the equation. Programs in which more than 25% of the doctoral candidates fail to graduate should be carefully screened when you make your final decision.

Preliminary or qualifying examinations, a second consideration in the complexities of your choice, are a series of structured tests that some programs require at the end of their first or second year. These examinations assume many forms, but generally they all attempt to test a candidate's knowledge of a wide range of areas in psychology—research methodology, learning, development, motivation, history, social, and personality. In some programs, only one attempt may be permitted to pass this examination (Scott & Silka, 1974). You should learn if the program requires "prelims" or "quals," whether multiple attempts are provided, and what percentage of students pass, before you make your final decision.

You should now be well acquainted with the importance of the decision criteria presented in Table 7-1 in your own life and well informed about the program's attractiveness on these criteria. If not, immediately request additional information on any of these for which you lack knowledge prior to making an informed choice of the program to attend.

The Financial Package

Note in Table 7-1 that the sixth and seventh most important selection factors are financial (tuition waiver and stipend amount). For many applicants, the financial aid offered by the school will probably assume an even higher priority in making final decisions. When an offer is made, establish if the program is offering a financial aid package. If so, does it cover tuition remission? Is it guaranteed for 4 years? Is it considered taxable at that institution? Does it provide health insurance? If you have a teaching or research assistantship, how many hours per week will this entail? Are you allowed to earn additional outside income?

On average, private universities are more expensive than public or state universities. Typically, the "in-state" versus "out-of-state" cost difference that operates in undergraduate education is not as salient in graduate education. That is because (1) once you begin study, you can establish residency there and pay in-state tuition after the first year, and (2) many financial aid packages include a tuition remission.

But graduate training is expensive, and external sources of financial support are slowly drying up. Consider, for instance, the average stipends and accumulated loans for Ph.D. psychology students over the years (Golding, Lang, Eymard, & Shadish, 1988). Back in the 1960s and 1970s the average graduate stipend was higher, and the typical student's accumulated loan lower, than in the 1990s, adjusted for inflation. In fact, the average stipend amount decreased 36% (controlled for inflation) over the past 20 years. About three-quarters of Ph.D. psychology candidates carry loans. Support is still available but not to the degree it once was—which accounts, in part, for your professors' fond memories of their "good ol' graduate days."

Federal support for graduate training has been eroding in all fields, including psychology. In 1972, for instance, almost 7% of all full-time graduate students in psychology held federally funded research assistantships. Twenty years later, federal sources supported only 4% of full-time graduate students in psychology

TABLE 7-2. Tuition Costs in Psychology by Insitution Type and Degree Level

	Institution type		Degree level	
	Public	Private	Doctoral	Master's
State residents	$2,976	$14,976	$4,980	$2,428
Nonstate residents	$7,619	$14,976	$10,705	$6,278

Note. Adapted from *Analyses of data from graduate study in psychology: 1997–98* by T. M. Murray & S. Williams, 1999, Washington, DC: American Psychological Association Research Office.

(Wicherski & Kohout, 1992). Similarly, almost 30% of Ph.D. recipients in clinical psychology back in the 1970s reported that federal fellowships and traineeships provided the major support for their graduate training. Twenty years later, that figure was down to 6% (Coyle & Bae, 1987).

Research supports the conclusion that today's graduate students are being asked to shoulder a larger share of their education. This is particularly true in Psy.D. programs, which generally fund proportionally fewer graduate students than Boulder model programs. Refer to the reports on individual programs for the percentage of a program's students who receive partial or full funding.

Table 7-2 shows the median tuition costs for psychology graduate students in 1998. The numbers demonstrate that tuition is largely a function of 3 variables: institution type, state residence, and degree level. Private universities uniformly charge higher graduate tuition than public institutions, just as is the case on the undergraduate level. Private universities, including non-university affiliated Psy.D. programs, routinely charge between $10,000 and $20,000 per year for tuition. Although your state residence does not influence tuition at private universities, it definitely reduces your tuition at public universities—from a median of $7,600 for non-state residents to $3,000 for state residents per year. Predictably, too, tuition is higher for doctoral programs than for master's programs. So, your annual tuition can range from $0 if you secure tuition remission, to $3,000 if you are a resident attending your state university, all the way up to $20,000 if you attend a private Psy.D. program.

Table 7-3 presents the assistantship stipends for psychology graduate students in 1998. As seen there, the median 9-month stipends for teaching and research assistantships were between $3,000 and $5,600 for master's students and between $5,500 and $8,400 for doctoral students. Stipends for doctoral students are consistently higher than those for master's students. Twelve-month assistantships provide more income, of course, than 9-month positions (Wicherski & Kohout, 1992). Traineeships, though less available than in years past, tend to pay the highest stipends.

Financial considerations include the tuition cost, available stipend, and living costs. The latter cannot be ignored: Although tuition costs may be equivalent in New York City and Kansas, the living costs are certainly not.

The Alternate List

Your fervent hope is to receive a telephone call early in April from the director of admissions or clinical training offering you acceptance into your top-rated program with generous financial aid. But this glorious dream may not happen; instead, the sobering reality is that many applicants will be rejected from several programs, will secure offers from programs lower on their list, or will receive offers without financial assistance. Many will also receive calls informing them that they have been "wait listed"—that is, placed on the alternate list.

As mentioned previously, ask the director of admissions where you stand on the alternate list—high, middle, or low. For your planning purposes, be politely assertive in probing further: "In typical years, what percentage of students with your position on the alternate list receive an admission offer? What percentage of the students admitted from the alternate list receive funding?" Without answers to these questions, you cannot render an informed decision on your other offers.

The admissions directors will, in all likelihood, arrange for you to be kept abreast of your admissions status until April 15th. They may telephone you or you may telephone them on occasion to determine the probability of admission.

TABLE 7-3. 1998 Median Assistantship Stipends in Psychology

	Doctoral students		Master's students	
	Public	Private	Public	Private
Teaching assistantship	$8,400	$5,490	$4,000	$5,610
Research assistantship	$8,451	$6,390	$4,000	$3,000
Fellowship/scholarship	$9,000	$6,040	$1,800	$2,700
Traineeship	$8,400	$9,900	$6,050	$7,500

Note. Adapted from *Analyses of data from graduate study in psychology: 1997–98* by T. M. Murray & S. Williams, 1999, Washington, DC: American Pyschological Association Research Office.

When speaking with the program representative try to impress upon him or her three key ideas. First, you are keenly interested in attending that program. Second, express your availability by stating you have not accepted another offer of admission. And third, if you have received another offer, inform the program accordingly; most schools desire people who are attractive to others. Enthusiasm, availability, and attractiveness frequently move students up the alternate list.

The tricky part of this process is how frequently an alternate should contact (by telephone or e-mail) the program representative. Too much contact will appear aggressive or desperate; too little, passive or complacent. Strike a balance by asking the program representative how often you may contact him or her without being irritating.

Decision Making

The choice of which offer to accept and which program to attend is a momentous one indeed. You, like 86% of students enrolling in graduate programs, will quickly discover that the decision-making process boils down to your sense of fit with a program (Kyle, 2000). A few fortunate souls may receive an early offer with excellent financial aid from their number one program. But most graduate school applicants will ultimately select the program that makes the "best" offer—an offer that needs to be seriously weighed on a host of the aforementioned and often conflicting considerations. The "April madness" abounds with such quandaries as: "Should I take the program with the best training but with no financial aid or the program with solid training and half tuition remission for four years?"; "Two programs have offered the same money, but the one that I prefer is 600 miles from my partner. What should I do?"; "My top program guaranteed me a teaching assistantship that requires 15 hours a week. My fourth choice is offering tuition remission and a fellowship. Any advice?"

Our advice centers on using systematic decision making. Begin by gathering all the salient data by interviewing program faculty and students, consulting published materials, and speaking with your mentors. Prioritize your primary reasons for selecting one program over another. Then develop a decision-making grid that will assist you in ranking your choices.

Two practical articles describe in detail how to apply decision-making techniques to choosing psychology programs and internships. Jacob's (1987) decision grid asks candidates to evaluate training programs along criteria that are important to them. You weigh those criteria that are more important to you correspondingly higher. You then tally the ratings for each training program to make the final decision. While it may sound a bit overintellectual, in practice we have found that the decision grid forces students to identify the criteria that they value most highly.

Stewart and Stewart (1996) describe a paired-comparison ranking technique, a method originally traced back to psychophysiological methods developed by Gustav Fechner. The first step of this technique is to select the relevant personal, professional, and practical criteria that you will use in comparing programs to one another. Consult the preceding pages to identify these criteria; more importantly, conduct an honest self-evaluation to determine which of these lie in your heart. The second step involves prioritizing these selection criteria. Do this by writing the name of each criterion on a single index card or piece of paper, and then forcing yourself to rank them in order. The third step entails generating a list of programs that will be compared to one another. We suggest that you use those programs that have accepted you or which have placed you on their waiting list.

The fourth step of the technique involves the actual pairwise comparison of the programs. Write the names of the graduate programs along one side of a large piece of paper and the selection criteria on the other side. Which of the training programs most clearly satisfies your criteria? Make a choice and allow no ties. For each criterion, put a hash mark across from the program that wins. The hash marks will be counted to determine your choice.

Although the final result will generally agree with what you expected, the more productive outcome of these two decision-making techniques may be that they force you to view your selection decision from multiple perspectives and to prioritize numerous criteria. To be sure, this is a complex method for a complex decision, but one that we and our students have repeatedly found surprisingly effective for making "impossible" choices more thoughtfully and systematically.

Finalizing Arrangements

An offer must eventually be formalized and specified in writing. Verbal offers and verbal acceptances are binding, but your acceptance of the offer should be in writing at the end of the process. Likewise, assistantships, tuition waivers, and stipends should be guaranteed in the written offer; respectfully insist that the financial arrangements be specified so that misunderstandings do not ensue. Should the offer be "contingent on expected funding," determine the odds of the funding coming through. No position is absolutely certain in life, but some are more certain than others.

Weighing offers, negotiating financial aid, and dealing with rejections make this a heady period. Be careful not to get caught up in the experience and forget the most important point: Accept one offer and confirm it in writing! One of our students (the affable Jean Willi) was offered admission to a prestigious doctoral program, with financial assistance. He carefully considered alternative offers, negotiated with other programs, leading to predictable delays. He awoke one morning in a cold sweat, realizing that he had turned down all other offers but had not formally accepted the offer of admission and financial package from his school of choice. He was in graduate school purgatory! Although the school was understanding and everything eventually worked out for Jean, because he missed the deadline, the school had the option of changing the financial aid package, or even revoking the offer of admission. The moral of the story: Don't pull a Willi! Be clear and decisive and put it in writing.

Once you have formally accepted an offer of admission in writing, two small matters of etiquette remain: (1) informing other programs who have accepted you, and (2) expressing your appreciation to those mentors who wrote letters of recommendation on your behalf and on their own time. A brief letter or thank-you note is an appropriate response (Keith-Spiegel, 1991). They will be interested in the outcome of your application process and may well join the ensuing celebration!

If Not Accepted

What happens if you are not accepted anywhere? The grim truth is that one-third to one-half of the entire applicant pool to APA-accredited clinical and counseling psychology programs will *not* make it in a given year (Korn, 1984). There are at least five alternatives:

1. *Contact the APA Education Directorate in early May and request a copy of the "Graduate School Openings List."* This document contains a list of graduate programs in psychology that still have openings for students in the fall. Although there are no clinical or counseling doctoral programs and only a few nonclinical doctoral programs on the list, you may find other programs of interest to you. To obtain a copy, call (202) 336-5710, fax (202) 216-7620, e-mail pwillingham@apa.org, or write Graduate Openings List, American Psychological Association, 750 First Street, NE, Washington, DC 20002-5963. The list is also posted on the APA Web site in May at www.apa.org/ed.

2. *Apply to master's programs in clinical or counseling psychology.* Degrees are frequent stepping stones to the doctorate in psychology. Although taking your master's at one institution and transferring to another for the doctorate is not as efficient as being admitted directly into a doctoral program, there are advantages nonetheless. One is that the acceptance odds are more favorable—41% for master's programs in clinical psychology and 53% for master's in counseling psychology on average (Kohout & Wicherski, 1993). A second advantage is that a few years of graduate training in psychology can dramatically improve your grade point average, GRE Psychology Test score, clinical acumen, and research skills. A third plus is an opportunity to confirm that psychology is the career for you. A cruel irony of baccalaureate recipients admitted directly into doctoral programs is that they have little direct contact with the field they claim as their lifelong career! A fourth advantage is exposure to twice the number of faculty supervisors and theoretical orientations. A fifth and final advantage is the flexible course offerings—part-time study and, frequently, night courses are available in master's programs (Actkinson, 2000).

Selecting a *quality* master's program in psychology may be a key to eventual admission into a doctoral clinical program. By all means try to avoid master's programs that have come to be pejoratively called "money mills." These programs exhibit most or all of the following features: accepting a very high percentage (75% plus) of applicants; offering courses only in the evening or largely by part-time faculty; providing no funded graduate assistantships; being reluctant or unwilling to state what percentage of their graduates go on to doctoral programs; declaring openly their disinterest in research; requiring little undergraduate preparation in psychology; and communicating greater interest in filling classroom seats than in attracting qualified students. By contrast, quality terminal master's programs in psychology can be roughly assessed by three criteria: exhibiting few of the aforementioned characteristics of "money mills"; holding a favorable reputation among the psychological community; and faculty producing published research. Gordon (1990) lists 20 American master's programs ranked highest in productivity in 15 APA journals; interested students are directed to that article.

In addition to the foregoing research-based article, we heartily recommend that you consult an extensive compilation of master's programs in psychology. The classic is APA's (2000) Graduate Study in Psychology, which lists hundreds of master's (and doctoral) programs in psychology throughout the United States and Canada. To order, call 1-800-374-2721 or fax 202-336-5502. A more recent source, consisting of over 260 master's programs, is *Programs in Psychology and Counseling Psychology* (Buskist & Mixon, 1998). To order, call 1-800-278-3525 or e-mail ablongwood@aol.com.

3. *Apply to doctoral programs that are not accredited by APA.* In general these programs fit into one of two categories. They may be very credible institutions that simply have not been around long enough to gain APA approval. Programs cannot apply for accreditation until they have graduated students, which takes several years. Usually these programs are planning on applying for accreditation as soon as they are eligible. However, there is a second category of institution not accredited by APA. These programs usually do not conform to APA standards and often do not even attempt to gain accreditation. The quality of these programs is often considerably lower than those of the APA-accredited programs. Because of their status, non-APA-accredited programs typically provide greater probabilities for acceptance. If you do choose to apply to such programs, by all means determine why they are not accredited, and whether their students are able to gain admission into credible internships and, later, to become licensed psychologists. You should refer to the most recent edition of APA's *Graduate Study in Psychology* to explore these and other programs.

4. *Decide against a doctorate in clinical or counseling psychology.* If your goal is to become a researcher or a psychotherapist, psychology is not your only option. Reexamine the other choices listed in Chapter 1 and consult your advisors to see if one of these options is suited to your needs.

5. *Apply again in a year or two to APA-accredited programs.* Knowing the criteria used by graduate schools, take a realistic look at what seem to be the limitations in your application. Many students continue to resubmit the same rejected application year after year to no avail; "doing more of the same" typically results in more of the same misery.

Another year can be an opportunity to remediate your weaknesses. Were your GREs low? Take a professional preparation course and retake the test. Was your GPA a bit low? Then take some additional courses or retake some old courses in which you did not perform your best to improve it. Take some graduate courses in psychology on a nonmatriculating basis to demonstrate your ability. Were you short on research skills? Then take one or two years and acquire a research position, paid or volunteer, in a psychology or psychiatry department. Did you lack significant clinical experience? Then spend a night or two a week working for a suicide hot line or find a job at a women's shelter. Were your letters of recommendation tepid or brief? Then acquaint yourself better with potential referees so they can write a positive and detailed letter.

Another year can also provide an opportunity to enhance your interview style or to acquire better matches with graduate faculty members. Some applicants find themselves in the position of perennial "bridesmaids" or "best men," not because their credentials were inadequate, but because their interview style or matching potential was a tad weak. Spend the extra months improving your interpersonal presentation and investigating programs that promise to be better fits with your interests.

In summary, reread this text and conduct a rigorous self-assessment of where you are and where you want to be. If you're still set on a career in clinical or counseling psychology, be prepared to take the time and energy to make yourself a better applicant. Especially if you are still in college and had planned to go straight on to graduate school, take time to gain some life experiences. Age and experience can work in your favor, and they will certainly help you better define your goals next time through the application process.

Two Final Words

Realism and persistence. Be realistic about your credentials, capacities, and acceptance odds. There are those applicants who refuse to accept the hard facts of the admission process and tragically resubmit the identically flawed application year after year to no avail. An honest evaluation of your credentials, perhaps with the assistance of an experienced professor, will enable you to strengthen your application, select more appropriate programs, or reevaluate your career decisions. This is not to dissuade or discourage you; it is realistic encouragement.

And be persistent! Many successful psychologists have required two or three tries to get into a doctoral program. Thousands of clinical and counseling psychologists have earned a master's degree at one institution before moving on to receive a doctorate at a different university. There is no shame in reaching for the stars; the real loss is not to reach at all.

We hope the information and suggestions contained in this *Insider's Guide* have been helpful to you. We wish you the best success in the application process and in graduate school.

REPORTS ON COMBINED PROFESSIONAL–SCIENTIFIC PSYCHOLOGY PROGRAMS

University at Buffalo/State University of New York

(counseling/school)
Department of Counseling, School, and Educational Psychology
Buffalo, NY 14260
phone#: (716) 645-2485
e-mail: stmeier@acsu.buffalo.edu
Web address: http://www.gse.buffalo.edu/DC/CEP/CEP_CP.htm

1	2	**3**	4	5	6	7

Clinically oriented — Equal emphasis — Research oriented

What percentage of your faculty subscribes to or practices in each of the following orientations?

Psychodynamic/Psychoanalytic	25%
Applied behavioral analysis/Radical behavioral	25%
Family systems/Systems	30%
Existential/Phenomenological/Humanistic	30%
Cognitive/Cognitive-behavioral	30%

What percentage of students applying for internship last year was accepted into APA-accredited internships? 100%

What courses are required for incoming students to have completed prior to enrolling?
None

Are there courses you recommend that are not mandatory?
Statistics

GRE mean (M), cutoff (C), or preferred (P)
Verbal 600 (M) Quantitative 600 (M)

GPA mean (M), cutoff (C), or preferred (P)
Overall GPA 3.3 (P)

Number of applications/admission offers/incoming students in 2001
60 applied/16 admission offers/10 incoming

% of students receiving:
Tuition waiver only: 0%
Assistantship/fellowship only: 0%
Both tuition waiver & assistantship/fellowship: 80%

Approximate percentage of incoming students who entered with a B.A./B.S. only: 80% **Master's:** 20%

Approximate percentage of students who are Women: 90% **Ethnic Minority:** 20%

Average years to complete the doctoral program (including internship): 5 years

Research areas	# Faculty	# Grants
assessment	1	0
family therapy	1	0
grief counseling	1	0
multicultural psychology	1	0
rehabilitation psychology	1	0
vocational psychology	1	0

Clinical opportunities
—

University of California–Santa Barbara

(counseling/clinical/school)
Department of Education
Santa Barbara, CA 93106
phone#: (805) 893-3375
e-mail: cosden@education.ucsb.edu
Web address: http://education.ucsb.edu/~ccspweb/

1	2	3	4	5	**6**	7

Clinically oriented — Equal emphasis — Research oriented

What percentage of your faculty subscribes to or practices in each of the following orientations?

Psychodynamic/Psychoanalytic	30%
Applied behavioral analysis/Radical behavioral	10%
Family systems/Systems	50%
Existential/Phenomenological/Humanistic	40%
Cognitive/Cognitive-behavioral	75%
Developmental	50%
Eclectic	100%

What percentage of students applying for internship last year was accepted into APA-accredited internships? 100%

What courses are required for incoming students to have completed prior to enrolling?
None

Are there courses you recommend that are not mandatory?
Human development, personality or abnormal psychology, individual differences, research design or statistics, physiological psychology, and measurement

GRE mean (M), cutoff (C), or preferred (P) score
Verbal 580 (M) Quantitative 550 (M)

GPA mean (M), cutoff (C), or preferred (P)
Overall GPA 3.0 (C), 3.4 (M) Psychology GPA 3.8 (M)
Junior/Senior GPA 3.76 (M)

Number of applications/admission offers/incoming students in 2001
237 applied/20 admission offers/10 incoming

% of students receiving:
Tuition waiver only: 0%
Assistantship/fellowship only: 20%
Both tuition waiver & assistantship/fellowship: 80%

Approximate percentage of incoming students who entered with a B.A./B.S.only: 80% **Master's:** 20%

Approximate percentage of students who are Women: 77% **Ethnic Minority:** 51%

Average years to complete the doctoral program (including internship): 6 years

Research areas	# Faculty	# Grants
autism	1	1
career development	2	0
clinical outcome	1	1
cross-cultural counseling	3	0
gender & identity schemas	1	0
high-risk families, children	4	4
minority risk factors	2	1

school programs	3	3
substance abuse	2	2

Clinical opportunities
autism
child abuse
community mental health
eating disorders
family
school

Florida State University

(counseling/school)
Psychological Services in Education Program
Department of Human Services and Studies
215 Stone Building
Tallahassee, FL 32306
phone#: (904) 644-1781
e-mail: gpeterso@admin.fsu.edu
Web address: http://www.fsu.edu/~counslg/programs.htm

1 2 3 4 **5** 6 7

Clinically oriented — Equal emphasis — Research oriented

What percentage of your faculty subscribes to or practices in each of the following orientations?

Psychodynamic/Psychoanalytic	15%
Applied behavioral analysis/Radical behavioral	15%
Family systems/Systems	75%
Existential/Phenomenological/Humanistic	15%
Cognitive/Cognitive-behavioral	100%

What percentage of students applying for internship last year was accepted into APA-accredited internships? 100%

What courses are required for incoming students to have completed prior to enrolling?
Requirements for a master's degree in counseling or a related discipline

Are there courses you recommend that are not mandatory?
Not specifically

GRE mean (M), cutoff (C), or preferred (P)
Verbal 550+ (P) Quantitative 550+ (P)

GPA mean (M), cutoff (C), or preferred (P)
Junior/Senior GPA 3.5 (P)

Number of applications/admission offers/incoming students in 2001
55 applied/8 admission offers/7 incoming

% of students receiving:
Tuition waiver only: 0%
Assistantship/fellowship only: 50%
Both tuition waiver & assistantship/fellowship: 50%

Approximate percentage of incoming students who entered with a B.A./B.S. only: 5% **Master's:** 95%

Approximate percentage of students who are Women: 54% **Ethnic Minority:** 20%

Average years to complete the doctoral program (including internship): 5.9 years

Research areas	**# Faculty**	**# Grants**
career development	3	2
counseling youth/prevention	2	3
school/community interventions	3	1

Clinical opportunities
adult learning and evaluation center (diagnose learning disabilities and prescribe treatments to adults)
full-service career center
human services center (general psychological services to 5-county area)

Hofstra University

(Clinical/School)
Department of Psychology
Hempstead, NY 11550
phone#: (516) 463-5662
e-mail: Psyjtc@hofstra.edu
Web address: http://www.hofstra.edu/Communities/?uri=/Graduate&bounce=/Graduate/SON U

1 2 3 **4** 5 6 7

Clinically oriented — Equal emphasis — Research oriented

What percentage of your faculty subscribes to or practices in each of the following orientations?

Psychodynamic/Psychoanalytic	5%
Applied behavioral analysis/Radical behavioral	50%
Family systems/Systems	0%
Existential/Phenomenological/Humanistic	0%
Cognitive/Cognitive-behavioral	45%

What percentage of students applying for internships last year was accepted into APA-accredited internships: 0% (all internships are part time)

What courses are required for incoming students to have completed prior to enrolling?
Statistics, research design

Are there courses you recommend that are not mandatory?
Yes

GRE mean (M), cutoff (C), or preferred (P)
Verbal 550 (P) Quantitative 550 (P)
Advanced Psychology 65th percentile

GPA mean (M), cutoff (C), or preferred (P)
Overall GPA 3.25 (P), 3.50 (M)
Psychology GPA 3.6 (P)

Number of applications/admission offers/incoming students in 2001
136 applied/42 admission offers/21 incoming

% of students receiving:
Tuition waiver only: 0%
Assistantship/fellowship only: 0%
Both tuition waiver & assistantship/fellowship: 60%

Approximate percentage of incoming students who entered with a B.A./B.S.only: 75% **Master's:** 25%

Approximate percentage of students who are Women: 80% **Ethnic Minority:** 10%

Average years to complete the doctoral program (including internship): 5 years

Research areas	# Faculty	# Grants
addictive behaviors (smoking, obesity, etc.)	3	1
anger disorders	2	0
attitudes and attitude change	1	0
behavior analysis	3	0
behavior modification (in industry, professional sports, depression, anxiety, social skills)	2	0
biofeedback	1	0
body image	2	0
communication of emotions	1	0
cross-cultural psychology	2	0
depression	1	0
family process/therapy	1	0
human error	1	0
infant/toddler development	1	0
normal and abnormal personalities	2	0
prevention of childhood disorders	2	0
psychotherapy for anger, guilt, fear, and anxiety	1	0
quantitative research methods	2	0
rational-emotive/behavior therapy for marital therapy	1	0
schizophrenia	2	1
self-report validity	1	0
sexual dysfunctions	1	0
verbal behavior	1	0
work attitudes and scholarly activities	1	0

Clinical opportunities
Professional services are offered to the community and to Hofstra University students.

James Madison University (Psy.D.)

(clinical/school/counseling)
School of Psychology
Harrisonburg, VA 22807-7401
phone#: (540) 568-2556
e-mail: shealycn@jmu.edu
Web address: http://cpp.jmu.edu/ClinicalPsyD/

1 2 **3** 4 5 6 7

Clinically oriented — Equal emphasis — Research oriented

What percentage of your faculty subscribes to or practices in each of the following orientations?

Psychodynamic/Psychoanalytic	20%
Applied behavioral analysis/Radical behavioral	0%
Family systems/Systems	40%
Existential/Phenomenological/Humanistic	20%
Cognitive/Cognitive-behavioral	20%

What percentage of students applying for internships last year was accepted into APA-accredited internships: 100%

What courses are required for incoming students to have completed prior to enrolling?
Students are required to have a master's degree in a psychology-related field.

Are there courses you recommend that are not mandatory?
—

GRE mean (M), cutoff (C), or preferred (P)
Verbal 550 (P) Quantitative 550 (P) Analytical 550 (P) Advanced Psychology 550 (P)

GPA mean (M), cutoff (C), or preferred (P)
Overall GPA 3.50 (P)

Number of applications/admission offers/incoming students in 2001
22 applied*/8 admission offers/6 incoming
*applicants must have Master's degree and professional experience

% of students receiving:
Tuition waiver only: 0%
Assistantship/fellowship only: 0%
Both tuition waiver & assistantship/fellowship: 100%

Approximate percentage of incoming students who entered with a B.A./B.S.only: 0% **Master's:** 100%

Approximate percentage of students who are Women: 60% **Ethnic Minority:** 20%

Average years to complete the doctoral program (including internship): 3.5 years

Research areas	# Faculty	# Grants
clinical training processes	3	0
family processes	3	0
social/skill development	4	0
traumatic brain injury	1	0
treatment outcomes	1	0
worldview/cultural issues	2	0

Clinical opportunities
attention deficit disorder
counseling center
family therapy
learning disabilities
multidisciplinary assessment
neuropsychology
outpatient private practice
school assessment

Northeastern University

(counseling/school)

Department of Counseling and Applied Educational Psychology
Bouve College of Health Sciences
203 Lake Hall
Boston, MA 02115
phone#: (617) 373-2485
e-mail: b.purnell@neu.edu
Web address: http://www.psych.neu.edu/Studies/grad/

1 2 3 4 **5** 6 7

Clinically oriented — Equal emphasis — Research oriented

What percentage of your faculty subscribes to or practices in each of the following orientations?

Psychodynamic/Psychoanalytic	10%
Applied behavioral analysis/Radical behavioral	20%
Family systems/Systems	20%
Existential/Phenomenological/Humanistic	20%
Cognitive/Cognitive-behavioral	30%

What percentage of students applying for internship last year was accepted into APA-accredited internships? 91%

What courses are required for incoming students to have completed prior to enrolling?
We require a master's degree in a field (applied preferred) of psychology

Are there courses you recommend that are not mandatory?
—

GRE mean (M), cutoff (C), or preferred (P)
Verbal 550 (P) Quantitative 550 (P) Analytical 550 (P)
Advanced Psychology 560 (P)

GPA mean (M), cutoff (C), or preferred (P)
Overall GPA 2.75 (P) Psychology GPA 3.0 (P)

Number of applications/admission offers/incoming students in 2001
68 applied/14 admission offers/9 incoming

% of students receiving:
Tuition waiver only: 50%
Assistantship/fellowship only: 50%
Both tuition waiver & assistantship/fellowship: 25%

Approximate percentage of incoming students who entered with a B.A./B.S. only: 0% **Master's:** 100%

Approximate percentage of students who are Women: 70% **Ethnic Minority:** 20%

Average years to complete the doctoral program (including internship): 5.5 years

Research areas	# Faculty	# Grants
consultation with telecommunication	1	1
counseling needs of minorities	1	1
early intervention	1	1
eating disorders	1	1
forensics in juvenile crime	1	1
impact of managed care on clinical training	1	0
leadership development	3	1
spatial ability and cognitive transfer	2	0
neuropsychological function	1	0

Clinical opportunities
Students have the opportunity to work with families, women, men, psychotics, chronically ill, autistic, etc. Training settings in the Boston area include all manners of ethnic and cultural diversity, medical, mental health, and private care facilities. Virtually everything and every kind of experience is available to students in a supervised setting.

Pace University (Psy.D.)

(school/clinical)

Department of Psychology
New York, NY 10038
phone#: (212) 346-1506
Web address: http://www.pace.edu

1 2 **3** 4 5 6 7

Clinically oriented — Equal emphasis — Research oriented

What percentage of your faculty subscribes to or practices in each of the following orientations?

Psychodynamic/Psychoanalytic	67%
Applied behavioral analysis/Radical behavioral	0%
Family systems/Systems	0%
Existential/Phenomenological/Humanistic	0%
Cognitive/Cognitive-behavioral	33%

What percentage of students applying for internship last year was accepted into APA-accredited internships? 75%

What courses are required for incoming students to have completed prior to enrolling?
General psychology, experimental psychology, statistics, developmental psychology, learning, personality, psychopathology

Are there courses you recommend that are not mandatory?
—

GRE mean (M), cutoff (C), or preferred (P)
—

GPA mean (M), cutoff (C), or preferred (P)
Overall GPA 3.5 (M)

Number of applications/admission offers/incoming students in 2001
175 applied/60 admission offers/24 incoming

% of students receiving:
Partial tuition scholarship: 25%
Assistantship/fellowship only: 25%
Both tuition waiver & assistantship/fellowship: 0%

Approximate percentage of incoming students who entered with a B.A./B.S. only: 88% **Master's:** 12%

Approximate percentage of students who are
Women: 85% **Ethnic Minority:** 17%

Average years to complete the doctoral program (including internship): 5.7 years

Research areas	# Faculty	# Grants
community psychology	1	0
gender	2	0
infant and early childhood	2	0
learning disabilities	1	0
learning	1	0
multicultural	2	0
psychometric	3	0
PTSD	1	0

Clinical opportunities
early childhood

University of Pennsylvania

(school/clinical)
Graduate School of Education
3700 Walnut Street
Philadelphia, PA 19104-6216
phone#: (215) 898-4176
e-mail: MaureenC@gse.upenn.edu
Web address: http://www.upenn.edu/gse/

1 2 3 4 5 6 **7**

Clinically oriented — Equal emphasis — Research oriented

What percentage of your faculty subscribes to or practices in each of the following orientations?
No information provided

What percentage of students applying for internship last year was accepted into APA-accredited internships?
The clinical training provided allows all students to obtain the Commonwealth of Pennsylvania certificate in school psychology.

What courses are required for incoming students to have completed prior to enrolling?
A master's degree in some form of applied psychology (e.g., counseling psychology, psychological services, etc.) is required prior to matriculation.

Are there courses you recommend that are not mandatory?
None

GRE mean (M), cutoff (C), or preferred (P) score
Verbal 630 (M) Quantitative 630 (M)
Advanced Psychology 600 (M)

GPA mean (M), cutoff (C), or preferred (P)
GPA 3.4 (M)

Number of applications/admission offers/incoming students in 2001
— applied/4 admission offers/4 incoming

% of students receiving:
Tuition waiver only: 0%
Assistantship/fellowship only: 25%
Both tuition waiver & assistantship/fellowship: 75%

Approximate percentage of incoming students who entered with a B.A./B.S. only: 0% **Master's:** 100%

Approximate percentage of students who are
Women: 99% **Ethnic Minority:** 8%

Average years to complete the doctoral program (including internship): 4 years

Research areas — **# Faculty** — **# Grants**
No information provided

Clinical opportunities
child
chronic illness
developmental disabilities
family
learning disabilities
sexual abuse

Utah State University

(clinical/counseling/school)
Department of Psychology
Logan, UT 84322
phone#: (435) 797-1460
e-mail: Anitab@coe.usu.edu
Web address: http://www.coe.usu.edu/psyc/

1 2 **3** 4 5 6 7

Clinically oriented — Equal emphasis — Research oriented

What percentage of your faculty subscribes to or practices in each of the following orientations?

Psychodynamic/Psychoanalytic	15%
Applied behavioral analysis/Radical behavioral	10%
Family systems/Systems	10%
Existential/Phenomenological/Humanistic	10%
Cognitive/Cognitive-behavioral	55%

What percentage of students applying for internship last year was accepted into APA-accredited internships? 100%

What courses are required for incoming students to have completed prior to enrolling?
General psychology, developmental psychology, analysis of behavior (learning), elementary statistics, personality, physiological, abnormal

Are there courses you recommend that are not mandatory?
No

GRE mean (M), cutoff (C), or preferred (P) score
Verbal 625 (M) Quantitative 625 (M)
Verbal + Quantitative 1100 (C)

GPA mean (M), cutoff (C), or preferred (P)
Junior/Senior GPA 3.7 (M)

Number of applications/admission offers/incoming students in 2001
49 applied/11 admission offers/9 incoming

% of students receiving:
Tuition waiver only: 0%
Assistantship/fellowship only: 0%
Both tuition waiver & assistantship/fellowship: 100%

Approximate percentage of incoming students who entered with a B.A./B.S. only: 72% **Master's:** 28%

Approximate percentage of students who are Women: 50% **Ethnic Minority:** 16%

Average years to complete the doctoral program (including internship): 6 years

Research areas	**# Faculty**	**# Grants**
addiction/substance abuse	1	1
behavioral medicine/health psychology	3	2
childhood/adolescent depression	2	1
Native American mental health	1	1
rural mental health	2	1
school behavioral assessment	2	1

Clinical opportunities
acute psychiatric inpatient
behavioral medicine
community mental health
disabilities
early intervention
eating disorders
Head Start
minority mental health
student counseling center

Yeshiva University (Psy.D.)

(school/clinical)
Ferkauf Graduate School of Psychology
Bronx, NY 10461
phone#: (718) 430-3945
e-mail: givner@aecom.yu.edu
Web address: http://www.yu.edu/ferkauf

1	**2**	3	4	5	6	7
Clinically oriented			Equal emphasis			Research oriented

What percentage of your faculty subscribes to or practices in each of the following orientations?

Psychodynamic/Psychoanalytic	50%
Applied behavioral analysis/Radical behavioral	15%
Family systems/Systems	20%
Existential/Phenomenological/Humanistic	0%
Cognitive/Cognitive-behavioral	40%

What percentage of students applying for internship last year was accepted into APA-accredited internships? 80%

What courses are required for incoming students to have completed prior to enrolling?
Statistics, abnormal psychology, experimental

Are there courses you recommend that are not mandatory?
Child development, physiological

GRE mean (M), cutoff (C), or preferred (P) score
Verbal 550 (M) Quantitative 580 (M)
Advanced Psychology 550 (P)

GPA mean (M), cutoff (C), or preferred (P)
Overall GPA 3.3 (M)

Number of applications/admission offers/incoming students in 2001
99 applied/28 admission offers/16 incoming

% of students receiving:
Tuition waiver only: 5%
Assistantship/fellowship only: 50%
Both tuition waiver & assistantship/fellowship: 0%

Approximate percentage of incoming students who entered with a B.A./B.S. only: 75% **Master's:** 25%

Approximate percentage of students who are Women: 90% **Ethnic Minority:** 10%

Average years to complete the doctoral program (including internship): 5.6 years

Research areas	**# Faculty**	**# Grants**
ADHD	2	0
attachment	3	0
behavioral interventions	1	0
early childhood	1	0
fathering	2	0
learning disabilities	2	0
multicultural issues	3	0
nontraditional families	2	0
professional issues	1	0
symbolic play	1	1

Clinical opportunities
adolescence
early childhood
family-school collaboration
parent training

Combined Professional–Scientific Psychology Program That Has Been Discontinued

University of Massachusetts–Amherst (school/counseling psychology)
Program continues as a school psychology Ph.D. program

REPORTS ON INDIVIDUAL CLINICAL PSYCHOLOGY PROGRAMS

Adelphi University

Institute of Advanced Psychological Studies
Garden City, NY 11530
phone#: (516) 877-4800
fax#: (516) 877-4805
Web address: http://www.adelphi.edu/study/courses-by-dept/grad/iaps/psi.shtml

1	**2**	3	4	5	6	7

Clinically oriented   Equal emphasis   Research oriented

What percentage of your faculty subscribes to or practices in each of the following orientations?

Psychodynamic/Psychoanalytic	100%
Applied behavioral analysis/Radical behavioral Systems	15%
Existential/Phenomenological/Humanistic	7%
Cognitive/Cognitive-behavioral	15%

What percentage of students applying for internship last year was accepted into APA-accredited internships? 97%

What courses are required for incoming students to have completed prior to enrolling?
Statistics, experimental psychology, developmental psychology, abnormal psychology

Are there courses you recommend that are not mandatory?
No

GRE mean (M), cutoff (C), or preferred (P) score
Verbal 600+ (P) Quantitative 600+ (P)
Advanced Psychology 600+ (P)

GPA mean (M), cutoff (C), or preferred (P)
Overall GPA 3.25+ (P) Psychology GPA 3.5+ (P)
Junior/Senior GPA 3.5+ (P)

Number of applications/admission offers/incoming students in 2001
200 applied/50 admission offers/25 incoming

% of students receiving:
(Partial) tuition waiver only: 50%
Assistantship/fellowship only: 0%
Both tuition waiver & assistantship/fellowship: 0%

Approximate percentage of incoming students who entered with a B.A./B.S. only: 67% **Master's:** 33%

Approximate percentage of students who are Women: 80% **Ethnic Minority:** 15%

Average years to complete the doctoral program (including internship): 6.5 years

Research areas	# Faculty	# Grants
change processes	2	0
equity in personal relationships	1	1
group process	2	0
health psychology	1	1
marriage	1	1
psychoanalysis	7	1
psychotherapy process	1	1

Clinical opportunities
addiction
child, adolescent, and family
group therapy
psychotherapy integration
short-term psychotherapy

Adler School of Professional Psychology (Psy.D.)

65 E. Wacker Place, #2100
Chicago, IL 60601-7203
phone#: (312) 201-5900
e-mail: information@adler.edu
Web address: http://www.adler.edu/

1	**2**	3	4	5	6	7

Clinically oriented   Equal emphasis   Research oriented

What percentage of your faculty subscribes to or practices in each of the following orientations?

Psychodynamic/Psychoanalytic	10%
Applied behavioral analysis/Radical behavioral	0%
Family systems/Systems	10%
Existential/Phenomenological/Humanistic	40%
Cognitive/Cognitive-behavioral	40%

What percentage of students applying for internship last year was accepted into APA-accredited internships? 20%

What courses are required for incoming students to have completed prior to enrolling?
Advanced abnormal psychology, general psychology, psychometrics, theories of personality, and others to total 18 credits

Are there courses you recommend that are not mandatory?
No

GRE mean (M), cutoff (C), or preferred (P) score
N/A

GPA mean (M), cutoff (C), or preferred (P)
Overall GPA 3.25 (C)

Number of applications/admission offers/incoming students in 2001
207 applied/63 admission offers/47 incoming

% of students receiving:
Tuition waiver only: 0%
Assistantship/fellowship only: 0%
Both tuition waiver & assistantship/fellowship: 0%

Approximate percentage of incoming students who entered with a B.A./B.S. only: 50% **Master's:** 50%

Approximate percentage of students who are Women: 65% **Ethnic Minority:** 20%

Average years to complete the doctoral program (including internship): 5.1 years

Research areas	# Faculty	# Grants
adult human development	1	0
disabled children and coping	2	0
neuropsychology of offenders	4	1

Clinical opportunities
Department of Corrections
developmental disabilities
halfway release programs for sex offenders
schools

University of Alabama

Department of Psychology
P. O. Box 870348
Tuscaloosa, AL 35487-5083
phone#: (205) 348-1919
e-mail: JMARTIN5GP.AS.UA.EDU
Web address: http://psychology.ua.edu/gradprog/clinical.html

1 2 3 4 **5** 6 7

Clinically oriented — Equal emphasis — Research oriented

What percentage of your faculty subscribes to or practices in each of the following orientations?

Psychodynamic/Psychoanalytic	0%
Applied behavioral analysis/Radical behavioral	10%
Family systems/Systems	10%
Existential/Phenomenological/Humanistic	50%
Cognitive/Cognitive-behavioral	80%

What percentage of students applying for internship last year was accepted into APA-accredited internships? 100%

What courses are required for incoming students to have completed prior to enrolling?
Undergrad statistics, research methods, abnormal psychology

Are there courses you recommend that are not mandatory?
No

GRE mean (M), cutoff (C), or preferred (P) score
Verbal 600 (P) Quantitative 600 (P) Analytical 600 (P)
Advanced Psychology 600 (P)

GPA mean (M), cutoff (C), or preferred (P)
Overall GPA 3.3 (P) Psychology GPA 3.5 (P)
Junior/Senior GPA 3.5 (P)

Number of applications/admission offers/incoming students in 1998–99
156 applied/20 admission offers/15 incoming

% of students receiving:
Tuition waiver only: 0%
Assistantship/fellowship only: 30%
Both tuition waiver & assistantship/fellowship: 70%

Approximate percentage of incoming students who entered with a B.A./B.S. only: 75% **Master's:** 25%

Approximate percentage of students who are Women: 80% **Ethnic Minority:** 20%

Average years to complete the doctoral program (including internship): 6 years

Research areas	# Faculty	# Grants
adult psychopathology	3	0
affective disorders/depression	2	1
aging	3	4
assessment	2	0
behavioral medicine	3	1
biofeedback	1	0
child clinical	3	1
clinical judgment	2	0
cross-cultural psychology	2	0
forensic	3	0
pain management	1	1
pediatric psychology	1	0
personality assessment	1	0
professional issues	3	0
psychotherapy process and outcome	2	0
social skills	3	0
violence/abuse	3	1

Clinical opportunities
AIDS
conduct disorder
forensic psychology
gerontology
pain management
parent–child interaction

University of Alabama at Birmingham

Department of Psychology
University Station
Birmingham, AL 35294
phone#: (205) 934-8723
e-mail: medpsych@uab.edu
Web address: http://main.uab.edu-show.asp?durki=9212

1 2 3 **4** 5 6 7

Clinically oriented — Equal emphasis — Research oriented

What percentage of your faculty subscribes to or practices in each of the following orientations?

Psychodynamic/Psychoanalytic	30%
Applied behavioral analysis/Radical behavioral	0%
Family systems/Systems	0%
Existential/Phenomenological/Humanistic	0%
Cognitive/Cognitive-behavioral	70%
Health psychology	100%

What percentage of students applying for internship last year was accepted into APA-accredited internships? 80%

What courses are required for incoming students to have completed prior to enrolling?
At least 18 credit hours of psychology, including statistics; at least 18 credit hours of life sciences

Are there courses you recommend that are not mandatory?
Psychopathology, learning, cognitive psychology, social psychology

GRE mean (M), cutoff (C), or preferred (P) score
Verbal + Quantitative 1250 (P)

GPA mean (M), cutoff (C), or preferred (P)
Overall GPA 3.5 (P) Psychology GPA 3.5 (P)
Junior/Senior GPA 3.5 (P)

Number of applications/admission offers/incoming students in 2001
76 applied/7 admission offers/ 6 incoming

% of students receiving:
Tuition waiver only: 0%
Assistantship/fellowship only: 75%
Both tuition waiver & assistantship/fellowship: 25%

Approximate percentage of incoming students who entered with a B.A./B.S. only: 80% **Master's:** 20%

Approximate percentage of students who are Women: 70% **Ethnic Minority:** 19%

Average years to complete the doctoral program (including internship): 6 years

Research areas	# Faculty	# Grants
aging	3	6
behavioral medicine	2	2
developmental disabilities	6	16
eating disorders	1	1
neuropsychology	3	2
psychophysiology	1	1
substance abuse	3	5

Clinical opportunities
behavioral medicine
neuropsychology

University at Albany/State University of New York

Department of Psychology
1400 Washington Avenue
Albany, NY 12222
phone#: (518) 442-4820
e-mail: e.wulfert@albany.edu
Web address: http://www.albany.edu/psy/clinical.html

1 2 3 4 5 6 **7**

Clinically oriented — Equal emphasis — Research oriented

What percentage of your faculty subscribes to or practices in each of the following orientations?

Psychodynamic/Psychoanalytic	0%
Applied behavioral analysis/Radical behavioral	30%
Family systems/Systems	0%
Existential/Phenomenological/Humanistic	0%
Cognitive/Cognitive-behavioral	70%

What percentage of students applying for internship last year was accepted into APA-accredited internships? 100%

What courses are required for incoming students to have completed prior to enrolling?
18 semester hours in psychology, including classes in statistics and experimental design

Are there courses you recommend that are not mandatory?
No

GRE mean (M), cutoff (C), or preferred (P) score
Verbal 600 (P) Quantitative 600 (P)
Advanced Psychology 600 (P)

GPA mean (M), cutoff (C), or preferred (P)
Overall GPA 3.0 (C) Psychology GPA 3.2 (C)

Number of applications/admission offers/incoming students in 2001
158 applied/20 admission offers/11 incoming

% of students receiving:
Tuition waiver only: 0%
Assistantship/fellowship only: 0%
Both tuition waiver & assistantship/fellowship: 100%

Approximate percentage of incoming students who entered with a B.A./B.S. only: 90% **Master's:** 10%

Approximate percentage of students who are Women: 70% **Ethnic Minority:** 6%

Average years to complete the doctoral program (including internship): 6.2 years

Research areas	# Faculty	# Grants
anxiety disorders	2	3
autism/developmental disabilities	1	2
behavioral medicine	2	3
children	3	1
eating disorders	1	0
neuropsychology	1	1
psychopathology	1	0
substance abuse/addiction	1	1

Clinical opportunities
addictive disorders
anxiety disorders
autism/developmental disabilities
behavioral medicine/health psychology
children
cross-cultural issues
eating disorders
neuropsychology

Alliant International University–Alameda (1997 Data)

Admissions Office
1005 Atlantic Avenue
Alameda, CA 94501
phone#: (510) 523-2300
e-mail: JZAPATA@mail.cspp.edu
Web address: http://www.alliant.edu/

1 **2** 3 4 5 6 7

Clinically oriented — Equal emphasis — Research oriented

What percentage of your faculty subscribes to or practices in each of the following orientations?

Psychodynamic/Psychoanalytic	30%
Applied behavioral analysis/Radical behavioral	0%
Family systems/Systems	25%
Existential/Phenomenological/Humanistic	15%
Cognitive/Cognitive-behavioral	10%

What courses are required for incoming students to have completed prior to enrolling?
Psychology courses: abnormal, statistics, experimental, physiological, learning theory, tests and measurements

Are there courses you recommend that are not mandatory?
—

GRE mean (M), cutoff (C), or preferred (P) score
GREs not required

GPA mean (M), cutoff (C), or preferred (P)
Overall GPA 3.0 (C) Psychology GPA 3.0 (C)

Number of applications/admission offers in 1997
126 applied/59 admission offers (Ph.D.)
283 applied/140 admission offers (Psy.D.)

% of students receiving:
Tuition waiver only: 0%
Assistantship/fellowship only: 0%
Both tuition waiver & assistantship/fellowship: 0%

Approximate percentage of incoming students who entered with a B.A./B.S. only: 80% **Master's:** 20%

Approximate percentage of students who are Women: 75% **Ethnic Minority:** 20%

Research areas	# Faculty	# Grants
family/child	9	0
health psychology	9	2
multicultural/community	7	1
psychodynamic	5	0
psychology of women	4	0

Clinical opportunities
We have over 100 practicum sites that specialize in almost all areas of psychology including inpatient, outpatient, and residential treatment programs for children, adolescents, and adults, hospitals specializing in behavioral health and neuropsychological populations, college counseling centers, mental health centers, forensic sites, and placements specializing in the treatment of specific ethnic minority populations, women, gays/lesbians, and the disabled.

Alliant International University–Alameda (Psy.D.) (1997 Data)

1005 Atlantic Avenue
Alameda, CA 94501
phone#: (510) 523-2300
Web address: http://www.alliant.edu/

1	**2**	3	4	5	6	7
Clinically oriented			Equal emphasis			Research oriented

What percentage of your faculty subscribes to or practices in each of the following orientations?

Psychodynamic/Psychoanalytic	70%
Applied behavioral analysis/Radical behavioral	0%
Family systems/Systems	50%
Existential/Phenomenological/Humanistic	25%
Cognitive/Cognitive-behavioral	30%

What courses are required for incoming students to have completed prior to enrolling?
A Bachelor's degree in psychology or courses on the following: statistics, tests and measurements, abnormal psychology, and learning, physiological psychology, or experimental psychology

Are there courses you recommend that are not mandatory?
No

GRE mean (M), cutoff (C), or preferred (P) score
GREs not required
If applicants do not have a Bachelor's in psychology, GRE Advanced Psychology score in the 80th percentile

GPA mean (M), cutoff (C), or preferred (P)
Overall GPA 3.0 Psychology GPA 3.0
Junior/Senior GPA 3.0

Number of applications/admission offers in 1997
126 applied/59 admission offers (Ph.D.)
273 applied/140 admission offers (Psy.D.)

% of students receiving:
Tuition waiver only: 0%
Assistantship/fellowship only: 0%
Both tuition waiver & assistantship/fellowship: 0%

Approximate percentage of incoming students who entered with a B.A./B.S. only: 80% **Master's:** 20%

Approximate percentage of students who are Women: 90% **Ethnic Minority:** 10%

Research areas	# Faculty	# Grants
—		

Clinical opportunities
A variety of practicum places is available throughout the Bay area and Northern California.

Alliant International University–Fresno (Ph.D. & Psy.D.)

5130 East Clinton Way
Fresno, CA 93727
phone#: (559) 456-2777
e-mail: Dtternand@mail.cspp.edu
Web address: http://www.alliant.edu/

1	**2***	3	4	**5****	6	7
Clinically oriented			Equal emphasis			Research oriented

*Psy.D. **Ph.D.

What percentage of your faculty subscribes to or practices in each of the following orientations?

Psychodynamic/Psychoanalytic	40%
Applied behavioral analysis/Radical behavioral	7%
Family systems/Systems	40%
Existential/Phenomenological/Humanistic	15%
Cognitive/Cognitive-behavioral	25%

What percentage of students applying for internship last year was accepted into APA-accredited internships? 65%

What courses are required for incoming students to have completed prior to enrolling?
Abnormal psychology, statistics, experimental or physiological psychology, learning theory, tests and measurement

Are there courses you recommend that are not mandatory?
None

GRE mean (M), cutoff (C), or preferred (P) score
GRE not required

GPA mean (M), cutoff (C), or preferred (P)
Overall GPA 3.0 (C) Psychology GPA 3.0 (C)

Number of applications/admission offers/incoming students in 2001
22 applied/9 admission offers/0 incoming (Ph.D.)
53 applied/26 admission offers/15 incoming (Psy.D.)

% of students receiving:
Tuition waiver only: 0%
Assistantship/fellowship only: 15%
Both tuition waiver & assistantship/fellowship: 15%

Approximate percentage of incoming students who entered with a B.A./B.S. only: 70% **Master's:** 30%

Approximate percentage of students who are Women: 67% **Ethnic Minority:** 15%

Average years to complete the doctoral program (including internship): 5 years (Ph.D.) 4 years (Psy.D.)

Research areas	**# Faculty**	**# Grants**
anxiety	1	0
attachment	1	0
domestic violence	3	1
eating disorders	2	1
family	4	2
forensic	3	0
health	2	0
neuropsychology	2	0
outcome studies	2	0
phenomenological studies	3	0
play therapy	3	1
psychotherapy research	2	0
Rorschach studies	1	0
schizophrenia	1	1
women's issues	4	0

Clinical opportunities
ADHD
adolescents
anxiety disorders
assessment
behavioral medicine
child assessment
diversity
domestic violence
eating disorders
family
forensic (adolescent & adult)
health neuropsychology
school-based intervention
sex offender treatment
women's issues

Alliant International University–Los Angeles (Ph.D.) (1997 Data)

Admissions Office
1000 South Fremont Avenue
Alhambra, CA 91803-1360
e-mail: mjscavio@ucl.edu
Web address: http://www.alliant.edu/

1	2	3	**4**	5	6	7
Clinically oriented			Equal emphasis			Research oriented

What percentage of your faculty subscribes to or practices in each of the following orientations?

Psychodynamic/Psychoanalytic	40%
Applied behavioral analysis/Radical behavioral	0%
Family systems/Systems	25%
Existential/Phenomenological/Humanistic	10%
Cognitive/Cognitive-behavioral	25%

What courses are required for incoming students to have completed prior to enrolling?
If no BA in psychology: statistics, tests & measurements, abnormal, and experimental or physiological or learning theory

Are there courses you recommend that are not mandatory?
Only if BA not in psychology

GRE mean (M), cutoff (C), or preferred (P)
80th percentile (if no BA in psychology and if no courses listed above)

GPA mean (M), cutoff (C), or preferred (P)
Overall GPA 3.0 Psychology GPA 3.0

Number of applications/admission offers in 1996
215 applied/40 admission offers

% of students receiving:
Tuition waiver only: 5%
Assistantship/fellowship only: 70%
Both tuition waiver & assistantship/fellowship: 2%

Approximate percentage of incoming students who entered with a B.A./B.S. only: 70% **Master's:** 30%

Approximate percentage of students who are
Women: 65% **Ethnic Minority:** 25%

Research areas	**# Faculty**	**# Grants**
clinical health	4	5
family systems	2	1
individual/child psychology	4	4
multicultural interventions	5	2
program evaluation	2	1
psychological assessment	2	0

Clinical opportunities
—

Alliant International University–Los Angeles (Psy.D.) (1997 Data)

1000 South Fremont Avenue
Alhambra, CA 91803
Web address: http://www.cspp.edu/catalog/9-b.htm

1	**2**	3	4	5	6	7

Clinically oriented — Equal emphasis — Research oriented

What percentage of your faculty subscribes to or practices in each of the following orientations?

Psychodynamic/Psychoanalytic	55%
Applied behavioral analysis/Radical behavioral	0%
Family systems/Systems	25%
Existential/Phenomenological/Humanistic	10%
Cognitive/Cognitive-behavioral	10%

What courses are required for incoming students to have completed prior to enrolling?
If no BA in psychology: statistics, tests and measurements, abnormal and experimental or physiological or learning theory

Are there courses you recommend that are not mandatory?
No

GRE mean (M), cutoff (C), or preferred (P) score
80% or better on GRE advanced psychology if BA is not in psychology

GPA mean (M), cutoff (C), or preferred (P)
Overall GPA 3.0 Psychology GPA 3.0

Number of applications/admission offers in 1997
600 applied/150 admission offers

% of students receiving:
Tuition waiver only: 2%
Assistantship/fellowship only: 70%
Both tuition waiver & assistantship/fellowship: 1%

Approximate percentage of incoming students who entered with a B.A./B.S. only: 65% **Master's:** 35%

Approximate percentage of students who are
Women: 65% **Ethnic Minority:** 25%

Research areas	**# Faculty**	**# Grants**
family systems	2	1
metaphysical theory	1	0
multicultural interactions	7	3
program evaluation	3	1
psychological assessment	2	0

Clinical opportunities
South Central Los Angeles Training Consortium

Alliant International University–San Diego (Ph.D.)

10455 Pomerado Road
San Diego, CA 92131-1799
phone#: (858) 635-4772
e-mail: admissions@alliant.edu
Web address: http://www.alliant.edu/

1	2	3	**4**	5	6	7

Clinically oriented — Equal emphasis — Research oriented

What percentage of your faculty subscribes to or practices in each of the following orientations?

Psychodynamic/Psychoanalytic	15%
Applied behavioral analysis/Radical behavioral	31%
Family systems/Systems	38%
Existential/Phenomenological/Humanistic	0%
Cognitive/Cognitive-behavioral	16%

What percentage of students applying for internship last year was accepted into APA-accredited internships? 60%

What courses are required for incoming students to have completed prior to enrolling?
Bachelor's degree in psychology. Others are required to take statistics, tests and measurement, abnormal psychology.

Are there courses you recommend that are not mandatory?
No

GRE mean (M), cutoff (C), or preferred (P) score
N/A

GPA mean (M), cutoff (C), or preferred (P)
Overall GPA 3.1 (C), 3.4 (M)

Number of applications/admission offers/incoming students in 2001
103 applied/52 admission offers/31 incoming

% of students receiving:
Tuition waiver only: 0%
Assistantship/fellowship only: 50%
Both tuition waiver & assistantship/fellowship: 50%

Approximate percentage of incoming students who entered with a B.A./B.S. only: 78% **Master's:** 22%

Approximate percentage of students who are
Women: 78% **Ethnic Minority:** 28%

Average years to complete the doctoral program (including internship): 6 years

Research areas	# Faculty	# Grants
adolescent psychopathology	3	0
childhood psychopathology	3	2
deafness	1	1
forensic psychology	1	0
health psychology	3	1
malingering	1	0
mood disorders	2	0
multicultural	4	0

Clinical opportunities
biofeedback
child custody evaluation
reproductive trauma
virtual reality

Alliant International University–San Diego (Psy.D.)

6160 Cornerstone Court, East
San Diego, CA 92121
phone#: (619) 623-2777
Web address: http://www.cspp.edu

1 **2** 3 4 5 6 7

Clinically oriented | Equal emphasis | Research oriented

What percentage of your faculty subscribes to or practices in each of the following orientations?

Psychodynamic/Psychoanalytic	35%
Applied behavioral analysis/Radical behavioral	10%
Family systems/Systems	25%
Existential/Phenomenological/Humanistic	5%
Cognitive/Cognitive-behavioral	25%

What percentage of students applying for internship last year was accepted into APA-accredited internships? 90%

What courses are required for incoming students to have completed prior to enrolling?
Bachelor of Arts in psychology. Other BAs are required to take statistics, tests and measurements, abnormal psychology

Are there courses you recommend that are not mandatory?
No

GRE mean (M), cutoff (C), or preferred (P) score
N/A

GPA mean (M), cutoff (C), or preferred (P)
Overall GPA 3.0 (C), 3.43 (M)

Number of applications/admission offers/incoming students in 2001
130 applied/65 admission offers/28 incoming

% of students receiving:
Partial tuition waiver only: 20%
Assistantship/fellowship only: 40%
Both tuition waiver & assistantship/fellowship: 30%

Approximate percentage of incoming students who entered with a B.A./B.S. only: 80% **Master's:** 20%

Approximate percentage of students who are Women: 79% **Ethnic Minority:** 28%

Average years to complete the doctoral program (including internship): 4.8 years

Research areas	# Faculty	# Grants
adolescent psychopathology	2	0
alcoholism	1	0
assessment	1	0
childhood psychopathology	3	3
forensic psychology	3	0
health psychology	4	2
malingering	1	0
mood disorders	3	0
multicultural psychopathology	3	2
rehabilitation psych (deafness)	2	1
reproductive trauma	1	0

Clinical opportunities
assessment
autism clinic
biofeedback clinic
custody evaluation clinic
domestic violence
forensic assessment
media and psychology
rehabilitation psychology
virtual reality intervention

American University

Department of Psychology
Washington, DC 20016
phone#: (202) 885-1716
e-mail: cweissb@american.edu
Web address: http://www.american.edu/academic.depts/cas/psych/doctoralprogs.html

1 2 3 4 **5** 6 7

Clinically oriented | Equal emphasis | Research oriented

What percentage of your faculty subscribes to or practices in each of the following orientations?

Psychodynamic/Psychoanalytic	15%
Applied behavioral analysis/Radical behavioral	0%
Family systems/Systems	0%
Existential/Phenomenological/Humanistic	15%
Cognitive/Cognitive-behavioral	70%

What percentage of students applying for internship last year was accepted into APA-accredited internships? 100%

What courses are required for incoming students to have completed prior to enrolling?
None

Are there courses you recommend that are not mandatory?
Psychology major, including experimental psychology, statistics

GRE mean (M), cutoff (C), or preferred (P) score
Verbal 600 (P) Quantitative 600 (P) Analytical 600 (P) Advanced Psychology 600 (P)

GPA mean (M), cutoff (C), or preferred (P)
Overall GPA 3.5+ (P) Psychology GPA 3.5 (P)

Number of applications/admission offers/incoming students in 2001
179 applied/13 admission offers/7 incoming

% of students receiving:
Tuition waiver only: 10%
Assistantship/fellowship only: 10%
Both tuition waiver & assistantship/fellowship: 40%

Approximate percentage of incoming students who entered with a B.A./B.S. only: 90% **Master's:** 10%

Approximate percentage of students who are Women: 90% **Ethnic Minority:** 20%

Average years to complete the doctoral program (including internship): 6.5 years

Research areas	**# Faculty**	**# Grants**
anxiety disorders	1	0
child	2	0
cognitive therapy	1	1
depression	1	0
eating disorders	1	0
neuropsychology testing	1	0
treatment cost effectiveness	1	1

Clinical opportunities
cognitive-behavior therapy
externships
family therapy
neuropsychological testing
person-centered therapy
psychodynamic therapy
psychological testing

Antioch/New England Graduate School (Psy.D.)

Department of Clinical Psychology
40 Avon Street
Keene, NH 03431
phone#: (603) 357-3122
e-mail: rpeterson@antiochne.edu
Web address: http://www.antiochue.edu/

1	2	**3**	4	5	6	7

Clinically oriented — Equal emphasis — Research oriented

What percentage of your faculty subscribes to or practices in each of the following orientations?

Psychodynamic/Psychoanalytic	20%
Applied behavioral analysis/Radical behavioral	10%
Family systems/Systems	10%
Existential/Phenomenological/Humanistic	10%
Cognitive/Cognitive-behavioral	20%
Integrative	30%

What percentage of students applying for internship last year was accepted into APA-accredited internships? 87%

What courses are required for incoming students to have completed prior to enrolling?
Undergraduate psychology major or master's in psychology (or related field)

Are there courses you recommend that are not mandatory?
No

GRE mean (M), cutoff (C), or preferred (P) score
Required

GPA mean (M), cutoff (C), or preferred (P)
Overall GPA 3.0 (P)

Number of applications/admission offers/incoming students in 2001
118 applied/58 admission offers/29 incoming

% of students receiving:
Tuition waiver only: 0%
Assistantship/fellowship only: 18%
Both tuition waiver & assistantship/fellowship: 0%

Approximate percentage of incoming students who entered with a B.A./B.S. only: 58% **Master's:** 42%

Approximate percentage of students who are Women: 64% **Ethnic Minority:** 6%

Average years to complete the doctoral program (including internship): 7.28 years

Research areas	**# Faculty**	**# Grants**
community services	2	0
health psychology	1	0
graduate training	1	0
multicultural psychology	1	0
outcome evaluation	2	0
women's issues	2	1

Clinical opportunities
AIDS
assessment
battering/abuse
behavioral medicine
child clinical psychology
cognitive/behavioral therapy
conduct disorders
family therapy
forensic
gay and lesbian
gerontology
group therapy
health psychology
neuropsychology/rehabilitation
personality disorders
psychodynamic
rural psychology
substance abuse
supervision

Argosy University–Honolulu Campus (Psy.D.)

400 Pacific Tower, 1001 Bishop Street
Honolulu, HI 96813
phone#: (808) 536-5555
e-mail: hawaii@argosyu.edu
Web address: http://www.argosyu.edu/

1	**2**	3	4	5	6	7

Clinically oriented — Equal emphasis — Research oriented

What percentage of your faculty subscribes to or practices in each of the following orientations?

Psychodynamic/Psychoanalytic	20%
Applied behavioral analysis/Radical behavioral	0%
Family systems/Systems	30%
Existential/Phenomenological/Humanistic	20%
Cognitive/Cognitive-behavioral	30%

What percentage of students applying for internship last year was accepted into APA-accredited internships? 89% (of those who applied to APA sites)

What courses are required for incoming students to have completed prior to enrolling?
Introduction to general psychology, abnormal psychology, tests and measurements, personality theories, research methods or statistics

Are there courses you recommend that are not mandatory?
—

GRE mean (M), cutoff (C), or preferred (P) score
N/A

GPA mean (M), cutoff (C), or preferred (P)
Overall GPA 3.25 (C)

Number of applications/admission offers/incoming students in 2001
154 applied/67 admission offers/32 incoming

% of students receiving:
Tuition waiver only: 2%
Assistantship/fellowship only: 5%
Both tuition waiver & assistantship/fellowship: 1%

Approximate percentage of incoming students who entered with a B.A./B.S. only: 65% **Master's:** 25% **Ph.D., J.D.:** 10%

Approximate percentage of students who are Women: 65% **Ethnic Minority:** 53%

Average years to complete the doctoral program (including internship): 5 years

Research areas	# Faculty	# Grants
brief dynamic psychotherapy	1	0
diversity education	2	0
gay/lesbian relationships	1	0
health psychology	1	0
neuropsychology	1	0
PTSD	1	1

Clinical opportunities
adolescent
day treatment and hospice programs
community mental health centers
developmental evaluation clinics
outpatient treatment centers
parole agencies
psychiatric, medical, and veterans hospitals
public and private schools
state courts, prisons
substance abuse

Argosy University–Twin Cities (Psy.D.)

School of Psychology
5503 Green Valley Drive
Minneapolis, MN 55437
phone#: (612) 921-9500
e-mail: admissions@aspp.edu
Web address: http://www.aspp.edu

1	2	3	4	5	6	7

Clinically oriented — Equal emphasis — Research oriented

What percentage of your faculty subscribes to or practices in each of the following orientations?

Psychodynamic/Psychoanalytic	10%
Applied behavioral analysis/Radical behavioral	30%
Family systems/Systems	20%
Existential/Phenomenological/Humanistic	10%
Cognitive/Cognitive-behavioral	30%

What percentage of students applying for internship last year was accepted into APA-accredited internships? 70%

What courses are required for incoming students to have completed prior to enrolling?
Intro, statistics, personality, tests & measures, abnormal psychology, 12 credits in undergraduate psychology, 3 credits in statistics

Are there courses you recommend that are not mandatory?
Biology

GRE mean (M), cutoff (C), or preferred (P)
Verbal 600 (P) Quantitative 600 (P) Analytical 600 (P)

GPA mean (M), cutoff (C), or preferred (P)
Overall GPA 3.25 (P) Psychology GPA 3.25 (P)
Junior/Senior GPA 3.25 (P)

Number of applications/admission offers/incoming students in 2001
240 applied/90 admission offers/45 incoming

% of students receiving:
Tuition waiver only: 8%
Assistantship/fellowship only: 21%
Both tuition waiver & assistantship/fellowship: 0%

Approximate percentage of incoming students who entered with a B.A./B.S. only: 70% **Master's:** 30%

Approximate percentage of students who are
Women: 80% **Ethnic Minority:** 20%

Average years to complete the doctoral program (including internship): 4.8 years

Research areas	**# Faculty**	**# Grants**
(not reported)		

Clinical opportunities
Behavioral medicine, pain clinic, geriatric clinic, eating disorders clinic, HIV-AIDS clinic, epilepsy clinic, ADHD clinic, forensic unit, sex offender units, biofeedback clinic

Argosy University–Washington, DC Campus (Psy.D.)

Department of Clinical Psychology
1550 Wilson Boulevard, Suite 600
Arlington, VA 22209
phone#: (703) 243-5300
e-mail: djacobs@aspp.edu
Web address: http://www.argosyu.edu/

1 **2** 3 4 5 6 7

Clinically oriented — Equal emphasis — Research oriented

What percentage of your faculty subscribes to or practices in each of the following orientations?

Psychodynamic/Psychoanalytic	30%
Applied behavioral analysis/Radical behavioral	0%
Family systems/Systems	10%
Existential/Phenomenological/Humanistic	20%
Cognitive/Cognitive-behavioral	40%

What percentage of students applying for internship last year was accepted into APA-accredited internships? 71%

What courses are required for incoming students to have completed prior to enrolling?
Introductory psychology, abnormal psychology, theories of personality, research methods or statistics, tests and measurements,

Are there courses you recommend that are not mandatory?
No

GRE mean (M), cutoff (C), or preferred (P) score
GRE is not required

GPA mean (M), cutoff (C), or preferred (P)
Overall GPA 3.25 (C)

Number of applications/admission offers/incoming students in 2001
304 applied/139 admission offers/74 incoming

% of students receiving:
Tuition waiver only: 0%
Assistantship/fellowship only: 10%
Both tuition waiver & assistantship/fellowship: 0%

Approximate percentage of incoming students who entered with a B.A./B.S. only: 69% **Master's:** 31%

Approximate percentage of students who are
Women: 75% **Ethnic Minority:** 26%

Average years to complete the doctoral program (including internship): 4.5 years

Research areas	**# Faculty**	**# Grants**
anxiety disorders	1	0
child sex abuse	1	0
forensic	2	0
health/neuropsychology/ behavioral medicine	4	0
personality disorders	1	0

Clinical opportunities
Students acquire practicum placements in a wide variety of community settings including forensic, behavioral medicine, neuropsychology, and child/family.

University of Arizona

Department of Psychology
Psychology Building
Tucson, AZ 85721
phone#: (520) 621-1867
e-mail: varda@u.arizona.edu
Web address: http://w3.arizona.edu/~psych/clinical.html

1 2 3 4 5 **6** 7

Clinically oriented — Equal emphasis — Research oriented

What percentage of your faculty subscribes to or practices in each of the following orientations?

Psychodynamic/Psychoanalytic	0%
Applied behavioral analysis/Radical behavioral	20%
Family systems/Systems	20%
Existential/Phenomenological/Humanistic	10%
Cognitive/Cognitive-behavioral	40%

What percentage of students applying for internship last year was accepted into APA-accredited internships? 100%

What courses are required for incoming students to have completed prior to enrolling?
B.A. or B.S. in psychology

Are there courses you recommend that are not mandatory?
No

GRE mean (M), cutoff (C), or preferred (P) score
Verbal 550 (M) Quantitative 550 (M)
Advanced Psychology 550 (M)

GPA mean (M), cutoff (C), or preferred (P)
Overall GPA 3.5 (P) Psychology GPA 3.5 (P)
Junior/Senior GPA 3.5 (P)

Number of applications/admission offers/incoming students in 2001
259 applied/11 admission offers/7 incoming

% of students receiving:
Tuition waiver only: 0%
Assistantship/fellowship only: 0%
Both tuition waiver & assistantship/fellowship: 100%

Approximate percentage of incoming students who entered with a B.A./B.S. only: 80% **Master's:** 20%

Approximate percentage of students who are Women: 60% **Ethnic Minority:** 20%

Average years to complete the doctoral program (including internship): 6 years

Research areas	# Faculty	# Grants
biofeedback	1	0
clinical neuropsychology	3	2
community psychology	1	0
depression	2	1
family systems	2	3
health psychology	4	4
mental health policy	2	2
personality assessment	1	0
sleep disorders	1	2
treatment outcome	3	2

Clinical opportunities
behavioral medicine
community psychology
couple and family therapy
depression
gerontology
neuropsychology/rehabilitation
sleep disorders

Arizona State University

Department of Psychology
Tempe, AZ 85287
phone#: (602) 965-7606
e-mail: laurie.chassin@asu.edu
Web address: http://www.asu.edu/clas/psych/clinical.html

1	2	3	4	5	**6**	7
Clinically oriented		Equal emphasis			Research oriented	

What percentage of your faculty subscribes to or practices in each of the following orientations?

Psychodynamic/Psychoanalytic	5%
Applied behavioral analysis/Radical behavioral	5%
Family systems/Systems	30%
Existential/Phenomenological/Humanistic	0%
Cognitive/Cognitive-behavioral	60%

What percentage of students applying for internship last year was accepted into APA-accredited internships? 100%

What courses are required for incoming students to have completed prior to enrolling?
B.A. in psychology or equivalent

Are there courses you recommend that are not mandatory?
No

GRE mean (M), cutoff (C), or preferred (P) score
Verbal 615 (M) Quantitative 725 (M)

GPA mean (M), cutoff (C), or preferred (P)
Overall GPA 3.6 (M)

Number of applications/admission offers/incoming students in 2001
210 applied/13 admission offers/6 incoming

% of students receiving:
Tuition waiver only: 0%
Assistantship/fellowship only: 0%
Both tuition waiver & assistantship/fellowship: 100%

Approximate percentage of incoming students who entered with a B.A./B.S. only: 90% **Master's:** 10%

Approximate percentage of students who are Women: 75% **Ethnic Minority:** 27%

Average years to complete the doctoral program (including internship): 7.3 years

Research areas	# Faculty	# Grants
adult psychopathology	4	1
aging/gerontology	3	2
behavioral medicine/health psychology	6	4
child clinical	8	7
community psychology	5	3
epidemiology	1	1
family interactions	1	1
gender roles	3	1
hispanic studies	5	2
minority mental health	5	2
personality assessment	2	1
prevention	6	5
psychoneuroimmunology	2	2
quantitative statistics	7	2
stress and coping	6	5
substance abuse	6	5

Clinical opportunities
behavioral analysis
behavioral medicine
child health psychology
family therapy
geropsychology
individual therapy
intellectual and academic assessment
interpersonal psychotherapy
marital/couples therapy
parenting groups
prevention programs

University of Arkansas

Department of Psychology
216 Memorial Hall
Fayetteville, AR 72701
phone#: (501) 575-4256
Web address: http://www.uark.edu/depts/psych/

1	2	3	**4**	5	6	7
Clinically oriented			Equal emphasis			Research oriented

What percentage of your faculty subscribes to or practices in each of the following orientations?

Psychodynamic/Psychoanalytic 0%
Applied behavioral analysis/Radical behavioral 15%
Family systems/Systems 30%
Existential/Phenomenological/Humanistic 15%
Cognitive/Cognitive-behavioral 70%

What percentage of students applying for internship last year was accepted into APA-accredited internships? 100%

What courses are required for incoming students to have completed prior to enrolling?
Applicants who have not taken a course in history and systems will be expected to take these courses upon arrival.

Are there courses you recommend that are not mandatory?
18 semester hours in psychology including statistics, learning, and experimental psychology

GRE mean (M), cutoff (C), or preferred (P) score
Verbal 500+ (P) Quantitative 500+ (P) Analytical 500+ (P)

GPA mean (M), cutoff (C), or preferred (P)
Overall GPA 2.7 (C), 3.0 (P)

Number of applications/admission offers/incoming students in 2001
60 applied/6 admission offers/6 incoming

% of students receiving:
Tuition waiver only: 0%
Assistantship/fellowship only: 0%
Both tuition waiver & assistantship/fellowship: 100%

Approximate percentage of incoming students who entered with a B.A./B.S. only: 80% **Master's:** 20%

Approximate percentage of students who are Women: 62% **Ethnic Minority:** 20%

Average years to complete the doctoral program (including internship): 5 years

Research areas	# Faculty	# Grants
child abuse	2	0
depression	2	0
eating disorders	1	0
neuropsychology	2	1
psychotherapy process	1	0
relational violence	3	0
sexual assault	3	1

Clinical opportunities
behavioral medicine
depression
sexual assault
violence

Auburn University

Department of Psychology
226 Thach
Auburn, AL 36849
phone#: (334) 844-6471
e-mail: BRYANGT@MAIL.AUBURN.EDU
Web address: http://www.auburn.edu/academic/liberal_arts/psychology/graduate.html

1	2	**3**	4	5	6	7
Clinically oriented			Equal emphasis			Research oriented

What percentage of your faculty subscribes to or practices in each of the following orientations?

Psychodynamic/Psychoanalytic 10%
Applied behavioral analysis/Radical behavioral 30%
Family systems/Systems 10%
Existential/Phenomenological/Humanistic 0%
Cognitive/Cognitive-behavioral 50%

What percentage of students applying for internship last year was accepted into APA-accredited internships? 100%

What courses are required for incoming students to have completed prior to enrolling?
14 semester hours in theoretical or experimental psychology and quantitative methods

Are there courses you recommend that are not mandatory?
No

GRE mean (M), cutoff (C), or preferred (P) score
Verbal + Quantitative 1203 (M)

GPA mean (M), cutoff (C), or preferred (P)
Overall GPA 3.56 (M)

Number of applications/admission offers/incoming students in 2001
88 applied/14 admission offers/8 incoming

% of students receiving:
Tuition waiver only: 0%
Assistantship/fellowship only: 100%
Both tuition waiver & assistantship/fellowship: 0%

Approximate percentage of incoming students who entered with a B.A./B.S. only: 70% **Master's:** 30%

Approximate percentage of students who are Women: 70% **Ethnic Minority:** 9%

Average years to complete the doctoral program (including internship): 6.5 years

Research areas	**# Faculty**	**# Grants**
anxiety disorders	2	1
child clinical/psychopathology	2	0
developmental disabilities	1	0
personality assessment	2	0
sexuality/deviation/dysfunction	1	1

Clinical opportunities
anxiety disorders
autism
hyperactivity
personality disorders
PTSD
victim/battering/abuse

Baylor University (Psy.D.)

Department of Psychology
P.O. Box 97334
Waco, TX 76798-7334
phone#: (254) 710-2811
e-mail: M_Rudd@Baylor.edu
Web address: http://www.baylor.edu/~Psychology

1 **2** 3 4 5 6 7

Clinically oriented — Equal emphasis — Research oriented

What percentage of your faculty subscribes to or practices in each of the following orientations?

Psychodynamic/Psychoanalytic	15%
Applied behavioral analysis/Radical behavioral	0%
Family systems/Systems	15%
Existential/Phenomenological/Humanistic	15%
Cognitive/Cognitive-behavioral	55%

What percentage of students applying for internship last year was accepted into APA-accredited internships? 100%

What courses are required for incoming students to have completed prior to enrolling?
None

Are there courses you recommend that are not mandatory?
Developmental psychology, psychopathology, statistics, biopsychology, personality, social

GRE mean (M), cutoff (C), or preferred (P) score
Verbal 630 (M) Quantitative 631 (M)

GPA mean (M), cutoff (C), or preferred (P)
Overall GPA 3.0 (P) Psychology GPA 3.3 (P)
Junior/Senior GPA 3.3 (P)

Number of applications/admission offers/incoming students in 2001
160 applied/16 admission offers/12 incoming

% of students receiving:
Tuition waiver only: 0%
Assistantship/fellowship only: 0%
Both tuition waiver & assistantship/fellowship: 100%

Approximate percentage of incoming students who entered with a B.A./B.S. only: 78% **Master's:** 22%

Approximate percentage of students who are Women: 78% **Ethnic Minority:** 11%

Average years to complete the doctoral program (including internship): 4 years

Research areas	**# Faculty**	**# Grants**
behavioral medicine	1	0
child psychopathology	2	0
cognitive therapy	3	0
depression	3	0
group therapy	1	0
personality assessment	3	0

Clinical opportunities
alcohol and drug dependence
anxiety disorders
behavioral medicine
child psychotherapy
community psychology
crisis intervention
eating disorders
family therapy
gerontology
group dynamics
group therapy
health psychology
impulse control
mood disorders
neuropsychology
personality disorder
play therapy
rural psychology
schizophrenia/psychoses
school/educational
sexual offenders
suicide prevention
victim/battering/abuse

Binghamton University/State University of New York

Department of Psychology
Vestal Parkway
Binghamton, NY 13901
phone#: (607) 777-2334
e-mail: randers@binghamton.edu
Web address: http://psychology.binghamton.edu/grad/gradprog.htm

1 2 3 4 **5** 6 7

Clinically oriented — Equal emphasis — Research oriented

What percentage of your faculty subscribes to or practices in each of the following orientations?

Psychodynamic/Psychoanalytic	0%
Applied behavioral analysis/Radical behavioral	10%
Family systems/Systems	0%

Existential/Phenomenological/Humanistic 0%
Cognitive/Cognitive-behavioral 90%

What percentage of students applying for internship last year was accepted into APA-accredited internships? 100%

What courses are required for incoming students to have completed prior to enrolling?
Equivalent of a psychology major, with knowledge of experimental psychology and research methods

Are there courses you recommend that are not mandatory?
No

GRE mean (M), cutoff (C), or preferred (P) score
Verbal 588 (M) Quantitative 677 (M) Analytical 735 (M)
Advanced Psychology 680 (M)

GPA mean (M), cutoff (C), or preferred (P)
Overall GPA 3.7 (M) Psychology GPA 3.5 (P)

Number of applications/admission offers/incoming students in 2001
98 applied/15 admission offers/8 incoming

% of students receiving:
Tuition waiver only: 0%
Assistantship/fellowship only: 0%
Both tuition waiver & assistantship/fellowship: 100%

Approximate percentage of incoming students who entered with a B.A./B.S. only: 90% **Master's:** 10%

Approximate percentage of students who are Women: 78% **Ethnic Minority:** 11%

Average years to complete the doctoral program (including internship): 6.7 years

Research areas	# Faculty	# Grants
adult psychopathology	5	0
anxiety disorders	2	1
assessment	4	0
behavioral medicine	1	1
child clinical	2	2
depression	1	1
developmental disabilities	2	1
hypnosis	1	0
learning disabilities	1	1
marital process and therapy	1	0
memory construction	1	0
neuropsychology	1	0
pain management	1	1
pediatric psychology	1	1
posttraumatic stress disorder/ trauma	2	0
prevention	3	1
psychophysiology	2	0
social skills	1	0
substance abuse	1	0

Clinical opportunities
adolescent delinquency
assessment
behavioral medicine
conduct disorder
developmental disabilities/autism
disorders of childhood
family therapy
marital therapy
neuropsychology
pain management
psychotherapy supervision
schizophrenia
school consultation
state prison
substance abuse

Biola University (Ph.D.)

Rosemead School of Psychology
13800 Biola Avenue
La Mirada, CA 90639
phone#: (562) 903-4752
e-mail: biola@admissions.edu
Web address: http://www.rosemead.edu/

1	2	**3**	4	5	6	7
Clinically oriented		Equal emphasis				Research oriented

What percentage of your faculty subscribes to or practices in each of the following orientations?
Psychodynamic/Psychoanalytic 39%
Applied behavioral analysis/Radical behavioral 0%
Family systems/Systems 17%
Existential/Phenomenological/Humanistic 10%
Cognitive/Cognitive-behavioral 34%

What percentage of students applying for internship last year was accepted into APA-accredited internships? 75%

What courses are required for incoming students to have completed prior to enrolling?
Introductory psychology, statistics, experimental psychology, abnormal psychology, personality, learning

Are there courses you recommend that are not mandatory?
Social psychology, history of psychology, physiological psychology, biology/zoology, developmental psychology

GRE mean (M), cutoff (C), or preferred (P) score
Verbal 600 (P) Quantitative 600 (P)
Advanced Psychology 500 (P)

GPA mean (M), cutoff (C), or preferred (P)
Overall GPA 3.5 (P) Psychology GPA 3.5 (P)
Junior/Senior GPA 3.0 (C)

Number of applications/admission offers/incoming students in 2001
120 applied/35 admission offers/25 incoming

% of students receiving:
Tuition waiver only: 2%
Assistantship/fellowship only: 60%
Both tuition waiver & assistantship/fellowship: 0%

Approximate percentage of incoming students who entered with a B.A./B.S. only: 78% **Master's:** 32%

Approximate percentage of students who are Women: 78% **Ethnic Minority:** 11%

Average years to complete the doctoral program (including internship): 6 years

Research areas	# Faculty	# Grants
cross-cultural adjustment	4	0
grief	1	0
neuropsychology	1	0
object relations	4	0
parenting behaviors	3	0

Clinical opportunities
diversity
couples and family therapy
psychology of religion
school/educational

Biola University (Psy.D.)

Rosemead School of Psychology
13800 Biola Avenue
La Mirada, CA 90639
phone#: (562) 903-4752
Web address: http://www.rosemead.edu/

1	2	**3**	4	5	6	7

Clinically oriented · Equal emphasis · Research oriented

What percentage of your faculty subscribes to or practices in each of the following orientations?

Psychodynamic/Psychoanalytic	39%
Applied behavioral analysis/Radical behavioral	0%
Family systems/Systems	17%
Existential/Phenomenological/Humanistic	10%
Cognitive/Cognitive-behavioral	34%

What percentage of students applying for internship last year was accepted into APA-accredited internships? 80%

What courses are required for incoming students to have completed prior to enrolling?
Introductory psychology, statistics, experimental psychology, abnormal psychology, personality, learning

Are there courses you recommend that are not mandatory?
Social psychology, history of psychology, physiological psychology, biology/zoology, developmental psychology

GRE mean (M), cutoff (C), or preferred (P) score
Verbal 600 (P) Quantitative 600 (P)
Advanced Psychology 500 (P)

GPA mean (M), cutoff (C), or preferred (P)
Overall GPA 3.5 (P) Psychology GPA 3.5 (P)
Junior/Senior GPA 3.0 (C)

Number of applications/admission offers/incoming students in 2001
116 applied/35 admission offers/23 incoming

% of students receiving:
Tuition waiver only: 5%
Assistantship/fellowship only: 60%
Both tuition waiver & assistantship/fellowship: 0%

Approximate percentage of incoming students who entered with a B.A./B.S. only: 58% **Master's:** 42%

Approximate percentage of students who are Women: 60% **Ethnic Minority:** 25%

Average years to complete the doctoral program (including internship): 6 years

Research areas	# Faculty	# Grants
cross-cultural adjustment	4	0
gender issues	2	1
grief	1	0
neuropsychology	1	1
object relations	4	0
parenting behaviors	3	0

Clinical opportunities
diversity
couples and family therapy
psychology of religion
school/educational

Boston University

Department of Psychology
64 Cummington Street
Boston, MA 02215
phone#: (617) 353-2587
e-mail: gagnej@bu.edu
Web address: http://www.bu.edu/psych/Clinical/clinmain.htm

1	2	3	4	**5**	6	7

Clinically oriented · Equal emphasis · Research oriented

What percentage of your faculty subscribes to or practices in each of the following orientations?

Psychodynamic/Psychoanalytic	17%
Applied behavioral analysis/Radical behavioral	0%
Family systems/Systems	17%
Existential/Phenomenological/Humanistic	0%
Cognitive/Cognitive-behavioral	48%
Neuropsychology	17%
Eclectic	20%

What percentage of students applying for internship last year was accepted into APA-accredited internships? 100%

What courses are required for incoming students to have completed prior to enrolling?
Introductory psychology, statistics, abnormal/clinical psychology, experimental

Are there courses you recommend that are not mandatory?
Broad liberal arts and science

GRE mean (M), cutoff (C), or preferred (P) score
Verbal + Quantitative 1370 (P)

GPA mean (M), cutoff (C), or preferred (P)
Overall GPA 3.3 (P) Psychology GPA 3.7 (P)
Junior/Senior GPA 3.7 (P)

Number of applications/admission offers/incoming students in 2001
410 applied/18 admission offers/13 incoming

% of students receiving:
Tuition waiver only: 0%
Assistantship/fellowship only: 0%
Both tuition waiver & assistantship/fellowship: 100%

Approximate percentage of incoming students who entered with a B.A./B.S. only: 90% **Master's:** 10%

Approximate percentage of students who are Women: 75% **Ethnic Minority:** 25%

Average years to complete the doctoral program (including internship): 6.5 years

Research areas	**# Faculty**	**# Grants**
affective disorders	2	2
anxiety disorders	7	5
community psychology	2	0
emotion	3	1
family	2	1
gender	1	0
gerontology	1	1
minority	1	0
neuropsychology	3	2
personality disorders	1	2
schizophrenia	1	1
substance abuse and addiction	1	1
victim/abuse	1	0
women's emotional health	1	0

Clinical opportunities
abuse/battering
adolescents
affective disorders
behavioral medicine
community psychology
couples therapy
dissociative disorders
eating disorders
family therapy
gerontology
neuropsychology
schizophrenia

Bowling Green State University

Department of Psychology
Bowling Green, OH 43403
phone#: (419) 372-2301
e-mail: khelm@bgnet.bgsu.edu
Web address: http://www.bgsu.edu/departments/psych/Facultyprograms.html/ZAreaClinical.html

1	2	3	**4**	5	6	7
Clinically oriented			Equal emphasis			Research oriented

What percentage of your faculty subscribes to or practices in each of the following orientations?

Psychodynamic/Psychoanalytic	12%
Applied behavioral analysis/Radical behavioral	0%
Family systems/Systems	25%
Existential/Phenomenological/Humanistic	12%
Cognitive/Cognitive-behavioral	50%

What percentage of students applying for internship last year was accepted into APA-accredited internships? 100%

What courses are required for incoming students to have completed prior to enrolling?
None

Are there courses you recommend that are not mandatory?
Science, math, statistics, introductory and advanced psychology courses, abnormal, abnormal, psychology lab courses

GRE mean (M), cutoff (C), or preferred (P) score
Verbal 550 (M) Quantitative 630 (M)
Advanced Psychology 630 (M)

GPA mean (M), cutoff (C), or preferred (P)
Overall GPA 3.66 (M) Psychology GPA 3.79 (M)

Number of applications/admission offers/incoming students in 2001
129 applied/7 admission offers/10 incoming

% of students receiving:
Tuition waiver only: 0%
Assistantship/fellowship only: 0%
Both tuition waiver & assistantship/fellowship: 100%

Approximate percentage of incoming students who entered with a B.A./B.S. only: 78% **Master's:** 22%

Approximate percentage of students who are Women: 91% **Ethnic Minority:** 27%

Average years to complete the doctoral program (including internship): 6.6 years

Research areas	**# Faculty**	**# Grants**
aggression	1	1
alcohol and substance abuse	1	1
behavioral medicine	3	1
child clinical psychology	2	1
child stress and adjustment	2	0
community psychology	2	1
developmental disabilities	1	0
family	3	0
neuropsychology	1	0
prevention	2	2
program evaluation	2	2
psychology of religion	1	1
school-based prevention	2	2
stress	2	0
weight management	1	0

Clinical opportunities
behavioral medicine
child clinical psychology
clinical health psychology
community mental health
community psychology
family
forensic psychology
minority mental health services

needs assessment/program evaluation
neuropsychology
school-based assessment/intervention
sexual/physical abuse of children

Brigham Young University

Clinical Psychology Ph.D. Program
284TLRB
Provo, UT 84602
phone#: (801) 378-4050
e-mail: clinical psychology@byu.edu
Web address: http://www.byu.edu/~psychweb/

1	2	**3**	4	5	6	7
Clinically oriented		Equal emphasis				Research oriented

What percentage of your faculty subscribes to or practices in each of the following orientations?

Psychodynamic/Psychoanalytic	50%
Applied behavioral analysis/Radical behavioral	20%
Family systems/Systems	20%
Existential/Phenomenological/Humanistic	50%
Cognitive/Cognitive-behavioral	80%

What percentage of students applying for internship last year was accepted into APA-accredited internships? 100%

What courses are required for incoming students to have completed prior to enrolling?
Introductory psychology, statistics, research design, personality, abnormal psychology, learning or cognition, tests and measurements

Are there courses you recommend that are not mandatory?
No

GRE mean (M), cutoff (C), or preferred (P) score
Verbal 600+ (P) Quantitative 600+ (P) Analytical 600 (P)

GPA mean (M), cutoff (C), or preferred (P)
Overall GPA 3.7 (P) Junior/Senior GPA 3.74 (P)

Number of applications/admission offers/incoming students in 2001
61 applied/11 admission offers/10 incoming

% of students receiving tuition waiver & assistantship/fellowship:
All 1st year students receive assistantships and a waiver for part of their tuition. All 2nd, 3rd, and 4th-year students are funded in work settings which are coordinated by the department and also receive a waiver for part of their tuition.

Approximate percentage of incoming students who entered with a B.A./B.S. only: 70% **Master's:** 30%

Approximate percentage of students who are Women: 44% **Ethnic Minority:** 7%

Average years to complete the doctoral program (including internship): 5.6 years

Research areas	**# Faculty**	**# Grants**
child/adolescent development	2	1
clinical assessment	2	0
clinical health psychology/ behavioral medicine	1	1
cultural diversity/gender issues	3	1
depression and cognitive behavioral therapy	1	1
eating disorders	1	1
group therapy, process and outcome	4	1
individual psychotherapy, process and outcome	3	1
measurement	2	1
neuropsychology	2	4
PTSD	1	1
psychopathology	2	0

Clinical opportunities
community mental health centers
neuropsychology rehabilitation units
private general hospitals—behavioral medicine, ER, psychiatric units
private practices
residential facilities for eating disorders
residential facilities for youths
school districts
state hospital
state prison
third world placements
university counseling centers—Utah and Hawaii

University of British Columbia

Department of Psychology
2316 West Mall, Douglas Kenny Building
Vancouver, British Columbia V6T 124, Canada
phone#: (604) 822-4156
e-mail: WLINDEN@CURTEX.PSYCH.UBC.CA
Web address: http://www.psych.ubc.ca

1	2	3	**4**	5	6	7
Clinically oriented			Equal emphasis			Research oriented

What percentage of your faculty subscribes to or practices in each of the following orientations?

Psychodynamic/Psychoanalytic	10%
Applied behavioral analysis/Radical behavioral	0%
Family systems/Systems	0%
Existential/Phenomenological/Humanistic	0%
Cognitive/Cognitive-behavioral	90%

What percentage of students applying for internship last year was accepted into APA-accredited internships? 100%

What courses are required for incoming students to have completed prior to enrolling?
None

Are there courses you recommend that are not mandatory?
Statistics, abnormal behavior, and a cross-section of other psychology courses

GRE mean (M), cutoff (C), or preferred (P) score
Verbal 80th percentile (P) Quantitative 80th percentile (P)
Analytic 80th percentile (P)

GPA mean (M), cutoff (C), or preferred (P)
Overall GPA 80% (P) Psychology GPA 80% (P)

Number of applications/admission offers/incoming students in 2001
109 applied/7 admission offers/7 incoming

% of students receiving:
Tuition waiver only: 0%
Assistantship/fellowship only: 100%
Both tuition waiver & assistantship/fellowship: 0%

Approximate percentage of incoming students who entered with a B.A./B.S. only: 95% **Master's:** 5%

Approximate percentage of students who are Women: 65% **Ethnic Minority:** 10%

Average years to complete the doctoral program (including internship): 6.4 years

Research areas	# Faculty	# Grants
anxiety disorders	2	3
attention-deficit disorder	1	2
behavioral medicine	3	7
eating disorders	1	1
health psychology	1	0
sexual dysfunction	1	1

Clinical opportunities
assessment
family therapy
forensic psychology
neuropsychology

University at Buffalo/State University of New York

Department of Psychology
Park Hall
Buffalo, NY 14260
phone#: (716) 645-3650, ext. #203
e-mail: meacham@acsu.buffalo.edu
Web address: http://www.wings.buffalo.edu/psychology/clinical/

1	2	3	4	5	**6**	7
Clinically oriented			Equal emphasis			Research oriented

What percentage of your faculty subscribes to or practices in each of the following orientations?

Psychodynamic/Psychoanalytic	0%
Applied behavioral analysis/Radical behavioral	25%
Family systems/Systems	0%
Existential/Phenomenological/Humanistic	0%
Cognitive/Cognitive-behavioral	75%

What percentage of students applying for internship last year was accepted into APA-accredited internships? 100%

What courses are required for incoming students to have completed prior to enrolling?
Introductory psychology, research methods, statistics

Are there courses you recommend that are not mandatory?
Good science background, abnormal psychology, cognitive psychology, social psychology, developmental psychology

GRE mean (M), cutoff (C), or preferred (P) score
Verbal 600 (P) Quantitative 600 (P)
Advanced Psychology 600 (P)

GPA mean (M), cutoff (C), or preferred (P)
Overall GPA 3.3 (P) Psychology GPA 3.5 (P)
Junior/Senior GPA 3.5 (P)

Number of applications/admission offers/incoming students in 2001
127 applied/20 admission offers/9 incoming

% of students receiving:
Tuition waiver only: 0%
Assistantship/fellowship only: 0%
Both tuition waiver & assistantship/fellowship: 100%

Approximate percentage of incoming students who entered with a B.A./B.S. only: 85% **Master's:** 15%

Approximate percentage of students who are Women: 75% **Ethnic Minority:** 23%

Average years to complete the doctoral program (including internship): 5 years

Research areas	# Faculty	# Grants
addictions	2	1
adolescent relationship dysfunction	—	—
anxiety disorders	2	1
attention-deficit disorder	1	2
behavioral medicine	1	0
childhood risk of psychopathology	—	—
depression	2	1
family	2	3
schizophrenia	1	1
sexual dysfunction	1	0

Clinical opportunities
ADHD
anxiety disorders
behavior modification
depression
family systems
sexual dysfunction

University of California–Berkeley

Department of Psychology
Berkeley, CA 94720
phone#: (510) 642-1382
e-mail: psychapp@socrates.berkeley.edu
Web address: http://psychology.berkeley.edu/clinical.html

1	2	3	4	5	**6**	7
Clinically oriented			Equal emphasis			Research oriented

What percentage of your faculty subscribes to or practices in each of the following orientations?

Psychodynamic/Psychoanalytic	14%
Applied behavioral analysis/Radical behavioral	0%
Family systems/Systems	43%
Existential/Phenomenological/Humanistic	0%
Cognitive/Cognitive-behavioral	43%

What percentage of students applying for internship last year was accepted into APA-accredited internships? 100%

What courses are required for incoming students to have completed prior to enrolling?
None

Are there courses you recommend that are not mandatory?
Research design and methods, breadth in psychology

GRE mean (M), cutoff (C), or preferred (P) score
Verbal 700 (M) Quantitative 650 (M) Analytical 650 (M)
Advanced psychology 730 (M)

GPA mean (M), cutoff (C), or preferred (P)
Overall GPA 3.60 (M)

Number of applications/admission offers/incoming students in 2001
346 applied/7 admission offers/6 incoming

% of students receiving:
Tuition waiver only: 0%
Assistantship/fellowship only: 25%
Both tuition waiver & assistantship/fellowship: 75%

Approximate percentage of incoming students who entered with a B.A./B.S. only: 80% **Master's:** 20%

Approximate percentage of students who are Women: 78% **Ethnic Minority:** 37%

Average years to complete the doctoral program (including internship): 6.6 years

Research areas	# Faculty	# Grants
ADHD externalizing behavior	1	2
classrooms, school, student achievement	1	0
emotion and aging	1	1
emotion and marriage	1	1
marriage and family	1	1
psychotherapy outcome	1	2
schizophrenia/depression	1	1

Clinical opportunities
—

University of California–Los Angeles

Department of Psychology
405 Hilgard Avenue
Los Angeles, CA 90095-1563
phone#: (310) 825-2617
e-mail: gradadm@psych.ucla.edu
Web address: http://www.psych.ucla.edu/Areas/#2

1	2	3	4	5	6	**7**
Clinically oriented			Equal emphasis			Research oriented

What percentage of your faculty subscribes to or practices in each of the following orientations?

Psychodynamic/Psychoanalytic	15%
Applied behavioral analysis/Radical behavioral	0%
Family systems/Systems	10%
Existential/Phenomenological/Humanistic	0%
Cognitive/Cognitive-behavioral	75%

What percentage of students applying for internship last year was accepted into APA-accredited internships? 95%

What courses are required for incoming students to have completed prior to enrolling?
Elementary statistics; two of the following: learning, physiological, or perception/information processing; two of the following: developmental, social, or personality/abnormal; one course in biology or zoology; two courses (physics and/or chemistry) although a course in anthropology, philosophy, or sociology may be substituted for one of the physical science courses; at least one math course, preferably calculus or probability; advanced statistics

Are there courses you recommend that are not mandatory?
Research design and methods, psychology research labs, independent research courses; a broad background in the mathematical, biological and social sciences

GRE mean (M), cutoff (C), or preferred (P) score
Verbal 670 (M) Quantitative 690 (M) Analytical 730 (M)
Advanced Psychology 740 (M)

GPA mean (M), cutoff (C), or preferred (P)
Overall GPA 3.69 (M)

Number of applications/admission offers/incoming students in 2001
273 applied/21 admission offers/11 incoming

% of students receiving:
Tuition waiver only: 0%
Assistantship/fellowship only: 0%
Both tuition waiver & assistantship/fellowship: 80%–90%

Approximate percentage of incoming students who entered with a B.A./B.S. only: 92% **Master's:** 8%

Approximate percentage of students who are Women: 60% **Ethnic Minority:** 40%

Average years to complete the doctoral program (including internship): 6.2 years

Research areas	# Faculty	# Grants
AIDS	1	1
adult affective disorders	1	2
anxiety disorders and treatment	1	2
child and adolescent psychotherapy	6	4
child psychopathology	8	5
child sexual abuse	1	1
children's health beliefs	1	1
couples and marital relationships	2	2
cross-cultural research	5	4
developmental disabilities	2	1

hypertension and stress in African-Americans	1	1
schizophrenia	2	3
stress and coping	2	2

Clinical opportunities
affective disorders
anxiety disorders
community psychology
couples/marital
developmental disabilities/autism
family/child
psychotherapy supervision

Carlos Albizu University–San Juan Campus (Psy.D.)

San Juan, PR 00902-3711
phone#: (787) 725-6500, ext. 52
e-mail: galtieri@albizu.edu
Web address: http://www.prip.ccas.edu/

1 2 **3** 4 5 6 7
Clinically oriented — Equal emphasis — Research oriented

What percentage of your faculty subscribes to or practices in each of the following orientations?

Psychodynamic/Psychoanalytic	20%
Applied behavioral analysis/Radical behavioral	10%
Family systems/Systems	30%
Existential/Phenomenological/Humanistic	10%
Cognitive/Cognitive-behavioral	30%

What percentage of students applying for internship last year was accepted into APA-accredited internships? 0%

What courses are required for incoming students to have completed prior to enrolling?
Experimental psychology, physiological psychology, abnormal psychology, statistics, personality theories

Are there courses you recommend that are not mandatory?
—

GRE mean (M), cutoff (C), or preferred (P) score
N/A

GPA mean (M), cutoff (C), or preferred (P)
Overall GPA 3.00 (C)

Number of applications/admission offers/incoming students in 2001
114 applied/92 admission offers/78 incoming

% of students receiving:
Tuition waiver only: 0%
Assistantship/fellowship only: 0%
Both tuition waiver & assistantship/fellowship: 0%

Approximate percentage of incoming students who entered with a B.A./B.S. only: 75% **Master's:** 25%

Approximate percentage of students who are Women: 82% **Ethnic Minority:** 99%

Average years to complete the doctoral program (including internship): 6 years

Research areas	# Faculty	# Grants
human sexuality	1	0
instrument validation	1	0
mood disorders	3	0
organ donation	1	0
sports psychology	1	0

Clinical opportunities
forensic psychology
sex abuse intervention and therapy
sexual disorders
sports psychology

Case Western Reserve University

Department of Psychology
Mather Memorial Building
11220 Bellflower Road
Cleveland, OH 44106
phone#: (216) 368-2686
e-mail: PSCL-DEPT
Web address: http://www.cwru.edu/artsci/pscl/grad/index.html

1 2 3 **4** 5 6 7
Clinically oriented — Equal emphasis — Research oriented

What percentage of your faculty subscribes to or practices in each of the following orientations?

Psychodynamic/Psychoanalytic	50%
Applied behavioral analysis/Radical behavioral	0%
Family systems/Systems	0%
Existential/Phenomenological/Humanistic	25%
Cognitive/Cognitive-behavioral	50%

What percentage of students applying for internship last year was accepted into APA-accredited internships? 100%

What courses are required for incoming students to have completed prior to enrolling?
Statistics, undergraduate psychology courses

Are there courses you recommend that are not mandatory?
Psychology major

GRE mean (M), cutoff (C), or preferred (P) score
Verbal + Quantitative 1200 (P)

GPA mean (M), cutoff (C), or preferred (P)
Overall GPA 3.0 (P)

Number of applications/admission offers/incoming students in 2001
109 applied/10 admission offers/5 incoming

% of students receiving:
Tuition waiver only: 80%
Assistantship/fellowship only: 0%
Both tuition waiver & assistantship/fellowship: 20%

Approximate percentage of incoming students who entered with a B.A./B.S. only: 90% **Master's:** 10%

Approximate percentage of students who are Women: 80% **Ethnic Minority:** 5%

Average years to complete the doctoral program (including internship): 6 years

Research areas	# Faculty	# Grants
aging	2	1
behavioral medicine/ health psychology	1	0
chronic mental illness	1	0
developmental disabilities	1	1
learning disabilities	1	0
memory	2	0
parent–child interaction	2	0
personality disorders	1	0
self-psychology	1	0
temperament	1	1

Clinical opportunities
affective disorders
anxiety disorders
developmental disabilities/autism
eating disorders
gerontology/Alzheimer's
obsessive–compulsive disorders
personality disorders
schizophrenia/psychosis

Catholic University of America

Department of Psychology
620 Michigan Avenue, NE
Washington, DC 20064
phone#: (202) 319-5729
e-mail: cua-psychology@cua.edu
Web address:
http://arts_sciences.cua.edu/psy/clprog.htm

1 2 3 **4** 5 6 7

Clinically oriented Equal emphasis Research oriented

What percentage of your faculty subscribes to or practices in each of the following orientations?

Psychodynamic/Psychoanalytic	25%
Applied behavioral analysis/Radical behavioral	0%
Family systems/Systems	50%
Existential/Phenomenological/Humanistic	50%
Cognitive/Cognitive-behavioral	75%

What percentage of students applying for internship last year was accepted into APA-accredited internships? 100%

What courses are required for incoming students to have completed prior to enrolling?
Introductory psychology, statistics, research methods

Are there courses you recommend that are not mandatory?
Research experience in psychology; abnormal psychology; personality; developmental psychology; social psychology

GRE mean (M), cutoff (C), or preferred (P) score
Verbal 600+ (P) Quantitative 600+ (P) Analytical 600+ (P) Advanced Psychology 600+ (P)

GPA mean (M), cutoff (C), or preferred (P)
Overall GPA 3.3+ (P) Psychology GPA 3.3+ (P) Junior/Senior GPA 3.5+ (P)

Number of applications/admission offers/incoming students in 2001
94 applied/12 admission offers/6 incoming

% of students receiving:
Tuition waiver only: 46%
Assistantship/fellowship only: 0%
Both tuition waiver & assistantship/fellowship: 38%

Approximate percentage of incoming students who entered with a B.A./B.S. only: 87% **Master's:** 13%

Approximate percentage of students who are Women: 76% **Ethnic Minority:** 13%

Average years to complete the doctoral program (including internship): 7 years

Research areas	# Faculty	# Grants
adolescence	4	0
adult psychopathology	5	1
affective disorders	5	0
anxiety disorders	3	0
assessment	2	1
child clinical	2	0
clinical training	3	0
cognition	3	0
couples	1	0
cross-cultural psychology	1	0
developmental	2	0
developmental psychopathology	2	0
emotions	3	0
emotion regulation	2	0
ethical issues	1	0
family	3	0
forensic	1	0
friendship	1	0
gender roles	3	0
group processes	2	0
interpersonal processes	4	0
parent–child interactions	2	0
personality assessment	2	0
personality disorders	1	0
psychotherapy integration	4	0
psychotherapy outcome	5	0
psychotherapy process	5	0
schizophrenia	1	0
self-efficacy	3	0
shyness	2	0
social cognition	2	0
social learning	2	0
stress and coping	3	0
suicide	3	0
supervision	3	0

Clinical opportunities
adult psychotherapy
assessment batteries
child and adult assessment

family therapy
group therapy
minority mental health
neuropsychology

Central Michigan University

Department of Psychology
Mt. Pleasant, MI 48859
phone#: (517) 774-6463
e-mail: RONAN1GF@MAIL.CMICH.EDU
Web address:
http://www.CHSBS.CMICH.EDU/Psychology/

1 2 3 **4** 5 6 7

Clinically oriented — Equal emphasis — Research oriented

What percentage of your faculty subscribes to or practices in each of the following orientations?

Psychodynamic/Psychoanalytic	29%
Applied behavioral analysis/Radical behavioral	0%
Family systems/Systems	14%
Existential/Phenomenological/Humanistic	0%
Cognitive/Cognitive-behavioral	57%

What percentage of students applying for internship last year was accepted into APA-accredited internships? 100%

What courses are required for incoming students to have completed prior to enrolling?
None

Are there courses you recommend that are not mandatory?
Statistics, experimental psychology, developmental psychology, abnormal psychology, theories of personality, tests and measurements

GRE mean (M), cutoff (C), or preferred (P) score
Verbal 566 (M) Quantitative 625 (M)

GPA mean (M), cutoff (C), or preferred (P)
Overall GPA 3.61 (M) Psychology GPA 3.87 (M)

Number of applications/admission offers/incoming students in 2001
69 applied/10 admission offers/8 incoming

% of students receiving:
Tuition waiver only: 20%
Assistantship/fellowship only: 0%
Both tuition waiver & assistantship/fellowship: 77%

Approximate percentage of incoming students who entered with a B.A./B.S. only: 75% **Master's:** 25%

Approximate percentage of students who are Women: 63% **Ethnic Minority:** 3%

Average years to complete the doctoral program (including internship): 6 years

Research areas	# Faculty	# Grants
anxiety disorders	1	1
assessment	1	1
children	1	0
diversity	1	0
health psychology	1	0
neuropsychology	1	0
severe psychopathology	1	0
violence and agression	1	0

Clinical opportunities
adult clinical
child clinical
cognitive-behavioral therapy
forensic psychology
neuropsychology/rehabilitation
parent–child interaction therapy
psychodynamic therapy
school-based interventions

Chicago School of Professional Psychology (Psy.D.)

47 West Polk
Chicago, IL 60605
phone#: (312) 786-9443
e-mail: admissions@csopp.edu
Web address: http://www.csopp.edu/cspp.html

1 **2** 3 4 5 6 7

Clinically oriented — Equal emphasis — Research oriented

What percentage of your faculty subscribes to or practices in each of the following orientations?

Psychodynamic/Psychoanalytic	30%
Applied behavioral analysis/Radical behavioral	10%
Family systems/Systems	20%
Existential/Phenomenological/Humanistic	15%
Cognitive/Cognitive-behavioral	25%

What percentage of students applying for internship last year was accepted into APA-accredited internships? 76%

What courses are required for incoming students to have completed prior to enrolling?
18 hours in psychology, including statistics, theories of personality, abnormal psychology

Are there courses you recommend that are not mandatory?
No

GRE mean (M), cutoff (C), or preferred (P) score
Verbal + Quantitative 1000 (P), 1015 (M)

GPA mean (M), cutoff (C), or preferred (P)
Overall GPA 3.35 (M), 3.0 (P)

Number of applications/admission offers/incoming students in 2001
176 applied/144 admission offers/60 incoming

% of students receiving:
Tuition waiver only: 9%
Assistantship/fellowship only: 21%
Both tuition waiver & assistantship/fellowship: 28%

Approximate percentage of incoming students who entered with a B.A./B.S. only: 61% **Master's:** 39%

Approximate percentage of students who are Women: 69% **Ethnic Minority:** 20%

Average years to complete the doctoral program (including internship): 5.5 years

Research areas	**# Faculty**	**# Grants**
—		

Clinical opportunities
administration
child and adolescent
community psychology
creative and expressive arts
cross-cultural/international
forensic
health
organizational
sexual orientation

University of Cincinnati

Department of Psychology
429 Dyer Hall
Cincinnati, OH 45221-0376
phone#: (513) 556-5580
e-mail: Paula.Shear@uc.edu
Web address: http://ucaswww.mcm.uc.edu/psychology/

1	2	3	4	5	**6**	7

Clinically oriented — Equal emphasis — Research oriented

What percentage of your faculty subscribes to or practices in each of the following orientations?

Psychodynamic/Psychoanalytic	20%
Applied behavioral analysis/Radical behavioral	10%
Family systems/Systems	5%
Existential/Phenomenological/Humanistic	10%
Cognitive/Cognitive-behavioral	55%

What percentage of students applying for internship last year was accepted into APA-accredited internships? 100%

What courses are required for incoming students to have completed prior to enrolling?
Preference given to applicants with coursework in psychology

Are there courses you recommend that are not mandatory?
Abnormal psychology, statistics and research methods

GRE mean (M), cutoff (C), or preferred (P) score
Verbal 600 (P) Quantitative 600 (P) Analytical 600 (P)
Advanced Psychology 600 (P)

GPA mean (M), cutoff (C), or preferred (P)
Overall GPA 3.0+ (C) Psychology GPA 3.0 (C)
Junior/Senior GPA 3.0 (C)

Number of applications/admission offers/incoming students in 2001
200 applied/20 admission offers/13 incoming

% of students receiving:
Tuition waiver only: 0%
Assistantship/fellowship only: 0%
Both tuition waiver & assistantship/fellowship: 100%

Approximate percentage of incoming students who entered with a B.A./B.S. only: 90% **Master's:** 10%

Approximate percentage of students who are Women: 75% **Ethnic Minority:** 25%

Average years to complete the doctoral program (including internship): 6 years

Research areas	**# Faculty**	**# Grants**
addictive behaviors	5	2
adolescence	2	1
adult development	1	1
child clinical	4	4
domestic abuse	2	1
health psychology	5	2
homelessness	2	1
neuropsychology	5	1
serious mental illness	3	2

Clinical opportunities
addictive behaviors
child clinical psychology
clinical neuropsychology
community mental health
developmental disorders
health psychology
serious mental illness
university counseling center

City University of New York at City College

Department of Psychology
138th Street and Covenant Avenue
New York, NY 10031
phone#: (212) 650-5674
e-mail: sbtuber@hotmail.com
Web address: http://www.ccny.cuny.edu/graduate_bulletin_97/Psychology.html

1	2	**3**	4	5	6	7

Clinically oriented — Equal emphasis — Research oriented

What percentage of your faculty subscribes to or practices in each of the following orientations?

Psychodynamic/Psychoanalytic	60%
Applied behavioral analysis/Radical behavioral	0%
Family systems/Systems	30%
Existential/Phenomenological/Humanistic	10%
Cognitive/Cognitive-behavioral	20%

What percentage of students applying for internship last year was accepted into APA-accredited internships? 100%

What courses are required for incoming students to have completed prior to enrolling?
Experimental, statistics

Are there courses you recommend that are not mandatory?
Abnormal, developmental

GRE mean (M), cutoff (C), or preferred (P)
Verbal 650 (M) Quantitative 600 (M) Analytic 600 (M)
Advanced Psychology 600 (M)

GPA mean (M), cutoff (C), or preferred (P)
Overall GPA 3.7 (M) Psychology GPA 3.8 (M) Junior/Senior GPA 3.8 (M)

Number of applications/admission offers/incoming students in 2001
275 applied/14 admission offers/12 incoming

% of students receiving:
Tuition waiver only: 10%
Assistantship/fellowship only: 20%
Both tuition waiver & assistantship/fellowship: 35%

Approximate percentage of incoming students who entered with a B.A./B.S. only: 80% **Master's:** 20%

Approximate percentage of students who are Women: 65% **Ethnic Minority:** 40%

Average years to complete the doctoral program (including internship): 6.5 years

Research areas	**# Faculty**	**# Grants**
African-American adolescents	1	0
attachment	3	1
object relations	4	1
social policies in mental health	1	0
racism	1	0
psychotherapy outcome	3	0

Clinical opportunities
child clinic
family clinic

Clark University

Frances L. Hiatt School of Psychology
950 Main Street
Worcester, MA 01610
phone#: (508) 793-7276
e-mail: wgrolnick@clarku.edu
Web address: http://www.clarku.edu

1 2 3 4 **5** 6 7

Clinically oriented — Equal emphasis — Research oriented

What percentage of your faculty subscribes to or practices in each of the following orientations?

Psychodynamic/Psychoanalytic	50%
Applied behavioral analysis/Radical behavioral	50%
Family systems/Systems	50%
Existential/Phenomenological/Humanistic	0%
Cognitive/Cognitive-behavioral	50%

What percentage of students applying for internship last year was accepted into APA-accredited internships? 100%

What courses are required for incoming students to have completed prior to enrolling?
Statistics, research design, abnormal psychology

Are there courses you recommend that are not mandatory?
Psychology major, substantial research experience

GRE mean (M), cutoff (C), or preferred (P) score
Verbal 650 (P) Quantitative 650 (P)
Advanced Psychology 700 (P)

GPA mean (M), cutoff (C), or preferred (P)
Overall GPA 3.5 (M)

Number of applications/admission offers/incoming students in 2001
145 applied/17 admission offers/4 incoming

% of students receiving:
Tuition waiver only: 40%
Assistantship/fellowship only: 0%
Both tuition waiver & assistantship/fellowship: 60%

Approximate percentage of incoming students who entered with a B.A./B.S. only: 90% **Master's:** 10%

Approximate percentage of students who are Women: 80% **Ethnic Minority:** 10%

Average years to complete the doctoral program (including internship): 10 years

Research areas	**# Faculty**	**# Grants**
adult psychopathology	1	1
affective disorders	1	0
assessment/diagnosis/classification	1	0
child abuse and children at-risk	1	0
child clinical/child psychopathology	2	0
family research/therapy	2	1
gender roles/sex differences	1	0
motivation	1	1
parent–child interaction	3	1
personality disorders	2	0
prevention	2	0
psychotherapy process and outcome	1	1
social learning	1	0

Clinical opportunities
childhood abuse
child therapy/assessment
couples/family therapy
systems therapy

University of Colorado

Department of Psychology
Muenzinger 244, Campus Box 345
Boulder, CO 80309-0345
phone#: (303) 492-8805
Web address: http://psych-www.colorado.edu/Graduate_Study/clinical_desc.html

1	2	3	4	5	**6**	7
Clinically oriented			Equal emphasis			Research oriented

What percentage of your faculty subscribes to or practices in each of the following orientations?

Psychodynamic/Psychoanalytic	30%
Applied behavioral analysis/Radical behavioral	13%
Family systems/Systems	25%
Existential/Phenomenological/Humanistic	25%
Cognitive/Cognitive-behavioral	40%

What courses are required for incoming students to have completed prior to enrolling?
Psychology or the equivalent (18 semester hours in psychology)

Are there courses you recommend that are not mandatory?
Psychological assessment, psychopathology, psychotherapy, research methods, statistics, developmental psychology, social psychology/personality, biological psychology

GRE mean (M), cutoff (C), or preferred (P) score
Verbal 600 (C) Quantitative 600 (C)
Advanced Psychology 600 (P)

GPA mean (M), cutoff (C), or preferred (P)
Overall GPA 3.0 (C), 3.5 (P) Psychology GPA 3.6 (P)
Junior/Senior GPA 3.6 (P)

Number of applications/admission offers/incoming students in 2001
137 applied/8 admission offers/4 incoming

% of students receiving:
Tuition waiver only: 0%
Assistantship/fellowship only: 0%
Both tuition waiver & assistantship/fellowship: 100%

Approximate percentage of incoming students who entered with a B.A./B.S. only: 83% **Master's:** 17%

Approximate percentage of students who are Women: 79% **Ethnic Minority:** 21%

Average years to complete the doctoral program (including internship): 6 years

Research areas	**# Faculty**	**# Grants**
adult psychopathology	3	1
affective disorders	3	1
applied behavioral analysis	1	1
assessment/diagnosis/classification	3	0
behavioral medicine	1	0
child clinical	2	1
community psychology	1	1
developmental	2	1
eating disorders	2	1
family research	2	2
gender roles	3	2
marriage/couples	2	0
parent–child interaction	3	2
personality disorders	3	1
prevention	4	1
psychoanalysis	1	0
psychotherapy outcome/process	3	0
schizophrenia	1	1
self-esteem	2	0
self-psychology	1	0
social skills	2	1
substance abuse	2	0
violence/abuse	1	1
women's studies	2	1

Clinical opportunities
adolescent delinquency
assessment
behavior therapy
cognitive therapy
conduct disorder
family therapy
infancy/postpartum
interpersonal treatment
psychodynamic psychotherapy
substance abuse

Columbia University, Teachers College

Clinical Psychology Program
525 West 120th Street
New York, NY 10027
phone#: (212) 678-3267
fax#: (212) 678-4048
e-mail: tcinfo@www.tc.columbia.edu
Web address: http://www.tc.columbia.edu/~academic/clinical/

1	2	3	**4**	5	6	7
Clinically oriented			Equal emphasis			Research oriented

What percentage of your faculty subscribes to or practices in each of the following orientations?

Psychodynamic/Psychoanalytic	80%
Applied behavioral analysis/Radical behavioral	0%
Family systems/Systems	0%
Existential/Phenomenological/Humanistic	0%
Cognitive/Cognitive-behavioral	20%

What percentage of students applying for internship last year was accepted into APA-accredited internships? 100%

What courses are required for incoming students to have completed prior to enrolling?
Statistics and 9 credits from among: experimental psychology, personality, history and systems, developmental psychology, or social psychology

Are there courses you recommend that are not mandatory?
Abnormal psychology

GRE mean (M), cutoff (C), or preferred (P) score
Verbal 650 (P) Quantitative 650 (P)
Advanced Psychology 650 (P)

GPA mean (M), cutoff (C), or preferred (P)
Overall GPA 3.6 (P)

Number of applications/admission offers/incoming students in 2001
210 applied/10 admission offers/8 incoming

% of students receiving:
Tuition waiver only: 70% (partial)
Assistantship/fellowship only: 0%
Both tuition waiver & assistantship/fellowship: 10%

Approximate percentage of incoming students who entered with a B.A./B.S. only: 40% **Master's:** 60%

Approximate percentage of students who are Women: 65% **Ethnic Minority:** 17%

Average years to complete the doctoral program (including internship): 7 years

Research areas	# Faculty	# Grants
altruism	1	0
child abuse	1	1
geriatrics	1	1
psychotherapy research	2	0
spirituality	1	1
stress and coping	1	2

Clinical opportunities
child therapy
psychodynamic/psychoanalytic therapy

Concordia University

Department of Psychology, PY 119-2
7141 Sherbrooke Street West
Montreal, Quebec H4B 1R6 Canada
phone#: (514) 848-2205
e-mail: black@vax2.concordia.ca
Web address: http://www.psychology.concordia.ca/department/graduate/clin-pro.html

1	2	3	4	**5**	6	7
Clinically oriented			Equal emphasis			Research oriented

What percentage of your faculty subscribes to or practices in each of the following orientations?

Psychodynamic/Psychoanalytic	25%
Applied behavioral analysis/Radical behavioral	0%
Family systems/Systems	25%
Existential/Phenomenological/Humanistic	0%
Cognitive/Cognitive-behavioral	50%

What percentage of students applying for internship last year was accepted into APA-accredited internships? 67%

What courses are required for incoming students to have completed prior to enrolling?
Honors (B.A./B.Sc.) in psychology

Are there courses you recommend that are not mandatory?
No

GRE mean (M), cutoff (C), or preferred (P) score
Verbal 600 (P) Quantitative 600 (P) Analytical 600 (P)
Advanced Psychology 700 (P)

GPA mean (M), cutoff (C), or preferred (P)
Overall GPA 3.8 (P) Psychology GPA 3.8 (P)

Number of applications/admission offers/incoming students in 2001
121 applied/17 admission offers/11 incoming

% of students receiving:
Tuition waiver only: 0%
Assistantship/fellowship only: 90%
Both tuition waiver & assistantship/fellowship: 10%

Approximate percentage of incoming students who entered with a B.A./B.S. only: 80% **Master's:** 20%

Approximate percentage of students who are Women: 80% **Ethnic Minority:** 15%

Research areas	# Faculty	# Grants
anxiety	2	2
behavioral medicine	1	1
developmental/infancy	4	4
developmental psychopathology	2	4
gender roles	2	1
health psychology	1	0
neuropsychology	2	5
schizophrenia	1	1
social competence	1	1

Clinical opportunities
adult
child/adolescent
cognitive/cognitive-behavioral
couples
family
psychodynamic

University of Connecticut

Department of Psychology
U-20, Babbidge Road
Storrs, CT 06269-1020
phone#: (860) 486-3528 (Admissions information)
e-mail: futuregr@psych.psy.uconn.edu
Web address: http://psych.uconn.edu/

1	2	3	4	**5**	6	7
Clinically oriented			Equal emphasis			Research oriented

What percentage of your faculty subscribes to or practices in each of the following orientations?

Psychodynamic/Psychoanalytic	12%
Applied behavioral analysis/Radical behavioral	0%
Family systems/Systems	12%
Existential/Phenomenological/Humanistic	12%
Cognitive-behavioral	64%

What percentage of students applying for internship last year was accepted into APA-accredited internships? 100%

What courses are required for incoming students to have completed prior to enrolling?
None

Are there courses you recommend that are not mandatory?
No

GRE mean (M), cutoff (C), or preferred (P) score
Verbal 630 (M) Quantitative 688 (M) Analytical 684 (M)
Advanced Psychology 659 (M)

GPA mean (M), cutoff (C), or preferred (P)
Overall GPA 3.75 (M)

Number of applications/admission offers/incoming students in 2001
189 applied/17 admission offers/9 incoming

% of students receiving:
Tuition waiver only: 0%
Assistantship/fellowship only: 0%
Both tuition waiver & assistantship/fellowship: 100%

Approximate percentage of incoming students who entered with a B.A./B.S. only: 87% **Master's:** 13%

Approximate percentage of students who are Women: 62% **Ethnic Minority:** 25%

Average years to complete the doctoral program (including internship): 5.6 years

Research areas	**# Faculty**	**# Grants**
adult psychopathology	1	0
anxiety disorders	2	1
autism	1	3
ethical issues	1	0
health psychology	2	1
hypnosis	1	1
neuropsychological assessment	2	2

Clinical opportunities
autistic children
corporate stress management
health psychology
neuroimaging
neuropsychological assessment
traumatic brain injury

Dalhousie University

Department of Psychology
Halifax, Nova Scotia B3H 4J1 Canada
phone #: (902) 494-1580
e-mail: beatrice@is.dal.ca
Web address: http://www.dal.ca/psychology/

1	2	3	4	**5**	6	7

Clinically oriented — Equal emphasis — Research oriented

What percentage of your faculty subscribes to or practices in each of the following orientations?

Psychodynamic/Psychoanalytic	0%
Applied behavioral analysis/Radical behavioral	0%
Family systems/Systems	0%
Existential/Phenomenological/Humanistic	0%
Cognitive/Cognitive-behavioral	100%

What percentage of students applying for internship last year was accepted into APA-accredited internships? 100%

What courses are required for incoming students to have completed prior to enrolling?
An honors degree in psychology

Are there courses you recommend that are not mandatory?
—

GRE mean (M), cutoff (C), or preferred (P) score
Verbal 680 (M) Quantitative 670 (M)

GPA mean (M), cutoff (C), or preferred (P)
Overall GPA 4.1 (M)

Number of applications/admission offers/incoming students in 2001
107 applied/7 admission offers/5 incoming

% of students receiving:
Tuition waiver only: 0%
Assistantship/fellowship only: 100%
Both tuition waiver & assistantship/fellowship: 0%

Approximate percentage of incoming students who entered with a B.A./B.S. only: 56% **Master's:** 44%

Approximate percentage of students who are Women: 73% **Ethnic Minority:** 13%

Average years to complete the doctoral program (including internship): 7 years

Research areas	**# Faculty**	**# Grants**
anxiety	1	4
cognitive process	1	3
depression	2	3
disruptive behavior/ peer relationships	2	1
forensic psychology	3	1
neuropsychology	1	1
pain in children	1	5

Clinical opportunities
—

University of Delaware

Department of Psychology
Newark, DE 19716
phone#: (302) 831-2271
e-mail: rkobak@udel.edu
Web address: http://www.psych.udel.edu/clinical/

1	2	3	4	5	**6**	7

Clinically oriented — Equal emphasis — Research oriented

What percentage of your faculty subscribes to or practices in each of the following orientations?

Psychodynamic/Psychoanalytic	12.5%
Applied behavioral analysis/Radical behavioral	12.5%
Family systems/Systems	12.5%
Existential/Phenomenological/Humanistic	12.5%
Cognitive/Cognitive-behavioral	75%

What percentage of students applying for internship last year was accepted into APA-accredited internships? 86%

What courses are required for incoming students to have completed prior to enrolling?
None

Are there courses you recommend that are not mandatory?
Statistics, biopsychology, abnormal psychology, history and systems, cognitive, developmental

GRE mean (M), cutoff (C), or preferred (P) score
Verbal 650 (P) Quantitative 650 (P)

GPA mean (M), cutoff (C), or preferred (P)
Overall GPA 3.5 (P) Psychology GPA 3.5 (P)

Number of applications/admission offers/incoming students in 2001
151 applied/5 admission offers/4 incoming

% of students receiving:
Tuition waiver only: 0%
Assistantship/fellowship only: 0%
Both tuition waiver & assistantship/fellowship: 100%

Approximate percentage of incoming students who entered with a B.A./B.S. only: 90% **Master's:** 10%

Approximate percentage of students who are Women: 75% **Ethnic Minority:** 10%

Average years to complete the doctoral program (including internship): 5 years

Research areas	**# Faculty**	**# Grants**
anxiety, stress, and coping	2	0
attachment theory	2	1
child clinical	4	5
developmental risk for pathology	4	4
emotions	4	0
foster care	1	2
personality	2	1
psychophysiology	3	1
psychotherapy	1	0

Clinical opportunities
anxiety disorders
child assessment
conduct disorder
developmental disabilities/autism
family therapy
neuropsychology/rehabilitation
pediatric
sexual assault/abuse

University of Denver (Ph.D.)

Department of Psychology
University Park
Denver, CO 80210
phone#: (303) 871-3803
e-mail: phoughta@nova.psy.du.edu
Web address: http://www.du.edu/psychology/CHILDCLINICALWHOLE.htm

1	2	3	4	**5**	6	7
Clinically oriented			Equal emphasis			Research oriented

What percentage of your faculty subscribes to or practices in each of the following orientations?

Psychodynamic/Psychoanalytic	30%
Applied behavioral analysis/Radical behavioral	10%
Family systems/Systems	10%
Existential/Phenomenological/Humanistic	0%
Cognitive/Cognitive-behavioral	50%

What percentage of students applying for internship last year was accepted into APA-accredited internships? 100%

What courses are required for incoming students to have completed prior to enrolling?
None

Are there courses you recommend that are not mandatory?
Statistics

GRE mean (M), cutoff (C), or preferred (P) score
Verbal + Quantitative 1250 (P)

GPA mean (M), cutoff (C), or preferred (P)
Overall GPA 3.0 (P)

Number of applications/admission offers in 1999
170 applied/8 admission offers

% of students receiving:
Tuition waiver only: 0%
Assistantship/fellowship only: 0%
Both tuition waiver & assistantship/fellowship: 100%

Approximate percentage of incoming students who entered with a B.A./B.S. only: 90% **Master's:** 10%

Approximate percentage of students who are Women: 75% **Ethnic Minority:** 33%

Research areas	**# Faculty**	**# Grants**
adolescent adjustment	2	2
behavioral genetics	1	1
child psychopathology	1	1
children's coping with abuse	1	0
dyslexia	1	3
family	1	0
marital	1	1
multicultural	1	1
neuropsychology	1	1
poverty	2	1
romantic relationships	1	1

Clinical opportunities
developmental disorders
family

inpatient adolescents
marital/couples
minority/cross-cultural
neuropsychology

University of Denver (Psy.D.)

School of Professional Psychology
2300 South Gaylord
Denver, CO 80208-0208
phone#: (303) 871-3873
e-mail: jfarmer@du.edu
Web address: http://www.du.edu/gspp/psyd.htm

1	**2**	3	4	5	6	7
Clinically oriented			Equal emphasis			Research oriented

What percentage of your faculty subscribes to or practices in each of the following orientations?

Psychodynamic/Psychoanalytic	40%
Applied behavioral analysis/Radical behavioral	20%
Family systems/Systems	20%
Existential/Phenomenological/Humanistic	10%
Cognitive/Cognitive-behavioral	10%

What percentage of students applying for internship last year was accepted into APA-accredited internships? 90%

What courses are required for incoming students to have completed prior to enrolling?
Statistics, learning theory, personality theory, experimental psychology, child psychology, abnormal psychology, history of psychology (or at least 90th percentile [660] on the Psychology Subject Test of the GREs)

Are there courses you recommend that are not mandatory?
Physiological psychology

GRE mean (M), cutoff (C), or preferred (P) score
Verbal 550–600 (P) Quantitative 500–550(P)

GPA mean (M), cutoff (C), or preferred (P)
Overall GPA 3.5 (P)

Number of applications/admission offers/incoming students in 2001
250 applied/45 admission offers/30 incoming

% of students receiving:
Tuition waiver only: 2%
Assistantship/fellowship only: 35%
Both tuition waiver & assistantship/fellowship: 5%

Approximate percentage of incoming students who entered with a B.A./B.S. only: 60% **Master's:** 39%

Approximate percentage of students who are Women: 76% **Ethnic Minority:** 11%

Average years to complete the doctoral program (including internship): 4 years

Research areas	# Faculty	# Grants
behavioral medicine/therapy	1	0
cognitive issues	1	0
couples and family therapy	2	0
forensic issues	2	0
multicultural issues	1	0

Clinical opportunities
assessment
behavioral medicine
cognitive therapy
forensic psychology
group therapy
hypnosis
psychodynamic/psychoanalytic therapy
psychotherapy supervision

DePaul University

Department of Psychology
2219 North Kenmore
Chicago, IL 60614
phone#: (773) 325-7780
e-mail: Lrobinson@WPPOST.DEPAUL.EDU
Web address: http://www.Depaul.edu

1	2	**3**	4	5	6	7
Clinically oriented			Equal emphasis			Research oriented

What percentage of your faculty subscribes to or practices in each of the following orientations?

Psychodynamic/Psychoanalytic	0%
Applied behavioral analysis/Radical behavioral	22%
Family systems/Systems	55%
Existential/Phenomenological/Humanistic	0%
Cognitive/Cognitive-behavioral	33%

What percentage of students applying for internship last year was accepted into APA-accredited internships? 100%

What courses are required for incoming students to have completed prior to enrolling?
24 semester hours in psychology, 3 semester hours of statistics, and 3 semester hours in experimental psychology

Are there courses you recommend that are not mandatory?
Science, computer, and math courses

GRE mean (M), cutoff (C), or preferred (P) score
Verbal 600 (M) Quantitative 620 (M)

GPA mean (M), cutoff (C), or preferred (P)
Overall GPA 3.5 (M) Psychology GPA 3.6 (M)

Number of applications/admission offers/incoming students in 2001
158 applied/15 admission offers/9 incoming

% of students receiving:
Tuition waiver only: 15%
Assistantship/fellowship only: 0%
Both tuition waiver & assistantship/fellowship: 85%

Approximate percentage of incoming students who entered with a B.A./B.S. only: 67% **Master's:** 33%

Approximate percentage of students who are Women: 70% **Ethnic Minority:** 40%

Average years to complete the doctoral program (including internship): 8.7 years

Research areas	# Faculty	# Grants
child abuse and neglect	1	1
community outreach	2	4
HIV/AIDS adolescent prevention	1	3
minority mental health	3	1
parent–child interaction	1	1
program evaluation	3	1
teenage pregnancy	2	1

Clinical opportunities
assessment
child and adolescent
community psychology
family therapy
group therapy
minority/cross-cultural

University of Detroit–Mercy

Department of Psychology
P. O. Box 19900
Detroit, MI 48219-3599
phone#: (313) 993-6220
e-mail: mccownja@udmercy.edu
Web address: http://udmercy.edu/psychology/

1 2 **3** 4 5 6 7

Clinically oriented — Equal emphasis — Research oriented

What percentage of your faculty subscribes to or practices in each of the following orientations?

Psychodynamic/Psychoanalytic	75%
Applied behavioral analysis/Radical behavioral	10%
Family systems/Systems	10%
Existential/Phenomenological/Humanistic	10%
Cognitive/Cognitive-behavioral	25%

What percentage of students applying for internship last year was accepted into APA-accredited internships? 85%

What courses are required for incoming students to have completed prior to enrolling?
Statistics, experimental, research methods, personality, abnormal psychology, research course

Are there courses you recommend that are not mandatory?
Physiological psychology

GRE mean (M), cutoff (C), or preferred (P) score
Verbal 550 (P) Quantitative 550 (P) Analytical 550 (P)

GPA mean (M), cutoff (C), or preferred (P)
Overall GPA 3.5 (P)

Number of applications/admission offers/incoming students in 2001
40 applied/12 admission offers/8 incoming

% of students receiving:
Tuition waiver only: 0%
Assistantship/fellowship only: 0%
Both tuition waiver & assistantship/fellowship: 30%
(all students in first 3 years of program)

Approximate percentage of incoming students who entered with a B.A./B.S. only: 75% **Master's:** 25%

Approximate percentage of students who are Women: 80% **Ethnic Minority:** 25%

Average years to complete the doctoral program (including internship): 6 years

Research areas	# Faculty	# Grants
critical incident response	2	0
helping behavior	1	0
information processing in schizophrenia	1	0
intellectual assessment using human figure drawings	1	0
marital and family relationships	2	0
posttraumatic stress disorder	2	0
psychiatric diagnosis, ethnicity, and clinical judgment	1	0
psychotherapy process and outcome	4	0
self-esteem/body image	2	0

Clinical opportunities
Practicums and internships are completed at one of over 30 agencies in the metropolitan area. Students are also encouraged to apply nationally for internship if their circumstances permit.

Drexel University

Department of Psychology
3141 Chestnut Street
Philadelphia, PA 19104
phone#: (215) 895-2455
Web address: http://www.psa.drexel.edu/

1 2 3 **4** 5 6 7

Clinically oriented — Equal emphasis — Research oriented

What percentage of your faculty subscribes to or practices in each of the following orientations?

Psychodynamic/Psychoanalytic	0%
Applied behavioral analysis/Radical behavioral	0%
Family systems/Systems	10%
Existential/Phenomenological/Humanistic	0%
Cognitive/Cognitive-behavioral	90%

What percentage of students applying for internship last year was accepted into APA-accredited internships? 100%

What courses are required for incoming students to have completed prior to enrolling?
None

Are there courses you recommend that are not mandatory?
Foundation courses in psychology

GRE mean (M), cutoff (C), or preferred (P) score
Verbal 600 (M) Quantitative 600 (M) Analytical 650 (M)
Advanced Psychology 650 (M)

GPA mean (M), cutoff (C), or preferred (P)
Overall GPA 3.75 (M)

Number of applications/admission offers/incoming students in 2001
130 applied/6 admission offers/5 incoming

% of students receiving:
Tuition waiver only: 0%
Assistantship/fellowship only: 0%
Both tuition waiver & assistantship/fellowship: 100%

Approximate percentage of incoming students who entered with a B.A./B.S. only: 70% **Master's:** 30%

Approximate percentage of students who are Women: 80% **Ethnic Minority:** 15%

Average years to complete the doctoral program (including internship): 5 years

Research areas	# Faculty	# Grants
dementia	2	0
health psychology/neuropsychology	3	0
medication management/older adults	1	0
pediatric psychology	2	1
traumatic brain injury	1	1

Clinical opportunities
anxiety disorders
behavioral medicine
eating disorders
neuropsychological assessment
TBI rehabilitation

Duke University

Department of Psychology
Durham, NC 27706
phone#: (919) 660-5711
e-mail: Beeymdre@Duke.edu
Web address: http://www.psych.duke.edu/grad.html

1 2 3 4 5 **6** 7

Clinically oriented — Equal emphasis — Research oriented

What percentage of your faculty subscribes to or practices in each of the following orientations?

Psychodynamic/Psychoanalytic	20%
Applied behavioral analysis/Radical behavioral	0%
Family systems/Systems	15%
Existential/Phenomenological/Humanistic	0%
Cognitive/Cognitive-behavioral	65%

What percentage of students applying for internship last year was accepted into APA-accredited internships? 100%

What courses are required for incoming students to have completed prior to enrolling?
None

Are there courses you recommend that are not mandatory?
Broad background, statistics, personality theory

GRE mean (M), cutoff (C), or preferred (P) score
Verbal + Quantitative 1350 (P)

GPA mean (M), cutoff (C), or preferred (P)
Overall GPA 3.5 (M)

Number of applications/admission offers/incoming students in 2001
250 applied/11 admission offers/7 incoming

% of students receiving:
Tuition waiver only: 0%
Assistantship/fellowship only: 0%
Both tuition waiver & assistantship/fellowship: 100%

Approximate percentage of incoming students who entered with a B.A./B.S. only: 90% **Master's:** 10%

Approximate percentage of students who are Women: 75% **Ethnic Minority:** 23%

Average years to complete the doctoral program (including internship): 5.5 years

Research areas	# Faculty	# Grants
affective disorders	3	2
behavioral medicine	4	6
conduct disorders	2	3
eating disorders	1	0
developmental psychopathology	5	5
neuropsychology	1	0
posttraumatic stress disorder	2	0
school/educational	5	2
sexual abuse	2	0
social cognition	2	2
social skills	3	2
stress and coping	6	6

Clinical opportunities
adolescents
affective disorders
behavioral cardiology
behavioral medicine
behavior disorders of children
child abuse
cognitive/dialectical behavior therapy
eating disorders
neuropsychology
pediatric psychology
posttraumatic stress disorder
public sector impairment treatment
school/educational
substance abuse

Emory University

Department of Psychology
Kilgo Circle
Atlanta, GA 30322
phone#: (404) 727-7456
e-mail:TLEGGE@EMORY.EDU
Web address: http://www.emory.edu/PSYCH/

1	2	3	4	5	**6**	7
Clinically oriented		Equal emphasis			Research oriented	

What percentage of your faculty subscribes to or practices in each of the following orientations?

Psychodynamic/Psychoanalytic	10%
Applied behavioral analysis/Radical behavioral	10%
Family systems/Systems	30%
Existential/Phenomenological/Humanistic	10%
Cognitive/Cognitive-behavioral	60%

What percentage of students applying for internship last year was accepted into APA-accredited internships? 100%

What courses are required for incoming students to have completed prior to enrolling?
No

Are there courses you recommend that are not mandatory?
Statistics, methodology

GRE mean (M), cutoff (C), or preferred (P) score
Verbal 600 (M) Quantitative 600 (M) Analytical 600 (M)

GPA mean (M), cutoff (C), or preferred (P)
Overall GPA 3.3 (M)

Number of applications/admission offers/incoming students in 2001
196 applied/31 admission offers/13 incoming

% of students receiving:
Tuition waiver only: 0%
Assistantship/fellowship only: 0%
Both tuition waiver & assistantship/fellowship: 100%

Approximate percentage of incoming students who entered with a B.A./B.S. only: 70% **Master's:** 30%

Approximate percentage of students who are Women: 85% **Ethnic Minority:** 10%

Average years to complete the doctoral program (including internship): 5 years

Research areas	# Faculty	# Grants
adolescent depression	2	0
attention-deficit disorder	1	1
behavior control	1	0
behavioral genetics	1	1
infant development	1	2
neuropsychology	2	0
personality theory	2	0
schizophrenia	2	1

Clinical opportunities
assessment
behavioral medicine
behavior therapy
cognitive therapy
neuropsychology

Fairleigh Dickinson University

Department of Psychology
Teaneck–Hackensack Campus
1000 River Road
Teaneck, NJ 07666
phone#: (201) 692-2315
e-mail: massoth@alpha.fdu.edu
Web address: http://www.fdu.edu/academic/depts/phdclinical.html

1	2	3	**4**	5	6	7
Clinically oriented		Equal emphasis			Research oriented	

What percentage of your faculty subscribes to or practices in each of the following orientations?

Psychodynamic/Psychoanalytic	60%
Applied behavioral analysis/Radical behavioral	10%
Family systems/Systems	15%
Existential/Phenomenological/Humanistic	20%
Cognitive/Cognitive-behavioral	60%

What percentage of students applying for internship last year was accepted into APA-accredited internships? 100%

What courses are required for incoming students to have completed prior to enrolling?
18 credits in psychology including statistics, introductory developmental, experimental, social

Are there courses you recommend that are not mandatory?
Psychopathology, physiological, assessment

GRE mean (M), cutoff (C), or preferred (P) score
Verbal 625 (M) Quantitative 600 (M) Analytical 625 (M)
Advanced Psychology 650 (M)

GPA mean (M), cutoff (C), or preferred (P)
Overall GPA 3.5 (M)

Number of applications/admission offers/incoming students in 2001
145 applied/26 admission offers/13 incoming

% of students receiving:
Tuition waiver only: 0%
Assistantship/fellowship only: 100% (can be taken as tuition remission)
Both tuition waiver & assistantship/fellowship: 0%

Approximate percentage of incoming students who entered with a B.A./B.S. only: 60% **Master's:** 40%

Approximate percentage of students who are Women: 66% **Ethnic Minority:** 20%

Average years to complete the doctoral program (including internship): 5.5 years

Research areas	# Faculty	# Grants
assessment	6	2
behavioral medicine	3	1
child clinical	4	2
community psychology	3	0
depression	1	0
eating disorders	1	0
ethical issues	2	0
forensic	2	0
minority issues	2	0
relationship	4	0
sexual abuse	3	0
statistics	2	0
stress-disasters	2	1
women's studies	4	0

Clinical opportunities
anxiety disorders
assessment
behavioral medicine
community psychology
family therapy
gerontology
minority populations
neuropsychology
substance abuse

Fielding Graduate Institute

School of Psychology
2112 Santa Barbara Street
Santa Barbara, CA 93105
phone#: (800) 340-1099
e-mail: admissions@fielding.edu
Web address: http://www.fielding.edu/

1	2	3	4	**5**	6	7
Clinically oriented			Equal emphasis			Research oriented

What percentage of your faculty subscribes to or practices in each of the following orientations?

Psychodynamic/Psychoanalytic	20%
Applied behavioral analysis/Radical behavioral	0%
Family systems/Systems	13%
Existential/Phenomenological/Humanistic	30%
Cognitive/Cognitive-behavioral	37%

What percentage of students applying for internship last year was accepted into APA-accredited internships? 60%

What courses are required for incoming students to have completed prior to enrolling?
A bachelor's equivalent of a psychology major

Are there courses you recommend that are not mandatory?
This is a networked distance learning organization only appropriate for adult students with professional experience.

GRE mean (M), cutoff (C), or preferred (P) score
Not used

GPA mean (M), cutoff (C), or preferred (P)
Overall GPA 3.0 (C)

Number of applications/admission offers/incoming students in 2001
255 applied/95 admission offers/86 incoming

% of students receiving:
Tuition waiver only: 0%
Assistantship/fellowship only: 0%
Both tuition waiver & assistantship/fellowship: 0%

Approximate percentage of incoming students who entered with a B.A./B.S. only: 20% **Master's:** 80%

Approximate percentage of students who are Women: 70% **Ethnic Minority:** 15%

Average years to complete the doctoral program (including internship): 8.8 years

Research areas
Concentrations available in health psychology and violence prevention

Clinical opportunities
Cognitive-behavioral, psychoanalytic, and TA-Gestalt training tracks

Finch University of Health Sciences, The Chicago Medical School

Department of Psychology
3333 Green Bay Road
North Chicago, IL 60064
phone#: (847) 578-3305
e-mail: CHINNI.CHILAMKURTI@FINCHCMS.EDU
Web address: http://www.finchcms.edu/psychology/PSY/htm

1	2	3	4	5	**6**	7
Clinically oriented			Equal emphasis			Research oriented

What percentage of your faculty subscribes to or practices in each of the following orientations?

Psychodynamic/Psychoanalytic	10%
Applied behavioral analysis/Radical behavioral	0%
Family systems/Systems	0%
Existential/Phenomenological/Humanistic	0%
Cognitive/Cognitive-behavioral	60%
Neuropsychology/Biological	30%

What percentage of students applying for internship last year was accepted into APA-accredited internships? 91%

What courses are required for incoming students to have completed prior to enrolling?
At least 15 credit hours of psychology, including a course in statistics and physiological psychology

Are there courses you recommend that are not mandatory?
No

GRE mean (M), cutoff (C), or preferred (P) score
Verbal 600 (P) Quantitative 600 (P) Analytical 600 (P)
Advanced Psychology 600 (P)

GPA mean (M), cutoff (C), or preferred (P)
Junior/Senior GPA 3.2 (P)

Number of applications/admission offers/incoming students in 2001
73 applied/34 admission offers/10 incoming

% of students receiving:
Tuition waiver only: 0%
Assistantship/fellowship only: 11%
Both tuition waiver & assistantship/fellowship: 70%

Approximate percentage of incoming students who entered with a B.A./B.S. only: 85% **Master's:** 15%

Approximate percentage of students who are Women: 77% **Ethnic Minority:** 20%

Average years to complete the doctoral program (including internship): 7.5 years

Research areas	# Faculty	# Grants
aging	1	1
anxiety disorders	1	0
behavioral medicine	3	2
neuropsychology	2	1
psychopathology	1	1
substance abuse	1	1

Clinical opportunities
anxiety disorders
behavioral medicine
behavioral pediatrics
clinical neuropsychology

University of Florida

Department of Clinical and Health Psychology
Box 100165 University of Florida Health Science Center
Gainesville, FL 32610
phone#: (352) 395-0455
e-mail: CARTER.HRP@MAIL.HEALTH.UFL.EDU
Web address: http://www.hp.ufl.edu/chp/gradprogram.html

1	2	3	**4**	5	6	7
Clinically oriented			Equal emphasis			Research oriented

What percentage of your faculty subscribes to or practices in each of the following orientations?

Psychodynamic/Psychoanalytic	20%
Applied behavioral analysis/Radical behavioral	10%
Family systems/Systems	60%
Existential/Phenomenological/Humanistic	20%
Cognitive/Cognitive-behavioral	80%

What percentage of students applying for internship last year was accepted into APA-accredited internships? 100%

What courses are required for incoming students to have completed prior to enrolling?
Statistics

Are there courses you recommend that are not mandatory?
Undergraduate courses in experimental psychology, developmental psychology, social psychology, personality, physiological, perception, statistics

GRE mean (M), cutoff (C), or preferred (P) score
Verbal 660 (P) Quantitative 660 (P)

GPA mean (M), cutoff (C), or preferred (P)
Junior/Senior GPA 3.6 (P)

Number of applications/admission offers/incoming students in 2001
266 applied/25 admission offers/15 incoming

% of students receiving:
Tuition waiver only: 0%
Assistantship/fellowship only: 0%
Both tuition waiver & assistantship/fellowship: 95% all students; 100% incoming

Approximate percentage of incoming students who entered with a B.A./B.S. only: 80% **Master's:** 20%

Approximate percentage of students who are Women: 78% **Ethnic Minority:** 20%

Average years to complete the doctoral program (including internship): 5.5 years

Research areas	# Faculty	# Grants
AIDS	1	1
anxiety disorders and emotions	2	3
child clinical psychology	3	3
clinical/medical psychology	3	3
neuropsychology	4	4
obesity treatment	1	1
pain	2	1
pediatric psychology	3	3
physician–patient communication	1	0

Clinical opportunities
anxiety
fear
medical psychology
neuropsychology
pain and stress
parent training'
pediatric consultation
weight loss

Florida Institute of Technology (Psy.D.)

School of Psychology
150 West University Boulevard
Melbourne, FL 32901
phone#: (407) 674-8105
e-mail: pfarber@fit.edu
Web address: http://www.fit.edu/AcadRes/psych/programs/clinical.html

1 2 **3** 4 5 6 7

Clinically oriented — Equal emphasis — Research oriented

What percentage of your faculty subscribes to or practices in each of the following orientations?

Psychodynamic/Psychoanalytic	10%
Applied behavioral analysis/Radical behavioral	10%
Family systems/Systems	20%
Existential/Phenomenological/Humanistic	20%
Cognitive/Cognitive-behavioral	40%

What percentage of students applying for internship last year was accepted into APA-accredited internships? 86%

What courses are required for incoming students to have completed prior to enrolling?
Statistics, learning, personality, physiological psychology, abnormal psychology, social psychology

Are there courses you recommend that are not mandatory?
A B.A. or B.S. in psychology

GRE mean (M), cutoff (C), or preferred (P) score
Verbal + Quantitative 1000 (P)

GPA mean (M), cutoff (C), or preferred (P)
Overall GPA 3.0 (P)

Number of applications/admission offers/incoming students in 2001
110 applied/42 admission offers/20 incoming

% of students receiving:
Tuition waiver only: 0%
Assistantship/fellowship only: 0%
Both tuition waiver & assistantship/fellowship: 30%

Approximate percentage of incoming students who entered with a B.A./B.S. only: 67% **Master's:** 33%

Approximate percentage of students who are Women: 70% **Ethnic Minority:** 15%

Average years to complete the doctoral program (including internship): 4 years

Research areas	# Faculty	# Grants
aging	2	0
eating disorders	1	1
family psychology	2	0
health psychology	3	0
neuropsychology	2	1
personality assessment	3	1
supervision	1	0
Vietnam veterans (posttraumatic stress syndrome)	1	1

Clinical opportunities
behavioral medicine/health psychology
eating disorders
family and marital therapy
neuropsychology
sexual abuse (offenders and victims)
substance abuse
Vietnam veterans (posttraumatic stress syndrome)

Florida State University

Department of Psychology
Tallahassee, FL 32306-1051
phone#: (850) 644-2499
e-mail: dilworth@psy.fsu.edu
Web address: http://www.psy.fsu.edu/

1 2 3 4 5 **6** 7

Clinically oriented — Equal emphasis — Research oriented

What percentage of your faculty subscribes to or practices in each of the following orientations?

Psychodynamic/Psychoanalytic	5%
Applied behavioral analysis/Radical behavioral	5%
Family systems/Systems	20%
Existential/Phenomenological/Humanistic	10%
Cognitive/Cognitive-behavioral	75%

What percentage of students applying for internship last year was accepted into APA-accredited internships? 100%

What courses are required for incoming students to have completed prior to enrolling?
Strong background in psychology and/or science

Are there courses you recommend that are not mandatory?
History and systems, research methods, developmental psychology, conditioning and learning, biological psychology, social psychology, personality, statistics, computer science

GRE mean (M), cutoff (C), or preferred (P) score
Verbal 600 (M) Quantitative 650 (M)

GPA mean (M), cutoff (C), or preferred (P)
Junior/Senior GPA 3.5 (M)

Number of applications/admission offers/incoming students in 2001
235 applied/12 admission offers/9 incoming

% of students receiving:
Tuition waiver only: 0%
Assistantship/fellowship only: 0%
Both tuition waiver & assistantship/fellowship: 100%

Approximate percentage of incoming students who entered with a B.A./B.S. only: 90% **Master's:** 10%

Approximate percentage of students who are Women: 75% **Ethnic Minority:** 17%

Average years to complete the doctoral program (including internship): 7 years

Research areas	# Faculty	# Grants
AIDS risk	1	0
aggression/violence	5	3
aging	2	1
alcohol and drug abuse	2	1
anxiety disorders	2	1
child and adolescent clinical/ psychopathology	4	5
depression	3	1
family interactions/therapy	3	0
forensic and correctional	5	3
gender roles/sex differences	2	0
personality assessment	4	1
psychopathy	3	2
psychophysiology of emotion	2	2
psychotherapy process and outcome	2	0
suicide	1	1

Clinical opportunities
adolescent delinquency
affective disorders/depression
anxiety disorders
assessment (child and adult)
forensic and correctional psychology
group therapy
marital/family therapy
minority/cross-cultural
neuropsychology/rehabilitation
schizophrenia/psychoses

Fordham University

Department of Psychology
Fordham Road and Southern Boulevard
Bronx, NY 10458
phone#: (718) 817-3782
fax#: (718) 817-3785
e-mail: cboyle@fordham.edu
Web address: http://www.fordham.edu/psychology/updated/index.html

1	2	3	**4**	5	6	7
Clinically oriented			Equal emphasis			Research oriented

What percentage of your faculty subscribes to or practices in each of the following orientations?

Psychodynamic/Psychoanalytic	20%
Applied behavioral analysis/Radical behavioral	10%
Family systems/Systems	20%
Existential/Phenomenological/Humanistic	10%
Cognitive/Cognitive-behavioral	40%

What percentage of students applying for internship last year was accepted into APA-accredited internships? 80%

What courses are required for incoming students to have completed prior to enrolling?
Statistics, experimental psychology, introductory psychology

Are there courses you recommend that are not mandatory?
No

GRE mean (M), cutoff (C), or preferred (P) score
Verbal 600 (C) Quantitative 600 (C)

GPA mean (M), cutoff (C), or preferred (P)
Overall GPA 3.0 (C) Psychology GPA 3.0 (C)

Number of applications/admission offers/incoming students in 2001
290 applied/25 admission offers/13 incoming

% of students receiving:
Tuition waiver only: 15%
Assistantship/fellowship only: 0%
Both tuition waiver & assistantship/fellowship: 50%

Approximate percentage of incoming students who entered with a B.A./B.S. only: 80% **Master's:** 20%

Approximate percentage of students who are Women: 66% **Ethnic Minority:** 20%

Average years to complete the doctoral program (including internship): 7.1 years

Research areas	# Faculty	# Grants
adolescent development	1	0
assessment	3	0
attachment relationships in couples	1	0
clinical child psychology	1	0
family systems	1	0
health psychology/behavioral medicine	1	0
MMPI	1	0
neuropsychology	1	0
parent–child relationships	2	0
personality disorders	1	0
prevention	1	0
social support	1	0
stress and coping	2	0
substance abuse	1	0

Clinical opportunities
Clinical externships available at numerous inpatient and outpatient specialty clinics in the New York metropolitan area. Appropriate training sites can be found in any area.

Forest Institute of Professional Psychology (Psy.D.)

2885 West Battlefield Road
Springfield, MO 65807
phone#: (417) 823-3477
e-mail: PRaleigh@forestinstitute.org (Director of Admissions); DCarpenter@forestinstitute.org (Graduate Training Director)
Web address: http://www.forestinstitute.org/

1	2	3	4	5	6	7
Clinically oriented			Equal emphasis			Research oriented

What percentage of your faculty subscribes to or practices in each of the following orientations?

Psychodynamic/Psychoanalytic	40%
Applied behavioral analysis/Radical behavioral	30%
Family systems/Systems	30%
Existential/Phenomenological/Humanistic	20%
Cognitive/Cognitive-behavioral	60%

What percentage of students applying for internship last year was accepted into APA-accredited internships? 25%

What courses are required for incoming students to have completed prior to enrolling?
Psy.D.: 18 hours of psychology
MA: 12 hours of psychology

Are there courses you recommend that are not mandatory?
General psychology, history and systems, abnormal psychology, theories of personality, statistics, biological sciences

GRE mean (M), cutoff (C), or preferred (P) score
Based on relationship to other variables

GPA mean (M), cutoff (C), or preferred (P)
Overall GPA 3.25 (C) Psychology GPA 3.0 (C)
Junior/Senior GPA 3.25 (C)

Number of applications/admission offers/incoming students in 2001
111 applied/76 admission offers/61 incoming

% of students receiving:
Tuition waiver only: 0%
Assistantship/fellowship only: 0%
Both tuition waiver & assistantship/fellowship: 0%

Approximate percentage of incoming students who entered with a B.A./B.S. only: 73% **Master's:** 27%

Approximate percentage of students who are Women: 58% **Ethnic Minority:** 11%

Average years to complete the doctoral program (including internship): 4 years

Research areas	# Faculty	# Grants
autoimmune disorders and psychological indices	2	1
electro-stimulation and stress	2	1
depression	2	1
pain management	2	0

Clinical opportunities
behavioral medicine
difficult child
gerontology
neuropsychology
pain management
parenting place
parenting skills classes
psychopharmacology
religion/psychology

Fuller Theological Seminary (Ph.D. & Psy.D.)

Graduate School of Psychology
180 North Oakland Avenue
Pasadena, CA 91101
phone#: (626) 584-5500
e-mail: LWagner@fuller.edu
Web address: http://www.fuller.edu/admiss/degrees/phdpsy.html and http://www.fuller.edu/admiss/degrees/psyd.html

1 2 3 **4** 5 6 7

Clinically oriented — Equal emphasis — Research oriented

What percentage of your faculty subscribes to or practices in each of the following orientations?

Psychodynamic/Psychoanalytic	30%
Applied behavioral analysis/Radical behavioral	0%
Family systems/Systems	30%
Existential/Phenomenological/Humanistic	10%
Cognitive/Cognitive-behavioral	30%

What percentage of students applying for internship last year was accepted into APA-accredited internships? 70%

What courses are required for incoming students to have completed prior to enrolling?
6 courses in psychology and a B.A. from an accredited school

Are there courses you recommend that are not mandatory?
Courses in the areas of abnormal, developmental, experimental, physiological, social psychology, statistics, tests and measures, learning, motivation, and personality

GRE mean (M), cutoff (C), or preferred (P) score
Verbal + Quantitative 1000 (C), 1100 (P), 1140 (M)

GPA mean (M), cutoff (C), or preferred (P)
Psychology GPA 3.0, 3.5 (P), 3.70 (M)

Number of applications/admission offers/incoming students in 2001
113 applied/66 admission offers/46 incoming

% of students receiving:
Tuition waiver only: 0%
Assistantship/fellowship only: 0%
Both tuition waiver & assistantship/fellowship: 0%

Approximate percentage of incoming students who entered with a B.A./B.S. only: 84.7% **Master's:** 15.3%

Approximate percentage of students who are Women: 63% **Ethnic Minority:** 28.7%

Average years to complete the doctoral program (including internship): 6 years

Research areas	# Faculty	# Grants
biopsychosocial	3	2
child clinical	2	1
cognition	1	0
cross-cultural psychology	2	0
depression	1	0
developmental	3	1

family	2	1
group processes	1	0
health psychology/behavioral medicine	3	0
hypnosis	0	0
marriages	1	0
neuropsychology	2	0
posttraumatic stress disorders	1	0
relaxation/biofeedback	2	0
religion	5	0
stress and coping	1	0
substance abuse	1	0

Clinical opportunities
assessment
chronic mental illness
family therapy
gerontology
group therapy
interpersonal psychotherapy
marital/couples therapy
neuropsychology/rehabilitation
supervision
victim/battering

Gallaudet University

Department of Psychology
8th and Florida Avenue, NE
Washington, DC 20002-3695
phone#: (202) 651-5540
e-mail: Patrick.Brice@Gallaudet.edu
Web address: http://www.gallaudet.edu/academics.html

1	2	**3**	4	5	6	7
Clinically oriented		Equal emphasis				Research oriented

What percentage of your faculty subscribes to or practices in each of the following orientations?

Psychodynamic/Psychoanalytic	60%
Applied behavioral analysis/Radical behavioral	20%
Family systems/Systems	0%
Existential/Phenomenological/Humanistic	20%
Cognitive/Cognitive-behavioral	40%

What percentage of students applying for internship last year was accepted into APA-accredited internships? 75%

What courses are required for incoming students to have completed prior to enrolling?
Major or minor in undergraduate psychology including statistics and experimental psychology

Are there courses you recommend that are not mandatory?
Development, social psychology, abnormal psychology, personality, learning, cognition, perception

GRE mean (M), cutoff (C), or preferred (P) score
Verbal 500 (P) Quantitative 500 (P) Analytical 500 (P)
Advanced Psychology is not required

GPA mean (M), cutoff (C), or preferred (P)
Overall GPA 3.00 (P) Psychology GPA 3.25 (P)

Number of applications/admission offers/incoming students in 2001
21 applied/9 admission offers/7 incoming

% of students receiving:
Tuition waiver only: 20%
Assistantship/fellowship only: 70%
Both tuition waiver & assistantship/fellowship: 5%

Approximate percentage of incoming students who entered with a B.A./B.S. only: 84% **Master's:** 16%

Approximate percentage of students who are
Women: 81% **Ethnic Minority:** 23%
Deaf or Hard of Hearing: 33% **Hearing:** 67%

Average years to complete the doctoral program (including internship): 6.2 years

Research areas	# Faculty	# Grants
adult development issues for deaf lesbians and gay men	1	0
assessment of attachment in deaf persons	2	1
assessment of attention in deaf children	1	0
assessment of depression in deaf clients	1	0
cognitive processing and memory in deaf persons	1	0
ethics in mental health and deafness	1	0
neuropsychological assessment of deaf clients	1	0
parental involvement with education of ethnic minority deaf children	1	1

Clinical opportunities
Assessment and therapy with deaf and hard of hearing clients through our multidisciplinary mental health clinic. More than 60 externship programs available in D.C. metropolitan area.

George Fox University (Psy.D.)

Graduate School of Clinical Psychology
Newburg, OR 97132-2697
phone#: (503) 554-2267
e-mail: jcain@georgefox.edu
Web address:
http://www.georgefox.edu/academic/grad/psyd

1	2	3	**4**	5	6	7
Clinically oriented			Equal emphasis			Research oriented

What percentage of your faculty subscribes to or practices in each of the following orientations?

Psychodynamic/Psychoanalytic	25%
Applied behavioral analysis/Radical behavioral	5%
Family systems/Systems	20%
Existential/Phenomenological/Humanistic	10%
Cognitive/Cognitive-behavioral	40%

What percentage of students applying for internship last year was accepted into APA-accredited internships? 54%

What courses are required for incoming students to have completed prior to enrolling?
18 semester hours or the equivalent (no specific courses required)

Are there courses you recommend that are not mandatory?
Personality, developmental, statistics, social, experimental, abnormal psychobiology

GRE mean (M), cutoff (C), or preferred (P) score
Verbal + Quantitative 1100 (P)

GPA mean (M), cutoff (C), or preferred (P)
Overall GPA 3.25 (P), 3.79 (M)

Number of applications/admission offers/incoming students in 2001
36 applied/26 admission offers/18 incoming

% of students receiving:
Tuition waiver only: 0%
Assistantship/fellowship only: 25%
Both tuition waiver & assistantship/fellowship: 0%

Approximate percentage of incoming students who entered with a B.A./B.S. only: 80% **Master's:** 20%

Approximate percentage of students who are Women: 56% **Ethnic Minority:** 11%

Average years to complete the doctoral program (including internship): 5.3 years

Research areas	# Faculty	# Grants
adjudicated youth	1	0
childhood memory	1	0
clinical supervision	1	0
long-distance school consultation	1	1
marriage relationships	1	0
memory assessment	1	0
shame	1	0
spirituality and mental health	1	0
Stroop effect	1	0

Clinical opportunities
corrections
CMH
inpatient hospital
military

George Mason University

Department of Psychology
4400 University Drive
Fairfax, VA 22030-4444
phone#: (703) 993-1342
e-mail: http://www.gmu.edu/departments/psychology/psychhp.html
Web address: http://www.gmu.edu/catalog/cas_psy3.htm#Psychology13

1	2	**3**	4	5	6	7
Clinically oriented		Equal emphasis				Research oriented

What percentage of your faculty subscribes to or practices in each of the following orientations?

Psychodynamic/Psychoanalytic	40%
Applied behavioral analysis/Radical behavioral	10%
Family systems/Systems	10%
Existential/Phenomenological/Humanistic	10%
Cognitive/Cognitive-behavioral	50%

What percentage of students applying for internship last year was accepted into APA-accredited internships? 92%

What courses are required for incoming students to have completed prior to enrolling?
Statistics, abnormal psychology, any laboratory science course

Are there courses you recommend that are not mandatory?
Tests and measurements/psychometrics

GRE mean (M), cutoff (C), or preferred (P) score
Verbal + Quantitative 1260 (M)

GPA mean (M), cutoff (C), or preferred (P)
Overall GPA 3.5 (M)

Number of applications/admission offers/incoming students in 2001
137 applied/22 admission offers/10 incoming

% of students receiving:
Tuition waiver only: 0%
Assistantship/fellowship only: 0%
Both tuition waiver & assistantship/fellowship: 100%

Approximate percentage of incoming students who entered with a B.A./B.S. only: 80% **Master's:** 20%

Approximate percentage of students who are Women: 80% **Ethnic Minority:** 9%

Average years to complete the doctoral program (including internship): 6 years

Research areas	# Faculty	# Grants
chronic mental illness/risk factors	1	1
cognition and affect (anxiety and depression)	2	0
media images of mental illness	1	1
parent–child interactions	2	1
personality—shame and guilt	1	1
self-efficacy	1	0
substance abuse	1	1
women's issues	1	0

Clinical opportunities
child/adult assessment
community consultation/education
group/marriage psychotherapy
individual adult psychotherapy

George Washington University (Ph.D.)

Department of Psychology
2125 G Street, NW
Washington, DC 20052
phone#: (202) 994-6544
e-mail: voilp@swis2.eivc.gwu.edu
Web address: http://www.gwu.edu/~clinpsyc

1 2 3 4 **5** 6 7

Clinically oriented — Equal emphasis — Research oriented

What percentage of your faculty subscribes to or practices in each of the following orientations?

Psychodynamic/Psychoanalytic	10%
Applied behavioral analysis/Radical behavioral	10%
Family systems/Systems	20%
Existential/Phenomenological/Humanistic	10%
Cognitive/Cognitive-behavioral	50%

What percentage of students applying for internship last year was accepted into APA-accredited internships? 100%

What courses are required for incoming students to have completed prior to enrolling?
At least a minor in psychology, statistics, research methods (or experimental course), basic psychology theory courses (from neuropsychology, physiological psychology, abnormal psychology, social psychology, learning, developmental psychology)

Are there courses you recommend that are not mandatory?
History and systems (if not taken must then take without credit)

GRE mean (M), cutoff (C), or preferred (P) score
Verbal 650 (P) Quantitative 650 (P) Analytical 650 (P)

GPA mean (M), cutoff (C), or preferred (P)
Overall GPA 3.5 (P)

Number of applications/admission offers/incoming students in 2001
180 applied/11 admission offers/7 incoming

% of students receiving:
Tuition waiver only: 0%
Assistantship/fellowship only: 0%
Both tuition waiver & assistantship/fellowship: 80%

Approximate percentage of incoming students who entered with a B.A./B.S. only: 80% **Master's:** 20%

Approximate percentage of students who are Women: 90% **Ethnic Minority:** 25%

Average years to complete the doctoral program (including internship): 6 years

Research areas	# Faculty	# Grants
adolescence	2	1
anxiety disorders	2	0
behavioral medicine	2	0
child/pediatrics	2	1
community	2	1
depression	1	0
family	1	1
health	2	1
minority mental health	2	2
relaxation/biofeedback	1	0
stress	2	0

Clinical opportunities
AIDS
adolescent delinquency
affective disorders/depression
anxiety disorders
assessment
behavioral medicine
conduct disorder
developmental disabilities/autism
dissociative disorder
eating disorders
family therapy
forensic psychology
gerontology/aging
group therapy
hyperactivity
impulse control/aggression
marital/couples therapy
minority/cross-cultural
neuropsychology/rehabilitation
obsessive–compulsive disorder
personality disorders
psychodynamic/psychoanalytic therapy
schizophrenia/psychoses
substance abuse
victim/battering abuse

George Washington University (Psy.D.)

Center for Professional Psychology
2300 M Street, NW, Suite 910
Washington, DC 20037
phone#: (202) 496-6260
e-mail: psyd@gwu.edu
Web address: http://www.gwu.edu/~psyd

1 2 **3** 4 5 6 7

Clinically oriented — Equal emphasis — Research oriented

What percentage of your faculty subscribes to or practices in each of the following orientations?

Psychodynamic/Psychoanalytic	90%
Applied behavioral analysis/Radical behavioral	0%
Family systems/Systems	0%
Existential/Phenomenological/Humanistic	0%
Cognitive/Cognitive-behavioral	10%

What percentage of students applying for internship last year was accepted into APA-accredited internships? 45%

What courses are required for incoming students to have completed prior to enrolling?
B.A./B.S.

Are there courses you recommend that are not mandatory?
Psychodynamic/psychoanalytic theory, personality development, psychodynamic/psychoanalytic therapy, cognitive development

GRE mean (M), cutoff (C), or preferred (P) score
Verbal 595 (M) Quantitative 558 (M) Analytical 637 (M)

GPA mean (M), cutoff (C), or preferred (P)
Overall GPA 3.5 (M), 3.0 (C)

Number of applications/admission offers/incoming students in 2001
260 applied/65 admission offers/45 incoming

% of students receiving:
Tuition waiver only: 33%
Assistantship/fellowship only: 0%
Both tuition waiver & assistantship/fellowship: 0%

Approximate percentage of incoming students who entered with a B.A./B.S. only: 63% **Master's:** 17%

Approximate percentage of students who are Women: 76% **Ethnic Minority:** 28%

Average years to complete the doctoral program (including internship): 4.3 years

Research areas	# Faculty	# Grants
adult psychopathology	4	0
child clinical	2	1
child development	2	2
community intervention	3	1
group process	3	0
infant and early childhood research	1	1
intellectual assessment	3	0
personality assessment	3	0

Clinical opportunities
assessment
clinical intervention with children
clinical outcome studies
developmental disorders
family therapy
learning disorders
psychotherapy
schizophrenia

University of Georgia

Department of Psychology
Athens, GA 30602
phone#: (706) 542-1787
e-mail: gradadm@arches.uga.edu
Web address: http://teach.psy.uga.edu/Dept/Programs/Clinical/clinical.htm

1	2	3	4	5	**6**	7
Clinically oriented		Equal emphasis			Research oriented	

What percentage of your faculty subscribes to or practices in each of the following orientations?

Psychodynamic/Psychoanalytic	0%
Applied behavioral analysis/Radical behavioral	0%
Family systems/Systems	0%
Existential/Phenomenological/Humanistic	0%
Cognitive/Cognitive-behavioral	100%

What percentage of students applying for internship last year was accepted into APA-accredited internships? 100%

What courses are required for incoming students to have completed prior to enrolling?
None

Are there courses you recommend that are not mandatory?
Abnormal psychology, statistics

GRE mean (M), cutoff (C), or preferred (P) score
Verbal 600 (P) Quantitative 600 (P)
Verbal + Quantitative 1200 (P)

GPA mean (M), cutoff (C), or preferred (P)
Overall GPA 3.5 (C)

Number of applications/admission offers/incoming students in 2001
139 applied/13 admission offers/8 incoming

% of students receiving:
Tuition waiver only: 0%
Assistantship/fellowship only: 0%
Both tuition waiver & assistantship/fellowship: 100%

Approximate percentage of incoming students who entered with a B.A./B.S. only: 87% **Master's:** 13%

Approximate percentage of students who are Women: 74% **Ethnic Minority:** 12%

Average years to complete the doctoral program (including internship): 5 years

Research areas	# Faculty	# Grants
AIDS	2	2
adolescence	1	1
adult psychopathology	1	0
affective disorder/depression	1	0
aggression	1	1
aging/gerontology	1	2
alcohol use and stress	1	1
anxiety disorders	1	0
applied behavioral analysis	1	0
battering	3	0
behavioral medicine	2	2
behavioral pharmacology	1	0
cardiovascular function and substance abuse	1	1
child clinical/child psychopathology	3	1
depression	2	0
developmental psychopathology	1	1
emotions	1	1
family/therapy/systems	2	3
interpersonal processes	1	2
marriage/couples	1	2
minority mental health	2	3
neuropsychology	2	1

pain management/control	1	0
parent–child interaction	3	4
pediatric psychology	1	1
prevention	4	3
psychology of women	1	0
schizophrenia/psychoses	1	1
stress and coping	2	1
violence/abuse/victim-offender	3	3
women's issues in therapy	1	0

Clinical opportunities
affective disorders/depression
anxiety disorders
assessment
behavior therapy
behavioral medicine
developmental disorders/autism
dissociative disorders
eating disorders
family therapy
hyperactivity
impulse control/aggression
marital/couples
minority/cross-cultural
neuropsychology
pediatric psychology
personality disorders
psychotherapy supervision
sex therapy
stress management
substance abuse
victim/battering/abuse

Georgia School of Professional Psychology (Psy.D.)

990 Hammond Drive, 11th Floor
Atlanta, GA 30328
phone#: (770) 671-1200 or (888) 671-4777
e-mail: jbinder@gspp.edu
Web address: http://www.aspp.edu/loc-ga.html

1	**2**	3	4	5	6	7
Clinically oriented			Equal emphasis			Research oriented

What percentage of your faculty subscribes to or practices in each of the following orientations?

Psychodynamic/Psychoanalytic	33%
Applied behavioral analysis/Radical behavioral	0%
Family systems/Systems	25%
Existential/Phenomenological/Humanistic	8%
Cognitive/Cognitive-behavioral	33%

What percentage of students applying for internship last year was accepted into APA-accredited internships? 97%

What courses are required for incoming students to have completed prior to enrolling?
General psychology, statistics, tests & measures, abnormal, and personality

Are there courses you recommend that are not mandatory?
No

GRE mean (M), cutoff (C), or preferred (P)
Verbal 500 (P) Quantitative 500 (P) Analytic 500 (P)
Advanced Psychology 500 (P)

GPA mean (M), cutoff (C), or preferred (P)
Overall GPA 3.25 (P) Psychology GPA 3.25 (P)
Junior/Senior GPA 3.25 (P)

Number of applications/admission offers/incoming students in 2001
268 applied/158 admission offers/82 incoming

% of students receiving:
Tuition waiver only: 0%
Assistantship/fellowship only: 15%
Both tuition waiver & assistantship/fellowship: 0%

Approximate percentage of incoming students who entered with a B.A./B.S. only: 95% **Master's:** 5%

Approximate percentage of students who are Women: 77% **Ethnic Minority:** 20%

Average years to complete the doctoral program (including internship): 5 years

Research areas	# Faculty	# Grants
geropsychology	2	0
multicultural issues	2	0
neuropsychology	2	1
pediatric psychology	2	0
psychological assessment	1	0
short-term, dynamic therapy	1	0
teenage sexuality	1	0

Clinical opportunities
adult psychotherap
child & adolescent psychotherapy
forensic psychology
neuropsychology
rehabilitation medicine
substance abuse rehabilitation

Georgia State University

Department of Psychology
University Plaza
Atlanta, GA 30303
phone#: (404) 651-2284
Web address: http://www.gsu.edu/~wwwpsy/

1	2	3	**4**	5	6	7
Clinically oriented			Equal emphasis			Research oriented

What percentage of your faculty subscribes to or practices in each of the following orientations?

Psychodynamic/Psychoanalytic	20%
Applied behavioral analysis/Radical behavioral	10%
Family systems/Systems	20%
Existential/Phenomenological/Humanistic	10%
Cognitive/Cognitive-behavioral	30%

What percentage of students applying for internship last year was accepted into APA-accredited internships? 100%

What courses are required for incoming students to have completed prior to enrolling?
Research methods, psychological statistics, and two additional Junior/Senior-level psychology courses

Are there courses you recommend that are not mandatory?
Abnormal psychology

GRE mean (M), cutoff (C), or preferred (P) score
Verbal + Quantitative 1200 (P)

GPA mean (M), cutoff (C), or preferred (P)
Overall GPA 3.5 (P)

Number of applications/admission offers/incoming students in 2001
247 applied/23 admission offers/11 incoming

% of students receiving:
Tuition waiver only: 0%
Assistantship/fellowship only: 0%
Both tuition waiver & assistantship/fellowship: 100%

Approximate percentage of incoming students who entered with a B.A./B.S. only: 90% **Master's:** 10%

Approximate percentage of students who are Women: 70% **Ethnic Minority:** 50%

Average years to complete the doctoral program (including internship): 7 years

Research areas	# Faculty	# Grants
acculturative stress	1	0
acquired brain injuries	2	0
adherence to therapy	1	0
attention deficit and hyperactivity disorder	1	1
cognitive therapy and depression	1	2
couples therapy	2	0
crime and delinquency	1	0
developmental disorders of learning and attention	1	0
eating disorders	1	3
early brain injury and visiospatial and attention skills	1	0
health influences on stress	1	0
HIV prevention	1	3
gender issues	1	1
imposter phenomenon	1	0
interpersonal skills training	1	0
multicultural issues	3	0
neuropsychology of aging, language, and memory	1	1
male parenting	1	1
parentification	1	0
reading/dyslexia	1	3
violence	2	1

Clinical opportunities
adjustment problems of adolescence and adulthood
anxiety disorders
behavior assessment
chronic health conditions
clinical-community psychology
clinical neuropsychology
depressive disorders
developmental disabilities
health psychology
HIV/AIDS prevention and therapy
individual, couples, family, and group therapy
neuropsychological assessment
personality assessment
personality disorders
psychopathology of childhood
psychosocial rehabilitation
psychotherapy supervision
violence prevention

University of Hartford (Psy.D.)

Graduate Institute of Professional Psychology
103 Woodland Street, 4th Floor
Hartford, CT 06105
phone#: (860) 520-1147/51
e-mail: DASINGER@UHAVAX.HARTFORD.EDU
Web address: http://uhavax.hartford.edu/~artsci/departments/html

1 **2** 3 4 5 6 7

Clinically oriented — Equal emphasis — Research oriented

What percentage of your faculty subscribes to or practices in each of the following orientations?

Psychodynamic/Psychoanalytic	32%
Applied behavioral analysis/Radical behavioral	16%
Family systems/Systems	16%
Existential/Phenomenological/Humanistic	16%
Cognitive/Cognitive-behavioral	16%

What percentage of students applying for internship last year was accepted into APA-accredited internships? 94%

What courses are required for incoming students to have completed prior to enrolling?
None

Are there courses you recommend that are not mandatory?
Psychology major, abnormal, social, research methods/experimental, personality theory, developmental, statistics

GRE mean (M), cutoff (C), or preferred (P) score
Verbal 550 (P) Quantitative 550 (P)
Advanced Psychology 550 (P)

GPA mean (M), cutoff (C), or preferred (P)
Overall GPA 3.0 (P) Psychology GPA 3.25 (P)

Number of applications/admission offers/incoming students in 2001
135 applied/62 admission offers/30 incoming

% of students receiving:
Tuition waiver only: 0%
Assistantship/fellowship only: 64%
Both tuition waiver & assistantship/fellowship: 0%

Approximate percentage of incoming students who entered with a B.A./B.S. only: 71% **Master's:** 29%

Approximate percentage of students who are Women: 74% **Ethnic Minority:** 21%

Average years to complete the doctoral program (including internship): 5.5 years

Research areas	# Faculty	# Grants
adolescent	1	0
aesthetics of therapy	1	1
community treatment	1	0
group therapy (therapist orientation)	1	0
mentoring women students	2	0
mother–daughter relationships	1	0
therapist–client match	1	0
therapy termination	1	0

Clinical opportunities
acute psychiatry/mental health
anxiety disorders
chronically mentally ill
mentally retarded adults
obsessive–compulsive disorder
70 other sites, including community mental health centers, hospital-based psychology departments, and residential schools

University of Hawaii at Manoa

Department of Psychology
2430 Campus Road
Honolulu, HI 96822
phone#: (808) 956-7644
e-mail: vkeough@hawaii.edu
Web address: http://www2.soc.hawaii.edu/psy/clinical.html

1	2	3	4	**5**	6	7
Clinically oriented			Equal emphasis			Research oriented

What percentage of your faculty subscribes to or practices in each of the following orientations?

Psychodynamic/Psychoanalytic	0%
Behavioral	36%
Family systems/Systems	0%
Existential/Phenomenological/Humanistic	0%
Cognitive/Cognitive-behavioral	45%

What percentage of students applying for internship last year was accepted into APA-accredited internships? 88%

What courses are required for incoming students to have completed prior to enrolling?
Psychology major or approximately 5 selected psychology courses

Are there courses you recommend that are not mandatory?
No

GRE mean (M), cutoff (C), or preferred (P) score
Verbal 600 (P) Quantitative 600 (P) Analytical 600 (P) Advanced Psychology 600 (P)

GPA mean (M), cutoff (C), or preferred (P)
Overall GPA 3.5 (P) Psychology GPA 3.75 (P) Junior/Senior GPA 3.5 (P)

Number of applications/admission offers/incoming students in 2001
100 applied/14 admission offers/9 incoming

% of students receiving:
Tuition waiver only: 0%
Assistantship/fellowship only: 0%
Both tuition waiver & assistantship/fellowship: 100%

Approximate percentage of incoming students who entered with a B.A./B.S. only: 80% **Master's:** 20%

Approximate percentage of students who are Women: 60% **Ethnic Minority:** 50%

Average years to complete the doctoral program (including internship): 7 years

Research areas	# Faculty	# Grants
anxiety	2	1
assessment	3	1
basic learning	1	0
behavioral medicine	1	1
childhood anxiety	1	1
clinical decision-making	1	0
cognitive assessment	2	0
cognitive-behavioral therapy	2	0
cross-cultural	2	1
data-based case management	1	1
depression	3	1
eating disorders	1	0
ethnic minority	2	1
health care compliance	1	0
intelligence	1	0
mental health service delivery	2	1
neurocognitive assessment	1	0
personaltiy	1	1
post traumatic stress disorder	2	1
psychopharmacology	1	0
schizophrenia	4	2

Clinical opportunities
aging
behavioral medicine
child behavior
cross-cultural
developmental disabilities
eating disorders
neuropsychology
rehabilitation psychology
school psychology
severely mentally ill

University of Houston

Department of Psychology
4800 Calhoun Road
Houston, TX 77204-5341
phone#: (713) 743-8600
e-mail: lprehm@mail.uh.edu
Web address: http://www.Psychology.uh.edu/GraduatePrograms/Clinical/

1	2	3	**4**	5	6	7
Clinically oriented			Equal emphasis			Research oriented

What percentage of your faculty subscribes to or practices in each of the following orientations?

Psychodynamic/Psychoanalytic	0%
Applied behavioral analysis/Radical behavioral	0%
Family systems/Systems	30%
Existential/Phenomenological/Humanistic	10%
Cognitive/Cognitive-behavioral	90%

What percentage of students applying for internship last year was accepted into APA-accredited internships? 100%

What courses are required for incoming students to have completed prior to enrolling?
None

Are there courses you recommend that are not mandatory?
Statistics, introductory psychology, history and systems, physiological psychology, abnormal psychology, experimental, social psychology, developmental psychology, methods

GRE mean (M), cutoff (C), or preferred (P) score
Verbal 615 (M) Quantitative 680 (M) Analytical 705 (M)

GPA mean (M), cutoff (C), or preferred (P)
Overall GPA 3.6 (M) Psychology GPA 3.7 (P)
Junior/Senior GPA 3.7 (P)

Number of applications/admission offers/incoming students in 2001
71 applied/17 admission offers/5 incoming

% of students receiving:
Tuition waiver only: 0%
Assistantship/fellowship only: 10%
Both tuition waiver & assistantship/fellowship: 90%

Approximate percentage of incoming students who entered with a B.A./B.S. only: 70% **Master's:** 30%

Approximate percentage of students who are Women: 75% **Ethnic Minority:** 8.5%

Research areas	# Faculty	# Grants
adult psychopathology	5	3
affective disorder/depression	1	1
anxiety disorder	1	0
child clinical	3	3
chronic mental illness	4	2
cross-cultural	1	1
family research/therapy	3	3
homelessness	1	1
marriage/couples	2	2
neuropsychology	3	2
parent–child interaction	4	3
schizophrenia/psychoses	4	2
sexual dysfunction	1	0
social skills	4	2

Clinical opportunities
adolescent delinquency
anxiety disorders
behavioral medicine
cognitive therapy
conduct disorder
couples therapy
depression
family therapy
interpersonal psychotherapy
minority/cross-cultural
neuropsychology
schizophrenia/psychoses
sex therapy
victim abuse

Howard University

Department of Psychology
520 Bryant Street, NW
Washington, DC 20059
phone#: (202) 806-6805
e-mail: DLewis.Jack@howard.edu
Web address: http://www.founders.howard.edu/gsas/progspec.html

1	2	3	**4**	5	6	7
Clinically oriented			Equal emphasis			Research oriented

What percentage of your faculty subscribes to or practices in each of the following orientations?

Psychodynamic/Psychoanalytic	30%
Applied behavioral analysis/Radical behavioral	0%
Family systems/Systems	20%
Existential/Phenomenological/Humanistic	20%
Cognitive/Cognitive-behavioral	30%

What percentage of students applying for internship last year was accepted into APA-accredited internships? 98%

What courses are required for incoming students to have completed prior to enrolling?
Psychology major, including the following: introductory psychology, statistics, abnormal psychology, experimental psychology

Are there courses you recommend that are not mandatory?
No

GRE mean (M), cutoff (C), or preferred (P) score
Required but not used for admission

GPA mean (M), cutoff (C), or preferred (P)
Overall GPA 3.5 (P) Psychology GPA 3.5 (P)
Junior/Senior GPA 3.5 (P)

Number of applications/admission offers/incoming students in 2001
74 applied/7 admission offers/6 incoming

% of students receiving:
Tuition waiver only: 0%
Assistantship/fellowship only: 0%
Both tuition waiver & assistantship/fellowship: 25%

Approximate percentage of incoming students who entered with a B.A./B.S. only: 50% **Master's:** 50%

Approximate percentage of students who are Women: 75% **Ethnic Minority:** 90%

Average years to complete the doctoral program (including internship): 6 years

Research areas	# Faculty	# Grants
adolescent development	3	2
behavioral medicine	3	3
clinical training	6	0
family therapy	2	0
minority mental health	4	4
neuropsychology	2	2
psychophysiology	1	0
suicide prevention	1	0

Clinical opportunities
anxiety disorders
behavioral medicine
child violence prevention
community psychology
crisis intervention
family
minority
neuropsychology
schizophrenia
victim/battering

University of Illinois at Chicago

Department of Psychology
1007 West Harrison
Chicago, IL 60680
phone#: (312) 996-1469
e-mail: robinm@uic.edu
Web address: http://www.uic.edu/depts/psych/clinical.html

1	2	3	4	5	**6**	7
Clinically oriented		Equal emphasis			Research oriented	

What percentage of your faculty subscribes to or practices in each of the following orientations?

Psychodynamic/Psychoanalytic	0%
Applied behavioral analysis/Radical behavioral	5%
Family systems/Systems	15%
Existential/Phenomenological/Humanistic	0%
Cognitive/Cognitive-behavioral	80%
Community psychology	40%

What percentage of students applying for internship last year was accepted into APA-accredited internships? 100%

What courses are required for incoming students to have completed prior to enrolling?
None

Are there courses you recommend that are not mandatory?
Statistics, science courses, independent research (for psychology majors), other research experience

GRE mean (M), cutoff (C), or preferred (P) score
Verbal 650 (P) Quantitative 650 (P)
Advanced Psychology 625 (P)

GPA mean (M), cutoff (C), or preferred (P)
Psychology GPA 4.6 on a 5-point scale (P)
Junior/Senior GPA 4.6 on a 5-point scale (P)

Number of applications/admission offers/incoming students in 2001
160 applied/10 admission offers/6 incoming

% of students receiving:
Tuition waiver only: 0%
Assistantship/fellowship only: 0%
Both tuition waiver & assistantship/fellowship: 100%

Approximate percentage of incoming students who entered with a B.A./B.S. only: 80% **Master's:** 20%

Approximate percentage of students who are Women: 75% **Ethnic Minority:** 20%

Average years to complete the doctoral program (including internship): 6.5 years

Research areas	# Faculty	# Grants
AIDS	2	1
adult psychopathology	2	2
aggression/conflict	1	1
community psychology	6	4
developmental disabilities	1	0
eating disorders	1	0
health psychology	3	3
schizophrenia	1	0

Clinical opportunities
adjustment reactions
anxiety and depression
eating disorders
emotional disorders among developmentally disabled
health-related behaviors
HIV prevention
marital therapy
preventive intervention with youth

University of Illinois at Urbana–Champaign

Department of Psychology
Psychology Building
603 East Daniel Street
Champaign, IL 61820
phone#: (217) 333-2169
e-mail: gradstdy@s.psych.uiuc.edu
Web address: http://www.psych.uiuc.edu/academics.graduate_handbook.html#clinical

1	2	3	4	5	**6**	7

Clinically oriented — Equal emphasis — Research oriented

What percentage of your faculty subscribes to or practices in each of the following orientations?

Psychodynamic/Psychoanalytic	18%
Applied behavioral analysis/Radical behavioral	18%
Family systems/Systems	27%
Existential/Phenomenological/Humanistic	27%
Cognitive/Cognitive-behavioral	63%

What percentage of students applying for internship last year was accepted into APA-accredited internships? 100%

What courses are required for incoming students to have completed prior to enrolling?
None

Are there courses you recommend that are not mandatory?
Psychology major, undergraduate statistics

GRE mean (M), cutoff (C), or preferred (P) score
Verbal 612 (M) Quantitative 699 (M) Subject 790 (M)

GPA mean (M), cutoff (C), or preferred (P)
Overall GPA 3.77 (M)

Number of applications/admission offers/incoming students in 2001
200 applied/16 admission offers/6 incoming

% of students receiving:
Tuition waiver only: 0%
Assistantship/fellowship only: 0%
Both tuition waiver & assistantship/fellowship: 100%

Approximate percentage of incoming students who entered with a B.A./B.S. only: 100% **Master's:** 0%

Approximate percentage of students who are Women: 83% **Ethnic Minority:** 50%

Average years to complete the doctoral program (including internship): 7.9 years

Research areas	**# Faculty**	**# Grants**
behavior genetics	1	0
children, law, and mental health policy	3	1
clinical neuropsychology	2	1
clinical psychophysiology	2	1
community psychology	4	1
emotion and psychopathology	5	3
marital/family/child	3	1
minority mental health	3	0
minority populations/mentoring	2	0
mutual-help organizations	1	0
psychotherapy/systems	1	0
schizophrenia	2	0
women's issues	3	2

Clinical opportunities
anxiety
child assessment
child protective services
community & economic development
community psychology
custody evaluations
feminist and women's issues
forensic evaluations
group therapy
individual adult psychotherapy
inpatient assessment/psychosis
juvenile justice services
marital and family/therapy
mutual help organizations
neighborhood organization
neuropsychological assessment
school consultation
school and educational settings and policy
voluntary organizations

Illinois Institute of Technology

Department of Psychology
IIT Center, LS252
Chicago, IL 60616
phone#: (312) 562-3503
e-mail: myoung@charlie.cns.iit.edu
Web address: http://www.iit.edu/colleges/psych/

1	2	3	**4**	5	6	7

Clinically oriented — Equal emphasis — Research oriented

What percentage of your faculty subscribes to or practices in each of the following orientations?

Psychodynamic/Psychoanalytic	0%
Applied behavioral analysis/Radical behavioral	15%
Family systems/Systems	25%
Existential/Phenomenological/Humanistic	0%
Cognitive/Cognitive-behavioral	65%

What percentage of students applying for internship last year was accepted into APA-accredited internships? 85%

What courses are required for incoming students to have completed prior to enrolling?
18 credits in psychology including experimental and statistics

Are there courses you recommend that are not mandatory?
No

GRE mean (M), cutoff (C), or preferred (P) score
Verbal 500 (P) Quantitative 500 (P)

GPA mean (M), cutoff (C), or preferred (P)
Overall GPA 3.3 (P) Psychology GPA 3.5 (P)

Number of applications/admission offers/incoming students in 2001
69 applied/27 admission offers/14 incoming

% of students receiving:
Tuition waiver only: 0%
Assistantship/fellowship only: 0%
Both tuition waiver & assistantship/fellowship: 20%

Approximate percentage of incoming students who entered with a B.A./B.S. only: 80% **Master's:** 20%

Approximate percentage of students who are Women: 60% **Ethnic Minority:** 20%

Average years to complete the doctoral program (including internship): 5.5 years

Research areas	**# Faculty**	**# Grants**
affective disorders	1	0
attention-deficit/hyperactivity disorder	1	0
behavioral medicine	1	0
child behavior	2	1
family	1	0
health	2	1
marital	1	1
pediatric	2	1
social support	1	0
sports psychology	1	0

Clinical opportunities
affective disorders
anxiety disorders
behavioral medicine
family
marital/couples
minority/cross-cultural
neuropsychology
pain
pediatric psychology
sports psychology
victim/battering/abuse

Illinois School of Professional Psychology–Chicago Campus (Psy.D.)

20 South Clark Street, Third Floor
Chicago, IL 60603
phone#: (312) 201-0200
Web address: http://www.aspp.edu/loc_chi.asp

1	**2**	3	4	5	6	7
Clinically oriented			Equal emphasis			Research oriented

What percentage of your faculty subscribes to or practices in each of the following orientations?

Psychodynamic/Psychoanalytic	35%
Applied behavioral analysis/Radical behavioral	0%
Family systems/Systems	20%
Existential/Phenomenological/Humanistic	15%
Cognitive/Cognitive-behavioral	20%

What percentage of students applying for internship last year was accepted into APA-accredited internships? 60%

What courses are required for incoming students to have completed prior to enrolling?
Introductory psychology, abnormal psychology, statistics, tests and measures, personality

Are there courses you recommend that are not mandatory?
No

GRE mean (M), cutoff (C), or preferred (P) score
Verbal 550 (P) Quantitative 550 (P) Analytical 550 (P)
Advanced Psychology 550 (P)

GPA mean (M), cutoff (C), or preferred (P)
Overall GPA 3.25(P) Psychology GPA 3.25(P)
Junior/Senior GPA 3.25(P)

Number of applications/admission offers/incoming students in 2001
280 applied/160 admission offers/65 incoming

% of students receiving:
Tuition waiver only: 0%
Assistantship/fellowship only: 0%
Both tuition waiver & assistantship/fellowship: 0%

Approximate percentage of incoming students who entered with a B.A./B.S. only: 55% **Master's:** 45%

Approximate percentage of students who are Women: 75% **Ethnic Minority:** 26%

Average years to complete the doctoral program (including internship): 5.7 years

Research areas	**# Faculty**	**# Grants**
behavioral medicine	2	0
eating disorders	1	0
graduate student development	2	1
mother–daughter cross-cultural patterns	1	0
sexual abuse	1	1
short-term psychotherapy	1	1
substance abuse	1	0
therapy of severe mental illness	1	1

Clinical opportunities
behavioral medicine
child and adolescent psychology
chronic mental illness
cognitive-behavioral psychotherapy
community psychology
couples
eating disorders
emergency crisis
ethnic-racial psychology
family psychology

forensic psychology
gay/lesbian/bisexual
gerontology
group therapy
health psychology
minority
neuropsychology
personality disorders
psychoanalytic psychotherapy
rehabilitation
religiously committed clients
school-based programs
sexual abuse
short-term psychotherapy
substance abuse
victim/abuse/battering

Illinois School of Professional Psychology–Chicago Northwest (Psy.D.)

Rolling Meadows, IL 60008
phone#: (847) 290-7400
e-mail: JWASNER@ASPP.EDU
Web address: http://www.aspp.edu/

1	2	**3**	4	5	6	7
Clinically oriented		Equal emphasis				Research oriented

What percentage of your faculty subscribes to or practices in each of the following orientations?

Psychodynamic/Psychoanalytic	17%
Applied behavioral analysis/Radical behavioral	8%
Family systems/Systems	17%
Existential/Phenomenological/Humanistic	25%
Cognitive/Cognitive-behavioral	17%

What percentage of students applying for internship last year was accepted into APA-accredited internships? 55%

What courses are required for incoming students to have completed prior to enrolling?
Introduction to psychology, abnormal psychology, tests and measurement, personality theory, introductory statistics

Are there courses you recommend that are not mandatory?
—

GRE mean (M), cutoff (C), or preferred (P) score
N/A

GPA mean (M), cutoff (C), or preferred (P)
Overall GPA 3.25 (C)

Number of applications/admission offers/incoming students in 2001
94 applied/40 admission offers/29 incoming

% of students receiving:
Tuition waiver only: 0%
Assistantship/fellowship only: 25%
Both tuition waiver & assistantship/fellowship: 0%

Approximate percentage of incoming students who entered with a B.A./B.S. only: 41% **Master's:** 59%

Approximate percentage of students who are Women: 77% **Ethnic Minority:** 14%

Average years to complete the doctoral program (including internship): 5.3 years

Research areas	# Faculty	# Grants
ADHD and child externalizing behaviors	1	0
cultural bias in psychological testing	1	0
effectiveness of process experiential therapy	1	0
family therapy effectiveness	1	0
men's perception of psychotherapy	1	0
multicultural training	2	0
psychotherapy process and outcome	2	1
stigma in mental illness identity	1	1
substance abuse program evaluation	1	1
treatment of domestic violence	2	0

Clinical opportunities
Numerous sites available; more than 200 practicum sites in greater Chicago area. Specialization sites include:
child and pediatric psychology
college counseling center
community mental health
family and marital counseling
forensics
inpatient psychiatric hospital, adult and adolescent rehabilitation
severely mentally ill
substance abuse

Immaculata College (Psy.D.)

Department of Graduate Psychology
Immaculata, PA 19345-0500
phone#: (610) 647-4400, ext. 3503
e-mail: jyalof@immaculata.edu

1	**2**	3	4	5	6	7
Clinically oriented		Equal emphasis				Research oriented

What percentage of your faculty subscribes to or practices in each of the following orientations?

Psychodynamic/Psychoanalytic	75%
Applied behavioral analysis/Radical behavioral	0%
Family systems/Systems	0%
Existential/Phenomenological/Humanistic	25%
Cognitive/Cognitive-behavioral	0%

What percentage of students applying for internship last year was accepted into APA-accredited internships? 50%

What courses are required for incoming students to have completed prior to enrolling?
Need M.A. in clinical or allied field, preferably

Are there courses you recommend that are not mandatory?
—

GRE mean (M), cutoff (C), or preferred (P) score
Verbal 600 (P) Quantitative 600 (P) Analytical 600 (P)

GPA mean (M), cutoff (C), or preferred (P)
Overall GPA 3.5 (P)

Number of applications/admission offers/incoming students in 2001
33 applied/19 admission offers/13 incoming

% of students receiving:
Tuition waiver only: 0%
Assistantship/fellowship only: 0%
Both tuition waiver & assistantship/fellowship: 0%

Approximate percentage of incoming students who entered with a B.A./B.S. only: 0% **Master's:** 100%

Approximate percentage of students who are Women: 73% **Ethnic Minority:** 8%

Average years to complete the doctoral program (including internship): 6 years

Research areas	# Faculty	# Grants
child-adolescent	2	0
development	2	0
existential-humanistic	1	0
gender	2	0
psychotherapy process	1	0
parenting	1	0
resilience and hopefulness	1	0
Rorschach	2	0
school psychology	2	0
sexism	1	0

Clinical opportunities
—

Indiana State University (Psy.D.)

Department of Psychology
Root Hall
Terre Haute, IN 47809
phone#: (812) 237-2445
e-mail: pyJudy@scifac.indstate.edu
Web address: http://web.indstate.edu/psych/clinical.html

1 2 3 **4** 5 6 7

Clinically oriented — Equal emphasis — Research oriented

What percentage of your faculty subscribes to or practices in each of the following orientations?

Psychodynamic/Psychoanalytic	10%
Applied behavioral analysis/Radical behavioral	10%
Family systems/Systems	10%
Existential/Phenomenological/Humanistic	0%
Cognitive/Cognitive-behavioral	70%

What percentage of students applying for internship last year was accepted into APA-accredited internships? 100%

What courses are required for incoming students to have completed prior to enrolling?
Introductory psychology, abnormal psychology, personality, experimental psychology, statistics, learning or cognition (24 credits in undergraduate psychology)

Are there courses you recommend that are not mandatory?
Physiological psychology

GRE mean (M), cutoff (C), or preferred (P) score
Verbal 500 (C), 575 (P) Quantitative 500 (C), 575 (P)
Analytical 500 (C), 575 (P)

GPA mean (M), cutoff (C), or preferred (P)
Overall Undergraduate GPA 3.0 (C)
Overall Graduate GPA 3.5 (C)

Number of applications/admission offers/incoming students in 2001
81 applied/14 admission offers/10 incoming

% of students receiving:
Tuition waiver only: 0%
Assistantship/fellowship only: 0%
Both tuition waiver & assistantship/fellowship: 100%

Approximate percentage of incoming students who entered with a B.A./B.S. only: 85% **Master's:** 15%

Approximate percentage of students who are Women: 50% **Ethnic Minority:** 10%

Average years to complete the doctoral program (including internship): 5.5 years

Research areas	# Faculty	# Grants
adult psychopathology	1	0
affective disorders/depression	2	0
anxiety disorders	1	0
assessment	1	0
behavioral medicine	2	1
child clinical psychopathology	2	0
clinical judgment	1	0
eating disorders	2	0
friendship/relationships/intimacy	1	0
gender roles	3	0
organizational/industrial	1	1
personality disorders	1	0
professional training	1	0
sexuality/deviation/dysfunction	1	0
stress and coping	2	0
substance abuse	1	0
women's studies	2	0

Clinical opportunities
behavioral medicine
group therapy
rural psychology
victim/battering/abuse

Indiana University

Department of Psychology
Bloomington, IN 47405
phone#: (812) 855-2311
e-mail: KJukes@indiana.edu
Web address: http://www.indiana.edu/~clinpsy

1	2	3	4	5	6	**7**
Clinically oriented			Equal emphasis			Research oriented

What percentage of your faculty subscribes to or practices in each of the following orientations?

Psychodynamic/Psychoanalytic	0%
Applied behavioral analysis/Radical behavioral	0%
Family systems/Systems	100%
Existential/Phenomenological/Humanistic	0%
Cognitive/Cognitive-behavioral	100%

What percentage of students applying for internship last year was accepted into APA-accredited internships? 100%

What courses are required for incoming students to have completed prior to enrolling?
Psychology major

Are there courses you recommend that are not mandatory?
Basic sciences, math

GRE mean (M), cutoff (C), or preferred (P) score
Verbal 652 (M) Quantitative 690 (M) Analytical 740 (M)

GPA mean (M), cutoff (C), or preferred (P)
Overall GPA 3.86 (M)

Number of applications/admission offers/incoming students in 2001
66 applied/6 admission offers/4 incoming

% of students receiving:
Tuition waiver only: 0%
Assistantship/fellowship only: 0%
Both tuition waiver & assistantship/fellowship: 100%

Approximate percentage of incoming students who entered with a B.A./B.S. only: 90% **Master's:** 10%

Approximate percentage of students who are Women: 76% **Ethnic Minority:** 21%

Average years to complete the doctoral program (including internship): 6.2 years

Research areas	**# Faculty**	**# Grants**
alcoholism/psychophysiology	1	1
behavioral genetics	4	2
child health interventions	1	1
childhood/temperament/family	3	3
health psychology	5	4
marital violence	1	1
mathematical models of causality	2	1
obsessive–compulsive disorder	1	0
prevention	1	0
schizophrenia	2	2
social gerontology	1	1
social information processing and social interaction	3	1

Clinical opportunities
anxiety disorders
assessment of health-related family adjustment problems
child and family therapy
community interventions
depression
marital violence/marital therapy
neuropsychology
obsessive–compulsive disorder
schizophrenia
school/Head Start consultation
sexual dysfunction
smoking cessation

Indiana University of Pennsylvania (Psy.D.)

Department of Psychology
201 Uhler Hall
Indiana, PA 15705
phone#: (412) 357-4519
e-mail: durobert@iup.edu
Web address: http://shade.grove.iup.edu:80/gradua/admit/catalog/natsciandmath.htmlx

1	2	**3**	4	5	6	7
Clinically oriented			Equal emphasis			Research oriented

What percentage of your faculty subscribes to or practices in each of the following orientations?

Psychodynamic/Psychoanalytic	5%
Applied behavioral analysis/Radical behavioral	25%
Family systems/Systems	30%
Existential/Phenomenological/Humanistic	5%
Cognitive/Cognitive-behavioral	40%

What percentage of students applying for internship last year was accepted into APA-accredited internships? 98%

What courses are required for incoming students to have completed prior to enrolling?
Introductory psychology, personality, statistics or methods, abnormal psychology

Are there courses you recommend that are not mandatory?
6 credits in other areas of psychology

GRE mean (M), cutoff (C), or preferred (P) score
Verbal 500 (P) Quantitative 500 (P) Analytical 500 (P)
Advanced Psychology 500 (P)

GPA mean (M), cutoff (C), or preferred (P)
Overall GPA 3.0 (P) Psychology GPA 3.0 (P)
Junior/Senior GPA 3.0 (P)

Number of applications/admission offers/incoming students in 2001
97 applied/22 admission offers/12 incoming

% of students receiving:
Tuition waiver only: 0%
Assistantship/fellowship only: 0%
Both tuition waiver & assistantship/fellowship: 100%

Approximate percentage of incoming students who entered with a B.A./B.S. only: 67% **Master's:** 33%

Approximate percentage of students who are Women: 60% **Ethnic Minority:** 16%

Average years to complete the doctoral program (including internship): 5 years

Research areas	# Faculty	# Grants
abortion	1	0
aging	1	0
behavioral medicine	1	0
clinical judgment	1	0
cross-cultural	2	0
death and dying	1	0
ethical issues	1	0
family therapy	3	0
gender roles	1	0
minority mental health	1	0
parent–child	1	0
prevention	1	0
professional issues	1	0
psychopathology	1	0
psychopharmacology	1	0
women's studies	3	0

Clinical opportunities
assessment
behavioral medicine
family therapy
stress and habit disorders

Indiana University–Purdue University Indianapolis

Clinical Rehabilitation Ph.D. Program
402 N. Blackford Street, LD124
Indianapolis, IN 46202-3275
phone#: (317) 274-6945
e-mail: gradpsy@IUPUI.edu
Web address: http://www.psynt.iupui.edu

1	2	3	4	5	**6**	7
Clinically oriented			Equal emphasis			Research oriented

What percentage of your faculty subscribes to or practices in each of the following orientations?

Psychodynamic/Psychoanalytic	0%
Applied behavioral analysis/Radical behavioral	0%
Family systems/Systems	5%
Existential/Phenomenological/Humanistic	5%
Cognitive/Cognitive-behavioral	90%

What percentage of students applying for internship last year was accepted into APA-accredited internships? 100%

What courses are required for incoming students to have completed prior to enrolling?
Tests & measurements, statistics, physiology, abnormal psychology

Are there courses you recommend that are not mandatory?
No

GRE mean (M), cutoff (C), or preferred (P) score
Verbal 600 (C) Quantitative 600 (C)
Advanced Psychology 600 (C)

GPA mean (M), cutoff (C), or preferred (P)
Overall GPA 3.2 (C)

Number of applications/admission offers/incoming students in 2001
37 applied/6 admission offers/3 incoming

% of students receiving:
Tuition waiver only: 0%
Assistantship/fellowship only: 0%
Both tuition waiver & assistantship/fellowship: 100%

Approximate percentage of incoming students who entered with a B.A./B.S. only: 90% **Master's:** 10%

Approximate percentage of students who are Women: 80% **Ethnic Minority:** 10%

Average years to complete the doctoral program (including internship): 7 years

Research areas	# Faculty	# Grants
health psychology	2	1
neuropsychology	2	2–3
psychobiology	3	5–6
severe mental illness	2	3–4

Clinical opportunities
adaptive educational services (students with disabilities)
adult behavioral medicine (community cancer care)
crisis intervention unit (Wishard)
hospice
neuropsychological assessment
neurorehabilitation intervention
pediatric behavioral medicine
severe mental illness
women's prison—female offenders with psychiatric and medical problems

University of Indianapolis (Psy.D.)

School of Psychological Sciences
1400 E. Hanna Avenue, Good Hall Room 109
Indianapolis, IN 46227-3697
phone#: (317) 788-3353
e-mail: sjwalker@uindy.edu or rholigrocki@uindy.edu
Web address: http://psych.uindy.edu/

1	2	**3**	4	5	6	7
Clinically oriented			Equal emphasis			Research oriented

What percentage of your faculty subscribes to or practices in each of the following orientations?

Psychodynamic/Psychoanalytic	25%
Applied behavioral analysis/Radical behavioral	12.5%
Family systems/Systems	12.5%
Existential/Phenomenological/Humanistic	12.5%
Cognitive/Cognitive-behavioral	37.5%

What percentage of students applying for internship last year was accepted into APA-accredited internships? 71%

What courses are required for incoming students to have completed prior to enrolling?
18 credit hours of psychology

Are there courses you recommend that are not mandatory?
Abnormal psychology, child/development, statistics, personality

GRE mean (M), cutoff (C), or preferred (P) score
Verbal 500 (P) Quantitative 500 (P) Analytical 500 (P)
Advanced Psychology 550 (P)

GPA mean (M), cutoff (C), or preferred (P)
Overall GPA 3.0 (C), 3.44 (M)

Number of applications/admission offers/incoming students in 2001
51 applied/32 admission offers/11 incoming

% of students receiving:
Tuition waiver only: 0%
Assistantship/fellowship only: 16%
Both tuition waiver & assistantship/fellowship: 0%

Approximate percentage of incoming students who entered with a B.A./B.S. only: 64% **Master's:** 36%

Approximate percentage of students who are Women: 78% **Ethnic Minority:** 2%

Average years to complete the doctoral program (including internship): 5 years

Research areas	**# Faculty**	**# Grants**
adult sibling relationships	1	0
child/family treatment outcome	1	0
intimate relationships	1	0
memory	1	0
multicultural mental health	1	1
parent-child relationships	2	1
posttraumatic stress disorders	1	0

Clinical opportunities
behavioral medicine
child/adolescent
forensics
neuropsychological assessment
pain management

University of Iowa

Department of Psychology
E-11 Seashore Hall
Iowa City, IA 52242-1407
phone#: (319) 335-2406
e-mail: la-clark@uiowa.edu
Web address: http://www.psychology.uiowa.edu/Training_Areas/clinical.html

1	2	3	4	5	**6**	7
Clinically oriented			Equal emphasis			Research oriented

What percentage of your faculty subscribes to or practices in each of the following orientations?

Psychodynamic/Psychoanalytic	0%
Applied behavioral analysis/Radical behavioral	0%
Family systems/Systems	0%
Existential/Phenomenological/Humanistic	0%
Cognitive/Cognitive-behavioral	100%

What percentage of students applying for internship last year was accepted into APA-accredited internships? 100%

What courses are required for incoming students to have completed prior to enrolling?
Statistics, abnormal psychology

Are there courses you recommend that are not mandatory?
Undergraduate psychology major, laboratory research, strong science background

GRE mean (M), cutoff (C), or preferred (P) score
Verbal 600 (P) Quantitative 600 (P) Analytical 600 (P)

GPA mean (M), cutoff (C), or preferred (P)
Overall GPA 3.5 (P) Psychology GPA 3.5 (P)
Junior/Senior GPA 3.5 (P)

Number of applications/admission offers/incoming students in 2001
140 applied/11 admission offers/5 incoming

% of students receiving:
Tuition waiver only: 0%
Assistantship/fellowship only: 80%
Both tuition waiver & assistantship/fellowship: 20%

Approximate percentage of incoming students who entered with a B.A./B.S. only: 80% **Master's:** 20%

Approximate percentage of students who are Women: 80% **Ethnic Minority:** 15%

Average years to complete the doctoral program (including internship): 5.9 years

Research areas	**# Faculty**	**# Grants**
behavioral medicine	3	2
child abuse	1	1
child psychopathology	1	1
deafness	1	0
depression	1	2
personality disorders	2	1
psychophysiology	1	1

Clinical opportunities
abuse
adult psychiatry
behavioral medicine
child/pediatric
deafness
neuropsychology

University of Kansas

Department of Psychology
426 Fraser Hall
Lawrence, KS 66045-2160
phone#: (785) 864-4195
e-mail: psycgrad@ukans.edu
Web address: http://www.ukans.edu/~psycgrad/index.html#Clinical

1	2	3	**4**	5	6	7

Clinically oriented — Equal emphasis — Research oriented

What percentage of your faculty subscribes to or practices in each of the following orientations?

Psychodynamic/Psychoanalytic	5%
Applied behavioral analysis/Radical behavioral	0%
Family systems/Systems	5%
Existential/Phenomenological/Humanistic	25%
Cognitive/Cognitive-behavioral	65%

What percentage of students applying for internship last year was accepted into APA-accredited internships? 100%

What courses are required for incoming students to have completed prior to enrolling?
18 hours of basic psychology

Are there courses you recommend that are not mandatory?
Basic psychology, including statistics

GRE mean (M), cutoff (C), or preferred (P) score
Not used

GPA mean (M), cutoff (C), or preferred (P)
Overall GPA 3.0 (C) Psychology GPA 3.5 (P)

Number of applications/admission offers/incoming students in 2001
134 applied/16 admission offers/10 incoming

% of students receiving:
Tuition waiver only: 0%
Assistantship/fellowship only: 70%
Both tuition waiver & assistantship/fellowship: 30%

Approximate percentage of incoming students who entered with a B.A./B.S. only: 80% **Master's:** 20%

Approximate percentage of students who are Women: 70% **Ethnic Minority:** 20%

Average years to complete the doctoral program (including internship): 6 years

Research areas	# Faculty	# Grants
adult psychopathology	2	0
affective disorders/depression	2	0
behavioral medicine/health	4	2
cancer	1	1
gender roles/sex differences	1	0
motivation	1	1
problem solving	2	0
rehabilitation	1	0
stress and coping	5	1
violence/abuse	1	0
women's studies	2	0

Clinical opportunities
anxiety disorders
behavioral medicine

Kent State University

Department of Psychology
Kent, OH 44242
phone#: (330) 672-3789
e-mail: jcrowthe@kent.edu
Web address: http://www.personal.kent.edu/~ksupsych/psych.htm

1	2	3	4	**5**	6	7

Clinically oriented — Equal emphasis — Research oriented

What percentage of your faculty subscribes to or practices in each of the following orientations?

Psychodynamic/Psychoanalytic	25%
Applied behavioral analysis/Radical behavioral	15%
Family systems/Systems	8%
Existential/Phenomenological/Humanistic	0%
Cognitive/Cognitive-behavioral	50%

What percentage of students applying for internship last year was accepted into APA-accredited internships? 90%

What courses are required for incoming students to have completed prior to enrolling?
None

Are there courses you recommend that are not mandatory?
Prefer 15–20 hours in psychology, including 1–2 statistics courses and at least 1 psychology class which has a lab associated with it

GRE mean (M), cutoff (C), or preferred (P) score
Verbal + Quantitative 1200 (P)

GPA mean (M), cutoff (C), or preferred (P)
Overall GPA 3.3 (C)

Number of applications/admission offers/incoming students in 2001
124 applied/21 admission offers/11 incoming

% of students receiving:
Tuition waiver only: 0%
Assistantship/fellowship only: 0%
Both tuition waiver & assistantship/fellowship: 100%

Approximate percentage of incoming students who entered with a B.A./B.S. only: 80% **Master's:** 20%

Approximate percentage of students who are Women: 70% **Ethnic Minority:** 19%

Average years to complete the doctoral program (including internship): 6 years

Research areas	# Faculty	# Grants
AIDS	2	1
anxiety in African-Americans	3	1
depression	1	0
eating disorders	1	0
family research	2	0
gerontology	1	0
MMPI	2	2
schizophrenia	1	1
stress and coping	4	2

Clinical opportunities
child/family therapy
eating disorders
forensic assessments
health psychology
marital therapy
neuropsychology
objective personality assessment
schizophrenia

University of Kentucky

Department of Psychology
Kastle Hall
Lexington, KY 40506-0044
phone#: (606) 257-6841
e-mail: rbaer@pop.uky.edu
Web address: http://www.uky.edu/AS/Psychology/clinical.html

1	2	3	4	**5**	6	7

Clinically oriented — Equal emphasis — Research oriented

What percentage of your faculty subscribes to or practices in each of the following orientations?

Psychodynamic/Psychoanalytic	20%
Applied behavioral analysis/Radical behavioral	20%
Family systems/Systems	20%
Existential/Phenomenological/Humanistic	0%
Cognitive/Cognitive-behavioral	100%

What percentage of students applying for internship last year was accepted into APA-accredited internships? 100%

What courses are required for incoming students to have completed prior to enrolling?
Experimental methodology, statistics

Are there courses you recommend that are not mandatory?
Abnormal psychology, tests & measures, personality

GRE mean (M), cutoff (C), or preferred (P) score
Verbal 650 (P) Quantitative 650 (P)

GPA mean (M), cutoff (C), or preferred (P)
Overall GPA 3.5 (P)

Number of applications/admission offers/incoming students in 2001
193 applied/12 admission offers/9 incoming

% of students receiving:
Tuition waiver only: 0%
Assistantship/fellowship only: 0%
Both tuition waiver & assistantship/fellowship: 100%
First 4 years in program in-state tuition is not always waived.

Approximate percentage of incoming students who entered with a B.A./B.S. only: 85% **Master's:** 15%

Approximate percentage of students who are Women: 60% **Ethnic Minority:** 25%

Average years to complete the doctoral program (including internship): 6.3 years

Research areas	# Faculty	# Grants
adolescent development	1	0
adult psychopathology	4	2
assessment/diagnosis/classification	4	0
behavioral medicine	2	0
child clinical	3	1
developmental psychopathology	1	0
eating disorders	1	0
forensic	1	0
neuropsychology	2	0
pain	1	1
personality assessment	3	0
personality disorders	2	0
psychoneuroimmunology	1	0
psychophysiology	2	0
substance abuse	4	3
violence/agression	1	1

Clinical opportunities
assessment
behavioral medicine
child
chronic mental illness
cognitive-behavioral therapies
community mental health
neuropsychology
orofacial pain

Loma Linda University (Ph.D.)

Department of Psychology
Loma Linda, CA 92350
phone#: (909) 558-8577 (Central Office)
e-mail: abradshaw@psych.llu.edu
Web address: http://www.llu.edu/llu/grad/programs

1	2	3	4	**5**	6	7

Clinically oriented — Equal emphasis — Research oriented

What percentage of your faculty subscribes to or practices in each of the following orientations?

Psychodynamic/Psychoanalytic	25%
Applied behavioral analysis/Radical behavioral	0%
Family systems/Systems	8%
Existential/Phenomenological/Humanistic	16%
Cognitive/Cognitive-behavioral	50%

What percentage of students applying for internship last year was accepted into APA-accredited internships? 60%

What courses are required for incoming students to have completed prior to enrolling?
History and systems, learning, personality theory, statistics, social psychology, developmental psychology

Are there courses you recommend that are not mandatory?
Computer literacy, math, research methods, anthropology, biology

GRE mean (M), cutoff (C), or preferred (P) score
Verbal 500 (C) Quantitative 500 (C) Analytical 500 (C)
Advanced Psychology 600+ (P)

GPA mean (M), cutoff (C), or preferred (P)
Overall GPA 3.5 (C)

Number of applications/admission offers/incoming students in 2001
26 applied/15 admission offers/11 incoming

% of students receiving:
Tuition waiver only: 17%
Assistantship/fellowship only: 0%
Both tuition waiver & assistantship/fellowship: 0%

Approximate percentage of incoming students who entered with a B.A./B.S. only: 82% **Master's:** 18%

Approximate percentage of students who are Women: 82% **Ethnic Minority:** 40%

Average years to complete the doctoral program (including internship): 6 years

Research areas	# Faculty	# Grants
adult health psychology	4	3
anxiety disorders	1	0
childhood sexual abuse	2	0
conflict resolution	1	0
ethical decision making	1	0
neurodegenerative diseases	1	0
pediatric health psychology	1	3
psychobiology	2	0
psychology and religion	2	0
psychotherapy process outcomes	1	0
PTSD	2	0
statistical methods	1	0

Clinical opportunities
adult behavioral medicine
community outpatient mental health
pediatric behavioral medicine

Loma Linda University (Psy.D.)

Department of Psychology
Loma Linda, CA 92350
phone#: (909) 558-8577 (central office)
e-mail: abradshaw@psych.llu.edu
Web address: http://www.llu.edu/llu/grad/programs/

1	2	**3**	4	5	6	7
Clinically oriented			Equal emphasis			Research oriented

What percentage of your faculty subscribes to or practices in each of the following orientations?

Psychodynamic/Psychoanalytic	25%
Applied behavioral analysis/Radical behavioral	0%
Family systems/Systems	8%
Existential/Phenomenological/Humanistic	16%
Cognitive/Cognitive-behavioral	50%

What percentage of students applying for internship last year was accepted into APA-accredited internships? 40%

What courses are required for incoming students to have completed prior to enrolling?
History and systems, learning, personality theory, statistics, social psychology, developmental psychology

Are there courses you recommend that are not mandatory?
Computer literacy, math, anthropology, biology

GRE mean (M), cutoff (C), or preferred (P) score
Verbal 500 (C) Quantitative 500 (C) Analytical 500 (C)
Advanced Psychology 600+ (P)

GPA mean (M), cutoff (C), or preferred (P)
Overall GPA 3.5 (M)

Number of applications/admission offers/incoming students in 2001
24 applied/13 admission offers/9 incoming

% of students receiving:
Tuition waiver only: 11%
Assistantship/fellowship only: 0%
Both tuition waiver & assistantship/fellowship: 0%

Approximate percentage of incoming students who entered with a B.A./B.S. only: 56% **Master's:** 44%

Approximate percentage of students who are Women: 61% **Ethnic Minority:** 37%

Average years to complete the doctoral program (including internship): 5 years

Research areas	# Faculty	# Grants
anxiety disorders	1	0
childhood sexual abuse	2	0
conflict resolution	1	0
ethical decision making	1	0
health psychology	4	3
neurodegenerative diseases	1	0
pediatric health psychology	1	3
posttraumatic stress disorder	2	0
psychobiology	2	0
psychology and religion	2	0

psychotherapy process outcome	1	0
statistics methods	1	0

Clinical opportunities
adult behavioral medicine
community outpatient
pediatric behavioral medicine

Long Island University

Department of Psychology
University Plaza
Brooklyn, NY 11201
phone#: (718) 488-1164
e-mail: nickp@viconet.com
Web address: http://www.liu.edu/cwis/bklyn/depts/psych/

1 2 3 **4** 5 6 7

Clinically oriented — Equal emphasis — Research oriented

What percentage of your faculty subscribes to or practices in each of the following orientations?

Psychodynamic/Psychoanalytic	60%
Applied behavioral analysis/Radical behavioral	5%
Family systems/Systems	20%
Existential/Phenomenological/Humanistic	20%
Cognitive/Cognitive-behavioral	30%

What percentage of students applying for internship last year was accepted into APA-accredited internships? 90%

What courses are required for incoming students to have completed prior to enrolling?
Experimental, statistics, abnormal, developmental

Are there courses you recommend that are not mandatory?
Social, history and systems, personality

GRE mean (M), cutoff (C), or preferred (P) score
Verbal 650 (M) Quantitative 630 (M) Analytical 630 (M)
Advanced Psychology 630 (M)

GPA mean (M), cutoff (C), or preferred (P)
Overall GPA 3.50 (M) Psychology GPA 3.60 (M)

Number of applications/admission offers/incoming students in 2001
175 applied/30 admission offers/15 incoming

% of students receiving:
Tuition waiver only: 4%
Both tuition waiver & assistantship/fellowship: 20%
Half tuition waiver & assistantship: 80%

Approximate percentage of incoming students who entered with a B.A./B.S. only: 50% **Master's:** 50%

Approximate percentage of students who are Women: 70% **Ethnic Minority:** 18%

Average years to complete the doctoral program (including internship): 6.5 years

Research areas	# Faculty	# Grants
aging and mental health	1	1
cultural/cross-cultural	1	0
developmental issues	1	1
developmental psychopathology	1	0
forensic issues	1	0
health psychology	1	1
neuropsychology	1	0
projective techniques	1	0
psychotherapy process	1	1
sociodevelopment	1	1
socioemotional development	1	0
trauma	1	1

Clinical opportunities
behavioral clinics
child clinics
college counseling
community MH
family therapy
homeless shelters
inpatient/outpatient
neuropsychology
substance abuse

Long Island University–C.W. Post Campus (Psy.D.)

Department of Psychology
College of Liberal Arts and Sciences
Brookville, NY 11548
phone#: (516) 299-2090
e-mail: doctoral.psychology@cwpost.liu.edu
Web address: http://www.cwpost.liunet.edu/cwis/cwp/clas/psyd

1 **2** 3 4 5 6 7

Clinically oriented — Equal emphasis — Research oriented

What percentage of your faculty subscribes to or practices in each of the following orientations?

Psychodynamic/Psychoanalytic	50%
Applied behavioral analysis/Radical behavioral	12%
Family systems/Systems	0%
Existential/Phenomenological/Humanistic	0%
Cognitive/Cognitive-behavioral	38%

What percentage of students applying for internship last year was accepted into APA-accredited internships? 100%

What courses are required for incoming students to have completed prior to enrolling?
18 credits of undergraduate psychology

Are there courses you recommend that are not mandatory?
No

GRE mean (M), cutoff (C), or preferred (P) score
Verbal 600 (P) Quantitative 600 (P) Analytical 600 (P)
Advanced psychology 600 (P)

GPA mean (M), cutoff (C), or preferred (P)
Overall GPA 3.25 (C)

Number of applications/admission offers/incoming students in 2001
177 applied/49 admission offers/18 incoming

% of students receiving:
Tuition waiver only: 25%
Assistantship/fellowship only: 40%
Both tuition waiver & assistantship/fellowship: 0%

Approximate percentage of incoming students who entered with a B.A./B.S. only: 75% **Master's:** 25%

Approximate percentage of students who are Women: 67% **Ethnic Minority:** 20%

Average years to complete the doctoral program (including internship): 5.5 years

Research areas	# Faculty	# Grants
anger management	1	0
attachment	1	1
developmental disabilities	1	0
marital violence	2	0
parent training	1	0
professional discipline	1	0
schizophrenia	1	0

Clinical opportunities
—

Louisiana State University

Department of Psychology
Audobon Hall
Baton Rouge, LA 70803
phone#: (225) 578-8745
fax#: (225) 578-4125

1 2 3 4 5 **6** 7

Clinically oriented — Equal emphasis — Research oriented

What percentage of your faculty subscribes to or practices in each of the following orientations?

Psychodynamic/Psychoanalytic	0%
Applied behavioral analysis/Radical behavioral	100%
Family systems/Systems	0%
Existential/Phenomenological/Humanistic	0%
Cognitive/Cognitive-behavioral	50%

What percentage of students applying for internship last year was accepted into APA-accredited internships? 100%

What courses are required for incoming students to have completed prior to enrolling?
None

Are there courses you recommend that are not mandatory?
Intro psych, stats, experimental, physiological psych, psychology of learning

GRE mean (M), cutoff (C), or preferred (P) score
Verbal 550 (P) Quantitative 550 (P)

GPA mean (M), cutoff (C), or preferred (P)
Overall GPA 3.2 (P) Psychology GPA 3.5 (P)

Number of applications/admission offers/incoming students in 2001
350 applied/12 admission offers/12 incoming

% of students receiving:
Tuition waiver only: 0%
Assistantship/fellowship only: 0%
Both tuition waiver & assistantship/fellowship: 100%

Approximate percentage of incoming students who entered with a B.A./B.S. only: 50% **Master's:** 50%

Approximate percentage of students who are Women: 75% **Ethnic Minority:** 10%

Average years to complete the doctoral program (including internship): 5 years

Research areas	# Faculty	# Grants
anxiety disorders	1	1
autism	1	1
depression	1	1
eating disorders	1	1
mental retardation	1	1
neuropsychology	1	0
parent skills training	1	0
psychophysiology	1	0
social skills	2	1
stress and coping	1	0

Clinical opportunities
anxiety disorders
autism
behavioral medicine
deafness disorder
eating disorders
family
mental retardation
neuropsychology
obsessive-compulsive
schizophrenia
school/educational

University of Louisville

Department of Psychology
Louisville, KY 40292
phone#: (502) 852-6775
e-mail: CAMASK@ULKYVM.louisville.edu
Web address: http://www.louisville.edu/a-s/psychology/clinical.html

1 2 3 4 **5** 6 7

Clinically oriented — Equal emphasis — Research oriented

What percentage of your faculty subscribes to or practices in each of the following orientations?

Psychodynamic/Psychoanalytic	0%
Interpersonal-ego relations	17%
Applied behavioral analysis/Radical behavioral	0%
Family systems/Systems	0%
Existential/Phenomenological/Humanistic	0%
Cognitive/Cognitive-behavioral	67%

What percentage of students applying for internship last year was accepted into APA-accredited internships? 100%

What courses are required for incoming students to have completed prior to enrolling?
None

Are there courses you recommend that are not mandatory?
History, abnormal, personality, social, statistics, physiological, learning

GRE mean (M), cutoff (C), or preferred (P) score
Verbal 655 (M) Quantitative 641 (M)

GPA mean (M), cutoff (C), or preferred (P)
Junior/Senior GPA 3.6 (M)

Number of applications/admission offers/incoming students in 2001
65 applied/27 admission offers/8 incoming

% of students receiving:
Tuition waiver only: 0%
Assistantship/fellowship only: 0%
Both tuition waiver & assistantship/fellowship: 100%

Approximate percentage of incoming students who entered with a B.A./B.S. only: 80% **Master's:** 20%

Approximate percentage of students who are Women: 62% **Ethnic Minority:** 12%

Average years to complete the doctoral program (including internship): 6 years

Research areas	**# Faculty**	**# Grants**
anxiety disorders	3	1
behavioral medicine	2	1
chronic mental illness	1	0
forensic psychology	1	0
gerontology/aging	2	0
stress and coping	2	0
substance abuse	1	0

Clinical opportunities
affective disorders
anxiety disorders
child clinical psychology
developmental disabilities
forensic psychology
gerontology/aging
health psychology
interpersonal psychotherapy

Loyola College in Maryland (Psy.D.)

Department of Psychology
Baltimore, MD 20210-2699
phone#: (410) 617-2696
e-mail: jlating@loyola.edu
Web address: http://www.loyola.edu/

1	**2**	3	4	5	6	7
Clinically oriented			Equal emphasis			Research oriented

What percentage of your faculty subscribes to or practices in each of the following orientations?

Psychodynamic/Psychoanalytic	15%
Applied behavioral analysis/Radical behavioral	10%
Family systems/Systems	10%
Existential/Phenomenological/Humanistic	0%
Cognitive/Cognitive-behavioral	65%

What percentage of students applying for internship last year was accepted into APA-accredited internships? 82%

What courses are required for incoming students to have completed prior to enrolling?
Introductory psychology, social psychology, statistics or research methods, abnormal psychology, personality theory, tests and measurements, learning theory or cognitive psychology

Are there courses you recommend that are not mandatory?
No

GRE mean (M), cutoff (C), or preferred (P) score
Verbal 518 (M) Quantitative 551 (M) Analytical 573 (M)

GPA mean (M), cutoff (C), or preferred (P)
Overall GPA 3.37 (M)

Number of applications/admission offers/incoming students in 2001
121 applied/27 admission offers/20 incoming

% of students receiving:
Tuition waiver only: 0%
Assistantship/fellowship only: 40%
Both tuition waiver & assistantship/fellowship: 0%

Approximate percentage of incoming students who entered with a B.A./B.S. only: 60% **Master's:** 40%

Approximate percentage of students who are Women: 82% **Ethnic Minority:** 16%

Average years to complete the doctoral program (including internship): 5.5 years

Research areas	**# Faculty**	**# Grants**
child psychopathology	2	0
domestic violence	1	0
ethics and legal issues	1	0
gambling	1	0
gerontology	1	0
health psychology	2	0
homophobia	1	0
multicultural	1	0
neuropsychology	1	0
nonverbal communication	1	0

psychotherapy outcomes	1	0
PTSD	2	1
sexuality	1	0
spirituality	1	0
social psychology	1	0
trichotillomania	1	0
women's issues	1	0

Clinical opportunities
behavioral medicine
child and family
eating disorders
juvenile forensics
Maryland School for the Blind
prison settings
stress and anxiety

Loyola University of Chicago

Department of Psychology
6525 North Sheridan Road
Chicago, IL 60626
phone#: (773) 508-6018
e-mail: DMORGAN@LUC.EDU
Web address: http://www.luc.edu/depts/psychology/grad/clinical.htm

1	2	3	4	**5**	6	7
Clinically oriented			Equal emphasis			Research oriented

What percentage of your faculty subscribes to or practices in each of the following orientations?

Psychodynamic/Psychoanalytic	27%
Applied behavioral analysis/Radical behavioral	0%
Family systems/Systems	18%
Existential/Phenomenological/Humanistic	27%
Cognitive/Cognitive-behavioral	27%

What percentage of students applying for internship last year was accepted into APA-accredited internships? 100%

What courses are required for incoming students to have completed prior to enrolling?
Research methods/experimental and statistics plus any six other psychology courses (24 hours, total)

Are there courses you recommend that are not mandatory?
No

GRE mean (M), cutoff (C), or preferred (P) score
Verbal 550 (C) Quantitative 550 (C)

GPA mean (M), cutoff (C), or preferred (P)
Overall GPA 3.2 (C)

Number of applications/admission offers/incoming students in 2001
195 applied/16 admission offers/7 incoming

% of students receiving:
Tuition waiver only: 0%
Assistantship/fellowship only: 0%
Both tuition waiver & assistantship/fellowship: 100%

Approximate percentage of incoming students who entered with a B.A./B.S. only: 90% **Master's:** 10%

Approximate percentage of students who are Women: 60% **Ethnic Minority:** 15%

Average years to complete the doctoral program (including internship): 7 years

Research areas	**# Faculty**	**# Grants**
AIDS	2	1
adult psychopathology	2	0
affective disorders	1	0
attention-deficit disorder	1	0
child clinical/psychopathology	5	3
community psychology	3	0
death/bereavement	2	0
ethical issues	1	0
minority mental health	3	2
personality	2	1
prevention	3	0
psychotherapy	4	1
sexuality/dysfunctions in African-American men	1	0
stress management/biofeedback	2	0
substance abuse	2	1

Clinical opportunities
adult psychotherapy
assessment (child and adult)
child behavioral
child clinical
eating disorders
health pscyhology
HIV/AIDS
neuropsychology (child and adolescent)
personality disorders
substance abuse
victims of assault

University of Maine

Department of Psychology, Room 301
5742 Little Hall
Orono, ME 04469-5742
phone#: (207) 581-2038
e-mail: SIGMON@UMIT.MAINE.EDU
Web address: http://inferno.asap.um.maine.edu/psy/graduateprogram/gradinfoclinical.html

1	2	3	4	**5**	6	7
Clinically oriented			Equal emphasis			Research oriented

What percentage of your faculty subscribes to or practices in each of the following orientations?

Psychodynamic/Psychoanalytic	0%
Applied behavioral analysis/Radical behavioral	20%
Family systems/Systems	0%
Existential/Phenomenological/Humanistic	0%
Cognitive/Cognitive-behavioral	80%

What percentage of students applying for internship last year was accepted into APA-accredited internships? 100%

What courses are required for incoming students to have completed prior to enrolling?
At least two or three advanced undergraduate psychology courses; background in natural sciences and mathematics

Are there courses you recommend that are not mandatory?
Learning, statistics, cognition

GRE mean (M), cutoff (C), or preferred (P) score
Verbal 550 (P) Quantitative 550 (P)
Advanced Psychology 550 (P)

GPA mean (M), cutoff (C), or preferred (P)
Overall GPA 3.5 (P)

Number of applications/admission offers/incoming students in 2001
85 applied/10 admission offers/5 incoming

% of students receiving:
Tuition waiver only: 0%
Assistantship/fellowship only: 0%
Both tuition waiver & assistantship/fellowship: 100% for the 1st-year students, 100% of the 2nd- to 4th-year students

Approximate percentage of incoming students who entered with a B.A./B.S. only: 75% **Master's:** 25%

Approximate percentage of students who are Women: 60% **Ethnic Minority:** 5%

Average years to complete the doctoral program (including internship): 6 years

Research areas	# Faculty	# Grants
anxiety disorders	2	0
behavioral medicine	1	0
children's regulation of affect	1	0
depression	1	0
psychotherapy outcome	3	0
social development	1	0
women's health	1	0

Clinical opportunities
ADHD
behavioral/developmental pediatrics
crisis/community
Head Start
inpatient psychotherapy
panic disorder
residential program for children at risk

University of Manitoba

Psychology Graduate Office P514
Duff Roblin Building
Winnipeg, Manitoba R3T 2N2, Canada
phone#: (204) 474-6377
fax #: (204) 474-7599
e-mail: inglislf@ms.umanitoba.ca
Web address: http://www.umanitoba.ca/faculties/arts/psychology/

1	2	3	**4**	5	6	7
Clinically oriented			Equal emphasis			Research oriented

What percentage of your faculty subscribes to or practices in each of the following orientations?

Psychodynamic/Psychoanalytic	10%
Applied behavioral analysis/Radical behavioral	20%
Clinical neuropsychology	14%
Family systems/Systems	20%
Existential/Phenomenological/Humanistic	10%
Cognitive/Cognitive-behavioral	30%

What percentage of students applying for internship last year was accepted into APA-accredited internships? 80%

What courses are required for incoming students to have completed prior to enrolling?
Eight half (3 credit hour) courses in psychology which include introductory psychology, research methods, and a second course in either research methods, statistics, or computer science

Are there courses you recommend that are not mandatory?
Psychological measurement and assessment; psychological tests or design and analysis for psychological experiments; physiological psychology or sensory processes

GRE mean (M), cutoff (C), or preferred (P) score
Verbal 573 (M) Quantitative 573 (M) Analytical 573 (M); subject score for one of the following: psychology, biology, zoology

GPA mean (M), cutoff (C), or preferred (P)
Junior/Senior GPA 3.0 (C)

Number of applications/admission offers/incoming students in 2001
49 applied/6 admission offers/3 incoming

% of students receiving:
Tuition waiver only: 0%
Assistantship/fellowship only: 25%
Both tuition waiver & assistantship/fellowship: 0%

Approximate percentage of incoming students who entered with a B.A./B.S. only: 25% **B.A. Honors:** 50% **Master's:** 25%

Approximate percentage of students who are Women: 77% **Ethnic Minority:** 10%

Average years to complete the doctoral program (including internship): 7 years

Research areas	# Faculty	# Grants
anxiety disorders	4	0
applied behavioral analysis	3	2
childhood psychopathology	1	0
chronic illness	1	1
chronic pain	1	0
clinical supervision	1	0
community psychology	1	0
compliance issues	2	0
developmental disabilities	3	0
eating disorders	2	0
health psychology	2	1
hypnosis	1	0

neuropsychology	2	1
offender/abuse	2	0
psychoneuroimmunology	1	0
psychopathology	1	0
psychotherapy outcome	3	0
schizophrenia	1	0
sports psychology	1	1
trauma effects	3	0
victim/abuse	3	0

Clinical opportunities
anxiety disorders
behavioral medicine
child/play therapy
clinical supervision
cognitive behavioral
community psychology
couples
eating disorders
developmental disabilities
family
health psychology
neuropsychology
obsessive-compulsive disorders
sports psychology
victim/battering/abuse

Marquette University

Psychology Department
P.O. Box 1881
Milwaukee, WI 53201-1881
phone#: (414) 288-7218
e-mail: Stephen.Saunders@mu.edu
Web address: http://www.marquette.edu/psyc/

1 2 3 **4** 5 6 7

Clinically oriented — Equal emphasis — Research oriented

What percentage of your faculty subscribes to or practices in each of the following orientations?

Psychodynamic/Psychoanalytic	30%
Applied behavioral analysis/Radical behavioral	10%
Family systems/Systems	30%
Existential/Phenomenological/Humanistic	10%
Cognitive/Cognitive-behavioral	70%

What percentage of students applying for internship last year was accepted into APA-accredited internships? 75%

What courses are required for incoming students to have completed prior to enrolling?
Research methods, statistics, developmental, abnormal, personality, social, cognition, neuroscience

Are there courses you recommend that are not mandatory?
History and systems

GRE mean (M), cutoff (C), or preferred (P) score
Verbal 525 (P) Quantitative 575 (P) Analytical 500 (P)

GPA mean (M), cutoff (C), or preferred (P)
Overall GPA 3.5 (P)

Number of applications/admission offers/incoming students in 2001
57 applied/12 admission offers/7 incoming

% of students receiving:
Tuition waiver only: 10%
Assistantship/fellowship only: 5%
Both tuition waiver & assistantship/fellowship: 50%

Approximate percentage of incoming students who entered with a B.A./B.S. only: 90% **Master's:** 10%

Approximate percentage of students who are Women: 75% **Ethnic Minority:** 20%

Average years to complete the doctoral program (including internship): 7 years

Research areas	# Faculty	# Grants
alcohol treatment	1	1
chaos theory	1	2
family conflict	2	1
help-seeking	1	1
memory problems	1	2
neuropsychology	2	0
psychotherapy research	3	0

Clinical opportunities
geriatric clinic
pediatric neuropsychology

University of Maryland

Department of Psychology
Biology–Psychology Building
College Park, MD 20742-4411
phone#: (301) 405-5866
e-mail: bpadgett@psyc.umd.edu
Web address: http://www.bsos.umd.edu/psyc/clinical.htm

1 2 3 4 5 **6** 7

Clinically oriented — Equal emphasis — Research oriented

What percentage of your faculty subscribes to or practices in each of the following orientations?

Psychodynamic/Psychoanalytic	10%
Applied behavioral analysis/Radical behavioral	20%
Family systems/Systems	30%
Existential/Phenomenological/Humanistic	0%
Cognitive/Cognitive-behavioral	40%

What percentage of students applying for internship last year was accepted into APA-accredited internships? 100%

What courses are required for incoming students to have completed prior to enrolling?
B.A. or B.S. in psychology or related areas

Are there courses you recommend that are not mandatory?
Statistics, laboratory courses in psychology

GRE mean (M), cutoff (C), or preferred (P) score
Verbal 550 (C), 600+ (P) Quantitative 550 (C), 600+ (P)
Analytical 650+ (P)

GPA mean (M), cutoff (C), or preferred (P)
Overall GPA 3.6

Number of applications/admission offers/incoming students in 2001
196 applied/14 admission offers/7 incoming

% of students receiving:
Tuition waiver only: 0%
Assistantship/fellowship only: 0%
Both tuition waiver & assistantship/fellowship: 100%

Approximate percentage of incoming students who entered with a B.A./B.S. only: 90% **Master's:** 10%

Approximate percentage of students who are Women: 75% **Ethnic Minority:** 44%

Average years to complete the doctoral program (including internship): 6.8 years

Research areas	# Faculty	# Grants
addictive behaviors	1	1
anxiety disorder	2	2
domestic violence	1	1
family therapy	2	0
marital interactions	1	0
personality and physiology	1	0
psychotherapy outcome	3	2
sequelae of sexual abuse	1	0
serious mental illnesses	2	1
social support	1	0

Clinical opportunities
Multiple opportunities in in-house training clinic, extern, and intern levels in inpatient, outpatient, and specialized settings

University of Maryland–Baltimore County

Department of Psychology
1000 Hilltop Circle
Baltimore, MD 21250
phone#: (410) 455-2567
e-mail: deluty@research.umbc.edu
Web address: http://psych.umbc.edu/

1	2	3	4	**5**	6	7
Clinically oriented		Equal emphasis				Research oriented

What percentage of your faculty subscribes to or practices in each of the following orientations?

Psychodynamic/Psychoanalytic	14%
Applied behavioral analysis/Radical behavioral	0%
Family systems/Systems	42%
Existential/Phenomenological/Humanistic	14%
Cognitive/Cognitive-behavioral	56%

What percentage of students applying for internship last year was accepted into APA-accredited internships? 90%

What courses are required for incoming students to have completed prior to enrolling?
Introductory psychology, experimental psychology, statistics, abnormal psychology

Are there courses you recommend that are not mandatory?
Personality, physiological, developmental

GRE mean (M), cutoff (C), or preferred (P) score
Verbal 600 (P) Quantitative 600 (P) Analytical 600 (P)
Advanced Psychology 600 (P)

GPA mean (M), cutoff (C), or preferred (P)
Overall GPA 3.5 (P) Psychology GPA 3.7 (P)
Junior/Senior GPA 3.5 (P)

Number of applications/admission offers/incoming students in 2001
96 applied/15 admission offers/8 incoming

% of students receiving:
Tuition waiver only: 0%
Assistantship/fellowship only: 0%
Both tuition waiver & assistantship/fellowship: 80%

Approximate percentage of incoming students who entered with a B.A./B.S. only: 83% **Master's:** 17%

Approximate percentage of students who are Women: 76% **Ethnic Minority:** 14%

Average years to complete the doctoral program (including internship): 6 years

Research areas	# Faculty	# Grants
addictive disorders	2	1
adult psychopathology	2	1
aggression	5	1
behavioral medicine	3	2
community psychology	2	1
eating disorders	1	0
interpersonal processes	3	0
psychology of religion	1	0
stress and coping	4	1
suicide	1	0
teen pregnancy	2	0
violence/abuse	5	1

Clinical opportunities
addictive disorders
affective disorders/depression
assessment
behavioral medicine
child clinical
community psychology
developmental psychopathology
eating disorders
family therapy
neuropsychology
schizophrenia/psychosis

University of Massachusetts at Amherst

Department of Psychology
Tobin Hall
Amherst, MA 01003
phone#: (413) 545-0662
e-mail: wisocki@psych.umass.edu
Web address: http://www.umass.edu/psychology/div4/index.html

1 2 3 **4** 5 6 7

Clinically oriented — Equal emphasis — Research oriented

What percentage of your faculty subscribes to or practices in each of the following orientations?

Psychodynamic/Psychoanalytic	50%
Applied behavioral analysis/Radical behavioral	0%
Family systems/Systems	10%
Existential/Phenomenological/Humanistic	10%
Cognitive/Cognitive-behavioral	30%

What percentage of students applying for internship last year was accepted into APA-accredited internships? 100%

What courses are required for incoming students to have completed prior to enrolling?
An undergraduate background in psychology which, at a minimum, consists of: introduction to psychology, statistics, methods, and three advanced subjects in psychology

Are there courses you recommend that are not mandatory?
No

GRE mean (M), cutoff (C), or preferred (P) score
Verbal 600 (C) Quantitative 600 (C)

GPA mean (M), cutoff (C), or preferred (P)
Overall GPA 3.5 (C)

Number of applications/admission offers/incoming students in 2001
324 applied/12 admission offers/7 incoming

% of students receiving:
Tuition waiver only: 0%
Assistantship/fellowship only: 0%
Both tuition waiver & assistantship/fellowship: 100%

Approximate percentage of incoming students who entered with a B.A./B.S. only: 100% **Master's:** 0%

Approximate percentage of students who are Women: 83% **Ethnic Minority:** 20%

Average years to complete the doctoral program (including internship): 5.6 years

Research areas	# Faculty	# Grants
aging/gerontology	2	0
child psychotherapy	4	2
eating disorders	1	0
family research	1	1
psychotherapy process	3	0
stress and coping	1	0

Clinical opportunities
behavior therapy
child and adolescent therapy
cultural diversity experience
geropsychology
psychoanalytic therapy
psychotherapy supervision

University of Massachusetts at Boston

Department of Psychology
Boston, MA 02125-3393
phone#: (617) 287-6340
e-mail: clinical.Psych@umb.edu
Web address: http://www.umb.edu/academic_programs/Graduate_Programs/Clinical_Psychology/Clini

1 2 3 **4** 5 6 7

Clinically oriented — Equal emphasis — Research oriented

What percentage of your faculty subscribes to or practices in each of the following orientations?

Psychodynamic/Psychoanalytic	75%
Applied behavioral analysis/Radical behavioral	0%
Family systems/Systems	50%
Existential/Phenomenological/Humanistic	25%
Cognitive/Cognitive-behavioral	30%

What percentage of students applying for internship last year was accepted into APA-accredited internships? 100%

What courses are required for incoming students to have completed prior to enrolling?
Statistics, research methods; 6 courses total in psychology

Are there courses you recommend that are not mandatory?
Development, abnormal, personality

GRE mean (M), cutoff (C), or preferred (P)
Verbal 600 (M), 650 (P) Quantitative 600 (M), 650 (P) Analytical 600 (M), 650 (P) Advanced Psychology 600 (M), 650 (P)

GPA mean (M), cutoff (C), or preferred (P)
Overall GPA 3.5 (M), 3.0 (C) Psychology GPA 3.5 (M), 3.5 (P), 3.0 (C) Junior/Senior GPA 3.5 (M), 3.5 (P)

Number of applications/admission offers/incoming students in 2001
274 applied/14 admission offers/8 incoming

% of students receiving:
Tuition waiver only: 0%
Assistantship/fellowship only: 0%
Both tuition waiver & assistantship/fellowship: 100%

Approximate percentage of incoming students who entered with a B.A./B.S. only: 100% **Master's:** 0%

Approximate percentage of students who are Women: 80% **Ethnic Minority:** 36%

Average years to complete the doctoral program (including internship): 6 years

Research areas	# Faculty	# Grants
cross-cultural	3	1
family	3	1
media and psychology	1	1
severe psychopathology	2	2
social stereotypes	1	0
trauma	4	1

Clinical opportunities

—

Massachusetts School of Professional Psychology (Psy.D.)

221 Rivermoor Street
Boston, MA 02132
phone#: (617) 327-6777
e-mail: admissions@mspp.edu
Web address: http://www.mspp.edu/

1 **2** 3 4 5 6 7

Clinically oriented — Equal emphasis — Research oriented

What percentage of your faculty subscribes to or practices in each of the following orientations?

Psychodynamic/Psychoanalytic	50%
Applied behavioral analysis/Radical behavioral	0%
Family systems/Systems	19%
Existential/Phenomenological/Humanistic	12%
Cognitive/Cognitive-behavioral	19%

What percentage of students applying for internship last year was accepted into APA-accredited internships? 60%

What courses are required for incoming students to have completed prior to enrolling?

Introduction to psychology, abnormal, developmental/child, personality theory

Are there courses you recommend that are not mandatory?

All psychology related

GRE mean (M), cutoff (C), or preferred (P) score

Verbal 575 (P) Quantitative 575 (P)

GPA mean (M), cutoff (C), or preferred (P)

Overall GPA 3.0 (P)

Number of applications/admission offers/incoming students in 2001

182 applied/78 admission offers/44 incoming

% of students receiving:

Tuition waiver only: 0%
Assistantship/fellowship only: 45%
Both tuition waiver & assistantship/fellowship: 0%

Approximate percentage of incoming students who entered with a B.A./B.S. only: 60% **Master's:** 40%

Approximate percentage of students who are Women: 68% **Ethnic Minority:** 12%

Average years to complete the doctoral program (including internship): 4.5 years

Research areas	# Faculty	# Grants
—		

Clinical opportunities

We have 160 sites per year in diverse areas. If your area is not covered, we will find a site.

McGill University

Department of Psychology
1205 Avenue Docteur Penfield
Montreal, Quebec H3A 1B1, Canada
phone#: (514) 398-6124
e-mail: gradapp@psych.mcgill.ca
Web address: http://www.psych.mcgill.ca

1 2 3 4 5 **6** 7

Clinically oriented — Equal emphasis — Research oriented

What percentage of your faculty subscribes to or practices in each of the following orientations?

Psychodynamic/Psychoanalytic	25%
Applied behavioral analysis/Radical behavioral	0%
Family systems/Systems	0%
Existential/Phenomenological/Humanistic	0%
Cognitive/Cognitive-behavioral	75%

What percentage of students applying for internship last year was accepted into APA-accredited internships? 100%

What courses are required for incoming students to have completed prior to enrolling?

None

Are there courses you recommend that are not mandatory?

No

GRE mean (M), cutoff (C), or preferred (P) score

Do not require GREs for non-native speakers of English

GPA mean (M), cutoff (C), or preferred (P)

Overall GPA 3.4 (P)

Number of applications/admission offers/incoming students in 2001

150 applied/9 admission offers/7 incoming

% of students receiving:

Tuition waiver only: 0%
Assistantship/fellowship only: 100%
Both tuition waiver & assistantship/fellowship: 0%

Approximate percentage of incoming students who entered with a B.A./B.S. only: 95% **Master's:** 5%

Approximate percentage of students who are Women: 60% **Ethnic Minority:** 10%

Average years to complete the doctoral program (including internship): 5 years

Research areas	**# Faculty**	**# Grants**
aggression	1	1
aging (including Alzheimer's)	2	1
assessment/diagnosis	2	0
attention-deficit disorder	1	1
behavior therapy	1	0
behavioral genetics	1	1
behavioral medicine	2	2
child	1	1
child psychopathology	1	1
cognitive information processing	1	0
depression	2	2
developmental	1	1
eating disorders	1	1
emotion	1	1
family	2	1
gender	1	0
health psychology	2	2
interpersonal relations	2	2
memory	2	1
neuropsychology	1	1
olfaction	1	0
personality	1	0
personality assessment	2	0
psychopathology	2	2
psychopharmacology	2	1
psychophysiology	2	1
psychotherapy process and outcome	1	0
sexual dysfunction	1	1
stress	1	1
substance abuse	1	1

Clinical opportunities
The McGill University Psychology Internship Consortium is closely associated with our graduate program in clinical psychology. The Consortium consists of departments of psychology in 3 university teaching hospitals, a children's hospital, and a psychiatric hospital.

MCP Hahnemann University of the Health Sciences

Department of Clinical & Health Psychology—MS626
Philadelphia, PA 19102-1192
phone#: (215) 762-7702
e-mail: Mike.Williams@drexel.edu
Web address: http://www.drexel.edu/

1	2	3	**4**	5	6	7
Clinically oriented			Equal emphasis			Research oriented

What percentage of your faculty subscribes to or practices in each of the following orientations?

Psychodynamic/Psychoanalytic	0%
Applied behavioral analysis/Radical behavioral	10%
Family systems/Systems	10%
Existential/Phenomenological/Humanistic	0%
Cognitive/Cognitive-behavioral	80%

What percentage of students applying for internship last year was accepted into APA-accredited internships? 95%

What courses are required for incoming students to have completed prior to enrolling?
Statistics, research design, abnormal psychology

Are there courses you recommend that are not mandatory?
No

GRE mean (M), cutoff (C), or preferred (P) score
Verbal 593 (M) Quantitative 678 (M) Analytical 667 (M)
Advanced Psychology 575 (M)

GPA mean (M), cutoff (C), or preferred (P)
Overall GPA 3.7 (M)

Number of applications/admission offers/incoming students in 2001
200 applied/40 admission offers/14 incoming

% of students receiving:
Tuition waiver only: 40%
Assistantship/fellowship only: 40%
Both tuition waiver & assistantship/fellowship: 40%

Approximate percentage of incoming students who entered with a B.A./B.S. only: 64.7% **Master's:** 35.3%

Approximate percentage of students who are Women: 88.2% **Ethnic Minority:** 29.4%

Average years to complete the doctoral program (including internship): 5 years

Research areas	**# Faculty**	**# Grants**
anxiety disorders	1	0
bipolar disorder	1	1
depression	1	0
developmental disabilities	2	1
diabetes	1	0
eating disorders	1	0
health	4	0
law psychology	2	0
marital violence	1	0
neuropsychology	1	0
prevention	1	0
psychooncology	2	2
schizophrenia	1	2
sex abuse	2	0

Clinical opportunities
adult psychiatry
cancer units
child psychiatry developmental disabilities
forensic assessment
heart transplant unit
neuropsychology
obesity
rehabilitation
severe mental illness
sex offenders

University of Memphis

Department of Psychology
Memphis, TN 38152
phone#: (901) 678-3015
e-mail: j.johnson@mail.psyc.memphis.edu
Web address: http://www.psych.memphis.edu/pages/clinical.htm

1	2	3	4	5	**6**	7

Clinically oriented — Equal emphasis — Research oriented

What percentage of your faculty subscribes to or practices in each of the following orientations?

Psychodynamic/Psychoanalytic	0%
Applied behavioral analysis/Radical behavioral	10%
Family systems/Systems	0%
Existential/Phenomenological/Humanistic	0%
Cognitive/Cognitive-behavioral	90%

What percentage of students applying for internship last year was accepted into APA-accredited internships? 100%

What courses are required for incoming students to have completed prior to enrolling?
12–18 credits including statistics and experimental psychology

Are there courses you recommend that are not mandatory?
No

GRE mean (M), cutoff (C), or preferred (P) score
Verbal 650 (P) Quantitative 650 (P)

GPA mean (M), cutoff (C), or preferred (P)
Overall GPA 3.6 (P) Psychology GPA 3.6 (P)
Junior/Senior GPA 3.5 (P)

Number of applications/admission offers/incoming students in 2001
123 applied/10 admission offers/6 incoming

% of students receiving:
Tuition waiver only: 0%
Assistantship/fellowship only: 0%
Both tuition waiver & assistantship/fellowship: 100%

Approximate percentage of incoming students who entered with a B.A./B.S. only: 80% **Master's:** 20%

Approximate percentage of students who are Women: 65% **Ethnic Minority:** 15%

Average years to complete the doctoral program (including internship): 5.6 years

Research areas	# Faculty	# Grants
behavioral medicine	5	4
child clinical	3	1
neuropsychology	2	1
psychopathology and psychotherapy	4	0

Clinical opportunities
affective disorders
anxiety disorders
behavioral medicine
cancer and emotional adjustment
developmental disabilities/autism
eating disorders
family therapy
gambling
inpatient psychology
minority/cross-cultural
neuropsychology/rehabilitation
school/educational
sleep disorders

University of Miami

Department of Psychology
P.O. Box 249229
Coral Gables, FL 33124
phone#: (305) 284-5222 (ext. 1 or 5)
e-mail: alagrecr@miami.edu
Web address: http://www.psy.miami.edu/Graduate/index.html

1	2	3	4	5	**6**	7

Clinically oriented — Equal emphasis — Research oriented

What percentage of your faculty subscribes to or practices in each of the following orientations?

Psychodynamic/Psychoanalytic	10%
Applied behavioral analysis/Radical behavioral	0%
Family systems/Systems	30%
Existential/Phenomenological/Humanistic	0%
Cognitive/Cognitive-behavioral	80%

What percentage of students applying for internship last year was accepted into APA-accredited internships? 100%

What courses are required for incoming students to have completed prior to enrolling?
Statistics, experimental psychology

Are there courses you recommend that are not mandatory?
Strong science background, especially biology, and mathematics

GRE mean (M), cutoff (C), or preferred (P) score
Verbal + Quantitative 1200 (P)

GPA mean (M), cutoff (C), or preferred (P)
Overall GPA 3.5 (P)

Number of applications/admission offers/incoming students in 2001
295 applied/22 admission offers/15 incoming

% of students receiving:
Tuition waiver only: 0%
Assistantship/fellowship only: 0%
Both tuition waiver & assistantship/fellowship: 100%

Approximate percentage of incoming students who entered with a B.A./B.S. only: 70% **Master's:** 30%

Approximate percentage of students who are Women: 70% **Ethnic Minority:** 24%

Average years to complete the doctoral program (including internship): 5 years

Research areas	**# Faculty**	**# Grants**
AIDS	6	2+
adult psychopathology	6	2+
affective disorders	2	1
cancer	3	1
cardiovascular disease	3	2+
child clinical psychology	5	2+
child psychopathology	5	2+
diabetes	3	2+
family therapy	2	1
health psychology	13	2+
hypertension	3	1
pediatric psychology	2	1
psychoneuroimmunology	6	2+
stress and coping	8	2+
trauma	3	2+

Clinical opportunities
abuse
AIDS
behavioral medicine
conduct disorder
developmental disabilities/autism
diabetes
family therapy
group therapy
marital therapy
minority/cross-cultural
neuropsychology
pediatrics
substance abuse

Miami University

Department of Psychology
Oxford, OH 45056
phone#: (513) 529-2400
e-mail: KNUDSORM@muohio.edu
Web address: http://muohio.edu/~psy3cwis/phdprogram.html

1	2	3	**4**	5	6	7
Clinically oriented			Equal emphasis			Research oriented

What percentage of your faculty subscribes to or practices in each of the following orientations?

Psychodynamic/Psychoanalytic	33%
Applied behavioral analysis/Radical behavioral	0%
Family systems/Systems	22%
Existential/Phenomenological/Humanistic	33%
Cognitive/Cognitive-behavioral	11%

What percentage of students applying for internship last year was accepted into APA-accredited internships? 100%

What courses are required for incoming students to have completed prior to enrolling?
One course in statistics

Are there courses you recommend that are not mandatory?
No

GRE mean (M), cutoff (C), or preferred (P) score
Verbal 600 (P) Quantitative 600 (P) Analytical 600 (P)

GPA mean (M), cutoff (C), or preferred (P)
Overall GPA 3.5 (P)

Number of applications/admission offers/incoming students in 2001
79 applied/18 admission offers/6 incoming

% of students receiving:
Tuition waiver only: 0%
Assistantship/fellowship only: 0%
Both tuition waiver & assistantship/fellowship: 100%

Approximate percentage of incoming students who entered with a B.A./B.S. only: 66.6% **Master's:** 33.3%

Approximate percentage of students who are Women: 71% **Ethnic Minority:** 29%

Average years to complete the doctoral program (including internship): 6 years

Research areas	**# Faculty**	**# Grants**
anxiety disorders	3	0
child psychopathology	2	0
dreams	1	0
family research	1	0
immigration/acculturation	2	0
narrative methodologies	2	0
personality disorders	1	0
psychotherapy process	3	0
trauma recovery	2	0

Clinical opportunities
assessment
conduct disorder
developmental disabilities
family therapy
hyperactivity
marital/couples therapy
neuropsychology
school-based mental health

University of Michigan

Department of Psychology
525 East University
Ann Arbor, MI 48109
phone#: (313) 764-6332
e-mail: duenas@umich.edu
Web address: http://www.umich.edu/~psycdept/

1	2	3	**4**	5	6	7
Clinically oriented			Equal emphasis			Research oriented

What percentage of your faculty subscribes to or practices in each of the following orientations?

Psychodynamic/Psychoanalytic	50%
Applied behavioral analysis/Radical behavioral	0%
Family systems/Systems	25%
Existential/Phenomenological/Humanistic	0%
Cognitive/Cognitive-behavioral	25%

What percentage of students applying for internship last year was accepted into APA-accredited internships? 100%

What courses are required for incoming students to have completed prior to enrolling?
None

Are there courses you recommend that are not mandatory?
Basic course work in psychology

GRE mean (M), cutoff (C), or preferred (P) score
Verbal 700 (M)(P) Quantitative 705 (M) Analytical 710 (M)

GPA mean (M), cutoff (C), or preferred (P)
Overall GPA 3.5 (P), 3.75 (M) Psychology GPA 3.9 (M)

Number of applications/admission offers/incoming students in 2001
350 applied/8 admission offers/6 incoming

% of students receiving:
Tuition waiver only: 0%
Assistantship/fellowship only: 0%
Both tuition waiver & assistantship/fellowship: 100%

Approximate percentage of incoming students who entered with a B.A./B.S. only: 90% **Master's:** 10%

Approximate percentage of students who are Women: 70% **Ethnic Minority:** 50%

Average years to complete the doctoral program (including internship): 6 years

Research areas	**# Faculty**	**# Grants**
adult survivors of incest	1	0
child abuse/neglect	1	0
childhood illness/family coping	1	0
childhood loss	2	2
chronic illness and coping (adult)	1	0
conscious/unconscious processes	1	0
divorce	1	1
dreams	1	0
family systems	4	1
family violence	2	2
health psychology (AIDS, polio, head injury)	2	0
homeless families	1	0
inner city children	4	2
life history research	1	0
low birthweight children	1	0
neuropsychology	6	0
peer relations/social skills in children	1	1
personality disorders	2	0
psychotherapy research	5	0
schizophrenia	1	0
social competence in children	2	0
substance abuse	2	2
TV violence	1	1

Clinical opportunities
adult
child and family

Michigan State University

Department of Psychology
East Lansing, MI 48824
phone#: (517) 432-9953
e-mail: mcvay@msu.edu
Web address: http://psychology.msu.edu/academic/clinical/

1	2	3	4	**5**	6	7
Clinically oriented			Equal emphasis			Research oriented

What percentage of your faculty subscribes to or practices in each of the following orientations?

Psychodynamic/Psychoanalytic	35%
Applied behavioral analysis/Radical behavioral	0%
Family systems/Systems	35%
Existential/Phenomenological/Humanistic	0%
Cognitive/Cognitive-behavioral	30%

What percentage of students applying for internship last year was accepted into APA-accredited internships? 78%

What courses are required for incoming students to have completed prior to enrolling?
12 hours of psychology courses at the bachelor's level

Are there courses you recommend that are not mandatory?
Quantitative methods, research design, advanced competence with the use of computer programs (SPSS, SYSTAT, etc.)

GRE mean (M), cutoff (C), or preferred (P) score
Verbal 600 (P) Quantitative 600 (P) Analytical 600 (P)
Advanced Psychology 600 (P)

GPA mean (M), cutoff (C), or preferred (P)
Overall GPA 3.4 (P) Psychology GPA 3.5 (P)
Junior/Senior GPA 3.5 (P)

Number of applications/admission offers/incoming students in 2001
148 applied/10 admission offers/6 incoming

% of incoming students receiving:
Tuition waiver only: 0%
Assistantship/fellowship only: 0%
Both tuition waiver & assistantship/fellowship: 100%

Approximate percentage of incoming students who entered with a B.A./B.S. only: 85% **Master's:** 15%

Approximate percentage of students who are Women: 83% **Ethnic Minority:** 33%

Average years to complete the doctoral program (including internship): 7 years

Research areas	# Faculty	# Grants
affective disorders/depression	2	1
aging/gerontology	1	1
child clinical	5	2
community psychology	3	0
cross-cultural issues	1	1
eating disorders	1	0
family research/systems	2	1
family violence	4	2
learning disabilities/ADHD	1	1
memory	1	1
neuropsychology	2	2
psychotherapy process	1	0
schizophrenia	1	1
sexual abuse	1	0
social skills/competence	1	1

Clinical opportunities
assessment (child, adult, aging)
community psychology
domestic violence
eating disorders
family therapy
gerontology/aging
minority/cross-cultural
neuropsychology
schizophrenia/psychosis

University of Minnesota

Department of Psychology
N218 Elliot Hall, 75 East River Road
Minneapolis, MN 55455
phone#: (612) 625-2546
e-mail: cspr@umn.edu
Web address: http://www.psych.umn.edu/psyareas/Clinical/clbrcindex.htm

1 2 3 4 5 **6** 7

Clinically oriented — Equal emphasis — Research oriented

What percentage of your faculty subscribes to or practices in each of the following orientations?

Psychodynamic/Psychoanalytic	17%
Applied behavioral analysis/Radical behavioral	17%
Family systems/Systems	0%
Existential/Phenomenological/Humanistic	0%
Cognitive/Cognitive-behavioral	83%

What percentage of students applying for internship last year was accepted into APA-accredited internships? 100%

What courses are required for incoming students to have completed prior to enrolling?
Statistics, abnormal psychology

Are there courses you recommend that are not mandatory?
No

GRE mean (M), cutoff (C), or preferred (P) score
Verbal 625 (C) Quantitative 625 (C)

GPA mean (M), cutoff (C), or preferred (P)
Overall GPA 3.5 (C)

Number of applications/admission offers/incoming students in 2001
133 applied/21 admission offers/9 incoming

% of students receiving:
Tuition waiver only: 0%
Assistantship/fellowship only: 0%
Both tuition waiver & assistantship/fellowship: 100%

Approximate percentage of incoming students who entered with a B.A./B.S. only: 95% **Master's:** 5%

Approximate percentage of students who are Women: 77% **Ethnic Minority:** 17%

Average years to complete the doctoral program (including internship): 6 years

Research areas	# Faculty	# Grants
affective disorders	2	1
anxiety disorders	2	1
behavioral genetics	4	4
cross-cultural psychology	1	0
developmental psychopathology	5	5
eating disorders	1	0
personality assessment	6	3
personality disorders	4	1
psychophysiology	2	2
responses to extreme stress	1	0
schizophrenia	2	0

Clinical opportunities
affective disorders
anxiety disorders
behavior therapy
childhood disorders and therapy
cognitive therapy
conduct disorder
crisis intervention
community psychology
eating disorders
family therapy
forensic psychology
gerontology/aging
hyperactivity/attention deficit disorder
long-term psychodynamic psychotherapy
neuropsychology
obsessive-compulsive disorder
panic disorder
psychotic disorders
schizophrenia
substance abuse

University of Mississippi

Department of Psychology
University, MS 38677
phone#: (662) 915-7383
e-mail: pydsh@olemiss.edu
Web address: http://www.olemiss.edu/depts/psychology/clinical_grad.html

1	2	3	4	**5**	6	7
Clinically oriented			Equal emphasis			Research oriented

What percentage of your faculty subscribes to or practices in each of the following orientations?

Psychodynamic/Psychoanalytic	0%
Applied behavioral analysis/Radical behavioral	29%
Family systems/Systems	29%
Existential/Phenomenological/Humanistic	0%
Cognitive/Cognitive-behavioral	71%

What percentage of students applying for internship last year was accepted into APA-accredited internships? 100%

What courses are required for incoming students to have completed prior to enrolling?
Introductory psychology, statistics, lab course

Are there courses you recommend that are not mandatory?
Physiological psychology, abnormal psychology, developmental psychology, and some grounding in biology/physiology/chemistry

GRE mean (M), cutoff (C), or preferred (P) score
Verbal 600 (P) Quantitative 600 (P)
Verbal + Quantitative 1200 (P)
Advanced Psychology 600 (P)

GPA mean (M), cutoff (C), or preferred (P)
Overall GPA 3.2 (P) Psychology GPA 3.5 (P)
Junior/Senior GPA 3.5 (P)

Number of applications/admission offers/incoming students in 2001
53 applied/13 admission offers/7 incoming

% of students receiving:
Tuition waiver only: 0%
Assistantship/fellowship only: 0%
Both tuition waiver & assistantship/fellowship: 100%

Approximate percentage of incoming students who entered with a B.A./B.S. only: 70% **Master's:** 30%

Approximate percentage of students who are Women: 58% **Ethnic Minority:** 23%

Average years to complete the doctoral program (including internship): 6 years

Research areas	**# Faculty**	**# Grants**
behavior problems in children	3	1
community psychology	2	0
compliance	2	0
eating disorders	1	0
menstrual pain/menstrual disorders	1	0
psychological assessment	1	0
posttraumatic stress disorder	1	0
race relations	3	0
rape	2	1
rural mental health	2	3
smoking cessation/addiction/substance abuse	1	0
social skills/competence	2	0

Clinical opportunities
child/adolescent
children's social skills
chronic mental illness
clinical assessment
community mental health
eating disorders
family/marital therapy
posttramatic stress disorder
smoking cessation
substance abuse/alcohol abuse

University of Missouri–Columbia

Department of Psychology
210 Alester Hall
Columbia, MO 65211
phone#: (573) 882-6860
e-mail: BellDolanD@Missouri.edu
Web address: http://web.missouri.edu/~psywww/clinical.htm

1	2	3	4	5	**6**	7
Clinically oriented			Equal emphasis			Research oriented

What percentage of your faculty subscribes to or practices in each of the following orientations?

Psychodynamic/Psychoanalytic	10%
Applied behavioral analysis/Radical behavioral	0%
Family systems/Systems	10%
Existential/Phenomenological/Humanistic	0%
Cognitive/Cognitive-behavioral	80%

What percentage of students applying for internship last year was accepted into APA-accredited internships? 100%

What courses are required for incoming students to have completed prior to enrolling?
None

Are there courses you recommend that are not mandatory?
Other sciences, statistics/mathematics

GRE mean (M), cutoff (C), or preferred (P) score
Verbal >600 (P) Quantitative >600 (P)

GPA mean (M), cutoff (C), or preferred (P)
Overall GPA 3.8 (M) Psychology GPA 3.9 (M)
Junior/Senior GPA 3.9 (M)

Number of applications/admission offers/incoming students in 2001
91 applied/9 admission offers/4 incoming

% of students receiving:
Tuition waiver only: 0%
Assistantship/fellowship only: 0%
Both tuition waiver & assistantship/fellowship: 100%

Approximate percentage of incoming students who entered with a B.A./B.S. only: 90% **Master's:** 10%

Approximate percentage of students who are Women: 70% **Ethnic Minority:** 17%

Average years to complete the doctoral program (including internship): 5.4 years

Research areas	# Faculty	# Grants
alcohol abuse	2	2
anxiety disorders	1	0
behavioral medicine/health psych	3	2
child anxiety/depression	2	1
child injury	1	1
child social interactions	1	0
community	1	1
eating disorders	1	0
family therapy	1	1
pediatric psychology	2	1
personality disorders	1	1
personality/psychopathology	2	2
sexual dysfunction	1	0

Clinical opportunities
adult and child, outpatient and inpatient
health psychology
medical center
rehabilitation psychology
research protocol assessment and prevention
state hospital
VA hospital

University of Missouri–St. Louis

Department of Psychology
8001 Natural Bridge Road
St. Louis, MO 63121
phone#: (314) 516-5391
Web address: http://www.umsl.edu/divisions/artscience/psychology/clinical/index.html

1	2	3	**4**	5	6	7
Clinically oriented			Equal emphasis			Research oriented

What percentage of your faculty subscribes to or practices in each of the following orientations?

Psychodynamic/Psychoanalytic	25%
Applied behavioral analysis/Radical behavioral	0%
Family systems/Systems	25%
Existential/Phenomenological/Humanistic	25%
Cognitive/Cognitive-behavioral	25%

What percentage of students applying for internship last year was accepted into APA-accredited internships? 100%

What courses are required for incoming students to have completed prior to enrolling?
A total of 24 undergraduate credits: introductory psychology, psychological statistics, research methods in psychology

Are there courses you recommend that are not mandatory?
Personality, social psychology, learning and motivation, history and systems, physiological psychology, developmental

GRE mean (M), cutoff (C), or preferred (P) score
Verbal + Quantitative 1200+ (P)
Analytical + Advanced Psychology 1200+ (P)

GPA mean (M), cutoff (C), or preferred (P)
Overall GPA 3.5 (P) Psychology GPA 3.75 (P)
Junior/Senior GPA 3.75 (P)

Number of applications/admission offers/incoming students in 2001
75 applied/13 admission offers/6 incoming

% of students receiving:
Tuition waiver only: 0%
Assistantship/fellowship only: 0%
Both tuition waiver & assistantship/fellowship: 100% in first 2 years

Approximate percentage of incoming students who entered with a B.A./B.S. only: 85% **Master's:** 15%

Approximate percentage of students who are Women: 80% **Ethnic Minority:** 22%

Average years to complete the doctoral program (including internship): 6.5 years

Research areas	# Faculty	# Grants
bereavement	1	0
caretakers of the elderly	1	1
child abuse	1	1
child and health	1	0
children's play	1	0
cross-cultural issues in mental health	1	1
psychology of women	2	0
racial identification	1	0
treatment of rape victims	1	1

Clinical opportunities
adult
children and families
feminist therapy
treatment of rape victims
psychotherapy with older populations

University of Montana

Department of Psychology
Missoula, MT 59812
phone#: (406) 243-4521
e-mail: PSYCGRAD@SELWAY.UMT.EDU
Web address: http://www.cas.umt.edu/psych/

1	2	3	**4**	5	6	7
Clinically oriented			Equal emphasis			Research oriented

What percentage of your faculty subscribes to or practices in each of the following orientations?

Psychodynamic/Psychoanalytic	25%
Applied behavioral analysis/Radical behavioral	12%
Family systems/Systems	25%
Existential/Phenomenological/Humanistic	12%
Cognitive/Cognitive-behavioral	50%

What percentage of students applying for internship last year was accepted into APA-accredited internships? 80%

What courses are required for incoming students to have completed prior to enrolling?
None

Are there courses you recommend that are not mandatory?
Yes

GRE mean (M), cutoff (C), or preferred (P) score
Verbal 630 (M) Quantitative 600 (M)
Advanced Psychology 600 (M)

GPA mean (M), cutoff (C), or preferred (P)
Overall GPA 3.75 (M)

Number of applications/admission offers/incoming students in 2001
84 applied/21 admission offers/7 incoming

% of students receiving:
Tuition waiver only: 0%
Assistantship/fellowship only: 36%
Both tuition waiver & assistantship/fellowship: 52%

Approximate percentage of incoming students who entered with a B.A./B.S. only: 85% **Master's:** 15%

Approximate percentage of students who are Women: 80% **Ethnic Minority:** 20%

Average years to complete the doctoral program (including internship): 6.5 years

Research areas	**# Faculty**	**# Grants**
assessment	1	0
attention-deficit disorder	1	0
behavioral medicine/health psychology	3	2
child clinical	2	1
child psychopathology	1	1
closed head injury	1	0
cognition	4	0
conditioning	3	0
eating disorders	1	1
emotion	4	1
gender issues	2	1
gifted	1	0
group therapy	1	0
learning	3	0
malingering	1	1
memory	2	0
neuropsychology	2	0
personality assessment	1	0
professional issues	1	0
program development	1	0
psychotherapy process and outcome	3	1
schizophrenia	1	0
school	1	0
statistics	1	0
stress and coping	1	0
substance abuse	2	1

Clinical opportunities
adolescent and child
attachment disorder
borderline personality disorder
community health
couples
depression
domestic violence
eating disorders
family
functional analytic therapy
interpersonal (IPT)
motivational interviewing
neuropsychology
pain management
prison populations
schizophrenia/psychoses
substance abuse
trauma

University of Nebraska–Lincoln

Department of Psychology
209 Burnett Hall
Lincoln, NE 68588
phone#: (402) 472-3229
e-mail: rbarnes1@unl.edu
Web address: http://www.unl.edu/psych

1	2	3	**4**	5	6	7
Clinically oriented			Equal emphasis			Research oriented

What percentage of your faculty subscribes to or practices in each of the following orientations?

Psychodynamic/Psychoanalytic	0%
Applied behavioral analysis/Radical behavioral	10%
Family systems/Systems	25%
Existential/Phenomenological/Humanistic	10%
Cognitive/Cognitive-behavioral	85%

What percentage of students applying for internship last year was accepted into APA-accredited internships? 100%

What courses are required for incoming students to have completed prior to enrolling?
Psychology major

Are there courses you recommend that are not mandatory?
Methodology and quantitative courses

GRE mean (M), cutoff (C), or preferred (P) score
Verbal 500 (C) Quantitative 500 (C)

GPA mean (M), cutoff (C), or preferred (P)
Overall GPA 3.6 (P) Psychology GPA 3.75 (P)

Number of applications/admission offers/incoming students in 2001
147 applied/10 admission offers/9 incoming

% of students receiving:
Tuition waiver only: 0%
Assistantship/fellowship only: 0%
Both tuition waiver & assistantship/fellowship: 100%

Approximate percentage of incoming students who entered with a B.A./B.S. only: 70% **Master's:** 30%

Approximate percentage of students who are Women: 65% **Ethnic Minority:** 30%

Average years to complete the doctoral program (including internship): 6.2 years

Research areas	# Faculty	# Grants
alcohol abuse/substance abuse	1	1
child abuse/family violence	4	2
child/adolescence	3	1
chronically mentally ill	1	1
forensic	3	2
neuropsychology	1	0
psychopathology	3	2
psychotherapy	3	1

Clinical opportunities
alcoholism
anxiety disorders
child abuse/family violence
chronically mentally ill
forensic
minority issues

University of Nevada–Reno

Department of Psychology
MSS 298
Reno, NV 89557
Web address: http://www.unr.edu/psych/clinical.html

1	2	3	**4**	5	6	7
Clinically oriented			Equal emphasis			Research oriented

What percentage of your faculty subscribes to or practices in each of the following orientations?
Psychodynamic/Psychoanalytic 0%
Applied behavioral analysis/Radical behavioral 50%
Family systems/Systems 33%
Existential/Phenomenological/Humanistic 0%
Cognitive/Cognitive-behavioral 33%

What percentage of students applying for internship last year was accepted into APA-accredited internships? 90%

What courses are required for incoming students to have completed prior to enrolling?
Abnormal psychology, statistics

Are there courses you recommend that are not mandatory?
Behavioral principles (e.g., behavior analysis, learning), research methodology

GRE mean (M), cutoff (C), or preferred (P) score
Verbal 500 (P) Quantitative 500 (P)
Advanced Psychology 500 (P)

GPA mean (M), cutoff (C), or preferred (P)
Overall GPA 3.2 (P) Psychology GPA 3.3 (P)

Number of applications/admission offers/incoming students in 2001
75 applied/10 admission offers/8 incoming

% of students receiving:
Tuition waiver only: 0%
Assistantship/fellowship only: 0%
Both tuition waiver & assistantship/fellowship: 100%

Approximate percentage of incoming students who entered with a B.A./B.S. only: 90% **Master's:** 10%

Approximate percentage of students who are Women: 66% **Ethnic Minority:** 17%

Average years to complete the doctoral program (including internship): 6.5 years

Research areas	# Faculty	# Grants
aging	1	2
anxiety disorders	2	0
behavior analysis	4	0
behavioral assessment	3	0
children	2	0
couples	1	0
drug & alcohol abuse	1	2
gerontology	1	2
incest survivors	2	0
minority mental health	1	0
prevention	4	2
sexual offenders	1	2
social skills	3	0
suicide	1	0
verbal behavior	4	0

Clinical opportunities
AIDS
anxiety disorders
behavioral health care
couples
depression
drug & alcohol abuse
gerontology
health care administration
incest survivors
posttraumatic stress disorder

University of New Mexico

Department of Psychology
Albuquerque, NM 87131
phone#: (505) 277-7512
e-mail: lsbell@unm.edu
Web address: http://www.unm.edu/~psych/gradprog.html#clinical

1	2	3	4	**5**	6	7
Clinically oriented			Equal emphasis			Research oriented

What percentage of your faculty subscribes to or practices in each of the following orientations?

Psychodynamic/Psychoanalytic	25%
Applied behavioral analysis/Radical behavioral	12.5%
Family systems/Systems	38%
Existential/Phenomenological/Humanistic	12.5%
Cognitive/Cognitive-behavioral	38%

What percentage of students applying for internship last year was accepted into APA-accredited internships? 80%

What courses are required for incoming students to have completed prior to enrolling?
Statistics, research methods, psychology major or equivalent course work

Are there courses you recommend that are not mandatory?
Basic science courses, laboratory courses, supervised research

GRE mean (M), cutoff (C), or preferred (P) score
Average of admitted students over the last 5 years:
Verbal 610 (M) Quantitative 642 (M) Analytical 630 (M)
Advanced Psychology 644 (M)
Average of admitted students for last year:
Verbal 663 (M) Quantitative 650 (M) Analytical 680 (M)
Advanced Psychology 693 (M)

GPA mean (M), cutoff (C), or preferred (P)
Average of admitted students over the last 5 years:
Overall GPA 3.8 (M)
Average of admitted students for last year:
Overall GPA 3.7 (M)

Number of applications/admission offers/incoming students in 2001
110 applied/9 admission offers/4 incoming

% of students receiving:
Tuition waiver only: 0%
Assistantship/fellowship only: 0%
Both tuition waiver & assistantship/fellowship: 100%

Approximate percentage of incoming students who entered with a B.A./B.S. only: 80% **Master's:** 20%

Approximate percentage of students who are Women: 70% **Ethnic Minority:** 15%

Average years to complete the doctoral program (including internship): 7 years

Research areas	# Faculty	# Grants
eating disorders	1	1
ethical issues	1	0
family interactions	1	3
minority issues	2	0
neuropsychology	2	4
pediatric psychology	1	0
stimulus equivalence	1	0
substance abuse	5	8

Clinical opportunities
behavioral medicine
inpatient/oupatient psychotherapy
neuropsychological assessment
pediatrics
personality assessment
school setting (children, adolescents, families, adults, couples)

New School for Social Research

Graduate Faculty, Department of Psychology
65 Fifth Avenue
New York, NY 10003
phone#: (212) 229-5727
e-mail: woodsm@newschool.edu
Web address: http://www.newschool.edu/gf/psy/gf_phdcl.htm

1	2	3	**4**	5	6	7
Clinically oriented			Equal emphasis			Research oriented

What percentage of your faculty subscribes to or practices in each of the following orientations?

Psychodynamic/Psychoanalytic	90%
Applied behavioral analysis/Radical behavioral	0%
Family systems/Systems	0%
Existential/Phenomenological/Humanistic	10%
Cognitive/Cognitive-behavioral	10%

What percentage of students applying for internship last year was accepted into APA-accredited internships? 100%

What courses are required for incoming students to have completed prior to enrolling?
There are no prerequisite courses for entry in the master's general psychology program. However, the clinical Ph.D. program requires the following: 3 100-level psych courses; 1 course in each of the following areas: personality, social, developmental; 2 clinical pscyhology courses (psychopathology I and II); 1 course in assessment of individual differences; 1 course for fulfillment of statistics requirement; 1 research methods course

Are there courses you recommend that are not mandatory?
Major in psychology

GRE mean (M), cutoff (C), or preferred (P) score
Verbal 612 (M) Quantitative 592 (M)

GPA mean (M), cutoff (C), or preferred (P)
GPA 3.4 (M)

Number of applications/admission offers/incoming students in 2001
20 applied/15 admission offers/15 incoming

% of students receiving:
Tuition waiver only: 17%
Assistantship/fellowship only: 14%
Both tuition waiver & assistantship/fellowship: 7%

Approximate percentage of incoming students who entered with a B.A./B.S. only: 0% **Master's:** 100%

Approximate percentage of students who are Women: 66% **Ethnic Minority:** 5.3%
Non-Resident Aliens: 6.6%

Average years to complete the doctoral program (including internship): 4.5 years

Research areas	**# Faculty**	**# Grants**
assessment/diagnosis	2	1
child clinical	1	1
developmental	1	0
emotions	2	0
memory	2	1
moral development	1	0
narrative methodologies	2	0
personality assessment	1	0
prevention	2	1
psychoanalysis	2	0
psychopathology	2	0
psychotherapy process and outcome	3	1

Clinical opportunities
We are located in downtown New York and are surrounded by a network of public and private clinics and hospitals. We also have a training clinic in collaboration with a major medical center.

New York University

Department of Psychology
The Psychology Building
6 Washington Place, Room 550
New York, NY 10003
phone#: (212) 998-7979
fax#: (212) 995-4292
e-mail: psychquery@psych.nyu.edu
Web address: http://psych.nyu.edu/dept/clinical.html

1 2 3 **4** 5 6 7

Clinically oriented — Equal emphasis — Research oriented

What percentage of your faculty subscribes to or practices in each of the following orientations?

Psychodynamic/Psychoanalytic	80%
Applied behavioral analysis/Radical behavioral	0%
Family systems/Systems	10%
Existential/Phenomenological/Humanistic	0%
Cognitive/Cognitive-behavioral	10%

What percentage of students applying for internship last year was accepted into APA-accredited internships? 100%

What courses are required for incoming students to have completed prior to enrolling?
Psychology major

Are there courses you recommend that are not mandatory?
Psychometrics, health psychology, neuropsychology

GRE mean (M), cutoff (C), or preferred (P) score
Verbal 695 (P) Quantitative 710 (P)

GPA mean (M), cutoff (C), or preferred (P)
Overall GPA 3.8 (P) Psychology GPA 3.7 (P)

Number of applications/admission offers/incoming students in 2001
482 applied/0 admission offers/0 incoming

% of students receiving:
Tuition waiver only: 0%
Assistantship/fellowship only: 100%
Both tuition waiver & assistantship/fellowship: 100%

Approximate percentage of incoming students who entered with a B.A./B.S. only: 100% **Master's:** 0%

Approximate percentage of students who are Women: 82% **Ethnic Minority:** 2%

Average years to complete the doctoral program (including internship): 6.25 years

Research areas	**# Faculty**	**# Grants**
adult psychopathology	3	0
affective disorders	5	0
child clinical	2	0
clinical judgment	1	0
family research/systems	2	0
psychoanalytic theory	3	0
psychology and minority issues	1	0
psychotherapy process and outcome	1	0
schizophrenia	1	0
transference	2	0
verbal communication	2	0

Clinical opportunities
assessment
child therapy
family therapy
psychodynamic therapy
psychotherapy supervision

University of North Carolina at Chapel Hill

Department of Psychology
Davie Hall 013A
Chapel Hill, NC 27514
phone#: (919) 962-5082
fax#: (919) 962-2537
Web address: http://www.unc.edu/depts/clinpsy/

1 2 3 4 **5** 6 7

Clinically oriented — Equal emphasis — Research oriented

What percentage of your faculty subscribes to or practices in each of the following orientations?

Psychodynamic/Psychoanalytic	20%
Applied behavioral analysis/Radical behavioral	0%
Family systems/Systems	20%
Existential/Phenomenological/Humanistic	20%
Cognitive/Cognitive-behavioral	40%

What percentage of students applying for internship last year was accepted into APA-accredited internships? 91%

What courses are required for incoming students to have completed prior to enrolling?
A psychology major or its equivalent (8 or more courses). These courses must include training in statistics.

Are there courses you recommend that are not mandatory?
No

GRE mean (M), cutoff (C), or preferred (P) score
Verbal + Quantitative 1350 (M)

GPA mean (M), cutoff (C), or preferred (P)
Psychology GPA 3.5 (M) Junior/Senior GPA 3.5 (M)

Number of applications/admission offers/incoming students in 2001
400 applied/11 admission offers/9 incoming

% of students receiving:
Tuition waiver only: 3%
Assistantship/fellowship only: 0%
Both tuition waiver & assistantship/fellowship: 95%

Approximate percentage of incoming students who entered with a B.A./B.S. only: 85% **Master's:** 15%

Approximate percentage of students who are Women: 64% **Ethnic Minority:** 20%

Average years to complete the doctoral program (including internship): 6 years

Research areas	**# Faculty**	**# Grants**
adolescent drug use	1	0
anxiety disorders	1	1
assessment	1	0
behavioral medicine	1	2
children's peer relationships	2	2
family systems/therapy	1	2
marriage/couples	1	1
neuropsychology of aging	2	0
rural–migrant families	1	1
schizophrenia	1	1
self-esteem/minority	1	0

Clinical opportunities
assessment
behavioral medicine
cognitive-behavioral
developmental disabilities
family therapy
marital therapy
pediatric
psychodynamic
victim/battering/abuse

University of North Carolina at Greensboro

Department of Psychology
296 Eberhart Building
Greensboro, NC 27412
phone#: (336) 334-5817
e-mail: R_Nelson@uncg.edu
Web address: http://www.uncg.edu/psy/grad/clinical/clinmain.htm

1	2	3	**4**	5	6	7
Clinically oriented			Equal emphasis			Research oriented

What percentage of your faculty subscribes to or practices in each of the following orientations?

Psychodynamic/Psychoanalytic	0%
Applied behavioral analysis/Radical behavioral	14%
Family systems/Systems	0%
Existential/Phenomenological/Humanistic	0%
Cognitive/Cognitive-behavioral	86%

What percentage of students applying for internship last year was accepted into APA-accredited internships? 80%

What courses are required for incoming students to have completed prior to enrolling?
Equivalent of undergraduate major in psychology which typically includes introductory psychology, statistics, and 4 other courses in psychology

Are there courses you recommend that are not mandatory?
Courses in psychology as a natural science (e.g., physiological psychology), abnormal psychology, statistics, learning/cognitive psychology

GRE mean (M), cutoff (C), or preferred (P) score
Verbal 600 (P) Quantitative 600 (P)
Advanced Psychology 600 (P)

GPA mean (M), cutoff (C), or preferred (P)
Overall GPA 3.2 (P) Psychology GPA 3.2 (P)
Junior/Senior GPA 3.2 (P)

Number of applications/admission offers/incoming students in 2001
128 applied/7 admission offers/5 incoming

% of students receiving:
Tuition waiver only: 0%
Assistantship/fellowship only: 25%
Both tuition waiver & assistantship/fellowship: 75%

Approximate percentage of incoming students who entered with a B.A./B.S. only: 100% **Master's:** 0%

Approximate percentage of students who are Women: 64% **Ethnic Minority:** 13%

Average years to complete the doctoral program (including internship): 5.7 years

Research areas	**# Faculty**	**# Grants**
ADHD	1	1
adolescents' externalizing disorder	1	0
behavioral analysis	1	0
behavioral assessment	1	0
children's internalizing disorder	1	0
children's social relationships	2	2
depression	1	0
personality disorders	1	0
schizophrenia	1	1

Clinical opportunities
university-based community clinic
university counseling center

University of North Dakota

Department of Psychology
Box 8380
Grand Forks, ND 58202
phone#: (701) 777-3451
e-mail: alan_kinp@UND.nodak.edu
Web address: http://www.und.nodak.edu/dept/clinpsy/

1	2	3	4	**5**	6	7

Clinically oriented — Equal emphasis — Research oriented

What percentage of your faculty subscribes to or practices in each of the following orientations?

Psychodynamic/Psychoanalytic	0%
Applied behavioral analysis/Radical behavioral	33%
Family systems/Systems	0%
Existential/Phenomenological/Humanistic	0%
Cognitive/Cognitive-behavioral	67%

What percentage of students applying for internship last year was accepted into APA-accredited internships? 100%

What courses are required for incoming students to have completed prior to enrolling?
Developmental, abnormal psychology, statistics, experimental or research methods

Are there courses you recommend that are not mandatory?
A background in social and natural sciences

GRE mean (M), cutoff (C), or preferred (P) score
Verbal 500 (C) Quantitative 500 (C)
Advanced Psychology 500 (C)

GPA mean (M), cutoff (C), or preferred (P)
Overall GPA 3.2 (C) Psychology GPA 3.5 (P)

Number of applications/admission offers/incoming students in 2001
52 applied/15 admission offers/8 incoming

% of students receiving:
Tuition waiver only: 0%
Assistantship/fellowship only: 0%
Both tuition waiver & assistantship/fellowship: 100%

Approximate percentage of incoming students who entered with a B.A./B.S. only: 100% **Master's:** 0%

Approximate percentage of students who are Women: 68% **Ethnic Minority:** 17%

Average years to complete the doctoral program (including internship): 6 years

Research areas	# Faculty	# Grants
adult psychopathology	1	0
anxiety disorders	1	0
applied behavioral analysis	2	0
behavioral medicine	3	0
community psychology	1	0
cross-cultural psychology	1	1
friendship/relationships	1	0
gender roles	2	0
minority mental health	1	0
pain management/control	1	0
personality assessment	1	0
personality disorders	1	0
psychophysiology	3	0
relaxation/biofeedback	1	0
rural psychology	1	1
stress and coping	1	0
substance abuse	1	0
women's studies	2	0

Clinical opportunities
affective disorders
anxiety disorders
assessment
behavioral medicine
community psychology
hypnosis
interpersonal psychotherapy
marital/couples therapy
minority/cross-cultural
obsessive–compulsive disorder
personality disorders
rational-emotive therapy
rural psychology
substance abuse
victim/battering abuse

University of North Texas

Department of Psychology
Box 13587
Denton, TX 76203
phone#: (940) 565-2652
e-mail: AMYG@UNT.EDU
Web address: http://www.psyc.unt.edu/

1	2	3	**4**	5	6	7

Clinically oriented — Equal emphasis — Research oriented

What percentage of your faculty subscribes to or practices in each of the following orientations?

Psychodynamic/Psychoanalytic	25%
Applied behavioral analysis/Radical behavioral	0%
Family systems/Systems	25%
Existential/Phenomenological/Humanistic	37%
Cognitive/Cognitive-behavioral	37%

What percentage of students applying for internship last year was accepted into APA-accredited internships? 100%

What courses are required for incoming students to have completed prior to enrolling?
Statistics, experimental, learning, and history and systems

Are there courses you recommend that are not mandatory?
Physiological psychology, social psychology, abnormal psychology, personality, tests and measurements

GRE mean (M), cutoff (C), or preferred (P) score
Verbal 500 (P) Quantitative 500 (P)

GPA mean (M), cutoff (C), or preferred (P)
Overall GPA 3.0 (P) Psychology GPA 3.5 (P)
Junior/Senior GPA 3.5 (P)

Number of applications/admission offers/incoming students in 2001
85 applied/17 admission offers/10 incoming

% of students receiving:
Tuition waiver only: 0%
Assistantship/fellowship only: 35%
Both tuition waiver & assistantship/fellowship: 25%

Approximate percentage of incoming students who entered with a B.A./B.S. only: 88% **Master's:** 12%

Approximate percentage of students who are Women: 75% **Ethnic Minority:** 15%

Average years to complete the doctoral program (including internship): 6 years

Research areas	# Faculty	# Grants
abuse	2	0
AIDS	1	0
affect management	1	0
aging	1	1
children	1	1
disaster intervention	2	0
forensics	2	1
malingering	2	2
neuropsychology	1	0
posttraumatic stress disorder	2	1
schizophrenia	2	1
stress	2	1

Clinical opportunities
attention-deficit disorder
children
depression
forensic psychology
neuropsychology
posttraumatic stress disorder

Northern Illinois University

Department of Psychology
DeKalb, IL 60115
phone#: (815) 753-0772
e-mail: MLOVEJOY@NIU.EDU
Web address: http://www.niu.edu/acad/psych/clinpsych.html

1 2 3 **4** 5 6 7

Clinically oriented — Equal emphasis — Research oriented

What percentage of your faculty subscribes to or practices in each of the following orientations?

Psychodynamic/Psychoanalytic	0%
Applied behavioral analysis/Radical behavioral	50%
Family systems/Systems	25%
Existential/Phenomenological/Humanistic	12%
Cognitive/Cognitive-behavioral	75%

What percentage of students applying for internship last year was accepted into APA-accredited internships? 83%

What courses are required for incoming students to have completed prior to enrolling?
None

Are there courses you recommend that are not mandatory?
Statistics, research methods, laboratory course, history

GRE mean (M), cutoff (C), or preferred (P) score
Verbal 600 (P) Quantitative 600 (P)

GPA mean (M), cutoff (C), or preferred (P)
Overall GPA 3.0 (P) Psychology GPA 3.5 (P)

Number of applications/admission offers/incoming students in 2001
111 applied/23 admission offers/8 incoming

% of students receiving:
Tuition waiver only: 0%
Assistantship/fellowship only: 0%
Both tuition waiver & assistantship/fellowship: 100%

Approximate percentage of incoming students who entered with a B.A./B.S. only: 75% **Master's:** 25%

Approximate percentage of students who are Women: 75% **Ethnic Minority:** 25%

Average years to complete the doctoral program (including internship): 6.8 years

Research areas	# Faculty	# Grants
adolescents	3	0
adult psychopathology	3	1
anxiety disorders	2	0
child sexual abuse	3	2
developmental psychopathology	5	1
emotion and psychotherapy	1	1
health psychology	3	0
pediatric psychology	1	0
physical abuse	3	1
prevention	3	3
psychometrics	4	2
psychotherapy	1	1
sexual aggression	1	0
suicide	1	0

Clinical opportunities
ADHD clinic
anxiety disorders
assessment
child psychotherapy
couples therapy
developmental disabilities
family therapy
group therapy
substance abuse
victim/battering/abuse

Northwestern University

Department of Psychology
102 Swift Hall, 2029 Sheridan Road
Evanston, IL 60208-2710
phone#: (847) 491-5190
e-mail: mineka@northwestern.edu
Web address: http://www.psych.northwestern.edu/Academics/Clinical/Clinical.htm

1	2	3	4	5	6	**7**
Clinically oriented			Equal emphasis			Research oriented

What percentage of your faculty subscribes to or practices in each of the following orientations?

Psychodynamic/Psychoanalytic	10%
Applied behavioral analysis/Radical behavioral	0%
Family systems/Systems	10%
Existential/Phenomenological/Humanistic	0%
Cognitive/Cognitive-behavioral	80%

What percentage of students applying for internship last year was accepted into APA-accredited internships? 100%

What courses are required for incoming students to have completed prior to enrolling?
None

Are there courses you recommend that are not mandatory?
Psychology major, undergraduate statistics

GRE mean (M), cutoff (C), or preferred (P) score
Verbal 700 (M) Quantitative 725 (M) Analytical 750 (M)
Advanced Psychology 750 (M)

GPA mean (M), cutoff (C), or preferred (P)
Overall GPA 3.5 (P) Psychology GPA 3.75 (P)
Junior/Senior GPA 4.0 (P)

Number of applications/admission offers/incoming students in 2001
100 applied/7 admission offers/3 incoming

% of students receiving:
Tuition waiver only: 0%
Assistantship/fellowship only: 0%
Both tuition waiver & assistantship/fellowship: 100%

Approximate percentage of incoming students who entered with a B.A./B.S. only: 90% **Master's:** 10%

Approximate percentage of students who are Women: 80% **Ethnic Minority:** 10%

Average years to complete the doctoral program (including internship): 6 years

Research areas	**# Faculty**	**# Grants**
anxiety	2	0
behavioral genetics	1	0
cognitive functioning	1	0
depression	1	0
personality	2	2
psychotherapy	1	1
schizophrenia	1	1

Clinical opportunities
anxiety disorders
behavioral medicine
couples
crisis intervention
depression
family
neuropsychology
psychosis

Northwestern University Medical School

Department of Psychiatry and Behavioral Sciences
Division of Psychology
Abbott Hall, Suite 1205
710 North Lakeshore Drive
Chicago, IL 60611
phone#: (312) 908-8262
e-mail: j-johnson6@northwestern.edu
Web address: http://www.clin.psych.NWU.edu

1	2	3	**4**	5	6	7
Clinically oriented			Equal emphasis			Research oriented

What percentage of your faculty subscribes to or practices in each of the following orientations?

Psychodynamic/Psychoanalytic	55%
Applied behavioral analysis/Radical behavioral	0%
Family systems/Systems	0%
Existential/Phenomenological/Humanistic	10%
Cognitive/Cognitive-behavioral	35%

What percentage of students applying for internship last year was accepted into APA-accredited internships? 100%

What courses are required for incoming students to have completed prior to enrolling?
Statistics, research designs, experimental, abnormal

Are there courses you recommend that are not mandatory?
Advanced statistics

GRE mean (M), cutoff (C), or preferred (P) score
Verbal 75th percentile (P)
Quantitative 75th percentile (P)
Advanced Psychology 75th percentile (P)

GPA mean (M), cutoff (C), or preferred (P)
Overall GPA 3.2 (P)

Number of applications/admission offers/incoming students in 2001
174 applied/12 admission offers/5 incoming

% of students receiving:
Tuition waiver only: 0%
Assistantship/fellowship only: 0%
Half tuition & research assistantship: 25%
Both tuition waiver & assistantship/fellowship: 75%

Approximate percentage of incoming students who entered with a B.A./B.S. only: 80% **Master's:** 20%

Approximate percentage of students who are
Women: 70% **Ethnic Minority:** 15%

Average years to complete the doctoral program (including internship): 6 years

Research areas	# Faculty	# Grants
adult psychopathology	1	0
aging	1	0
chronic mental illness	3	1
eating disorders	2	2
mental health services and policy	2	5
neuropsychology	2	1
personality	1	0
psychosocial oncology	1	1
psychotherapy process and outcome	1	0
sexuality	2	0

Clinical opportunities
adult psychiatric clinic
behavioral medicine
chronic mental illness
chronic pain
developmental disorders
eating disorders
neuropsychology
student mental health

Nova Southeastern University (Ph.D.)

Dean, Center for Psychological Studies
3301 College Avenue
Fort Lauderdale, FL 33314
phone#: (954) 262-5700
e-mail: cpsinfo@nova.edu
Web address: http://www.cps.nova.edu

1	2	3	4	**5**	6	7
Clinically oriented			Equal emphasis			Research oriented

What percentage of your faculty subscribes to or practices in each of the following orientations?

Psychodynamic/Psychoanalytic	22%
Applied behavioral analysis/Radical behavioral	3%
Family systems/Systems	9%
Existential/Phenomenological/Humanistic	3%
Cognitive/Cognitive-behavioral	63%

What percentage of students applying for internship last year was accepted into APA-accredited internships? 91%

What courses are required for incoming students to have completed prior to enrolling?
18 credits in psychology and 3 credits in statistics

Are there courses you recommend that are not mandatory?
Calculus, intermediate statistics, experimental psychology, and hard rather than soft courses in psychology, biology, and philosophy

GRE mean (M), cutoff (C), or preferred (P) score
Verbal 563 (M) Quantitative 599 (M) Analytical 635 (M)
Advanced Psychology 631 (M)

GPA mean (M), cutoff (C), or preferred (P)
Overall GPA 3.0 (C), 3.49 (M) Graduate GPA 3.5 (C)

Number of applications/admission offers/incoming students in 2001
— applied/— admission offers/17 incoming

% of students receiving:
Tuition waiver only: 0%
Assistantship/fellowship only: 24%
Both tuition waiver & assistantship/fellowship: 24%

Approximate percentage of incoming students who entered with a B.A./B.S. only: 84% **Master's:** 16%

Approximate percentage of students who are
Women: 84% **Ethnic Minority:** 16%

Average years to complete the doctoral program (including internship): 5 years

Research areas	# Faculty	# Grants
AIDS	1	1
alcohol/substance abuse	4	2
anxiety disorders	1	0
behavior therapy	8	0
biofeedback	2	0
child/adolescent depression	2	0
child/adolescent psychotherapy	3	0
child neuropsychology	4	0
community mental health	4	0
cross-cultural counseling	2	0
domestic/interpersonal violence	2	0
forensic psychology	3	0
gerontology	2	1
health psychology	7	1
long-term mental illness	2	0
MMPI-2	1	0
neuropsychology	5	0
posttraumatic stress disorder	4	1
psychoanalysis	2	0
psychology of men	1	0
survivors of sexual abuse/assault	2	0
trauma and victimization	7	0

Clinical opportunities
anxiety disorders
behavioral modification
biofeedback
child/adolescent assessment and treatment
child/adolescent depression
community support services
crisis assessment and intervention
day treatment
depression
dual diagnosis
family and multifamily therapy
forensic evaluation and testimony
geriatric
group therapy
interpersonal violence
medication management
multilingual services

neuropsychological assessment and evaluation
pain management
parenting skills training
psychodynamic psychotherapy
psychological consultation
psychological testing
serious emotional disturbance
skills treatment and enhancement program (STEP)
stress management
student counseling
substance abuse

Nova Southeastern University (Psy.D.)

Dean, Center for Psychological Studies
3301 College Avenue
Fort Lauderdale, FL 33314
phone#: (954) 262-5700
e-mail: cpsinfo@cps.acast.nova.edu
web page: www.cps.nova.edu

1	**2**	3	4	5	6	7

Clinically oriented — Equal emphasis — Research oriented

What percentage of your faculty subscribes to or practices in each of the following orientations?

Psychodynamic/Psychoanalytic	22%
Applied behavioral analysis/Radical behavioral	3%
Family systems/Systems	9%
Existential/Phenomenological/Humanistic	3%
Cognitive/Cognitive-behavioral	63%

What percentage of students applying for internship last year was accepted into APA-accredited internships? 60%

What courses are required for incoming students to have completed prior to enrolling?
18 credits in psychology and 3 credits in statistics

Are there courses you recommend that are not mandatory?
Experimental psychology; hard rather than soft courses in psychology, biology, and philosophy

GRE mean (M), cutoff (C), or preferred (P) score
Verbal 493 (M) Quantitative 530 (M) Analytical 557 (M)
Advanced Psychology 569 (M)

GPA mean (M), cutoff (C), or preferred (P)
Overall GPA 3.0 (C), 3.4 (M) Graduate GPA 3.5 (C)

Number of applications/admission offers/incoming students in 2001
— applied/— admission offers/71 incoming

% of students receiving:
Tuition waiver only: 0%
Assistantship/fellowship only: 24%
Both tuition waiver & assistantship/fellowship: 24%

Approximate percentage of incoming students who entered with a B.A./B.S. only: 96% **Master's:** 4%

Approximate percentage of students who are Women: 85% **Ethnic Minority:** 21%

Average years to complete the doctoral program (including internship): 4 years

Research areas	# Faculty	# Grants
AIDS	1	1
alcohol/substance abuse	4	2
anxiety disorders	1	0
behavior therapy	8	0
biofeedback	2	0
child/adolescent depression	2	0
child/adolescent psychotherapy	3	0
child neuropsychology	4	0
cross-cultural counseling	2	0
domestic/interpersonal violence	2	0
forensic psychology	3	0
gerontology	2	1
health psychology	7	0
long-term mental illness	2	0
MMPI-2	1	0
neuropsychology	5	0
posttraumatic stress disorder	4	1
psychoanalysis	2	0
psychology of men	1	0
survivors of sexual abuse/assault	2	0
trauma and victimization	7	0

Clinical opportunities
alcohol and other drug abuse
anxiety disorders
behavioral modification
biofeedback
child/adolescent traumatic stress and depression
community support services
crisis assessment and intervention
day treatment
depression
dual diagnosis and day treatment
family and multifamily treatment
forensic evaluation and testimony
geriatric residential treatment
group therapy
interpersonal violence
medication management
multilingual services
neuropsychological assessment and evaluation
pain management
parenting skills and training
psychodynamic psychotherapy
psychological consultation
psychological testing
serious emotional disturbance
skills treatment and enhancement program (STEP)
stress management
student counseling
trauma resolution

Ohio State University

Department of Psychology
142 Townshend Hall
1885 Neil Avenue Mall
Columbus, OH 43210
phone#: (614) 292-4112
e-mail: sexton.3@osu.edu
Web address: http://www.psy.ohio_state.edu/

1 2 3 4 5 6 **7**

Clinically oriented — Equal emphasis — Research oriented

What percentage of your faculty subscribes to or practices in each of the following orientations?

Psychodynamic/Psychoanalytic	14%
Applied behavioral analysis/Radical behavioral	0%
Family systems/Systems	0%
Existential/Phenomenological/Humanistic	0%
Cognitive/Cognitive-behavioral	86%

What percentage of students applying for internship last year was accepted into APA-accredited internships? 100%

What courses are required for incoming students to have completed prior to enrolling?
Experimental psychology, abnormal psychology, statistics, personality

Are there courses you recommend that are not mandatory?
Psychophysiology

GRE mean (M), cutoff (C), or preferred (P) score
Verbal 600 (P) Quantitative 600 (P)
Advanced Psychology 600 (P)

GPA mean (M), cutoff (C), or preferred (P)
Psychology GPA 3.5 (P)
Junior/Senior GPA 3.5 (P)

Number of applications/admission offers/incoming students in 2001
118 applied/12 admission offers/8 incoming

% of students receiving:
Tuition waiver only: 0%
Assistantship/fellowship only: 0%
Both tuition waiver & assistantship/fellowship: 100%

Approximate percentage of incoming students who entered with a B.A./B.S. only: 85% **Master's:** 15%

Approximate percentage of students who are Women: 74% **Ethnic Minority:** 20%

Average years to complete the doctoral program (including internship): 6 years

Research areas	# Faculty	# Grants
anxiety disorders	1	2
cardiovascular health	2	3
child psychopathology	1	1
childhood anxiety	1	1
eating disorders	1	0
oncology	1	2
personality	1	0

Clinical opportunities
anxiety disorder
autism
childhood anxiety
childhood depression
crisis intervention
eating disorders
family
gerontology
health psychology
neuropsychology
oncology
sex therapy

Ohio University

Department of Psychology
Athens, Ohio 45701-2979
phone#: (740) 593-1707
Web address: http://www.ohiou.edu/~psydept/programs/clinicalpsy.htm

1 2 3 **4** 5 6 7

Clinically oriented — Equal emphasis — Research oriented

What percentage of your faculty subscribes to or practices in each of the following orientations?

Psychodynamic/Psychoanalytic	20%
Applied behavioral analysis/Radical behavioral	0%
Family systems/Systems	30%
Existential/Phenomenological/Humanistic	0%
Cognitive/Cognitive-behavioral	50%

What percentage of students applying for internship last year was accepted into APA-accredited internships? 100%

What courses are required for incoming students to have completed prior to enrolling?
27 quarter hours of undergraduate psychology, introductory psychology, experimental psychology, statistics

Are there courses you recommend that are not mandatory?
Computer science, abnormal psychology, personality

GRE mean (M), cutoff (C), or preferred (P) score
Verbal + Quantitative 1100 (P)

GPA mean (M), cutoff (C), or preferred (P)
Overall GPA 3.5 (C) Psychology GPA 3.5 (C)

Number of applications/admission offers/incoming students in 2001
139 applied/40 admission offers/11 incoming

% of students receiving:
Tuition waiver only: 0%
Assistantship/fellowship only: 0
Both tuition waiver & assistantship/fellowship: 100%

Approximate percentage of incoming students who entered with a B.A./B.S. only: 73% **Master's:** 27%

Approximate percentage of students who are
Women: 70% **Ethnic Minority:** 5%

Average years to complete the doctoral program (including internship): 6 years

Research areas	**# Faculty**	**# Grants**
adult psychopathology	2	0
family and child	3	0
health psychology	4	3
psychotherapy	2	2
sexual assault	1	2

Clinical opportunities
adult inpatient and outpatient
child and family
neuropsychological assessment
pain management
substance abuse
tension headaches

Oklahoma State University

Department of Psychology
215 North Murray Hall
Stillwater, OK 74078
phone#: (405) 744-6983
e-mail: FRANKLC@OKSTATE.EDU
Web address: http://psychology.okstate.edu/pages/clinical.html

1 2 3 4 **5** 6 7

Clinically oriented — Equal emphasis — Research oriented

What percentage of your faculty subscribes to or practices in each of the following orientations?

Psychodynamic/Psychoanalytic	0%
Applied behavioral analysis/Radical behavioral	12.5%
Family systems/Systems	12.5%
Existential/Phenomenological/Humanistic	0%
Cognitive/Cognitive-behavioral	75%

What percentage of students applying for internship last year was accepted into APA-accredited internships? 100%

What courses are required for incoming students to have completed prior to enrolling?
Introductory psychology, statistics, experimental psychology

Are there courses you recommend that are not mandatory?
Abnormal psychology, history and systems

GRE mean (M), cutoff (C), or preferred (P) score
Verbal 600 (P) Quantitative 550 (P)
Advanced Psychology 550 (P)

GPA mean (M), cutoff (C), or preferred (P)
Overall GPA 3.2 (P)

Number of applications/admission offers/incoming students in 2001
96 applied/11 admission offers/9 incoming

% of students receiving:
Tuition waiver only: 0%
Assistantship/fellowship only: 0%
Both tuition waiver & assistantship/fellowship: 100%

Approximate percentage of incoming students who entered with a B.A./B.S. only: 100% **Master's:** 0%

Approximate percentage of students who are
Women: 66% **Ethnic Minority:** 34%

Average years to complete the doctoral program (including internship): 6.4 years

Research areas	**# Faculty**	**# Grants**
anxiety disorders	1	0
health psychology	2	0
pediatric psychology	2	0
sexual abuse	1	0
substance abuse	1	0

Clinical opportunities
anxiety disorder
behavioral medicine
family therapy
marital therapy

University of Oregon

Department of Psychology
Eugene, OR 97403
phone#: (541) 346-5060
e-mail: gradsec@psych.uoregon.edu
Web address: http://psychweb.uoregon.edu/

1 2 3 4 **5** 6 7

Clinically oriented — Equal emphasis — Research oriented

What percentage of your faculty subscribes to or practices in each of the following orientations?

Psychodynamic/Psychoanalytic	0%
Applied behavioral analysis/Radical behavioral	20%
Family systems/Systems	20%
Existential/Phenomenological/Humanistic	0%
Cognitive/Cognitive-behavioral	55%

What percentage of students applying for internship last year was accepted into APA-accredited internships? 100%

What courses are required for incoming students to have completed prior to enrolling?
Good background in psychology

Are there courses you recommend that are not mandatory?
Research, statistics or math background

GRE mean (M), cutoff (C), or preferred (P) score
All of GRE scores should be in the high 600 or 700 range or higher

GPA mean (M), cutoff (C), or preferred (P)
Overall GPA 3.5 (P)

Number of applications/admission offers/incoming students in 2001
309 applied/9 admission offers/5 incoming

% of students receiving:
Tuition waiver only: 0%
Assistantship/fellowship only: 0%
Both tuition waiver & assistantship/fellowship: 100%

Approximate percentage of incoming students who entered with a B.A./B.S. only: 75% **Master's:** 25%

Approximate percentage of students who are Women: 60% **Ethnic Minority:** 16%

Average years to complete the doctoral program (including internship): 5 years

Research areas	# Faculty	# Grants
affective disorders	3	2
anxiety disorders	2	2
developmental psychopathology	2	1
life stress	1	0
neuropsychology	2	2

Clinical opportunities
anxiety disorders
depression
marital
neuropsychology

University of Ottawa

School of Psychology
Lamoureux Hall
145 Jean–Jaques Lussier
Ottawa, Ontario K1N 6N5, Canada
phone#: (613) 562-5801
Web address: http://aix1.uottawa.ca/academic/socsci/psych/

1	2	3	**4**	5	6	7

Clinically oriented — Equal emphasis — Research oriented

What percentage of your faculty subscribes to or practices in each of the following orientations?

Psychodynamic/Psychoanalytic	5%
Applied behavioral analysis/Radical behavioral	0%
Family systems/Systems	20%
Existential/Phenomenological/Humanistic	25%
Cognitive/Cognitive-behavioral	50%

What percentage of students applying for internship last year was accepted into APA-accredited internships? 80%

What courses are required for incoming students to have completed prior to enrolling?
Canadian Honors B.A. degree or its equivalent (60 credits in psychology, plus research experience similar to the honors thesis)

Are there courses you recommend that are not mandatory?
History and systems

GRE mean (M), cutoff (C), or preferred (P) score
GRE is not required for admission

GPA mean (M), cutoff (C), or preferred (P)
Overall GPA 8 on a scale of 10

Number of applications/admission offers/incoming students in 2001
125 applied/14 admission offers/9 incoming

% of students receiving:
Tuition waiver only: 0%
Assistantship/fellowship only: 20%
Both tuition waiver & assistantship/fellowship: 50%

Approximate percentage of incoming students who entered with a B.A./B.S. only: 85% **Master's:** 15%

Approximate percentage of students who are Women: 82% **Ethnic Minority:** —

Average years to complete the doctoral program (including internship): 6.5 years

Research areas	# Faculty	# Grants
adult psychopathology	1	0
behavior problems in children	3	2
family functioning	1	1
forensic psychology	1	0
health psychology	1	0
marital therapy	1	0
psychotherapy and counselling	3	0
social development of children	3	2

Clinical opportunities
—

Pacific Graduate School of Psychology

Department of Clinical Psychology
935 East Meadow
Palo Alto, CA 94303
phone#: (415) 843-3419
e-mail: admissions@pysp.edu
Web address: http://www.pgsp.edu/njacademic.html

1	2	3	**4**	5	6	7

Clinically oriented — Equal emphasis — Research oriented

What percentage of your faculty subscribes to or practices in each of the following orientations?

Psychodynamic/Psychoanalytic	40%
Applied behavioral analysis/Radical behavioral	0%
Family systems/Systems	20%
Existential/Phenomenological/Humanistic	0%
Cognitive/Cognitive-behavioral	40%

What percentage of students applying for internship last year was accepted into APA-accredited internships? 92%

What courses are required for incoming students to have completed prior to enrolling?
Statistics, personality or abnormal, developmental psychology, physiological psychology

Are there courses you recommend that are not mandatory?
Solid academic background

GRE mean (M), cutoff (C), or preferred (P) score
Verbal + Quantitative 1130 (P)

GPA mean (M), cutoff (C), or preferred (P)
Undergraduate GPA 3.0 (P) Graduate GPA 3.3 (P)

Number of applications/admission offers/incoming students in 2001
253 applied/149 admission offers/36 incoming

% of students receiving:
Tuition waiver only: 0%
Assistantship/fellowship only: 19%
Both tuition waiver & assistantship/fellowship: 0%

Approximate percentage of incoming students who entered with a B.A./B.S. only: 70% **Master's:** 30%

Approximate percentage of students who are Women: 69% **Ethnic Minority:** 25%

Average years to complete the doctoral program (including internship): 6.5 years

Research areas	# Faculty	# Grants
adult psychopathology	7	0
assessment	5	0
child and adolescent development	4	0
culture	4	0
health psychology	2	0
neuropsychology	2	0
substance abuse	1	0

Clinical opportunities
AIDS
assessment
child psychology
family
health psychology
minority
neuropsychology

Pacific University (Psy.D.)

Department of Clinical Psychology
School of Professional Psychology
2004 Pacific Avenue
Forest Grove, OR 97116
phone#: (503) 359-2240
e-mail: admissions@pacificu.edu (Admissions)
Web address: http://www.pacificu.edu/academics/spp.html

1 2 3 **4** 5 6 7

Clinically oriented — Equal emphasis — Research oriented

What percentage of your faculty subscribes to or practices in each of the following orientations?

Psychodynamic/Psychoanalytic	25%
Applied behavioral analysis	25%
Family systems/Systems	10%
Existential/Phenomenological/Humanistic	5%
Cognitive/Cognitive-behavioral	65%

What percentage of students applying for internship last year was accepted into APA-accredited internships? 30%

What courses are required for incoming students to have completed prior to enrolling?
A strong undergraduate background in psychology

Are there courses you recommend that are not mandatory?
No

GRE mean (M), cutoff (C), or preferred (P) score
Verbal 550 (P) Quantitative 550 (P) Analytical 550 (P)
Advanced Psychology 600 (P)

GPA mean (M), cutoff (C), or preferred (P)
Junior/Senior GPA 3.0 (P)

Number of applications/admission offers/incoming students in 2001
122 applied/73 admission offers/38 incoming

% of students receiving:
Tuition waiver only: 19%
Assistantship/fellowship only: 18%
Both tuition waiver & assistantship/fellowship: 4%

Approximate percentage of incoming students who entered with a B.A./B.S. only: 76% **Master's:** 24%

Approximate percentage of students who are Women: 65% **Ethnic Minority:** 14%

Average years to complete the doctoral program (including internship): 5.5 years

Research areas	# Faculty	# Grants
abuse	2	1
anger arousal	2	0
assessment	6	0
children	5	1
gender roles	2	0
minority/cross-cultural	2	0
posttraumatic stress disorders	1	0
psychology of women	3	1
supervision	2	0

Clinical opportunities
The school maintains a large psychological service center in downtown Portland.

University of Pennsylvania

Department of Psychology
3815 Walnut Street
Philadelphia, PA 19104
phone#: (215) 898-5663
e-mail: ruth@Psych.upenn.edu
Web address: http://www.psych.upenn.edu/grad.html

1 2 3 4 5 **6** 7

Clinically oriented — Equal emphasis — Research oriented

What percentage of your faculty subscribes to or practices in each of the following orientations?

Psychodynamic/Psychoanalytic	16%
Applied behavioral analysis/Radical behavioral	16%
Family systems/Systems	0%
Existential/Phenomenological/Humanistic	16%
Cognitive/Cognitive-behavioral	50%

What percentage of students applying for internship last year was accepted into APA-accredited internships? 100%

What courses are required for incoming students to have completed prior to enrolling?
None

Are there courses you recommend that are not mandatory?
Statistics

GRE mean (M), cutoff (C), or preferred (P)
Verbal 680 (P) Quantitative 700 (P) Analytical 700 (P)
Advanced Psychology 700 (P)

GPA mean (M), cutoff (C), or preferred (P)
Overall GPA 3.5 (P) Psychology GPA 3.5 (P)

Number of applications/admission offers/incoming students in 2001
200 applied/7 admission offers/3 incoming

% of students receiving:
Tuition waiver only: 0%
Assistantship/fellowship only: 0%
Both tuition waiver & assistantship/fellowship: 100%

Approximate percentage of incoming students who entered with a B.A./B.S. only: 80% **Master's:** 20%

Approximate percentage of students who are Women: 50% **Ethnic Minority:** 15%

Average years to complete the doctoral program (including internship): 6 years

Research areas	# Faculty	# Grants
anxiety disorders	1	3
depression	2	3
family/community	1	1
psychodynamic treatment	1	2
psychopharmacology	1	1
substance abuse	1	1

Clinical opportunities
cognitive therapy
neuropsychology
psychodynamic therapy

Pennsylvania State University

Department of Psychology
417 Bruce V. Moore Building
University Park, PA 16802
phone#: (814) 863-1751
e-mail: kac8@psu.edu
Web address: http://psych.la.psu.edu/clinical.htm

1	2	3	**4**	5	6	7
Clinically oriented			Equal emphasis			Research oriented

What percentage of your faculty subscribes to or practices in each of the following orientations?

Psychodynamic/Psychoanalytic	30%
Applied behavioral analysis/Radical behavioral	0%
Family systems/Systems	20%
Existential/Phenomenological/Humanistic	10%
Cognitive/Cognitive-behavioral	40%

What percentage of students applying for internship last year was accepted into APA-accredited internships? 90%

What courses are required for incoming students to have completed prior to enrolling?
No course requirements. Broad psychology background preferred.

Are there courses you recommend that are not mandatory?
Statistics and methodology

GRE mean (M), cutoff (C), or preferred (P) score
Verbal 600 (P) Quantitative 600 (P)

GPA mean (M), cutoff (C), or preferred (P)
Overall GPA 3.5 (P) Psychology GPA 3.7 (P)
Junior/Senior GPA 3.7 (P)

Number of applications/admission offers/incoming students in 2001
215 applied/21 admission offers/13 incoming

% of students receiving:
Tuition waiver only: 0%
Assistantship/fellowship only: 0%
Both tuition waiver & assistantship/fellowship: 99%

Approximate percentage of incoming students who entered with a B.A./B.S. only: 90% **Master's:** 10%

Approximate percentage of students who are Women: 65% **Ethnic Minority:** 35%

Average years to complete the doctoral program (including internship): 6.7 years

Research areas	# Faculty	# Grants
AIDS	1	0
adult psychopathology	5	3
affective disorders	3	0
anxiety disorders	3	1
behavioral medicine	2	0
child clinical/child psychopathology	4	2
cognition/information processing	1	0
cross-cultural psychology	1	1
developmental/childhood and adolescence	4	2
developmental disabilities	1	0
emotions	3	0
family research/therapy	2	0
forensic	1	0
hypnosis	1	0
marriage/couples	1	0
minority mental health	2	0
neuropsychology	3	0
parent–child interactions	4	0

personality assessment	2	0
personality development	2	0
personality disorders	2	0
psychoanalysis/psychodynamics	3	0
psychology of religion	1	0
psychophysiology	3	1
psychotherapy process and outcome	3	2
relaxation/biofeedback	1	0
rural psychology	1	0
violence/abuse	1	0

Clinical opportunities
Since we serve as a mental health center for this area, we offer a broad range of clinical experiences involving a variety of psychopathologies. The only significant area in which we do not offer experience in our clinic is with drug and alcohol dependence.

Pepperdine University (Psy.D.)

Department of Psychology
Graduate School of Education and Psychology
400 Corporate Pointe
Culver City, CA 90230
phone#: (310) 568-5600
e-mail: csaunder@pepperdine.edu
Web address: http://gsep.pepperdine.edu/gsep

1 2 **3** 4 5 6 7

Clinically oriented — Equal emphasis — Research oriented

What percentage of your faculty subscribes to or practices in each of the following orientations?

Psychodynamic/Psychoanalytic	20%
Applied behavioral analysis/Radical behavioral	4%
Family systems/Systems	12%
Existential/Phenomenological/Humanistic	12%
Cognitive/Cognitive-behavioral	52%

What percentage of students applying for internship last year was accepted into APA-accredited internships? 85%

What courses are required for incoming students to have completed prior to enrolling?
Applicants for doctoral study should possess a master's degree in psychology or a closely related field that reflects a master's-level foundation of knowledge in the following domains: biological aspects of behavior; cognitive and affective aspects of behavior; social aspects of behavior; psychological measurement; research methodology; and techniques of data analysis.

Are there courses you recommend that are not mandatory?
No

GRE mean (M), cutoff (C), or preferred (P) score
Verbal 600 (P) Quantitative 600 (P)
Advanced Psychology 600 (P)

GPA mean (M), cutoff (C), or preferred (P)
Overall GPA 3.16 (M) Master's GPA 3.85 (M)

Number of applications/admission offers/incoming students in 2001
95 applied/46 admission offers/26 incoming

% of students receiving:
Partial scholarship: 80%
Assistantship/fellowship only: 2%
Both tuition waiver & assistantship/fellowship: 0%

Approximate percentage of incoming students who entered with a B.A./B.S. only: 0% **Master's:** 100%

Approximate percentage of students who are Women: 74% **Ethnic Minority:** 20%

Average years to complete the doctoral program (including internship): 4.8 years

Research areas	# Faculty	# Grants
ADHD	—	—
program evaluation	—	—
psychotherapy process and outcome	—	—
PTSD	—	—

Clinical opportunities
ADHD
adolescence
AIDS
aging
assessment
behavior therapy
behavioral medicine (oncology)
child clinical
chronically mentally ill
community
family
forensic
group
inpatient
marital
neuropsychology
PTSD
rehabilitation
religious
schizophrenia
substance abuse

University of Pittsburgh

Department of Psychology
455 Langley Hall
Pittsburgh, PA 15260
phone#: (412) 624-4502
e-mail: psych+@pitt.edu
Web address: http://www.pitt.edu/~psych

1 2 3 4 5 **6** 7

Clinically oriented — Equal emphasis — Research oriented

What percentage of your faculty subscribes to or practices in each of the following orientations?

Psychodynamic/Psychoanalytic	0%
Applied behavioral analysis/Radical behavioral	0%
Family systems/Systems	30%

Existential/Phenomenological/Humanistic	0%
Cognitive/Cognitive-behavioral	70%

What percentage of students applying for internship last year was accepted into APA-accredited internships? 100%

What courses are required for incoming students to have completed prior to enrolling?
None

Are there courses you recommend that are not mandatory?
Basic psychology courses, including research methods and statistics; background in biology, math, and computer science

GRE mean (M), cutoff (C), or preferred (P) score
Verbal 650 (M) Quantitative 690 (M) Analytical 695 (M)
Advanced Psychology 727 (M)

GPA mean (M), cutoff (C), or preferred (P)
Overall GPA 3.5 (P), 3.7 (M) Psychology GPA 3.5 (P)
Junior/Senior GPA 3.5 (P)

Number of applications/admission offers/incoming students in 2001
212 applied/13 admission offers/7 incoming

% of students receiving:
Tuition waiver only: 0%
Assistantship/fellowship only: 0%
Both tuition waiver & assistantship/fellowship: 100%

Approximate percentage of incoming students who entered with a B.A./B.S. only: 90% **Master's:** 10%

Approximate percentage of students who are Women: 72% **Ethnic Minority:** 11%

Average years to complete the doctoral program (including internship): 8 years

Research areas	# Faculty	# Grants
adult psychopathology	7	17
attention deficit disorder	1	2
behavioral genetics	2	3
behavioral medicine/health psychology	9	30
behavioral oncology	2	2
cardiovascular behavioral medicine	3	11
child/family/developmental psychopathology	7	18
child clinical	7	18
developmental	7	18
disaster/trauma	1	1
emotion	1	4
mood disorders	4	7
obesity/eating disorders	1	3
parent–child interactions	4	7
posttraumatic stress disorder	1	1
psychoneuroimmunology	3	5
schizophrenia	1	1
stress and coping	2	5
substance abuse/addictions/ psychopharmacology	5	15

Clinical opportunities
affective disorders/depression
anxiety disorders
assessment (preschool, school age, and adult)
attention-deficit disorder
behavioral medicine
child treatment
cognitive-behavioral therapy
conduct disorder
eating disorders
emergency room assessment
family therapy
gay/lesbian
inpatient
neuropsychological assessment
pain management
parent training
personality disorders
posttraumatic stress disorder
schizophrenia
smoking cessation
substance abuse
victim/violence/sexual abuse
weight management

Purdue University

Department of Psychological Sciences
West Lafayette, IN 47907
phone#: (765) 494-6982
e-mail: jcc@psych.purdue.edu
Web address: http://www.psych.purdue.edu/Clinical/index.html

1 2 3 4 **5** 6 7

Clinically oriented — Equal emphasis — Research oriented

What percentage of your faculty subscribes to or practices in each of the following orientations?

Psychodynamic/Psychoanalytic	10%
Applied behavioral analysis/Radical behavioral	0%
Family systems/Systems	0%
Existential/Phenomenological/Humanistic	0%
Cognitive/Cognitive-behavioral	90%

What percentage of students applying for internship last year was accepted into APA-accredited internships? 100%

What courses are required for incoming students to have completed prior to enrolling?
Some background in psychology, especially methodology and statistics

Are there courses you recommend that are not mandatory?
Science and mathematics, statistics and research experience with a university researcher

GRE mean (M), cutoff (C), or preferred (P) score
Verbal + Quantitative 1100

GPA mean (M), cutoff (C), or preferred (P)
Overall GPA 3.2 out of a 4.0 scale

Number of applications/admission offers/incoming students in 2001
230 applied/10 admission offers/8 incoming

% of students receiving:
Tuition waiver only: 0%
Assistantship/fellowship only: 0%
Both tuition waiver & assistantship/fellowship: 100%

Approximate percentage of incoming students who entered with a B.A./B.S. only: 85% **Master's:** 15%

Approximate percentage of students who are Women: 65% **Ethnic Minority:** 10%

Average years to complete the doctoral program (including internship): 6.9 years

Research areas	# Faculty	# Grants
addictive disorders/ substance abuse	1	2
affective disorders	1	0
anxiety disorders	1	0
ADHD	1	3
child clinical	2	1
emotion	1	1
ethnicity	2	0
temperament	1	0

Clinical opportunities
advanced child
anxiety
ADHD
depression
ODD
pervasive problem solving

Queen's University

Department of Psychology
Kingston, Ontario K7L 3N6, Canada
phone#: (613) 533-6004
e-mail: Leachj@psyc.queensu.ca
Web address: http://pavlov.psyc.queensu.ca/

1	2	3	4	5	**6**	7
Clinically oriented			Equal emphasis			Research oriented

What percentage of your faculty subscribes to or practices in each of the following orientations?

Psychodynamic/Psychoanalytic	1%
Applied behavioral analysis/Radical behavioral	20%
Family systems/Systems	10%
Existential/Phenomenological/Humanistic	20%
Cognitive/Cognitive-behavioral	90%

What percentage of students applying for internship last year was accepted into APA-accredited internships? 100%

What courses are required for incoming students to have completed prior to enrolling?
Undergraduate thesis required; history and systems; biological, cognitive-affective; social; (2) abnormal psychology

Are there courses you recommend that are not mandatory?
No

GRE mean (M), cutoff (C), or preferred (P)
Verbal 580 (M) Quantitative 620 (M) Analytic 650 (M)
Advanced Psychology 730 (M)

GPA mean (M), cutoff (C), or preferred (P)
Psychology GPA 3.8 (M)

Number of applications/admission offers/incoming students in 2001
103 applied/12 admission offers/6 incoming

% of students receiving:
Tuition waiver only: 0%
Assistantship/fellowship only: 90%
Both tuition waiver & assistantship/fellowship: 0%

Approximate percentage of incoming students who entered with a B.A./B.S. (Honors) only: 90% **Master's:** 10%

Approximate percentage of students who are Women: 82% **Ethnic Minority:** 0%

Average years to complete the doctoral program (including internship): 6 years

Research areas	# Faculty	# Grants
—		

Clinical opportunities
child and family
children and adolescents
developmental disabilities
education
forensic
geriatric
inpatient and outpatient facilities
neuropsychology
rehabilitation
young offenders

University of Rhode Island

Department of Psychology
Chafee Center
Kingston, RI 02881
phone#: (401) 874-2193
e-mail: morokorf@URI.edu
Web address: http://www.uri.edu/

1	2	3	**4**	5	6	7
Clinically oriented			Equal emphasis			Research oriented

What percentage of your faculty subscribes to or practices in each of the following orientations?

Psychodynamic/Psychoanalytic	10%
Applied behavioral analysis/Radical behavioral	0%
Family systems/Systems	40%

Existential/Phenomenological/Humanistic	30%
Cognitive/Cognitive-behavioral	50%
Feminist	10%

What percentage of students applying for internship last year was accepted into APA-accredited internships? 100%

What courses are required for incoming students to have completed prior to enrolling?
Sufficient background in undergraduate psychology courses

Are there courses you recommend that are not mandatory?
Psychological tests and measurements

GRE mean (M), cutoff (C), or preferred (P) score
Verbal + Quantitative 1200 (P)

GPA mean (M), cutoff (C), or preferred (P)
Undergraduate GPA 3.25 (P)

Number of applications/admission offers/incoming students in 2001
195 applied/17 admission offers/10 incoming

% of students receiving:
Tuition waiver only: 0%
Assistantship/fellowship only: 22%
Both tuition waiver & assistantship/fellowship: 83.3%

Approximate percentage of incoming students who entered with a B.A./B.S. only: 66% **Master's:** 33%

Approximate percentage of students who are Women: 66% **Ethnic Minority:** 16%

Average years to complete the doctoral program (including internship): 5 years

Research areas	**# Faculty**	**# Grants**
behavioral medicine/health psychology	3	9
child clinical	1	0
clinical judgment	1	0
community psychology	1	4
family research	2	1
multicultural issues	1	0

Clinical opportunities
child therapy
community psychology
family therapy
health psychology
marriage and couples therapy
sex therapy

University of Rochester

Department of Psychology
River Station
Rochester, NY 14627
phone#: (716) 275-8704
e-mail: gilbert@scp.rochester.edu
Web address: http://www.psych.rochester.edu/scp/

1	2	3	4	**5**	6	7
Clinically oriented		Equal emphasis				Research oriented

What percentage of your faculty subscribes to or practices in each of the following orientations?

Psychodynamic/Psychoanalytic	33%
Applied behavioral analysis/Radical behavioral	33%
Family systems/Systems	0%
Existential/Phenomenological/Humanistic	33%
Cognitive/Cognitive-behavioral	33%

What percentage of students applying for internship last year was accepted into APA-accredited internships? 100%

What courses are required for incoming students to have completed prior to enrolling?
Equivalent of psychology major

Are there courses you recommend that are not mandatory?
No

GRE mean (M), cutoff (C), or preferred (P) score
Verbal 660 (M) Quantitative 620 (M)
Advanced Psychology 730 (M)
There are no cutoffs or preferred scores

GPA mean (M), cutoff (C), or preferred (P)
Overall GPA 3.8 (M)

Number of applications/admission offers/incoming students in 2001
111 applied/7 admission offers/3 incoming

% of students receiving:
Tuition waiver only: 0%
Assistantship/fellowship only: 0%
Both tuition waiver & assistantship/fellowship: 100%

Approximate percentage of incoming students who entered with a B.A./B.S. only: 75% **Master's:** 25%

Approximate percentage of students who are Women: 75% **Ethnic Minority:** 25%

Research areas	**# Faculty**	**# Grants**
attention-deficit disorder	1	2
child abuse	1	3
gender & psychopathology	1	0
motivation	1	2
neuropsychology	3	0
prevention	2	2

Clinical opportunities
attention-deficit disorder
autism
child mistreatment/abuse
psychodynamic therapy
smoking prevention

Rutgers University (Ph.D.)

Department of Psychology
Graduate School of Arts and Sciences
New Brunswick, NJ 08903
Web address: http://psych.rutgers.edu/program_areas/clin/clin.html

1	2	3	4	**5**	6	7
Clinically oriented			Equal emphasis			Research oriented

What percentage of your faculty subscribes to or practices in each of the following orientations?

Psychodynamic/Psychoanalytic	12.5%
Applied behavioral analysis/Radical behavioral	12.5%
Family systems/Systems	0%
Existential/Phenomenological/Humanistic	0%
Cognitive/Cognitive-behavioral	75%

What percentage of students applying for internship last year was accepted into APA-accredited internships? 100%

What courses are required for incoming students to have completed prior to enrolling?
A major in psychology or equivalent courses

Are there courses you recommend that are not mandatory?
No

GRE mean (M), cutoff (C), or preferred (P) score
Verbal 600 (P) Quantitative 600 (P)
Advanced Psychology 600 (P)

GPA mean (M), cutoff (C), or preferred (P)
Overall GPA 3.74 (M) Psychology GPA 3.5 (P)
Junior/Senior GPA 3.5 (P)

Number of applications/admission offers/incoming students in 2001
256 applied/10 admission offers/8 incoming

% of students receiving:
Tuition waiver only: 0%
Assistantship/fellowship only: 0%
Both tuition waiver & assistantship/fellowship: 100%

Approximate percentage of incoming students who entered with a B.A./B.S. only: 85% **Master's:** 15%

Approximate percentage of students who are Women: 86% **Ethnic Minority:** 25%

Average years to complete the doctoral program (including internship): 5.5 years

Research areas	# Faculty	# Grants
applied behavioral analysis	2	0
autism	1	1
behavioral medicine	4	5
depression	2	0
developmental psychopathology	1	1
eating disorders	1	1
ethical issues	1	0
marriage/couples	3	2
philosophical issues	2	0
prevention	2	1
program design and evaluation	1	1
psychotherapy process and outcome	5	3
somatization disorders	1	1
substance abuse	3	5

Clinical opportunities
AIDS
adolescent delinquency
affective disorders
anxiety disorders
assessment
behavioral medicine
community psychology
conduct disorder
depression
developmental disabilities
eating disorders
family therapy
forensic psychology
gerontology
group therapy
hyperactivity
hypnosis
impulse control
infancy/postpartum
interpersonal psychotherapy
marital/couples therapy
minority
neuropsychology
obsessive–compulsive disorder
personality disorders
psychodynamic/psychoanalytic therapy
rational–emotive psychotherapy
schizophrenia
school psychology
sex therapy
substance abuse
victim/abuse

Rutgers University (Psy.D.)

Graduate School of Applied and Professional Psychology
152 Frelinghuysen Road
Piscataway, NJ 08854-8085
phone#: (732) 445-2004
e-mail: zatkow@gsapp.rutgers.edu
Web address: http://www.gsappweb.rutgers.edu/

1	2	**3**	4	5	6	7
Clinically oriented			Equal emphasis			Research oriented

What percentage of your faculty subscribes to or practices in each of the following orientations?

Psychodynamic/Psychoanalytic	35%
Applied behavioral analysis/Radical behavioral	10%
Family systems/Systems	20%
Existential/Phenomenological/Humanistic	10%
Cognitive/Cognitive-behavioral	25%

What percentage of students applying for internship last year was accepted into APA-accredited internships? 100%

What courses are required for incoming students to have completed prior to enrolling?
Statistics, abnormal psychology, psychophysiological psychology, experimental psychology, introductory psychology

Are there courses you recommend that are not mandatory?
Tests and measurements, developmental psychology, personality, learning theory, social psychology, comparative psychology, perception, motivation, history and systems

GRE mean (M), cutoff (C), or preferred (P) score
GRE general and subject in psychology required, but we do not have specific mean, cutoff, or preferred scores

GPA mean (M), cutoff (C), or preferred (P)
Overall GPA 3.5 (M)

Number of applications/admission offers/incoming students in 2001
323 applied/27 admission offers/15 incoming

% of students receiving:
Tuition waiver only: 0%
Scholarships: 60%
Both tuition waiver & assistantship/fellowship: 40%

Approximate percentage of incoming students who entered with a B.A./B.S. only: 33% **Master's:** 67%

Approximate percentage of students who are Women: 60% **Ethnic Minority:** 33%

Average years to complete the doctoral program (including internship): 4.5 years

Research areas	# Faculty	# Grants
adolescence	4	1
adoption	1	1
anxiety depressive disorders	3	1
applied and behavioral analysis	1	1
autism	1	1
community	2	1
developmental disabilities	3	2
diagnosis and classification	2	0
dissociative disorders	1	0
eating disorders	1	1
empirically supported treatment research	2	1
ethical issues	1	0
family/marriage/couples	4	2
feminist theory and psychology	1	0
mental health policy	2	1
mind/body/health	1	0
multicultural issues	2	0
organizational psychology	2	0
personality disorders	2	0
philosophy and psychology	5	1
program design and evaluation	1	0
psychiatric disabilities	1	1
psychoanalytic theory	7	1
psychology and the arts	1	0
psychophysiological disorders	1	0
psychotherapy process and outcome	3	0
severe mental illness	2	1
social learning theory	1	1
substance abuse	4	4

Clinical opportunities
AIDS
adolescent delinquency
affective disorders
anxiety disorders
assessment
behavioral medicine
community psychology
conduct disorder
developmental disabilities
dissociative disorder
eating disorders
family therapy
forensic psychology
gerontology
group therapy
hyperactivity
hypnosis
impulse control
infancy/postpartum
interpersonal psychotherapy
marital/couples therapy
minority
neuropsychology
obsessive–compulsive disorder
organizational psychology
personality disorders
psychodynamic/psychoanalytic therapy
rational-emotive psychotherapy
schizophrenia
school psychology
sex therapy
substance abuse
victim/abuse

St. John's University

Department of Psychology
Grand Central and Utopia Parkways
Jamaica, NY 11439
phone#: (718) 990-6369
Web address: http://www.stjohns.edu/academics/sjc/depts/psychology/doctorate.html

1	2	3	**4**	5	6	7
Clinically oriented			Equal emphasis			Research oriented

What percentage of your faculty subscribes to or practices in each of the following orientations?

Psychodynamic/Psychoanalytic	50%
Applied behavioral analysis/Radical behavioral	0%
Family systems/Systems	10%
Existential/Phenomenological/Humanistic	0%
Cognitive/Cognitive-behavioral	50%

What percentage of students applying for internship last year was accepted into APA-accredited internships? 100%

What courses are required for incoming students to have completed prior to enrolling?
Introductory psychology, statistics, experimental laboratory

Are there courses you recommend that are not mandatory?
No

GRE mean (M), cutoff (C), or preferred (P) score
Verbal 500 (P) Quantitative 500 (P)
Advanced Psychology 500 (P)

GPA mean (M), cutoff (C), or preferred (P)
Overall GPA 3.0 (P) Psychology GPA 3.0 (P)

Number of applications/admission offers/incoming students in 2001
186 applied/29 admission offers/12 incoming

% of incoming students receiving:
Tuition waiver only: 0%
Assistantship/fellowship only: 12%
Both tuition waiver & assistantship/fellowship: 70%

Approximate percentage of incoming students who entered with a B.A./B.S. only: 70% **Master's:** 30%

Approximate percentage of students who are Women: 94% **Ethnic Minority:** 6%

Average years to complete the doctoral program (including internship): 7 years

Research areas	# Faculty	# Grants
anxiety disorders	1	0
bilingualism	1	0
gender issues	2	0
health psychology	3	1
minority mental health	3	0
moral development	1	0
physiological psychology	1	1
psychotherapy research	1	0
schizophrenia	2	0
smoking cessation	2	0
stress management	2	1

Clinical opportunities
cognitive-behavioral therapy
family therapy
group therapy
geropsychology
neuropsychological assessment
psychodynamic/psychoanalytic therapy

St. Louis University

Department of Psychology
221 North Grand Boulevard
St. Louis, MO 63103
phone#: (314) 977-2278
Web address: http://www.slu.edu/colleges/AS/PSY/Grad.html

1	2	3	**4**	5	6	7
Clinically oriented			Equal emphasis			Research oriented

What percentage of your faculty subscribes to or practices in each of the following orientations?

Psychodynamic/Psychoanalytic	30%
Applied behavioral analysis/Radical behavioral	0%
Family systems/Systems	25%
Existential/Phenomenological/Humanistic	30%
Cognitive/Cognitive-behavioral	50%

What percentage of students applying for internship last year was accepted into APA-accredited internships? 100%

What courses are required for incoming students to have completed prior to enrolling?
Introductory psychology, statistics, abnormal psychology, and 6 upper division psychology courses

Are there courses you recommend that are not mandatory?
Personality, learning, social psychology, physiological psychology, developmental psychology

GRE mean (M), cutoff (C), or preferred (P) score
Verbal 550 (P) Quantitative 550 (P) Analytical 550 (P)

GPA mean (M), cutoff (C), or preferred (P)
Overall GPA 3.5 (P) Psychology GPA 3.7 (P)
Junior/Senior GPA 3.5 (P)

Number of applications/admission offers/incoming students in 2001
125 applied/10 admission offers/8 incoming

% of students receiving:
Tuition waiver only: 0%
Assistantship/fellowship only: 0%
Tuition waiver & assistantship/fellowship: 100% for first year only

Approximate percentage of incoming students who entered with a B.A./B.S. only: 75% **Master's:** 25%

Approximate percentage of students who are Women: 60% **Ethnic Minority:** 25%

Average years to complete the doctoral program (including internship): 5 years

Research areas	# Faculty	# Grants
abuse/violence	2	1
adjustment	2	0
assessment	3	0
child/adolescent	2	0
community	1	0
depression	2	0
ethical issues	3	0
family	3	0
personality disorders	2	0
professional issues	3	0
stress and coping	2	0

Clinical opportunities
anxiety
assessment
clinical neuropsychology
ethnic diversity
family therapy
hyperactivity
learning disabilities

marital
parent skills training
personality disorders
psychodynamic therapy
victims of abuse and assault

San Diego State University/University of California–San Diego

College of Sciences/School of Medicine
San Diego, CA 92182
phone#: (619) 594-2246
e-mail: akienle@psychology.sdsu.edu
Web address: http://www.psychology.sdsu.edu/doctoral/

1	2	3	4	5	**6**	7
Clinically oriented			Equal emphasis			Research oriented

What percentage of your faculty subscribes to or practices in each of the following orientations?

Psychodynamic/Psychoanalytic	10%
Applied behavioral analysis/Radical behavioral	30%
Family systems/Systems	5%
Existential/Phenomenological/Humanistic	5%
Cognitive/Cognitive-behavioral	50%

What percentage of students applying for internship last year was accepted into APA-accredited internships? 100%

What courses are required for incoming students to have completed prior to enrolling?
None

Are there courses you recommend that are not mandatory?
Psychology major or 18 semester hours in psychology including: personality, abnormal, social, statistics, testing, experimental with lab, physiological, perception and learning, biology, mathematics, linguistics, computer science, medical physics

GRE mean (M), cutoff (C), or preferred (P) score
Verbal 600 (P) Quantitative 600 (P)
Verbal + Quantitative 1252 (M) Analytical 600 (P)
Advanced Psychology 600 (P)

GPA mean (M), cutoff (C), or preferred (P)
Overall GPA 3.56 (M), 3.5 (P) Psychology GPA 3.75 (M), 3.5 (P) Junior/Senior GPA 3.5 (P)

Number of applications/admission offers/incoming students in 2001
277 applied/18 admission offers/14 incoming

% of students receiving:
Tuition waiver only: 0%
Assistantship/fellowship only: 0%
Tuition waiver & assistantship/fellowship: 100%

Approximate percentage of incoming students who entered with a B.A./B.S. only: 85% **Master's:** 15%

Approximate percentage of students who are Women: 66% **Ethnic Minority:** 18%

Average years to complete the doctoral program (including internship): 6 years

Research areas	**# Faculty**	**# Grants**
AIDS	7	1
aging	8	1
Alzheimer's/dementia	6	0
anxiety	4	1
applied behavioral analysis	4	0
autism	2	0
behavioral medicine		
cancer	4	0
cardiovascular disease	4	1
exercise	2	1
pain	2	0
PNI	3	0
women's health	3	0
bereavement	2	0
biofeedback	1	0
child, marriage, and family	5	0
childhood brain damage	2	0
chronic disease	4	1
cognition and memory	13	0
cognitive psychology/therapy	2	0
community psychology	1	0
cross-cultural psychology	10	0
decision making	1	0
depression	3	2
developmental neuropsychology	7	0
developmental psychopathology	3	0
gender issues	2	0
information processing	4	0
interpersonal psychology	1	0
neuropsychological testing	2	1
nutrition	3	0
posttraumatic stress disorder	1	0
problem solving	1	0
psychological testing	4	0
psychology of humor	1	0
psychopathology	3	0
psychopharmacology	6	2
psychophysiology	5	0
psychotherapy process and outcome	4	0
schizophrenia/psychosis	7	2
sexuality	1	0
sleep	4	0
smoking	7	1
social skills training	1	0
social support	2	0
statistics	4	0
stress and coping	13	0
substance abuse	12	5

Clinical opportunities
anxiety disorders
behavioral medicine
child and family therapy
cognitive therapy
neuropsychology
school psychology

University of Saskatchewan

Department of Psychology
Saskatoon, Saskatchewan S7N 5A5, Canada
e-mail: carl.vonbaeyer@usask.ca
Web address: http://www.usask.ca/psychology/

1	2	3	**4**	5	6	7
Clinically oriented			Equal emphasis			Research oriented

What percentage of your faculty subscribes to or practices in each of the following orientations?

Psychodynamic/Psychoanalytic	25%
Applied behavioral analysis/Radical behavioral	0%
Family systems/Systems	10%
Existential/Phenomenological/Humanistic	10%
Cognitive/Cognitive-behavioral	55%

What percentage of students applying for internship last year was accepted into APA-accredited internships? 80%

What courses are required for incoming students to have completed prior to enrolling?
An honors degree or its equivalent, including statistics, research methods, and an honors thesis

Are there courses you recommend that are not mandatory?
Basic area courses, for example, biological basis, social, personality

GRE mean (M), cutoff (C), or preferred (P) score
Verbal 550 (P) Quantitative 550 (P) Analytical 550 (P)
Advanced Psychology 550 (P)

GPA mean (M), cutoff (C), or preferred (P)
Overall GPA 80% (P) Psychology GPA 80% (P)
Junior/Senior GPA 80% (P)

Number of applications/admission offers/incoming students in 2001
61 applied/8 admission offers/5 incoming

% of students receiving:
Tuition waiver only: 0%
Assistantship/fellowship only: 100%
Tuition waiver & assistantship/fellowship: 0%

Approximate percentage of incoming students who entered with a B.A./B.S. only: 80% **Master's:** 20%

Approximate percentage of students who are Women: 75% **Ethnic Minority:** 5%

Average years to complete the doctoral program (including internship): 7.4 years

Research areas	# Faculty	# Grants
bereavement	1	0
forensic/psychopathy	3	2
metaphor/narrative	1	1
neuropsychology (FAS & attention)	2	2
pain	1	1
psychobiography	1	0
psychotherapy process	2	1
sexual abuse of children	1	1

Clinical opportunities
adult psychotherapy
behavioral medicine
developmental disabilities
inpatient forensic
neuropsychology
young offenders

Simon Fraser University

Department of Psychology
Burnaby, British Columbia V5A 1S6, Canada
phone#: (604) 291-3354
e-mail: tarcea@sfu.ca
Web address: http://www.sfu.ca/psychology/

1	2	3	**4**	5	6	7
Clinically oriented			Equal emphasis			Research oriented

What percentage of your faculty subscribes to or practices in each of the following orientations?

Psychodynamic/Psychoanalytic	40%
Applied behavioral analysis/Radical behavioral	20%
Family systems/Systems	10%
Existential/Phenomenological/Humanistic	0%
Cognitive/Cognitive-behavioral	30%

What percentage of students applying for internship last year was accepted into APA-accredited internships? 75%

What courses are required for incoming students to have completed prior to enrolling?
24 semester hours in experimental areas and statistics

Are there courses you recommend that are not mandatory?
Psychology honors program

GRE mean (M), cutoff (C), or preferred (P) score
Verbal 604 (M) Quantitative 668 (M) Analytical 669 (M)
Advanced Psychology 751 (M)

GPA mean (M), cutoff (C), or preferred (P)
Overall GPA 3.73 (M) Psychology GPA 3.73 (M)

Number of applications/admission offers/incoming students in 2001
109 applied/9 admission offers/6 incoming

% of students receiving:
Tuition waiver only: 0%
Assistantship/fellowship only: 75%
Both tuition waiver & assistantship/fellowship: 0%

Approximate percentage of incoming students who entered with a B.A./B.S. only: 100% **Master's:** 0%

Approximate percentage of students who are Women: 67% **Ethnic Minority:** 11%

Average years to complete the doctoral program (including internship): 7.6 years

Research areas	# Faculty	# Grants
aging	1	0
behavioral medicine	2	0
child clinical	1	1
child psychopathology	3	1
cognition	1	1
cognitive therapy	1	1
depression	1	0
developmental	2	2
emotion	1	1
family	1	1
forensic	3	3
gender	1	0
individual differences	1	0
marital	1	0
neuropsychology	1	0
psychopathology	2	2
sex offenders	1	0
stress and coping	1	0
violence and abuse	1	0

University of South Carolina

Department of Psychology
Columbia, SC 29208
phone#: (803) 777-4137
e-mail: doris@gwin.sc.edu
Web address: http:/www.cla.sc.edu/PSYC/ccprog.htm

1 2 3 **4** 5 6 7

Clinically oriented | Equal emphasis | Research oriented

What percentage of your faculty subscribes to or practices in each of the following orientations?

Psychodynamic/Psychoanalytic	20%
Applied behavioral analysis/Radical behavioral	30%
Family systems/Systems	20%
Existential/Phenomenological/Humanistic	10%
Cognitive/Cognitive-behavioral	30%

What percentage of students applying for internship last year was accepted into APA-accredited internships? 100%

What courses are required for incoming students to have completed prior to enrolling?
18 hours in psychology, including statistics

Are there courses you recommend that are not mandatory?
Research methods, learning, biopsychology, abnormal, social, developmental, personality

GRE mean (M), cutoff (C), or preferred (P) score
Verbal 600 (P) Quantitative 600 (P) Analytical 600 (P)
Advanced Psychology 600 (P)

GPA mean (M), cutoff (C), or preferred (P)
Overall GPA 3.5 (P) Psychology GPA 3.7 (P)
Junior/Senior GPA 3.7 (P)

Number of applications/admission offers/incoming students in 2001
150 applied/16 admission offers/10 incoming

% of students receiving:
Tuition waiver only: 0%
Assistantship/fellowship only: 0%
Both tuition waiver & assistantship/fellowship: 100%

Approximate percentage of incoming students who entered with a B.A./B.S. only: 70% **Master's:** 30%

Approximate percentage of students who are Women: 65% **Ethnic Minority:** 25%

Average years to complete the doctoral program (including internship): 6 years

Research areas	# Faculty	# Grants
citizen participation	1	0
community coalition development	1	1
conduct disorders	1	1
coping with cancer	1	1
families of chronically mentally ill	1	0
marital relationships	4	0
prevention (racism/cross-cultural intolerance)	5	3
self-help intervention	2	0
self-perception in minority youth	1	1
violence/rape/battering	1	1

Clinical opportunities
community psychology
family therapy
neuropsychology

University of South Dakota

Department of Psychology
Vermillion, SD 57069
phone#: (605) 677-5353
e-mail: byutrzen@usd.edu
Web address: http://www.usd.edu/psyc/ctp/CTP.html

1 2 3 **4** 5 6 7

Clinically oriented | Equal emphasis | Research oriented

What percentage of your faculty subscribes to or practices in each of the following orientations?

Psychodynamic/Psychoanalytic	30%
Applied behavioral analysis/Radical behavioral	0%
Family systems/Systems	30%
Existential/Phenomenological/Humanistic	10%
Cognitive/Cognitive-behavioral	100%

What percentage of students applying for internship last year was accepted into APA-accredited internships? 100%

What courses are required for incoming students to have completed prior to enrolling?
18 semester hours in psychology within a distribution among standard coursework in general and experimental psychology

Are there courses you recommend that are not mandatory?
Research design, statistics, history/systems, learning/memory, abnormal psychology, physiological

GRE mean (M), cutoff (C), or preferred (P) score
Verbal 520 (M) Quantitative 556 (M) Analytical 577 (M)
Advanced Psychology 595 (M)

GPA mean (M), cutoff (C), or preferred (P)
Overall GPA 3.0 (C) Psychology GPA 3.0 (C)

Number of applications/admission offers/incoming students in 2001
67 applied/15 admission offers/9 incoming

% of students receiving:
Tuition waiver only: 0%
Assistantship/fellowship only: 100%
Both tuition waiver & assistantship/fellowship: 0%

Approximate percentage of incoming students who entered with a B.A./B.S. only: 80% **Master's:** 20%

Approximate percentage of students who are Women: 67% **Ethnic Minority:** 33%

Average years to complete the doctoral program (including internship): 6 years

Research areas	# Faculty	# Grants
aging	2	0
child clinical	3	0
cross-cultural	10	2
depression	2	0
disaster mental health	5	2
ethics	1	0
family violence	2	0
health psychology	2	0
psychosis/serious mental illness	2	0
rural community psychology	4	0
visual impairment/computer application	1	0

Clinical opportunities
crisis intervention
disaster mental health
minority/cross-cultural (specific emphasis in American Indian mental health)
rural/community psychology
severe mental illness

University of South Florida

Department of Psychology
4202 Fowler Avenue, PCP 4118G
Tampa, FL 33620
phone#: (813) 974-2492
e-mail: phares@luna.cas.usf.edu
Web address: http://www.cas.usf.edu/psychology/clin/index.html

1 2 3 4 5 **6** 7

Clinically oriented — Equal emphasis — Research oriented

What percentage of your faculty subscribes to or practices in each of the following orientations?

Psychodynamic/Psychoanalytic	0%
Applied behavioral analysis/Radical behavioral	10%
Family systems/Systems	20%
Existential/Phenomenological/Humanistic	0%
Cognitive/Cognitive-behavioral	70%

What percentage of students applying for internship last year was accepted into APA-accredited internships? 83%

What courses are required for incoming students to have completed prior to enrolling?
None

Are there courses you recommend that are not mandatory?
Research design, statistics

GRE mean (M), cutoff (C), or preferred (P) score
Verbal 600 (P) Quantitative 600 (P)

GPA mean (M), cutoff (C), or preferred (P)
Junior/Senior GPA 3.0 (C)

Number of applications/admission offers/incoming students in 2001
235 applied/17 admission offers/9 incoming

% of students receiving:
Tuition waiver only: 0%
Assistantship/fellowship only: 0%
Both tuition waiver & assistantship/fellowship: 100%

Approximate percentage of incoming students who entered with a B.A./B.S. only: 89% **Master's:** 11%

Approximate percentage of students who are Women: 71% **Ethnic Minority:** 30%

Average years to complete the doctoral program (including internship): 6.5 years

Research areas	# Faculty	# Grants
adult neuropsychology	1	0
aggression/anger	2	0
behavioral genetics	1	0
behavioral medicine/health psychology	5	6
child/adolescent psychopathology	3	0
depression	1	0
eating disorders	1	1
family dysfunction	2	1
marital/sexual dysfunction	1	0
personality assessment	2	0
substance abuse	3	6

Clinical opportunities
adult neuropsychology
anger control
behavioral medicine
child and adolescent disorders
eating disorders
family dysfunction
forensic evaluation
intellectual assessment
marital/sexual
depression/anxiety
personality assessment
psychosocial oncology
substance abuse

University of Southern California

Department of Psychology
University Park, SGM 501
Los Angeles, CA 90089-1061
phone#: (213) 740-2219
Web address: http://www.usc.edu/dept/LAS/psychology/clinical.html

1	2	3	4	5	**6**	7
Clinically oriented		Equal emphasis			Research oriented	

What percentage of your faculty subscribes to or practices in each of the following orientations?

Psychodynamic/Psychoanalytic	0%
Applied behavioral analysis/Radical behavioral	20%
Family systems/Systems	20%
Existential/Phenomenological/Humanistic	0%
Cognitive/Cognitive-behavioral	80%

What percentage of students applying for internship last year was accepted into APA-accredited internships? 87%

What courses are required for incoming students to have completed prior to enrolling?
None are required

Are there courses you recommend that are not mandatory?
Introductory psychology, elementary statistics, research methods or experimental psychology, and courses in biology, physical and social sciences mathematics

GRE mean (M), cutoff (C), or preferred (P) score
Verbal 630 (M) Quantitative 650 (M)

GPA mean (M), cutoff (C), or preferred (P)
Overall GPA 3.55 (M)

Number of applications/admission offers/incoming students in 2001
243 applied/17 admission offers/11 incoming

% of students receiving:
Tuition waiver only: 0%
Assistantship/fellowship only: 0%
Both tuition waiver & assistantship/fellowship: 100%

Approximate percentage of incoming students who entered with a B.A./B.S. only: 50% **Master's:** 50%

Approximate percentage of students who are Women: 67% **Ethnic Minority:** 31%

Average years to complete the doctoral program (including internship): 6 years

Research areas	# Faculty	# Grants
adolescent substance abuse	1	0
alcohol use/abuse	2	1
behavioral medicine	2	1
child psychopathology	3	2
childhood victimization	1	1
clinical neuroscience/experimental psychopathology	3	1
cognitive behavioral therapy/assessment	2	1
gerontology	2	2
marital & family research/abuse	1	1

Clinical opportunities
community
gerontology
marital/family
minority mental health

Southern Illinois University

Department of Psychology
Life Science Building II, Room 281
Carbondale, IL 62901
phone#: (618) 453-3564 (graduate program secretary)
e-mail: DOLLNGR@SIU.EDU
Web address: http://www.siu.edu/departments/cola/psycho/clinical.html

1	2	3	**4**	5	6	7
Clinically oriented			Equal emphasis			Research oriented

What percentage of your faculty subscribes to or practices in each of the following orientations?

Psychodynamic/Psychoanalytic	10%
Applied behavioral analysis/Radical behavioral	0%
Family systems	0%
Existential/Phenomenological/Humanistic	0%
Cognitive/Cognitive-behavioral	90%

What percentage of students applying for internship last year was accepted into APA-accredited internships? 100%

What courses are required for incoming students to have completed prior to enrolling?
None

Are there courses you recommend that are not mandatory?
History and systems, tests and measurements, abnormal psychology, personality, learning

GRE mean (M), cutoff (C), or preferred (P) score
Verbal 600 (P) Quantitative 600 (P)
Advanced Psychology 600 (P)

GPA mean (M), cutoff (C), or preferred (P)
Overall GPA 3.5 (P), 3.0 (C) Psychology GPA 3.75 (P)

Number of applications/admission offers/incoming students in 2001
— applied/— admission offers/8 incoming

% of students receiving:
Tuition waiver only: 0%
Assistantship/fellowship only: 0%
Both tuition waiver & assistantship/fellowship: 100%

Approximate percentage of incoming students who entered with a B.A./B.S. only: 85% **Master's:** 15%

Approximate percentage of students who are Women: 69% **Ethnic Minority:** 28%

Average years to complete the doctoral program (including internship): 7.5 years

Research areas	# Faculty	# Grants
abuse	2	0
abortion issues	1	0
AIDS attitudes	1	0
adolescent issues	1	0
anxiety disorders	1	0
assessment	8	0
behavioral genetics	1	0
behavioral medicine	2	0
child clinical	5	0
child sexual abuse	1	0
clinical judgment	1	0
community psychology	1	0
delinquency	1	1
depression	1	0
family systems	1	0
gender roles	1	0
learning disabilities	2	0
marital	1	0
neuropsychology	2	0
pediatric psychology	1	0
personality (five-factor model)	3	0
personality assessment	4	0
psychology of religion	1	0
relationships	2	0
sleep (child)	1	0
smoking	1	1
stress, coping, and social support	1	0

Clinical opportunities
family therapy
forensic psychology
juvenile corrections
neuropsychology/rehabilitation
severe psychopathology
sexual abuse
substance abuse

University of Southern Mississippi

Department of Psychology
Box 5025 Southern Station
Hattiesburg, MS 39406-5025
phone#: (601) 266-4587
e-mail: psych.grad.admissions@usm.edu
Web address: http://www.dept.usm.edu/~psy/clinical/home.htm

1	2	3	**4**	5	6	7
Clinically oriented			Equal emphasis			Research oriented

What percentage of your faculty subscribes to or practices in each of the following orientations?

Psychodynamic/Psychoanalytic	25%
Applied behavioral analysis/Radical behavioral	0%
Family systems/Systems	0%
Existential/Phenomenological/Humanistic	12%
Cognitive/Cognitive-behavioral	62%

What percentage of students applying for internship last year was accepted into APA-accredited internships? 100%

What courses are required for incoming students to have completed prior to enrolling?
None

Are there courses you recommend that are not mandatory?
Experimental, statistics, history and systems

GRE mean (M), cutoff (C), or preferred (P) score
Verbal + Quantitative 1100 (P)

GPA mean (M), cutoff (C), or preferred (P)
Overall GPA 3.5 (P)

Number of applications/admission offers/incoming students in 2001
65 applied/10 admission offers/7 incoming

% of students receiving:
Tuition waiver only: 0%
Assistantship/fellowship only: 0%
Both tuition waiver & assistantship/fellowship: 100%

Approximate percentage of incoming students who entered with a B.A./B.S. only: 60% **Master's:** 40%

Approximate percentage of students who are Women: 50% **Ethnic Minority:** 20%

Average years to complete the doctoral program (including internship): 5.3 years

Research areas	# Faculty	# Grants
children's behavioral disorders	1	0
experimental psychopathology	2	2
neuropsychology	1	0
psychophysiology/health	2	0
social/clinical	1	0
suicide	1	0

Clinical opportunities
child clinical psychology
health psychology
neuropsychology
suicide prevention

Spalding University (Psy.D.)

Department of Psychology
851 South Fourth Street
Louisville, KY 40203
phone#: (502) 585-7127
e-mail: esimpson@spalding.edu
Web address: http://www.spalding.edu/ugrad/psychology/default.htm

1	**2**	3	4	5	6	7
Clinically oriented			Equal emphasis			Research oriented

What percentage of your faculty subscribes to or practices in each of the following orientations?

Psychodynamic/Psychoanalytic	10%
Applied behavioral analysis/Radical behavioral	20%
Family systems/Systems	22%
Existential/Phenomenological/Humanistic	20%
Cognitive/Cognitive-behavioral	10%

What percentage of students applying for internship last year was accepted into APA-accredited internships? 100%

What courses are required for incoming students to have completed prior to enrolling?
18 hours of undergraduate work.

Are there courses you recommend that are not mandatory?
Undergraduate research, physiological psychology

GRE mean (M), cutoff (C), or preferred (P) score
Verbal 550 (M), 500 (C) Quantitative 590 (M), 500 (C)
Analytical 630 (M), 500 (C)

GPA mean (M), cutoff (C), or preferred (P)
Overall GPA 3.5 (M), 3.8 (P) Psychology GPA 3.5 (P)

Number of applications/admission offers/incoming students in 2001
78 applied/42 admission offers/26 incoming

% of students receiving:
Tuition waiver only: 0%
Assistantship/fellowship only: 16%
Both tuition waiver & assistantship/fellowship: 0%

Approximate percentage of incoming students who entered with a B.A./B.S. only: 74% **Master's:** 26%

Approximate percentage of students who are Women: 72% **Ethnic Minority:** 9%

Average years to complete the doctoral program (including internship): 6 years

Research areas	**# Faculty**	**# Grants**
child development	1	0
clinical supervision	1	0
health psychology	2	0
program evaluation	1	0
sociobiology	1	0
sports psychology	2	0

Clinical opportunities
family/systems psychology
health psychology

Stony Brook University/State University of New York

Department of Psychology
Stony Brook, NY 11794-2500
phone#: (516) 632-7830
e-mail: DKlein@notes.CC.SUNYSB.EDU
Web address: http://www.psychology.SUNYSB.edu

1	2	3	4	5	**6**	7
Clinically oriented			Equal emphasis			Research oriented

What percentage of your faculty subscribes to or practices in each of the following orientations?

Psychodynamic/Psychoanalytic	0%
Applied behavioral analysis/Radical behavioral	13%
Family systems/Systems	0%
Existential/Phenomenological/Humanistic	0%
Cognitive/Cognitive-behavioral	87%

What percentage of students applying for internship last year was accepted into APA-accredited internships? 67%

What courses are required for incoming students to have completed prior to enrolling?
None

Are there courses you recommend that are not mandatory?
Statistics, introductory psychology, experimental with lab, abnormal psychology, research methods

GRE mean (M), cutoff (C), or preferred (P) score
Verbal 650 (P) Quantitative 650 (P) Analytical 650 (P)
Advanced Psychology 650 (P)

GPA mean (M), cutoff (C), or preferred (P)
Overall GPA 3.5 (P)

Number of applications/admission offers/incoming students in 2001
220 applied/13 admission offers/8 incoming

% of students receiving:
Tuition waiver only: 0%
Assistantship/fellowship only: 0%
Both tuition waiver & assistantship/fellowship: 100%

Approximate percentage of incoming students who entered with a B.A./B.S. only: 83% **Master's:** 17%

Approximate percentage of students who are Women: 70% **Ethnic Minority:** 10%

Average years to complete the doctoral program (including internship): 6 years

Research areas	**# Faculty**	**# Grants**
affective disorders	1	1
developmental disabilities	1	1
marriage/spousal abuse	1	1
pain	1	0
parent–child interactions	1	1
problem solving	1	0
psychotherapy process and outcome	1	0
reading difficulties	1	1

Clinical opportunities
psychological center, marital clinic, university hospital, student counseling center, various community agencies

Suffolk University

Department of Psychology
Boston, MA 02114-4280
phone#: (617) 573-8293
e-mail: phd@acad.suffolk.edu
Web address: http://www.cas.suffolk.edu/psych/ndonovan/psych.htm

1	2	3	**4**	5	6	7
Clinically oriented			Equal emphasis			Research oriented

What percentage of your faculty subscribes to or practices in each of the following orientations?

Psychodynamic/Psychoanalytic	43%
Applied behavioral analysis/Radical behavioral	14%
Family systems/Systems	71%
Existential/Phenomenological/Humanistic	43%
Cognitive/Cognitive-behavioral	86%

What percentage of students applying for internship last year was accepted into APA-accredited internships? 82%

What courses are required for incoming students to have completed prior to enrolling?
5 courses in psychology including statistics, research methods

Are there courses you recommend that are not mandatory?
Biological psychology

GRE mean (M), cutoff (C), or preferred (P) score
Verbal 528 (M) Quantitative 585 (M) Analytical 631 (M)
Advanced Psychology 590 (M)

GPA mean (M), cutoff (C), or preferred (P)
Overall GPA 3.53 (M)

Number of applications/admission offers/incoming students in 2001
72 applied/28 admission offers/14 incoming

% of students receiving:
Tuition waiver only: 0%
Assistantship/fellowship only: 100%
Both tuition waiver & assistantship/fellowship: 0%

Approximate percentage of incoming students who entered with a B.A./B.S. only: 75% **Master's:** 25%

Approximate percentage of students who are Women: 72% **Ethnic Minority:** 3%

Average years to complete the doctoral program (including internship): 5.3 years

Research areas	# Faculty	# Grants
acculturation of immigrants/minorities	1	0
African-American identity, development	1	0
cognitive development	1	0
consumer psychology	1	0
couples and family issues	1	0
cross-cultural psychology	1	0
cyberpsychology	1	1
developmental psychology	1	0
eating disorders	1	0
educational psychology	1	0
ego development	1	0
emotions	2	0
empathy	1	0
gender studies	1	0
health behavior	1	0
late adolescent and adult development	2	0
motor development	1	0
narrative development	1	0
nature of affect	1	0
neuropsychology	2	0
parent psychopathology	1	0
personality psychology	2	0
psychology of family	2	0
psychology of sports	1	0
psychotherapy	2	0
teaching of psychology	1	0
visitor studies	1	0

Clinical opportunities
—

Syracuse University

Department of Psychology
430 Huntington Hall
Syracuse, NY 13244-2340
phone#: (315) 443-2760
e-mail: samaisto@psych.syr.edu
Web address: http://psychweb.syr.edu/Programs/clinmain.htm

1	2	3	4	**5**	6	7
Clinically oriented			Equal emphasis			Research oriented

What percentage of your faculty subscribes to or practices in each of the following orientations?

Psychodynamic/Psychoanalytic	0%
Applied behavioral analysis/Radical behavioral	0%
Family systems/Systems	17%
Existential/Phenomenological/Humanistic	0%
Cognitive/Cognitive-behavioral	83%

What percentage of students applying for internship last year was accepted into APA-accredited internships? 100%

What courses are required for incoming students to have completed prior to enrolling?
15 credits of psychology courses, statistics, laboratory course

Are there courses you recommend that are not mandatory?
Numerous laboratory courses, research experience, science courses

GRE mean (M), cutoff (C), or preferred (P) score
Verbal 550 (P) Quantitative 550 (P)

GPA mean (M), cutoff (C), or preferred (P)
Overall GPA 3.4 (P) Psychology GPA 3.6 (P)

Number of applications/admission offers/incoming students in 2001
98 applied/7 admission offers/3 incoming

% of students receiving:
Tuition waiver only: 0%
Assistantship/fellowship only: 0%
Both tuition waiver & assistantship/fellowship: 100%

Approximate percentage of incoming students who entered with a B.A./B.S. only: 80% **Master's:** 20%

Approximate percentage of students who are Women: 65% **Ethnic Minority:** 15%

Average years to complete the doctoral program (including internship): 6 years

Research areas	# Faculty	# Grants
developmental psychopathology	1	1
family	1	1
psychophysiology	1	0
sexual health, AIDS prevention	2	2
substance abuse	2	5

Clinical opportunities
addictions
anxiety disorders
behavioral medicine
community psychology
couples
crisis intervention
family
neuropsychology
school/educational

Temple University

Department of Psychology
Broad and Montgomery Streets
Philadelphia, PA 19122
phone#: (215) 204-1561
Web address: http://www.temple.edu/psychology/CLIN.html

1	2	3	4	5	**6**	7
Clinically oriented			Equal emphasis			Research oriented

What percentage of your faculty subscribes to or practices in each of the following orientations?

Psychodynamic/Psychoanalytic	10%
Applied behavioral analysis/Radical behavioral	10%
Family systems/Systems	20%
Existential/Phenomenological/Humanistic	10%
Cognitive/Cognitive-behavioral	75%

What percentage of students applying for internship last year was accepted into APA-accredited internships? 100%

What courses are required for incoming students to have completed prior to enrolling?
Abnormal psychology, introductory psychology, statistics

Are there courses you recommend that are not mandatory?
No

GRE mean (M), cutoff (C), or preferred (P) score
Verbal + Quantitative 1300 (M)

GPA mean (M), cutoff (C), or preferred (P)
GPA 3.54 (M)

Number of applications/admission offers/incoming students in 2001
Approximately 300 applied/13 admission offers/8 incoming

% of students receiving:
Tuition waiver only: 0%
Assistantship/fellowship only: 0%
Both tuition waiver & assistantship/fellowship: 100%

Approximate percentage of incoming students who entered with a B.A./B.S. only: 80% **Master's:** 20%

Approximate percentage of students who are Women: 68% **Ethnic Minority:** 9%

Average years to complete the doctoral program (including internship): 6 years

Research areas	# Faculty	# Grants
anxiety	3	5
child/adolescent psychopathology	2	2
child psychological therapy	2	2
depression	3	2
divorce	1	0
emotions and psychopathology	1	0
family psychology	2	0
trauma/rape victims	1	1

Clinical opportunities
anxiety disorders in children, adult social phobia, a generic on-campus clinic and many specialty clinics in a large urban area

University of Tennessee

Department of Psychology
Austin Peay Psychology Building
Knoxville, TN 37996-0900
phone#: (423) 974-2165
e-mail: cjogle@utk.edu
Web address: http://www.utk.edu/~jlawler/

1	2	3	**4**	5	6	7
Clinically oriented			Equal emphasis			Research oriented

What percentage of your faculty subscribes to or practices in each of the following orientations?

Psychodynamic/Psychoanalytic	37%
Applied behavioral analysis/Radical behavioral	25%
Family systems/Systems	38%
Existential/Phenomenological/Humanistic	12%
Cognitive/Cognitive-behavioral	25%

What percentage of students applying for internship last year was accepted into APA-accredited internships? 71%

What courses are required for incoming students to have completed prior to enrolling?
None

Are there courses you recommend that are not mandatory?
No

GRE mean (M), cutoff (C), or preferred (P) score
Verbal 650 (P) Quantitative 650 (P)
Advanced Psychology 630 (P)

GPA mean (M), cutoff (C), or preferred (P)
Overall GPA 3.5 (P)

Number of applications/admission offers/incoming students in 2001
77 applied/9 admission offers/9 incoming

% of students receiving:
Tuition waiver only: 0%
Assistantship/fellowship only: 0%
Both tuition waiver & assistantship/fellowship: 100%

Approximate percentage of incoming students who entered with a B.A./B.S. only: 60% **Master's:** 40%

Approximate percentage of students who are Women: 60% **Ethnic Minority:** 5%

Average years to complete the doctoral program (including internship): 5.5 years

Research areas	# Faculty	# Grants
adult psychopathology	4	0
developmental psychopathology	3	2
health psychology	2	0

Clinical opportunities
conduct disordered children
dysfunctional families
long-term psychotherapy
personality disorders
sexual deviation

Texas A&M University

Department of Psychology
College Station, TX 77843-4235
phone#: (979) 845-2581
e-mail: DKS@PSYC.TAMU.EDU
Web address: http://psychweb.tamu.edu/programs/clinical/clinical%20/psychology.html

1 2 3 **4** 5 6 7

Clinically oriented — Equal emphasis — Research oriented

What percentage of your faculty subscribes to or practices in each of the following orientations?

Psychodynamic/Psychoanalytic	25%
Applied behavioral analysis/Radical behavioral	0%
Family systems/Systems	10%
Existential/Phenomenological/Humanistic	15%
Cognitive/Cognitive-behavioral	50%

What percentage of students applying for internship last year was accepted into APA-accredited internships? 100%

What courses are required for incoming students to have completed prior to enrolling?
Introductory statistics, abnormal psychology, and at least 3 other psychology courses including a course in a core basic experimental area

Are there courses you recommend that are not mandatory?
No

GRE mean (M), cutoff (C), or preferred (P) score
Verbal 600 (P) Quantitative 600 (P) Analytical 600 (P)

GPA mean (M), cutoff (C), or preferred (P)
Overall GPA 3.5 (P)

Number of applications/admission offers/incoming students in 2001
150 applied/8 admission offers/5 incoming

% of students receiving:
Tuition waiver only: 0%
Assistantship/fellowship only: 0%
Both tuition waiver & assistantship/fellowship: 100%

Approximate percentage of incoming students who entered with a B.A./B.S. only: 70% **Master's:** 30%

Approximate percentage of students who are Women: 70% **Ethnic Minority:** 30%

Average years to complete the doctoral program (including internship): 5 years

Research areas	# Faculty	# Grants
addictive disorders	1	1
aging	2	1
anxiety disorders	3	1
assessment	3	0
child behavior disorders	4	3
health psychology	2	1
marital/family studies	5	3
psychopathology	2	1
psychotherapy	7	2

Clinical opportunities
community
family
forensic
neuropsychology
rural psychology
substance abuse

University of Texas at Austin

Department of Psychology
Austin, TX 78712
phone#: (512) 471-3393
e-mail: gradoffice@psy.utexas.edu
Web address: http://www.psy.utexas.edu/psy/clinical/ctp.html

1 2 3 4 5 **6** 7

Clinically oriented — Equal emphasis — Research oriented

What percentage of your faculty subscribes to or practices in each of the following orientations?

Psychodynamic/Psychoanalytic	0%
Applied behavioral analysis/Radical behavioral	0%
Family systems/Systems	0%
Existential/Phenomenological/Humanistic	25%
Cognitive/Cognitive-behavioral	75%

What percentage of students applying for internship last year was accepted into APA-accredited internships? 100%

What courses are required for incoming students to have completed prior to enrolling?
None

Are there courses you recommend that are not mandatory?
Abnormal psychology, biopsychology, research methods, statistics

GRE mean (M), cutoff (C), or preferred (P) score
Verbal + Quantitative 1200 (C), 1300 (P)

GPA mean (M), cutoff (C), or preferred (P)
Psychology GPA 3.6 (M)

Number of applications/admission offers/incoming students in 2001
243 applied/6 admission offers/5 incoming

% of students receiving:
Tuition waiver only: 0%
Assistantship/fellowship only: 0%
Both tuition waiver & assistantship/fellowship: 100%

Approximate percentage of incoming students who entered with a B.A./B.S. only: 90% **Master's:** 10%

Approximate percentage of students who are Women: 57% **Ethnic Minority:** 11%

Average years to complete the doctoral program (including internship): 6.7 years

Research areas	**# Faculty**	**# Grants**
anxiety	1	1
attention-deficit hyperactivity disorder	1	1
cross-cultural	1	0
eating disorders	1	1
epidemiology	1	0
health psychology	1	1
neuropsychology	1	1
sexual dysfunction	1	1
stress and coping	1	1
substance abuse	1	1

Clinical opportunities
alcoholism
anxiety disorders
community
crisis intervention
family
gay/lesbian
marital
neuropsychology
obsessive-compulsive disorder
personality disorders
schizophrenia

University of Texas Southwestern Medical Center at Dallas

Graduate Program in Clinical Psychology
5323 Harry Hines Boulevard
Dallas, Texas 75390-9044
phone#: (214) 648-5277
e-mail: Alyce.Cadena@utsouthwestern.edu
Web address: http://www.utsouthwestern.edu/clinicalpsych

1	2	3	**4**	5	6	7
Clinically oriented			Equal emphasis			Research oriented

What percentage of your faculty subscribes to or practices in each of the following orientations?

Psychodynamic/Psychoanalytic	30%
Applied behavioral analysis/Radical behavioral	10%
Family systems/Systems	20%
Existential/Phenomenological/Humanistic	5%
Cognitive/Cognitive-behavioral	35%

What percentage of students applying for internship last year was accepted into APA-accredited internships? 100%

What courses are required for incoming students to have completed prior to enrolling?
Introduction to psychology, learning, statistics; a bachelor's degree or its equivalent

Are there courses you recommend that are not mandatory?
Developmental, physiological, experimental

GRE mean (M), cutoff (C), or preferred (P) score
Verbal + Quantitative 1200 (P)

GPA mean (M), cutoff (C), or preferred (P)
Overall GPA 3.5 (P)

Number of applications/admission offers/incoming students in 2001
127 applied/15 admission offers/12 incoming

% of students receiving:
Tuition waiver only: 0%
Assistantship/fellowship: 100% (in 3rd semester of 1st year through end of 4th year)
Both tuition waiver & assistantship/fellowship: 11.6%

Approximate percentage of incoming students who entered with a B.A./B.S. only: 64% **Master's:** 36%

Approximate percentage of students who are Women: 70% **Ethnic Minority:** 20%

Average years to complete the doctoral program (including internship): 4.5 years

Research areas	**# Faculty**	**# Grants**
Alzheimer's	1	1
child depression	2	1
community mental health	1	0
cultural issues in psychology	2	0
depression	3	3
developmental psychology	1	1
health psychology	3	3

health services research	1	1
learning disabilities	1	0
neurobiological aspects of psychological disorders	2	2
neuropsychological profiles associated with medical disease	2	2
pain management	1	1
pediatric psychology	1	0
rehabilitation psychology	1	1
sleep disorders	1	1

Clinical opportunities
affective disorders
behavioral psychology
clinical child
community mental health
deafness
developmental disabilities
family therapy
forensic psychology
health/medical psychology
inpatient psychiatry
neuropsychology
outpatient psychotherapy
personality disorders
primary care clinic consultation
psychiatric emergency care
rehabilitation psychology
sleep disorders
vocational assessment/counseling

Texas Tech University

Department of Psychology
P.O. Box 42501
Lubbock, TX 79409
phone#: (806) 742-3711
fax#: (806) 742-0818
e-mail: steph.harter@ttu.edu
Web address: http://www.psychology.ttu.edu/

1	2	3	**4**	5	6	7
Clinically oriented			Equal emphasis			Research oriented

What percentage of your faculty subscribes to or practices in each of the following orientations?

Psychodynamic/Psychoanalytic	29%
Applied behavioral analysis/Radical behavioral	14%
Family systems/Systems	57%
Existential/Phenomenological/Humanistic	14%
Cognitive/Cognitive-behavioral	86%

What percentage of students applying for internship last year was accepted into APA-accredited internships? 100%

What courses are required for incoming students to have completed prior to enrolling?
18 semester hours of psychology

Are there courses you recommend that are not mandatory?
Statistics, abnormal psychology, developmental psychology, physiological psychology, and a research course such as experimental design or independent research with a faculty member

GRE mean (M), cutoff (C), or preferred (P) score
Verbal 599 (M) Quantitative 662 (M)

GPA mean (M), cutoff (C), or preferred (P)
Overall GPA 3.69 (M)

Number of applications/admission offers/incoming students in 2001
72 applied/14 admission offers/8 incoming

% of students receiving:
Tuition waiver only: 0%
Assistantship/fellowship only: 0%
Both tuition waiver & assistantship/fellowship: 100%

Approximate percentage of incoming students who entered with a B.A./B.S. only: 86% **Master's:** 14%

Approximate percentage of students who are Women: 71% **Ethnic Minority:** 9%

Average years to complete the doctoral program (including internship): 6.24 years

Research areas	**# Faculty**	**# Grants**
addictions	1	1
behavioral assessment	1	1
child depression and anxiety	1	1
child maltreatment and abuse	3	2
clinical decision making and de-biasing strategies	1	1
cognitive-behavioral therapies	2	1
community interventions	1	0
eating disorders	1	0
ethnic minority/cultural issues	1	0
high-risk youth	1	1
informant discrepancies/rater biases in child assessment	1	1
MMPI/MMPI-2	1	0
neuropsychological assessment	1	0
nightmares, personality, and psychopathology	1	0
parenting	1	0
personal meaning-making processes	2	2
Rorschach	1	1
single subject design, time series regression, dynamic factor analysis	1	0
Spanish-speaking families	1	0
teachers' evaluations of children's problems	2	0
trauma	2	0

Clinical opportunities
Extensive opportunities with diverse populations are available.

University of Toledo

Department of Psychology
2801 West Bancroft Street
Toledo, OH 43606-3390
phone#: (419) 530-2721
e-mail: mtaylor2@pop3.utoledo.edu
Web address: http://www.utoledo.edu/psychology/clinic.html

1	2	3	**4**	5	6	7
Clinically oriented			Equal emphasis			Research oriented

What percentage of your faculty subscribes to or practices in each of the following orientations?

Psychodynamic/Psychoanalytic	25%
Applied behavioral analysis/Radical behavioral	0%
Family systems/Systems	13%
Existential/Phenomenological/Humanistic	13%
Cognitive/Cognitive-behavioral	13%
Neuropsychology	13%

What percentage of students applying for internship last year was accepted into APA-accredited internships? 100%

What courses are required for incoming students to have completed prior to enrolling?
Psychology major, including experimental, statistics

Are there courses you recommend that are not mandatory?
Topical seminars

GRE mean (M), cutoff (C), or preferred (P) score
Verbal 550 (P) Quantitative 550 (P)
Better than 70th percentile

GPA mean (M), cutoff (C), or preferred (P)
Psychology GPA 3.5 (P)

Number of applications/admission offers/incoming students in 2001
73 applied/11 admission offers/6 incoming

% of students receiving:
Tuition waiver only: 0%
Assistantship/fellowship only: 0%
Both tuition waiver & assistantship/fellowship: 100%

Approximate percentage of incoming students who entered with a B.A./B.S. only: 90% **Master's:** 10%

Approximate percentage of students who are Women: 75% **Ethnic Minority:** 25%

Average years to complete the doctoral program (including internship): 5.5 years

Research areas	**# Faculty**	**# Grants**
ADHD/LD	2	0
child/adolescent psychopathology	3	1
chronic mental illness	1	1
neuropsychology	1	0
posttraumatic stress syndrome	1	0
psychotherapy research	2	0
qualitative research	1	0

Clinical opportunities
child abuse/neglect
college adjustment problems
family/conjoint therapy
neuropsychology
process-experimental therapy

University of Tulsa

Department of Psychology
Tulsa, OK 74104
phone#: (918) 631-2248
e-mail: allan-harkness@utulsa.edu
Web address: http://www.cas.utulsa.edu/psych/

1	2	3	4	**5**	6	7
Clinically oriented			Equal emphasis			Research oriented

What percentage of your faculty subscribes to or practices in each of the following orientations?

Psychodynamic/Psychoanalytic	20%
Applied behavioral analysis/Radical behavioral	20%
Family systems/Systems	0%
Existential/Phenomenological/Humanistic	10%
Cognitive/Cognitive-behavioral	50%

What percentage of students applying for internship last year was accepted into APA-accredited internships? 100%

What courses are required for incoming students to have completed prior to enrolling?
Abnormal psychology, statistics, research methods, assessment, core psychology courses

Are there courses you recommend that are not mandatory?
Advanced courses in psychology core areas

GRE mean (M), cutoff (C), or preferred (P) score
Verbal 650 (M) Quantitative 650 (M)

GPA mean (M), cutoff (C), or preferred (P)
GPA 3.5 (M)

Number of applications/admission offers/incoming students in 2001
39 applied/8 admission offers/6 incoming

% of students receiving:
Tuition waiver only: 10%
Assistantship/fellowship only: 0%
Both tuition waiver & assistantship/fellowship: 40%

Approximate percentage of incoming students who entered with a B.A./B.S. only: 80% **Master's:** 20%

Approximate percentage of students who are Women: 55% **Ethnic Minority:** 15%

Average years to complete the doctoral program (including internship): 6 years

Research areas	**# Faculty**	**# Grants**
child clinical	1	0
clinical assessment	3	0

clinical gerontology	1	0
community psychology	1	2
depression	1	0
forensic psychology	1	1
life-span development	2	0
marital communication	0	0
neuropsychology	1	1
personality disorders	2	0
posttraumatic stress disorder	1	0
stress	3	1

Clinical opportunities
Practicum program is community-based with access to 18 general and specialty clinics.

Uniformed Services University of Health Sciences

4301 Jones Bridge Road
Bethesda, MD 20814-4799
phone#: (301) 295-3270
e-mail: mfeuerstein@usuhs.mil
Web address: http://www.usuhs.mil

1 2 3 **4** 5 6 7

Clinically oriented — Equal emphasis — Research oriented

What percentage of your faculty subscribes to or practices in each of the following orientations?

Psychodynamic/Psychoanalytic	10%
Applied behavioral analysis/Radical behavioral	0%
Family systems/Systems	10%
Existential/Phenomenological/Humanistic	10%
Cognitive/Cognitive-behavioral	80%

What percentage of students applying for internship last year was accepted into APA-accredited internships? 100%

What courses are required for incoming students to have completed prior to enrolling?
None

Are there courses you recommend that are not mandatory?
Basic undergraduate sequence of courses in psychology

GRE mean (M), cutoff (C), or preferred (P) score
Verbal 650 (P) Quantitative 650 (P) Analytical 650 (P)

GPA mean (M), cutoff (C), or preferred (P)
GPA 3.5 (M)

Number of applications/admission offers/incoming students in 2001
30 applied/2 admission offers/2 incoming

% of students receiving:
Tuition waiver only: 0%
Assistantship/fellowship only: 0%
Both tuition waiver & assistantship/fellowship: 100%

Approximate percentage of incoming students who entered with a B.A./B.S. only: 25% **Master's:** 75%

Approximate percentage of students who are
Women: 60% **Ethnic Minority:** 8%

Average years to complete the doctoral program (including internship): 5 years

Research areas	# Faculty	# Grants
neuropsychology	1	0
obesity and eating disorders	1	1
occupational health psychology—stress and pain in the workplace	1	4
sexual dysfunction	1	1
stress and appetitive behaviors	1	3
stress and cardiovascular disease	1	1

Clinical opportunities
children and adolescent
employee assistance program
forensic psychology
medical center
military teaching hospitals
occupational health (for police, fire fighters, secret service)
substance abuse
VA hospitals

University of Utah

Department of Psychology
380 S 1530 E, Room 502
Salt Lake City, UT 84112
phone#: (801) 581-6126
e-mail: Catalan@psych.utah.edu
Web address: http://www.psych.utah.edu

1 2 3 **4** 5 6 7

Clinically oriented — Equal emphasis — Research oriented

What percentage of your faculty subscribes to or practices in each of the following orientations?

Psychodynamic/Psychoanalytic	35%
Applied behavioral analysis/Radical behavioral	0%
Family systems/Systems	15%
Existential/Phenomenological/Humanistic	0%
Cognitive/Cognitive-behavioral	50%

What percentage of students applying for internship last year was accepted into APA-accredited internships? 100%

What courses are required for incoming students to have completed prior to enrolling?
Undergraduate degree in psychology or its equivalent, including statistics, research design and abnormal psychology

Are there courses you recommend that are not mandatory?
Advanced statistics and research design

GRE mean (M), cutoff (C), or preferred (P) score
Verbal 600 (P) Quantitative 600 (P) Analytical 600 (P)
Advanced Psychology 600 (P)

GPA mean (M), cutoff (C), or preferred (P)
Overall GPA 3.0 (P) Psychology GPA 3.0 (P)
Junior/Senior GPA 3.0 (P)

Number of applications/admission offers/incoming students in 2001
90 applied/7 admission offers/5 incoming

% of students receiving:
Tuition waiver only: 0%
Assistantship/fellowship only: 0%
Both tuition waiver & assistantship/fellowship: 100%

Approximate percentage of incoming students who entered with a B.A./B.S. only: 50% **Master's:** 50%

Approximate percentage of students who are Women: 75% **Ethnic Minority:** 12%

Average years to complete the doctoral program (including internship): 6.5 years

Research areas	# Faculty	# Grants
adolescent psychology	1	1
adult psychopathology	3	1
autism	1	1
behavioral medicine	2	2
child clinical	1	1
developmental	1	1
family research	2	3
forensic	1	0
personality assessment	2	0
personality disorders	2	0
sexuality	1	1
stress and coping	2	2

Clinical opportunities
adolescent psychopathology and psychotherapy
behavioral medicine
family therapy
forensic psychology
inpatient psychiatry
interpersonal psychotherapy
personality disorders
rational–emotive therapy
sex therapy/sexuality

Vanderbilt University–Department of Psychology

111 21st Avenue South
Nashville, TN 37240
phone#: (615) 322-0080
e-mail: burnspm@ctruax.vanderbilt.edu
Web address: http://www.vanderbilt.edu/AnS/psychology/clinical/clin.html#program

1 2 3 4 5 **6** 7

Clinically oriented — Equal emphasis — Research oriented

What percentage of your faculty subscribes to or practices in each of the following orientations?

Psychodynamic/Psychoanalytic	0%
Applied behavioral analysis/Radical behavioral	5%
Family systems/Systems	5%
Existential/Phenomenological/Humanistic	0%
Cognitive/Cognitive-behavioral	90%

What percentage of students applying for internship last year was accepted into APA-accredited internships? 100%

What courses are required for incoming students to have completed prior to enrolling?
None

Are there courses you recommend that are not mandatory?
Abnormal psychology

GRE mean (M), cutoff (C), or preferred (P) score
Verbal 650 (P) Quantitative 650 (P)

GPA mean (M), cutoff (C), or preferred (P)
Overall GPA 3.5 (P) Psychology GPA 3.5 (P)

Number of applications/admission offers/incoming students in 2001
90 applied/3 admission offers/2 incoming

% of students receiving:
Tuition waiver only: 0%
Assistantship/fellowship only: 0%
Both tuition waiver & assistantship/fellowship: 100%

Approximate percentage of incoming students who entered with a B.A./B.S. only: 90% **Master's:** 10%

Approximate percentage of students who are Women: 60% **Ethnic Minority:** 10%

Average years to complete the doctoral program (including internship): 6.5 years

Research areas	# Faculty	# Grants
aging	1	0
assessment (with computers)	2	0
clinical judgment	1	0
depression	4	2
eating	1	1
emotion	4	2
gender issues	1	0
health psychology	1	0
neuropsychology	4	2
personality assessment	1	0
prevention	1	0
psychoneuroimmunology	1	0
psychopathology	5	1
psychophysiology	1	1
schizophrenia	1	1
statistics	1	0
stress and coping	2	0
therapy process and outcome	1	1

Clinical opportunities
affective disorders
anxiety disorders
behavioral medicine
impulse control
neuropsychology
personality disorders
schizophrenia

Vanderbilt University–Peabody College

Department of Psychology and Human Development
Box 512
Nashville, TN 37203
phone#: (615) 322-8141
e-mail: JudyGarber@Vanderbilt.edu
Web address: http://peabody.vanderbilt.edu/depts/psych_and_hd/general/gradover.html

1	2	3	4	5	**6**	7

Clinically oriented — Equal emphasis — Research oriented

What percentage of your faculty subscribes to or practices in each of the following orientations?

Psychodynamic/Psychoanalytic	10%
Applied behavioral analysis/Radical behavioral	10%
Family systems/Systems	30%
Existential/Phenomenological/Humanistic	0%
Cognitive/Cognitive-behavioral	50%

What percentage of students applying for internship last year was accepted into APA-accredited internships? 100%

What courses are required for incoming students to have completed prior to enrolling?
None

Are there courses you recommend that are not mandatory?
Statistics

GRE mean (M), cutoff (C), or preferred (P) score
Verbal 650 (M) Quantitative 700 (M) Analytical 700 (M)
Advanced Psychology 700 (M)

GPA mean (M), cutoff (C), or preferred (P)
Overall GPA 3.72 (M) Psychology GPA 3.87 (M)

Number of applications/admission offers/incoming students in 1999
167 applied/5 admission offers/— incoming

% of students receiving:
Tuition waiver only: 0%
Assistantship/fellowship only: 0%
Both tuition waiver & assistantship/fellowship: 100%

Approximate percentage of incoming students who entered with a B.A./B.S. only: 90% **Master's:** 10%

Approximate percentage of students who are Women: 75% **Ethnic Minority:** 10%

Average years to complete the doctoral program (including internship): 5.5 years

Research areas	# Faculty	# Grants
adult psychopathology	1	0
affective disorders	4	6
child clinical	7	6
child psychopathology	6	6
cognition	3	1
cross-cultural	3	0
eating disorders	1	0
externalizing disorders	3	2
family research	6	3
prevention	2	0

Clinical opportunities
affective disorders
cognitive-behavioral therapy
developmental disabilities
family therapy
neuropsychology
pediatric psychology
school-based interventions

University of Vermont

Department of Psychology
John Dewey Hall
Burlington, VT 05405
phone#: (802) 656-2670
e-mail: esther.rothblum@uvm.edu
Web address: http://www.uvm.edu/~psych/PsychAtUVM/Grad96.html#Clinical

1	2	3	**4**	5	6	7

Clinically oriented — Equal emphasis — Research oriented

What percentage of your faculty subscribes to or practices in each of the following orientations?

Psychodynamic/Psychoanalytic	20%
Applied behavioral analysis/Radical behavioral	10%
Family systems/Systems	10%
Existential/Phenomenological/Humanistic	0%
Cognitive/Cognitive-behavioral	60%

What percentage of students applying for internship last year was accepted into APA-accredited internships? 100%

What courses are required for incoming students to have completed prior to enrolling?
Psychology major or equivalent including general psychology, statistics, research design, and at least 3 other psychology courses

Are there courses you recommend that are not mandatory?
No

GRE mean (M), cutoff (C), or preferred (P) score
Verbal 650 (P) Quantitative 650 (P) Analytical 650 (P)
Advanced Psychology 650 (P)

GPA mean (M), cutoff (C), or preferred (P)
Overall GPA 3.5 (P) Psychology GPA 3.5 (P)
Junior/Senior GPA 3.5 (P)

Number of applications/admission offers/incoming students in 2001
219 applied/— admission offers/6 incoming

% of students receiving:
Tuition waiver only: 0%
Assistantship/fellowship only: 70%
Both tuition waiver & assistantship/fellowship: 30%

Approximate percentage of incoming students who entered with a B.A./B.S. only: 66% **Master's:** 33%

Approximate percentage of students who are Women: 75% **Ethnic Minority:** 25%

Average years to complete the doctoral program (including internship): 5 years

Research areas	# Faculty	# Grants
adolescent treatment	2	1
anxiety disorders	2	0
child psychopathology	3	2
eating disorders	1	0
health psychology/behavioral medicine	4	2
lesbian/gay issues	1	0
prevention	2	1
sex offenders/abuse	3	2

Clinical opportunities
adolescent psychotherapy
anxiety disorders
behavioral medicine
childhood disorders
chronically mentally ill
depression
eating disorders
family therapy
HIV/AIDS
mental retardation
neuropsychology
prevention
substance abuse

University of Victoria

Department of Psychology
Victoria, British Columbia V8W 3P5, Canada
phone#: (250) 721-7525
e-mail: ptaylor@uvic.ca
Web address: http://www.uvic.ca/psyc/clinical/

1 2 3 **4** 5 6 7

Clinically oriented | Equal emphasis | Research oriented

What percentage of your faculty subscribes to or practices in each of the following orientations?

Psychodynamic/Psychoanalytic	40%
Applied behavioral analysis/Radical behavioral	5%
Family systems/Systems	30%
Existential/Phenomenological/Humanistic	15%
Cognitive/Cognitive-behavioral	40%

What percentage of students applying for internship last year was accepted into APA- (or CPA-) accredited internships? 80%

What courses are required for incoming students to have completed prior to enrolling?
"A" level grades for one full year of coursework in 4 areas: social psychology, biological psychology, cognitive psychology, developmental or abnormal psychology

Are there courses you recommend that are not mandatory?
Additional special topics in clinical psychology selections

GRE mean (M), cutoff (C), or preferred (P)
Verbal 690 (M) Quantitative 650 (M) Analytic 680 (M)

GPA mean (M), cutoff (C), or preferred (P)
Overall GPA 7.5 (M) Psychology GPA 7.5 (M)

Number of applications/admission offers/incoming students in 2001
104 applied/8 admission offers/3 incoming

% of students receiving:
Tuition waiver only: 0%
Assistantship/fellowship only: 95%
Both tuition waiver & assistantship/fellowship: 0%

Approximate percentage of incoming students who entered with a B.A./B.S. only: 90% **Master's:** 10%

Approximate percentage of students who are Women: 75% **Ethnic Minority:** 10%

Average years to complete the doctoral program (including internship): 6.5 years

Research areas	# Faculty	# Grants
attention-deficit disorder	1	1
childhood sexual abuse	2	1
epilepsy	1	1
families and divorce	1	1
traumatic brain injury	2	2

Clinical opportunities
adolescent and adult forensic
adult psychiatric
adult rehabilitation
child and adult mental health
child inpatient
pediatric and adult neuropsychology

University of Virginia–Department of Human Services

Curry School of Education
P.O. Box 400270
Charlottesville, VA 22904-4270
phone#: (804) 924-7472
e-mail: clin-psych@virginia.edu
Web address: http://curry.edschool.virginia.edu/go/clinpsych/

1 2 3 **4** 5 6 7

Clinically oriented | Equal emphasis | Research oriented

What percentage of your faculty subscribes to or practices in each of the following orientations?

Psychodynamic/Psychoanalytic	33%
Applied behavioral analysis/Radical behavioral	0%
Family systems/Systems	55%
Existential/Phenomenological/Humanistic	0%
Cognitive/Cognitive-behavioral	55%

What percentage of students applying for internship last year was accepted into APA-accredited internships? 100%

What courses are required for incoming students to have completed prior to enrolling?
None

Are there courses you recommend that are not mandatory?
Undergraduate statistics, child development, learning, abnormal psychology, physiological psychology/ biopsychology, social psychology

GRE mean (M), cutoff (C), or preferred (P) score
Verbal 600 (M) Quantitative 664 (M) Analytical 660 (M)
Advanced Psychology 643 (M)

GPA mean (M), cutoff (C), or preferred (P)
Overall GPA 3.5 (M) Psychology GPA 3.7 (M)
Junior/Senior GPA 3.7 (M)

Number of applications/admission offers/incoming students in 2001
148 applied/14 admission offers/8 incoming

% of students receiving:
Tuition waiver only: 0%
Assistantship/fellowship only: 0%
Both tuition waiver & assistantship/fellowship: 100%

Approximate percentage of incoming students who entered with a B.A./B.S. only: 80% **Master's:** 20%

Approximate percentage of students who are Women: 74% **Ethnic Minority:** 33%

Average years to complete the doctoral program (including internship): 5.5 years

Research areas	# Faculty	# Grants
adolescent females	2	1
adolescent suicide	1	0
child clinical	4	4
cognitive/learning disorders	3	1
forensic psychology	1	1
incarcerated populations	2	1
multicultural issues	1	0
parenting behavior	2	0
test development	3	0
treatment outcome	2	0
youth violence	3	2

Clinical opportunities
crisis intervention
developmental psychopathology
family therapy
forensic psychology
infant, child, and family assessment and intervention
neuropsychology
parenting/parent–child interaction
school interventions
school psychology
systems consultation

University of Virginia–Department of Psychology

College of Arts and Sciences
102 Gilmer Hall
Charlottesville, VA 22903-2477
phone#: (804) 982-4750
Web address: http://www.virginia.edu/~psych/

1	2	3	4	5	**6**	7

Clinically oriented — Equal emphasis — Research oriented

What percentage of your faculty subscribes to or practices in each of the following orientations?

Psychodynamic/Psychoanalytic	25%
Applied behavioral analysis/Radical behavioral	0%
Family systems/Systems	25%
Existential/Phenomenological/Humanistic	0%
Cognitive/Cognitive-behavioral	50%

What percentage of students applying for internship last year was accepted into APA-accredited internships? 100%

What courses are required for incoming students to have completed prior to enrolling?
B.A. in psychology or equivalent

Are there courses you recommend that are not mandatory?
Abnormal psychology, statistics

GRE mean (M), cutoff (C), or preferred (P) score
Verbal 620 (P) Quantitative 620 (P) Analytical 620 (P)
Advanced Psychology 620 (P)

GPA mean (M), cutoff (C), or preferred (P)
Overall GPA 3.5 (P)

Number of applications/admission offers/incoming students in 2001
300 applied/8 admission offers/6 incoming

% of students receiving:
Tuition waiver only: 0%
Assistantship/fellowship only: 0%
Both tuition waiver & assistantship/fellowship: 100%

Approximate percentage of incoming students who entered with a B.A./B.S. only: 70% **Master's:** 30%

Approximate percentage of students who are Women: 75% **Ethnic Minority:** 25%

Average years to complete the doctoral program (including internship): 6 years

Research areas	# Faculty	# Grants
adult psychopathology	3	3
anxiety/obsessive–compulsive disorders	1	0
behavioral genetics	2	1
child clinical/psychopathology	5	5
community psychology	3	3
developmental adolescence	3	3
epidemiology	2	1
family research/systems	2	2
minority mental health	2	2

neuropsychology	1	0
personality disorders	2	1
prevention	3	2
schizophrenia/psychosis	2	0
violence/abuse/victim–offender	4	2

Clinical opportunities
anxiety disorders
obsessive–compulsive disorder
behavioral medicine
community psychology
depression
family therapy
forensic psychology
marital/couples therapy
neuropsychology
pediatric psychology
psychology/law
schizophrenia/psychosis
victim/battering/abuse

Virginia Commonwealth University

Department of Psychology
808 West Franklin Street
Richmond, VA 23284-2018
phone#: (804) 828-1158 (admissions)
e-mail: clin-psy@vcu.edu
Web address: http://www.vcu.edu/hasweb/psy/clin.html

1 2 3 4 **5** 6 7

Clinically oriented — Equal emphasis — Research oriented

What percentage of your faculty subscribes to or practices in each of the following orientations?

Psychodynamic/Psychoanalytic	0%
Applied behavioral analysis/Radical behavioral	0%
Family systems/Systems	10%
Existential/Phenomenological/Humanistic	0%
Cognitive/Cognitive-behavioral	75%
Interpersonal	15%

What percentage of students applying for internship last year was accepted into APA-accredited internships? 100%

What courses are required for incoming students to have completed prior to enrolling?
18 hours of psychology including general psychology, history and systems, experimental psychology, statistics

Are there courses you recommend that are not mandatory?
We recommend as much psychology, statistics, and other science courses as possible.

GRE mean (M), cutoff (C), or preferred (P) score
Verbal 580 (M) Quantitative 650 (M)
Advanced Psychology 650 (M)

GPA mean (M), cutoff (C), or preferred (P)
Overall GPA 3.5 (M) Psychology GPA 3.5 (P)
Junior/Senior GPA 3.5 (P)

Number of applications/admission offers/incoming students in 2001
128 applied/12 admission offers/9 incoming

% of students receiving:
Tuition waiver only: 0%
Assistantship/fellowship only: 0%
Both tuition waiver & assistantship/fellowship: 100%

Approximate percentage of incoming students who entered with a B.A./B.S. only: 80% **Master's:** 20%

Approximate percentage of students who are Women: 70% **Ethnic Minority:** 25%

Average years to complete the doctoral program (including internship): 5.8 years

Research areas	# Faculty	# Grants
adolescent	4	3
anxiety	2	0
behavioral medicine	4	3
child clinical/pediatric	4	3
community	3	2
emotion	1	0
divorce	1	0
forensic psychology	1	0
minority/cross-cultural	2	1
pregnancy issues	1	1
psychopathology	1	1
psychophysiology	2	0
psychotherapy	1	1
stress and coping	3	0
substance abuse	2	1

Clinical opportunities
assessment and testing
behavioral medicine
child and adult anxiety
child pediatric
children of divorce
chronic mental illness
community psychology
correctional psychology
inpatient
neuropsychology
pain management
school
substance abuse
unipolar mood disorder

Virginia Consortium Program in Clinical Psychology (Psy.D.)

Pembroke Two/Suite 301
287 Independence Blvd.
Virginia Beach, VA 23462
phone#: (757) 518-2550
e-mail: npwats@wm.edu
Web address: http://www.VCpcp.odu.edu/VCpcp

1 2 **3** 4 5 6 7

Clinically oriented — Equal emphasis — Research oriented

What percentage of your faculty subscribes to or practices in each of the following orientations?

Psychodynamic/Psychoanalytic	17%
Applied behavioral analysis/Radical behavioral	17%
Family systems/Systems	28%
Existential/Phenomenological/Humanistic	3%
Cognitive/Cognitive-behavioral	35%

What percentage of students applying for internship last year was accepted into APA-accredited internships? 100%

What courses are required for incoming students to have completed prior to enrolling?
B.A. in psychology or equivalent

Are there courses you recommend that are not mandatory?
Statistics, research methods

GRE mean (M), cutoff (C), or preferred (P) score
Verbal 491 (M) Quantitative 532 (M) Analytical 567 (M)
Advanced Psychology 536 (M)

GPA mean (M), cutoff (C), or preferred (P)
Undergraduate GPA 3.45 (M) Graduate GPA 3.67 (M)

Number of applications/admission offers/incoming students in 2001
128 applied/20 admission offers/10 incoming

% of students receiving:
Tuition waiver only: 0%
Assistantship/fellowship only: 0%
Both tuition waiver & assistantship/fellowship: 97%

Approximate percentage of incoming students who entered with a B.A./B.S. only: 60% **Master's:** 40%

Approximate percentage of students who are Women: 78% **Ethnic Minority:** 22%

Average years to complete the doctoral program (including internship): 5 years

Research areas	# Faculty	# Grants
ADHD	1	1
behavior therapy	1	0
body image	1	1
child/clinical	1	0
childhood trauma	1	0
community	1	1
comprehension	1	1
depression	1	0
developmental psychopathology	1	0
dissociative disorders	1	0
domestic violence	1	0
eating disorders	1	0
family	1	0
gender issues	1	0
group processes	1	0
HIV/AIDS	1	0
humor	1	0
learning	1	0
mathematical problem solving	1	0
minority issues	2	0
neuropsychology	1	1
personal constructs	1	0
personality assessment/outcome	2	2
prevention	1	1
psychoanalysis	1	0
psychotherapy	1	0
relationships	1	0
religion	1	0
schizophrenia	1	0
sleep disorders	1	1
social behavior	1	0
stereotypes	1	0
testing/assessment	1	0
women's issues	1	0

Clinical opportunities
ADHD
alcohol/substance abuse
Alzheimer's disease
anxiety disorders
behavioral medicine
bipolar disorder
brain tumor/traumatic injury
cerebral palsy
congential/neuro conditions
dementias
depression
epilepsy
family therapy
individual therapy
learning disabilities
marital/couples therapy
mental retardation
neuropsychology
Parkinson's disease
pediatric psychology
obssessive-compulsive disorder
schizophrenia/psychosis
sexual abuse
sickle cell disease
sleep disorders
stroke
Tourette's disorder

Virginia Polytechnic Institute and State University

Department of Psychology
5088 Derring Hall
Blacksburg, VA 24061-0436
phone#: (540) 231-6275
e-mail: RSW.NETT@VT.EDU
Web address: http://www.vt.edu/CollegesDepts.html

1 2 3 4 5 **6** 7
Clinically oriented — Equal emphasis — Research oriented

What percentage of your faculty subscribes to or practices in each of the following orientations?

Psychodynamic/Psychoanalytic	0%
Applied behavioral analysis/Radical behavioral	5%
Family systems/Systems	20%
Existential/Phenomenological/Humanistic	0%
Cognitive/Cognitive-behavioral	100%

What percentage of students applying for internship last year was accepted into APA-accredited internships? 100%

What courses are required for incoming students to have completed prior to enrolling?
Introductory psychology, research methods, statistics, learning, history and systems

Are there courses you recommend that are not mandatory?
Abnormal psychology, social psychology, developmental psychology, personality

GRE mean (M), cutoff (C), or preferred (P) score
Verbal 600 (P) Quantitative 600 (P)

GPA mean (M), cutoff (C), or preferred (P)
Overall GPA 3.25 (P) Psychology GPA 3.25 (P)
Junior/Senior GPA 3.25 (P)

Number of applications/admission offers/incoming students in 2001
115 applied/13 admission offers/8 incoming

% of students receiving:
Tuition waiver only: 0%
Assistantship/fellowship only: 0%
Both tuition waiver & assistantship/fellowship: 90%

Approximate percentage of incoming students who entered with a B.A./B.S. only: 80% **Master's:** 20%

Approximate percentage of students who are Women: 75% **Ethnic Minority:** 15%

Average years to complete the doctoral program (including internship): 6.1 years

Research areas	**# Faculty**	**# Grants**
AIDS	2	1
affective disorders/depression	2	0
anxiety disorders	3	1
attention-deficit disorder	1	0
autism	1	0
behavioral medicine	3	2
child clinical	3	2
eating disorders	1	0
gender roles	2	0
hypnosis	1	1
marriage/couples	1	0
minority mental health	2	1
neuropsychology	2	0
pain management	2	0
parent–child interaction	2	1
pediatric psychology	1	1
prevention	4	3
psychotherapy outcome	2	1
shyness	1	0
social skills	3	0
stress and coping	1	0
substance abuse	2	2

Clinical opportunities
AIDS
affective disorders
anxiety disorders
attention-deficit/hyperactivity disorder
behavioral medicine
child clinical
conduct disorder
consultation
data management systems
gerontology
marital/couples therapy
neuropsychology
prevention in the community
substance abuse
systems management

University of Washington

Department of Psychology
Seattle, WA 98195
Web address: http://depts.washington.edu/psych/

1	2	3	4	5	**6**	7
Clinically oriented			Equal emphasis			Research oriented

What percentage of your faculty subscribes to or practices in each of the following orientations?

Psychodynamic/Psychoanalytic	10%
Applied behavioral analysis/Radical behavioral	10%
Family systems/Systems	30%
Existential/Phenomenological/Humanistic	0%
Cognitive/Cognitive-behavioral	60%

What percentage of students applying for internship last year was accepted into APA-accredited internships? 100%

What courses are required for incoming students to have completed prior to enrolling?
None

Are there courses you recommend that are not mandatory?
Abnormal/psychopathology, biological bases of behavior, developmental, statistics, learning & motivation, social psychology

GRE mean (M), cutoff (C), or preferred (P) score
Verbal 600 (P) Quantitative 600 (P) Analytical 600 (P)
Advanced Psychology 600 (P)

GPA mean (M), cutoff (C), or preferred (P)
Overall GPA 3.5 (P) Psychology GPA 3.5 (P)
Junior/Senior GPA 3.5 (P)

Number of applications/admission offers/incoming students in 2001
271 applied/15 admission offers/12 incoming

% of students receiving:
Tuition waiver only: 0%
Assistantship/fellowship only: 0%
Both tuition waiver & assistantship/fellowship: 90%

Approximate percentage of incoming students who entered with a B.A./B.S. only: 85% **Master's:** 15%

Approximate percentage of students who are Women: 65% **Ethnic Minority:** 20%

Average years to complete the doctoral program (including internship): 6 years

Research areas	# Faculty	# Grants
autism	1	1
child emotional development	3	3
cognitive therapy	4	1
couples	2	1
depression	3	1
minority	5	4
psychology process	1	1
sports medicine	2	0
spouse abuse	2	1
substance abuse	3	3
suicide	1	1

Clinical opportunities
autism
community psychology
couples
family
minority
personality disorders
sports psychology
substance abuse

Washington State University

Department of Psychology
Pullman, WA 99164-4820
phone#: (509) 335-2631
Web address: http://www.wsu.edu/psychology/clinical.htm

1	2	3	**4**	5	6	7
Clinically oriented			Equal emphasis			Research oriented

What percentage of your faculty subscribes to or practices in each of the following orientations?

Psychodynamic/Psychoanalytic	13%
Applied behavioral analysis/Radical behavioral	13%
Family systems/Systems	0%
Existential/Phenomenological/Humanistic	0%
Cognitive/Cognitive-behavioral	74%

What percentage of students applying for internship last year was accepted into APA-accredited internships? 100%

What courses are required for incoming students to have completed prior to enrolling?
None

Are there courses you recommend that are not mandatory?
Physiology, abnormal, social, developmental, personality, statistics, research methods

GRE mean (M), cutoff (C), or preferred (P) score
Verbal + Quantitative 1200 (M)

GPA mean (M), cutoff (C), or preferred (P)
Overall GPA 3.7 (M)

Number of applications/admission offers/incoming students in 2001
108 applied/8 admission offers/7 incoming

% of students receiving:
Tuition waiver only: 0%
Assistantship/fellowship only: 0%
Both tuition waiver & assistantship/fellowship: 100%

Approximate percentage of incoming students who entered with a B.A./B.S. only: 90% **Master's:** 10%

Approximate percentage of students who are Women: 71% **Ethnic Minority:** 15%

Average years to complete the doctoral program (including internship): 5.5 years

Research areas	# Faculty	# Grants
adult and child neuropsychology	2	1
adult psychopathology	3	2
behavioral medicine/health psychology	3	1
child clinical	4	1
community psychology	1	1

Clinical opportunities
adult and child inpatient
adult and child neuropsychological assessment
adult and child psychotherapy
health psychology

Washington University

Department of Psychology
Lindell and Skinker Boulevards
St. Louis, MO 63130
phone#: (314) 935-6520
e-mail: RMKURTZ@ARTSCI.WUSTL.edu
Web address: http://www.psych.wustl.edu/clinical/

1	2	3	4	5	6	**7**
Clinically oriented			Equal emphasis			Research oriented

What percentage of your faculty subscribes to or practices in each of the following orientations?

Psychodynamic/Psychoanalytic	36%
Applied behavioral analysis/Radical behavioral	0%
Family systems/Systems	0%
Existential/Phenomenological/Humanistic	9%
Cognitive/Cognitive-behavioral	55%

What percentage of students applying for internship last year was accepted into APA-accredited internships? 100%

What courses are required for incoming students to have completed prior to enrolling?
24 credits of psychology and 30 credits in the physical, biological, and social sciences; courses in experimental psychology (with laboratory), and a course in quantitative methods

Are there courses you recommend that are not mandatory?
History and systems

GRE mean (M), cutoff (C), or preferred (P) score
Verbal 620 (M) Quantitative 690 (M) Analytical 710 (M)
Advanced Psychology 680 (M)

GPA mean (M), cutoff (C), or preferred (P)
Overall GPA 3.65 (M) Psychology GPA 3.8 (M)
Junior/Senior GPA 3.8 (M)

Number of applications/admission offers/incoming students in 2001
101 applied/11 admission offers/5 incoming

% of students receiving:
Tuition waiver only: 0%
Assistantship/fellowship only: 0%
Both tuition waiver & assistantship/fellowship: 100%

Approximate percentage of incoming students who entered with a B.A./B.S. only: 98% **Master's:** 2%

Approximate percentage of students who are Women: 80% **Ethnic Minority:** 25%

Average years to complete the doctoral program (including internship): 6 years

Research areas	# Faculty	# Grants
aging/gerontology	2	3
health psychology	3	10
hypnosis	1	0
neuropsychology	2	3

Clinical opportunities
A psychological services center, as well as a wide range of other practicum agencies throughout the St. Louis area, are used. The student's particular interests, as well as the need for diverse training, are considered in placement at these various agencies.

University of Waterloo

Department of Psychology
Waterloo, Ontario N2L 3G1 Canada
phone#: (519) 885-1211, ext. #2548
e-mail: steffy@watserv1.uwaterloo.ca
Web address: http://www.arts.uwaterloo.ca/psychology/gradprog/gradhandbook.html#div-clinical

1	2	3	4	**5**	6	7

Clinically oriented — Equal emphasis — Research oriented

What percentage of your faculty subscribes to or practices in each of the following orientations?

Psychodynamic/Psychoanalytic	20%
Applied behavioral analysis/Radical behavioral	5%
Family systems/Systems	0%
Existential/Phenomenological/Humanistic	5%
Cognitive/Cognitive-behavioral	70%

What percentage of students applying for internship last year was accepted into APA-accredited internships? 100%

What courses are required for incoming students to have completed prior to enrolling?
Basic statistics, research design, research courses, undergraduate thesis or equivalent

Are there courses you recommend that are not mandatory?
History of psychology

GRE mean (M), cutoff (C), or preferred (P) score
Verbal 628 (M) Quantitative 674 (M) Analytical 730 (M)
Advanced Psychology 702 (M)

GPA mean (M), cutoff (C), or preferred (P)
Overall GPA B+ (P) Psychology GPA A– (P)
Junior/Senior GPA A– (P)

Number of applications/admission offers/incoming students in 2001
105 applied/7 admission offers/6 incoming

% of students receiving:
Tuition waiver only: 0%
Assistantship/fellowship only: 100%
Both tuition waiver & assistantship/fellowship: 0%

Approximate percentage of incoming students who entered with a B.A./B.S. only: 75% **Master's:** 25%

Approximate percentage of students who are Women: 80% **Ethnic Minority:** 13%

Average years to complete the doctoral program (including internship): 6.5 years

Research areas	# Faculty	# Grants
attention-deficit disorders	1	1
cognitive-behavior therapy	3	3
depression	1	0
hypnosis	1	1
learning disabilities	1	0

Clinical opportunities
child/adolescent/adult
family
hypnosis
neuropsychology
school/educational

Wayne State University

Department of Psychology
71 West Warren
Detroit, MI 48202
phone#: (313) 577-2800
e-mail: AAllen@Sun.science.wayne.edu
Web address: http://www.science.wayne.edu/~psych/areas/clinical/cl_gradinfo.html

1	2	3	4	**5**	6	7

Clinically oriented — Equal emphasis — Research oriented

What percentage of your faculty subscribes to or practices in each of the following orientations?

Psychodynamic/Psychoanalytic	0%
Applied behavioral analysis/Radical behavioral	0%
Family systems/Systems	20%
Existential/Phenomenological/Humanistic	0%
Cognitive/Cognitive-behavioral	80%

What percentage of students applying for internship last year was accepted into APA-accredited internships? 100%

What courses are required for incoming students to have completed prior to enrolling?
18 quarter hours (12 semester hours) in psychology, including experimental psychology (with laboratory experience) and statistical methods

Are there courses you recommend that are not mandatory?
Undergraduate courses in mathematics and life sciences

GRE mean (M), cutoff (C), or preferred (P) score
Verbal 650 (M) Quantitative 650 (M)

GPA mean (M), cutoff (C), or preferred (P)
Overall GPA 2.0 (C), 3.75 (M)

Number of applications/admission offers/incoming students in 2001
96 applied/21 admission offers/8 incoming

% of students receiving:
Tuition waiver only: 10%
Assistantship/fellowship only: 50%
Both tuition waiver & assistantship/fellowship: 33%

Approximate percentage of incoming students who entered with a B.A./B.S. only: 80% **Master's:** 20%

Approximate percentage of students who are Women: 70% **Ethnic Minority:** 10%

Average years to complete the doctoral program (including internship): 7.6 years

Research areas	# Faculty	# Grants
behavioral medicine	2	2
community psychology	2	2
neuropsychology	2	2
risk factors/family	1	2
schizophrenia	1	0

Clinical opportunities
behavioral medicine
community psychology
neuropsychology
schizophrenia

West Virginia University

Department of Psychology
114 Oglebay Hall
Morgantown, WV 26506-6040
phone#: (304) 293-2001, ext. # 628
e-mail: dswinney@mail.WVU.edu
Web address: http://www.as.wvu.edu/psyc/

1	2	3	4	**5**	6	7
Clinically oriented			Equal emphasis			Research oriented

What percentage of your faculty subscribes to or practices in each of the following orientations?

Psychodynamic/Psychoanalytic	0%
Applied behavioral analysis/Radical behavioral	50%
Family systems/Systems	0%
Existential/Phenomenological/Humanistic	0%
Cognitive/Cognitive-behavioral	50%

What percentage of students applying for internship last year was accepted into APA-accredited internships? 100%

What courses are required for incoming students to have completed prior to enrolling?
None

Are there courses you recommend that are not mandatory?
Psychology major or related field, research, clinical experience

GRE mean (M), cutoff (C), or preferred (P) score
Verbal 500 (P) Quantitative 500 (P)
Advanced Psychology 500 (P)

GPA mean (M), cutoff (C), or preferred (P)
Overall GPA 3.5 (P) Psychology GPA 3.5 (P)

Number of applications/admission offers/incoming students in 2001
157 applied/9 admission offers/8 incoming

% of students receiving:
Tuition waiver only: 0%
Assistantship/fellowship only: 0%
Both tuition waiver & assistantship/fellowship: 100%

Approximate percentage of incoming students who entered with a B.A./B.S. only: 70% **Master's:** 30%

Approximate percentage of students who are Women: 70% **Ethnic Minority:** 8%

Average years to complete the doctoral program (including internship): 6 years

Research areas	# Faculty	# Grants
anxiety disorders	2	0
attention deficit/ hyperactivity disorder	2	1
behavioral dentistry	1	0
behavioral medicine	4	2
cardiovascular reactivity	1	0
child behavior disorders	1	0
developmental disabilities	1	0
ethnic minority issues	1	0
forensics	1	0

gerontology	1	0
hypertension	1	2
pain	1	0
pediatric psychology	2	3
posttraumatic stress disorder	1	0

Clinical opportunities
anxiety disorders (adults and children)
behavioral dentistry
behavioral medicine (adults and children)
burn trauma
developmental disabilities
eating disorders
forensic psychology
gerontology
parent training
school interventions
victim/battering/abuse

Western Michigan University

Department of Psychology
Kalamazoo, MI 49008
phone#: (616) 387-8340
e-mail: alison.levine@wmich.edu
Web address: http://www.wmich.edu/psychology/psychframe.html

1 2 3 **4** 5 6 7

Clinically oriented — Equal emphasis — Research oriented

What percentage of your faculty subscribes to or practices in each of the following orientations?

Psychodynamic/Psychoanalytic	0%
Applied behavioral analysis/Radical behavioral	57%
Family systems/Systems	14%
Existential/Phenomenological/Humanistic	0%
Cognitive/Cognitive-behavioral	100%

What percentage of students applying for internship last year was accepted into APA-accredited internships? 100%

What courses are required for incoming students to have completed prior to enrolling?
Psychology major at an accredited institution

Are there courses you recommend that are not mandatory?
Basic course in behavioral principles/theory

GRE mean (M), cutoff (C), or preferred (P) score
Verbal 500 (C) Quantitative 500 (C)

GPA mean (M), cutoff (C), or preferred (P)
Overall GPA 3.2 (C) Psychology GPA 3.5 (P)

Number of applications/admission offers/incoming students in 2001
70 applied/7 admission offers/7 incoming

% of students receiving:
Tuition waiver only: 0%
Assistantship/fellowship only: 0%
Both tuition waiver & assistantship/fellowship: 62%

Approximate percentage of incoming students who entered with a B.A./B.S. only: 50% **Master's:** 50%

Approximate percentage of students who are Women: 67% **Ethnic Minority:** 9%

Average years to complete the doctoral program (including internship): 5.5 years

Research areas	# Faculty	# Grants
AIDS prevention/education	1	1
anxiety disorders/PTSD	2	1
attention-deficit disorder	1	1
behavioral medicine	3	2
program evaluation	1	0
sexual deviations and dysfunctions	1	0

Clinical opportunities
attention-deficit disorder
autism/developmental disabilities
domestic violence
forensic mental health
function-based treatment
posttraumatic stress disorder
refugee mental health
school refusal

University of Western Ontario

Department of Psychology
London, Ontario N6A 5C2, Canada
phone#: (519) 661-2064
e-mail: vmvandom@uwo.ca
Web address: http://www.ssc.uwo.ca/psychology/clinical

1 2 3 4 5 **6** 7

Clinically oriented — Equal emphasis — Research oriented

What percentage of your faculty subscribes to or practices in each of the following orientations?

Psychodynamic/Psychoanalytic	35%
Applied behavioral analysis/Radical behavioral	5%
Family systems/Systems	10%
Existential/Phenomenological/Humanistic	5%
Cognitive/Cognitive-behavioral	45%

What percentage of students applying for internship last year was accepted into APA-accredited internships? 90%

What courses are required for incoming students to have completed prior to enrolling?
—

Are there courses you recommend that are not mandatory?
Abnormal psychology, statistics, history and systems of psychology

GRE mean (M), cutoff (C), or preferred (P) score
Verbal 621 (M) Quantitative 663 (M)
Advanced Psychology 704 (M)

GPA mean (M), cutoff (C), or preferred (P)
Overall GPA B+ (C) Psychology GPA A– (C)
Overall GPA A (M) Psychology GPA A (M)

Number of applications/admission offers/incoming students in 2001
140 applied/11 admission offers/6 incoming

% of students receiving:
Tuition waiver only: 0%
Assistantship/fellowship only: 0%
Both tuition waiver & assistantship/fellowship: 100%

Approximate percentage of incoming students who entered with a B.A./B.S. only: 80% **Master's:** 20%

Approximate percentage of students who are Women: 81% **Ethnic Minority:** —

Average years to complete the doctoral program (including internship): 7 years

Research areas	**# Faculty**	**# Grants**
applied assessment	1	0
attachment in infancy	2	1
cognitive deficits in schizophrenia	1	1
depression	1	1
drug addiction	1	1
emotion and cognition	1	0
family violence	1	1
health psychology	4	2
humor	2	0
menopause	1	0
pain	1	1
physical and sexual abuse	1	1
psychology of physical symptoms	1	1
psychopharmacology	1	0
stress and coping	3	0

Clinical opportunities
anxiety disorders
behavioral medicine
career counseling and development
child behavior and emotion
child forensics
inpatient psychiatry
mood disorders
outpatient psychiatry
pediatric health psychology
rehabilitation

Wheaton College (Psy.D.)

Department of Psychology
Wheaton, IL 60187-5593
phone#: (630) 752-7053
e-mail: Robert.J.Gregory@wheaton.edu
Web address: http://www.wheaton.edu/

1	2	**3**	4	5	6	7
Clinically oriented		Equal emphasis			Research oriented	

What percentage of your faculty subscribes to or practices in each of the following orientations?

Psychodynamic/Psychoanalytic	25%
Applied behavioral analysis/Radical behavioral	0%
Family systems/Systems	33%
Existential/Phenomenological/Humanistic	0%
Cognitive/Cognitive-behavioral	42%

What percentage of students applying for internship last year was accepted into APA-accredited internships? 65%

What courses are required for incoming students to have completed prior to enrolling?
Introduction to psychology, theories of personality, physiological psychology, abnormal psychology, research/statistics

Are there courses you recommend that are not mandatory?
Developmental, cognition, social

GRE mean (M), cutoff (C), or preferred (P) score
Verbal 500 (M) Quantitative 550 (M) Analytical 550 (M)
Advanced Psychology 560 (M)

GPA mean (M), cutoff (C), or preferred (P)
Overall GPA 3.0 (C)

Number of applications/admission offers/incoming students in 2001
65 applied/31 admission offers/23 incoming

% of students receiving:
Tuition waiver only: 0%
Assistantship/fellowship only: 0%
Both tuition waiver & assistantship/fellowship: 0%

Approximate percentage of incoming students who entered with a B.A./B.S. only: 65% **Master's:** 35%

Approximate percentage of students who are Women: 52% **Ethnic Minority:** 25%

Average years to complete the doctoral program (including internship): 5 years

Research areas	**# Faculty**	**# Grants**
church-psychology collaboration	3	1
family transitions	1	0
gender research	1	1
geropsychology issues	1	0
meta-analysis	1	0
parent training (Hispanic & African American)	1	1
rural psychology	2	0
spirituality and psychology	2	0

Clinical opportunities
Chicago and suburban area has great variety of offerings.

Widener University (Psy.D.)

Institute for Graduate Clinical Psychology
301 East 19th Street
Chester, PA 19013
phone#: (610) 499-1208
e-mail: ellen.t.madison@widener.edu
Web address: http://muse.widener.edu/Graduate-Psychology/index.html

1	2	3	4	5	6	7
Clinically oriented			Equal emphasis			Research oriented

What percentage of your faculty subscribes to or practices in each of the following orientations?

Psychodynamic/Psychoanalytic	40%
Applied behavioral analysis/Radical behavioral	0%
Family systems/Systems	20%
Existential/Phenomenological/Humanistic	10%
Cognitive/Cognitive-behavioral	30%

What percentage of students applying for internship last year was accepted into APA-accredited internships? 100%

What courses are required for incoming students to have completed prior to enrolling?
Introduction to psychology, statistics

Are there courses you recommend that are not mandatory?
Research design, elementary statistics

GRE mean (M), cutoff (C), or preferred (P) score
Verbal 600 (P) Quantitative 600 (P)

GPA mean (M), cutoff (C), or preferred (P)
Overall GPA 3.3 (P)

Number of applications/admission offers/incoming students in 2001
216 applied/66 admission offers/37 incoming

% of students receiving:
Tuition waiver only: 43%
Assistantship/fellowship only: 0%
Both tuition waiver & assistantship/fellowship: 43%

Approximate percentage of incoming students who entered with a B.A./B.S. only: 91% **Master's:** 8%

Approximate percentage of students who are Women: 75% **Ethnic Minority:** 14%

Average years to complete the doctoral program (including internship): 5 years

Research areas	**# Faculty**	**# Grants**
assessment/diagnosis	1	0
early childhood	1	0
learning disabilities	1	0
problem solving	2	0
stress and coping	2	0

Clinical opportunities
assessment
couples therapy
family therapy
forensic psychology
group therapy
neuropsychology
psychoanalytic/psychodynamic therapy
school psychology certification—state level
sex therapy

University of Windsor

Department of Psychology
Windsor, Ontario N9B 3P4, Canada
phone#: (519) 253-3000
fax#: (519) 973-7021
e-mail: bzakoor@uwindsor.ca
Web address: http://www.uwindsor.ca/psychology

1	2	**3**	4	5	6	7
Clinically oriented			Equal emphasis			Research oriented

What percentage of your faculty subscribes to or practices in each of the following orientations?

Psychodynamic/Psychoanalytic	45%
Applied behavioral analysis/Radical behavioral	15%
Family systems/Systems	15%
Existential/Phenomenological/Humanistic	30%
Cognitive/Cognitive-behavioral	25%

What percentage of students applying for internship last year was accepted into APA-accredited internships? 100%

What courses are required for incoming students to have completed prior to enrolling?
Statistics, experimental method, human learning, abnormal, honors thesis or equivalent

Are there courses you recommend that are not mandatory?
No

GRE mean (M), cutoff (C), or preferred (P)
Verbal 60th percentile Quantitative 60th percentile
Analytical 60th percentile
Advanced Psychology 60th percentile

GPA mean (M), cutoff (C), or preferred (P)
Overall GPA 3.25 (P) Psychology GPA 3.5 (P)
Junior/Senior GPA 3.5 (P)

Number of applications/admission offers/incoming students in 2001
146 applied/32 admission offers/13 incoming

% of students receiving:
Tuition waiver only: 20%
Assistantship/fellowship only: 95%
Both tuition waiver & assistantship/fellowship: 20%

Approximate percentage of incoming students who entered with a B.A./B.S. only: 90% **Master's:** 10%

Approximate percentage of students who are Women: 60% **Ethnic Minority:** 10%

Average years to complete the doctoral program (including internship): 7 years

Research areas	# Faculty	# Grants
addiction	2	1
child research	3	2
community psychology	2	2
eating disorders	2	1
gambling behavior	1	1
neuropsychological	4	4
psychotherapy research	3	1
service/training neurobiofeedback	1	1

Clinical opportunities

We have a Psychological Service Center which serves the campus and general community. Extensive training in psychotherapy is available at the PSC. In addition we have numerous training sites for practica and internships in the Detroit area. We presently have students placed in 7 sites in the Detroit Medical Center consortium. These training sites offer exceptional training in all aspects of clinical psychology. In total we have students train in more than 40 internship and practica sites in Canada and the USA.

University of Wisconsin–Madison

Department of Psychology
W.J. Brogden Psychology Building
1202 West Johnson Street
Madison, WI 53706
phone#: (608) 262-2079
e-mail: jpnewman@facstaff.wisc.edu
Web address: http://www.wisc.edu/grad/catalog//etsci/psycho.html#heading/

1 2 3 4 5 6 **7**

Clinically oriented — Equal emphasis — Research oriented

What percentage of your faculty subscribes to or practices in each of the following orientations?

Psychodynamic/Psychoanalytic	50%
Applied behavioral analysis/Radical behavioral	0%
Family systems/Systems	10%
Existential/Phenomenological/Humanistic	10%
Cognitive/Cognitive-behavioral	80%
Motivational/Interviewing	10%
Child	10%

Note: Some faculty endorsed more than one orientation, some only one, and some endorsed none.

What percentage of students applying for internship last year was accepted into APA-accredited internships? 100%

What courses are required for incoming students to have completed prior to enrolling?

Psychology major or related field training

Are there courses you recommend that are not mandatory?

No

GRE mean (M), cutoff (C), or preferred (P) score

Verbal + Quantitative 1400 (M)
Verbal + Quantitative 1200 (C)

GPA mean (M), cutoff (C), or preferred (P)

GPA 3.69 (M) GPA 3.00 (C)

Number of applications/admission offers/incoming students in 2001

220 applied/6 admission offers/3 incoming

% of students receiving:

Tuition waiver only: 0%
Assistantship/fellowship only: 0%
Both tuition remission (out of state portion only) & assistantship/fellowship: 100%

Approximate percentage of incoming students who entered with a B.A./B.S. only: 100% **Master's:** 0%

Approximate percentage of students who are Women: 57% **Ethnic Minority:** 10%

Average years to complete the doctoral program (including internship): 5.5 years

Research areas	# Faculty	# Grants
affective disorders	4	8
developmental psychopathology	2	7
health	2	4
personality disorders: psychopathy	1	2
psychotherapy	1	2
schizophrenia and other psychotic disorders	2	2
self-concept	1	0
substance abuse	2	4

Clinical opportunities

addictive disorders
assessment (IQ, objective, psychophysiological, neuropsychological)
assessment of forensic populations
assessment of schizophrenia, first-degree relatives of schizophrenics, and at-risk populations
brief dynamic psychotherapy
cognitive therapy for affective and anxiety disorders
families/couples therapy
inpatient therapy
self-concept
therapy with criminal offenders

University of Wisconsin–Milwaukee

Department of Psychology
P.O. Box 413
Milwaukee, WI 53201
phone#: (414) 224-5521
e-mail: ejs@csd.uwm.edu
Web address: http://www.uwm.edu/Dept/Psychology/clinical.htm

1 2 3 **4** 5 6 7

Clinically oriented — Equal emphasis — Research oriented

What percentage of your faculty subscribes to or practices in each of the following orientations?

Psychodynamic/Psychoanalytic	9%
Applied behavioral analysis/Radical behavioral	18%
Family systems/Systems	46%
Existential/Phenomenological/Humanistic	9%
Cognitive/Cognitive-behavioral	18%

What percentage of students applying for internship last year was accepted into APA-accredited internships? 100%

What courses are required for incoming students to have completed prior to enrolling?
B.A.or B.S. in psychology or equivalent

Are there courses you recommend that are not mandatory?
Laboratory courses in psychology

GRE mean (M), cutoff (C), or preferred (P) score
Verbal 598 (M) Quantitative 643 (M)
Verbal + Quantitative 1241 (M) Analytical 702 (M)
Advanced Psychology 640 (M)

GPA mean (M), cutoff (C), or preferred (P)
Overall GPA 3.37 (M) Psychology GPA 3.40 (M)
Junior/Senior GPA 3.37 (M)

Number of applications/admission offers/incoming students in 2001
61 applied/10 admission offers/5 incoming

% of students receiving:
Tuition waiver only: 0%
Assistantship/fellowship only: 0%
Both tuition waiver & assistantship/fellowship: 100%

Approximate percentage of incoming students who entered with a B.A./B.S. only: 88% **Master's:** 12%

Approximate percentage of students who are Women: 80% **Ethnic Minority:** 14%

Average years to complete the doctoral program (including internship): 6.5 years

Research areas	# Faculty	# Grants
alcohol and substance abuse	1	0
cognitive-behavior therapy	3	0
developmental	2	0
health psychology/behavioral medicine	3	0
neuropsychology	2	2
obsessive–compulsive disorder	2	0

Clinical opportunities
behavioral medicine
child and adult neuropsychology
child development
inpatient psychiatric
premature infants and their families—stress

The Wright Institute (Psy.D.)

2728 Durant Avenue
Berkeley, CA 94704
phone#: (510) 841-9230
e-mail: info@wrightinst.edu
Web address: http://www.wrightinst.edu

1	**2**	3	4	5	6	7
Clinically oriented			Equal emphasis			Research oriented

What percentage of your faculty subscribes to or practices in each of the following orientations?

Psychodynamic/Psychoanalytic	65%
Applied behavioral analysis/Radical behavioral	0%
Family systems/Systems	20%
Existential/Phenomenological/Humanistic	10%
Cognitive/Cognitive-behavioral	5%

What percentage of students applying for internship last year was accepted into APA-accredited internships? 80%

What courses are required for incoming students to have completed prior to enrolling?
None

Are there courses you recommend that are not mandatory?
Personality theory, abnormal psychology, statistics

GRE mean (M), cutoff (C), or preferred (P) score
—

GPA mean (M), cutoff (C), or preferred (P)
Overall GPA 3.0 (P) Psychology GPA 3.0 (P)

Number of applications/admission offers/incoming students in 2001
225 applied/100 admission offers/50 incoming

% of students receiving:
Tuition waiver only: 0%
Assistantship/fellowship only: 18%
Both tuition waiver & assistantship/fellowship: 0%

Approximate percentage of incoming students who entered with a B.A./B.S. only: 60% **Master's:** 40%

Approximate percentage of students who are Women: 80% **Ethnic Minority:** 20%

Average years to complete the doctoral program (including internship): 5.5 years

Research areas	# Faculty	# Grants
cognition and consciousness	1	0
cross-cultural psychology	3	0
gender studies	3	0
infant/parent psychotherapy outcome	3	0
parenting	3	0
step-families	1	0
substance abuse	2	1

Clinical opportunities
AIDS
affect disorders
assessment
child assessment
child psychopathology
couples therapy
crisis intervention
family therapy
forensic populations
gay and lesbian
group therapy
minority
neuropsychology
pediatric/developmental
personality disorders

psychodynamic
schizophrenia
substance abuse
university counseling

Wright State University (Psy.D.)

School of Professional Psychology
3640 Colonel Glenn Highway
Dayton, OH 45435
phone#: (937) 775-3492
e-mail: sopp1@wright.edu
Web address: http://www.wright.edu/sopp/

1	**2**	3	4	5	6	7
Clinically oriented			Equal emphasis			Research oriented

What percentage of your faculty subscribes to or practices in each of the following orientations?

Psychodynamic/Psychoanalytic	8%
Applied behavioral analysis/Radical behavioral	8%
Family systems/Systems	24%
Existential/Phenomenological/Humanistic	8%
Cognitive/Cognitive-behavioral	20%

What percentage of students applying for internship last year was accepted into APA-accredited internships? 100%

What courses are required for incoming students to have completed prior to enrolling?
Introductory psychology, introductory statistics, abnormal psychology, experimental psychology, developmental psychology, physiological psychology

Are there courses you recommend that are not mandatory?
Learning, tests and measurements, multicultural issues, gender issues, personality theory, social psychology

GRE mean (M), cutoff (C), or preferred (P) score
Verbal + Quantitative 1200 (P)

GPA mean (M), cutoff (C), or preferred (P)
Overall GPA 3.5 (P) Junior/Senior GPA 3.0 (P)

Number of applications/admission offers/incoming students in 2001
290 applied/35 admission offers/26 incoming

% of students receiving:
Tuition waiver only: 38%
Assistantship/fellowship only: 57%
Both tuition waiver & assistantship/fellowship: 5%

Approximate percentage of incoming students who entered with a B.A./B.S. only: 75% **Master's:** 25%

Approximate percentage of students who are Women: 64% **Ethnic Minority:** 40% **Disabled:** 5%

Average years to complete the doctoral program (including internship): 5 years

Research areas	**# Faculty**	**# Grants**
domestic violence	1	1
family therapy	3	1
gender issues	1	0
health psychology	2	1
hearing impaired	1	1
managed care	1	1
minority mental health	3	0
multicultural issues	3	2
peace psychology	1	0
professional issues	1	0
social skills	3	3
violence reduction	1	2

Clinical opportunities
brief therapy/cognitive behavioral therapy
child/adolescent
community psychology
crisis intervention
deafness
family
forensic psychology
health psychology
marital/couples
multicultural issues
multidisciplinary teams
neuropsychology
victim/battering/abuse
violence reduction

University of Wyoming

Department of Psychology
Box 3415 University Station
Laramie, WY 82071
phone#: (307) 766-6303
e-mail: psyc.uw@uwyo.edu
Web address: http://www.uwyo.edu/psyc

1	2	3	4	**5**	6	7
Clinically oriented			Equal emphasis			Research oriented

What percentage of your faculty subscribes to or practices in each of the following orientations?

Psychodynamic/Psychoanalytic	20%
Applied behavioral analysis/Radical behavioral	50%
Family systems/Systems	10%
Existential/Phenomenological/Humanistic	20%
Cognitive/Cognitive-behavioral	25%

What percentage of students applying for internship last year was accepted into APA-accredited internships? 100%

What courses are required for incoming students to have completed prior to enrolling?
None

Are there courses you recommend that are not mandatory?
Statistics, 30–45 psychology credits, research experience

GRE mean (M), cutoff (C), or preferred (P) score
Verbal + Quantitative 1200 (P)
Advanced Psychology 600 (P)

GPA mean (M), cutoff (C), or preferred (P)
Overall GPA 3.2 (P) Psychology GPA 3.2 (P)
Junior/Senior GPA 3.2 (P)

Number of applications/admission offers/incoming students in 2001
No students were admitted for 2001—program being restructured—visit Web page for details.

% of students receiving:
100% of students in years 1–3 receive at least 1 semester of assistantship plus tuition waiver

Approximate percentage of incoming students who entered with a B.A./B.S. only: 75% **Master's:** 25%

Approximate percentage of students who are Women: 60% **Ethnic Minority:** 5%

Research areas	# Faculty	# Grants
child abuse/delinquency prevention	2	2
depression	1	0
family violence	1	0
HIV/AIDS prevention	1	3
mental retardation	2	1
primary care	3	1
psychology and the law	2	3
self-regulation/self-efficacy	2	0
substance abuse	3	3

Clinical opportunities
adult/child inpatient and residential
developmental disabilities
empirically supported psychotherapies
forensic/correctional
mood/anxiety disorders
primary/interdisciplinary care
rural/community health care

Yale University

Department of Psychology
P.O. Box 208205
New Haven, CT 06520-8205
phone#: (203) 432-4505
e-mail: Jerome.Singer@yale.edu
Kelly.Brownell@yale.edu
Mitchell.Prinsetein@yale.edu
Web address: http://www.yale.edu/psychology/

1 2 3 4 5 **6** 7

Clinically oriented — Equal emphasis — Research oriented

What percentage of your faculty subscribes to or practices in each of the following orientations?

Psychodynamic/Psychoanalytic	20%
Applied behavioral analysis/Radical behavioral	0%
Family systems/Systems	30%
Existential/Phenomenological/Humanistic	0%
Cognitive/Cognitive-behavioral	50%

What percentage of students applying for internship last year was accepted into APA-accredited internships? 100%

What courses are required for incoming students to have completed prior to enrolling?
None

Are there courses you recommend that are not mandatory?
Broad psychology background, undergraduate psychology major

GRE mean (M), cutoff (C), or preferred (P) score
Verbal 710 (M) Quantitative 725 (M) Analytical 750 (M)

GPA mean (M), cutoff (C), or preferred (P)
Overall GPA 3.85 (M)

Number of applications/admission offers/incoming students in 2001
300 applied/4 admission offers/4 incoming

% of students receiving:
Tuition waiver only: 0%
Assistantship/fellowship only: 0%
Both tuition waiver & assistantship/fellowship: 100%

Approximate percentage of incoming students who entered with a B.A./B.S. only: 100% **Master's:** 0%

Approximate percentage of students who are Women: 65% **Ethnic Minority:** 10%

Average years to complete the doctoral program (including internship): 6 years

Research areas	# Faculty	# Grants
adult psychopathology	2	3
antisocial behavior in childhood	2	3
anxiety disorders	1	0
children's imagination processes	1	1
depression	1	1
eating disorders	1	2
psychotherapy process	2	1
television viewing in childhood	1	1

Clinical opportunities
anxiety disorders
child psychotherapy
conduct disorders
couples
eating disorders
health psychology
interpersonal psychotherapy

Yeshiva University (Psy.D.)

Department of Psychology
Ferkauf Graduate School of Psychology
1300 Morris Park Avenue
Bronx, NY 10461
phone#: (718) 430-3850
e-mail: gill@aecom.yu.edu
Web address: http://www.yu.edu/ferkauf/clinical.htm

1 **2** 3 4 5 6 7

Clinically oriented — Equal emphasis — Research oriented

What percentage of your faculty subscribes to or practices in each of the following orientations?

Psychodynamic/Psychoanalytic	30%
Applied behavioral analysis/Radical behavioral	10%
Family systems/Systems	40%
Existential/Phenomenological/Humanistic	20%
Cognitive/Cognitive-behavioral	40%

What percentage of students applying for internship last year was accepted into APA-accredited internships? 95%

What courses are required for incoming students to have completed prior to enrolling?
Introductory psychology, statistics, abnormal psychology, experimental psychology, physiological psychology, personality

Are there courses you recommend that are not mandatory?
No

GRE mean (M), cutoff (C), or preferred (P) score
Verbal 600 (M) Quantitative 600 (C)
Advanced Psychology 550 (P)

GPA mean (M), cutoff (C), or preferred (P)
Overall GPA 3.0 (C) Psychology GPA 3.0 (C)

Number of applications/admission offers/incoming students in 2001
184 applied/58 admission offers/21 incoming

% of students receiving:
Tuition waiver only: 0%
Assistantship/fellowship only: 70%
Both tuition waiver & assistantship/fellowship: 0%

Approximate percentage of incoming students who entered with a B.A./B.S. only: 85% **Master's:** 15%

Approximate percentage of students who are Women: 73% **Ethnic Minority:** 15%

Average years to complete the doctoral program (including internship): 5 years

Research areas	**# Faculty**	**# Grants**
AIDS/HIV	2	1
anxiety disorders	3	0
child psychopathology	2	0
chronic illness	1	1
depression	3	0
early childhood intervention	1	0
eating disorders	2	0
ethnicity and identity	2	0
family therapy	4	0
infant–mother interaction	1	0
pain	2	0
pediatric psychology	1	0
psychoanalytic therapy	5	0
psychotherapy process and outcome	3	0
sleep disorders/nightmares	1	0
stress and coping	4	1
substance abuse	1	2
suicide	1	0
teenage pregnancy	1	0

Clinical opportunities
anxiety disorders
at-risk adolescents
behavioral medicine
child treatment
cognitive-behavioral medicine
family therapy
group therapy
marital/couples
parent training
psychodynamic therapy
psychoeducational assessment

York University—Adult Clinical Program

Department of Psychology
Toronto, Ontario M3J 1P3, Canada
phone#: (416) 736-2100, ext. 33132
e-mail: stouk@yorku.ca
Web address: http://www.yorku.ca/grads/

1	2	3	**4**	5	6	7
Clinically oriented			Equal emphasis			Research oriented

What percentage of your faculty subscribes to or practices in each of the following orientations?

Psychodynamic/Psychoanalytic	25%
Applied behavioral analysis/Radical behavioral	0%
Family systems/Systems	6%
Existential/Phenomenological/Humanistic	38%
Cognitive/Cognitive-behavioral	31%

What percentage of students applying for internship last year was accepted into APA-accredited internships? 40%

What courses are required for incoming students to have completed prior to enrolling?
Introductory psychology, physical/neuropsychology, organizational/social/groups, research design and statistics analysis, learning/perception/emotion/motivation, personality/abnormal/individual differences

Are there courses you recommend that are not mandatory?
Multicultural psychology, sex-roles, tests and measurements

GRE mean (M), cutoff (C), or preferred (P) score
Verbal 563 (M) Quantitative 559 (M) Analytical 611 (M)
Advanced Psychology 674 (M)

GPA mean (M), cutoff (C), or preferred (P)
Overall GPA A– (M)

Number of applications/admission offers/incoming students in 2001
132 applied/14 admission offers/11 incoming

% of students receiving:
Tuition waiver only: N/A
Assistantship/fellowship only: 34%
Both tuition waiver & assistantship/fellowship: N/A

Approximate percentage of incoming students who entered with a B.A./B.S. only: 100% **Master's:** 0%

Approximate percentage of students who are
Women: 79% **Ethnic Minority:** N/A

Average years to complete the doctoral program (including internship): 6 years

Research areas	# Faculty	# Grants
alcohol and substance abuse	1	3
anxiety disorders	2	2
depression	3	3
family and groups	1	0
grief and trauma	1	0
health with a focus on cardiovascular disease	1	3
memory and cognition in aging and dementia	1	2
personality factors in mental, physical, and neuropsychological health	2	0
pyschotherapy process and outcome	4	3
schizophrenia	1	0
stress and coping	1	1

Clinical opportunities
alcohol and substance abuse
anxiety disorders
depression
eating disorders
health psychology

York University—Clinical-Developmental Area

Department of Psychology
Toronto, Ontario M3J 1P3, Canada
phone#: (416) 736-2100
e-mail: cdarea@yorku.ca
Web address: http://www.yorku.ca/dept/psych/grad/areas.htm

1 2 3 **4** 5 6 7

Clinically oriented | Equal emphasis | Research oriented

What percentage of your faculty subscribes to or practices in each of the following orientations?

Psychodynamic/Psychoanalytic	10%
Applied behavioral analysis/Radical behavioral	10%
Family systems/Systems	75%
Existential/Phenomenological/Humanistic	0%
Cognitive/Cognitive-behavioral	75%

What courses are required for incoming students to have completed prior to enrolling?
Honors degree in psychology

Are there courses you recommend that are not mandatory?
—

GRE mean (M), cutoff (C), or preferred (P) score
Verbal 530 (M) Quantitative 620 (M)
Advanced Psychology 670 (M)

GPA mean (M), cutoff (C), or preferred (P)
Overall GPA B+ (C) Psychology GPA B+ (C), A (P)
Junior/Senior GPA B+ (C), A (P)

Number of applications/admission offers/incoming students in 2001
102 applied/10 admission offers/7 incoming

% of students receiving:
Tuition waiver only: 0%
Assistantship/fellowship only: 100%
Both partial tuition waiver & assistantship/fellowship: 100%

Approximate percentage of incoming students who entered with a B.A./B.S. only: 90% **Master's:** 10%

Approximate percentage of students who are
Women: 80% **Ethnic Minority:** 18%

Average years to complete the doctoral program (including internship): 6.5 years

Research areas	# Faculty	# Grants
adolescent peer relations	3	3
aggression-child and adolescence	3	3
bullying and victimization	2	1
child abuse	3	2
child testimony	1	2
cognitive and language development	1	0
history of psychology	1	0
pervasive developmental delay (autism, deafness, developmental disability)	2	1
problem-solving/emotion	1	0
stress and coping	1	0
teen violence	2	2
underachievement	1	1

Clinical opportunities
children's rehabilitation center
dual diagnosis clinic
gender disorder clinic
learning disability clinic
mental health centers
psychiatric clinics
school boards

Clinical Programs Not Providing Information

Alliant International University/California School of Professional Psychology–Alameda (Ph.D. and Psy.D.; 1997 data provided)

Alliant International University/California School of Professional Psychology–Los Angeles (Ph.D. and Psy.D.; 1997 data provided)

Carlos Albizu University–Miami (Psy.D.)

Carlos Albizu University–San Juan (Ph.D.; data provided for the Psy.D. program)

REPORTS ON INDIVIDUAL COUNSELING PSYCHOLOGY PROGRAMS

University of Akron

Department of Psychology and
Department of Counseling and Special Education
Akron, OH 44325-4301
phone#: (330) 972-7280 or (330) 972-7777
e-mail: dmt5@uakron.edu
Web address: http://www.uakron.edu/psychology/COUNSEL.HTM

1	2	3	**4**	5	6	7
Clinically oriented			Equal emphasis			Research oriented

What percentage of your faculty subscribes to or practices in each of the following orientations?

Psychodynamic/Psychoanalytic	10%
Applied behavioral analysis/Radical behavioral	0%
Family systems/Systems	30%
Existential/Phenomenological/Humanistic	10%
Cognitive/Cognitive-behavioral	50%

What percentage of students applying for internship last year was accepted into APA-accredited internships? 81%

What courses are required for incoming students to have completed prior to enrolling?
The program has two tracks: one track (Department of Psychology) admits students with a bachelor's degree in psychology; the other track (Department of Counseling and Special Education) admits students with a master's degree in counseling.

Are there courses you recommend that are not mandatory?
No

GRE mean (M), cutoff (C), or preferred (P)
1100 recommended

GPA mean (M), cutoff (C), or preferred (P)
Overall GPA 3.25 (M)

Number of applications/admission offers/incoming students in 2001
80 applied/14 admission offers/11 incoming

% of students receiving:
Tuition waiver only: 20%
Assistantship/fellowship only: 0%
Both tuition waiver & assistantship/fellowship: 80%

Approximate percentage of incoming students who entered with a B.A./B.S. only: 50% **Master's:** 50%

Approximate percentage of students who are Women: 70% **Ethnic Minority:** 10%

Average years to complete the doctoral program (including internship): 6 years

Research areas	# Faculty	# Grants
family	2	0
multicultural issues	2	0
personality assessment	2	0
suicide	2	0
vocational counseling	2	0
women's issues	3	0

Clinical opportunities
child and adolescent service center
clinic for child study and family therapy
community mental health center
VA medical center

University at Albany/State University of New York

Division of Counseling Psychology
Department of Education and Counseling Psychology
ED 220
Albany, NY 12222
phone#: (518) 442-5040
e-mail: mfriedlander@uamail.albany.edu
Web address: http://www.albany.edu/counseling_psych

1	2	3	**4**	5	6	7
Clinically oriented			Equal emphasis			Research oriented

What percentage of your faculty subscribes to or practices in each of the following orientations?

Psychodynamic/Psychoanalytic	20%
Applied behavioral analysis/Radical behavioral	0%
Family systems/Systems	20%
Existential/Phenomenological/Humanistic	20%
Cognitive/Cognitive-behavioral	40%

What percentage of students applying for internship last year was accepted into APA-accredited internships? 100%

What courses are required for incoming students to have completed prior to enrolling?
Intro. theory (can be completed here), undergraduate/graduate preparation in basic psychology (18 credits minimum)

Are there courses you recommend that are not mandatory?
No

GRE mean (M), cutoff (C), or preferred (P)
Verbal + Quantitative 1150 (M)
Analytical and Advanced Psychology not considered

GPA mean (M), cutoff (C), or preferred (P)
Overall GPA 3.5 (M) Psychology GPA 3.6 (M)

Number of applications/admission offers/incoming students in 2001
85 applied/20 admission offers/8 incoming

% of students receiving:
Tuition waiver only: 0%
Assistantship/fellowship only: 0%
Both tuition waiver & assistantship/fellowship: 100%

Approximate percentage of incoming students who entered with a B.A./B.S. only: 50% **Master's:** 50%

Approximate percentage of students who are Women: 75% **Ethnic Minority:** 22%

Average years to complete the doctoral program (including internship): 6 years

Research areas	# Faculty	# Grants
career development	2	0
cross-cultural	4	2
family dynamics	1	0
family therapy	1	0
methodology	2	0
psychotherapy process	1	0
social phobia	1	1
supervision	2	0
women's issues	2	0

Clinical opportunities

adolescent residential treatment center
college and university counseling centers
community agencies
county mental health clinics including general and substance abuse clinics and adolescent units
inpatient units at state psychiatric center and private general hospitals
neuropsychology rehabilitation center
private psychiatric hospital
rehabilitation hospital
various units at V. A. hospitals, including primary care, outpatient, day treatment, substance abuse, inpatient psychiatry

Arizona State University

Division of Psychology and Education
Arizona State University
Tempe, AZ 85287-0611
phone#: (480) 965-6339
e-mail: dpe@asu.edu
Web address: http://seamonkey.cd.asu.edu/~gail/programs/cpy1.htm

1	2	3	**4**	5	6	7
Clinically oriented			Equal emphasis			Research oriented

What percentage of your faculty subscribes to or practices in each of the following orientations?

Psychodynamic/Psychoanalytic	30%
Applied behavioral analysis/Radical behavioral	0%
Family systems/Systems	10%
Existential/Phenomenological/Humanistic	30%
Cognitive/Cognitive-behavioral	30%

What percentage of students applying for internship last year was accepted into APA-accredited internships? 80%

What courses are required for incoming students to have completed prior to enrolling?
No specific courses

Are there courses you recommend that are not mandatory?
Psychology or related background.

GRE mean (M), cutoff (C), or preferred (P)
Verbal 600 (P) Quantitative 600 (P)

GPA mean (M), cutoff (C), or preferred (P)
Overall GPA 3.5 (P) Junior/Senior GPA 3.5 (P)

Number of applications/admission offers/incoming students in 2001
147 applied/19 admission offers/12 incoming

% of students receiving:
Tuition waiver only: 0%
Assistantship/fellowship only: 0%
Both tuition waiver & assistantship/fellowship: 100%

Approximate percentage of incoming students who entered with a B.A./B.S. only: 35% **Master's:** 65%

Approximate percentage of students who are Women: 65% **Ethnic Minority:** 25%

Average years to complete the doctoral program (including internship): 5 years

Research areas	# Faculty	# Grants
career development and counseling	3	0
cognitive appraisal	1	0
cognitive-behavioral interventions	1	0
consultation	2	0
counseling the gifted and talented	2	1
counseling process	4	0
counseling women and minorities	5	1
culture sensitivity training and counselor's race ethics	4	0
experimental methodology	2	0
family enrichment	1	0
gender issues in counseling	2	0
group counseling	1	0
health psychology	1	0
HIV	1	0
international issues	1	0
interpersonal models of personality and therapy	3	0
psychology of women	2	0
social psychological approaches to counseling	2	0
suicidology	1	0
training and supervision	4	0
values and decision making	1	0

Clinical opportunities
varied

Auburn University

Department of Counseling and Counseling Psychology
Auburn, AL 36849-5218
phone#: (334) 844-5160
e-mail: ccp@mail.auburn.edu
Web address: http://www.auburn.edu/ccp

1	2	3	**4**	5	6	7
Clinically oriented			Equal emphasis			Research oriented

What percentage of your faculty subscribes to or practices in each of the following orientations?

Psychodynamic/Psychoanalytic	33%
Applied behavioral analysis/Radical behavioral	0%
Family systems/Systems	0%
Existential/Phenomenological/Humanistic	33%
Cognitive/Cognitive-behavioral	33%

What percentage of students applying for internship last year was accepted into APA-accredited internships? 67%

What courses are required for incoming students to have completed prior to enrolling?
None

Are there courses you recommend that are not mandatory?
No

GRE mean (M), cutoff (C), or preferred (P)
Verbal + Quantitative 1100 plus (P) Analytical not required
Advanced Psychology not required

GPA mean (M), cutoff (C), or preferred (P)
Overall GPA 3.3 (M)

Number of applications/admission offers/incoming students in 2001
45 applied/11 admission offers/5 incoming

% of students receiving:
Tuition waiver only: 0%
Assistantship/fellowship only: 0%
Both tuition waiver & assistantship/fellowship: 100%

Approximate percentage of incoming students who entered with a B.A./B.S. only: 45% **Master's:** 55%

Approximate percentage of students who are Women: 65% **Ethnic Minority:** 20%

Average years to complete the doctoral program (including internship): 5.5 years

Research areas	**# Faculty**	**# Grants**
alternative methods	1	0
gay/lesbian/bisexual themes	2	0
professional issues/ethics	3	0
psychometrics	2	0
substance abuse prevention	3	1

Clinical opportunities
mental health center (outpatient)
substance abuse unit (inpatient and outpatient)
university counseling center

Ball State University

Department of Counseling Psychology and Guidance Services
Muncie, IN 47306
phone#: (765) 285-8040
fax#: (765) 285-2067
e-mail: SBOWMAN@BSU.EDU
Web address: http://www.bsu.edu/web/counselingpsych/

1	2	3	**4**	5	6	7
Clinically oriented			Equal emphasis			Research oriented

What percentage of your faculty subscribes to or practices in each of the following orientations?

Psychodynamic/Psychoanalytic	15%
Applied behavioral analysis/Radical behavioral	0%
Family systems/Systems	35%
Existential/Phenomenological/Humanistic	20%
Cognitive/Cognitive-behavioral	30%

What percentage of students applying for internship last year was accepted into APA-accredited internships? 95%

What courses are required for incoming students to have completed prior to enrolling?
Counseling theories, counseling techniques (pre-practicum), practicum, one other counseling course

Are there courses you recommend that are not mandatory?
No

GRE mean (M), cutoff (C), or preferred (P)
Verbal 550 (M) Quantitative 550 (M)
Analytical not considered
Advanced Psychology 550 (M)

GPA mean (M), cutoff (C), or preferred (P)
Overall Master's GPA 3.87 (M)

Number of applications/admission offers/incoming students in 2001
40 applied/14 admission offers/9 incoming

% of students receiving:
Tuition waiver only: 0%
Assistantship/fellowship only: 0%
Both tuition waiver & assistantship/fellowship: 100%

Approximate percentage of incoming students who entered with a B.A./B.S. only: 0% **Master's:** 100%

Approximate percentage of students who are Women: 80% **Ethnic Minority:** 20%

Average years to complete the doctoral program (including internship): 4.5 years

Research areas	**# Faculty**	**# Grants**
behavioral medicine/wellness	1	0
career/vocational	4	0
child/adolescent	2	0
clinical judgment	1	1
multicultural	3	0
organizational/EAP	1	0
social psychology applications	2	0
vocational rehabilitation	2	1
women's identity	2	0

Clinical opportunities
departmental mental health clinic
gerontology
oncology
university counseling center

Boston College

Department of Counseling, Developmental and Educational Psychology
School of Education
Chestnut Hill, MA 02167
phone#: (617) 552-4710 or (617) 552-4214
e-mail: gsoe@bc.edu
Web address: http://www.bc.edu/bc_org/avp/soe/counselpsy/doctorate.html

1 2 3 4 **5** 6 7

Clinically oriented — Equal emphasis — Research oriented

What percentage of your faculty subscribes to or practices in each of the following orientations?

Psychodynamic/Psychoanalytic	40%
Applied behavioral analysis/Radical behavioral	0%
Family systems/Systems	40%
Existential/Phenomenological/Humanistic	10%
Cognitive/Cognitive-behavioral	10%

What percentage of students applying for internship last year was accepted into APA-accredited internships? 100%

What courses are required for incoming students to have completed prior to enrolling?
Statistics, counseling theories, principles and techniques of counseling, and 200 hour practicum

Are there courses you recommend that are not mandatory?
Group counseling, career development, psychological testing, developmental psychology, personality theory (graduate courses at master's level)

GRE mean (M), cutoff (C), or preferred (P)
Verbal 570 (M) Quantitative 585 (M) Analytical 610 (M)

GPA mean (M), cutoff (C), or preferred (P)
Overall GPA 3.30 (M)

Number of applications/admission offers/incoming students in 2001
100 applied/7 admission offers/6 incoming

% of students receiving:
Tuition waiver only: 0%
Assistantship/fellowship only: 0%
Both tuition waiver & assistantship/fellowship: 90%

Approximate percentage of incoming students who entered with a B.A./B.S. only: 0% **Master's:** 100%

Approximate percentage of students who are Women: 79% **Ethnic Minority:** 52%

Average years to complete the doctoral program (including internship): 7.2 years

Research areas	# Faculty	# Grants
adolescent development	2	0
ethical sensitivity	1	1
gender roles	2	0
homelessness	1	1
integrative services	3	2
multicultural issues	3	0
risk and resilience	4	3
school-to-work transition	3	3
violence prevention (community and marital)	3	2

Clinical opportunities
acute psychiatric inpatient
child inpatient unit
college counseling center
community mental health
school based mental health clinic
violence prevention/intervention

Brigham Young University

Department of Counseling Psychology and Special Education
Provo, UT 84602-5093
phone#: (801) 378-4839
e-mail: Ron_Bingham@byu.edu
Web address: http://www.byu.edu/CSE/

1 2 3 **4** 5 6 7

Clinically oriented — Equal emphasis — Research oriented

What percentage of your faculty subscribes to or practices in each of the following orientations?

Psychodynamic/Psychoanalytic	10%
Applied behavioral analysis/Radical behavioral	0%
Family systems/Systems	5%
Existential/Phenomenological/Humanistic	30%
Cognitive/Cognitive-behavioral	55%

What percentage of students applying for internship last year was accepted into APA-accredited internships? 50%

What courses are required for incoming students to have completed prior to enrolling?
A master's degree in counseling, psychology, or closely related area

Are there courses you recommend that are not mandatory?
Statistics

GRE mean (M), cutoff (C), or preferred (P)
Verbal 500 (P) Quantitative 500 (P) Analytical 500 (P)

GPA mean (M), cutoff (C), or preferred (P)
Overall GPA 3.5 (M)

Number of applications/admission offers/incoming students in 2001
22 applied/7 admission offers/6 incoming

% of students receiving:
Tuition waiver only: 0%
Assistantship/fellowship only: 0%
Both tuition waiver & assistantship/fellowship: 100%

Approximate percentage of incoming students who entered with a B.A./B.S. only: 0% **Master's:** 100%

Approximate percentage of students who are Women: 40% **Ethnic Minority:** 15%

Average years to complete the doctoral program (including internship): 5 years

Research areas	# Faculty	# Grants
crisis intervention	1	1
mental health and spirituality	6	3
mental health in schools	2	1
multicultural counseling	2	2
Native-American vocational development	2	1
outcome research	3	2
women's issues	2	1

Clinical opportunities
eating disorders
family clinic

Colorado State University

Department of Psychology
Fort Collins, CO 80523
phone#: (970) 491-6363
e-mail: wendyann@LAMAR.colostate.edu
Web address: http://www.colostate.edu/Depts/Psychology/couns.html

1 2 **3** 4 5 6 7

Clinically oriented — Equal emphasis — Research oriented

What percentage of your faculty subscribes to or practices in each of the following orientations?

Psychodynamic/Psychoanalytic	0%
Applied behavioral analysis/Radical behavioral	0%
Family systems/Systems	20%
Existential/Phenomenological/Humanistic	0%
Cognitive/Cognitive-behavioral	80%

What percentage of students applying for internship last year was accepted into APA-accredited internships? 100%

What courses are required for incoming students to have completed prior to enrolling?
None

Are there courses you recommend that are not mandatory?
Learning, personality, history and systems, developmental, abnormal, statistics

GRE mean (M), cutoff (C), or preferred (P)
Verbal 603 (M) Quantitative 657 (M)
Advanced Psychology 656 (M)

GPA mean (M), cutoff (C), or preferred (P)
Overall GPA 3.61 (M)

Number of applications/admission offers/incoming students in 2001
184 applied/8 admission offers/5 incoming

% of students receiving:
Tuition waiver only: 0%
Assistantship/fellowship only: 0%
Both tuition waiver & assistantship/fellowship: 100%

Approximate percentage of incoming students who entered with a B.A./B.S. only: 100% **Master's:** 0%

Approximate percentage of students who are Women: 80% **Ethnic Minority:** 20%

Average years to complete the doctoral program (including internship): 6 years

Research areas	# Faculty	# Grants
AIDS/HIV education	1	0
adolescent issues	1	1
aggression (anger research and reduction)	1	1
anxiety (reduction)	1	1
assessment (including ethnic/minority issues)	3	1
attention-deficit/hyperactivity disorder	1	0
behavioral medicine	1	0
body image beating disturbances	1	0
child issues (behavior problems and custody)	3	0
cognitive issues	2	0
college teaching	1	0
educational outcomes	1	1
emotional disorders	1	0
ethics	1	0
family relations	1	0
forensic psychology	2	1
health psychology	5	0
interpersonal relationships	1	0
learning disabilities	1	0
men's issues	1	0
multicultural issues	6	3
parent–child interaction	1	0
psychopathology (including child)	3	0
psychotherapy process (behavior therapy)	1	0
sexual orientation issues	1	0
stress and coping processes	2	0
substance abuse	4	3
supervision and training	2	0
violence/abuse	2	0
vocational psychology	2	0
women's issues	3	0

Clinical opportunities
family stress center
inpatient psychiatry
university counseling center

Columbia University, Teachers College (Ph.D. & Ed.D.)

Program in Counseling Psychology
New York, NY 10027
phone#: (212) 678-3257
e-mail: rtcio@columbia.edu
Web address: http://www.tc.columbia.edu/new-home/department/counseling/

1 2 3 4 **5** 6 7

Clinically oriented Equal emphasis Research oriented

What percentage of your faculty subscribes to or practices in each of the following orientations?

Psychodynamic/Psychoanalytic	15%
Applied behavioral analysis/Radical behavioral	0%
Family systems/Systems	40%
Existential/Phenomenological/Humanistic	35%
Cognitive/Cognitive-behavioral	15%

What percentage of students applying for internship last year was accepted into APA-accredited internships? 100%

What courses are required for incoming students to have completed prior to enrolling?
Master's degree or equivalent

Are there courses you recommend that are not mandatory?
Yes

GRE mean (M), cutoff (C), or preferred (P)
Verbal 570 (P) Quantitative 570 (P)

GPA mean (M), cutoff (C), or preferred (P)
Overall GPA 3.0 (P) Psychology GPA 3.0 (P)

Number of applications/admission offers/incoming students in 2001
140 applied/10 admission offers/5 incoming

% of students receiving:
Tuition waiver only: 50%
Assistantship/fellowship only: 25%
Both tuition waiver & assistantship/fellowship: 25%

Approximate percentage of incoming students who entered with a B.A./B.S. only: 10% **Master's:** 90%

Approximate percentage of students who are Women: 80% **Ethnic Minority:** 30%

Average years to complete the doctoral program (including internship): 6 years

Research areas	# Faculty	# Grants
group processes	1	0
identity	1	1
racial identity	2	0
sexual harassment	1	0
women and leadership	1	0

Clinical opportunities
—

University of Denver

College of Education
Denver, CO 80208
phone#: (303) 871-2480
e-mail: KKITCHEN@DU.EDU
Web address: http://www.du.edu/education/counseling/programs.html

1 2 3 **4** 5 6 7

Clinically oriented Equal emphasis Research oriented

What percentage of your faculty subscribes to or practices in each of the following orientations?

Psychodynamic/Psychoanalytic	25%
Applied behavioral analysis/Radical behavioral	0%
Family systems/Systems	15%
Existential/Phenomenological/Humanistic	25%
Cognitive/Cognitive-behavioral	35%

What percentage of students applying for internship last year was accepted into APA-accredited internships? 100%

What courses are required for incoming students to have completed prior to enrolling?
None

Are there courses you recommend that are not mandatory?
Learning, personality theory

GRE mean (M), cutoff (C), or preferred (P)
Verbal 580 (P) Quantitative 580 (P)

GPA mean (M), cutoff (C), or preferred (P)
Overall GPA 3.75 (P)

Number of applications/admission offers/incoming students in 2001
90 applied/15 admission offers/9 incoming

% of students receiving:
Tuition waiver only: 30%
Assistantship/fellowship only: 60%
Both tuition waiver & assistantship/fellowship: 10%

Approximate percentage of incoming students who entered with a B.A./B.S. only: 10% **Master's:** 90%

Approximate percentage of students who are Women: 70% **Ethnic Minority:** 10%

Average years to complete the doctoral program (including internship): 5 years

Research areas	# Faculty	# Grants
adolescent substance abuse	1	1
adult cognitive development	1	1
coping mechanisms (Parkinson's patients)	1	1
ethics	1	0
group counseling	1	0
multicultural counseling	1	1
worker job satisfaction	1	1

Clinical opportunities
Placements working with racial and ethnic minorities

University of Florida

Department of Psychology
Gainesville, FL 32611
phone#: (352) 392-0601
e-mail: CMTUCKER@UFL.EDU
Web address: http://www.PSYCH.UFL.EDU

1	2	3	**4**	5	6	7

Clinically oriented Equal emphasis Research oriented

What percentage of your faculty subscribes to or practices in each of the following orientations?

Psychodynamic/Psychoanalytic	10%
Applied behavioral analysis/Radical behavioral	15%
Family systems/Systems	30%
Existential/Phenomenological/Humanistic	15%
Cognitive/Cognitive-behavioral	30%

What percentage of students applying for internship last year was accepted into APA-accredited internships? 100%

What courses are required for incoming students to have completed prior to enrolling?
Undergraduate 4-year degree in psychology or related field

Are there courses you recommend that are not mandatory?
Statistics, research design/methods, personality, abnormal

GRE mean (M), cutoff (C), or preferred (P)
Verbal 500 (C), 600 (P), 645 (M)
Quantitative 500 (C), 600 (P), 620 (M)
Analytical and Advanced Psychology not typically used as an indicator

GPA mean (M), cutoff (C), or preferred (P)
Overall GPA 3.5 + (P), 3.75 (M)
Psychology GPA 3.5 + (P), 3.90 (M)
Junior/Senior GPA 3.5 + (P), 3.80 (M)

Number of applications/admission offers/incoming students in 2001
150 applied/12 admission offers/7 incoming

% of students receiving:
Tuition waiver only: 0%
Assistantship/fellowship only: 0%
Both tuition waiver & assistantship/fellowship: 40%
All students are currently funded by grant, teaching assistantship, or campus placement.

Approximate percentage of incoming students who entered with a B.A./B.S. only: 60% **Master's:** 40%

Approximate percentage of students who are Women: 65% **Ethnic Minority:** 35%

Average years to complete the doctoral program (including internship): 6 years

Research areas	**# Faculty**	**# Grants**
behavioral medicine	1	1
career/vocational	1	0
constructivist psychology	2	0
eating disorders	1	0
gender and emotion	1	0
sexuality	1	0
women's issues	1	0

Clinical opportunities
assessment (inpatient psychiatric)
career counseling center
couples clinic
crisis intervention center
eating disorder's clinic
ethnic counseling clinic
forensics hospital/prison
gerontology rotation
rape awareness resource program
substance abuse clinic

Fordham University

Division of Psychological and Educational Services
New York, NY 10023
phone#: (212) 636-6460
e-mail: mkeitel@fordham.edu
Web address: http://www.fordham.edu/gse/pes.htm#pes_dcp

1	2	3	**4**	5	6	7

Clinically oriented Equal emphasis Research oriented

What percentage of your faculty subscribes to or practices in each of the following orientations?

Psychodynamic/Psychoanalytic	25%
Applied behavioral analysis/Radical behavioral	20%
Family systems/Systems	16%
Existential/Phenomenological/Humanistic	50%
Cognitive/Cognitive-behavioral	100%

What percentage of students applying for internship last year was accepted into APA-accredited internships? 100%

What courses are required for incoming students to have completed prior to enrolling?
Should have 5 undergraduate psychology courses completed before enrollment

Are there courses you recommend that are not mandatory?
Qualitative research methods

GRE mean (M), cutoff (C), or preferred (P)
Verbal 600 (P) Quantitative 600 (P) Analytical 600 (P)
Advanced Psychology 600 (P)

GPA mean (M), cutoff (C), or preferred (P)
Overall GPA 3.5 (P) Psychology GPA 3.5 (P)
Junior/Senior GPA 3.5 (P)

Number of applications/admission offers/incoming students in 2001
140 applied/15 admission offers/9 incoming

% of students receiving:
Tuition waiver only: 0%
Assistantship/fellowship only: 0%
Both tuition waiver & assistantship/fellowship: 32%

Approximate percentage of incoming students who entered with a B.A./B.S. only: 50% **Master's:** 50%

Approximate percentage of students who are Women: 75% **Ethnic Minority:** 23%

Average years to complete the doctoral program (including internship): 5 years

Research areas	# Faculty	# Grants
career development	2	1
criminal behavior	1	0
health psychology	1	0
multicultural counseling	4	0
supervision	2	0

Clinical opportunities
College counseling centers, community mental health centers, and hospitals where students complete practica

University of Georgia

Department of Counseling and Human Development Services
Athens, GA 30602
phone#: (706) 542-1812
e-mail: couns@uga.cc.uga.edu
Web address: http://www.coe.uga.edu/echd/

1	2	3	**4**	5	6	7
Clinically oriented			Equal emphasis			Research oriented

What percentage of your faculty subscribes to or practices in each of the following orientations?

Psychodynamic/Psychoanalytic	25%
Applied behavioral analysis/Radical behavioral	0%
Family systems/Systems	20%
Existential/Phenomenological/Humanistic	25%
Cognitive/Cognitive-behavioral	30%

What percentage of students applying for internship last year was accepted into APA-accredited internships? 90%

What courses are required for incoming students to have completed prior to enrolling?
Research methods, descriptive statistics, interpersonal relationships, individual assessment, vocational development, theories of counseling, individual counseling practicum, group counseling or group process (master's degree required), multicultural counseling

Are there courses you recommend that are not mandatory?
No

GRE mean (M), cutoff (C), or preferred (P)
Verbal + Quantitative 1100 (P)

GPA mean (M), cutoff (C), or preferred (P)
Overall GPA 3.0 (P)

Number of applications/admission offers/incoming students in 2001
40 applied/11 admission offers/7 incoming

% of students receiving:
Tuition waiver only: 10% (out-of-state)
Assistantship/fellowship only: 0%
Both tuition waiver & assistantship/fellowship: 90%

Approximate percentage of incoming students who entered with a B.A./B.S. only: 0% **Master's:** 100%

Approximate percentage of students who are Women: 75% **Ethnic Minority:** 40%

Average years to complete the doctoral program (including internship): 5 years

Research areas	# Faculty	# Grants
attributions and therapy	2	0
empowering schools/developmental	2	1
juvenile delinquency/aggression	2	1
men's development/gender	1	0
multicultural development and counseling	2	0
preventing violence and aggression in schools	1	2
school counselor education	2	0
substance abuse	1	0
young adult development	2	0

Clinical opportunities
University counseling and testing center (separate from general, in-house clinic)

Georgia State University

Department of Counseling and Psychological Services
Atlanta, GA 30303
phone#: (404) 651-2550
e-mail: gsu.cps.edu
Web address: http://www.gsu.edu/~wwwaae/phdcpy.html

1	2	3	**4**	5	6	7
Clinically oriented			Equal emphasis			Research oriented

What percentage of your faculty subscribes to or practices in each of the following orientations?

Psychodynamic/Psychoanalytic	12%
Applied behavioral analysis/Radical behavioral	0%
Family systems/Systems	13%
Existential/Phenomenological/Humanistic	50%
Cognitive/Cognitive-behavioral	25%

What percentage of students applying for internship last year was accepted into APA-accredited internships? 50%

What courses are required for incoming students to have completed prior to enrolling?
M.A. in counseling or clinical psychology

Are there courses you recommend that are not mandatory?
No

GRE mean (M), cutoff (C), or preferred (P)
Verbal 640 (M) Quantitative 600 (M) Analytical 630 (M)
Advanced Psychology 625 (M)

GPA mean (M), cutoff (C), or preferred (P)
Overall GPA 3.42 (M)

Number of applications/admission offers/incoming students in 2001
50 applied/8 admission offers/6 incoming

% of students receiving:
Tuition waiver only: 0%
Assistantship/fellowship only: 0%
Both tuition waiver & assistantship/fellowship: 100%

Approximate percentage of incoming students who entered with a B.A./B.S. only: 0% **Master's:** 100%

Approximate percentage of students who are Women: 60% **Ethnic Minority:** 26%

Average years to complete the doctoral program (including internship): 5 years

Research areas	# Faculty	# Grants
marital adjustment	3	0
multicultural attitudes	2	1
stress/coping	3	0

Clinical opportunities
behavior therapy center
family education center

University of Houston

Department of Educational Psychology
Houston, TX 77004-5874
phone#: (713) 743-5019
e-mail: EPSY@UH.EDU
Web address: htttp://www.coe.uh.edu/coe_kiosk/epsy/doctoral/source/coupsy_program.html#1

1 2 3 4 **5** 6 7

Clinically oriented — Equal emphasis — Research oriented

What percentage of your faculty subscribes to or practices in each of the following orientations?

Psychodynamic/Psychoanalytic	33%
Applied behavioral analysis/Radical behavioral	0%
Family systems/Systems	33%
Existential/Phenomenological/Humanistic	0%
Cognitive/Cognitive-behavioral	33%

What percentage of students applying for internship last year was accepted into APA-accredited internships? 67%

What courses are required for incoming students to have completed prior to enrolling?
A master's degree in counseling or closely related field is typically required.

Are there courses you recommend that are not mandatory?
No

GRE mean (M), cutoff (C), or preferred (P)
Verbal 500 (C) Quantitative 540 (C) Analytical 500 (C)
These scores represent the departmental guidelines; however, exceptions to the cutoff scores have been made when an applicant provides clear evidence of academic potential.

GPA mean (M), cutoff (C), or preferred (P)
Overall master's GPA 3.5 (C) (on last 60 hours, including graduate work)

Number of applications/admission offers/incoming students in 2001
50 applied/12 admission offers/9 incoming

% of students receiving:
Tuition waiver only: 0%
Assistantship/fellowship only: 5%
Both tuition waiver & assistantship/fellowship: 20%

Approximate percentage of incoming students who entered with a B.A./B.S. only: 0% **Master's:** 100%

Approximate percentage of students who are Women: 85% **Ethnic Minority:** 12%

Average years to complete the doctoral program (including internship): 5.5 years

Research areas	# Faculty	# Grants
ADHD in children and adolescents	1	1
adult survivors of childhood trauma	1	1
gender identity and psychological well-being in men	1	0
cross-cultural counseling	1	0
process issues in counseling	1	0
emotionally disturbed adolescents	1	0

Clinical opportunities
Child guidance center; family therapy; crisis intervention program for children and their families; university counseling center; VA hospital with a variety of rotations including substance abuse, gerontology, family therapy, chronic inpatient, behavioral medicine, forensic, postttraumatic stress disorder

University of Illinois at Urbana–Champaign

Department of Educational Psychology
Champaign, IL 61820
phone#: (888) 843-3779
Web address: http://www.ed.uiuc.edu/EDPSY/counseling/index.html

1 2 3 4 5 **6** 7

Clinically oriented — Equal emphasis — Research oriented

What percentage of your faculty subscribes to or practices in each of the following orientations?

Psychodynamic/Psychoanalytic	0%
Applied behavioral analysis/Radical behavioral	0%
Family systems/Systems	0%
Existential/Phenomenological/Humanistic	0%
Cognitive/Cognitive-behavioral	0%
Eclectic	100%

What percentage of students applying for internship last year was accepted into APA-accredited internships? 100%

What courses are required for incoming students to have completed prior to enrolling?
None

Are there courses you recommend that are not mandatory?
Undergraduate psychology degree

GRE mean (M), cutoff (C), or preferred (P)
Verbal 600 (C) Quantitative 600 (C)

GPA mean (M), cutoff (C), or preferred (P)
Overall GPA 3.5 (C)

Number of applications/admission offers/incoming students in 2001
50 applied/8 admission offers/5 incoming

% of students receiving:
Tuition waiver only: 0%
Assistantship/fellowship only: 0%
Both tuition waiver & assistantship/fellowship: 100%

Approximate percentage of incoming students who entered with a B.A./B.S. only: 95% **Master's:** 5%

Approximate percentage of students who are Women: 90% **Ethnic Minority:** 10%

Average years to complete the doctoral program (including internship): 5.5 years

Research areas	# Faculty	# Grants
adolescent aggression	1	1
eating disorders	1	1
ethnic/racial identity	2	0
personality assessment	1	1
racial and sexual harassment	1	1
racism	2	2
vocational psychology	2	1
women's career development	1	0

Clinical opportunities
African-American psychology
breast and cervical cancer control
cancer survivorship
medically underserved Latina populations
sexual violence

Indiana University

Department of Counseling and Educational Psychology
Wright Education Building, Room 4003
Bloomington, IN 47405
phone#: (812) 856-8300
e-mail: chatomp@indiana.edu
Web address: http://www.indiana.edu/~counsel

1	2	3	**4**	5	6	7

Clinically oriented — Equal emphasis — Research oriented

What percentage of your faculty subscribes to or practices in each of the following orientations?

Psychodynamic/Psychoanalytic	0%
Applied behavioral analysis/Radical behavioral	10%
Family systems/Systems	30%
Existential/Phenomenological/Humanistic	30%
Cognitive/Cognitive-behavioral	30%

What percentage of students applying for internship last year was accepted into APA-accredited internships? 90%

What courses are required for incoming students to have completed prior to enrolling?
We look at overall preparation without concern for specific courses

Are there courses you recommend that are not mandatory?
Statistics and research methods

GRE mean (M), cutoff (C), or preferred (P)
Verbal 522 (M) Quantitative 545 (M) Analytical 622 (M)

GPA mean (M), cutoff (C), or preferred (P)
Overall Undergraduate GPA 3.26
Overall Graduate GPA 3.74

Number of applications/admission offers/incoming students in 2001
100 applied/8 admission offers/6 incoming

% of students receiving:
Tuition waiver only: 0%
Assistantship/fellowship only: 0%
Both tuition waiver & assistantship/fellowship: 90%

Approximate percentage of incoming students who entered with a B.A./B.S. only: 5% **Master's:** 95%

Approximate percentage of students who are Women: 65% **Ethnic Minority:** 30%

Average years to complete the doctoral program (including internship): 4 years

Research areas	# Faculty	# Grants
at-risk youth	1	0
counselor training	5	0
elementary school counseling	1	0
group counseling	4	0
human sexuality	3	0
marriage and family counseling	3	0
multicultural counseling	2	0
women's vocational behavior	1	0

Clinical opportunities
—

Indiana State University

Department of Counseling
Terre Haute, IN 47809
phone#: (812) 237-2832
e-mail: egshuff@befac.indstate.edu
Web address: http://web.indstate.edu/soe/soecoun/

1	2	**3**	4	5	6	7

Clinically oriented — Equal emphasis — Research oriented

What percentage of your faculty subscribes to or practices in each of the following orientations?

Psychodynamic/Psychoanalytic	10%
Applied behavioral analysis/Radical behavioral	0%

Family systems/Systems	30%
Existential/Phenomenological/Humanistic	40%
Cognitive/Cognitive-behavioral	30%

What percentage of students applying for internship last year was accepted into APA-accredited internships? 100%

What courses are required for incoming students to have completed prior to enrolling?
Bachelor's degree and master's degree in counseling/psychology, including graduate courses in techniques of counseling, practicum, psychological assessment, and career development

Are there courses you recommend that are not mandatory?
No

GRE mean (M), cutoff (C), or preferred (P)
Verbal 500 (C) Quantitative 500 (C) Analytical 500 (C)
Advanced Psychology 500 (C)

GPA mean (M), cutoff (C), or preferred (P)
Overall Undergraduate GPA 2.5 (C)
Overall Graduate GPA 3.5 (C)

Number of applications/admission offers/incoming students in 2001
17 applied/11 admission offers/7 incoming

% of students receiving:
Tuition waiver only: 0%
Assistantship/fellowship only: 0%
Both tuition waiver & assistantship/fellowship: 89%

Approximate percentage of incoming students who entered with a B.A./B.S. only: 0% **Master's:** 100%

Approximate percentage of students who are Women: 57% **Ethnic Minority:** 12%

Average years to complete the doctoral program (including internship): 5 years

Research areas	# Faculty	# Grants
AIDS/HIV	1	3
Adlerian therapy	1	0
career development/assessment	3	0
counseling/supervision process	3	0
family therapy	3	1
men's studies	2	0
personality assessment	1	0
program evaluation	1	1
school counseling	2	2
values/learning skills	1	0

Clinical opportunities
community mental health centers
local hospitals and community medical health centers
marriage and family therapy clinic
prison/penitentiary population
university counseling center
VA medical center

University of Iowa

Division of Psychological and Quantitative Foundations
Iowa City, IA 52242
phone#: (319) 335-5639
e-mail: daniel-clay@uiowa.edu
Web address: http://www.uiowa.edu/~coe2/divisions/pandq/counspsych/index.htm

1	2	3	**4**	5	6	7
Clinically oriented			Equal emphasis			Research oriented

What percentage of your faculty subscribes to or practices in each of the following orientations?

Psychodynamic/Psychoanalytic	25%
Applied behavioral analysis/Radical behavioral	0%
Family systems/Systems	25%
Existential/Phenomenological/Humanistic	0%
Cognitive/Cognitive-behavioral	50%

What percentage of students applying for internship last year was accepted into APA-accredited internships? 33%

What courses are required for incoming students to have completed prior to enrolling?
None are required but we encourage as much core psychology as possible

Are there courses you recommend that are not mandatory?
See above

GRE mean (M), cutoff (C), or preferred (P)
Verbal 600 (P) Quantitative 600 (P)

GPA mean (M), cutoff (C), or preferred (P)
Overall GPA 3.00 (P)

Number of applications/admission offers/incoming students in 2001
56 applied/9 admission offers/5 incoming

% of students receiving:
Tuition waiver only: 0%
Assistantship/fellowship only: 40%
Both tuition waiver & assistantship/fellowship: 60%

Approximate percentage of incoming students who entered with a B.A./B.S. only: 50% **Master's:** 50%

Approximate percentage of students who are Women: 60% **Ethnic Minority:** 35%

Average years to complete the doctoral program (including internship): 5.6 years

Research areas	# Faculty	# Grants
child and adolescent health psychology	1	1
college student suicide	1	0
ethics	2	1
multicultural issues	2	1
psychosocial oncology	2	1
public health	3	2

Clinical opportunities
community mental health
hospital

prison
university counseling center
VA medical center
women's center

Iowa State University

Department of Psychology
Ames, IA 50011-3180
phone#: (515) 294-1743
e-mail: dle@iastate.edu
Web address: http://psych-server.iastate.edu

1	2	3	4	**5**	6	7
Clinically oriented			Equal emphasis			Research oriented

What percentage of your faculty subscribes to or practices in each of the following orientations?

Psychodynamic/Psychoanalytic	0%
Applied behavioral analysis/Radical behavioral	0%
Family systems/Systems	20%
Existential/Phenomenological/Humanistic	20%
Cognitive/Cognitive-behavioral	60%

What percentage of students applying for internship last year was accepted into APA-accredited internships? 100%

What courses are required for incoming students to have completed prior to enrolling?
A minimum of 15 credits in psychology including statistics, psychological measurement, psychopathology, developmental psychology, counseling or psychotherapy, research methods

Are there courses you recommend that are not mandatory?
Most successful applicants have a diversified psychology major (30–40 semester hours)

GRE mean (M), cutoff (C), or preferred (P)
Verbal 600 (P), 610 (M) Quantitative 600 (P), 640 (M)
Analytical 600 (P), 615 (M)
Advanced Psychology 600 (P), 620 (M)

GPA mean (M), cutoff (C), or preferred (P)
Overall GPA 3.5 (P), 3.6 (M) Psychology GPA 3.5 (P), 3.7 (M) Junior/Senior GPA 3.5 (P), 3.8 (M)

Number of applications/admission offers/incoming students in 2001
51 applied/12 admission offers/4 incoming

% of students receiving:
Tuition waiver only: 0%
Assistantship/fellowship only: 0%
Both tuition waiver & assistantship/fellowship: 80%

Approximate percentage of incoming students who entered with a B.A./B.S. only: 75% **Master's:** 25%

Approximate percentage of students who are Women: 66% **Ethnic Minority:** 4%

Average years to complete the doctoral program (including internship): 6.5 years

Research areas	# Faculty	# Grants
ethics and legal issues in counseling	1	0
gender roles	2	0
meta analysis-counseling process and outcome	2	0
sex offenders	1	0
social support in intimate relationships	1	1
vocational development of women in science	1	1
vocational interest assessment	3	1

Clinical opportunities
child and adolescent treatment centers
community mental health center
inpatient psychiatry
patient/family services in general medical hospital
private psychological practice
university counseling center
VA medical center

University of Kansas

Department of Psychology and Research in Education
Counseling Psychology Program
Lawrence, KS 66045
phone#: (913) 864-3931
e-mail: jlicht@ku.edu
Web address: http://www.soe.ukans.edu/depts/pre/

1	2	3	**4**	5	6	7
Clinically oriented			Equal emphasis			Research oriented

What percentage of your faculty subscribes to or practices in each of the following orientations?

Psychodynamic/Psychoanalytic	0%
Applied behavioral analysis/Radical behavioral	0%
Family systems/Systems	20%
Existential/Phenomenological/Humanistic	20%
Cognitive/Cognitive-behavioral	60%

What percentage of students applying for internship last year was accepted into APA-accredited internships? 100%

What courses are required for incoming students to have completed prior to enrolling?
None

Are there courses you recommend that are not mandatory?
Basic courses in psychology (e.g., social psychology, personality, abnormal psychology, experimental psychology)

GRE mean (M), cutoff (C), or preferred (P)
Verbal 560 (M) Quantitative 600 (M) Analytical 660 (M)
Advanced Psychology not required

GPA mean (M), cutoff (C), or preferred (P)
Overall GPA 3.6 (M)

Number of applications/admission offers/incoming students in 2001
58 applied/12 admission offers/6 incoming

% of students receiving:
Tuition waiver only: 0%
Assistantship/fellowship only: 0%
Both tuition waiver & assistantship/fellowship: 75%

Approximate percentage of incoming students who entered with a B.A./B.S. only: 75% **Master's:** 25%

Approximate percentage of students who are Women: 67% **Ethnic Minority:** 16%

Average years to complete the doctoral program (including internship): 5.5 years

Research areas	# Faculty	# Grants
hope	1	1
interactional processes	1	1
learning styles	1	0
positive psychology	1	1
vocational indecision	1	0

Clinical opportunities
—

University of Kentucky

Department of Educational and Counseling Psychology
Lexington, KY 40506
phone#: (606) 257-7881
e-mail: sllaws0@pop.uky.edu
Web address: http://www.uky.edu/Education/edphead.html

1	2	3	4	5	**6**	7

Clinically oriented — Equal emphasis — Research oriented

What percentage of your faculty subscribes to or practices in each of the following orientations?

Psychodynamic/Psychoanalytic	0%
Applied behavioral analysis/Radical behavioral	30%
Family systems/Systems	20%
Existential/Phenomenological/Humanistic	10%
Cognitive/Cognitive-behavioral	40%

What percentage of students applying for internship last year was accepted into APA-accredited internships? 80%

What courses are required for incoming students to have completed prior to enrolling?
None

Are there courses you recommend that are not mandatory?
Prefer master's degree in behavioral science

GRE mean (M), cutoff (C), or preferred (P)
Verbal + Quantitative 1055 (M)

GPA mean (M), cutoff (C), or preferred (P)
Overall GPA 3.4 (M) Psychology GPA 3.6 (M)
Junior/Senior GPA 3.5 (M)

Number of applications/admission offers/incoming students in 2001
38 applied/14 admission offers/11 incoming

% of students receiving:
Tuition waiver only: 0%
Assistantship/fellowship only: 45%
Both tuition waiver & assistantship/fellowship: 25%

Approximate percentage of incoming students who entered with a B.A./B.S. only: 0% **Master's:** 100%

Approximate percentage of students who are Women: 60% **Ethnic Minority:** 25%

Average years to complete the doctoral program (including internship): 4.6 years

Research areas	# Faculty	# Grants
behavioral	2	0
family	2	0
gender	2	1
multicultural	2	2

Clinical opportunities
community mental health center
counseling center
federal medical center (prison)
residential treatment facility
rural mental health centers
VA hospital

Lehigh University

Education and Human Services
Bethlehem, PA 18015-4792
phone#: (610) 758-3250
Web address: http://www.lehigh.edu/~ineduc/CP/CPdesc.html

1	2	3	4	**5**	6	7

Clinically oriented — Equal emphasis — Research oriented

What percentage of your faculty subscribes to or practices in each of the following orientations?

Psychodynamic/Psychoanalytic	25%
Applied behavioral analysis/Radical behavioral	0%
Family systems/Systems	25%
Existential/Phenomenological/Humanistic	25%
Cognitive/Cognitive-behavioral	25%

What percentage of students applying for internship last year was accepted into APA-accredited internships? 100%

What courses are required for incoming students to have completed prior to enrolling?
None

Are there courses you recommend that are not mandatory?
Psychology related

GRE mean (M), cutoff (C), or preferred (P)
Verbal 550 (M) Quantitative 550 (M) Analytical 550 (M)

GPA mean (M), cutoff (C), or preferred (P)
Overall GPA 3.7 (M)

Number of applications/admission offers/incoming students in 2001
80 applied/10 admission offers/5 incoming

% of students receiving:
Tuition waiver only: 10%
Assistantship/fellowship only: 0%
Both tuition waiver & assistantship/fellowship: 90%

Approximate percentage of incoming students who entered with a B.A./B.S. only: 50% **Master's:** 50%

Approximate percentage of students who are Women: 70% **Ethnic Minority:** 40%

Average years to complete the doctoral program (including internship): 6 years

Research areas	# Faculty	# Grants
cross-cultural	1	1
family systems	1	1
supervision/training	1	1
vocational psychology	1	1

Clinical opportunities
—

University of Louisville

Department of Educational and Counseling Psychology
Louisville, KY 40292
phone#: (502) 852-6884
e-mail: KKIRBY@louisville.edu

1	2	3	**4**	5	6	7
Clinically oriented			Equal emphasis			Research oriented

What percentage of your faculty subscribes to or practices in each of the following orientations?

Psychodynamic/Psychoanalytic	50%
Applied behavioral analysis/Radical behavioral	25%
Family systems/Systems	25%
Existential/Phenomenological/Humanistic	0%
Cognitive/Cognitive-behavioral	50%

What percentage of students applying for internship last year was accepted into APA-accredited internships? 100%

What courses are required for incoming students to have completed prior to enrolling?
30 hours MA in counseling psychology or psychology plus abnormal psychology, human or lifespan development, statistics or methodology, social psychology

Are there courses you recommend that are not mandatory?
Psycholinguistics, sociology, anthropology, psychology (general and clinical)

GRE mean (M), cutoff (C), or preferred (P)
Verbal 500 (C) Quantitative 500 (C) Analytical 600 (P)

GPA mean (M), cutoff (C), or preferred (P)
Overall GPA 3.9 (M), 3.0 (C), 3.5 (P)

Number of applications/admission offers/incoming students in 2001
15 applied/6 admission offers/3 incoming

% of students receiving:
Tuition waiver only: 10%
Assistantship/fellowship only: 10%
Both tuition waiver & assistantship/fellowship: 10%

Approximate percentage of incoming students who entered with a B.A./B.S. only: 0% **Master's:** 100%

Approximate percentage of students who are Women: 70% **Ethnic Minority:** 17%

Average years to complete the doctoral program (including internship): 6 years

Research areas	# Faculty	# Grants
depression	1	1
divorce adjustment	1	2
drug and alcohol abuse	1	1
evolutionary psychology	—	—
GBLT issues	1	1
school adjustment of special populations	1	0
school violence	1	2
stress and parenting	1	0

Clinical opportunities
child developmental disabilities
child treatment center

Loyola University of Chicago

Department of Counseling Psychology
1014 Ridge Road
Wilmette, IL 60091
phone#: (847) 853-3310
e-mail: SBROWN@LUC.EDU
Web address: http://www.luc.edu/schools/education/cpsy/conspsyc.htm

1	2	3	**4**	5	6	7
Clinically oriented			Equal emphasis			Research oriented

What percentage of your faculty subscribes to or practices in each of the following orientations?

Psychodynamic/Psychoanalytic	14%
Applied behavioral analysis/Radical behavioral	0%
Family systems/Systems	30%
Existential/Phenomenological/Humanistic	14%
Cognitive/Cognitive-behavioral	42%

What percentage of students applying for internship last year was accepted into APA-accredited internships? 100%

What courses are required for incoming students to have completed prior to enrolling?
Master's degree in counseling, psychology, or related field

Are there courses you recommend that are not mandatory?
No

GRE mean (M), cutoff (C), or preferred (P)
Verbal 500 (P) Quantitative 500 (P) Analytical 500 (P)
Advanced Psychology 500 (P)

GPA mean (M), cutoff (C), or preferred (P)
Overall GPA 3.5 (P) Psychology GPA 3.5 (P)
Junior/Senior GPA 3.5 (P)

Number of applications/admission offers/incoming students in 2001
60 applied/12 admission offers/9 incoming

% of students receiving:
Tuition waiver only: 0%
Assistantship/fellowship only: 0%
Both tuition waiver & assistantship/fellowship: 98%

Approximate percentage of incoming students who entered with a B.A./B.S. only: 0% **Master's:** 100%

Approximate percentage of students who are Women: 60% **Ethnic Minority:** 40%

Average years to complete the doctoral program (including internship): 6 years

Research areas	# Faculty	# Grants
adolescent risk behavior	1	1
child/adolescent development	1	4
counseling process	1	0
counseling supervision	1	0
multicultural counseling	2	0
vocational psychology	1	1

Clinical opportunities
Opportunities in the greater Chicago area include hospitals, clinics, and universities.

University of Maryland

Department of Psychology and Department of Counseling and Personnel Services
College Park, MD 20742
Web address: http://www.bsos.umd.edu/psyc/counsel.htm

1 2 3 4 **5** 6 7

Clinically oriented — Equal emphasis — Research oriented

What percentage of your faculty subscribes to or practices in each of the following orientations?

Psychodynamic/Psychoanalytic	38%
Applied behavioral analysis/Radical behavioral	0%
Family systems/Systems	0%
Existential/Phenomenological/Humanistic	0%
Cognitive/Cognitive-behavioral	12%
Interpersonal	12%
Feminist	12%
Integrative	25%

What percentage of students applying for internship last year was accepted into APA-accredited internships? 100%

What courses are required for incoming students to have completed prior to enrolling?
No specific courses but we require that students have a minimum of 15 credits of coursework in psychology, including statistics

Are there courses you recommend that are not mandatory?
—

GRE mean (M), cutoff (C), or preferred (P)
Verbal 600 (P) Quantitative 600 (P) Analytical 600 (P)
A total of 1150 for the Verbal and Quantitative scores with neither below 550 (C)

GPA mean (M), cutoff (C), or preferred (P)
Overall Undergraduate GPA 3.5 (P)
Junior/Senior GPA 3.5 (P) Overall Master's GPA 3.75 (P)

Number of applications/admission offers/incoming students in 2001
138 applied/13 admission offers/8 incoming

% of students receiving:
Tuition waiver only: 0%
Assistantship/fellowship only: 0%
Both tuition waiver & assistantship/fellowship: 100%

Approximate percentage of incoming students who entered with a B.A./B.S. only: 50% **Master's:** 50%

Approximate percentage of students who are Women: 75% **Ethnic Minority:** 35%

Average years to complete the doctoral program (including internship): 6 years

Research areas	# Faculty	# Grants
AIDS/HIV	1	0
career counseling	4	0
counseling process	3	0
the counseling relationship	2	0
countertransference	2	0
dreams (their use in therapy)	1	0
health issues	1	0
multicultural issues	4	1
supervision/training	2	0
vocational psychology	3	1

Clinical opportunities
Multicultural, group, individual, consultation, career, and supervision practica

University of Memphis

Department of Counseling, Educational Psychology, and Research
Ball Education Building, Rm. 100
Memphis, TN 38152
phone#: (901) 678-2841
e-mail: slease@memphis.edu
Web address: http://www.people.memphis.edu/~coe_cepr/

1 2 3 **4** 5 6 7

Clinically oriented — Equal emphasis — Research oriented

What percentage of your faculty subscribes to or practices in each of the following orientations?

Psychodynamic/Psychoanalytic	17%
Applied behavioral analysis/Radical behavioral	17%
Family systems/Systems	67%
Existential/Phenomenological/Humanistic	50%
Cognitive/Cognitive-behavioral	83%
Feminist	33%
Constructivist	17%
Social learning	50%

What percentage of students applying for internship last year was accepted into APA-accredited internships? 100%

What courses are required for incoming students to have completed prior to enrolling?
Master's degree in counseling, psychology, or related area

Are there courses you recommend that are not mandatory?
Psychological assessment, psychopathology

GRE mean (M), cutoff (C), or preferred (P)
Verbal 570 (M) Quantitative 570 (M)

GPA mean (M), cutoff (C), or preferred (P)
Overall GPA 3.89 (M), 3.5 (C)

Number of applications/admission offers/incoming students in 2001
31 applied/15 admission offers/8 incoming

% of students receiving:
Tuition waiver only: 0%
Assistantship/fellowship only: 0%
Both tuition waiver & assistantship/fellowship: 100%

Approximate percentage of incoming students who entered with a B.A./B.S. only: 0% **Master's:** 100%

Approximate percentage of students who are Women: 70% **Ethnic Minority:** 20%

Average years to complete the doctoral program (including internship): 4.3 years

Research areas	# Faculty	# Grants
AIDS/HIV counseling and education	2	1
at-risk families and children	2	1
consultation	1	1
counseling gays, lesbians, and bisexuals	3	1
crisis/trauma	2	0
disabled persons	2	0
international psychology	1	1
multicultural counseling and supervision	2	0
psychological resources (e.g., resilience)	2	0
professional development	2	0
vocational psychology	1	0

Clinical opportunities
adolescents/children
assessment
domestic violence
forensic psychology
inpatients/outpatients
substance abuse unit
university students

University of Miami

Department of Psychology
P.O. Box 248065
Coral Gables, FL 33124
phone#: (305) 284-3001
e-mail: MCROSBUR@UMIAMI.IR.MIAMI.EDU
Web address: http://www.education.miami.edu/

1	2	3	**4**	5	6	7
Clinically oriented			Equal emphasis			Research oriented

What percentage of your faculty subscribes to or practices in each of the following orientations?

Psychodynamic/Psychoanalytic	15%
Applied behavioral analysis/Radical behavioral	0%
Family systems/Systems	60%
Existential/Phenomenological/Humanistic	40%
Cognitive/Cognitive-behavioral	70%

What percentage of students applying for internship last year was accepted into APA-accredited internships? 100%

What courses are required for incoming students to have completed prior to enrolling?
Standard curriculum for master's in counseling

Are there courses you recommend that are not mandatory?
No

GRE mean (M), cutoff (C), or preferred (P)
Verbal 610 (M) Quantitative 600 (M)

GPA mean (M), cutoff (C), or preferred (P)
Overall GPA 3.4 (M) Psychology GPA 3.9 (M)

Number of applications/admission offers/incoming students in 2001
80 applied/8 admission offers/6 incoming

% of students receiving:
Tuition waiver only: 0%
Assistantship/fellowship only: 0%
Both tuition waiver & assistantship/fellowship: 100%

Approximate percentage of incoming students who entered with a B.A./B.S. only: 25% **Master's:** 75%

Approximate percentage of students who are Women: 60% **Ethnic Minority:** 30%

Average years to complete the doctoral program (including internship): 6 years

Research areas	# Faculty	# Grants
counseling process	1	0
ethnic minorities	1	0
families	2	1
health psychology	2	1

Clinical opportunities
Tailor to students' interests

Michigan State University

Department of Counseling, Educational Psychology and Special Education
East Lansing, MI 48824
phone#: (517) 355-8502
e-mail: KGR1@MSU.EDU
Web address: http://ed-web3.educ.msu.edu/CEPSE/cp/default.htm

1	2	3	4	**5**	6	7

Clinically oriented — Equal emphasis — Research oriented

What percentage of your faculty subscribes to or practices in each of the following orientations?

Psychodynamic/Psychoanalytic	30%
Applied behavioral analysis/Radical behavioral	0%
Family systems/Systems	30%
Existential/Phenomenological/Humanistic	20%
Cognitive/Cognitive-behavioral	20%

What percentage of students applying for internship last year was accepted into APA-accredited internships? 75%

What courses are required for incoming students to have completed prior to enrolling?
MA/MS degree in counseling or a related area that requires a counseling/clinical practicum experience

Are there courses you recommend that are not mandatory?
Statistics, measurement

GRE mean (M), cutoff (C), or preferred (P)
Verbal 550 (P) Quantitative 550 (P) Analytical 550 (P)

GPA mean (M), cutoff (C), or preferred (P)
Overall Master's GPA 3.3 + (P)

Number of applications/admission offers/incoming students in 2001
56 applied/11 admission offers/4 incoming

% of students receiving:
Tuition waiver only: 0%
Assistantship/fellowship only: 0%
Both tuition waiver & assistantship/fellowship: 88%

Approximate percentage of incoming students who entered with a B.A./B.S. only: 0% **Master's:** 100%

Approximate percentage of students who are Women: — **Ethnic Minority:** —

Average years to complete the doctoral program (including internship): 5 years

Research areas	# Faculty	# Grants
close relationships	2	0
college adjustment	1	3
gender issues	1	0
minority/urban counseling and development	2	1
perfectionism	1	0
rehab counseling	1	1

Clinical opportunities
Multi-Ethnic Counseling Center Alliance (MECCA)

University of Minnesota—Department of Educational Psychology

129 Burton Hall
Minneapolis, MN 55455
phone#: (612) 624-6827
e-mail: cspp-adm@umn.edu
Web address: http://www.education.umn.edu/edpsych/cspp

1	2	3	**4**	5	6	7

Clinically oriented — Equal emphasis — Research oriented

What percentage of your faculty subscribes to or practices in each of the following orientations?

Psychodynamic/Psychoanalytic	25%
Applied behavioral analysis/Radical behavioral	10%
Family systems/Systems	30%
Existential/Phenomenological/Humanistic	35%
Cognitive/Cognitive-behavioral	30%

What percentage of students applying for internship last year was accepted into APA-accredited internships? 90%

What courses are required for incoming students to have completed prior to enrolling?
None

Are there courses you recommend that are not mandatory?
Foundational courses in undergraduate psychology

GRE mean (M), cutoff (C), or preferred (P)
Verbal 560 (M) Quantitative 640 (M)

GPA mean (M), cutoff (C), or preferred (P)
Overall GPA 3.6 (M)

Number of applications/admission offers/incoming students in 2001
57 applied/6 admission offers/6 incoming

% of students receiving:
Tuition waiver only: 25%
Assistantship/fellowship only: 25%
Both tuition waiver & assistantship/fellowship: 50%

Approximate percentage of incoming students who entered with a B.A./B.S. only: 15% **Master's:** 85%

Approximate percentage of students who are Women: 60% **Ethnic Minority:** 30%

Average years to complete the doctoral program (including internship): 5 years

Research areas	# Faculty	# Grants
burnout prevention	1	0
career development	1	0
genetic counseling	1	2
high-risk adolescents	1	1
international counseling	4	0

master therapist	1	0
multicultural counseling	1	0
multicultural integrative therapy	1	0
prevention	1	0
school counseling	2	1
substance abuse	1	1
supervision	2	0
therapist/counselor development	1	0
therapy outcome	1	0

Clinical opportunities
Multiple practicum sites in the Twin Cities

University of Minnesota—Department of Psychology

75 East River Road
Minneapolis, MN 55455
phone#: (612) 625-3873
e-mail: counpsy@umn.edu
Web address: http://www.psych.umn.edu/psyareas/Counseling/counsel.htm

1 2 3 4 5 6 **7**

Clinically oriented — Equal emphasis — Research oriented

What percentage of your faculty subscribes to or practices in each of the following orientations?

Psychodynamic/Psychoanalytic	33%
Applied behavioral analysis/Radical behavioral	0%
Family systems/Systems	0%
Existential/Phenomenological/Humanistic	0%
Cognitive/Cognitive-behavioral	66%

What percentage of students applying for internship last year was accepted into APA-accredited internships? 100%

What courses are required for incoming students to have completed prior to enrolling?
Prefer applicants with a broad base of scientific or empirical training in psychology with a background in statistics

Are there courses you recommend that are not mandatory?
See above

GRE mean (M), cutoff (C), or preferred (P)
Verbal 583 (M) Quantitative 640 (M)
Analytical and Advanced Psychology not applicable

GPA mean (M), cutoff (C), or preferred (P)
Overall GPA 3.92 (M) Psychology GPA 3.91 (M)
Junior/Senior GPA not applicable

Number of applications/admission offers/incoming students in 2001
58 applied/6 admission offers/4 incoming

% of students receiving:
Tuition waiver only: 0%
Assistantship/fellowship only: 0%
Both tuition waiver & assistantship/fellowship: 100%

Approximate percentage of incoming students who entered with a B.A./B.S. only: 100% **Master's:** 0%

Approximate percentage of students who are Women: 61% **Ethnic Minority:** 25%

Average years to complete the doctoral program (including internship): 6 years

Research areas	# Faculty	# Grants
Asian-American identity and family	1	1
career development and choice	1	1
interest measurement	1	1
interpersonal relations	1	1
issues related to organ transplants	1	0
multicultural counseling	1	0
occupational health psychology	1	0
personality and adjustment	1	0
rape interventions	1	0
values and work adjustment	1	0

Clinical opportunities
We use about 15 locations as practica and advanced practica locations. The sites are matched with students' interests and with the goal of providing them with diversity in experience over a 3- to 4-year period.

University of Missouri–Columbia

Department of Educational and Counseling Psychology
Columbia, MO 65211-2130
phone#: (573) 882-7731
e-mail: ecpgrad@tiger.coe.missouri.edu
Web address: http://tiger.coe.missouri.edu/~ecp/

1 2 3 **4** 5 6 7

Clinically oriented — Equal emphasis — Research oriented

What percentage of your faculty subscribes to or practices in each of the following orientations?

Psychodynamic/Psychoanalytic	23%
Applied behavioral analysis/Radical behavioral	8%
Family systems/Systems	8%
Existential/Phenomenological/Humanistic	17%
Cognitive/Cognitive-behavioral	58%

What percentage of students applying for internship last year was accepted into APA-accredited internships? 93%

What courses are required for incoming students to have completed prior to enrolling?
No specific courses

Are there courses you recommend that are not mandatory?
No

GRE mean (M), cutoff (C), or preferred (P)
Verbal 600 (P) Quantitative 600 (P)

GPA mean (M), cutoff (C), or preferred (P)
Overall GPA 3.0 (C)

Number of applications/admission offers/incoming students in 2001
100 applied/12 admission offers/7 incoming

% of students receiving:
Tuition waiver only: 0%
Assistantship/fellowship only: 0%
Both tuition waiver & assistantship/fellowship: 100%

Approximate percentage of incoming students who entered with a B.A./B.S. only: 25% **Master's:** 75%

Approximate percentage of students who are Women: 60% **Ethnic Minority:** 35%

Average years to complete the doctoral program (including internship): 6.45 years

Research areas	# Faculty	# Grants
career development	5	2
counseling process	3	0
counseling supervision	3	0
group process	2	0
multicultural counseling	5	1
problem solving	2	0
scale construction	6	0

Clinical opportunities
family counseling center
intensive cognitive-behavioral outpatient center
learning disabilities clinic
psychiatric clinic
psychology clinic
Rusk Rehabilitation Center
state hospital
state prison
university counseling center
university career planning and placement center
university medical clinics
VA hospital
women's center

University of Missouri–Kansas City

Division of Counseling Psychology and Counseling Education
Kansas City, MO 64110
phone#: (816) 235-2722
e-mail: CPCE@SMTPGATE.UMKC.EDU
Web address: http://cctr.umkc.edu/dept/education/dius/cpce/index.html

1 2 3 **4** 5 6 7

Clinically oriented — Equal emphasis — Research oriented

What percentage of your faculty subscribes to or practices in each of the following orientations?

Psychodynamic/Psychoanalytic	10%
Applied behavioral analysis/Radical behavioral	5%
Family systems/Systems	20%
Existential/Phenomenological/Humanistic	25%
Cognitive/Cognitive-behavioral	40%

What percentage of students applying for internship last year was accepted into APA-accredited internships? 100%

What courses are required for incoming students to have completed prior to enrolling?
Undergraduate psychology major or master's degree in counseling or psychology

Are there courses you recommend that are not mandatory?
No

GRE mean (M), cutoff (C), or preferred (P)
Verbal + Quantitative 1000 (C)
Advanced Psychology not required

GPA mean (M), cutoff (C), or preferred (P)
Overall Undergraduate GPA 2.75 (C)
Overall Master's GPA 3.5 (C)

Number of applications/admission offers/incoming students in 2001
60 applied/20 admission offers/10 incoming

% of students receiving:
Tuition waiver only: 0%
Assistantship/fellowship only: 0%
Both tuition waiver & assistantship/fellowship: 100%

Approximate percentage of incoming students who entered with a B.A./B.S. only: 16% **Master's:** 84%

Approximate percentage of students who are Women: 67% **Ethnic Minority:** 16%

Average years to complete the doctoral program (including internship): 6.5 years

Research areas	# Faculty	# Grants
AIDS	2	1
behavioral medicine	4	0
cross-cultural perspectives of counseling	4	0
family systems theory	1	0
health psychology	3	0
interpersonal relations	3	0
professional issues	3	0
psychopathology prevention	3	0
psychotherapy process	3	0
sexuality	1	0
sports psychology	1	0
stress and coping	1	0
substance abuse	1	0
supervision	2	0
vocational interests	1	0

Clinical opportunities
—

University of Nebraska–Lincoln

Department of Educational Psychology
114 Teachers College Hall
Lincoln, NE 68588-0345
phone#: (402) 472-2223
e-mail: mretzlaff@unl.edu
Web address: http://www.unl.edu/edpsych/deptinfo.html

1	2	3	**4**	5	6	7

Clinically oriented — Equal emphasis — Research oriented

What percentage of your faculty subscribes to or practices in each of the following orientations?

Psychodynamic/Psychoanalytic	20%
Applied behavioral analysis/Radical behavioral	0%
Family systems/Systems	20%
Existential/Phenomenological/Humanistic	20%
Cognitive/Cognitive-behavioral	40%

What percentage of students applying for internship last year was accepted into APA-accredited internships? 100%

What courses are required for incoming students to have completed prior to enrolling?
Master's in counseling or closely related field

Are there courses you recommend that are not mandatory?
—

GRE mean (M), cutoff (C), or preferred (P)
Verbal 500 (C) Quantitative 500 (C)

GPA mean (M), cutoff (C), or preferred (P)
Overall GPA 3.5 (M)

Number of applications/admission offers/incoming students in 2001
42 applied/7 admission offers/5 incoming

% of students receiving:
Tuition waiver only: 0%
Assistantship/fellowship only: 0%
Both tuition waiver & assistantship/fellowship: 90%

Approximate percentage of incoming students who entered with a B.A./B.S. only: 0% **Master's:** 100%

Approximate percentage of students who are Women: 70% **Ethnic Minority:** 36%

Average years to complete the doctoral program (including internship): 5 years

Research areas	# Faculty	# Grants
family counseling	1	0
multicultural issues	2	0
psychological assessment	2	0
vocational	1	0

Clinical opportunities
family counseling
multicultural counseling
psychological assessment
vocational counseling

New Mexico State University

Department of Counseling and Educational Psychology
MSC 3CEP
P.O. Box 30001
Las Cruces, NM 88003-8001
phone#: (505) 646-2121
e-mail: cepdept@nmsu.edu
Web address: http://_education.nmsu.edu

1	2	3	**4**	5	6	7

Clinically oriented — Equal emphasis — Research oriented

What percentage of your faculty subscribes to or practices in each of the following orientations?

Psychodynamic/Psychoanalytic	12.5%
Applied behavioral analysis/Radical behavioral	12.5%
Family systems/Systems	12.5%
Existential/Phenomenological/Humanistic	50%
Cognitive/Cognitive-behavioral	12.5%

What percentage of students applying for internship last year was accepted into APA-accredited internships? 67%

What courses are required for incoming students to have completed prior to enrolling?
Human development, multicultural psychology, organization and administration or professional issues in counseling, counseling theory and techniques, family therapy, group work, career/life planning and vocational assessment, counseling research, diagnosis and treatment planning, addictions counseling

Are there courses you recommend that are not mandatory?
No

GRE mean (M), cutoff (C), or preferred (P)
Verbal 500 (P) Quantitative 500 (P) Analytical 500 (P)

GPA mean (M), cutoff (C), or preferred (P)
GPA 3.0 (C) 3.76 (M)

Number of applications/admission offers/incoming students in 2001
25 applied/10 admission offers/5 incoming

% of students receiving:
Tuition waiver only: 0%
Assistantship/fellowship only: 100%
Both tuition waiver & assistantship/fellowship: 0%

Approximate percentage of incoming students who entered with a B.A./B.S. only: 0% **Master's:** 100%

Approximate percentage of students who are Women: 56% **Ethnic Minority:** 48%

Average years to complete the doctoral program (including internship): 5 years

Research areas	# Faculty	# Grants
acculturation	3	0
Adlerian psychology	1	0
career	1	0
family systems	1	0
gender	2	0

identity/phenotype	3	0
multicultural curriculum development	1	0
relationship enhancement	1	0

Clinical opportunities
community organizations
families
groups
low income
minorities
rural
substance abuse
vocational career development

New York University

School of Education
Counseling Psychology
Department of Applied Psychology
East Building, 4th Floor
239 Greene Street
New York, NY 10003
phone#: (212) 998-5559
Web address: http://www.nyu.edu/education/appsych/

1	2	3	**4**	5	6	7
Clinically oriented			Equal emphasis			Research oriented

What percentage of your faculty subscribes to or practices in each of the following orientations?

Psychodynamic/Psychoanalytic	50%
Applied behavioral analysis/Radical behavioral	0%
Family systems/Systems	13%
Existential/Phenomenological/Humanistic	25%
Cognitive/Cognitive-behavioral	13%

What percentage of students applying for internship last year was accepted into APA-accredited internships? 100%

What courses are required for incoming students to have completed prior to enrolling?
18 credits of prerequisites in psychology at undergraduate or graduate level. Not necessary to complete prerequisites before enrollment.

Are there courses you recommend that are not mandatory?
In general, basic areas in psychology course work are recommended

GRE mean (M), cutoff (C), or preferred (P)
Preferred minimum score on combined Verbal + Quantitative 1000

GPA mean (M), cutoff (C), or preferred (P)
Overall GPA 3.0 (C)

Number of applications/admission offers/incoming students in 2001
130 applied/7 admission offers/4 incoming

% of students receiving:
Tuition waiver only: 0%
Assistantship/fellowship only: 5%
Both tuition waiver & assistantship/fellowship: 0%

Approximate percentage of incoming students who entered with a B.A./B.S. only: 0% **Master's:** 100%

Approximate percentage of students who are Women: 80% **Ethnic Minority:** 10%

Research areas	# Faculty	# Grants
group process	1	0
multicultural counseling and assessment	2	2
psychoanalytic constructs	1	0
psychopathology and differential diagnosis	1	0
religion and spirituality	1	0
women's development	2	0
work as a developmental context	1	0

Clinical opportunities
Wide range of specialized practica and externship sites are available in the New York metropolitan area.

University of North Dakota

Department of Counseling
Box 8255
Grand Forks, ND 58202-8255
phone#: (701) 777-2729
fax#: (701) 777-3184
e-mail: sujacobs@badlands.nodak.edu
Web address: http://www.und.edu/dept/grad/depts/coun/

1	2	3	**4**	5	6	7
Clinically oriented			Equal emphasis			Research oriented

What percentage of your faculty subscribes to or practices in each of the following orientations?

Psychodynamic/Psychoanalytic	40%
Applied behavioral analysis/Radical behavioral	20%
Family systems/Systems	20%
Existential/Phenomenological/Humanistic	40%
Cognitive/Cognitive-behavioral	50%
Feminist	50%

What percentage of students applying for internship last year was accepted into APA-accredited internships? 100%

What courses are required for incoming students to have completed prior to enrolling?
Counseling methods, research methods, 20 semester hours of undergraduate psychology including statistics, research methods, abnormal psychology, developmental psychology, and general psychology

Are there courses you recommend that are not mandatory?
Master's level practicum, 60 hours supervised practice

GRE mean (M), cutoff (C), or preferred (P)
Verbal 540 (M), 500+ (P) Quantitative 562 (M), 500+ (P)
Analytical 557 (M), 500+ (P)
Advanced Psychology 632 (M), 500+ (P)

GPA mean (M), cutoff (C), or preferred (P)
Overall Undergraduate GPA 3.3 (M)
Junior/Senior GPA 3.5 (M)
Overall Master's GPA 3.5 (P), 3.8 (M)

Number of applications/admission offers/incoming students in 2001
21 applied/14 admission offers/6 incoming

% of students receiving:
Tuition waiver only: 0%
Assistantship/fellowship only: 6%
Both tuition waiver & assistantship/fellowship: 94%

Approximate percentage of incoming students who entered with a B.A./B.S. only: 50% **Master's:** 50%

Approximate percentage of students who are Women: 66% **Ethnic Minority:** 20%

Average years to complete the doctoral program (including internship): 4.5 years

Research areas	**# Faculty**	**# Grants**
career development	2	2
conflict resolution	1	0
gay, lesbian, bisexual issues	1	0
gender and intimacy	1	0
gender issues in supervision	1	0
impact of disaster and trauma	2	0
international student adjustment	1	0
men and depression	2	0
Native American career development	1	0
social support and chronic illness	1	0
student self-efficacy	1	0
supervisor strategies	2	0
vocational interests testing	1	1
women/career development	1	0

Clinical opportunities
Fieldwork placements at a variety of community and academic settings

University of North Texas

Department of Psychology
NT Box 13587
Denton, TX 76203-3587
phone#: (940) 565-2671
e-mail: AMYG@UNT.EDU
Web address: http://www.psyc.unt.edu/counsel.htm

1	2	3	**4**	5	6	7
Clinically oriented			Equal emphasis			Research oriented

What percentage of your faculty subscribes to or practices in each of the following orientations?

Psychodynamic/Psychoanalytic	35%
Applied behavioral analysis/Radical behavioral	0%
Family systems/Systems	45%
Existential/Phenomenological/Humanistic	20%
Cognitive/Cognitive-behavioral	45%

What percentage of students applying for internship last year was accepted into APA-accredited internships? 100%

What courses are required for incoming students to have completed prior to enrolling?
Statistics, experimental, cognition/learning theory or history and systems

Are there courses you recommend that are not mandatory?
Social psychology, physiological psychology, tests and measurements

GRE mean (M), cutoff (C), or preferred (P)
Verbal 500 (C) Quantitative 500 (C)

GPA mean (M), cutoff (C), or preferred (P)
Overall GPA 3.0 or 3.5 on last 60 hours (C)
Psychology GPA 3.5 (C)

Number of applications/admission offers/incoming students in 2001
70 applied/22 admission offers/11 incoming

% of students receiving:
Tuition waiver only: 0%
Assistantship/fellowship only: 40%
Both tuition waiver & assistantship/fellowship: 0%

Approximate percentage of incoming students who entered with a B.A./B.S. only: 75% **Master's:** 25%

Approximate percentage of students who are Women: 65% **Ethnic Minority:** 2%

Average years to complete the doctoral program (including internship): 7.7 years

Research areas	**# Faculty**	**# Grants**
counseling and therapy	6	0
eating disorders	3	0
gerontology	1	1
marriage and family	3	0
minority and cross-cultural	2	1
professional issues	4	0
sports psychology	2	1
vocational development	3	0

Clinical opportunities
university counseling and testing center
psychology clinic
external agencies after completing required on-campus practica

University of Northern Colorado (Psy.D.)

Division of Professional Psychology
Greeley, CO 80639
phone#: (970) 351-2209
e-mail: bjohnson@coe.unco.edu
Web address: http://www.unco.edu

1	2	3	**4**	5	6	7

Clinically oriented — Equal emphasis — Research oriented

What percentage of your faculty subscribes to or practices in each of the following orientations?

Psychodynamic/Psychoanalytic	0%
Applied behavioral analysis/Radical behavioral	10%
Family systems/Systems	20%
Existential/Phenomenological/Humanistic	35%
Cognitive/Cognitive-behavioral	35%

What percentage of students applying for internship last year was accepted into APA-accredited internships? 80%

What courses are required for incoming students to have completed prior to enrolling?
A master's degree is required in a related field of applied psychology

Are there courses you recommend that are not mandatory?
No

GRE mean (M), cutoff (C), or preferred (P)
Verbal 500 (P) Quantitative 500 (P) Analytical 500 (P)
Recommended GRE Total 1500

GPA mean (M), cutoff (C), or preferred (P)
Overall GPA 3.25

Number of applications/admission offers/incoming students in 2001
30 applied/6 admission offers/6 incoming

% of students receiving:
Tuition waiver only: 0%
Assistantship/fellowship only: 25%
Both tuition waiver & assistantship/fellowship: 25%

Approximate percentage of incoming students who entered with a B.A./B.S. only: 0% **Master's:** 100%

Approximate percentage of students who are Women: 70% **Ethnic Minority:** 10%

Average years to complete the doctoral program (including internship): 5 years

Research areas	**# Faculty**	**# Grants**
ADHD	1	0
counseling process	2	0
eating disorders	2	0
family dynamics	2	1
multicultural	2	0

Clinical opportunities
clinical hypnosis
marriage and family
neuropsychological assessment
play therapy
supervision

University of Notre Dame

Department of Psychology
Notre Dame, IN 46556
phone#: (219) 631-6650
fax#: (219) 631-8883
e-mail: JudyA.Spiro.2@nd.edu
Web address: http://www.nd.edu:80/~psych/counseling/index.htm

1	2	3	4	5	**6**	7

Clinically oriented — Equal emphasis — Research oriented

What percentage of your faculty subscribes to or practices in each of the following orientations?

Psychodynamic/Psychoanalytic	20%
Applied behavioral analysis/Radical behavioral	10%
Family systems/Systems	20%
Existential/Phenomenological/Humanistic	30%
Cognitive/Cognitive-behavioral	20%

What percentage of students applying for internship last year was accepted into APA-accredited internships? 100%

What courses are required for incoming students to have completed prior to enrolling?
Undergraduate psychology major, statistics, methodology, and some research experience

Are there courses you recommend that are not mandatory?
No

GRE mean (M), cutoff (C), or preferred (P)
Verbal + Quantitative 1100 (C)

GPA mean (M), cutoff (C), or preferred (P)
Overall GPA 3.2 (C) Psychology GPA 3.4 (C)

Number of applications/admission offers/incoming students in 2001
128 applied/5 admission offers/4 incoming

% of students receiving:
Tuition waiver only: 0%
Assistantship/fellowship only: 0%
Both tuition waiver & assistantship/fellowship: 100%

Approximate percentage of incoming students who entered with a B.A./B.S. only: 90% **Master's:** 10%

Approximate percentage of students who are Women: 70% **Ethnic Minority:** 20%

Average years to complete the doctoral program (including internship): 6 years

Research areas	**# Faculty**	**# Grants**
behavioral medicine	1	1
child depression	1	1
conduct disorders	1	0
ethics	2	0
narrative psychology	1	1

Clinical opportunities
local community mental health center
university counseling center

Ohio State University

Department of Psychology
Columbus, OH 43210
phone#: (614) 292-5303
e-mail: walsh.1@osu.edu
Web address: http://www.psy.ohiostate.edu/counsel.html

1	2	3	**4**	5	6	7
Clinically oriented			Equal emphasis			Research oriented

What percentage of your faculty subscribes to or practices in each of the following orientations?

Psychodynamic/Psychoanalytic	10%
Applied behavioral analysis/Radical behavioral	10%
Family systems/Systems	10%
Existential/Phenomenological/Humanistic	30%
Cognitive/Cognitive-behavioral	50%

What percentage of students applying for internship last year was accepted into APA-accredited internships? 100%

What courses are required for incoming students to have completed prior to enrolling?
20 credit hours in psychology

Are there courses you recommend that are not mandatory?
Statistics

GRE mean (M), cutoff (C), or preferred (P)
Verbal 600 (P) Quantitative 600 (P)
Advanced Psychology 600 (P)

GPA mean (M), cutoff (C), or preferred (P)
Overall GPA 3.25 (C)

Number of applications/admission offers/incoming students in 2001
150 applied/14 admission offers/8 incoming

% of students receiving:
Tuition waiver only: 0%
Assistantship/fellowship only: 0%
Both tuition waiver & assistantship/fellowship: 95%

Approximate percentage of incoming students who entered with a B.A./B.S. only: 75% **Master's:** 25%

Approximate percentage of students who are Women: 70% **Ethnic Minority:** 47%

Average years to complete the doctoral program (including internship): 5 years

Research areas	# Faculty	# Grants
counseling process	2	0
counseling supervision	2	0
cross-cultural research	4	0
health psychology	2	0
person environment assessment	3	0
psychology of women	2	0
social influence processes	2	0
vocational psychology	4	0

Clinical opportunities
rehabilitation medicine
various counseling centers
VA outpatient clinic

University of Oklahoma

Department of Educational Psychology
Norman, OK 73019-0260
phone#: (405) 325-5974
e-mail: cstoltenberg@ou.edu
Web address: http://www.ou.edu/education/cpp/cpprog.html

1	2	3	**4**	5	6	7
Clinically oriented			Equal emphasis			Research oriented

What percentage of your faculty subscribes to or practices in each of the following orientations?

Psychodynamic/Psychoanalytic	15%
Applied behavioral analysis/Radical behavioral	0%
Family systems/Systems	60%
Existential/Phenomenological/Humanistic	16%
Cognitive/Cognitive-behavioral	70%

What percentage of students applying for internship last year was accepted into APA-accredited internships? 100%

What courses are required for incoming students to have completed prior to enrolling?
College algebra (or equivalent), 2 semesters of English grammar and composition, 18 semester hours in psychology or related area

Are there courses you recommend that are not mandatory?
No

GRE mean (M), cutoff (C), or preferred (P)
Verbal 550 (M) Quantitative 600 (M) Analytical 600 (M)

GPA mean (M), cutoff (C), or preferred (P)
Overall GPA 3.00 (C) Junior/Senior GPA 3.25 (C)

Number of applications/admission offers/incoming students in 2001
80 applied/16 admission offers/8 incoming

% of students receiving:
Tuition waiver only: 0%
Assistantship/fellowship only: 0%
Both tuition waiver & assistantship/fellowship: 80%

Approximate percentage of incoming students who entered with a B.A./B.S. only: 12.5% **Master's:** 87.5%

Approximate percentage of students who are Women: 60% **Ethnic Minority:** 18%

Average years to complete the doctoral program (including internship): 5 years

Research areas	# Faculty	# Grants
assessment	2	0
career issues	2	0

child treatment	3	0
clinical supervision	3	0
counseling process and outcomes	4	1
gender issues	1	0
health psychology	3	0
marriage and family issues	4	0
multicultural counseling	4	0

Clinical opportunities
child abuse and neglect clinics
child study center
community mental health clinics
correctional facilities
Indian health service clinic
psychiatric hospitals
rehabilitation clinics
university counseling center
VA hospital

Oklahoma State University

School of Applied Health and Educational Psychology
Stillwater, OK 74078
phone#: (405) 744-6040
e-mail: miville@okstate.edu
Web address: http://www.okstate.edu/education/sahep/psychcore.html

1	2	3	**4**	5	6	7
Clinically oriented			Equal emphasis			Research oriented

What percentage of your faculty subscribes to or practices in each of the following orientations?

Psychodynamic/Psychoanalytic	10%
Applied behavioral analysis/Radical behavioral	0%
Family systems/Systems	30%
Existential/Phenomenological/Humanistic	30%
Cognitive/Cognitive-behavioral	90%

What percentage of students applying for internship last year was accepted into APA-accredited internships? 100%

What courses are required for incoming students to have completed prior to enrolling?
Master's degree in psychology or related area

Are there courses you recommend that are not mandatory?
None

GRE mean (M), cutoff (C), or preferred (P)
Verbal 500 (P) Quantitative 500 (P) Analytical 500 (P)

GPA mean (M), cutoff (C), or preferred (P)
Overall Undergraduate GPA 2.5 (C)
Overall Master's GPA 3.5 (C)

Number of applications/admission offers/incoming students in 2001
100 applied/13 admission offers/11 incoming

% of students receiving:
Tuition waiver only: 10%
Assistantship/fellowship only: 0%
Both tuition waiver & assistantship/fellowship: 90%

Approximate percentage of incoming students who entered with a B.A./B.S. only: 27% **Master's:** 73%

Approximate percentage of students who are Women: 60% **Ethnic Minority:** 30%

Average years to complete the doctoral program (including internship): 4.5 years

Research areas	# Faculty	# Grants
American Indian issues	3	3
at-risk youth	2	1
career issues	4	1
health psychology	2	1
LGBT issues	1	1
multicultural issues	4	5
professional issues	2	1
psychological assessment	1	0
rural mental health	1	0
sports psychology	1	0
supervision	3	0
women/gender issues	2	0

Clinical opportunities
domestic violence center
correctional psychology unit
hospitals
Indian health services
inpatient unit
marriage and family clinic
pain clinics
physician's office
rural mental health clinic
women's health center
youth services

University of Oregon

Counseling Psychology Program
5251 University of Oregon
Eugene, OR 97403-5251
phone#: (541) 346-2456
e-mail: counpsy@oregon.uoregon.edu
Web address: http://interact.uoregon.edu/counseling/

1	2	3	4	**5**	6	7
Clinically oriented			Equal emphasis			Research oriented

What percentage of your faculty subscribes to or practices in each of the following orientations?

Psychodynamic/Psychoanalytic	25%
Applied behavioral analysis/Radical behavioral	0%
Family systems/Systems	25%
Existential/Phenomenological/Humanistic	75%
Cognitive/Cognitive-behavioral	100%

What percentage of students applying for internship last year was accepted into APA-accredited internships? 100%

What courses are required for incoming students to have completed prior to enrolling?
No specific courses required

Are there courses you recommend that are not mandatory?
—

GRE mean (M), cutoff (C), or preferred (P)
Verbal 560 (P) Quantitative 560 (P)

GPA mean (M), cutoff (C), or preferred (P)
Overall 3.5 (P)

Number of applications/admission offers/incoming students in 2001
125 applied/10 admission offers/9 incoming

% of students receiving:
Tuition waiver only: 0%
Assistantship/fellowship only: 0%
Both tuition waiver & assistantship/fellowship: 100%

Approximate percentage of incoming students who entered with a B.A./B.S. only: 80% **Master's:** 20%

Approximate percentage of students who are Women: 75% **Ethnic Minority:** 47%

Average years to complete the doctoral program (including internship): 5.5 years

Research areas	# Faculty	# Grants
child & family psychology	1	3
prevention research	2	1
social support and interactions	3	0
treatment outcomes	2	0
vocational	1	0

Clinical opportunities
child-family
community prevention
counseling centers
inpatient settings
VA

Our Lady of the Lake University (Psy.D.)

Graduate Admissions Office
School of Education and Clinical Studies
411 SW 24th Street
San Antonio, TX 78207-4689
phone#: (210) 431-3914
e-mail: BOBEM@lake.ollusa.edu
Web address: http://www.ollusa.edu/

1 **2** 3 4 5 6 7
Clinically oriented — Equal emphasis — Research oriented

What percentage of your faculty subscribes to or practices in each of the following orientations?

Psychodynamic/Psychoanalytic	20%
Applied behavioral analysis/Radical behavioral	0%
Family systems/Systems	60%
Existential/Phenomenological/Humanistic	0%
Cognitive/Cognitive-behavioral	20%

What percentage of students applying for internship last year was accepted into APA-accredited internships? 90%

What courses are required for incoming students to have completed prior to enrolling?
Master's degree in psychology or closely related area

Are there courses you recommend that are not mandatory?
No

GRE mean (M), cutoff (C), or preferred (P)
Verbal 558 Quantitative 550
No cutoffs

GPA mean (M), cutoff (C), or preferred (P)
Overall GPA 3.67, 3.5 (C)

Number of applications/admission offers/incoming students in 2001
32 applied/11 admission offers/7 incoming

% of students receiving:
Tuition waiver only: 10%
Assistantship/fellowship only: 0%
Both tuition waiver & assistantship/fellowship: 22%

Approximate percentage of incoming students who entered with a B.A./B.S. only: 0% **Master's:** 100%

Approximate percentage of students who are Women: 63% **Ethnic Minority:** 20%

Average years to complete the doctoral program (including internship): 7 years

Research areas	# Faculty	# Grants
brief therapy	3	1
ethics	1	0
reimbursement issues	1	0

Clinical opportunities
community counseling service, Spanish-speaking population
Shertz-Cibilo School District, school-age population

Pennsylvania State University

Department of Counselor Education, Counseling Psychology, and Rehabilitation Services
University Park, PA 16802
phone#: (814) 865-8304
e-mail: jak2@psu.edu
Web address: http://www.ed.psu.edu/counsed/cnpsy/index.html

1 2 3 **4** 5 6 7
Clinically oriented — Equal emphasis — Research oriented

What percentage of your faculty subscribes to or practices in each of the following orientations?

Psychodynamic/Psychoanalytic	31%
Applied behavioral analysis/Radical behavioral	0%
Family systems/Systems	0%
Existential/Phenomenological/Humanistic	50%
Cognitive/Cognitive-behavioral	19%

What percentage of students applying for internship last year was accepted into APA-accredited internships? 100%

What courses are required for incoming students to have completed prior to enrolling?
Recommended: theories of counseling/psychotherapy, assessment/testing, statistics/research design, career counseling, multicultural counseling, group counseling/psychotherapy, counselor skills training/prepracticum counseling practicum

Are there courses you recommend that are not mandatory?
No

GRE mean (M), cutoff (C), or preferred (P)
Verbal 550 (M) Quantitative 550 (M)

GPA mean (M), cutoff (C), or preferred (P)
Overall Master's GPA 3.33 (P)

Number of applications/admission offers/incoming students in 2001
58 applied/12 admission offers/6 incoming

% of students receiving:
Tuition waiver only: 0%
Assistantship/fellowship only: 0%
Both tuition waiver & assistantship/fellowship: 100%

Approximate percentage of incoming students who entered with a B.A./B.S. only: 0% **Master's:** 100%

Approximate percentage of students who are Women: 70% **Ethnic Minority:** 39%

Average years to complete the doctoral program (including internship): 5 years

Research areas	# Faculty	# Grants
perfectionism	1	0
prevention	1	0
psychotherapy	1	0
racial identity	1	0

Clinical opportunities
—

University of St. Thomas (Psy.D.)

Graduate Department of Professional Psychology
MPL451, 1000 La Salle Avenue
Minneapolis, MN 55403-2005
phone#: (651) 962-4650
e-mail: GradPsych@St.Thomas.Edu
Web address: http://www.St.Thomas.Edu/

1	**2**	3	4	5	6	7
Clinically oriented			Equal emphasis			Research oriented

What percentage of your faculty subscribes to or practices in each of the following orientations?

Psychodynamic/Psychoanalytic	0%
Applied behavioral analysis/Radical behavioral	0%
Family systems/Systems	50%
Existential/Phenomenological/Humanistic	0%
Cognitive/Cognitive-behavioral	50%

What percentage of students applying for internship last year was accepted into APA-accredited internships? 1%

What courses are required for incoming students to have completed prior to enrolling?
Students must complete a 45-credit M.A. program in counseling psychology or equivalent

Are there courses you recommend that are not mandatory?
Abnormal psychology, psychological statistics, research design, personality theory, developmental psychology

GRE mean (M), cutoff (C), or preferred (P)
MAT 60 (P) (M)

GPA mean (M), cutoff (C), or preferred (P)
Overall GPA 3.2 (M)

Number of applications/admission offers/incoming students in 2001
43 applied/18 admission offers/18 incoming

% of students receiving:
Tuition waiver only: 0%
Assistantship/fellowship only: 16%
Both tuition waiver & assistantship/fellowship: 0%

Approximate percentage of incoming students who entered with a B.A./B.S. only: 0% **Master's:** 100%

Approximate percentage of students who are Women: 80% **Ethnic Minority:** 13%

Average years to complete the doctoral program (including internship): 5.5 years

Research areas	# Faculty	# Grants
anxiety disorders	2	1
cultural sensitive therapy	2	0
eating disorders	2	0
geropsychology	1	0
interprofessional ethics	1	0
licensure and regulatory boards	1	0
master therapists	1	0
religion and psychotherapy	1	0

Clinical opportunities
anxiety disorders
eating disorders
family therapy

Seton Hall University

Counseling Psychology Program
College of Education
400 S. Orange Avenue
South Orange, NJ 07079
phone#: (973) 275-2740
e-mail: palmerla@shu.edu
Web address: http://education/shu.edu/

1	2	3	**4**	5	6	7

Clinically oriented | Equal emphasis | Research oriented

What percentage of your faculty subscribes to or practices in each of the following orientations?

Psychodynamic/Psychoanalytic	25%
Applied behavioral analysis/Radical behavioral	0%
Family systems/Systems	0%
Existential/Phenomenological/Humanistic	37%
Cognitive/Cognitive-behavioral	43%

What percentage of students applying for internship last year was accepted into APA-accredited internships? 15%

What courses are required for incoming students to have completed prior to enrolling?
Group counseling, abnormal psychology, test and measurement, counseling skills

Are there courses you recommend that are not mandatory?
No

GRE mean (M), cutoff (C), or preferred (P)
Verbal 470 (M) Quantitative 515 (M) Analytical 577 (M)

GPA mean (M), cutoff (C), or preferred (P)
Overall GPA 3.2 (M)

Number of applications/admission offers/incoming students in 2001
60 applied/6 admission offers/5 incoming

% of students receiving:
Tuition waiver only: 0%
Assistantship/fellowship only: 90%
Both tuition waiver & assistantship/fellowship: 0%

Approximate percentage of incoming students who entered with a B.A./B.S. only: 10% **Master's:** 90%

Approximate percentage of students who are Women: 66% **Ethnic Minority:** 30%

Average years to complete the doctoral program (including internship): 5 years

Research areas	# Faculty	# Grants
career development	2	9
multicultural counseling	1	0
neuropsychology	1	0
psychological trauma	1	0
resiliency	1	0
student well-being	1	0

Clinical opportunities
The university does not run any specialty clinics. The program has developed an extensive offering of diverse clinical training opportunities in the greater New York area.

University of Southern California

Division of Counseling Psychology
503 WPH
Los Angeles, CA 90089-0031
phone#: (213) 740-3267
e-mail: Goodyea@usc.edu
Web address: http://www.usc.edu/dept/couns_psych/

1	2	3	4	**5**	6	7

Clinically oriented | Equal emphasis | Research oriented

What percentage of your faculty subscribes to or practices in each of the following orientations?

Psychodynamic/Psychoanalytic	0%
Applied behavioral analysis/Radical behavioral	0%
Family systems/Systems	0%
Existential/Phenomenological/Humanistic	20%
Cognitive/Cognitive-behavioral	0%
Integrative/Eclectic	80%

What percentage of students applying for internship last year was accepted into APA-accredited internships? 80%

What courses are required for incoming students to have completed prior to enrolling?
None

Are there courses you recommend that are not mandatory?
No

GRE mean (M), cutoff (C), or preferred (P)
Verbal 600 (P) Quantitative 600 (P)
Verbal + Quantitative 1300 (M)

GPA mean (M), cutoff (C), or preferred (P)
Overall GPA 3.0 (C)

Number of applications/admission offers/incoming students in 2001
110 applied/10 admission offers/8 incoming

% of students receiving:
Tuition waiver only: 0%
Assistantship/fellowship only: 0%
Both tuition waiver & assistantship/fellowship: 25%

Approximate percentage of incoming students who entered with a B.A./B.S. only: 35% **Master's:** 65%

Approximate percentage of students who are Women: 70% **Ethnic Minority:** 40%

Average years to complete the doctoral program (including internship): 6.3 years

Research areas	# Faculty	# Grants
Asian-American mental health issues	1	0
clinical supervision processes	1	0

Latino mental health issues	3	0
sexual behavior	2	0
substance abuse	1	1

Clinical opportunities
Practicum is at Kednen Community Health Center (all students) plus at least one university counseling center and another site of the student's choice.

Southern Illinois University

Department of Psychology
Carbondale, IL 62901
phone#: (618) 453-3564
e-mail: sharonr@siu.edu (graduate secretary)
byanico@siu.edu (program director)
Web address: http://www.siu.edu/~psyc/counseling.html

1	2	3	**4**	5	6	7
Clinically oriented			Equal emphasis			Research oriented

What percentage of your faculty subscribes to or practices in each of the following orientations?

Psychodynamic/Psychoanalytic	17%
Applied behavioral analysis/Radical behavioral	0%
Family systems/Systems	0%
Existential/Phenomenological/Humanistic	67%
Cognitive/Cognitive-behavioral	33%

What percentage of students applying for internship last year was accepted into APA-accredited internships? 100%

What courses are required for incoming students to have completed prior to enrolling?
—

Are there courses you recommend that are not mandatory?
At least one statistics course; if student was not an undergraduate psychology major, we look for coursework in core areas of psychology (e.g., history and systems, abnormal, personality, cognitive, social, physiological)

GRE mean (M), cutoff (C), or preferred (P)
Verbal 603 (M) Quantitative 621 (M) Analytical 682 (M)

GPA mean (M), cutoff (C), or preferred (P)
Overall GPA 3.0 (C) Psychology GPA 3.62 (M)

Number of applications/admission offers/incoming students in 2001
42 applied/11 admission offers/7 incoming

% of students receiving:
Tuition waiver only: 0%
Assistantship/fellowship only: 0%
Both tuition waiver & assistantship/fellowship: 100%

Approximate percentage of incoming students who entered with a B.A./B.S. only: 85% **Master's:** 15%

Approximate percentage of students who are Women: 70% **Ethnic Minority:** 34%

Average years to complete the doctoral program (including internship): 5.5 years

Research areas	**# Faculty**	**# Grants**
academic disidentification	1	0
academic self-concept, achievement and motivation	1	0
adjustment to brain injury/disability	1	0
career assessment and counseling	2	2
career choice and development	2	1
caregiver burden	1	1
counseling supervision	2	0
disaster management/crisis intervention	1	0
expectations about counseling	2	0
gender and cultural influences on therapy	3	0
health psychology	1	0
human sexual behavior	1	0
occupational stress and health	1	0
personality assessment	1	0
psychological measurement	1	0
psychological student development	1	0
qualitative research methodology	1	0
racial/ethnic identity	2	0
research training	1	0
self-efficacy	1	0
sexual harassment	1	0
spiritual/religious issues	1	0
stress and coping	2	0
technology in counseling	1	0
women in management	1	0
workplace violence	1	0

Clinical opportunities
career development
clinical center, marriage and family practicum
local community mental health centers (rural mental health)
state correctional system (medium security facility)
student health service
university counseling center
VA hospital
vocational rehabilitation
wellness center: substance abuse unit, stress management unit, sexuality counseling unit

University of Southern Mississippi

Department of Psychology
Hattiesburg, MS 39406-5012
phone#: (601) 266-4602
Web address: http://www-dept.usm.edu/~psy/counseling/overview.htm

1	2	3	4	**5**	6	7
Clinically oriented			Equal emphasis			Research oriented

What percentage of your faculty subscribes to or practices in each of the following orientations?

Psychodynamic/Psychoanalytic	20%
Applied behavioral analysis/Radical behavioral	0%
Family systems/Systems	10%
Existential/Phenomenological/Humanistic	20%
Cognitive/Cognitive-behavioral	50%

What percentage of students applying for internship last year was accepted into APA-accredited internships? 100%

What courses are required for incoming students to have completed prior to enrolling?
None

Are there courses you recommend that are not mandatory?
Statistics, personality theory, human growth and development, learning theory

GRE mean (M), cutoff (C), or preferred (P)
Verbal 600 (M) Quantitative 600 (M)

GPA mean (M), cutoff (C), or preferred (P)
Overall GPA 3.50 (M) Overall Master's GPA 3.80 (M)

Number of applications/admission offers/incoming students in 2001
50 applied/10 admission offers/6 incoming

% of students receiving:
Tuition waiver only: 0%
Assistantship/fellowship only: 0%
Both tuition waiver & assistantship/fellowship: 100%

Approximate percentage of incoming students who entered with a B.A./B.S. only: 40% **Master's:** 60%

Approximate percentage of students who are Women: 65% **Ethnic Minority:** 15%

Average years to complete the doctoral program (including internship): 4 years

Research areas	# Faculty	# Grants
alcohol and drugs	1	0
anger	1	0
attachment	3	0
body image	1	0
child sexual abuse	1	0
consultation	1	0
eating disorders	1	0
empirically supported treatments	2	0
forgiveness	1	0
minority/multicultural	3	0
psychological separation	2	0
suicide	1	0

Clinical opportunities
behavioral medicine
child sexual abuse
eating disorders
psychological assessment center
training clinic
university counseling center
university medical center
VA hospital

Stanford University

School of Education
Stanford, CA 94305
phone#: (650) 723-2115
e-mail: jdk@stanford.edu
Web address: http://www.stanford.edu/dept/SUSE/programs/pse_cont.html

1	2	3	**4**	5	6	7
Clinically oriented			Equal emphasis			Research oriented

What percentage of your faculty subscribes to or practices in each of the following orientations?

Psychodynamic/Psychoanalytic	0%
Applied behavioral analysis/Radical behavioral	0%
Family systems/Systems	0%
Existential/Phenomenological/Humanistic	0%
Cognitive/Cognitive-behavioral	100%

What percentage of students applying for internship last year was accepted into APA-accredited internships? 100%

What courses are required for incoming students to have completed prior to enrolling?
—

Are there courses you recommend that are not mandatory?
Psychology background helpful but not required. A master's degree and some relevant counseling experience is strongly preferred.

GRE mean (M), cutoff (C), or preferred (P)
No score requirements

GPA mean (M), cutoff (C), or preferred (P)
No score requirements

Number of applications/admission offers/incoming students in 2001
100 applied/3 admission offers/2 incoming

% of students receiving:
Tuition waiver only: 0%
Assistantship/fellowship only: 25%
Both tuition waiver & assistantship/fellowship: 75%

Approximate percentage of incoming students who entered with a B.A./B.S. only: 10% **Master's:** 90%

Approximate percentage of students who are Women: 67% **Ethnic Minority:** 35%

Average years to complete the doctoral program (including internship): 5 years

Research areas	# Faculty	# Grants
career development	1	1
minority mental health	1	1

Clinical opportunities
—

Temple University

Counseling Psychology Program
2nd Floor Weiss Hall (265-63)
Philadelphia, PA 19122-6085
phone#: (215) 204-3253
e-mail:Tucnpsy@Temple.edu
Web address: http://WWW.TEMPLE.EDU/education/counspsych

1	2	**3**	4	5	6	7
Clinically oriented		Equal emphasis				Research oriented

What percentage of your faculty subscribes to or practices in each of the following orientations?

Psychodynamic/Psychoanalytic	0%
Applied behavioral analysis/Radical behavioral	20%
Family systems/Systems	20%
Existential/Phenomenological/Humanistic	20%
Cognitive/Cognitive-behavioral	40%

What percentage of students applying for internship last year was accepted into APA-accredited internships? 78%

What courses are required for incoming students to have completed prior to enrolling?
We prefer an undergraduate major in psychology. Students are required to have a master's degree in counseling or a related clinical degree.

Are there courses you recommend that are not mandatory?
See above

GRE mean (M), cutoff (C), or preferred (P)
Verbal 500 (P) Quantitative 500 (P)

GPA mean (M), cutoff (C), or preferred (P)
Overall Undergraduate GPA 3.00 (P)
Overall Master's GPA 3.5 (P) Psychology GPA 3.50 (P)
Junior/Senior GPA 3.00 (P)

Number of applications/admission offers/incoming students in 2001
50 applied/16 admission offers/10 incoming

% of students receiving:
Tuition waiver only: 0%
Assistantship/fellowship only: 10%
Both tuition waiver & assistantship/fellowship: 50%

Approximate percentage of incoming students who entered with a B.A./B.S. only: 0% **Master's:** 100%

Approximate percentage of students who are Women: 70% **Ethnic Minority:** 40%

Average years to complete the doctoral program (including internship): 5.7 years

Research areas	**# Faculty**	**# Grants**
cognitive and behavioral change	3	3
family psychology and therapy	1	0
health psychology	—	—
minority and diversity issues	2	0
training and supervision	2	0

Clinical opportunities
adult, children, and family clinic
third-year practicum
vocational counseling clinic

University of Tennessee (1999 Data)

Counselor Education and Counseling Psychology Unit
College of Education
Knoxville, TN 37996
phone#: (423) 974-5131
e-mail: hector@utkux.utcc.utk.edu
Web address: http://www.coe.utk.edu/units/counselor.html

1	2	3	**4**	5	6	7
Clinically oriented			Equal emphasis			Research oriented

What percentage of your faculty subscribes to or practices in each of the following orientations?

Psychodynamic/Psychoanalytic	0%
Applied behavioral analysis/Radical behavioral	0%
Family systems/Systems	14%
Existential/Phenomenological/Humanistic	29%
Cognitive/Cognitive-behavioral	43%

What percentage of students applying for internship last year was accepted into APA-accredited internships? 100%

What courses are required for incoming students to have completed prior to enrolling?
None

Are there courses you recommend that are not mandatory?
No

GRE mean (M), cutoff (C), or preferred (P)
Score of 1000 on any two of Verbal, Quantitative, or Analytical Advanced Psychology (C)

GPA mean (M), cutoff (C), or preferred (P)
Overall GPA 3.91 (M)

Number of applications/admission offers in 1997
79 applied/6 admission offers

% of students receiving:
Tuition waiver only: 0%
Assistantship/fellowship only: 0%
Both tuition waiver & assistantship/fellowship: 70%

Approximate percentage of incoming students who entered with a B.A./B.S. only: 25% **Master's:** 75%

Approximate percentage of students who are Women: 58% **Ethnic Minority:** 13%

Research areas	**# Faculty**	**# Grants**
careers	2	0
counseling process	2	0
ethics	1	0

group process	1	0
teaching statistics	1	0

Clinical opportunities

—

Tennessee State University

Department of Psychology
Nashville, TN 37209-1561
phone#: (615) 963-5141
e-mail: pknox@tnstate.edu
Web address: http://www.tnstate.edu/psy/

1 2 **3** 4 5 6 7

Clinically oriented — Equal emphasis — Research oriented

What percentage of your faculty subscribes to or practices in each of the following orientations?

Psychodynamic/Psychoanalytic	42%
Applied behavioral analysis/Radical behavioral	14%
Family systems/Systems	14%
Existential/Phenomenological/Humanistic	14%
Cognitive/Cognitive-behavioral	14%

What percentage of students applying for internship last year was accepted into APA-accredited internships? 50%

What courses are required for incoming students to have completed prior to enrolling?
Learning; statistics and research methodology; counseling theories; physiological psychology; intelligence, aptitude, and achievement testing; personality theory; master's-level practicum

Are there courses you recommend that are not mandatory?
No

GRE mean (M), cutoff (C), or preferred (P)
Verbal 500 (P) Quantitative 500 (P)

GPA mean (M), cutoff (C), or preferred (P)
Overall GPA 3.25 (M)

Number of applications/admission offers/incoming students in 2001
22 applied/10 admission offers/8 incoming

% of students receiving:
Tuition waiver only: 0%
Assistantship/fellowship only: 13%
Both tuition waiver & assistantship/fellowship: 4%

Approximate percentage of incoming students who entered with a B.A./B.S. only: 0% **Master's:** 100%

Approximate percentage of students who are Women: 71% **Ethnic Minority:** 38%

Average years to complete the doctoral program (including internship): — years

Research areas	**# Faculty**	**# Grants**
decision making	1	0
eating disorders	2	1
family	1	1
multicultural concerns	2	1

Clinical opportunities
adult, child, and adolescent psychiatry
behavioral health
forensics

Texas A&M University

Department of Educational Psychology
College Station, TX 77843
phone#: (409) 845-1833
e-mail: c-wagner@tamu.edu
Web address: http://www.coe.tamu.edu/~edpsy/

1 2 3 **4** 5 6 7

Clinically oriented — Equal emphasis — Research oriented

What percentage of your faculty subscribes to or practices in each of the following orientations?

Psychodynamic/Psychoanalytic	50%
Applied behavioral analysis/Radical behavioral	0%
Family systems/Systems	25%
Existential/Phenomenological/Humanistic	0%
Cognitive/Cognitive-behavioral	25%

What percentage of students applying for internship last year was accepted into APA-accredited internships? 100%

What courses are required for incoming students to have completed prior to enrolling?
None

Are there courses you recommend that are not mandatory?
Yes

GRE mean (M), cutoff (C), or preferred (P)
1000 (C)

GPA mean (M), cutoff (C), or preferred (P)
Overall GPA 3.5 (C)

Number of applications/admission offers/incoming students in 2001
60 applied/16 admission offers/10 incoming

% of students receiving:
Tuition waiver only: 10%
Assistantship/fellowship only: 85%
Both tuition waiver & assistantship/fellowship: 5%

Approximate percentage of incoming students who entered with a B.A./B.S. only: 0% **Master's:** 100%

Approximate percentage of students who are Women: 50% **Ethnic Minority:** 20%

Average years to complete the doctoral program (including internship): 5 years

Research areas	**# Faculty**	**# Grants**
child service	2	1
gender issues	2	0
gerontology	1	0
multicultural issues	2	0
therapy process/outcome	2	0

Clinical opportunities
departmental clinic
student counseling centers
women's and adolescent prisons
various units at hospitals and V.A. centers

University of Texas at Austin

Department of Educational Psychology
D 5800
Austin, TX 78712
phone#: (512) 471-4409
e-mail: stephanie.rude@mail.utexas.edu
Web address: http://www.edb.utexas.edu/coe/depts/edp/gs/counseling.html

1 2 3 4 **5** 6 7

Clinically oriented — Equal emphasis — Research oriented

What percentage of your faculty subscribes to or practices in each of the following orientations?

Psychodynamic/Psychoanalytic	12.5%
Applied behavioral analysis/Radical behavioral	0%
Family systems/Systems	12.5%
Existential/Phenomenological/Humanistic	12.5%
Cognitive/Cognitive-behavioral	12.5%

What percentage of students applying for internship last year was accepted into APA-accredited internships? 95%

What courses are required for incoming students to have completed prior to enrolling?
6 hours in psychology

Are there courses you recommend that are not mandatory?
No

GRE mean (M), cutoff (C), or preferred (P)
Verbal + Quantitative 1280 (M)

GPA mean (M), cutoff (C), or preferred (P)
Overall GPA 3.5 (M)

Number of applications/admission offers/incoming students in 2001
109 applied/19 admission offers/10 incoming

% of students receiving:
Tuition waiver only: 18%
Assistantship/fellowship only: 18%
Both tuition waiver & assistantship/fellowship: 0%

Approximate percentage of incoming students who entered with a B.A./B.S. only: 50% **Master's:** 50%

Approximate percentage of students who are Women: 70% **Ethnic Minority:** 20%

Average years to complete the doctoral program (including internship): 6 years

Research areas	**# Faculty**	**# Grants**
depression (cognitive-behavioral methods)	1	0
family issues	1	0
multicultural/cross-cultural issues	2	1
psychoanalysis	1	0
psychology of women	1	0

Clinical opportunities
adolescent and adult inpatient and outpatient
child guidance clinics
community practicum
inpatient units at state and V. A. hospitals
long-term outpatient psychotherapy clinic
university counseling centers

Texas Tech University

Department of Psychology
Lubbock, TX 79409
phone#: (806) 742-3701
e-mail: scook@ttu.edu
Web address: http://www.ttu.edu/~psy/template.php?page=graduate/counseling/counseling

1 2 3 **4** 5 6 7

Clinically oriented — Equal emphasis — Research oriented

What percentage of your faculty subscribes to or practices in each of the following orientations?

Psychodynamic/Psychoanalytic	20%
Applied behavioral analysis/Radical behavioral	0%
Family systems/Systems	10%
Existential/Phenomenological/Humanistic	35%
Cognitive/Cognitive-behavioral	35%

What percentage of students applying for internship last year was accepted into APA-accredited internships? 86%

What courses are required for incoming students to have completed prior to enrolling?
18 undergraduate hours in psychology and 1 statistics course

Are there courses you recommend that are not mandatory?
No

GRE mean (M), cutoff (C), or preferred (P)
Verbal 556 (M) Quantitative 635 (M)

GPA mean (M), cutoff (C), or preferred (P)
Overall GPA 3.75 (M)

Number of applications/admission offers/incoming students in 2001
71 applied/10 admission offers/7 incoming

% of students receiving:
Tuition waiver only: 0%
Assistantship/fellowship only: 0%
Both tuition waiver & assistantship/fellowship: 100%

Approximate percentage of incoming students who entered with a B.A./B.S. only: 80% **Master's:** 20%

Approximate percentage of students who are Women: 64% **Ethnic Minority:** 15%

Average years to complete the doctoral program (including internship): 6 years

Research areas	# Faculty	# Grants
behavioral addictions	1	0
cardiac rehabilitation	1	0
coping and stress	2	0
depression	1	0
family	2	0
forensic/correctional	1	0
gender and women	2	0
group therapy	—	—
relationships	1	0
religion	1	0
sexual behavior	1	0
vocational	1	0

Clinical opportunities
departmental outpatient psychology clinic
pain clinic
psychiatric prison unit
university counseling center

Texas Woman's University

Department of Psychology and Philosophy
P.O. Box 425470
Denton, TX 76204
phone#: (940) 898-2303
e-mail: F_NUTT@twu.edu
Web address: http://www.twu.edu/as/psyphil/cppc/phdcurr.html

1 2 3 **4** 5 6 7

Clinically oriented — Equal emphasis — Research oriented

What percentage of your faculty subscribes to or practices in each of the following orientations?

Psychodynamic/Psychoanalytic	10%
Applied behavioral analysis/Radical behavioral	10%
Family systems/Systems	50%
Existential/Phenomenological/Humanistic	100%
Cognitive/Cognitive-behavioral	40%

What percentage of students applying for internship last year was accepted into APA-accredited internships? 100%

What courses are required for incoming students to have completed prior to enrolling?
Introduction to general psychology, life span development, statistics, learning, experimental psychology, history and systems of psychology

Are there courses you recommend that are not mandatory?
—

GRE mean (M), cutoff (C), or preferred (P)
Verbal 500 (C) Quantitative 500 (C)

GPA mean (M), cutoff (C), or preferred (P)
Psychology GPA 3.5 (C) Junior/Senior GPA 3.0 (C)

Number of applications/admission offers/incoming students in 2001
60 applied/10 admission offers/8 incoming

% of students receiving:
Tuition waiver only: 0%
Assistantship/fellowship only: 0%
Both tuition waiver & assistantship/fellowship: 20%

Approximate percentage of incoming students who entered with a B.A./B.S. only: 50% **Master's:** 50%

Approximate percentage of students who are Women: 89% **Ethnic Minority:** 21%

Average years to complete the doctoral program (including internship): 5.75 years

Research areas	# Faculty	# Grants
career development	3	1
ethics and regulation	2	0
gender issues	4	0
infidelity	1	1
marital issues	3	0
sexual harassment	3	1

Clinical opportunities
12 agency settings in the Dallas-Fort Worth metropolitan area

University of Utah

Department of Educational Psychology
1705E Campus Center Drive, Room 327
Salt Lake City, UT 84112-9255
phone#: (801) 581-7148
e-mail: morrow@ed.utah.edu
Web address: http://www.gse.utah.edu/edpsy/Doccouns.htm

1 2 3 **4** 5 6 7

Clinically oriented — Equal emphasis — Research oriented

What percentage of your faculty subscribes to or practices in each of the following orientations?

Psychodynamic/Psychoanalytic	0%
Applied behavioral analysis/Radical behavioral	0%
Family systems/Systems	10%
Existential/Phenomenological/Humanistic	30%
Cognitive/Cognitive-behavioral	40%
Feminist/Multicultural	20%

What percentage of students applying for internship last year was accepted into APA-accredited internships? 80%

What courses are required for incoming students to have completed prior to enrolling?
Undergraduate and/or previous graduate preparation in psychology is required but no specific courses are required.

Are there courses you recommend that are not mandatory?
General/experimental psychology, personality, developmental, physiological, normal and abnormal behavior, elementary statistics, research methods, social psychology, and learning

GRE mean (M), cutoff (C), or preferred (P)
Verbal 605 (M) Quantitative 593 (M) Analytical 581 (M)
Advanced Psychology not required

GPA mean (M), cutoff (C), or preferred (P)
Overall GPA 3.40 (M) Junior/Senior GPA 3.57 (M)

Number of applications/admission offers/incoming students in 2001
70 applied/9 admission offers/8 incoming

% of students receiving:
Tuition waiver only: 0%
Assistantship/fellowship only: 0%
Both tuition waiver & assistantship/fellowship: 88% [reduced tuition (1/2)]

Approximate percentage of incoming students who entered with a B.A./B.S. only: 50% **Master's:** 50%

Approximate percentage of students who are Women: 75% **Ethnic Minority:** 32%

Average years to complete the doctoral program (including internship): 6.5 years

Research areas	# Faculty	# Grants
abuse	3	0
applied gerontology	1	2
ethical issues	1	0
evaluation of counseling services	1	0
lesbian, gay, bisexual career development	1	2
multicultural counseling	2	0

Clinical opportunities
community mental health center
drug and alcohol treatment clinic
ethnic student center
family medicine health services center (outpatient medical)
gerontology services center
sexual abuse treatment unit (victims and perpetrators)
university counseling center
VA medical center (inpatient)
women's resource center

Virginia Commonwealth University

Department of Psychology
Richmond, VA 23284-2018
phone#: (804) 828-1193
Web address: http://www.has.vcu.edu/psy/counseling/index.html

1	2	3	**4**	5	6	7
Clinically oriented			Equal emphasis			Research oriented

What percentage of your faculty subscribes to or practices in each of the following orientations?

Psychodynamic/Psychoanalytic	40%
Applied behavioral analysis/Radical behavioral	0%
Family systems/Systems	30%
Existential/Phenomenological/Humanistic	20%
Cognitive/Cognitive-behavioral	30%

What percentage of students applying for internship last year was accepted into APA-accredited internships? 100%

What courses are required for incoming students to have completed prior to enrolling?
18 undergraduate credit hours in psychology, including statistics, experimental methods, and introductory psychology

Are there courses you recommend that are not mandatory?
No

GRE mean (M), cutoff (C), or preferred (P)
Verbal 600 (P) Quantitative 600 (P)

GPA mean (M), cutoff (C), or preferred (P)
Overall GPA 3.2 (P) Psychology GPA 3.8 (P)
Junior/Senior GPA 3.8 (P)

Number of applications/admission offers/incoming students in 2001
112 applied/12 admission offers/8 incoming

% of students receiving:
Tuition waiver only: 0%
Assistantship/fellowship only: 0%
Both tuition waiver & assistantship/fellowship: 90%

Approximate percentage of incoming students who entered with a B.A./B.S. only: 75% **Master's:** 25%

Approximate percentage of students who are Women: 70% **Ethnic Minority:** 25%

Average years to complete the doctoral program (including internship): 5.5 years

Research areas	# Faculty	# Grants
career development and decision making	1	1
community psychology	3	0
family psychology	1	0
family violence and substance abuse interventions	1	1
forgiveness and reconciliation	1	1
group dynamics	1	0
health psychology	6	3
marital and family enrichment	1	1
organizational behavior	1	1
parenting	2	0
religious values	1	0
stress and coping	5	1
teaching of life skills	1	1

Clinical opportunities
on-campus community mental health center
university counseling center
Opportunities at external agencies (after completing required on-campus practica) include child treatment center, community mental health center, federal correctional center, rehabilitation medicine unit, state juvenile correctional system, state psychiatric hospital, substance abuse treatment facility, VA hospital, workplace training and consultation center.

Washington State University

Department of Educational Leadership and Counseling Psychology
Pullman, WA 99164
phone#: (509) 335-7016
e-mail: McNeill@mail.wsu.edu
Web address: http://www.educ.wsu.edu/ELCP/Counseling_Psych/phdcopsy/index.html

1	2	3	**4**	5	6	7
Clinically oriented			Equal emphasis			Research oriented

What percentage of your faculty subscribes to or practices in each of the following orientations?

Psychodynamic/Psychoanalytic	0%
Applied behavioral analysis/Radical behavioral	0%
Family systems/Systems	10%
Existential/Phenomenological/Humanistic	40%
Cognitive/Cognitive-behavioral	50%

What percentage of students applying for internship last year was accepted into APA-accredited internships? 100%

What courses are required for incoming students to have completed prior to enrolling?
None

Are there courses you recommend that are not mandatory?
No

GRE mean (M), cutoff (C), or preferred (P)
Verbal 515 (M) Quantitative 552 (M) Analytical 554 (M)

GPA mean (M), cutoff (C), or preferred (P)
Overall GPA 3.43 (M), 3.0 (P) Psychology GPA 3.0 (P)
Junior/Senior GPA 3.0 (P)
Overall Master's GPA 3.85 (M), 3.0 (P)

Number of applications/admission offers/incoming students in 2001
69 applied/12 admission offers/7 incoming

% of students receiving:
Tuition waiver only: 0%
Assistantship/fellowship only: 60%
Both tuition waiver & assistantship/fellowship: 25%

Approximate percentage of incoming students who entered with a B.A./B.S. only: 50% **Master's:** 50%

Approximate percentage of students who are Women: 75% **Ethnic Minority:** 60%

Average years to complete the doctoral program (including internship): 4.5 years

Research areas	**# Faculty**	**# Grants**
attentional problems	2	1
measurement/assessment	3	1
multicultural	3	1
social influence	1	0
supervision	1	0
vocational	2	0

Clinical opportunities
—

West Virginia University

Department of Counseling, Rehabilitation Counseling, and Counseling Psychology
P.O. Box 6122
Morgantown, WV 26506-6122
phone#: (304) 293-3807
e-mail: CRKALOD@WVNVM.WVNET.EDU
Web address: http://www.wvu.edu/~hre/departments/crc/index.htm

1	2	**3**	4	5	6	7
Clinically oriented			Equal emphasis			Research oriented

What percentage of your faculty subscribes to or practices in each of the following orientations?

Psychodynamic/Psychoanalytic	20%
Applied behavioral analysis/Radical behavioral	0%
Family systems/Systems	20%
Existential/Phenomenological/Humanistic	40%
Cognitive/Cognitive-behavioral	20%

What percentage of students applying for internship last year was accepted into APA-accredited internships? 87%

What courses are required for incoming students to have completed prior to enrolling?
Master's degree in counseling or clinical psychology or a related field

Are there courses you recommend that are not mandatory?
Supervised field experience

GRE mean (M), cutoff (C), or preferred (P)
Verbal 590 (M) Quantitative 560 (M)

GPA mean (M), cutoff (C), or preferred (P)
Overall GPA 3.0 (P), 3.25 (M)
Overall Graduate GPA 3.75 (M)

Number of applications/admission offers/incoming students in 2001
50 applied/10 admission offers/4 incoming

% of students receiving:
Tuition waiver only: 2%
Assistantship/fellowship only: 0%
Both tuition waiver & assistantship/fellowship: 98%

Approximate percentage of incoming students who entered with a B.A./B.S. only: 0% **Master's:** 100%

Approximate percentage of students who are Women: 55% **Ethnic Minority:** 15%

Average years to complete the doctoral program (including internship): 5 years

Research areas	# Faculty	# Grants
clinical models of supervision	1	0
conflict resolution and medication	1	0
consulting models	1	0
eating disorders	1	1
group counseling	1	0
injured athletes	1	0
personality assessment	1	0
premature termination from counseling	1	0
psychiatric rehabilitation	1	0
psychology of disability	1	0
psychology and mental health	3	0
psychotherapeutic techniques	3	0
rehab counseling and psychology	3	0
self-efficacy and health	2	0
vocational counseling	4	0

Clinical opportunities
community agencies
correctional facilities
VA hospital

Western Michigan University

Department of Counselor Education
and Counseling Psychology
3102 Sangren Hall
Kalamazoo, MI 49008-5195
phone#: (616) 387-5100
Web address: http://www.wmich.edu/cecp/programs/doccp.html

1	2	3	4	**5**	6	7
Clinically oriented			Equal emphasis			Research oriented

What percentage of your faculty subscribes to or practices in each of the following orientations?

Psychodynamic/Psychoanalytic	13%
Applied behavioral analysis/Radical behavioral	0%
Family systems/Systems	25%
Existential/Phenomenological/Humanistic	88%
Cognitive/Cognitive-behavioral	88%

What percentage of students applying for internship last year was accepted into APA-accredited internships? 100%

What courses are required for incoming students to have completed prior to enrolling?
—

Are there courses you recommend that are not mandatory?
Psychology or social science major

GRE mean (M), cutoff (C), or preferred (P)
Verbal + Quantitative 1000 (P)
Advanced Psychology is required for applicants with only a Bachelor's degree

GPA mean (M), cutoff (C), or preferred (P)
Overall Graduate GPA 3.25 (P)
Overall Undergraduate GPA 3.0 (P)

Number of applications/admission offers/incoming students in 2001
50 applied/13 admission offers/8 incoming

% of students receiving:
Tuition waiver only: 0%
Assistantship/fellowship only: 60%
Both tuition waiver & assistantship/fellowship: 40%

Approximate percentage of incoming students who entered with a B.A./B.S. only: 10% **Master's:** 90%

Approximate percentage of students who are Women: 65% **Ethnic Minority:** 40%

Average years to complete the doctoral program (including internship): 5 years

Research areas	# Faculty	# Grants
—		

Clinical opportunities
—

University of Wisconsin–Madison

Department of Counseling Psychology
321 Education Building, 1000 Bascom Mall
Madison, WI 53706
phone#: (608) 263-2746
e-mail: counpsych@education.wisc.edu
Web address: http://www.education.wisc.edu/CP

1	2	3	4	**5**	6	7
Clinically oriented			Equal emphasis			Research oriented

What percentage of your faculty subscribes to or practices in each of the following orientations?

Psychodynamic/Psychoanalytic	30%
Applied behavioral analysis/Radical behavioral	0%
Family systems/Systems	10%
Existential/Phenomenological/Humanistic	40%
Cognitive/Cognitive-behavioral	30%
Multicultural	100%

What percentage of students applying for internship last year was accepted into APA-accredited internships? 60%

What courses are required for incoming students to have completed prior to enrolling?
Master's degree in counseling or admitted with deficiencies, including multicultural counseling and career psychology

Are there courses you recommend that are not mandatory?
No

GRE mean (M), cutoff (C), or preferred (P)
Verbal 550+ (P) Quantitative 550+ (P)
Analytical 550+ (P) Advanced Psychology 550+ (P)

GPA mean (M), cutoff (C), or preferred (P)
Junior/Senior GPA 3.6 (M)

Number of applications/admission offers/incoming students in 2001
54 applied/12 admission offers/8 incoming

% of students receiving:
Tuition waiver only: 0%
Assistantship/fellowship only: 10%
Both tuition waiver & assistantship/fellowship: 30%

Approximate percentage of incoming students who entered with a B.A./B.S. only: 5% **Master's:** 95%

Approximate percentage of students who are Women: 75% **Ethnic Minority:** 50%

Average years to complete the doctoral program (including internship): 6 years

Research areas	# Faculty	# Grants
academic retention	2	0
career development	2	0
clinical supervision	1	1
corporate systems	1	0
ethnic identity	4	2
gender	4	0
group	1	0
multidisciplinary environments	2	1
multiethnic/cultural environments	5	3
process-outcome	3	0
school counseling	2	2
other	1	1

Clinical opportunities
counseling psychology

University of Wisconsin–Milwaukee

Urban Education Doctoral Program
P.O. Box 413
Milwaukee, WI 53201
Nadya Fouad, Training Director
phone#: (414) 229-4729
e-mail: nadya@uwm.edu
Web address: http://www.uwm.edu/Dept/EdPysch/counpg.html

1	2	3	4	5	**6**	7
Clinically oriented			Equal emphasis			Research oriented

What percentage of your faculty subscribes to or practices in each of the following orientations?

Psychodynamic/Psychoanalytic	15%
Applied behavioral analysis/Radical behavioral	0%
Family systems/Systems	15%
Existential/Phenomenological/Humanistic	0%
Cognitive/Cognitive-behavioral	70%

What percentage of students applying for internship last year was accepted into APA-accredited internships? 100%

What courses are required for incoming students to have completed prior to enrolling?
Group counseling, listening skills, statistics, multicultural counseling, theories of counseling, cognition, career development, personality
Note: These are required master's courses; if students do not have these courses, they can complete when in the doctoral program.

Are there courses you recommend that are not mandatory?
—

GRE mean (M), cutoff (C), or preferred (P)
Verbal 520 (M) Quantitative 530 (M) Analytical 560 (M)

GPA mean (M), cutoff (C), or preferred (P)
Overall GPA 3.5 (M)

Number of applications/admission offers/incoming students in 2001
25 applied/7 admission offers/5 incoming

% of students receiving:
Tuition waiver only: 0%
Assistantship/fellowship only: 50%
Both tuition waiver & assistantship/fellowship: 0%

Approximate percentage of incoming students who entered with a B.A./B.S. only: 0% **Master's:** 100%

Approximate percentage of students who are Women: 75% **Ethnic Minority:** 25%

Average years to complete the doctoral program (including internship): 5 years

Research areas	# Faculty	# Grants
family therapy and systems theory	1	1
hypnosis and hypnotizability	1	0
pediatric behavioral health	1	0
vocational development	2	2

Clinical opportunities
children's hospital
community mental health agencies
family services

Counseling Psychology Programs Not Providing Information

McGill University

University of Tennessee (1999 data provided)

APPENDIX A
TIME LINE

Freshman and Sophomore Years

1. Take the core psychology courses—introduction, statistics, research methods/experimental, abnormal, physiological.
2. Find out about faculty interests and research.
3. Make preliminary contact with faculty members whose research interests you.
4. Explore volunteer opportunities in clinical settings.
5. Investigate various career choices.
6. Join psychology student organizations and become an active member.
7. Attend departmental colloquia and social gatherings.
8. Enroll in courses helpful for graduate school, including biological sciences, mathematics, writing, and public speaking.
9. Learn to use library and electronic resources, such as scholarly journals and PsycLit.
10. Consider participating in your university's honors program, if you qualify.

Junior Year

1. Take more advanced psychology courses, for example, cognitive, developmental, psychological testing.
2. Begin clinical work, both volunteer and practicum.
3. Volunteer for research with faculty and begin researching a potential honors thesis/independent project.
4. Continue contact with faculty and upperclassmen.
5. Enroll in professional organizations, for example, student affiliate of American Psychological Association or American Psychological Society.
6. Apply for membership in your local Psi Chi chapter.
7. Draft a curriculum vitae to determine your strengths and weaknesses.
8. Attend a state or regional psychology convention.
9. Peruse graduate school bulletins and catalogues to acquaint yourself with typical requirements, offerings, and policies.
10. Surf the Web. Become comfortable with leading Web sites on graduate school admissions.
11. Begin a file for your curriculum vita/resume and place reminders of your activities and accomplishments in it.
12. Try to focus your interests in particular research areas, theoretical orientations, and clinical populations.
13. Consider serving as an officer in one of the student organizations on campus.

Application Year

June–August

1. Continue to acquire research competencies, clinical experiences—about 20–40.
2. Surf the Web and begin to gather information from program Web sites.
3. Begin to narrow down potential schools to 20–40.
4. Prepare for the GREs.
5. Consider taking the GRE General Test if you are prepared; this will afford ample time to retake them in the fall if necessary.

6. Investigate financial aid opportunities for graduate students.
7. Set aside money for the cost of the GREs and applications.

August–September

1. Download program information and applications from program Web sites and/or write to schools for information and applications.
2. Receive information packets and read through them.
3. Consult with advisors regarding various programs, application procedures, faculty of interest, etc.
4. Continue to study diligently for the GREs.
5. Update your curriculum vitae.
6. Investigate possible financial aid opportunities.
7. Begin a file in your institution's Office of Career Services/Planning.
8. Gather applications for salient fellowships and scholarships.

September–October

1. Take the GRE General Test.
2. Register for the GRE Psychology Subject Test administered in November and December.
3. Choose a short list of schools using the worksheets.
4. Record the deadlines for submitting each application.
5. Choose the faculty at each school that most interest you.
6. Research your area of interest, focusing on the work of faculty with whom you would like to work.
7. Write to faculty expressing interest in their work (if appropriate).
8. Request a copy of your own transcript and inspect it for any errors or omissions.

October–November

1. Take the GRE Psychology Subject Test.
2. Take the MAT (only if necessary).
3. Prepare letters to your recommenders, including a complete vitae or resume.
4. Request letters of recommendation.
5. Arrange for the registrar to send your transcripts to schools.
6. Begin first drafts of your personal statement.
7. Gather information on financial aid and loans available to graduate students.

November–December

1. Complete applications.
2. Maintain a photocopy of each application for your records.
3. If the opportunity arises, visit professors with whom you have been in contact.
4. Submit applications.
5. Verify that the applications and all necessary materials have been received.
6. Request ETS forward your GRE scores to the appropriate institutions.

January–March

1. Wait patiently.
2. Insure that all of your letters of recommendation have been sent.
3. Be prepared for surprise telephone interviews.
4. Practice and prepare for interviews.
5. Travel to interviews as invited.
6. Develop contingency plans if not accepted into any programs.

April–May

1. If other programs make early offers, call your top choices to determine the current status of your application.
2. Accept an offer of admission and promptly turn down less-preferred offers.
3. Send official transcripts with Spring term grades to the program you plan to attend.
4. If not accepted to any schools, refer to Chapter 7.

APPENDIX B

WORKSHEET FOR CHOOSING SCHOOLS

		Research			Clinical			
Area of Interest	School	# Faculty	Funded	Rank	Orientation	Res/ Clin	Rank	Self-Rating

APPENDIX B: WORKSHEET FOR CHOOSING SCHOOLS

		Research			Clinical			
Area of Interest	School	# Faculty	Funded	Rank	Orienta-tion	Res/Clin	Rank	Self-Rating

APPENDIX C

WORKSHEET FOR ASSESSING PROGRAM CRITERIA

School	Self-Rating	Courses	GRE-V	GRE-Q	GRE-S	GPA	Research	Clinical	Compete	**Total**

APPENDIX D

WORKSHEET FOR MAKING FINAL CHOICES

School	School Criteria	Research	Clinical	Theoretical Orientation	Financial Aid	Quality of Life

APPENDIX E

RESEARCH AREAS

	# Faculty	# Grants
Acquired Immune Deficiency Syndrome/HIV		
Arizona State University (Co)	1	0
Binghamton University/State University of New York (Cl)	1	1
Colorado State University (Co)	1	0
DePaul University (Cl)	1	3
Florida State University (Cl)	1	0
Georgia State University (Cl)	1	3
Indiana State University (Co)	1	0
Kent State University (Cl)	1	1
Loyola University of Chicago (Cl)	2	1
Nova Southeastern University (Ph.D. & Psy.D.) (Cl)	1	1
Pennsylvania State University (Cl)	1	0
San Diego State University/University of California–San Diego (Cl)	7	1
Southern Illinois University (Cl)	1	0
Syracuse University (Cl)	2	2
University of California–Los Angeles (Cl)	1	1
University of Florida (Cl)	1	1
University of Georgia (Cl)	2	1
University of Illinois at Chicago (Cl)	2	1
University of Maryland (Co)	1	0
University of Memphis (Co)	2	1
University of Miami (Cl)	6	2+
University of Missouri–Kansas City (Co)	2	1
University of North Texas (Cl)	1	0
University of Wyoming (Cl)	1	3
Virginia Consortium Program in Clinical Psychology (Cl)	1	0
Virginia Polytechnic Institute and State University (Cl)	2	1
Western Michigan University (Cl)	1	1
Yeshiva University (Cl)	2	1
Adjustment		
Biola University (Ph.D.) (Cl)	4	0
Biola University (Psy.D.) (Cl)	4	0
Bowling Green State University (Cl)	2	0
Michigan State University (Co)	1	3
St. Louis University (Cl)	2	0
University of Minnesota (Co)	1	0
Yale University (Cl)	1	1
Adolescent/At-Risk Adolescent		
Alliant International University–San Diego (Ph.D. & Psy.D.) (Cl)	5	0
Ball State University (Co)	2	0
Catholic University of America (Cl)	4	0
Emory University (Cl)	2	0
Florida State University (Cl)	4	5
George Fox University (Cl)	1	0
George Washington University (Ph.D.) (Cl)	2	1
Georgia School of Professional Psychology (Cl)	1	0
Immaculata College (Cl)	2	0
Indiana University (Co)	1	0
Loyola University of Chicago (Co)	1	1
Northern Illinois University (Cl)	3	0
Nova Southeastern University (Ph.D. & Psy.D.) (Cl)	2	1
Oklahoma State University (Co)	2	1
Rutgers University (Psy.D.) (Cl)	4	1
St. Louis University (Cl)	2	0
Suffolk University (Cl)	2	0
Southern Illinois University (Cl)	3	1
Temple University (Cl)	2	1
Texas Tech University (Cl)	1	1
University at Buffalo/State University of New York (Cl)	—	—
University of Cincinnati	2	1
University of Denver (Ph.D.) (Cl)	2	2
University of Georgia (Cl)	1	0
University of Hartford (Cl)	1	0
University of Houston (Co)	1	1
University of Kentucky (Cl)	1	0
University of Minnesota–Deptartment of Educational Psychology (Co)	1	1
University of Nebraska–Lincoln (Cl)	3	1

Note. Cl, Clinical; Co, Counseling; Cm, combined professional–scientific psychology programs.

	# Faculty	# Grants
University of North Carolina at Chapel Hill (Cl)	1	0
University of North Carolina at Greensboro (Cl)	1	0
University of South Florida (Cl)	2	0
University of Southern California (Cl)	1	0
University of Toledo (Cl)	2	0
University of Utah (Cl)	1	1
University of Vermont (Cl)	2	1
University of Virginia–Department of Human Services (Cl)	3	1
University of Wyoming (Cl)	2	2
Utah State University (Cm)	2	1
Virginia Commonwealth University (Cl)	4	3
York University–Clinical-Developmental Area (Cl)	3	3

Affective Disorders/Depression/ Mood Disorders

Alliant International University–San Diego (Ph.D. & Psy.D.) (Cl)	5	0
American University (Cl)	1	0
Baylor University (Psy.D.) (Cl)	3	0
Binghamton University/State University of New York (Cl)	1	1
Boston University (Cl)	2	2
Carlos Albizu University–San Juan (Psy.D.) (Cl)	3	0
Catholic University of America (Cl)	5	0
Clark University (Cl)	1	0
Colorado State University (Co)	1	0
Dalhousie University (Cl)	2	3
Duke University (Cl)	3	2
Fairleigh Dickinson University (Cl)	1	0
Florida State University (Cl)	3	1
Forest Institute of Professional Psychology (Cl)	2	1
Fuller Theological Seminary (Ph.D. & Psy.D.) (Cl)	1	0
Gallaudet University (Cl)	1	1
George Washington University (Ph.D.) (Cl)	1	0
Georgia State University (Cl)	1	0
Hofstra University (Cm)	1	0
Illinois Institute of Technology (Cl)	1	0
Indiana State University (Cl)	2	0
Kent State University (Cl)	1	0
Louisiana State University (Cl)	1	1
Loyola University of Chicago (Cl)	1	0
McGill University (Cl)	2	2
MCP Hahnemann University of the Health Sciences (Cl)	2	1
Michigan State University (Cl)	2	1
New York University (Cl)	5	0
Northwestern University (Cl)	1	0
Ohio State University (Cl)	1	0
Pennsylvania State University (Cl)	3	0
Purdue University (Cl)	1	0
Rutgers University (Ph.D.) (Cl)	2	0
St. Louis University (Cl)	2	0
San Diego State University/University of California–San Diego (Cl)	3	2
Simon Fraser University (Cl)	1	0
Southern Illinois University (Cl)	1	1
Stony Brook University/State University of New York (Cl)	1	1
Temple University (Cl)	3	2
Texas Tech University (Cl)	1	1
Texas Tech University (Co)	1	0
University of Alabama (Cl)	2	1
University of Arizona (Cl)	2	1
University of Arkansas (Cl)	2	0
University at Buffalo/State University of New York (Cl)	2	1
University of California–Los Angeles (Cl)	1	2
University of Colorado (Cl)	3	1
University of Georgia (Cl)	3	0
University of Hawaii at Manoa (Cl)	3	1
University of Houston (Cl)	1	1
University of Iowa (Cl)	1	2
University of Kansas (Cl)	2	0
University of Louisville (Co)	1	1
University of Maine (Cl)	1	0
University of Miami (Cl)	3	1
University of Minnesota (Cl)	2	1
University of North Carolina at Greensboro (Cl)	1	0
University of North Dakota (Co)	3	1
University of Oregon (Cl)	3	2
University of Pennsylvania (Cl)	2	3
University of Pittsburgh (Cl)	4	7
University of South Dakota (Cl)	2	0
University of South Florida (Cl)	1	0
University of Texas at Austin (Co)	1	0
University of Texas Southwestern Medical Center at Dallas (Cl)	5	4
University of Tulsa (Cl)	1	0
University of Washington (Cl)	3	1
University of Waterloo (Cl)	1	0
University of Western Ontario (Cl)	1	1
University of Wisconsin–Madison (Cl)	4	8
University of Wyoming (Cl)	1	0
Vanderbilt University–Deptartment of Psychology (Cl)	4	2
Vanderbilt University–Peabody College (Cl)	4	6
Virginia Consortium Program in Clinical Psychology (Cl)	1	0
Virginia Polytechnic Institute and State University (Cl)	2	0
Washington State University (Cl)	1	0
Yale University (Cl)	1	1
Yeshiva University (Cl)	3	0
York University–Adult Clinical Program (Cl)	3	3

Aging/Gerontology

Arizona State University (Cl)	3	2
Boston University (Cl)	1	1
Case Western Reserve University (Cl)	2	1
Columbia University, Teachers College (Cl)	1	1

	# Faculty	# Grants
Drexel University (Cl)	1	0
Finch University of Health Sciences, The Chicago Medical School (Cl)	1	1
Florida Institute of Technology (Cl)	2	0
Florida State University (Cl)	2	1
Georgia School of Professional Psychology (Cl)	2	0
Indiana University (Cl)	1	1
Indiana University of Pennsylvania (Cl)	1	0
Kent State University (Cl)	1	0
Long Island University (Cl)	1	1
Loyola College in Maryland (Cl)	1	0
McGill University (Cl)	2	1
Michigan State University (Cl)	1	1
Northwestern University Medical School (Cl)	1	0
Nova Southeastern University (Ph.D. & Psy.D.) (Cl)	2	1
San Diego State University/University of California–San Diego (Cl)	14	1
Simon Fraser University (Cl)	1	0
Texas A&M University (Cl)	2	1
Texas A&M University (Co)	1	0
University of Alabama (Cl)	3	4
University of Alabama at Birmingham (Cl)	3	6
University of California–Berkeley (Cl)	1	1
University of Georgia (Cl)	1	1
University of Louisville (Cl)	2	0
University of Massachusetts at Amherst (Cl)	2	0
University of Missouri–St. Louis (Cl)	1	4
University of Nevada–Reno (Cl)	2	3
University of North Carolina at Chapel Hill (Cl)	2	0
University of North Texas (Cl)	1	1
University of North Texas (Co)	1	1
University of St. Thomas (Co)	1	0
University of South Dakota (Cl)	2	0
University of Southern California (Cl)	2	2
University of Texas Southwestern Medical Center at Dallas (Cl)	1	1
University of Tulsa (Cl)	1	0
University of Utah (Co)	1	2
Vanderbilt University–Department of Psychology (Cl)	1	0
Washington University (Cl)	2	3
West Virginia University (Cl)	1	0
Wheaton College (Cl)	1	0
York University–Adult Clinical Program (Cl)	1	2

Aggression/Anger Control

Bowling Green State University (Cl)	1	1
Colorado State University (Co)	1	1
Florida State University (Cl)	5	3
Hofstra University (Cm)	2	0
Long Island University–C.W. Post Campus (Cl)	1	0
McGill University (Cl)	1	1
Northern Illinois University (Cl)	1	0
Pacific University (Cl)	2	0
University of Georgia (Cl)	1	1
University of Georgia (Co)	2	1
University of Illinois at Chicago (Cl)	1	1
University of Illinois at Urbana–Champaign (Co)	1	1
University of Maryland–Baltimore County (Cl)	5	1
University of South Florida (Cl)	2	0
University of Southern Mississippi (Co)	1	0
York University–Clinical-Developmental Area (Cl)	5	4

Anxiety Disorders/Panic Disorders

Alliant International University–Fresno (Ph.D. & Psy.D.) (Cl)	1	0
American University (Cl)	1	0
Argosy University–Washington, DC Campus (Cl)	1	0
Auburn University (Cl)	2	1
Binghamton University/State University of New York (Cl)	2	1
Boston University (Cl)	7	5
Catholic University of America (Cl)	3	0
Central Michigan University (Cl)	1	1
Colorado State University (Co)	1	1
Concordia University (Cl)	2	2
Dalhousie University (Cl)	1	4
Finch University of Health Sciences, The Chicago Medical School (Cl)	1	0
Florida State University (Cl)	3	1
George Washington University (Cl)	2	0
Indiana State University (Psy.D.) (Cl)	1	0
Indiana University–Purdue University Indianapolis (Cl)	2	1
Kent State University (Cl)	3	1
Loma Linda University (Ph.D. & Psy.D.) (Cl)	1	0
Louisiana State University (Cl)	1	1
Loyola College in Maryland (Cl)	1	0
MCP Hahnemann University of the Health Sciences (Cl)	1	0
Miami University (Cl)	3	0
Northern Illinois University (Cl)	2	0
Northwestern University (Cl)	2	0
Nova Southeastern University (Ph.D. & Psy.D.) (Cl)	1	0
Oklahoma State University (Cl)	1	0
Pennsylvania State University (Cl)	3	1
Purdue University (Cl)	1	0
Rutgers University (Psy.D.) (Cl)	3	1
St. John's University (Cl)	1	0
San Diego State University/University of California–San Diego (Cl)	4	1
Southern Illinois University (Cl)	1	0
Temple University (Cl)	3	5
Texas A&M University (Cl)	3	1
Texas Tech University (Cl)	1	1
University at Albany/State University of New York (Cl)	2	3
University at Albany/State University of New York (Co)	1	0

	# Faculty	# Grants
University at Buffalo/State University of New York (Cl)	2	1
University of British Columbia (Cl)	2	3
University of California–Los Angeles (Cl)	1	2
University of Connecticut (Cl)	2	1
University of Delaware (Cl)	2	0
University of Florida (Cl)	2	3
University of Georgia (Cl)	1	0
University of Hawaii at Manoa (Cl)	3	2
University of Houston (Cl)	1	0
University of Iowa (Co)	1	0
University of Louisville (Cl)	3	1
University of Maine (Cl)	2	0
University of Manitoba (Cl)	4	0
University of Maryland (Cl)	2	2
University of Minnesota (Cl)	2	1
University of Missouri–Columbia (Cl)	1	0
University of Nevada–Reno (Cl)	2	0
University of North Carolina at Chapel Hill (Cl)	1	1
University of North Dakota (Cl)	1	0
University of Oregon (Cl)	2	2
University of Pennsylvania (Cl)	1	3
University of St. Thomas (Co)	2	1
University of Texas at Austin (Cl)	1	1
University of Vermont (Cl)	2	0
University of Virginia–Department of Psychology (Cl)	1	0
Virginia Commonwealth University (Cl)	2	0
Virginia Polytechnic Institute and State University (Cl)	3	1
West Virginia University (Cl)	2	0
Western Michigan University (Cl)	2	1
Yale University (Cl)	1	0
Yeshiva University (Psy.D.) (Cl)	3	0
York University–Adult Clinical Program (Cl)	2	2

Assessment/Diagnosis

Alliant International University–Los Angeles (Ph.D. & Psy.D.) (Cl)	2	0
Alliant International University–San Diego (Psy.D.) (Cl)	1	0
Binghamton University/State University of New York (Cl)	4	0
Brigham Young University (Cl)	2	0
Catholic University of America (Cl)	2	1
Central Michigan University (Cl)	1	1
Clark University (Cl)	1	0
Colorado State University (Co)	3	1
Fairleigh Dickinson University (Cl)	6	2
Fordham University (Cl)	3	0
Gallaudet University (Cl)	4	2
George Fox University (Cl)	1	0
George Washington University (Psy.D.) (Cl)	3	0
Georgia School of Professional Psychology (Cl)	1	0
Indiana State University (Psy.D.) (Cl)	1	0
McGill University (Cl)	2	0
New School for Social Research (Cl)	2	1
New York University (Co)	2	2
Ohio State University (Co)	3	0
Oklahoma State University (Co)	1	0
Pacific Graduate School of Psychology (Cl)	5	0
Pacific University (Cl)	6	0
Rutgers University (Psy.D.) (Cl)	2	0
St. Louis University (Cl)	3	0
San Diego State University/University of California–San Diego (Cl)	4	0
Southern Illinois University (Cl)	8	0
Texas A&M University (Cl)	3	0
Texas Tech University (Cl)	1	1
University of Alabama (Cl)	2	0
University at Buffalo/State University of New York (Co)	1	0
University of Colorado (Cl)	3	0
University of Detroit–Mercy (Cl)	1	0
University of Hawaii at Manoa (Cl)	6	1
University of Kentucky (Cl)	4	0
University of Mississippi (Cl)	1	0
University of Montana (Cl)	1	0
University of Nebraska–Lincoln (Co)	2	0
University of Nevada–Reno (Cl)	3	0
University of North Carolina at Chapel Hill (Cl)	1	0
University of North Carolina at Greensboro (Cl)	1	0
University of Oklahoma (Co)	2	0
University of Tulsa (Cl)	3	0
University of Western Ontario (Cl)	1	0
Vanderbilt University–Department. of Psychology (Cl)	2	0
Virginia Consortium Program in Clinical Psychology (Cl)	1	0
Washington State University (Co)	3	1
Widener University (Cl)	1	0
Yeshiva University (Cm)	2	0

Attachment

Alliant International University–Fresno (Ph.D. & Psy.D.) (Cl)	1	0
City University of New York at City College (Cl)	3	1
Long Island University–C.W. Post Campus (Cl)	1	0
University of Delaware (Cl)	2	1
University of Southern Mississippi (Co)	3	0
Yeshiva University (Cm)	3	0

Attention-Deficit/Hyperactivity Disorder

Colorado State University (Co)	1	0
Emory University (Cl)	1	1
Georgia State University (Cl)	1	1
Illinois Institute of Technology (Cl)	1	0
Illinois School of Professional Psychology–Chicago Northwest (Cl)	1	0
Loyola University of Chicago (Cl)	1	0
McGill University (Cl)	1	1
Michigan State University (Cl)	2	1

	# Faculty	# Grants
Pepperdine University (Cl)	—	—
Purdue University (Cl)	1	3
University at Buffalo/State University of New York (Cl)	1	2
University of British Columbia (Cl)	1	2
University of California–Berkeley (Cl)	1	2
University of Houston (Co)	1	1
University of Montana (Cl)	1	0
University of North Carolina at Greensboro (Cl)	1	1
University of Northern Colorado (Co)	1	0
University of Pittsburgh (Cl)	1	2
University of Rochester (Cl)	1	2
University of Texas at Austin (Cl)	1	1
University of Toledo (Cl)	2	0
University of Victoria (Cl)	1	1
University of Waterloo (Cl)	1	1
Virginia Consortium Program in Clinical Psychology (Cl)	1	1
Virginia Polytechnic Institute and State University (Cl)	1	0
Washington State University (Co)	2	1
West Virginia University (Cl)	2	1
Western Michigan University (Cl)	1	1
Yeshiva University (Cm)	2	0

Attitudes and Values

Arizona State University (Co)	1	0
Hofstra University (Cm)	2	0
Immaculata College (Cl)	1	0
Indiana State University (Co)	1	0
Southern Illinois University (Cl)	1	0

Autism/Pervasive Developmental Disorder

Louisiana State University (Cl)	1	1
Rutgers University (Ph.D.) (Cl)	1	1
Rutgers University (Psy.D.) (Cl)	1	1
San Diego State University/University of California–San Diego (Cl)	2	0
University at Albany/State University of New York (Cl)	1	2
University at Buffalo/State University of New York (Cl)	1	0
University of California–Santa Barbara (Cm)	1	1
University of Connecticut (Cl)	1	3
University of Utah (Cl)	1	1
University of Washington (Cl)	1	1
Virginia Polytechnic Institute and State University (Cl)	1	0
York University–Clinical-Developmental Area (Cl)	2	1

Behavior Therapy/ Applied Behavioral Analysis

Hofstra University (Cm)	3	0
McGill University (Cl)	1	0
Nova Southeastern University (Ph.D. & Psy.D.) (Cl)	8	0
Rutgers University (Ph.D.) (Cl)	2	0
Rutgers University (Psy.D.) (Cl)	1	1
San Diego State University/University of California–San Diego (Cl)	4	0
University of Colorado (Cl)	1	1
University of Denver (Psy.D.) (Cl)	1	0
University of Georgia (Cl)	1	0
University of Kentucky (Co)	2	0
University of Manitoba (Cl)	3	2
University of Nevada–Reno (Cl)	4	0
University of North Carolina at Greensboro (Cl)	1	0
University of North Dakota (Cl)	2	0
Virginia Consortium Program in Clinical Psychology (Cl)	1	0
Yeshiva University (Cl)	1	0

Behavioral Genetics

Emory University (Cl)	1	1
Indiana University (Cl)	4	2
McGill University (Cl)	1	1
Northwestern University (Cl)	1	0
Southern Illinois University (Cl)	1	0
University of Denver (Ph.D.) (Cl)	1	1
University of Illinois at Urbana–Champaign (Cl)	1	0
University of Minnesota (Cl)	4	4
University of Pittsburgh (Cl)	2	3
University of South Florida (Cl)	1	0
University of Virginia (Cl)	2	1

Behavioral Medicine/Health Psychology

Adelphi University (Cl)	1	1
Alliant International University–Alameda (Ph.D. & Psy.D.) (Cl)	9	2
Alliant International University–Fresno (Ph.D. & Psy.D.) (Cl)	2	0
Alliant International University–Los Angeles (Ph.D.) (Cl)	4	5
Alliant International University–San Diego (Ph.D. & Psy.D.) (Cl)	7	3
Antioch/New England Graduate School (Cl)	1	0
Argosy University–Honolulu Campus (Cl)	1	0
Argosy University–Washington, DC Campus (Cl)	4	0
Arizona State University (Cl)	6	4
Arizona State University (Co)	1	0
Ball State University (Co)	1	0
Baylor University (Cl)	1	0
Binghamton University/State University of New York (Cl)	1	1
Bowling Green State University (Cl)	3	1
Brigham Young University (Cl)	1	1
Carlos Albizu University–San Juan (Psy.D.) (Cl)	1	0
Case Western Reserve University (Cl)	1	0
Catholic University of America (Cl)	1	0

	# Faculty	# Grants
Central Michigan University (Cl)	1	0
Colorado State University (Co)	5	0
Concordia University (Cl)	2	2
Drexel University (Cl)	3	0
Duke University (Cl)	4	6
Fairleigh Dickinson University (Cl)	3	1
Fielding Graduate Institute (Cl)	—	—
Finch University of Health Sciences, The Chicago Medical School (Cl)	3	2
Florida Institute of Technology (Cl)	3	0
Fordham University (Cl)	1	0
Fordham University (Co)	1	0
Fuller Theological Seminary (Ph.D. & Psy.D.) (Cl)	3	0
George Washington University (Ph.D.) (Cl)	4	1
Howard University (Cl)	3	3
Illinois Institute of Technology (Cl)	3	1
Illinois School of Professional Psychology–Chicago Campus (Cl)	2	0
Indiana State University (Cl)	2	1
Indiana University (Cl)	5	4
Indiana University of Pennsylvania (Cl)	1	0
Indiana University–Purdue University Indianapolis (Cl)	2	1
Loma Linda University (Ph.D. & Psy.D.) (Cl)	5	6
Long Island University (Cl)	1	1
Loyola College in Maryland (Cl)	2	0
McGill University (Cl)	4	4
MCP Hahnemann University of the Health Sciences (Cl)	7	2
Northern Illinois University	3	0
Northwestern University Medical School (Cl)	1	1
Nova Southeastern University (Ph.D. & Psy.D.) (Cl)	7	0
Ohio State University (Cl)	3	4
Ohio State University (Co)	2	0
Ohio University (Cl)	4	3
Oklahoma State University (Cl)	2	0
Oklahoma State University (Co)	2	1
Pacific Graduate School of Psychology (Cl)	2	0
Pennsylvania State University (Cl)	2	0
Rutgers University (Ph.D.) (Cl)	4	5
Rutgers University (Psy.D.) (Cl)	1	0
St. John's University (Cl)	3	1
San Diego State University/University of California–San Diego (Cl)	22	3
Simon Fraser University (Cl)	2	0
Southern Illinois University (Cl)	2	0
Southern Illinois University (Co)	1	0
Spalding University (Cl)	2	0
Suffolk University (Cl)	1	0
Temple University (Co)	—	—
Texas A&M University (Cl)	2	1
Texas Tech University (Cl)	1	0
Uniformed Services University of Health Sciences (Cl)	2	5
University of Alabama (Cl)	3	1
University of Alabama at Birmingham (Cl)	2	2
University at Albany/State University of New York (Cl)	2	3
University at Buffalo/State University of New York (Cl)	1	0
University of Arizona (Cl)	4	1
University of British Columbia (Cl)	3	7
University of Cincinnati (Cl)	5	2
University of Colorado (Cl)	1	0
University of Connecticut (Cl)	2	1
University of Denver (Psy.D.) (Cl)	1	0
University of Florida (Cl)	3	3
University of Florida (Co)	1	1
University of Georgia (Cl)	2	0
University of Georgia (Co)	1	0
University of Hawaii at Manoa (Cl)	1	1
University of Illinois at Chicago (Cl)	3	3
University of Iowa (Cl)	3	2
University of Iowa (Co)	6	4
University of Kansas (Cl)	5	3
University of Kentucky (Cl)	2	0
University of Kentucky (Co)	2	0
University of Louisville (Cl)	2	1
University of Maine (Cl)	1	0
University of Manitoba (Cl)	2	1
University of Maryland–Baltimore County (Cl)	3	2
University of Maryland (Co)	1	0
University of Memphis (Cl)	5	4
University of Miami (Cl)	3	6
University of Miami (Co)	2	1
University of Michigan (Cl)	2	0
University of Minnesota–Department of Psychology (Co)	2	0
University of Mississippi (Cl)	1	0
University of Missouri–Columbia (Cl)	3	2
University of Missouri–Kansas City (Co)	7	0
University of Montana (Cl)	3	2
University of North Carolina at Chapel Hill (Cl)	1	2
University of North Dakota (Cl)	3	0
University of North Dakota (Co)	1	0
University of Notre Dame (Co)	1	1
University of Oklahoma (Co)	3	0
University of Ottawa (Cl)	1	0
University of Pittsburgh (Cl)	14	43
University of Rhode Island (Cl)	3	9
University of South Dakota (Cl)	2	0
University of South Florida (Cl)	5	6
University of Southern California (Cl)	2	1
University of Tennessee (Cl)	2	0
University of Texas at Austin (Cl)	1	1
University of Texas Southwestern Medical Center at Dallas (Cl)	4	4
University of Utah (Cl)	2	2
University of Vermont (Cl)	4	2
University of Western Ontario (Cl)	4	2
University of Wisconsin–Madison (Cl)	2	4
University of Wisconsin–Milwaukee (Cl)	3	0
Utah State University (Cm)	3	2
Vanderbilt University (Cl)	1	0
Virginia Commonwealth University (Cl)	4	3
Virginia Commonwealth University (Co)	6	3

	# Faculty	# Grants
Virginia Polytechnic Institute and State University (Cl)	3	2
Washington State University (Cl)	3	1
Washington University (Cl)	3	10
Wayne State University (Cl)	2	2
West Virginia University (Cl)	6	4
West Virginia University (Co)	2	0
Western Michigan University (Cl)	3	2
Wright State University (Cl)	2	1
York University–Adult Clinical Program (Cl)	1	3

Biofeedback/Relaxation

Fuller Theological Seminary (Ph.D. & Psy.D.) (Cl)	2	0
George Washington University (Ph.D.) (Cl)	1	0
Hofstra University (Cm)	1	0
Loyola University of Chicago (Cl)	2	0
Nova Southeastern University (Ph.D. & Psy.D.) (Cl)	2	0
Pennsylvania State University (Cl)	1	0
San Diego State University/University of California–San Diego (Cl)	1	0
University of Alabama (Cl)	1	0
University of Arizona (Cl)	1	0
University of North Dakota (Cl)	1	0
University of Windsor (Cl)	1	1

Biopsychology

Fuller Theological Seminary (Ph.D. & Psy.D.) (Cl) (biopsychosocial)	3	2
Indiana University–Purdue University Indianapolis (Cl)	3	6
Loma Linda University (Ph.D. & Psy.D.) (Cl)	2	0
Spalding University (Cl) (sociobiology)	1	0

Brain Injury/Head Injury

Drexel University (Cl)	1	1
Georgia State University (Cl)	3	0
James Madison University (Cm)	1	0
San Diego State University/University of California–San Diego (Cl)	2	0
Southern Illinois University (Co)	1	0
University of Montana (Cl)	1	0
University of Victoria (Cl)	2	2

Child Abuse/Neglect/Sexual Abuse

Alliant International University–San Diego (Psy.D.) (Cl)	2	1
Argosy University–Washington, DC Campus (Cl)	1	0
Clark University (Cl)	1	0
Columbia University, Teachers College (Cl)	1	1
DePaul University (Cl)	1	1
Loma Linda University (Ph.D. & Psy.D.) (Cl)	2	0
Northern Illinois University (Cl)	1	2
Southern Illinois University (Cl)	1	0
State University of New York at Buffalo (Cl)	1	1
Texas Tech University (Cl)	3	2
University of Arkansas (Cl)	2	0
University of California–Los Angeles (Cl)	1	1
University of Denver (Ph.D.) (Cl)	1	0
University of Iowa (Cl)	1	1
University of Michigan (Cl)	1	0
University of Missouri–St. Louis (Cl)	1	1
University of Nebraska–Lincoln (Cl)	4	2
University of Rochester (Cl)	1	3
University of Saskatchewan (Cl)	1	1
University of Southern California (Cl)	1	1
University of Southern Mississippi (Co)	1	0
University of Wyoming (Cl)	2	2
Virginia Consortium Program in Clinical Psychology (Cl)	1	0
York University–Clinical-Developmental Area (Cl)	3	2

Child/Child Clinical/Pediatric

Adler School of Professional Psychology (Cl)	2	0
Alliant International University–Alameda (Ph.D. & Psy.D.) (Cl)	9	0
Alliant International University–Fresno (Ph.D. & Psy.D.) (Cl)	3	1
Alliant International University–Los Angeles (Ph.D.) (Cl)	4	4
Alliant International University–San Diego (Ph.D.) (Cl)	3	2
American University (Cl)	2	0
Arizona State University (Cl)	8	7
Auburn University (Cl)	2	0
Ball State University (Co)	2	0
Binghamton University/State University of New York (Cl)	3	3
Bowling Green State University (Cl)	5	2
Catholic University of America (Cl)	2	0
Central Michigan University (Cl)	1	0
Clark University (Cl)	2	0
Drexel University (Cl)	2	1
Fairleigh Dickinson University (Cl)	4	2
Fordham University (Cl)	1	0
Fuller Theological Seminary (Ph.D. & Psy.D.) (Cl)	2	1
George Washington University (Ph.D. & Psy.D.) (Cl)	2	1
Georgia School of Professional Psychology (Cl)	2	0
Hofstra University (Cm)	2	0
Illinois Institute of Technology (Cl)	4	2
Immaculata College (Cl)	2	0
Indiana State University (Cl)	2	0
Indiana University (Cl)	3	4
Loma Linda University (Ph.D. & Psy.D.) (Cl)	1	3
Loyola University of Chicago (Cl)	5	3

	# Faculty	# Grants
McGill University (Cl)	1	1
Michigan State University (Cl)	5	2
New School for Social Research (Cl)	1	1
New York University (Cl)	2	0
Northern Illinois University (Cl)	1	0
Ohio State University (Cl)	1	0
Ohio University (Cl)	3	0
Oklahoma State University (Cl)	2	0
Pace University (Psy.D.) (Cm)	2	0
Pacific University (Cl)	5	1
Purdue University (Cl)	2	1
St. Louis University (Cl)	2	0
San Diego State University/University of California–San Diego (Cl)	5	0
Simon Fraser University (Cl)	1	1
Southern Illinois University (Cl)	5	0
Temple University (Cl)	2	2
Texas A&M University (Cl)	4	3
Texas A&M University (Co)	2	1
Texas Tech University (Cl)	2	2
University of Alabama (Cl)	3	1
University at Albany/State University of New York (Cl)	3	1
University of California–Los Angeles (Cl)	7	5
University of California–Santa Barbara (Cm)	4	2
University of Cincinnati (Cl)	4	4
University of Colorado (Cl)	2	1
University of Delaware (Cl)	4	5
University of Florida (Cl)	6	6
University of Georgia (Cl)	3	0
University of Houston (Cl)	3	3
University of Illinois at Urbana–Champaign (Cl)	6	2
University of Kentucky (Cl)	3	1
University of Maine (Cl)	1	0
University of Massachusetts at Amherst (Cl)	4	2
University of Memphis (Co)	2	1
University of Miami (Cl)	5	2+
University of Michigan (Cl)	8	4
University of Mississippi (Cl)	3	1
University of Missouri–Columbia (Cl)	6	3
University of Missouri–St. Louis (Cl)	2	0
University of Montana (Cl)	2	1
University of Nebraska–Lincoln (Cl)	3	1
University of Nevada–Reno (Cl)	2	0
University of New Mexico (Cl)	1	0
University of North Carolina at Chapel Hill (Cl)	2	2
University of North Carolina at Greensboro (Cl)	1	0
University of North Texas (Cl)	1	1
University of Notre Dame (Co)	1	0
University of Oklahoma (Co)	3	0
University of Oregon (Co)	1	3
University of Ottawa (Cl)	3	2
University of Pittsburgh (Cl)	7	18
University of Rhode Island (Cl)	1	0
University of South Dakota (Cl)	3	0
University of Texas Southwestern Medical Center at Dallas (Cl)	1	0
University of Tulsa (Cl)	1	0
University of Utah (Cl)	1	1
University of Virginia–Department of Human Services (Cl)	4	4
University of Virginia–Department of Psychology (Cl)	5	5
University of Windsor (Cl)	2	2
University of Wisconsin–Milwaukee	1	0
Vanderbilt University–Peabody College (Cl)	7	6
Virginia Commonwealth University (Cl)	4	3
Virginia Consortium Program in Clinical Psychology (Cl)	1	0
Virginia Polytechnic Institute and State University (Cl)	4	2
Washington State University (Cl)	4	1
West Virginia University (Cl)	2	3
Widener University (Cl)	1	0
Yale University (Cl)	2	3
Yeshiva University (Cm)	1	0
Yeshiva University (Cl)	1	0

Chronic Illness

University of Manitoba (Cl)	1	1
Yeshiva University (Cl)	1	1

Chronic/Severe Mental Illness

Case Western Reserve University (Cl)	1	0
George Mason University (Cl)	1	1
Indiana University–Purdue University Indianapolis (Cl)	2	3–4
Northwestern University Medical School (Cl)	3	1
Nova Southeastern University (Ph.D. & Psy.D.) (Cl)	2	0
Rutgers University (Psy.D.) (Cl)	2	1
University of Cincinnati (Cl)	3	2
University of Houston (Cl)	4	2
University of Louisville (Cl)	1	0
University of Maryland (Cl)	2	1
University of Massachusetts at Boston (Cl)	2	2
University of Nebraska–Lincoln (Cl)	1	1
University of South Carolina (Cl)	1	0
University of South Dakota (Cl)	2	0
University of Toledo (Cl)	1	1

Clinical Judgment/Decision Making

Ball State University (Co)	1	1
Indiana State University (Cl)	1	0
Indiana University of Pennsylvania (Cl)	1	0
James Madison University (Psy.D.) (Cm)	3	0
Loma Linda University (Ph.D. & Psy.D.) (Cl)	1	0
New York University (Cl)	1	0
San Diego State University/University of California–San Diego (Cl)	1	0
Southern Illinois University (Cl)	1	0
Tennessee State University (Co)	1	0
Texas Tech University (Cl)	1	1
University of Alabama (Cl)	2	0

	# Faculty	# Grants
University of Detroit–Mercy (Cl)	1	0
University of Hawaii at Manoa (Cl)	1	0
University of Rhode Island (Cl)	1	0
Vanderbilt University, Department of Psychology (Cl)	1	0

Cognition/Social Cognition

Arizona State University (Co)	1	0
Binghamton University/State University of New York (Cl)	1	0
Case Western Reserve University (Cl)	2	0
Catholic University of America (Cl)	3	0
Colorado State University (Co)	2	0
Dalhousie University (Cl)	1	3
Duke University (Cl)	2	2
Fuller Theological Seminary (Ph.D. & Psy.D.) (Cl)	1	0
Gallaudet University (Cl)	1	1
George Mason University (Cl)	2	0
Indiana University (Cl)	1	0
Marquette University (Cl)	1	2
McGill University (Cl)	3	1
Michigan State University (Cl)	2	1
New School for Social Research (Cl)	2	1
Northeastern University (Cm)	2	0
Northwestern University (Cl)	1	0
Nova Southeastern University (Ph.D. & Psy.D.) (Cl)	1	0
Pennsylvania State University (Cl)	1	0
Rutgers University (Psy.D.) (Cl)	1	1
San Diego State University/University of California–San Diego (Cl)	17	0
Suffolk University (Cl)	1	0
University of Denver (Co)	1	1
University of Denver (Psy.D.) (Cl)	1	0
University of Hawaii at Manoa (Cl)	2	0
University of Indianapolis (Cl)	1	0
University of Montana (Cl)	6	0
University of Western Ontario (Cl)	2	1
Vanderbilt University–Peabody College (Cl)	3	1
Virginia Commonwealth University (Co)	1	1
Washington State University (Co)	2	1
Wright Institute (Cl)	1	0

Cognitive Therapy/ Cognitive-Behavioral Therapy

American University (Cl)	1	1
Arizona State University (Co)	1	0
Baylor University (Cl)	3	0
Brigham Young University (Cl)	1	1
George Fox University (Cl)	2	6
Georgia State University (Cl)	1	2
San Diego State University/University of California–San Diego (Cl)	2	0
Simon Fraser University (Cl)	1	1
Temple University (Co)	3	3
Texas Tech University (Cl)	2	1
University of Hawaii at Manoa (Cl)	2	0
University of Southern California (Cl)	2	1
University of Washington (Cl)	4	1
University of Waterloo (Cl)	3	3
University of Wisconsin–Milwaukee (Cl)	3	0
York Univeristy–Clinical-Developmental Area (Cl)	1	0

Community Psychology

Alliant International University–Alameda (Ph.D. & Psy.D.) (Cl)	7	1
Antioch/New England Graduate School (Cl)	2	0
Arizona State University (Cl)	5	3
Boston University (Cl)	2	0
Bowling Green State University (Cl)	2	1
DePaul University (Cl)	2	4
Fairleigh Dickinson University (Cl)	3	0
Florida State University (Cm)	2	1
George Washington University (Ph.D.) (Cl)	2	1
George Washington University (Psy.D.) (Cl)	3	1
Loyola University of Chicago (Cl)	3	0
Michigan State University (Cl)	3	0
Nova Southeastern University (Ph.D. & Psy.D.) (Cl)	4	0
Pace University (Psy.D.) (Cm)	1	0
Rutgers University (Psy.D.) (Cl)	2	1
St. Louis University (Cl)	1	0
San Diego State University/University of California–San Diego (Cl)	1	0
Southern Illinois University (Cl)	1	0
Texas Tech University (Cl)	1	0
University of Arizona (Cl)	1	0
University of Colorado (Cl)	1	1
University of Hartford (Cl)	1	0
University of Illinois at Chicago (Cl)	6	4
University of Illinois at Urbana–Champaign (Cl)	5	1
University of Manitoba (Cl)	1	0
University of Maryland–Baltimore County (Cl)	2	1
University of Mississippi (Cl)	2	0
University of Missouri–Columbia (Cl)	1	1
University of North Dakota (Cl)	1	0
University of Pennsylvania (Cl)	1	1
University of Rhode Island (Cl)	1	4
University of South Carolina (Cl)	2	1
University of South Dakota (Cl)	6	1
University of Texas Southwestern Medical Center at Dallas (Cl)	1	0
University of Tulsa (Cl)	1	2
University of Virginia–Department of Psychology (Cl)	3	3
University of Windsor (Cl)	3	2
Virginia Commonwealth University (Cl)	3	2
Virginia Commonwealth University (Co)	3	0
Virginia Consortium Program in Clinical Psychology (Cl)	1	1
Washington State University (Cl)	1	0
Wayne State University (Cl)	2	2

	# Faculty	# Grants

Conduct Disorder

Duke University (Cl)	2	3
University of North Carolina at Greensboro (Cl)	1	0
University of South Carolina (Cl)	1	1

Conflict Mediation/Resolution

Loma Linda University (Ph.D. & Psy.D.) (Cl)	1	0
University at Albany/State University of New York (Co)	1	0
University of North Dakota (Co)	1	0

Consultation

Arizona State University (Co)	2	0
Northeastern University (Cm)	1	1
University of Memphis (Co)	1	1
University of Southern Mississippi (Co)	1	0
West Virginia University (Co)	1	0

Crisis Intervention

Brigham Young University (Co)	1	1
Southern Illinois University (Co)	1	0
University of Detroit–Mercy (Cl)	2	0

Deafness/Hearing Impairment

Alliant International University–San Diego (Ph.D. & Psy.D.) (Cl)	3	2
Gallaudet University (Cl)	9	2
University of Iowa (Cl)	1	0
Wright State University (Cl)	1	1
York University–Clinical-Developmental Area (Cl)	2	1

Death and Dying/Bereavement

Biola University (Ph.D.) (Cl)	1	0
Biola University (Psy.D.) (Cl)	1	0
Indiana University of Pennsylvania (Cl)	1	0
Loyola University of Chicago (Cl)	2	0
San Diego State University/University of California–San Diego (Cl)	2	0
University at Buffalo/State University of New York (Co)	1	0
University of Michigan (Cl)	2	2
University of Missouri–St. Louis (Cl)	1	0
University of Saskatchewan (Cl)	1	0

Developmental (Adult)

Adler School of Professional Psychology (Cl)	1	0

Developmental (Child and Adolescent)

Boston College (Co)	2	0
Brigham Young University (Cl)	2	1
Catholic University of America (Cl)	2	0
Colorado State University (Co)	1	1
Fordham University (Cl)	1	0
Fuller Theological Seminary (Ph.D. & Psy.D.) (Cl)	3	1
George Washington University (Psy.D.) (Cl)	2	2
Hofstra University (Cm)	1	0
Howard University (Cl)	3	2
Immaculata College (Cl)	4	0
Long Island University (Cl)	1	1
Loyola University of Chicago (Co)	1	4
McGill University (Cl)	1	1
New School for Social Research (Cl)	1	0
Pacific Graduate School of Psychology (Cl)	4	0
Pennsylvania State University (Cl)	4	2
Simon Fraser University (Cl)	2	2
Spalding University (Cl)	1	0
Stony Brook University/State University of New York (Cl)	1	1
Suffolk University (Cl)	5	0
University of Cincinnati (Cl)	1	1
University of Colorado (Cl)	2	1
University of Georgia (Co)	2	0
University of Ottawa (Cl)	3	2
University of Pittsburgh (Cl)	7	18
University of Texas Southwestern Medical Center at Dallas (Cl)	1	1
University of Tulsa (Cl)	2	0
University of Utah (Cl)	1	1
University of Virginia (Cl)	3	3
University of Washington (Cl)	3	3
University of Wisconsin–Milwaukee (Cl)	2	0
Virginia Commonwealth University (Cl)	2	2
Yale University (Cl)	1	1

Developmental Disabilities/ Mental Retardation

Auburn University (Cl)	1	0
Binghamton University/State University of New York (Cl)	2	1
Bowling Green State University (Cl)	1	0
Case Western Reserve University (Cl)	1	1
George Washington University (Psy.D.) (Cl)	2	2
Long Island University–C.W. Post Campus (Cl)	1	0
Louisiana State University (Cl)	1	1
MCP Hahnemann University of the Health Sciences (Cl)	2	1
Pennsylvania State University (Cl)	1	0
Rutgers University (Psy.D.) (Cl)	4	3
Stony Brook University/State University of New York (Cl)	1	1
University of Alabama at Birmingham (Cl)	6	16

	# Faculty	# Grants
University at Albany/State University of New York (Cl)	1	2
University of California–Los Angeles (Cl)	2	1
University of Illinois at Chicago (Cl)	1	0
University of Manitoba (Cl)	3	0
University of Wyoming (Cl)	2	1
Virginia Consortium Program in Clinical Psychology (Cl)	1	0
West Virginia University (Cl)	1	0
York University–Clinical-Developmental Area (Cl)	2	1

Disaster/Trauma

Fairleigh Dickinson University (Cl)	2	0
Long Island University (Cl)	1	1
Miami University (Cl)	2	0
Nova Southeastern University (Ph.D. & Psy.D) (Cl)	7	0
Seton Hall University (Co)	1	0
Temple University (Cl) (rape)	1	1
Texas Tech University (Cl)	2	0
University of Manitoba (Cl)	3	0
University of Massachusetts at Boston (Cl)	4	1
University of Memphis (Co)	2	0
University of Miami (Cl)	3	2+
University of North Dakota (Co)	2	0
University of North Texas (Cl)	2	0
University of Pittsburgh (Cl)	1	1
University of South Dakota (Cl)	5	2
York University–Adult Clinical Program (Cl)	1	0

Dissociative Disorders

Central Michigan University (Cl)	1	1
Rutgers University (Psy.D.) (Cl)	1	0
Virginia Consortium Program in Clinical Psychology (Cl)	1	0

Divorce/Child Custody

Colorado State University (Co)	3	0
Temple University (Cl)	1	0
University of Louisville (Co)	1	2
University of Michigan (Cl)	1	1
University of Victoria (Cl)	1	1
Virginia Commonwealth University (Cl)	1	0

Dreams

Miami University (Cl)	1	0
University of Maryland (Co)	1	0
University of Michigan (Cl)	1	0

Eating Disorders/Body Image

Alliant International University–Fresno (Ph.D. & Psy.D.) (Cl)	2	1
American University (Cl)	1	0
Brigham Young University (Cl)	1	1
Colorado State University (Co)	1	0
Duke University (Cl)	1	0
Fairleigh Dickinson University (Cl)	1	0
Florida Institute of Technology (Cl)	1	1
Georgia State University (Cl)	1	3
Hofstra University (Cm)	2	0
Illinois School of Professional Psychology–Chicago Campus (Cl)	1	0
Indiana State University (Cl)	2	0
Kent State University (Cl)	1	0
Louisiana State University (Cl)	1	1
McGill University (Cl)	1	1
MCP Hahnemann University of the Health Sciences (Cl)	1	0
Michigan State University (Cl)	1	0
Northeastern University (Cm)	1	1
Northwestern University Medical School (Cl)	2	2
Ohio State University (Cl)	1	0
Rutgers University (Ph.D.) (Cl)	1	1
Rutgers University (Psy.D.) (Cl)	1	1
Suffolk University (Cl)	1	0
Tennessee State University (Co)	2	1
Texas Tech University (Cl)	1	0
Uniformed Services University of Health Sciences (Cl)	1	1
University of Alabama at Birmingham (Cl)	1	1
University at Albany/State University of New York (Cl)	1	0
University of Arkansas (Cl)	1	0
University of British Columbia (Cl)	1	1
University of Colorado (Cl)	2	1
University of Detroit–Mercy (Cl)	2	0
University of Florida (Co)	1	1
University of Hawaii at Manoa (Cl)	1	0
University of Kentucky (Cl)	1	0
University of Illinois at Chicago (Cl)	1	0
University of Illinois at Urbana–Champaign (Co)	1	1
University of Manitoba (Cl)	2	0
University of Maryland–Baltimore County (Cl)	1	0
University of Massachusetts at Amherst (Cl)	1	0
University of Minnesota (Cl)	1	0
University of Mississippi (Cl)	1	0
University of Missouri–Columbia (Cl)	1	0
University of Montana (Cl)	1	1
University of New Mexico (Cl)	1	1
University of North Texas (Co)	3	0
University of Northern Colorado (Co)	2	3
University of Pittsburgh (Cl)	1	3
University of St. Thomas (Co)	2	0
University of South Florida (Cl)	1	1
University of Southern Mississippi (Co)	2	0
University of Texas at Austin (Cl)	1	1
University of Vermont (Cl)	2	0
University of Windsor (Cl)	2	1
Vanderbilt University–Department of Psychology (Cl)	1	1
Vanderbilt University–Peabody College (Cl)	1	0

	# Faculty	# Grants
Virginia Consortium Program in Clinical Psychology (Cl)	2	1
Virginia Polytechnic Institute and State University (Cl)	1	0
West Virginia University (Co)	1	1
Yale University (Cl)	1	2
Yeshiva University (Cl)	2	0

Emotion

	# Faculty	# Grants
Boston University (Cl)	3	1
Catholic University of America (Cl)	5	0
Florida State University (Cl)	2	2
Hofstra University (Cm)	1	0
Long Island University (Cl) (socioemotional development)	1	0
McGill University (Cl)	1	1
New School for Social Research (Cl)	2	0
Northern Illinois University (Cl)	1	1
Pennsylvania State University (Cl)	3	0
Purdue University (Cl)	1	1
Simon Fraser University (Cl)	1	1
Suffolk University (Cl)	3	0
Temple University (Cl)	1	0
University of California–Berkeley (Cl)	1	1
University of Delaware (Cl)	4	0
University of Florida (Cl)	1	3
University of Florida (Co)	1	0
University of Georgia (Cl)	1	1
University of Illinois at Urbana–Champaign (Cl)	5	2
University of Montana (Cl)	4	1
University of North Texas (Cl)	1	0
University of Pittsburgh (Cl)	1	4
University of Western Ontario (Cl)	1	0
Vanderbilt University–Department of Psychology (Cl)	4	2
Virginia Commonwealth University (Cl)	1	0
York University–Clincal-Developmental Area (Cl)	1	0

Epidemiology

	# Faculty	# Grants
Arizona State University (Cl)	1	1
University of Kansas (Co)	1	1
University of Texas at Austin (Cl)	1	0
University of Virginia (Cl)	2	1

Ethical Issues

	# Faculty	# Grants
Arizona State University (Co)	1	0
Boston College (Co)	1	1
Catholic University of America (Cl)	1	0
Colorado State University (Co)	1	0
Fairleigh Dickinson University (Cl)	2	0
Gallaudet University (Cl)	1	0
Indiana University of Pennsylvania (Cl)	1	0
Iowa State University (Co)	1	0
Loma Linda University (Ph.D. & Psy.D.) (Cl)	1	0
Loyola College in Maryland (Cl)	1	0
Loyola University of Chicago (Cl)	1	0
Our Lady of the Lake University (Co)	1	0
Rutgers University (Ph.D.) (Cl)	1	0
Rutgers University (Psy.D.) (Cl)	1	0
St. Louis University (Cl)	3	0
Temple University (Co)	1	0
Texas Woman's University (Co)	2	
University of Connecticut (Cl)	1	0
University of Denver (Co)	1	0
University of Iowa (Co)	2	1
University of New Mexico (Cl)	1	0
University of Notre Dame (Co)	2	0
University of St. Thomas (Co)	1	0
University of South Dakota (Cl)	1	0
University of Tennessee (Co)	1	0
University of Utah (Co)	1	0

Family/Family Therapy/Systems

	# Faculty	# Grants
Alliant International University–Alameda (Ph.D. & Psy.D.) (Cl)	9	0
Alliant International University–Fresno (Ph.D. & Psy.D.) (Cl)	4	2
Alliant International University–Los Angeles (Ph.D. & Psy.D.) (Cl)	2	1
Arizona State University (Cl)	1	1
Arizona State University (Co)	1	0
Boston University (Cl)	2	1
Bowling Green State University (Cl)	3	0
Catholic University of America (Cl)	3	0
Clark University (Cl)	2	1
Colorado State University (Co)	1	0
Florida Institute of Technology (Cl)	2	0
Florida State University (Cl)	3	0
Fordham University (Cl)	1	0
Fuller Theological Seminary (Ph.D. & Psy.D.) (Cl)	2	1
George Washington University (Cl)	1	1
Hofstra University (Cm)	1	0
Howard University (Cl)	2	0
Illinois Institute of Technology (Cl)	1	0
Illinois School of Professional Psychology–Chicago Northwest (Cl)	1	0
Indiana State University (Co)	3	1
Indiana University (Cl)	1	1
Indiana University (Co)	3	0
Indiana University of Pennsylvania (Cl)	3	0
James Madison University (Cm)	3	0
Kent State University (Cl)	2	0
Lehigh University (Co)	1	1
Marquette University (Cl)	2	1
McGill University (Cl)	2	1
Miami University (Cl)	1	0
Michigan State University (Cl)	6	3
New Mexico State University (Co)	1	0
New York University (Cl)	2	0
Ohio University (Cl)	3	1
Pennsylvania State University (Cl)	2	0
Pepperdine University (Cl)	0	0
Rutgers University (Psy.D.) (Cl)	4	2
St. Louis University (Cl)	3	0
San Diego State University/University of California–San Diego (Cl)	5	0

	# Faculty	# Grants
Simon Fraser University (Cl)	1	1
Southern Illinois University (Cl)	1	0
Suffolk University (Cl)	3	0
Syracuse University (Cl)	1	1
Temple University (Cl)	2	0
Temple University (Co)	1	0
Tennessee State University (Co)	1	1
Texas A&M University (Cl)	5	3
Texas Tech University (Co)	2	0
University at Albany/State University of New York (Co)	2	0
University of Akron (Co)	2	0
University of Arizona (Cl)	2	2
University at Buffalo/State University of New York (Cl)	2	3
University at Buffalo/State University of New York (Co)	1	0
University of California–Berkeley (Cl)	1	1
University of California–Santa Barbara (Cm)	4	4
University of Colorado (Cl)	2	2
University of Denver (Ph.D.) (Cl)	1	0
University of Denver (Psy.D.) (Cl)	2	0
University of Detroit–Mercy (Cl)	2	0
University of Georgia (Cl)	2	3
University of Houston (Cl)	3	3
University of Illinois at Urbana–Champaign (Cl)	5	1
University of Indianapolis (Cl)	1	0
University of Kentucky (Co)	2	0
University of Maryland (Cl)	2	0
University of Massachusetts at Amherst (Cl)	1	1
University of Massachusetts at Boston (Cl)	3	1
University of Memphis (Co)	2	1
University of Miami (Cl)	1	1
University of Miami (Co)	2	1
University of Michigan (Cl)	8	3
University of Missouri–Columbia (Cl)	1	1
University of Missouri–Kansas City (Co)	1	0
University of New Mexico (Cl)	1	3
University of North Carolina at Chapel Hill (Cl)	1	2
University of North Texas (Co)	3	0
University of Northern Colorado (Co)	2	1
University of Oklahoma (Co)	4	0
University of Oregon (Co)	1	3
University of Ottawa (Cl)	1	1
University of Pennsylvania (Cl)	1	1
University of Rhode Island (Cl)	2	1
University of South Florida (Cl)	2	1
University of Southern California (Cl)	1	1
University of Texas at Austin (Co)	1	0
University of Utah (Cl)	2	3
University of Virginia (Cl)	2	2
University of Wisconsin–Milwaukee (Co)	1	1
University of Wyoming (Cl)	2	0
Vanderbilt University–Peabody College (Cl)	6	3
Virginia Commonwealth University (Co)	2	1
Virginia Consortium Program in Clinical Psychology (Cl)	1	0
Wayne State University (Cl)	1	2
Wheaton College (Cl)	1	0
Wright Institute (Cl)	1	0
Wright State University (Cl)	3	1
Yeshiva University (Cm)	2	0
Yeshiva University (Cl)	4	0
York University–Adult Clinical Program (Cl)	1	0

Forensic

Alliant International University–Fresno (Ph.D. & Psy.D.) (Cl)	3	0
Alliant International University–San Diego (Ph.D. & Psy.D.) (Cl)	4	0
Argosy University–Washington, DC Campus (Cl)	2	0
Catholic University of America (Cl)	1	0
Colorado State University (Co)	2	1
Dalhousie University (Cl)	3	1
Fairleigh Dickinson University (Cl)	2	0
Florida State University (Cl)	5	3
Long Island University (Cl)	1	0
Northeastern University (Cm)	1	1
Nova Southeastern University (Ph.D. & Psy.D.) (Cl)	3	0
Pennsylvania State University (Cl)	1	0
Simon Fraser University (Cl)	3	3
Texas Tech University (Co)	1	0
University of Alabama (Cl)	3	0
University of Denver (Psy.D.) (Cl)	2	0
University of Kentucky (Cl)	1	0
University of Louisville (Cl)	1	0
University of Nebraska–Lincoln (Cl)	3	2
University of North Texas (Cl)	2	1
University of Ottawa (Cl)	1	0
University of Saskatchewan (Cl)	3	2
University of Tulsa (Cl)	1	1
University of Utah (Cl)	1	0
University of Virginia–Department of Human Services (Cl)	1	1
Virginia Commonwealth University (Cl)	1	0
West Virginia University (Cl)	1	0

Forgiveness

University of Southern Mississippi (Co)	1	0
Virginia Commonwealth University (Co)	1	1

Gay/Lesbian/Bisexuality

Argosy University–Honolulu Campus (Cl)	1	0
Auburn University (Co)	2	0
Gallaudet University (Cl)	1	0
Loyola College in Maryland (Cl)	1	0
Oklahoma State University (Co)	1	1
University of Louisville (Co)	1	1
University of Memphis (Co)	3	1
University of North Dakota (Co)	1	0
University of Utah (Co)	1	2
University of Vermont (Cl)	1	0
Virginia Commonwealth University (Co)	1	0

Gender Roles/Sex Differences

	# Faculty	# Grants
Arizona State University (Cl)	3	1
Arizona State University (Co)	2	0
Biola University (Psy.D.) (Cl)	2	1
Boston College (Co)	2	0
Boston University (Cl)	1	0
Brigham Young University (Cl)	3	1
Catholic University of America (Cl)	3	0
Clark University (Cl)	1	0
Colorado State University (Co)	1	0
Concordia University (Cl)	2	1
Florida State University (Cl)	2	0
Georgia State University (Cl)	1	1
Illinois School of Professional Psychology–Chicago Northwest (Cl)	1	0
Immaculata College (Cl)	3	0
Indiana State University (Co)	2	0
Indiana State University (Cl)	3	0
Indiana University of Pennsylvania (Cl)	1	0
Iowa State University (Co)	2	0
McGill University (Cl)	1	0
Michigan State University (Co)	1	0
New Mexico State University (Co)	2	0
Nova Southeastern University (Ph.D. & Psy.D.) (Cl)	1	0
Oklahoma State University (Co)	2	0
Pace University (Psy.D.) (Cm)	2	0
Pacific University (Cl)	2	0
Rutgers University (Psy.D.) (Cl)	1	0
St. John's University (Cl)	2	0
San Diego State University/University of California–San Diego (Cl)	2	0
Simon Fraser University (Cl)	1	0
Southern Illinois University (Cl)	2	0
Southern Illinois University (Co)	3	0
Suffolk University (Cl)	1	0
Texas A&M University (Co)	2	0
Texas Tech University (Co)	2	0
Texas Woman's University (Co)	4	0
University of California–Santa Barbara (Cm)	1	0
University of Colorado (Cl)	3	2
University of Florida (Co)	1	0
University of Georgia (Co)	1	0
University of Houston (Co)	1	0
University of Kansas (Cl)	1	0
University of Kentucky (Co)	2	1
University of Montana (Cl)	2	1
University of North Dakota (Cl)	2	0
University of North Dakota (Co)	4	0
University of Oklahoma (Co)	1	0
University of Rochester (Cl)	1	0
University of Wisconsin–Madison (Co)	4	0
Vanderbilt University–Department of Psychology (Cl)	1	0
Virginia Consortium Program in Clinical Psychology (Cl)	1	0
Virginia Polytechnic Institute and State University (Cl)	2	0
Wheaton College (Cl)	1	1
Wright Institute (Cl)	3	0
Wright State University (Cl)	1	0

Group Process and Therapy

	# Faculty	# Grants
Adelphi University (Cl)	2	0
Arizona State University (Co)	1	0
Baylor University (Cl)	1	0
Brigham Young University (Cl)	4	1
Catholic University of America (Cl)	2	0
Columbia University, Teachers College (Ph.D. & Ed.D.) (Co)	1	0
Fuller Theological Seminary (Ph.D. & Psy.D.) (Cl)	1	0
George Washington University (Psy.D.) (Cl)	3	0
Indiana University (Co)	4	0
New York University (Co)	1	0
Ohio State University (Co)	2	0
Texas Tech University (Co)	1	0
University of Denver (Co)	1	0
University of Hartford (Cl)	1	0
University of Missouri–Columbia (Co)	2	0
University of Montana (Cl)	1	0
University of Tennessee (Co)	1	0
University of Wisconsin–Madison (Co)	1	0
Virginia Commonwealth University (Co)	1	0
Virginia Consortium Program in Clinical Psychology (Cl)	1	0
Washington State University (Co)	1	0
West Virginia University (Co)	1	0

Homelessness

	# Faculty	# Grants
Boston College (Co)	1	1
University of Cincinnati (Cl)	2	1
University of Houston (Cl)	1	1
University of Michigan (Cl)	1	0

Humor

	# Faculty	# Grants
San Diego State University/University of California–San Diego (Cl)	1	0
University of Western Ontario (Cl)	2	0

Hypnosis

	# Faculty	# Grants
Binghamton University/State University of New York (Cl)	1	0
Fuller Theological Seminary (Cl)	0	0
Pennsylvania State University (Cl)	1	0
University of Connecticut (Cl)	1	1
University of Manitoba (Cl)	1	0
University of Waterloo (Cl)	1	1
University of Wisconsin–Milwaukee (Co)	1	0
Virginia Polytechnic Institute and State University (Cl)	1	1
Washington State University (Cl)	1	0
Washington University (Cl)	1	0

Infancy

	# Faculty	# Grants
Concordia University (Cl)	4	4
Emory University (Cl)	1	2
George Washington University (Psy.D.) (Cl)	1	1
Pace University (Psy.D.) (Cm)	2	0
University of Western Ontario (Cl)	2	1

Interpersonal Relations/Processes

	# Faculty	# Grants
Adelphi University (Cl)	1	1
Arizona State University (Cl)	1	1
Arizona State University (Co)	3	0
Catholic University of America (Cl)	4	0
Colorado State University (Co)	1	0
Fairleigh Dickinson University (Cl)	4	0
Georgia State University (Cl)	1	1
Indiana State University (Cl)	1	0
Indiana University (Cl)	3	1
James Madison University (Cm)	4	0
McGill University (Cl)	2	2
Michigan State University (Co)	2	0
New Mexico State University (Co)	1	0
San Diego State University/University of California–San Diego (Cl)	1	0
Southern Illinois University (Cl)	2	0
Texas Tech University (Co)	1	0
University of Cincinnati (Cl)	2	0
University of Denver (Ph.D.) (Cl)	1	1
University of Georgia (Cl)	1	2
University of Hartford (Cl)	1	0
University of Indianapolis (Cl)	2	0
University of Kansas (Co)	1	1
University of Maryland–Baltimore County (Cl)	3	0
University of Michigan (Cl)	1	1
University of Minnesota–Department of Psychology (Co)	1	1
University of Missouri–Kansas City (Co)	3	0
University of New Mexico (Cl)	1	2
University of North Carolina at Chapel Hill (Cl)	2	1
University of North Carolina at Greensboro (Cl)	3	2
University of North Dakota (Cl)	1	0
University of Oregon (Co)	3	0
Virginia Consortium Program in Clinical Psychology (Cl)	1	0

Intervention

	# Faculty	# Grants
Alliant International University–Los Angeles (Ph.D.) (Cl)	5	2
Northeastern University (Cm)	1	1
University of Minnesota–Department of Psychology (Co)	1	1

Learning

	# Faculty	# Grants
Loyola College in Maryland (Cl)	1	0
Pace University (Psy.D.) (Cm)	1	0
University of Hawaii at Manoa (Cl)	1	0
University of Kansas (Co)	1	0
University of Montana (Cl)	3	0
Virginia Consortium Program in Clinical Psychology (Cl)	1	0

Learning Disabilities/Disorders

	# Faculty	# Grants
Binghamton University/State University of New York (Cl)	1	1
Case Western Reserve University (Cl)	1	0
Colorado State University (Co)	1	0
Georgia State University (Cl)	2	3
Michigan State University (Cl)	1	1
Pace University (Psy.D.) (Cm)	1	0
Southern Illinois University (Cl)	2	0
Stony Brook University/State University of New York (Cl)	1	1
University of Denver (Ph.D.) (Cl)	1	3
University of Texas Southwestern Medical Center at Dallas (Cl)	1	0
University of Virginia–Department of Human Services (Cl)	3	1
University of Waterloo (Cl)	1	0
Widener University (Psy.D.) (Cl)	1	0
Yeshiva University (Cm)	2	0
York University–Clinical-Developmental Area (Cl)	1	0

Legal Issues/Law Psychology

	# Faculty	# Grants
Alliant International University–San Diego (Ph.D. & Psy.D.) (Cl)	1	0
George Washington University (Psy.D.) (Cl)	2	0
Iowa State University (Co)	1	0
Loyola College in Maryland (Cl)	1	0
MCP Hahnemann University of the Health Sciences (Cl)	2	0
Northwestern University Medical School (Cl)	2	5
University of Arizona (Cl)	2	2
University of Illinois–Urbana–Champaign (Cl)	3	2
University of St. Thomas (Co)	1	0
University of Southern Mississippi (Co)	3	0
University of Wyoming (Cl)	2	3

Life History Research/Psychobiography

	# Faculty	# Grants
University of Michigan (Cl)	1	0
University of Saskatchewan (Cl)	1	0

Malingering/Somatoform Disorders

	# Faculty	# Grants
Alliant International University–San Diego (Ph.D. & Psy.D.) (Cl)	1	0

	# Faculty	# Grants
Rutgers University (Ph.D.) (Cl)	1	1
University of Montana (Cl)	1	1
University of North Texas (Cl)	2	2

Managed Care/Health Care

Northeastern University (Cm)	1	0
University of Hawaii at Manoa (Cl)	1	0
Wright State University (Psy.D.) (Cl)	1	1

Marriage/Couples

Adelphi University (Cl)	1	1
Binghamton University/State University of New York (Cl)	1	0
Catholic University of America (Cl)	1	0
Fordham University (Cl)	1	0
Fuller Theological Seminary (Ph.D. & Psy.D.) (Cl)	1	0
George Fox University (Cl)	1	0
Georgia State University (Cl)	2	0
Hofstra University (Cm)	1	0
Illinois Institute of Technology (Cl)	1	1
Indiana University (Cl)	1	1
Indiana University (Co)	3	0
Long Island University–C.W. Post Campus (Cl)	2	0
MCP Hahnemann University of the Health Sciences (Cl)	1	0
Pennsylvania State University (Cl)	1	0
Rutgers University (Ph.D.) (Cl)	3	2
Rutgers University (Psy.D.) (Cl)	1	1
San Diego State University/University of California–San Diego (Cl)	5	0
Simon Fraser University (Cl)	1	0
Southern Illinois University (Cl)	1	0
Stony Brook University/State University of New York (Cl)	1	1
Suffolk University (Cl)	1	0
Texas A&M University (Cl)	5	3
Texas Woman's University (Co)	4	1
University of California–Berkeley (Cl)	2	1
University of California–Los Angeles (Cl)	2	2
University of Colorado (Cl)	2	0
University of Denver (Ph.D.) (Cl)	2	2
University of Denver (Psy.D.) (Cl)	1	0
University of Detroit–Mercy (Cl)	2	0
University of Georgia (Cl)	1	1
University of Houston (Cl)	2	2
University of Illinois at Urbana–Champaign (Cl)	5	1
University of Indianapolis (Cl)	1	0
University of Maryland (Cl)	1	0
University of Nevada–Reno (Cl)	1	0
University of North Carolina at Chapel Hill (Cl)	1	1
University of North Texas (Co)	3	0
University of Oklahoma (Co)	4	0
University of Ottawa (Cl)	1	0
University of South Carolina (Cl)	3	0
University of South Florida (Cl)	1	0
University of Southern California (Cl)	1	1
University of Tulsa (Cl)	0	0
University of Washington (Cl)	2	1
Virginia Commonwealth University (Co)	1	1
Virginia Polytechnic Institute and State University (Cl)	1	0

Media and Psychology

George Mason University (Cl)	1	1
University of Massachusetts at Boston (Cl)	1	1

Minority/Cross-Cultural

Alliant International University–Alameda (Ph.D. & Psy.D.) (Cl)	7	1
Alliant International University–Los Angeles (Ph.D. & Psy.D.) (Cl)	5	2
Alliant International University–San Diego (Psy.D.) (Cl)	3	2
Alliant International University–San Diego (Ph.D.) (Cl)	4	0
Antioch/New England Graduate School (Cl)	1	0
Arizona State University (Cl)	10	4
Arizona State University (Co)	4	1
Ball State University (Co)	3	0
Biola University (Ph.D.) (Cl)	4	0
Biola University (Psy.D.) (Cl)	4	0
Boston College (Co)	3	0
Boston University (Cl)	1	0
Brigham Young University (Co)	4	3
Catholic University of America (Cl)	1	0
Central Michigan University (Cl)	1	0
City University of New York at City College (Cl)	2	0
Colorado State University (Co)	6	3
Columbia University, Teachers College (Ph.D. & Ed.D.) (Co)	2	0
DePaul University (Cl)	3	1
Fairleigh Dickinson University (Cl)	2	0
Fordham University (Co)	4	0
Fuller Theological Seminary (Ph.D. & Psy.D.) (Cl)	2	0
Gallaudet University (Cl)	1	1
George Washington University (Ph.D.) (Cl)	2	1
Georgia School of Professional Psychology (Cl)	3	0
Georgia State University (Co)	3	0
Hofstra University (Cm)	2	0
Howard University (Cl)	4	4
Illinois School of Professional Psychology–Chicago Campus (Cl)	1	0
Illinois School of Professional Psychology–Chicago Northwest (Cl)	3	0
Indiana University (Co)	3	0
Indiana University of Pennsylvania (Cl)	3	0
James Madison University (Cm)	2	0
Kent State University (Cl)	1	1
Lehigh University (Co)	1	1
Long Island University (Cl)	1	1

	# Faculty	# Grants
Loyola College in Maryland (Cl)	1	0
Loyola University of Chicago (Cl)	3	2
Loyola University of Chicago (Co)	2	0
Miami University (Cl)	2	0
Michigan State University (Cl)	1	1
Michigan State University (Co)	2	1
New Mexico State University (Co)	4	0
New York University (Cl)	1	0
New York University (Co)	2	2
Northeastern University (Cm)	1	1
Nova Southeastern University (Ph.D. & Psy.D.) (Cl)	2	0
Ohio State University (Co)	4	0
Oklahoma State University (Co)	7	8
Pace University (Psy.D.) (Cm)	2	0
Pacific Graduate School of Psychology (Cl)	4	0
Pacific University (Cl)	2	0
Pennsylvania State University (Cl)	3	1
Pennsylvania State University (Co)	1	0
Purdue University (Cl)	2	0
Rutgers University (Psy.D.) (Cl)	2	0
St. John's University (Cl)	3	0
San Diego State University/University of California–San Diego (Cl)	10	0
Seton Hall University (Co)	1	0
Southern Illinois University (Co)	2	0
Stanford University (Co)	1	1
Suffolk University (Cl)	3	0
Temple University (Co)	2	0
Tennessee State University (Co)	2	1
Texas A&M University (Co)	2	0
Texas Tech University (Cl)	3	0
University of Akron (Co)	2	0
University of Alabama (Cl)	2	0
University at Albany/State University of New York (Co)	4	2
University at Buffalo/State University of New York (Co)	1	0
University of California–Los Angeles (Cl)	6	5
University of California–Santa Barbara (Cm)	5	1
University of Denver (Ph.D.) (Cl)	1	1
University of Denver (Psy.D.) (Cl)	1	0
University of Denver (Co)	1	1
University of Georgia (Cl)	1	0
University of Georgia (Co)	2	0
University of Hawaii at Manoa (Cl)	4	2
University of Houston (Cl)	1	1
University of Houston (Co)	1	0
University of Illinois at Urbana–Champaign (Cl)	5	0
University of Illinois at Urbana–Champaign (Co)	5	3
University of Indianapolis (Cl)	1	1
University of Iowa (Co)	2	1
University of Kentucky (Co)	2	2
University of Maryland (Co)	4	1
University of Massachusetts at Boston (Cl)	3	1
University of Memphis (Co)	2	0
University of Miami (Co)	1	0
University of Minnesota (Cl)	1	0
University of Minnesota–Department of Educational Psychology (Co)	6	1
University of Minnesota–Department of Psychology (Co)	2	1
University of Mississippi (Cl)	3	0
University of Missouri–Columbia (Co)	5	1
University of Missouri–Kansas City (Co)	4	0
University of Missouri–St. Louis (Cl)	2	1
University of Nebraska–Lincoln (Co)	2	0
University of Nevada–Reno (Cl)	4	2
University of New Mexico (Cl)	3	0
University of North Carolina at Chapel Hill (Cl)	1	0
University of North Dakota (Cl)	2	1
University of North Dakota (Co)	1	0
University of North Texas (Co)	2	1
University of Northern Colorado (Co)	2	0
University of Oklahoma (Co)	4	0
University of Rhode Island (Cl)	1	0
University of St. Thomas (Co)	2	0
University of South Carolina (Cl)	6	4
University of South Dakota (Cl)	10	2
University of Southern California (Co)	4	0
University of Southern Mississippi (Co)	3	0
University of Texas at Austin (Cl)	1	0
University of Texas at Austin (Co)	2	1
University of Texas Southwestern Medical Center at Dallas (Cl)	2	0
University of Utah (Co)	2	0
University of Virginia–Department of Human Services (Cl)	1	0
University of Virginia–Department of Psychology (Cl)	2	1
University of Washington (Cl)	5	4
University of Wisconsin–Madison (Co)	9	5
Utah State University (Cm)	1	1
Vanderbilt University–Peabody College (Cl)	3	0
Virginia Commonwealth University (Cl)	2	1
Virginia Consortium Program in Clinical Psychology (Cl)	2	0
Virginia Polytechnic Institute and State University (Cl)	2	1
Washington State University (Co)	3	1
West Virginia University (Cl)	1	0
Wheaton College (Cl)	1	1
Wright Institute (Cl)	3	0
Wright State University (Cl)	6	2
Yeshiva University (Cl)	2	0
Yeshiva University (Cm)	3	0

Moral Development

New School for Social Research (Cl)	1	0
St. John's University (Cl)	1	0

Motivation

Clark University (Cl)	1	1
University of Kansas (Cl)	1	1
University of Rochester (Cl)	1	2

	# Faculty	# Grants

Narrative Psychology/Methodology

Miami University (Cl)	2	0
New School for Social Research (Cl)	2	0
Suffolk University (Cl)	1	0
University of Notre Dame (Co)	1	1
University of Saskatchewan (Cl)	1	1

Neuropsychology

Adler School of Professional Psychology (Cl)	4	1
Alliant International University–Fresno (Ph.D. & Psy.D.) (Cl)	2	0
American University (Cl)	1	0
Argosy University–Honolulu Campus (Cl)	1	0
Argosy University–Washington, DC Campus (Cl)	4	0
Binghamton University/State University of New York (Cl)	1	0
Biola University (Ph.D.) (Cl)	1	0
Biola University (Psy.D.) (Cl)	1	1
Boston University (Cl)	3	2
Bowling Green State University (Cl)	1	0
Brigham Young University (Cl)	2	4
Central Michigan University (Cl)	1	0
Concordia University (Cl)	2	5
Dalhousie University (Cl)	1	1
Drexel University (Cl)	3	0
Duke University (Cl)	1	0
Emory University (Cl)	2	0
Finch University of Health Sciences, The Chicago Medical School (Cl)	2	1
Florida Institute of Technology (Cl)	2	1
Fordham University (Cl)	1	0
Fuller Theological Seminary (Ph.D. & Psy.D.) (Cl)	2	0
Gallaudet University (Cl)	1	1
George Fox University (Cl)	1	0
Georgia School of Professional Psychology (Cl)	2	1
Georgia State University (Cl)	1	1
Howard University (Cl)	2	2
Indiana University–Purdue University Indianapolis (Cl)	2	2
Loma Linda University (Ph.D. & Psy.D.) (Cl)	1	0
Long Island University (Cl)	1	0
Louisiana State University (Cl)	1	0
Loyola College in Maryland (Cl)	1	0
Marquette University (Cl)	2	0
McGill University (Cl)	1	1
MCP Hahnemann University of the Health Sciences (Cl)	1	0
Michigan State University (Cl)	2	2
Northeastern University (Cm)	1	0
Northwestern University Medical School (Cl)	2	2
Nova Southeastern University (Ph.D. & Psy.D.) (Cl)	9	0
Pacific Graduate School of Psychology (Cl)	2	0
Pennsylvania State University (Cl)	3	0
San Diego State University/University of California–San Diego (Cl)	9	1
Seton Hall University (Co)	1	0
Simon Fraser University (Cl)	1	0
Southern Illinois University (Cl)	2	0
Suffolk University (Cl)	2	0
Texas Tech University (Cl)	1	0
Uniformed Services University of Health Sciences (Cl)	1	0
University of Alabama at Birmingham (Cl)	3	2
University at Albany/State University of New York (Cl)	1	1
University of Arizona (Cl)	3	2
University of Arkansas (Cl)	2	1
University of Cincinnati (Cl)	5	1
University of Connecticut (Cl)	2	2
University of Denver (Ph.D.) (Cl)	1	1
University of Florida (Cl)	4	4
University of Georgia (Cl)	2	1
University of Houston (Cl)	3	2
University of Illinois at Urbana–Champaign (Cl)	2	1
University of Kentucky (Cl)	2	0
University of Manitoba (Cl)	2	1
University of Memphis (Cl)	2	1
University of Michigan (Cl)	6	0
University of Montana (Cl)	2	0
University of Nebraska–Lincoln (Cl)	1	0
University of New Mexico (Cl)	2	4
University of North Carolina at Chapel Hill (Cl)	2	0
University of North Texas (Cl)	1	0
University of Oregon (Cl)	2	2
University of Rochester (Cl)	3	0
University of South Florida (Cl)	1	0
University of Southern California (Cl)	3	1
University of Southern Mississippi (Cl)	1	0
University of Texas at Austin (Cl)	1	1
University of Texas Southwestern Medical Center at Dallas (Cl)	4	4
University of Toledo (Cl)	1	0
University of Tulsa (Cl)	1	1
University of Virginia (Cl)	1	0
University of Windsor (Cl)	4	4
University of Wisconsin–Milwaukee (Cl)	2	2
Vanderbilt University–Department of Psychology (Cl)	4	2
Virginia Consortium Program in Clinical Psychology (Cl)	1	1
Virginia Polytechnic Institute and State University (Cl)	2	0
Washington State University (Cl)	2	1
Washington University (Cl)	2	3
Wayne State University (Cl)	2	2

Object Relations

Biola University (Ph.D.) (Cl)	4	0
Biola University (Psy.D.) (Cl)	4	0

Obsessive–Compulsive Disorder

	# Faculty	# Grants
Finch University of Health Sciences, The Chicago Medical School (Cl)	1	0
Indiana University (Cl)	1	0
University of Virginia (Cl)	1	0
University of Wisconsin–Milwaukee (Cl)	2	0

Organizational

	# Faculty	# Grants
Ball State University (Co)	1	0
Indiana State University (Cl)	1	1
Rutgers University (Psy.D.) (Cl)	2	0
Virginia Commonwealth University (Co)	1	1

Pain Management

	# Faculty	# Grants
Binghamton University/State University of New York (Cl)	1	1
Dalhousie University (Cl)	1	5
Forest Institute of Professional Psychology (Cl)	2	0
Stony Brook University/State University of New York (Cl)	1	0
Uniformed Services University of Health Sciences (Cl)	1	4
University of Alabama (Cl)	1	1
University of Florida (Cl)	2	1
University of Georgia (Cl)	1	0
University of Kentucky (Cl)	1	1
University of Manitoba (Cl)	1	0
University of North Dakota (Cl)	1	0
University of Saskatchewan (Cl)	1	1
University of Texas Southwestern Medical Center at Dallas (Cl)	1	1
University of Western Ontario (Cl)	1	1
Virginia Polytechnic Institute and State University (Cl)	2	0
West Virginia University (Cl)	1	0
Yeshiva University (Cl)	2	0

Parent–Child Interactions/Parenting

	# Faculty	# Grants
Biola University (Ph.D.) (Cl)	3	0
Biola University (Psy.D.) (Cl)	3	0
Case Western Reserve University (Cl)	2	0
Catholic University of America (Cl)	2	0
Clark University (Cl)	3	1
Colorado State University (Co)	1	0
DePaul University (Cl)	1	1
Fordham University (Cl)	2	0
Gallaudet University (Cl)	1	1
George Mason University (Cl)	2	1
Georgia State University (Cl)	2	1
Illinois School of Professional Psychology–Chicago Campus (Cl)	2	1
Immaculata College (Cl)	1	0
Indiana University of Pennsylvania (Cl)	1	0
Long Island University–C.W. Post Campus (Cl)	1	0
Louisiana State University (Cl)	1	0
Pennsylvania State University (Cl)	4	0
Stony Brook University/State University of New York (Cl)	1	1
Texas Tech University (Cl)	1	0
University of Colorado (Cl)	3	2
University of Delaware (Cl)	1	2
University of Georgia (Cl)	3	4
University of Houston (Cl)	4	3
University of Indianapolis (Cl)	2	1
University of Louisville (Co)	1	0
University of Pittsburgh (Cl)	4	7
University of Virginia–Department of Human Services (Cl)	2	0
Virginia Commonwealth University (Co)	2	0
Virginia Polytechnic Institute and State University (Cl)	2	1
Wheaton College (Cl)	1	0
Wright Institute (Cl)	3	0
Yeshiva University (Cm)	2	0
Yeshiva University (Cl)	1	0

Perfectionism

	# Faculty	# Grants
Michigan State University (Co)	1	0
Pennsylvania State University (Co)	1	0

Personality Assessment

	# Faculty	# Grants
Arizona State University (Cl)	2	1
Auburn University (Cl)	2	0
Baylor University (Psy.D.) (Cl)	3	0
Catholic University of America (Cl)	2	0
Florida Institute of Technology (Cl)	3	1
Florida State University (Cl)	4	1
Fordham University (Cl)	1	0
George Washington University (Psy.D.) (Cl)	3	0
Indiana State University (Co)	1	0
Kent State University (Cl)	2	2
McGill University (Cl)	2	0
New School for Social Research (Cl)	1	0
Nova Southeastern University (Ph.D. & Psy.D.) (Cl)	1	0
Pennsylvania State University (Cl)	2	0
Southern Illinois University (Cl)	4	0
Southern Illinois University (Co)	1	0
Texas Tech University (Cl)	2	0
University of Akron (Co)	2	0
University of Alabama (Cl)	1	0
University of Arizona (Cl)	2	0
University of Illinois at Urbana–Champaign	1	1
University of Kentucky (Cl)	3	0
University of Minnesota (Cl)	6	3
University of Montana (Cl)	1	0
University of North Dakota (Cl)	1	0
University of South Florida (Cl)	2	0
University of Utah (Cl)	2	0
Vanderbilt University–Department of Psychology (Cl)	1	0
Virginia Consortium Program in Clinical Psychology (Cl)	2	2
West Virginia University (Co)	1	0

Personality Disorders

	# Faculty	# Grants
Argosy University–Washington, DC Campus (Cl)	1	0
Boston University (Cl)	1	2
Case Western Reserve University (Cl)	1	0
Catholic University of America (Cl)	1	0
Clark University (Cl)	2	0
Fordham University (Cl)	1	0
Indiana State University (Cl)	1	0
Pennsylvania State University (Cl)	2	0
Rutgers University (Psy.D.) (Cl)	2	0
St. Louis University (Cl)	2	0
University of Colorado (Cl)	3	1
University of Iowa (Cl)	2	1
University of Kentucky (Cl)	2	0
University of Miami (Cl)	1	0
University of Michigan (Cl)	2	0
University of Minnesota (Cl)	4	1
University of Missouri–Columbia (Cl)	1	1
University of North Carolina at Greensboro (Cl)	1	0
University of North Dakota (Cl)	1	0
University of Tulsa (Cl)	2	0
University of Utah (Cl)	2	0
University of Virginia–Department of Psychology (Cl)	2	1
University of Wisconsin–Madison (Cl)	1	2
Vanderbilt University–Peabody College (Cl)	3	2

Personality/Temperament

	# Faculty	# Grants
Case Western Reserve University (Cl)	1	1
Columbia University, Teachers College (Ph.D. & Ed.D.) (Co)	1	1
Emory University (Cl)	2	0
George Mason University (Cl)	1	1
Hofstra University (Cm)	2	0
Loyola University of Chicago (Cl)	2	1
McGill University (Cl)	1	0
Northwestern University (Cl)	2	2
Northwestern University Medical School (Cl)	1	0
Ohio State University (Cl)	1	0
Pennsylvania State University (Cl)	2	0
Purdue University (Cl)	1	0
Simon Fraser University (Cl)	1	0
Southern Illinois University (Cl)	4	0
Suffolk University (Cl)	2	0
University at Albany/State University of New York (Co)	2	1
University of Delaware (Cl)	2	1
University of Hawaii at Manoa (Cl)	1	1
University of Maryland (Cl)	1	0
University of Minnesota–Department of Psychology (Co)	1	0
York University–Adult Clinical Program (Cl)	2	0

Philosophical Issues

	# Faculty	# Grants
Rutgers University (Psy.D.) (Cl)	5	1
Rutgers University (Ph.D.) (Cl)	2	0

Positive Psychology/Resilience

	# Faculty	# Grants
Boston College (Co)	4	3
Immaculata College (Cl)	1	0
Seton Hall University (Co)	1	0
University of Kansas (Co)	1	1
University of Memphis (Co)	2	0

Posttraumatic Stress Disorder

	# Faculty	# Grants
Argosy University–Honolulu Campus (Cl)	1	1
Binghamton University/State University of New York (Cl)	2	0
Brigham Young University (Cl)	1	1
Duke University (Cl)	2	0
Florida Institute of Technology (Psy.D.) (Cl)	1	1
Fuller Theological Seminary (Ph.D. & Psy.D.) (Cl)	1	0
Loma Linda University (Ph.D. & Psy.D.) (Cl)	2	0
Loyola College in Maryland (Cl)	2	1
Nova Southeastern University (Ph.D. & Psy.D.) (Cl)	4	1
Pace University (Psy.D.) (Cm)	1	0
Pacific University (Psy.D.) (Cl)	1	0
Pepperdine University (Cl)	—	—
San Diego State University/University of California–San Diego (Cl)	1	0
University of Detroit–Mercy (Cl)	2	0
University of Hawaii at Manoa (Cl)	2	1
University of Indianapolis (Cl)	1	0
University of Mississippi (Cl)	1	0
University of North Texas (Cl)	2	1
University of Pittsburgh (Cl)	1	1
University of Toledo (Cl)	1	0
University of Tulsa (Cl)	1	0
West Virginia University (Cl)	1	0
Western Michigan University (Cl)	2	1

Pregnancy

	# Faculty	# Grants
Alliant International University–San Diego (Ph.D. & Psy.D.) (Cl)	1	0
DePaul University (Cl)	2	1
Indiana University of Pennsylvania (Cl)	1	0
Southern Illinois University (Cl)	1	0
University of Maryland–Baltimore County (Cl)	2	0
Virginia Commonwealth University (Cl)	1	1
Yeshiva University (Cl)	1	0

Prevention

	# Faculty	# Grants
Arizona State University (Cl)	6	5
Binghamton University/State University of New York (Cl)	3	1

	# Faculty	# Grants
Boston College (Co)	2	1
Bowling Green State University (Cl)	2	2
Clark University (Cl)	2	0
Fielding Graduate Institute (Cl)	—	—
Fordham University (Cl)	1	0
Hofstra University (Cm)	2	0
Indiana University (Cl)	1	0
Indiana University of Pennsylvania (Cl)	1	0
Loyola University of Chicago (Cl)	3	0
MCP Hahnemann University of Health Sciences (Cl)	1	0
New School for Social Research (Cl)	2	1
Northern Illinois University (Cl)	3	3
Pennsylvania State University (Co)	1	0
Rutgers University (Ph.D.)(Cl)	2	1
University of Colorado (Cl)	4	1
University of Georgia (Cl)	4	3
University of Minnesota–Department of Educational Psychology (Co)	1	0
University of Nevada–Reno (Cl)	1	1
University of Oregon (Co)	2	1
University of Rochester (Cl)	2	2
University of South Carolina (Cl)	4	0
University of Vermont (Cl)	2	1
University of Virginia (Cl)	3	2
Vanderbilt University–Department of Psychology (Cl)	1	0
Vanderbilt University, Peabody College (Cl)	2	0
Virginia Consortium Program in Clinical Psychology (Cl)	1	1
Virginia Polytechnic Institute and State University (Cl)	4	3

Problem Solving

San Diego State University/University of California–San Diego (Cl)	4	0
Stony Brook University/State University of New York (Cl)	1	0
University of Kansas (Cl)	2	0
University of Missouri–Columbia (Co)	2	0
Virginia Consortium Program in Clinical Psychology (Cl)	1	0
Widener University (Cl)	2	0
York University–Clinical-Developmental Area (Cl)	1	0

Professional Issues/Training

American University (Cl)	1	1
Antioch/New England Graduate School (Cl)	1	0
Arizona State University (Co)	9	0
Auburn University (Co)	3	0
Catholic University of America (Cl)	3	0
City University of New York at City College (Cl)	1	0
Howard University (Cl)	6	0
Illinois School of Professional Psychology–Chicago Campus (Cl)	2	1
Indiana State University (Cl)	1	0
Indiana University (Co)	5	0
Indiana University of Pennsylvania (Cl)	1	0
James Madison University (Cm)	3	0
Long Island University–C.W. Post Campus (Cl)	1	0
Oklahoma State University (Co)	2	1
Our Lady of the Lake University (Co)	1	0
St. Louis University (Cl)	3	0
Southern Illinois University (Co)	2	0
Temple University (Co)	2	0
University of Alabama (Cl)	3	0
University of Georgia (Co)	4	0
University of Memphis (Co)	2	0
University of Minnesota–Department of Educational Psychology (Co)	1	0
University of Missouri–Kansas City (Co)	3	0
University of Montana (Cl)	1	0
University of North Texas (Co)	4	0
University of St. Thomas (Co)	1	0
University of Tennessee (Co)	1	0
University of Wisconsin–Madison (Co)	1	0
Wright State University (Cl)	1	0
Yeshiva University (Cm)	1	0

Program Evaluation

Alliant International University–Los Angeles (Ph.D. & Psy.D.) (Cl)	2	1
Bowling Green State University (Cl)	2	2
DePaul University (Cl)	3	1
Indiana State University (Co)	1	1
Pepperdine University (Cl)	—	—
Rutgers University (Ph.D.) (Cl)	1	1
Rutgers University (Psy.D.) (Cl)	1	1
Spalding University (Cl)	1	0
Texas Tech University (Co)	1	0
University of Montana (Cl)	1	0

Psychoanalysis/Psychodynamics

Adelphi University (Cl)	7	1
Alliant International University–Alameda (Ph.D. & Psy.D.) (Cl)	5	0
Georgia School of Professional Psychology (Cl)	1	0
Indiana State University (Co)	1	0
Long Island University (Cl)	1	0
New School for Social Research (Cl)	2	0
New York University (Cl)	3	0
New York University (Co)	1	0
Nova Southeastern University (Ph.D. & Psy.D.) (Cl)	2	0
Pennsylvania State University (Cl)	3	0
Rutgers University (Psy.D.) (Cl)	7	1
University of Colorado (Cl)	1	0
University of Maryland (Co)	2	0
University of Pennsylvania (Cl)	1	2
University of Texas at Austin (Co)	1	0
Virginia Consortium Program in Clinical Psychology (Cl)	1	0
Yeshiva University (Cl)	5	0

Psychometrics/Measurement

	# Faculty	# Grants
Auburn University (Co)	2	0
Brigham Young University (Cl)	2	1
Carlos Albizu University–San Juan (Cl)	1	0
Hofstra University (Cm)	1	0
Illinois School of Professional Psychology–Chicago Northwest (Psy.D.) (Cl)	1	0
Northern Illinois University (Cl)	4	2
Pace University (Psy.D.) (Cm)	3	0
Southern Illinois University (Co)	1	0
Texas Tech University (Cl)	1	0
University of Minnesota–Department of Psychology (Co)	1	1
University of Missouri–Columbia (Co)	6	0
University of Virginia–Department of Human Services (Cl)	3	0

Psychoneuroimmunology

	# Faculty	# Grants
Arizona State University (Cl)	2	2
Forest Institute of Professional Psychology (Cl)	2	1
University of Iowa (Cl)	1	1
University of Kentucky (Cl)	1	0
University of Manitoba (Cl)	1	0
University of Miami (Cl)	6	1
University of Pittsburgh (Cl)	3	5
Vanderbilt University–Department of Psychology (Cl)	1	0

Psychopathology–Adult Psychopathology

	# Faculty	# Grants
Arizona State University (Cl)	4	1
Binghamton University/State University of New York (Cl)	5	0
Brigham Young University (Cl)	2	0
Catholic University of America (Cl)	5	1
Central Michigan University (Cl)	1	0
Clark University (Cl)	1	1
Colorado State University (Co)	3	0
Finch University of Health Sciences, The Chicago Medical School (Cl)	1	1
Florida State University (Cl)	3	2
George Washington University (Psy.D.) (Cl)	4	0
Indiana State University (Cl)	1	0
Indiana University of Pennsylvania (Cl)	1	0
Indiana University–Purdue University Indianapolis (Cl)	2	4
Loyola University of Chicago (Cl)	2	0
McGill University (Cl)	2	2
New School for Social Research (Cl)	2	0
New York University (Cl)	3	0
New York University (Co)	1	0
Northern Illinois University (Cl)	3	1
Northwestern University Medical School (Cl)	1	0
Nova Southeastern University (Cl)	2	0
Ohio University (Cl)	2	0
Pacific Graduate School of Psychology (Cl)	7	0
Pennsylvania State University (Cl)	5	3
Rutgers University (Psy.D.) (Cl)	1	1
San Diego State University/University of California–San Diego (Cl)	3	0
Simon Fraser University (Cl)	2	2
Temple University (Cl)	1	0
Texas A&M University (Cl)	2	1
Texas Tech University (Cl)	1	0
University of Alabama (Cl)	3	0
University at Albany/State University of New York (Cl)	1	0
University of Colorado (Cl)	3	1
University of Connecticut (Cl)	1	0
University of Georgia (Cl)	1	0
University of Houston (Cl)	5	3
University of Illinois at Chicago (Cl)	2	2
University of Illinois at Urbana–Champaign (Cl)	5	3
University of Kansas (Cl)	2	0
University of Kentucky (Cl)	4	0
University of Manitoba (Cl)	1	0
University of Maryland (Cl)	2	1
University of Maryland–Baltimore County (Cl)	2	1
University of Massachusetts–Boston (Cl)	2	2
University of Miami (Cl)	6	2
University of Missouri–Columbia (Cl)	2	2
University of Missouri–Kansas City (Co)	3	0
University of Nebraska–Lincoln (Cl)	3	2
University of North Dakota (Cl)	1	0
University of Ottawa (Cl)	1	0
University of Pittsburgh (Cl)	7	17
University of Southern Mississippi (Cl)	2	2
University of Tennessee (Cl)	4	0
University of Utah (Cl)	3	1
University of Virginia (Cl)	3	3
Vanderbilt University–Department of Psychology (Cl)	5	1
Vanderbilt University–Peabody College (Cl)	1	0
Virginia Commonwealth University (Cl)	1	1
Washington State University (Cl)	3	2
Yale University (Cl)	2	3

Psychopathology–Child/Developmental

	# Faculty	# Grants
Alliant International University–San Diego (Ph.D. and Psy.D.) (Cl)	6	5
Auburn University (Cl)	2	0
Baylor University (Cl)	2	0
Brigham Young University (Cl)	2	0
Catholic University of America (Cl)	2	0
Clark University (Cl)	2	0
Concordia University (Cl)	2	4
Duke University (Cl)	5	5
Florida State University (Cl)	4	5
George Fox University (Cl)	1	0
Indiana State University (Psy.D.) (Cl)	2	0
Long Island University (Cl)	1	0
Loyola College in Maryland (Cl)	2	0
Loyola University of Chicago (Cl)	5	3
McGill University (Cl)	1	1

	# Faculty	# Grants
Miami University (Cl)	2	0
Northern Illinois University (Cl)	5	1
Nova Southeastern University (Ph.D. & Psy.D.) (Cl)	2	0
Ohio State University (Cl)	1	1
Pennsylvania State University (Cl)	4	2
Rutgers University (Ph.D.) (Cl)	1	1
San Diego State University/University of California–San Diego (Cl)	3	0
Simon Fraser University (Cl)	3	1
Syracuse University (Cl)	1	1
Temple University (Cl)	2	2
University at Buffalo/State University of New York (Cl)	—	—
University of California–Los Angeles (Cl)	8	5
University of Delaware (Cl)	4	4
University of Denver (Ph.D.) (Cl)	1	1
University of Georgia (Cl)	5	0
University of Hawaii at Manoa (Cl)	2	0
University of Houston (Co)	1	1
University of Iowa (Cl)	1	1
University of Kentucky (Cl)	1	0
University of Manitoba (Cl)	1	0
University of Miami (Cl)	7	3+
University of Minnesota (Cl)	5	5
University of Montana (Cl)	1	1
University of Notre Dame (Co)	2	1
University of Oregon (Cl)	2	1
University of Pittsburgh (Cl)	7	18
University of South Florida (Cl)	3	0
University of Southern California (Cl)	3	2
University of Southern Mississippi (Cl)	1	0
University of Tennessee (Cl)	3	2
University of Toledo (Cl)	3	1
University of Vermont (Cl)	3	2
University of Wisconsin–Madison (Cl)	2	7
Utah State University (Cm)	2	1
Vanderbilt University–Peabody College (Cl)	6	6
Virginia Consortium Program in Clinical Psychology (Cl)	1	0
West Virginia University (Cl)	1	0
Yeshiva University (Cl)	2	0

Psychopharmacology

	# Faculty	# Grants
Indiana University of Pennsylvania (Psy.D.) (Cl)	1	0
McGill University (Cl)	2	1
San Diego State University/University of California–San Diego (Cl)	6	2
University of Georgia (Cl)	1	0
University of Hawaii at Manoa (Cl)	1	0
University of Pennsylvania (Cl)	1	1
University of Pittsburgh (Cl)	4	14
University of Western Ontario (Cl)	1	0

Psychophysiology

	# Faculty	# Grants
Binghamton University/State University of New York (Cl)	2	0
Florida State University (Cl)	2	2
Howard University (Cl)	1	0
Indiana University (Cl)	1	2
Louisiana State University (Cl)	1	0
McGill University (Cl)	2	1
Ohio State University (Cl)	2	2
Pennsylvania State University (Cl)	3	1
Rutgers University (Psy.D.) (Cl)	1	0
St. John's University (Cl)	1	1
San Diego State University/University of California–San Diego (Cl)	5	0
Syracuse University (Cl)	1	0
University of Alabama at Birmingham (Cl)	1	1
University of Delaware (Cl)	3	1
University of Illinois at Urbana–Champaign (Cl)	2	1
University of Iowa (Cl)	1	0
University of Kentucky (Cl)	2	0
University of Maryland (Cl)	2	0
University of Minnesota (Cl)	2	2
University of North Dakota (Cl)	3	0
University of Pittsburgh (Cl)	4	13
University of Southern Mississippi (Cl)	2	0
Vanderbilt University–Department. of Psychology (Cl)	1	1
Virginia Commonwealth University (Cl)	2	0

Psychotherapy/Process and Outcome

	# Faculty	# Grants
Adelphi University (Cl)	1	1
Alliant International University–Fresno (Ph.D. & Psy.D.) (Cl)	2	0
Alliant International University–San Diego (Psy.D.) (Cl)	1	0
Antioch/New England Graduate School (Cl)	2	0
Argosy University–Honolulu Campus (Cl)	1	0
Arizona State University (Co)	4	0
Brigham Young University (Co)	3	2
Catholic University of America (Cl)	5	0
City University of New York at City College (Cl)	3	0
Clark University (Cl)	1	1
Colorado State University (Co)	1	0
Columbia University, Teachers College (Cl)	2	0
Florida State University (Cl)	2	0
Georgia State University (Cl)	1	0
Hofstra University (Cm)	1	0
Illinois School of Professional Psychology–Chicago Campus (Cl)	3	2
Illinois School of Professional Psychology–Chicago Northwest (Cl)	1	0
Immaculata College (Cl)	1	0
Iowa State University (Co)	2	0
James Madison University (Cm)	1	0
Loma Linda University (Ph.D. & Psy.D.) (Cl)	1	0
Long Island University (Cl)	1	1

	# Faculty	# Grants
Loyola College in Maryland (Cl)	1	0
Loyola University of Chicago (Cl)	4	1
Loyola University of Chicago (Co)	1	0
Marquette University (Cl)	3	0
McGill University (Cl)	1	0
Miami University (Cl)	3	0
Michigan State University (Cl)	1	0
New School for Social Research (Cl)	3	1
New York University (Cl)	1	0
Northern Illinois University (Cl)	1	1
Northwestern University (Cl)	1	1
Northwestern University Medical School (Cl)	1	0
Nova Southeastern University (Ph.D. & Psy.D.) (Cl)	3	0
Ohio State University (Co)	2	0
Ohio University (Cl)	2	2
Pennsylvania State University (Cl)	3	2
Pennsylvania State University (Co)	1	0
Pepperdine University (Cl)	—	—
Rutgers University (Ph.D.) (Cl)	5	3
Rutgers University (Psy.D.) (Cl)	5	1
St. John's University (Cl)	1	0
San Diego State University/University of California–San Diego (Cl)	4	0
Southern Illinois University (Co)	3	0
Stony Brook University/State University of New York (Cl)	1	0
Suffolk University (Cl)	2	0
Texas A&M University (Cl)	7	2
Texas A&M University (Co)	2	0
University of Alabama (Cl)	2	0
University at Albany/State University of New York (Co)	1	0
University of Arizona (Cl)	3	2
University of Arkansas (Cl)	1	0
University of California–Berkeley (Cl)	1	2
University of California–Santa Barbara (Cm)	1	1
University of Colorado (Cl)	3	0
University of Delaware (Cl)	1	0
University of Detroit–Mercy (Cl)	4	0
University of Georgia (Co)	2	0
University of Hartford (Cl)	4	1
University of Illinois at Urbana–Champaign (Cl)	1	0
University of Kansas (Co)	1	1
University of Maine (Cl)	3	0
University of Manitoba (Cl)	3	0
University of Maryland (Cl)	3	2
University of Maryland (Co)	4	0
University of Massachusetts at Amherst (Cl)	3	0
University of Memphis (Cl)	4	0
University of Miami (Co)	1	0
University of Michigan (Cl)	5	0
University of Minnesota–Department of Educational Psychology (Co)	2	0
University of Missouri–Columbia (Co)	3	0
University of Missouri–Kansas City (Co)	3	0
University of Montana (Cl)	3	1
University of Nebraska–Lincoln (Cl)	3	1
University of North Texas (Co)	6	0
University of Northern Colorado (Co)	2	0
University of Oklahoma (Co)	4	1
University of Oregon (Co)	2	0
University of Ottawa (Cl)	3	0
University of St. Thomas (Co)	1	0
University of San Francisco (Co)	3	0
University of Saskatchewan (Cl)	2	1
University of Southern Mississippi (Co)	2	0
University of Tennessee (Co)	2	0
University of Toledo (Cl)	2	0
University of Virginia–Department of Human Services (Cl)	2	0
University of Washington (Cl)	1	1
University of Windsor (Cl)	3	1
University of Wisconsin–Madison (Cl & Co)	4	2
Vanderbilt University–Department of Psychology (Cl)	1	1
Virginia Commonwealth University (Cl)	1	1
Virginia Consortium Program in Clinical Psychology (Cl)	1	0
Virginia Polytechnic Institute and State University (Cl)	2	1
West Virginia University (Co)	3	0
Wright Institute (Cl)	3	0
Yale University (Cl)	2	1
Yeshiva University (Psy.D.) (Cl)	3	0
York University–Adult Clinical Program (Cl)	4	3

Rehabilitation

	# Faculty	# Grants
Alliant International University–San Diego (Ph.D.) (Cl)	2	1
Ball State University (Co)	2	1
Michigan State University (Co)	1	1
University at Buffalo/State University of New York (Co)	1	0
University of Kansas (Cl)	1	0
University of Texas Southwestern Medical Center at Dallas (Cl)	1	1
West Virginia University (Co)	4	0

Religion/Spirituality

	# Faculty	# Grants
Bowling Green State University (Cl)	1	1
Brigham Young University (Co)	6	3
Columbia University, Teachers College (Cl)	1	1
Fuller Theological Seminary (Ph.D. & Psy.D.) (Cl)	5	0
George Fox University (Cl)	1	0
Loma Linda University (Ph.D. & Psy.D.) (Cl)	2	0
Loyola College in Maryland (Cl)	1	0
New York University (Co)	1	0
Pennsylvania State University (Cl)	1	0
Southern Illinois University (Cl)	1	0
Southern Illinois University (Co)	1	0
Texas Tech University (Co)	1	0
University of Maryland–Baltimore County (Cl)	1	0
University of St. Thomas (Co)	1	0

	# Faculty	# Grants
Virginia Commonwealth University (Co)	1	0
Virginia Consortium Program in Clinical Psychology (Cl)	1	0
Wheaton College (Cl)	5	1

Research Methodology

Arizona State University (Co)	2	0
Hofstra University (Cm)	2	0
Southern Illinois University (Co)	1	0
Texas Tech University (Cl)	1	0
University at Albany/State University of New York (Co)	2	0
University of Toledo (Cl)	1	0
Wheaton College (Cl)	1	0

Rorschach

Alliant International University–Fresno (Ph.D.) (Cl)	1	0
Immaculata College (Cl)	2	0
Texas Tech University (Cl)	1	1

Rural Mental Health/Psychology

Oklahoma State University (Co)	1	0
Pennsylvania State University (Cl)	1	0
University of Mississippi (Cl)	2	3
University of North Carolina at Chapel Hill (Cl)	1	1
University of North Dakota (Cl)	1	1
University of South Dakota (Cl)	4	0
Utah State University (Cm)	2	1
Wheaton College (Cl)	2	0

Schizophrenia/Psychoses

Alliant International University–Fresno (Ph.D. & Psy.D.) (Cl)	1	1
Boston University (Cl)	1	1
Catholic University of America (Cl)	1	0
Concordia University (Cl)	1	1
Emory University (Cl)	2	1
Hofstra University (Cm)	2	1
Indiana University (Cl)	2	2
Kent State University (Cl)	2	1
Long Island University–C.W. Post Campus (Cl)	1	0
MCP Hahnemann University of the Health Sciences (Cl)	1	2
Michigan State University (Cl)	1	1
New York University (Cl)	1	0
Northwestern University (Cl)	1	1
St. John's University (Cl)	2	0
San Diego State University/University of California–San Diego (Cl)	7	2
University at Buffalo/State University of New York (Cl)	1	1
University of California–Berkeley (Cl)	1	1
University of California–Los Angeles (Cl)	2	3
University of Colorado (Cl)	1	1
University of Detroit–Mercy (Cl)	1	0
University of Georgia (Cl)	1	1
University of Hawaii at Manoa (Cl)	4	2
University of Houston (Cl)	4	2
University of Illinois at Chicago (Cl)	1	0
University of Illinois at Urbana–Champaign (Cl)	2	0
University of Manitoba (Cl)	1	0
University of Michigan (Cl)	1	0
University of Minnesota (Cl)	2	0
University of Montana (Cl)	1	0
University of North Carolina at Chapel Hill (Cl)	1	1
University of North Carolina at Greensboro (Cl)	1	1
University of North Texas (Cl)	2	1
University of Pittsburgh (Cl)	1	1
University of Virginia–Department of Psychology (Cl)	2	0
University of Western Ontario (Cl)	1	1
University of Wisconsin–Madison (Cl)	2	2
Vanderbilt University–Department of Psychology (Cl)	1	1
Virginia Consortium Program in Clinical Psychology (Cl)	1	0
Wayne State University (Cl)	1	0
York University (Cl)	1	0

School/Education

Bowling Green State University (Cl)	2	2
Brigham Young University (Co)	2	1
Colorado State University (Co)	2	1
Duke University (Cl)	5	2
Florida State University (Cm)	3	1
George Fox University (Cl)	1	1
Immaculata College (Cl)	2	0
Indiana State University (Co)	2	2
Indiana University (Co)	1	0
New Mexico State University (Co)	1	0
Southern Illinois University (Co)	3	0
Suffolk University (Cl)	1	0
Texas Tech University (Cl)	2	0
University of California–Berkeley (Cl)	1	0
University of California–Santa Barbara (Cm)	3	3
University of Georgia (Co)	2	1
University of Kansas (Co)	1	0
University of Louisville (Co)	1	0
University of Minnesota–Department of Educational Psychology (Co)	2	1
University of Montana (Cl)	1	0
University of Wisconsin–Madison (Co)	4	2
Utah State University (Cm)	2	1

Self-Esteem/Self-Efficacy

Catholic University of America (Cl)	3	0
George Mason University (Cl)	1	0
Southern Illinois University (Co)	1	0
Suffolk University (Cl)	1	0
University of Colorado (Cl)	2	0
University of North Carolina at Chapel Hill (Cl)	1	0

	# Faculty	# Grants
University of North Dakota (Co)	1	0
University of Wisconsin–Madison (Cl)	1	0
University of Wyoming (Cl)	2	0
West Virginia University (Cl)	3	0
West Virginia University (Co)	2	0

Self Psychology

Case Western Reserve University (Cl)	1	0
University of Colorado (Cl)	1	0

Sexuality/Dysfunction and Deviation

Auburn University (Cl)	1	0
Brigham Young University (Cl)	1	0
Carlos Albizu University–San Juan (Cl)	1	0
Colorado State University (Co)	1	0
Georgia School of Professional Psychology (Cl)	1	0
Hofstra University (Cm)	1	0
Immaculata College (Cl)	1	0
Indiana State University (Cl)	1	0
Indiana University (Co)	3	0
Iowa State University (Co)	1	0
Loyola College in Maryland (Cl)	1	0
Loyola University of Chicago (Cl)	1	0
McGill University (Cl)	1	1
Northwestern University Medical School (Cl)	2	0
San Diego State University/University of California–San Diego (Cl)	1	0
Simon Fraser University (Cl)	1	0
Southern Illinois University (Co)	1	0
Texas Tech University (Co)	1	0
Uniformed Services University of Health Sciences (Cl)	1	1
University of British Columbia (Cl)	1	1
University at Buffalo/State University of New York (Cl)	1	0
University of Florida (Co)	1	0
University of Houston (Cl)	1	0
University of Missouri–Columbia (Cl)	1	0
University of Missouri–Kansas City (Co)	1	0
University of Nevada–Reno (Cl)	1	2
University of Southern California (Co)	2	0
University of Texas at Austin (Cl)	1	1
University of Utah (Cl)	1	1
University of Vermont (Cl)	3	2
Western Michigan University (Cl)	1	0

Shyness

Catholic University of America (Cl)	2	0
Virginia Polytechnic Institute and State University (Cl)	1	0

Sleep Disorders

San Diego State University/University of California–San Diego (Cl)	4	0
University of Arizona (Cl)	1	2
University of Texas Southwestern Medical Center at Dallas (Cl)	1	1
Virginia Consortium Program in Clinical Psychology (Cl)	1	1
Yeshiva University (Cl)	1	0

Social Learning

Catholic University of America (Cl)	2	0
Rutgers University (Psy.D.) (Cl)	1	1
Clark University (Cl)	1	0
Long Island University (Cl)	1	1
University of Georgia (Cl)	1	0

Social Psychological Approaches

Arizona State University (Co)	2	0
Ball State University (Co)	2	0
Loyola College in Maryland (Cl)	1	0
University of Maine (Cl)	1	0
University of Southern Mississippi (Cl)	1	0

Social Skills/Competence

Binghamton University/State University of New York (Cl)	1	0
Concordia University (Cl)	1	1
Duke University (Cl)	3	2
James Madison University (Cm)	—	—
Louisiana State University (Cl)	2	1
Michigan State University (Cl)	1	1
San Diego State University/University of California–San Diego (Cl)	1	0
University of Alabama (Cl)	3	0
University of Colorado (Cl)	2	1
University of Houston (Cl)	4	2
University of Michigan (Cl)	3	1
University of Mississippi (Cl)	4	0
University of Nevada–Reno (Cl)	3	0
University of Ottawa (Cl)	1	1
Virginia Commonwealth University (Co)	1	1
Virginia Consortium Program in Clinical Psychology (Cl)	2	1
Virginia Polytechnic Institute and State University (Cl)	3	0
Wright State University (Cl)	3	3
York University–Clinical-Developmental Area (Cl)	3	3

Social Support

Fordham University (Cl)	1	0
Illinois Institute of Technology (Cl)	1	0
Iowa State University (Co)	1	1
San Diego State University/University of California–San Diego (Cl)	2	0
Southern Illinois University (Cl)	1	0
University of Maryland (Cl)	1	0
University of North Dakota (Co)	1	0
University of Oregon (Co)	3	0
University of Pittsburgh (Cl)	1	2

Speech and Language/Verbal Behavior

	# Faculty	# Grants
Hofstra University (Cm)	1	0
New York University (Cl)	2	0
St. John's University (Cl)	1	0
Stony Brook University/State University of New York (Cl)	1	1
University of Nevada–Reno (Cl)	4	0
York University–Clinical-Developmental Area (Cl)	1	0

Sports Psychology

	# Faculty	# Grants
Carlos Albizu University–San Juan (Cl)	1	0
Illinois Institute of Technology (Cl)	1	0
Oklahoma State University (Co)	1	0
Spalding University (Cl)	2	0
Suffolk University (Cl)	1	0
University of Manitoba (Cl)	1	1
University of Missouri–Kansas City (Co)	1	0
University of North Texas (Co)	2	1
University of Washington (Cl)	2	0
West Virginia University (Co)	1	0

Statistics

	# Faculty	# Grants
Arizona State University (Cl)	7	2
Fairleigh Dickinson University (Cl)	2	0
Indiana University (Cl)	2	1
Loma Linda University (Ph.D. & Psy.D.) (Cl)	1	0
San Diego State University/University of California–San Diego (Cl)	4	0
University of Montana (Cl)	1	0
Vanderbilt University–Department of Psychology (Cl)	1	0

Stereotypes

	# Faculty	# Grants
University of Massachusetts–Boston (Cl)	1	0
Virginia Consortium Program in Clinical Psychology (Cl)	1	0

Stress and Coping

	# Faculty	# Grants
Arizona State University (Cl)	6	5
Bowling Green State University (Cl)	3	0
Catholic University of America (Cl)	3	0
Colorado State University (Co)	2	0
Columbia University, Teachers College (Cl)	1	2
Duke University (Cl)	6	6
Fairleigh Dickinson University (Cl)	2	1
Fordham University (Cl)	2	0
Forest Institute of Professional Psychology (Cl)	2	1
Fuller Theological Seminary (Ph.D. & Psy.D.) (Cl)	1	0
George Washington University (Ph.D.) (Cl)	2	0
Georgia State University (Cl)	3	1
Georgia State University (Co)	2	0
Indiana State University (Cl)	2	0
Kent State University (Cl)	4	2
Louisiana State University (Cl)	1	0
Loyola University of Chicago (Cl)	2	0
McGill University (Cl)	1	1
St. John's University (Cl)	2	1
St. Louis University (Cl)	2	0
San Diego State University/University of California–San Diego (Cl)	13	0
Simon Fraser University (Cl)	1	0
Southern Illinois University (Cl)	1	0
Southern Illinois University (Co)	3	0
Texas Tech University (Co)	2	0
Uniformed Services University of Health Sciences (Cl)	3	8
University of California–Los Angeles (Cl)	2	2
University of Delaware (Cl)	2	0
University of Denver (Co)	1	1
University of Georgia (Cl)	2	1
University of Kansas (Cl)	5	1
University of Louisville (Cl)	2	0
University of Maryland–Baltimore County (Cl)	4	1
University of Massachusetts at Amherst (Cl)	1	0
University of Miami (Cl)	8	2
University of Michigan (Cl)	2	0
University of Minnesota (Cl)	1	0
University of Missouri–Kansas City (Co)	1	0
University of Montana (Cl)	1	0
University of North Dakota (Cl)	1	0
University of North Texas (Cl)	2	1
University of Oregon (Cl)	1	0
University of Pittsburgh (Cl)	2	5
University of South Carolina (Cl)	1	1
University of Texas at Austin (Cl)	1	1
University of Tulsa (Cl)	3	1
University of Utah (Cl)	2	2
University of Western Ontario (Cl)	3	0
Vanderbilt University–Department of Psychology (Cl)	2	0
Virginia Commonwealth University (Cl)	3	0
Virginia Commonwealth University (Co)	5	1
Virginia Polytechnic Institute and State University (Cl)	1	0
Widener University (Cl)	2	0
Yeshiva University (Cl)	4	1
York University–Adult Clinical Program (Cl)	1	1
York University–Clinical-Developmental Area (Cl)	1	0

Substance Abuse/Addictive Behaviors

	# Faculty	# Grants
Alliant International University–San Diego (Psy.D.) (Cl)	1	0
Arizona State University (Cl)	6	5
Auburn University (Co)	3	1
Binghamton University/State University of New York (Cl)	1	0
Boston University (Cl)	1	1

	# Faculty	# Grants
Colorado State University (Co)	4	3
Finch University of Health Sciences, The Chicago Medical School (Cl)	1	1
Florida State University (Cl)	2	1
Fordham University (Cl)	1	0
Fuller Theological Seminary (Ph.D. & Psy.D.) (Cl)	1	0
George Mason University (Cl)	1	1
Hofstra University (Cm)	3	1
Illinois School of Professional Psychology–Chicago Campus (Cl)	1	1
Illinois School of Professional Psychology–Chicago Northwest (Cl)	1	1
Indiana State University (Cl)	1	0
Indiana University (Cl)	1	1
Loyola College in Maryland (Cl)	1	0
Loyola University of Chicago (Cl)	2	1
Marquette University (Cl)	1	1
McGill University (Cl)	1	1
Nova Southeastern University (Ph.D. & Psy.D.) (Cl)	4	2
Oklahoma State University (Cl)	1	0
Pacific Graduate School of Psychology (Cl)	1	0
Purdue University (Cl)	1	2
Rutgers University (Ph.D.) (Cl)	3	5
Rutgers University (Psy.D.) (Cl)	4	4
St. John's University (Cl)	2	0
San Diego State University/University of California–San Diego (Cl)	19	6
Southern Illinois University (Cl)	1	1
Syracuse University (Cl)	2	5
Texas A&M University (Cl)	1	1
Texas Tech University (Cl)	1	0
Texas Tech University (Co)	1	0
Uniformed Services University of Health Sciences (Cl)	1	3
University of Alabama at Birmingham (Cl)	3	5
University at Albany/State University of New York (Cl)	1	1
University at Buffalo/State University of New York (Cl)	2	1
University of California–Santa Barbara (Cm)	2	2
University of Cincinnati (Cl)	5	2
University of Colorado (Cl)	2	0
University of Denver (Co)	1	1
University of Georgia (Cl)	1	1
University of Georgia (Co)	1	0
University of Kentucky (Cl)	4	3
University of Louisville (Cl)	1	0
University of Louisville (Co)	1	1
University of Maryland (Cl)	1	1
University of Maryland–Baltimore County (Cl)	2	1
University of Michigan (Cl)	2	2
University of Minnesota–Department of Educational Psychology (Co)	1	1
University of Mississippi (Cl)	1	0
University of Missouri–Columbia (Cl)	2	2
University of Missouri–Kansas City (Co)	1	0
University of Montana (Cl)	2	1
University of Nebraska–Lincoln (Cl)	1	1
University of Nevada–Reno (Cl)	1	2
University of New Mexico (Cl)	5	8
University of North Carolina at Chapel Hill (Cl)	1	0
University of North Dakota (Cl)	1	0
University of Pennsylvania (Cl)	1	1
University of Pittsburgh (Cl)	5	15
University of South Florida (Cl)	3	6
University of Southern California (Cl)	2	1
University of Southern California (Co)	1	1
University of Southern Mississippi (Co)	1	0
University of Texas at Austin (Cl)	1	1
University of Washington (Cl)	3	3
University of Western Ontario (Cl)	1	1
University of Windsor (Cl)	3	2
University of Wisconsin–Madison (Cl)	2	4
University of Wisconsin–Milwaukee (Cl)	1	0
University of Wyoming (Cl)	3	3
Utah State University (Cm)	1	1
Virginia Commonwealth University (Cl)	2	1
Virginia Commonwealth University (Co)	1	1
Virginia Consortium Program in Clinical Psychology (Cl)	1	1
Virginia Polytechnic Institute and State University (Cl)	2	2
Wright Institute (Cl)	2	1
Yeshiva University (Cl)	1	2
York University–Adult Clinical Program (Cl)	1	3

Suicide

Arizona State University (Co)	1	0
Catholic University of America (Cl)	3	0
Florida State University (Cl)	1	1
Howard University (Cl)	1	0
Northern Illinois University (Cl)	1	0
University of Akron (Co)	2	0
University of Iowa (Co)	1	0
University of Maryland–Baltimore County (Cl)	1	0
University of Nevada–Reno (Cl)	1	0
University of Southern Mississippi (Cl)	1	0
University of Southern Mississippi (Co)	1	0
University of Washington (Cl)	1	1
Yeshiva University (Cl)	1	0

Supervision/Mentoring

Arizona State University (Co)	4	0
Catholic University of America (Cl)	3	0
Colorado State University (Co)	2	0
Florida Institute of Technology (Cl)	1	0
Fordham University (Co)	2	0
George Fox University (Cl)	1	0
Indiana State University (Co)	3	0
Lehigh University (Co)	1	1
Loyola University of Chicago (Co)	1	0
Ohio State University (Co)	2	0
Oklahoma State University (Co)	3	0
Pacific University (Cl)	2	0

	# Faculty	# Grants
Southern Illinois University (Co)	2	0
Spalding University (Cl)	1	0
University at Albany/State University of New York (Co)	2	0
University of Manitoba (Cl)	1	0
University of Maryland (Co)	2	0
University of Minnesota–Department of Educational Psychology (Co)	2	0
University of Missouri–Columbia (Co)	3	0
University of Missouri–Kansas City (Co)	2	0
University of North Dakota (Co)	3	0
University of Oklahoma (Co)	3	0
University of Southern California (Co)	1	0
University of Wisconsin–Madison (Co)	1	1
Washington State University (Co)	1	0
West Virginia University (Co)	1	0

Telehealth/Technology

	# Faculty	# Grants
Argosy University–Honolulu Campus (Cl)	2	0
Southern Illinois University (Co)	1	0
Suffolk University (Cl)	1	1

Violence/Abuse/Sexual Abuse

	# Faculty	# Grants
Alliant International University–Fresno (Ph.D. & Psy.D.) (Cl)	3	1
Boston College (Co)	3	2
Boston University (Cl)	1	0
Central Michigan University (Cl)	2	0
Colorado State University (Co)	2	0
Columbia University, Teachers College (Co)	1	0
Duke University (Cl)	2	0
Fairleigh Dickinson University (Cl)	3	0
Fielding Graduate Institute (Cl)	—	—
Florida State University (Cl)	5	3
Georgia State University (Cl)	2	1
Illinois School of Professional Psychology–Chicago Campus (Cl)	2	0
Illinois School of Professional Psychology–Chicago Northwest (Cl)	2	0
Indiana University (Cl)	1	1
Loma Linda University (Ph.D. & Psy.D.) (Cl)	2	0
Long Island University–C.W. Post Campus (Cl)	2	0
Loyola College in Maryland (Cl)	1	0
MCP Hahnemann University of the Health Sciences (Cl)	3	0
Michigan State University (Cl)	1	0
Northern Illinois University (Cl)	3	1
Nova Southeastern University (Ph.D. & Psy.D.) (Cl)	7	0
Ohio University (Cl)	1	2
Oklahoma State University (Cl)	1	0
Pacific University (Cl)	2	1
Pennsylvania State University (Cl)	1	0
St. Louis University (Cl)	2	1
Simon Fraser University (Cl)	1	0
Southern Illinois University (Cl)	2	0
Southern Illinois University (Co)	2	0
Stony Brook University/State University of New York (Cl)	1	1
Temple University (Cl)	1	1
Texas Women's University (Co)	3	1
University of Alabama (Cl)	3	1
University of Arkansas (Cl)	6	1
University of Cincinnati (Cl)	2	1
University of Colorado (Cl)	1	1
University of Georgia (Cl)	6	3
University of Georgia (Co)	1	2
University of Houston (Co)	1	1
University of Illinois at Urbana–Champaign (Co)	1	1
University of Kansas (Cl)	1	0
University of Kentucky (Cl)	1	1
University of Louisville (Co)	1	2
University of Manitoba (Cl)	5	0
University of Maryland (Cl)	2	1
University of Maryland–Baltimore County (Cl)	5	1
University of Michigan (Cl)	4	3
University of Mississippi (Cl)	2	1
University of Missouri–St. Louis (Cl)	1	1
University of Nebraska–Lincoln (Cl)	4	2
University of Nevada–Reno (Cl)	2	0
University of North Texas (Cl)	2	0
University of South Carolina (Cl)	1	1
University of South Dakota (Cl)	2	0
University of Southern California (Cl)	1	1
University of Utah (Co)	3	0
University of Victoria (Cl)	2	1
University of Virginia–Department of Human Services (Cl)	3	2
University of Virginia–Department of Psychology (Cl)	4	2
University of Washington (Cl)	2	1
University of Western Ontario (Cl)	2	2
University of Wyoming (Cl)	1	0
Virginia Commonwealth University (Co)	1	1
Virginia Consortium Program in Clinical Psychology (Cl)	1	0
Wright State University (Cl)	2	3
York University–Clinical-Developmental Area (Cl)	2	2

Vocational Interests/Career Development

	# Faculty	# Grants
Arizona State University (Co)	5	1
Ball State University (Co)	4	0
Boston College (Co)	3	3
Colorado State University (Co)	2	0
Florida State University (Cm)	3	2
Fordham University (Co)	2	1
Indiana State University (Co)	3	0
Indiana University (Co)	1	0
Iowa State University (Co)	3	1
Lehigh University (Co)	1	1
Loyola University of Chicago (Co)	1	1
New Mexico State University (Co)	1	0
New York University (Co)	1	0
Ohio State University (Co)	4	0

Oklahoma State University (Co)	4	1
Seton Hall University (Co)	2	9
Southern Illinois University (Co)	4	3
Stanford University (Co)	1	1
Texas Tech University (Co)	1	0
Texas Woman's University (Co)	3	1
University of Akron (Co)	2	0
University at Albany/State University of New York (Co)	2	0
University at Buffalo/State University of New York (Co)	1	0
University of California–Santa Barbara (Cm)	2	0
University of Denver (Co)	1	1
University of Florida (Co)	1	0
University of Illinois at Urbana–Champaign (Co)	2	1
University of Kansas (Co)	1	0
University of Maryland (Co)	7	1
University of Memphis (Co)	3	0
University of Minnesota–Department of Educational Psychology (Co)	3	1
University of Minnesota–Department of Psychology (Co)	2	1
University of Missouri–Columbia (Co)	5	2
University of Missouri–Kansas City (Co)	4	0
University of Nebraska–Lincoln (Co)	1	0
University of North Dakota (Co)	5	3
University of North Texas (Co)	3	0
University of Oklahoma (Co)	2	0
University of Oregon (Co)	1	0
University of Tennessee (Co)	2	0
University of Utah (Co)	1	2
University of Wisconsin–Madison (Co)	2	0
University of Wisconsin–Milwaukee (Co)	2	2
Virginia Commonwealth University (Co)	1	1
Washington State University (Co)	2	0
West Virginia University (Co)	4	0

Weight Management

Bowling Green University (Cl)	1	0
University at Buffalo/State University of New York (Cl)	1	2
University of Florida (Cl)	1	0

Women's Studies/Issues

Alliant International University–Alameda (Ph.D. & Psy.D.) (Cl)	4	0
Alliant International University–Fresno (Ph.D. & Psy.D.) (Cl)	4	0
Alliant International University–San Diego (Ph.D. & Psy.D.) (Cl)	2	1
Antioch/New England Graduate School (Cl)	2	1
Arizona State University (Co)	5	1
Ball State University (Co)	2	0
Boston University (Cl)	1	0
Brigham Young University (Co)	2	1
Colorado State University (Co)	3	0
Columbia University, Teachers College (Ph.D. & Ed.D.) (Co)	1	0
Fairleigh Dickinson University (Cl)	4	0
George Mason University (Cl)	1	0
Illinois School of Professional Psychology–Chicago Campus (Cl)	1	0
Indiana State University (Cl)	2	0
Indiana University (Co)	1	0
Indiana University of Pennsylvania (Cl)	3	0
Iowa State University (Co)	1	1
Loyola College in Maryland (Cl)	1	0
New York University (Co)	2	0
Ohio State University (Co)	2	0
Oklahoma State University (Co)	2	0
Pacific University (Cl)	3	1
Southern Illinois University (Co)	1	0
Texas Tech University (Co)	3	0
University at Albany/State University of New York (Co)	2	0
University of Akron (Co)	3	0
University of Colorado (Cl)	2	1
University of Florida (Co)	1	0
University of Georgia (Cl)	2	0
University of Hartford (Cl)	2	0
University of Illinois at Urbana–Champaign (Cl)	3	2
University of Illinois at Urbana–Champaign (Co)	1	0
University of Kansas (Cl)	2	0
University of Maine (Cl)	1	0
University of Memphis (Co)	2	0
University of Minnesota–Department of Educational Psychology (Co)	1	0
University of Missouri–St. Louis (Cl)	3	1
University of North Dakota (Cl)	2	0
University of North Dakota (Co)	1	0
University of Texas at Austin (Co)	1	0
University of Western Ontario (Cl)	1	0
Virginia Consortium Program in Clinical Psychology (Cl)	1	0

Miscellaneous

Adlerian psychology–New Mexico State University (Co)	1	0
adoption–Rutgers University (Psy.D.) (Cl)	1	1
adult survivors of incest–University of Michigan (Cl)	1	0
alternative methods–Auburn University (Co)	1	0
altruism–Columbia University, Teachers College (Cl)	1	0
behavior control–Emory University (Cl)	1	0
behavioral dentistry–West Virginia University (Cl)	1	0
brief therapy–Our Lady of the Lake University (Co)	3	1
burnout prevention–University of Minnesota–Department of Educational Psychology (Co)	1	0
caregiver burden–Southern Illinois University (Co)	1	1
change processes–Adelphi University (Cl)	2	0
chaos theory–Marquette University (Cl)	1	2

child testimony–York University–Clinical-Developmental Area (Cl)	1	0
compliance–University of Manitoba (Cl)	2	0
comprehension–Virginia Consortium Program in Clinical Psychology (Cl)	1	1
conditioning–University of Montana (Cl)	3	0
conscious/unconscious processes–University of Michigan (Cl)	1	0
constructivist psychology–University of Florida (Co)	2	0
consumer psychology–Suffolk University (Cl)	1	0
counseling youth/prevention–Florida State University (Cm)	2	1
crime and delinquency–Georgia State University (Cl)	1	0
data-based case management–University of Hawaii at Manoa (Cl)	1	1
disabilities/disabled persons–University of Memphis (Co)	2	0
empathy–Suffolk University (Cl)	1	0
epilepsy–University of Victoria (Cl)	1	1
evaluation of counseling services–University of Utah (Co)	1	0
evolutionary psychology–University of Louisville (Co)	—	—
Eye Movement Desensitization and Reprocessing–Central Michigan University (Cl)	1	0
FAS & attention–University of Saskatchewan (Cl)	2	2
genetic counseling–University of Minnesota–Department of Educational Psychology (Cl)	1	2
gifted/talented children–Arizona State University (Co)	2	1
help-seeking–Marquette University (Cl)	1	1
history of psychology–York University–Clinical-Developmental Area (Cl)	1	0
human error–Hofstra University (Cm)	1	0
identity phenotype–New Mexico State University (Co)	3	0
imposter phenomenon–Georgia State University (Cl)	1	0
incarcerated populations–University of Virginia–Department of Human Services (Cl)	2	1
integrative services–Boston College (Co)	3	2
intelligence–University of Hawaii at Manoa (Cl)	1	0
international psychology–University of Memphis (Co)	1	1
international student adjustment–University of North Dakota (Cl)	1	0
leadership development–Northeastern University (Cm)	3	1
mental health policy–Rutgers University (Psy.D.) (Cl)	2	1
mental health service delivery–University of Hawaii at Manoa (Cl)	2	1
metaphysical theory–Alliant International University–Los Angeles (Psy.D.) (Cl)	1	0
multidisciplinary environments–University of Wisconsin–Madison (Co)	1	1
nightmares–Texas Tech University (Cl)	1	0
nonverbal communication–Loyola College in Maryland (Cl)	1	0
nutrition–San Diego State University/University of California–San Diego (Cl)	1	0
object relations–City University of New York at City College (Cl)	4	1
olfaction–McGill University (Cl)	1	0
peace psychology–Wright State University (Psy.D.) (Cl)	1	0
personal constructs–Virginia Consortium Program in Clinical Psychology (Cl)	1	0
personal meaning-making processes–Texas Tech University (Cl)	2	2
phenomenology–Alliant International University–Fresno (Ph.D. & Psy.D.) (Cl)	3	0
poverty–University of Denver (Ph.D.) (Cl)	2	1
primary care–University of Wyoming (Cl)	3	1
psychological separation–University of Southern Mississippi (Co)	2	0
psychology and the arts–Rutgers (Psy.D.) (Cl)	1	0
psychology of physical symptoms–University of Western Ontario (Cl)	1	1
rational-emotive therapy–Hofstra University (Cm)	1	0
self-help intervention–University of South Carolina (Cl)	2	0
shame–George Fox University (Cl)	1	0
stimulus equivalence–University of New Mexico (Cl)	1	0
student well being–Seton Hall University (Co)	1	0
symbolic play–Yeshiva University (Cm)	1	1
teaching of psychology–Suffolk University (Cl)	1	0
underachievement–York University–Clinical-Developmental Area (Cl)	1	0
visitor studies–Suffolk University (Cl)	1	0

APPENDIX F

SPECIALTY CLINICS AND PRACTICA SITES

Acquired Immune Deficiency Syndrome/HIV

Antioch/New England Graduate School (Cl)
Argosy University–Twin Cities (Cl)
George Washington University (Ph.D.) (Cl)
Georgia State University (Cl)
Loyola University of Chicago (Cl)
Pacific Graduate School of Psychology (Cl)
Pepperdine University (Cl)
Rutgers University (Ph.D.) (Cl)
Rutgers University (Psy.D.) (Cl)
University of Alabama (Cl)
University of Illinois at Chicago (Cl)
University of Miami (Cl)
University of Nevada–Reno (Cl)
University of Vermont (Cl)
Virginia Polytechnic Institute and State University (Cl)
Wright Institute (Cl)

Adolescent Psychotherapy/ At-Risk Adolescents/Delinquency

Alliant International University–Alameda (Ph.D. & Psy.D.) (Cl)
Alliant International University–Fresno (Ph.D. & Psy.D.) (Cl)
Argosy University–Honolulu Campus (Cl)
Binghamton University/State University of New York (Cl)
Boston University (Cl)
Brigham Young University (Cl)
Concordia University (Cl)
Duke University (Cl)
Florida State University (Cl)
George Washington University (Ph.D. & Psy.D.) (Cl)
Georgia School of Professional Psychology (Cl)
Georgia State University (Cl)
Iowa State University (Co)
Oklahoma State University (Co)
Pepperdine University (Psy.D.) (Cl)
Queen's University (Cl)
Rutgers University (Ph.D.) (Cl)
Rutgers University (Psy.D.) (Cl)
Southern Illinois University (Cl)
Tenessee State University (Co)
Uniformed Services University of Health Sciences (Cl)
University of Akron (Co)
University at Albany/State University of New York (Co)
University of Colorado (Cl)
University of Denver (Ph.D.) (Cl)
University of Houston (Cl)
University of Indianapolis (Cl)
University of Massachusetts at Amherst (Cl)
University of Memphis (Co)
University of Montana (Cl)
University of Saskatchewan (Cl)
University of South Florida (Cl)
University of Utah (Cl)
University of Vermont (Cl)
University of Waterloo (Cl)
Yeshiva University (Cl & Cm)

Affective Disorders/ Depression/Mood Disorders

Baylor University (Cl)
Boston University (Cl)
Case Western Reserve University (Cl)
Duke University (Cl)
Florida State University (Cl)
George Washington University (Ph.D.) (Cl)
Georgia State University (Cl)
Illinois Institute of Technology (Cl)
Indiana University (Cl)
Northwestern University (Cl)
Nova Southeastern University (Ph.D. & Psy.D.) (Cl)
Purdue University (Cl)
Rutgers University (Ph.D.) (Cl)
Rutgers University (Psy.D.) (Cl)
University of Arizona (Cl)
University of Arkansas (Cl)
University at Buffalo/State University of New York (Cl)

Note. Cl, Clinical; Co, Counseling; Cm, combined professional–scientific psychology programs.

University of California–Los Angeles (Cl)
University of Illinois at Chicago (Cl)
University of Georgia (Cl)
University of Louisville (Cl)
University of Manitoba (Cl)
University of Maryland–Baltimore County (Cl)
University of Memphis (Cl)
University of Minnesota (Cl)
University of Nevada–Reno (Cl)
University of North Dakota (Cl)
University of North Texas (Cl)
University of Oregon (Cl)
University of Pittsburgh (Cl)
University of South Florida (Cl)
University of Texas Southwestern Medical Center at Dallas (Cl)
University of Vermont (Cl)
University of Virginia–Department of Psychology (Cl)
University of Western Ontario (Cl)
University of Wyoming (Cl)
Vanderbilt University–Department of Psychology (Cl)
Virginia Commonwealth University (Cl)
Virginia Consortium Program in Clinical Psychology (Cl)
Virginia Polytechnic Institute and State University (Cl)
Wright Institute (Cl)
York University–Adult Clinical Program (Cl)

Aging/Gerontology

Antioch/New England Graduate School (Cl)
Argosy University–Twin Cities (Cl)
Arizona State University (Cl)
Ball State University (Co)
Baylor University (Psy.D.) (Cl)
Boston University (Cl)
Case Western Reserve University (Cl)
Fairleigh Dickinson University (Cl)
Forest Institute of Professional Psychology (Cl)
Fuller Theological Seminary (Ph.D. & Psy.D.) (Cl)
George Washington University (Ph.D.)(Cl)
Illinois School of Professional Psychology–Chicago Campus (Cl)
Marquette University (Cl)
Michigan State University (Cl)
Nova Southeastern University (Ph.D. & Psy.D.) (Cl)
Ohio State University (Cl)
Pepperdine University (Cl)
Queen's University (Cl)
Rutgers University (Ph.D.) (Cl)
Rutgers University (Psy.D.) (Cl)
St. John's University (Cl)
University of Alabama (Cl)
University at Albany/State University of New York (Co)
University of Arizona (Cl)
University of Florida (Co)
University of Hawaii at Manoa (Cl)
University of Houston (Co)
University of Louisville (Cl)
University of Massachusetts at Amherst (Cl)
University of Minnesota (Cl)
University of Missouri–St. Louis (Cl)
University of Nevada–Reno (Cl)
University of Southern California (Cl)
University of Utah (Co)
Virginia Consortium Program in Clinical Psychology (Cl)
Virginia Polytechnic Institute and State University (Cl)
West Virginia University (Cl)

Anxiety Disorders/Panic Disorders

Alliant International University–Fresno (Ph.D. & Psy.D.) (Cl)
Auburn University (Cl)
Baylor University (Psy.D.) (Cl)
Case Western Reserve University (Cl)
Drexel University (Cl)
Fairleigh Dickinson University (Cl)
Finch University of Health Sciences, The Chicago Medical School (Cl)
Florida State University (Cl)
George Washington University (Ph.D.) (Cl)
Georgia State University (Cl)
Howard University (Cl)
Illinois Institute of Technology (Cl)
Indiana University (Cl)
Louisiana State University (Cl)
Loyola College in Maryland (Cl)
Northern Illinois University (Cl)
Northwestern University (Cl)
Nova Southeastern University (Ph.D. & Psy.D.) (Cl)
Ohio State University (Cl)
Oklahoma State University (Cl)
Purdue University (Cl)
Rutgers University (Ph.D.) (Cl)
Rutgers University (Psy.D.) (Cl)
St. Louis University (Cl)
San Diego State University/University of California–San Diego (Cl)
Syracuse University (Cl)
Temple University (Cl)
University at Albany/State University of New York (Cl)
University at Buffalo/State University of New York (Cl)
University of California–Los Angeles (Cl)
University of Delaware (Cl)
University of Florida (Cl)
University of Hartford (Cl)
University of Houston (Cl)
University of Illinois at Chicago (Cl)
University of Illinois at Urbana–Champaign (Cl)
University of Kansas (Cl)
University of Louisville (Cl)
University of Maine (Cl)
University of Manitoba (Cl)
University of Memphis (Cl)
University of Minnesota (Cl)
University of Nebraska–Lincoln (Cl)
University of Nevada–Reno (Cl)
University of North Dakota (Cl)
University of Oregon (Cl)
University of Pittsburgh (Cl)
University of St. Thomas (Co)
University of South Florida (Cl)
University of Texas at Austin (Cl)
University of Vermont (Cl)
University of Virginia–Department of Psychology (Cl)
University of Western Ontario (Cl)
University of Wyoming (Cl)
Vanderbilt University–Department of Psychology (Cl)

Virginia Commonwealth University (Cl)
Virginia Consortium Program in Clinical Psychology (Cl)
Virginia Polytechnic Institute and State University (Cl)
West Virginia University (Cl)
Yale University (Cl)
Yeshiva University (Cl)
York University–Adult Clinical Program (Cl)

Assessment/Testing

Alliant International University–Fresno (Ph.D. & Psy.D.) (Cl)
Alliant International University–San Diego (Psy.D.) (Cl)
American University (Cl)
Antioch/New England Graduate School (Psy.D.) (Cl)
Arizona State University (Cl)
Binghamton University/State University of New York (Cl)
Bowling Green State University (Cl)
Catholic University of America (Cl)
DePaul University (Cl)
Emory University (Cl)
Fairleigh Dickinson University (Cl)
Florida State University (Cl)
Fuller Theological Seminary (Ph.D. & Psy.D.) (Cl)
Gallaudet University (Cl)
George Mason University (Cl)
George Washington University (Ph.D. & Psy.D.) (Cl)
Georgia State University (Cl)
Indiana University of Pennsylvania (Cl)
James Madison University (Cm)
Kent State University (Cl)
Loyola University of Chicago (Cl)
Miami University (Cl)
Michigan State University (Cl)
New York University (Cl)
Northern Illinois University (Cl)
Nova Southeastern University (Ph.D. & Psy.D.) (Cl)
Pacific Graduate School of Psychology (Cl)
Pepperdine University (Cl)
Rutgers University (Ph.D.) (Cl)
Rutgers University (Psy.D.) (Cl)
St. Louis University (Cl)
University of British Columbia (Cl)
University of Colorado (Cl)
University of Delaware (Cl)
University of Denver (Psy.D.) (Cl)
University of Florida (Co)
University of Georgia (Cl)
University of Georgia (Co)
University of Illinois at Urbana–Champaign (Cl)
University of Kentucky (Cl)
University of Maryland–Baltimore County (Cl)
University of Memphis (Co)
University of Mississippi (Cl)
University of Missouri–Columbia (Cl)
University of Nebraska–Lincoln (Cl)
University of Nebraska–Lincoln (Co)
University of New Mexico (Cl)
University of North Carolina at Chapel Hill (Cl)
University of North Dakota (Cl)
University of North Texas (Co)
University of Pittsburgh (Cl)
University of South Florida (Cl)
University of Southern Mississippi (Co)
University of Virginia–Department of Human Services (Cl)
University of Wisconsin–Madison (Cl)
Virginia Commonwealth University (Cl)
Widener University (Cl)
Wright Institute (Cl)

Attention-Deficit/Hyperactivity Disorder

Alliant International University–Fresno (Ph.D. & Psy.D.) (Cl)
Argosy University–Twin Cities (Cl)
Auburn University (Cl)
George Washington University (Ph.D.) (Cl)
James Madison University (Cm)
Miami University (Cl)
Northern Illinois University (Cl)
Pepperdine University (Cl)
Purdue University (Cl)
Rutgers University (Ph.D.) (Cl)
Rutgers University (Psy.D.) (Cl)
St. Louis University (Cl)
University at Buffalo/State University of New York (Cl)
University of Georgia (Cl)
University of Maine (Cl)
University of Minnesota (Cl)
University of North Texas (Cl)
University of Pittsburgh (Cl)
University of Rochester (Cl)
Virginia Consortium Program in Clinical Psychology (Cl)
Virginia Polytechnic Institute and State University (Cl)
Western Michigan University (Cl)

Behavioral Medicine/Health Psychology

Alliant International University–Fresno (Ph.D. & Psy.D.) (Cl)
Antioch/New England Graduate School (Cl)
Argosy University–Twin Cities (Cl)
Argosy University–Washington, DC Campus (Cl)
Arizona State University (Cl)
Ball State University (Co)
Baylor University (Cl)
Binghamton University/State University of New York (Cl)
Boston University (Cl)
Bowling Green State University (Cl)
Chicago School of Professional Psychology (Cl)
Drexel University (Cl)
Duke University (Cl)
Emory University (Cl)
Fairleigh Dickinson University (Cl)
Finch University of Health Sciences, The Chicago Medical School (Cl)
Florida Institute of Technology (Cl)
Forest Institute of Professional Psychology (Cl)
George Washington University (Ph.D.) (Cl)
Georgia State University (Cl)
Howard University (Cl)
Illinois Institute of Technology (Cl)
Illinois School of Professional Psychology–Chicago Campus (Cl)
Indiana State University (Cl)
Indiana University (Cl)
Indiana University of Pennsylvania (Cl)
Indiana University–Purdue University Indianapolis (Cl)
Kent State University (Cl)
Loma Linda University (Ph.D. & Psy.D.) (Cl)

Louisiana State University (Cl)
Loyola College in Maryland (Cl)
Loyola University of Chicago (Cl)
MCP Hahnemann University of the Health Sciences (Cl)
Northwestern University (Cl)
Northwestern University Medical School (Cl)
Nova Southeastern University (Ph.D. & Psy.D.) (Cl)
Ohio State University (Cl)
Ohio University (Cl)
Oklahoma State University (Cl)
Pacific Graduate School of Psychology (Cl)
Pepperdine University (Cl)
Rutgers University (Ph.D.) (Cl)
Rutgers University (Psy.D.) (Cl)
San Diego State University/University of California–San Diego (Cl)
Spalding University (Cl)
Syracuse University (Cl)
Tennessee State University (Co)
University of Alabama at Birmingham (Cl)
University at Albany/State University of New York (Cl)
University at Albany/State University of New York (Co)
University of Arizona (Cl)
University of Arkansas (Cl)
University of Cincinnati (Cl)
University of Connecticut (Cl)
University of Denver (Psy.D.) (Cl)
University of Florida (Cl)
University of Georgia (Cl)
University of Hawaii at Manoa (Cl)
University of Houston (Co)
University of Illinois at Chicago (Cl)
University of Illinois at Urbana–Champaign (Co)
University of Indianapolis (Cl)
University of Iowa (Cl)
University of Kansas (Cl)
University of Kentucky (Cl)
University of Louisville (Cl)
University of Manitoba (Cl)
University of Maryland–Baltimore County (Cl)
University of Memphis (Cl)
University of Miami (Cl)
University of Missouri–Columbia (Cl)
University of Nevada–Reno (Cl)
University of New Mexico (Cl)
University of North Carolina at Chapel Hill (Cl)
University of North Dakota (Cl)
University of Pennsylvania (Cm) (chronic illness)
University of Pittsburgh (Cl)
University of Rhode Island (Cl)
University of Saskatchewan (Cl)
University of South Florida (Cl)
University of Southern Mississippi (Cl)
University of Southern Mississippi (Co)
University of Texas Southwestern Medical Center at Dallas (Cl)
University of Utah (Cl)
University of Vermont (Cl)
University of Virginia–Department of Psychology (Cl)
University of Western Ontario (Cl)
University of Wisconsin–Milwaukee (Cl)
Utah State University (Cm)
Vanderbilt University–Department of Psychology (Cl)
Virginia Commonwealth University (Cl)
Virginia Consortium Program in Clinical Psychology (Cl)
Virginia Polytechnic Institute and State University (Cl)
Washington State University (Cl)
Wayne State University (Cl)
West Virginia University (Cl) (including burn trauma)
Wright State University (Cl)
Yale University (Cl)
Yeshiva University (Cl)
York University–Adult Clinical Program (Cl)

Biofeedback

Alliant International University–San Diego (Ph.D. & Psy.D.) (Cl)
Argosy University–Twin Cities (Cl)
Nova Southeastern University (Ph.D. & Psy.D.) (Cl)

Child/Pediatric

Adelphi University (Cl)
Alliant International University–Alameda (Ph.D. & Psy.D.) (Cl)
Antioch/New England Graduate School (Cl)
Argosy University–Honolulu Campus(Cl)
Argosy University–Washington, DC Campus (Cl)
Arizona State University (Cl)
Baylor University (Cl)
Binghamton University–State University of New York (Cl)
Boston College (Co)
Bowling Green State University (Cl)
Central Michigan University (Cl)
Chicago School of Professional Psychology (Cl)
City University of New York at City College (Cl)
Clark University (Cl)
Columbia University, Teachers College (Cl)
Concordia University (Cl)
DePaul University (Cl)
Duke University (Cl)
Finch University of Health Sciences, The Chicago Medical School (Cl)
Fuller Theological Seminary (Ph.D. & Psy.D.) (Cl)
George Washington University (Ph.D.)
Georgia School of Professional Psychology (Cl)
Georgia State University (Cl)
Illinois Institute of Technology (Cl)
Illinois School of Professional Psychology–Chicago Campus (Cl)
Illinois School of Professional Psychology–Chicago Northwest (Cl)
Indiana University (Cl)
Iowa State University (Co)
Kent State University (Cl)
Long Island University (Cl)
Loyola College in Maryland (Cl)
Loyola University of Chicago (Cl)
McGill University (Cl)
MCP Hahnemann University of the Health Sciences (Cl)
New York University (Cl)
Northern Illinois University (Cl)
Nova Southeastern University (Ph.D. & Psy.D.) (Cl)
Ohio State University (Cl)
Ohio University (Cl)
Pace University (Psy.D.) (Cm)

Pacific Graduate School of Psychology (Cl)
Pepperdine University (Cl)
Purdue University (Cl)
Queen's University (Cl)
San Diego State University/University of California–San Diego (Cl)
Southern Illinois University (Cl)
Temple University (Cl & Co)
Tennessee State University (Co)
Uniformed Services University of Health Sciences (Cl)
University of Akron (Co)
University at Albany–State University of New York (Cl)
University of California–Los Angeles (Cl)
University of Cincinnati (Cl)
University of Delaware (Cl)
University of Florida (Cl)
University of Georgia (Cl)
University of Hawaii at Manoa (Cl)
University of Houston (Co)
University of Illinois at Urbana–Champaign (Cl)
University of Indianapolis (Cl)
University of Iowa (Cl)
University of Kentucky (Cl)
University of Louisville (Cl)
University of Louisville (Co)
University of Maine (Cl)
University of Manitoba (Cl)
University of Maryland–Baltimore County (Cl)
University of Massachusetts at Amherst (Cl)
University of Memphis (Co)
University of Miami (Cl)
University of Michigan (Cl)
University of Minnesota (Cl)
University of Mississippi (Cl)
University of Missouri–Columbia (Cl)
University of Missouri–St. Louis (Cl)
University of Montana (Cl)
University of New Mexico (Cl)
University of North Carolina at Chapel Hill (Cl)
University of North Texas (Cl)
University of Northern Colorado (Co) (play therapy)
University of Oklahoma (Co)
University of Oregon (Co)
University of Pennsylvania (Cm)
University of Pittsburgh (Cl)
University of Rhode Island (Cl)
University of Rochester (Cl)
University of South Florida (Cl)
University of Southern Mississippi (Cl)
University of Texas at Austin (Co)
University of Texas Southwestern Medical Center at Dallas (Cl)
University of Vermont (Cl)
University of Virginia–Department of Human Services (Cl)
University of Virginia–Department of Psychology (Cl)
University of Waterloo (Cl)
University of Western Ontario (Cl)
University of Wisconsin–Milwaukee (Cl)
University of Wisconsin–Milwaukee (Co)
Vanderbilt University–Peabody College (Cl)
Virginia Commonwealth University (Cl)
Virginia Commonwealth University (Co)
Virginia Consortium Program in Clinical Psychology (Cl)
Virginia Polytechnic Institute and State University (Cl)
Wright Institute (Cl)
Wright State University (Cl)
Yale University (Cl)
Yeshiva University (Cl & Cm)
York University–Clinical-Developmental Area (Cl)

Chronic/Severe Mental Illness

Fuller Theological Seminary (Ph.D. & Psy.D.) (Cl)
Illinois School of Professional Psychology–Chicago Campus (Cl)
Illinois School of Professional Psychology–Chicago Northwest (Cl)
Indiana University–Purdue University Indianapolis (Cl)
MCP Hahnemann University of the Health Sciences (Cl)
Northeastern University (Cm)
Northwestern University Medical School (Cl)
Nova Southeastern University (Ph.D. & Psy.D.) (Cl)
Pepperdine University (Cl)
Southern Illinois University (Cl)
University of Cincinnati (Cl)
University of Hartford (Cl)
University of Hawaii at Manoa (Cl)
University of Kentucky (Cl)
University of Mississippi (Cl)
University of Nebraska–Lincoln (Cl)
University of South Dakota (Cl)
University of Vermont (Cl)
Virginia Commonwealth University (Cl)

Cognitive/Cognitive-Behavioral Therapy

American University (Cl)
Antioch/New England Graduate School (Cl)
Arizona State University (Cl) (behavioral analysis)
Central Michigan University (Cl)
Concordia University (Cl)
Duke University (Cl)
Emory University (Cl)
Fielding Graduate Institute (Cl)
Georgia State University (Co)
Illinois School of Professional Psychology–Chicago Campus (Cl)
Long Island University (Cl)
Nova Southeastern University (Ph.D. & Psy.D.) (Cl)
Pepperdine University (Cl)
St. John's University (Cl)
San Diego State University/University of California–San Diego (Cl)
University at Buffalo/State University of New York (Cl)
University of Colorado (Cl)
University of Denver (Psy.D.) (Cl)
University of Georgia (Cl)
University of Houston (Cl)
University of Kentucky (Cl)
University of Maine (Cl)
University of Manitoba (Cl)
University of Massachusetts at Amherst (Cl)
University of Minnesota (Cl)
University of Missouri–Columbia (Co)
University of North Carolina at Chapel Hill (Cl)
University of Pennsylvania (Cl)
University of Pittsburgh (Cl)

University of Texas Southwestern Medical Center at Dallas (Cl)
University of Wisconsin–Madison (Cl)
Vanderbilt University–Peabody College (Cl)
Wright State University (Cl)
Yeshiva University (Cl)

Community Psychology

Argosy University–Honolulu Campus (Cl)
Auburn University (Co)
Baylor University (Cl)
Brigham Young University (Cl)
Boston College (Co)
Boston University (Cl)
Bowling Green State University (Cl)
Chicago School of Professional Psychology (Cl)
DePaul University (Cl)
Fairleigh Dickinson University (Cl)
Florida State University (Cm)
Fordham University (Co)
George Fox University (Cl)
George Mason University (Cl)
Georgia State University (Cl)
Howard University (Cl)
Illinois School of Professional Psychology–Chicago Campus (Cl)
Illinois School of Professional Psychology–Chicago Northwest (Cl)
Indiana State University (Co)
Indiana University (Cl)
Iowa State University (Co)
James Madison University (Cm)
Loma Linda University (Ph.D. & Psy.D.) (Cl)
Long Island University (Cl)
Michigan State University (Cl)
New Mexico State University (Co)
Nova Southeastern University (Cl)
Our Lady of the Lake University (Co)
Pacific University (Cl)
Pennsylvania State University (Cl)
Pepperdine University (Cl)
Rutgers University (Ph.D.) (Cl)
Rutgers University (Psy.D.) (Cl)
Stony Brook University/State University of New York (Cl)
Syracuse University (Cl)
Texas A&M University (Cl)
University of Akron (Co)
University at Albany/State University of New York (Co)
University of Arizona (Cl)
University of California–Los Angeles (Cl)
University of California–Santa Barbara (Cm)
University of Cincinnati (Cl)
University of Illinois at Urbana–Champaign (Cl)
University of Iowa (Co)
University of Kentucky (Cl)
University of Kentucky (Co)
University of Maine (Cl)
University of Manitoba (Cl)
University of Maryland (Cl)
University of Maryland–Baltimore County (Cl)
University of Minnesota (Cl)
University of Mississippi (Cl)
University of Montana (Cl)
University of North Carolina at Greensboro (Cl)
University of North Dakota (Cl)
University of Notre Dame (Co)
University of Oklahoma (Co)
University of Oregon (Co)
University of Rhode Island (Cl)
University of South Carolina (Cl)
University of South Dakota (Cl)
University of Southern California (Cl)
University of Texas at Austin (Cl)
University of Texas at Austin (Co)
University of Texas Southwestern Medical Center at Dallas (Cl)
University of Utah (Co)
University of Virginia–Department of Psychology (Cl)
University of Washington (Cl)
University of Wisconsin–Milwaukee (Co)
Utah State University (Cm)
Virginia Commonwealth University (Cl)
Virginia Commonwealth University (Co)
Virginia Polytechnic Institute and State University (Cl)
Wayne State University (Cl)
West Virginia University (Co)
Wright State University (Cl)

Conduct Disorder

Antioch/New England Graduate School (Cl)
Binghamton University/State University of New York (Cl)
Forest Institute of Professional Psychology (Cl)
George Washington University (Ph.D.) (Cl)
Miami University (Cl)
Rutgers University (Ph.D.) (Cl)
Rutgers University (Psy.D.) (Cl)
University of Alabama (Cl)
University of Colorado (Cl)
University of Delaware (Cl)
University of Houston (Cl)
University of Miami (Cl)
University of Minnesota (Cl)
University of Pittsburgh (Cl)
University of Tennessee (Cl)
Virginia Polytechnic Institute and State University (Cl)
Yale University (Cl)

Consultation

University of Virginia–Department of Human Services (Cl)
Virginia Polytechnic Institute and State University (Cl)

Correctional Psychology/Prisons

Adler School of Professional Psychology (Cl)
Argosy University–Honolulu Campus (Cl)
Binghamton University/State University of New York (Cl)
Brigham Young University (Cl & Co)
George Fox University (Cl)
Indiana State University (Co)
Indiana University–Purdue University Indianapolis (Cl)
Loyola College in Maryland (Cl)
Nova Southeastern University (Ph.D. & Psy.D.) (Cl)
Oklahoma State University (Co)
Southern Illinois University (Cl)
Southern Illinois University (Co)

Texas A&M University (Co)
Texas Tech University (Co)
University of Florida (Co)
University of Illinois at Urbana–Champaign (Cl)
University of Iowa (Co)
University of Kentucky (Co)
University of Missouri–Columbia (Co)
University of Montana (Cl)
University of Oklahoma (Co)
University of Wisconsin–Madison (Cl)
University of Wyoming (Cl)
Virginia Commonwealth University (Cl & Co)
West Virginia University (Co)

Crisis Intervention

Baylor University (Cl)
Howard University (Cl)
Illinois School of Professional Psychology–Chicago Campus (Cl)
Indiana University–Purdue University Indianapolis (Cl)
Northwestern University (Cl)
Nova Southeastern University (Ph.D. & Psy.D.) (Cl)
Ohio State University (Cl)
Syracuse University (Cl)
University of Florida (Co)
University of Houston (Co)
University of Maine (Cl)
University of Minnesota (Cl)
University of South Dakota (Cl)
University of Texas at Austin (Cl)
University of Virginia–Department of Human Services (Cl)
Wright Institute (Cl)
Wright State University (Cl)

Deafness

Alliant International University–San Diego (Psy.D.) (Cl)
Gallaudet University (Cl)
Louisiana State University (Cl)
University of Iowa (Cl)
University of Texas Southwestern Medical Center at Dallas (Cl)
Wright State University (Cl)

Developmental Disabilities/Autism

Adler School of Professional Psychology (Cl)
Alliant International University–San Diego (Ph.D. & Psy.D.) (Cl)
Argosy University–Honolulu Campus (Cl)
Auburn University (Cl)
Binghamton University/State University of New York (Cl)
Brigham Young University (Cl)
Case Western Reserve University (Cl)
George Washington University (Ph.D. & Psy.D.)(Cl)
Georgia State University (Cl)
Louisiana State University (Cl)
MCP Hahnemann University of the Health Sciences (Cl)
Miami University (Cl)
Northeastern University (Cm)
Northern Illinois University (Cl)
Northwestern University Medical School (Cl)
Ohio State University (Cl)
Queen's University (Cl)
Rutgers University (Ph.D.) (Cl)
Rutgers University (Psy.D.) (Cl)
University at Albany/State University of New York (Cl)
University of California–Los Angeles (Cl)
University of California–Santa Barbara (Cm)
University of Cincinnati (Cl) (developmental disorders)
University of Connecticut (Cl)
University of Delaware (Cl)
University of Denver (Ph.D.) (Cl)
University of Georgia (Cl)
University of Hawaii at Manoa (Cl)
University of Illinois at Chicago (Cl)
University of Louisville (Co)
University of Manitoba (Cl)
University of Memphis (Cl)
University of Miami (Cl)
University of North Carolina at Chapel Hill (Cl)
University of Pennsylvania (Cm)
University of Rochester (Cl)
University of Saskatchewan (Cl)
University of Texas Southwestern Medical Center at Dallas (Cl)
University of Wyoming (Cl)
Vanderbilt University–Peabody College (Cl)
West Virginia University (Cl)

Disabilities/Disabled Persons

Adler School of Professional Psychology (Cl)
Alliant International University–Alameda (Ph.D. & Psy.D.) (Cl)
Loyola College in Maryland (Cl)
University of Louisville (Cl)
Utah State University (Cm)

Disaster/Trauma

Nova Southeastern University (Ph.D. & Psy.D.) (Cl)
University of Connecticut (Cl)
University of Montana (Cl)
University of South Dakota (Cl)
Virginia Consortium Program in Clinical Psychology (Cl)

Dissociative Disorder/ Multiple Personality Disorder

Boston University (Cl)
George Washington University (Ph.D.) (Cl)
Rutgers University (Psy.D.) (Cl)
University of Georgia (Cl)
University of Hartford (Cl)

Divorce/Child Custody

Alliant International University–San Diego (Ph.D. & Psy.D.) (Cl)
University of Illinois at Urbana–Champaign (Ph.D.) (Cl)
Virginia Commonwealth University (Cl)

Dual Diagnosis Clinic

Nova Southeastern University (Ph.D. & Psy.D.) (Cl)
York University–Clinical-Developmental Area (Cl)

Eating Disorders/Body Image

Alliant International University–Fresno (Ph.D. & Psy.D.) (Cl)
Argosy University–Twin Cities (Cl)
Arizona State University (Cl)
Baylor University (Cl)
Boston University (Cl)
Brigham Young University (Cl & Co)
Case Western Reserve University (Cl)
Drexel University (Cl)
Duke University (Cl)
Florida Institute of Technology (Cl)
George Washington University (Ph.D.) (Cl)
Illinois School of Professional Psychology–Chicago Campus (Cl)
Kent State University (Cl)
Louisiana State University (Cl)
Loyola College in Maryland (Cl)
Loyola University of Chicago (Cl)
Michigan State University (Cl)
Northwestern University Medical School (Cl)
Ohio State University (Cl)
Rutgers University (Ph.D. & Psy.D.) (Cl)
University at Albany/State University of New York (Cl)
University of California–Santa Barbara (Cm)
University of Florida (Co)
University of Georgia (Cl)
University of Hawaii at Manoa (Cl)
University of Illinois at Chicago (Cl)
University of Manitoba (Cl)
University of Maryland–Baltimore County (Cl)
University of Memphis (Cl)
University of Minnesota (Cl)
University of Mississippi (Cl)
University of Montana (Cl)
University of St. Thomas (Co)
University of South Florida (Cl)
University of Southern Mississippi (Co)
University of Vermont (Cl)
Utah State University (Cm)
West Virginia University (Cl)
Yale University (Cl)
York University–Adult Clinical Program (Cl)

Family Therapy/Systems

Adelphi University (Cl)
Alliant International University–Fresno (Ph.D. & Psy.D.) (Cl)
American University (Cl)
Antioch/New England Graduate School (Cl)
Argosy University–Washington, DC Campus (Cl)
Arizona State University (Cl)
Baylor University (Cl)
Binghamton University/State University of New York (Cl)
Biola University (Ph.D.) (Cl)
Biola University (Psy.D.) (Cl)
Boston University (Cl)
Bowling Green State University (Cl)
Brigham Young University (Cl & Co)
Catholic University of America (Cl)
City University of New York at City College (Cl)
Clark University (Cl)
Colorado State University (Co)
Concordia University (Cl)
DePaul University (Cl)
Fairleigh Dickinson University (Cl)
Florida Institute of Technology (Psy.D.) (Cl)
Florida State University (Cl)
Fuller Theological Seminary (Ph.D. & Psy.D.) (Cl)
George Washington University (Ph.D. & Psy.D.) (Cl)
Georgia State University (Cl)
Howard University (Cl)
Illinois Institute of Technology (Cl)
Illinois School of Professional Psychology–Chicago Campus (Cl)
Illinois School of Professional Psychology–Chicago Northwest (Cl)
Indiana State University (Co)
Indiana University (Cl)
Indiana University of Pennsylvania (Cl)
Iowa State University (Co)
James Madison University (Cm)
Kent State University (Cl)
Long Island University (Cl)
Louisiana State University (Cl)
Loyola College in Maryland (Cl)
Miami University (Cl)
Michigan State University (Cl)
New Mexico State University (Co)
New York University (Cl)
Northeastern University (Cm)
Northern Illinois University (Cl)
Northwestern University (Cl)
Nova Southeastern University (Ph.D. & Psy.D.) (Cl)
Ohio State University (Cl)
Ohio University (Cl)
Oklahoma State University (Cl)
Oklahoma State University (Co)
Pacific Graduate School of Psychology (Cl)
Pepperdine University (Cl)
Queen's University (Cl)
Rutgers University (Ph.D.) (Cl)
Rutgers University (Psy.D.) (Cl)
St. John's University (Cl)
St. Louis University (Cl)
San Diego State University/University of California–San Diego (Cl)
Southern Illinois University (Cl)
Southern Illinois University (Co)
Spalding University (Psy.D.) (Cl)
Syracuse University (Cl)
Texas A&M University (Cl)
University of Akron (Co)
University of British Columbia (Cl)
University at Buffalo/State University of New York (Cl)
University of California–Los Angeles (Cl)
University of California–Santa Barbara (Cm)
University of Colorado (Cl)
University of Delaware (Cl)
University of Denver (Ph.D.) (Cl)
University of Georgia (Cl)
University of Houston (Co)
University of Illinois at Urbana–Champaign (Cl)
University of Manitoba (Cl)
University of Maryland–Baltimore County (Cl)
University of Memphis (Cl)
University of Miami (Cl)

University of Michigan (Cl)
University of Minnesota (Cl)
University of Mississippi (Cl)
University of Missouri–Columbia (Co)
University of Missouri–St. Louis (Cl)
University of Montana (Cl)
University of Nebraska–Lincoln (Co)
University of New Mexico (Cl)
University of North Carolina at Chapel Hill (Cl)
University of Northern Colorado (Co)
University of Oregon (Co)
University of Pennsylvania (Cm)
University of Pittsburgh (Cl)
University of Pittsburgh (Co)
University of Rhode Island (Cl)
University of St. Thomas (Co)
University of South Carolina (Cl)
University of South Florida (Cl)
University of Southern California (Cl)
University of Tennessee (Cl)
University of Texas at Austin (Cl)
University of Texas Southwestern Medical Center at Dallas (Cl)
University of Toledo (Cl)
University of Utah (Cl)
University of Utah (Co)
University of Vermont (Cl)
University of Virginia–Department of Human Services (Cl)
University of Virginia–Department of Psychology (Cl)
University of Washington (Cl)
University of Waterloo (Cl)
University of Wisconsin–Milwaukee (Cl)
University of Wisconsin–Milwaukee (Co)
Vanderbilt University–Peabody College (Cl)
Virginia Consortium Program in Clinical Psychology (Cl)
Widener University (Cl)
Wright Institute (Cl)
Wright State University (Cl)
Yeshiva University (Cl)
Yeshiva University (Cm)

Forensic

Alliant International University–Alameda (Ph.D. & Psy.D.) (Cl)
Alliant International University–Fresno (Ph.D. & Psy.D.) (Cl)
Alliant International University–San Diego (Psy.D.) (Cl)
Antioch/New England Graduate School (Cl)
Argosy University–Twin Cities (Cl)
Argosy University–Washington, DC Campus (Cl)
Bowling Green State University (Cl)
Brigham Young University (Cl)
Carlos Albizu University–San Juan (Cl)
Central Michigan University (Cl)
Chicago School of Professional Psychology (Cl)
Dalhousie University (Cl)
Florida State University (Cl)
George Washington University (Ph.D.)(Cl)
Georgia School of Professional Psychology (Cl)
Illinois School of Professional Psychology–Chicago Campus (Cl)
Illinois School of Professional Psychology–Chicago Northwest (Cl)
Kent State University (Cl)
Loyola College in Maryland (Cl)
MCP Hahnemann University of the Health Sciences (Cl)
Nova Southeastern University (Ph.D. & Psy.D.) (Cl)
Pepperdine University (Cl)
Queen's University (Cl)
Rutgers University (Ph.D.) (Cl)
Rutgers University (Psy.D.) (Cl)
Southern Illinois University (Cl)
Tennessee State University (Co)
Texas A&M University (Cl)
Uniformed Services University of Health Sciences (Cl)
University of Alabama (Cl)
University of British Columbia (Cl)
University of Denver (Psy.D.) (Cl)
University of Florida (Co)
University of Houston (Co)
University of Illinois at Urbana–Champaign (Cl)
University of Indianapolis (Cl)
University of Louisville (Cl)
University of Memphis (Co)
University of Minnesota (Cl)
University of Nebraska–Lincoln (Cl)
University of North Texas (Cl)
University of Saskatchewan (Cl)
University of South Florida (Cl)
University of Texas Southwestern Medical Center at Dallas (Cl)
University of Utah (Cl)
University of Victoria (Cl)
University of Virginia–Department of Human Services (Cl)
University of Virginia–Department of Psychology (Cl)
University of Washington (Cl)
University of Western Ontario (Cl)
University of Wisconsin–Madison (Cl)
University of Wyoming (Cl)
West Virginia University (Cl)
Wright Institute (Cl)
Wright State University (Cl)

Gay/Lesbian/Bisexual/Transgender

Alliant International University–Alameda (Ph.D. & Psy.D.) (Cl)
Antioch/New England Graduate School (Cl)
Chicago School of Professional Psychology (Cl)
Illinois School of Professional Psychology–Chicago Campus (Cl)
University of Pittsburgh (Cl)
University of Texas at Austin (Cl)
Wright Institute (Cl)

Group Therapy

Adelphi University (Cl)
Antioch/New England Graduate School (Cl)
Baylor University (Cl)
Catholic University of America (Cl)
DePaul University (Cl)
Florida State University (Cl)
Fuller Theological Seminary (Ph.D. & Psy.D.) (Cl)
George Mason University (Cl)
George Washington University (Ph.D.) (Cl)
Georgia State University (Cl)

Illinois School of Professional Psychology–Chicago Campus (Cl)
Indiana State University (Cl)
New Mexico State University (Co)
Northern Illinois University (Cl)
Nova Southeastern University (Ph.D. & Psy.D.) (Cl)
Pepperdine University (Cl)
Rutgers University (Ph.D.) (Cl)
Rutgers University (Psy.D.) (Cl)
St. John's University (Cl)
University of Denver (Psy.D.) (Cl)
University of Illinois at Urbana–Champaign (Cl)
University of Maryland (Co)
University of Miami (Cl)
University of Wisconsin–Madison (Cl)
Widener University (Cl)
Wright Institute (Cl)
Yeshiva University (Cl)

Hospice

Argosy University–Honolulu Campus (Cl)
Indiana University–Purdue University (Cl)

Humanistic/Experiential Therapy

American University (Cl)
Fielding Graduate Institute (Cl)
University of Toledo (Cl)

Hypnosis

Rutgers University (Ph.D.) (Cl)
Rutgers University (Psy.D.) (Cl)
University of Denver (Psy.D.) (Cl)
University of North Dakota (Cl)
University of Northern Colorado (Co)
University of Waterloo (Cl)

Impulse Control/Aggression/ Anger Control

Baylor University (Cl)
Dalhousie University (Cl)
George Washington University (Ph.D.) (Cl)
Rutgers University (Ph.D.) (Cl)
Rutgers University (Psy.D.) (Cl)
University of Georgia (Cl)
University of South Florida (Cl)
Vanderbilt University–Department of Psychology (Cl)

Infancy/Postpartum

Rutgers University (Ph.D.) (Cl)
Rutgers University (Psy.D.) (Cl)
University of Colorado (Cl)

Inpatient Psychology/Psychiatry

Alliant International University–Alameda (Ph.D. & Psy.D.) (Cl)
Boston College (Co)
Brigham Young University (Cl)
Colorado State University (Co)
Fordham University (Co)
George Fox University (Cl)
Illinois School of Professional Psychology–Chicago Northwest (Cl)
Indiana State University (Co)
Iowa State University (Co)
Long Island University (Cl)
Loyola University of Chicago (Co)
McGill University (Cl)
MCP Hahnemann University of the Health Sciences (Cl)
New School for Social Research (Cl)
Northeastern University (Cm)
Northwestern University Medical School (Cl)
Ohio University (Cl)
Oklahoma State University (Co)
Pepperdine University (Psy.D.) (Cl)
Queen's University (Cl)
Stony Brook University/State University of New York (Cl)
Tennessee State University (Co)
Uniformed Services University of Health Sciences (Cl)
University at Albany/State University of New York (Co)
University of Denver (Ph.D.) (Cl)
University of Florida (Co)
University of Hartford (Cl)
University of Houston (Co)
University of Illinois at Urbana–Champaign (Cl)
University of Iowa (Cl)
University of Iowa (Co)
University of Kentucky (Co)
University of Maine (Cl)
University of Maryland (Cl)
University of Memphis (Co)
University of Missouri–Columbia (Cl)
University of Missouri–Columbia (Co)
University of New Mexico (Cl)
University of Oklahoma (Co)
University of Oregon (Co)
University of Pittsburgh (Cl)
University of Pittsburgh (Co)
University of Southern Mississippi (Cl)
University of Texas at Austin (Co)
University of Texas Southwestern Medical Center at Dallas (Cl)
University of Utah (Cl)
University of Victoria (Cl)
University of Western Ontario (Cl)
University of Wisconsin–Madison (Cl)
University of Wisconsin–Milwaukee (Cl)
University of Wyoming (Cl)
Utah State University (Cm)
Virginia Commonwealth University (Cl)
Washington State University (Cl)

Learning Disabilities

Florida State University (Cl)
George Washington University (Psy.D.) (Cm)
James Madison University (Cm)
St. Louis University (Cl)
University of Missouri–Columbia (Co)
University of Pennsylvania (Cm)
Virginia Consortium Program in Clinical Psychology (Cl)
York University–Clinical-Developmental Area (Cl)

Marital/Couples

Arizona State University (Cl)
Binghamton University/State University of New York (Cl)
Biola University (Ph.D.) (Cl)
Biola University (Psy.D.) (Cl)
Boston University (Cl)
Chicago School of Professional Psychology (Cl)
Clark University (Cl)
Concordia University (Cl)
Florida Institute of Technology (Cl)
Florida State University (Cl)
Fuller Theological Seminary (Ph.D. & Psy.D.) (Cl)
George Mason University (Cl)
George Washington University (Ph.D.) (Cl)
Georgia State University (Cl)
Illinois Institute of Technology (Cl)
Illinois School of Professional Psychology–Chicago Campus (Cl)
Illinois School of Professional Psychology–Chicago Northwest (Cl)
Indiana State University (Co)
Indiana University (Cl)
Kent State University (Cl)
Miami University (Cl)
Northern Illinois University (Cl)
Northwestern University (Cl)
Oklahoma State University (Cl)
Oklahoma State University (Co)
Pepperdine University (Cl)
Rutgers University (Ph.D.) (Cl)
Rutgers University (Psy.D.) (Cl)
St. Louis University (Cl)
Southern Illinois University (Co)
Stony Brook University/State University of New York (Cl)
Syracuse University (Cl)
University of Arizona (Cl)
University of California–Los Angeles (Cl)
University of Denver (Ph.D.) (Cl)
University of Florida (Co)
University of Georgia (Cl)
University of Illinois at Chicago (Cl)
University of Illinois at Urbana–Champaign (Cl)
University of Manitoba (Cl)
University of Maryland (Co)
University of Miami (Cl)
University of Mississippi (Cl)
University of Montana (Cl)
University of Nevada–Reno (Cl)
University of New Mexico (Cl)
University of North Carolina at Chapel Hill (Cl)
University of North Dakota (Cl)
University of Northern Colorado (Co)
University of Oregon (Cl)
University of Pennsylvania (Cm)
University of Rhode Island (Cl)
University of South Florida (Cl)
University of Southern California (Cl)
University of Texas at Austin (Cl)
University of Virginia–Department of Psychology (Cl)
University of Washington (Cl)
Virginia Consortium Program in Clinical Psychology (Cl)
Virginia Polytechnic Institute and State University (Cl)
Widener University (Cl)
Wright Institute (Cl)
Wright State University (Cl)
Yale University (Cl)
Yeshiva University (Cl)

Mental Retardation

Louisiana State University (Cl)
University of Hartford (Cl)
University of Vermont (Cl)
Virginia Consortium Program in Clinical Psychology (Cl)

Minority/Cross-Cultural

Alliant International University–Alameda (Ph.D. & Psy.D.) (Cl)
Alliant International University–Fresno (Ph.D. & Psy.D.) (Cl)
Bowling Green State University (Cl)
Catholic University of America (Cl)
Chicago School of Professional Psychology (Cl)
DePaul University (Cl)
Fairleigh Dickinson University (Cl)
Florida State University (Cl)
George Washington University (Ph.D.) (Cl)
Howard University (Cl)
Illinois Institute of Technology (Cl)
Illinois School of Professional Psychology–Chicago Campus (Cl)
Michigan State University (Cl)
Michigan State University (Co)
New Mexico State University (Co)
Northeastern University (Cm)
Nova Southeastern University (Ph.D. & Psy.D.) (Cl)
Oklahoma State University (Co)
Our Lady of the Lake University (Co)
Pacific Graduate School of Psychology (Cl)
Rutgers University (Ph.D.) (Cl)
Rutgers University (Psy.D.) (Cl)
St. Louis University (Cl)
University at Albany/State University of New York (Cl)
University of Denver (Co)
University of Denver (Ph.D.) (Cl)
University of Florida (Co)
University of Georgia (Cl)
University of Hawaii at Manoa (Cl)
University of Houston (Cl)
University of Illinois at Urbana–Champaign (Co)
University of Maryland (Co)
University of Massachusetts at Amherst (Cl)
University of Memphis (Cl)
University of Miami (Cl)
University of Nebraska–Lincoln (Cl)
University of Nebraska–Lincoln (Co)
University of North Dakota (Cl)
University of Oklahoma (Co)
University of South Dakota (Cl)
University of Southern California (Cl)
University of Utah (Co)
University of Washington (Cl)
Utah State University (Cm)
Wright Institute (Cl)
Wright State University (Cl)

Neuropsychology/Clinical Neuropsychology/Brain Injury

Alliant International University–Alameda (Ph.D. & Psy.D.) (Cl)
Alliant International University–Fresno (Ph.D. & Psy.D.) (Cl)
American University (Cl)
Antioch/New England Graduate School (Cl)
Argosy University, Washington, DC Campus (Cl)
Baylor University (Cl)
Binghamton University/State University of New York (Cl)
Boston University (Cl)
Bowling Green State University (Cl)
Brigham Young University (Cl)
Catholic University of America (Cl)
Central Michigan University (Cl)
Drexel University (Cl)
Duke University (Cl)
Emory University (Cl)
Fairleigh Dickinson University (Cl)
Finch University of Health Sciences, The Chicago Medical School (Cl)
Florida Institute of Technology (Cl)
Florida State University (Cl)
Forest Institute of Professional Psychology (Cl)
Fuller Theological Seminary (Ph.D. & Psy.D.) (Cl)
George Washington University (Cl)
Georgia School of Professional Psychology (Cl)
Georgia State University (Cl)
Howard University (Cl)
Illinois Institute of Technology (Cl)
Illinois School of Professional Psychology–Chicago Campus (Cl)
Indiana University (Cl)
Indiana University–Purdue University Indianapolis (Cl)
James Madison University (Cm)
Kent State University (Cl)
Long Island University (Cl)
Louisiana State University (Cl)
Loyola University of Chicago (Cl)
Marquette University (Cl)
MCP Hahnemann University of the Health Sciences (Cl)
Michigan State University (Cl)
Northwestern University (Cl)
Northwestern University Medical School (Cl)
Nova Southeastern (Ph.D. & Psy.D.) (Cl)
Ohio State University (Cl)
Ohio University (Cl)
Pacific Graduate School of Psychology (Cl)
Pepperdine University (Cl)
Queen's University (Cl)
Rutgers University (Ph.D.) (Cl)
Rutgers University (Psy.D.) (Cl)
St. John's University (Cl)
St. Louis University (Cl)
San Diego State University/University of California–San Diego (Cl)
Southern Illinois University (Cl)
Syracuse University (Cl)
Texas A&M University (Cl)
Texas Tech University (Co)
University of Alabama at Birmingham (Cl)
University at Albany/State University of New York (Cl)
University at Albany/State University of New York (Co)
University of Arizona (Cl)
University of British Columbia (Cl)
University of Cincinnati (Cl)
University of Connecticut (Cl)
University of Delaware (Cl)
University of Denver (Ph.D.) (Cl)
University of Florida (Cl)
University of Georgia (Cl)
University of Hawaii at Manoa (Cl)
University of Houston (Cl)
University of Illinois at Urbana–Champaign (Cl)
University of Indianapolis (Cl)
University of Iowa (Cl)
University of Kentucky (Cl)
University of Manitoba (Cl)
University of Maryland–Baltimore County (Cl)
University of Memphis (Cl)
University of Miami (Cl)
University of Minnesota (Cl)
University of Montana (Cl)
University of North Texas (Cl)
University of Northern Colorado (Co)
University of Oregon (Cl)
University of Pennsylvania (Cl)
University of Pittsburgh (Cl)
University of Saskatchewan (Cl)
University of South Carolina (Cl)
University of South Florida (Cl)
University of Southern Mississippi (Cl)
University of Texas at Austin (Cl)
University of Texas Southwestern Medical Center at Dallas (Cl)
University of Toledo (Cl)
University of Vermont (Cl)
University of Victoria (Cl)
University of Virginia–Department of Human Services (Cl)
University of Virginia–Department of Psychology (Cl)
University of Waterloo (Cl)
University of Wisconsin–Madison (Cl)
University of Wisconsin–Milwaukee (Cl)
Vanderbilt University–Department of Psychology (Cl)
Virginia Commonwealth University (Cl)
Virginia Consortium Program in Clinical Psychology (Cl)
Virginia Polytechnic Institute and State University (Cl)
Washington State University (Cl)
Wayne State University (Cl)
Widener University (Cl)
Wright Institute (Cl)
Wright State University (Cl)

Obsessive–Compulsive Disorder

Case Western Reserve University (Cl)
George Washington University (Cl)
Indiana University (Cl)
Louisiana State University (Cl)
Rutgers University (Ph.D.) (Cl)
Rutgers University (Psy.D.) (Cl)
University of Hartford (Cl)
University of Manitoba (Cl)
University of Minnesota (Cl)
University of North Dakota (Cl)
University of Texas at Austin (Cl)

University of Virginia–Department of Psychology (Cl)
Virginia Consortium Program in Clinical Psychology (Cl)

Organizational

Chicago School of Professional Psychology (Cl)
Rutgers University (Psy.D.) (Cl)

Pain Management

Argosy University–Twin Cities (Cl)
Binghamton University/State University of New York (Cl)
Forest Institute of Professional Psychology (Cl)
Illinois Institute of Technology (Cl)
Nova Southeastern University (Ph.D. & Psy.D.) (Cl)
Ohio University (Cl)
Oklahoma State University (Co)
University of Alabama (Cl)
University of Florida (Cl)
University of Indianapolis (Cl)
University of Kentucky (Cl)
University of Montana (Cl)
University of Pittsburgh (Cl)
Virginia Commonwealth University (Cl)

Parent–Child Interaction/Parent Training

Arizona State University (Cl)
Central Michigan University (Cl)
Forest Institute of Professional Psychology (Cl)
Nova Southeastern University (Ph.D. & Psy.D.) (Cl)
St. Louis University (Cl)
University of Alabama (Cl)
University of Florida (Cl)
University of Pittsburgh (Cl)
University of Virginia–Department of Human Services (Cl)
West Virginia University (Cl)
Yeshiva University (Cl & Cm)

Personality Disorders

Antioch/New England Graduate School (Cl)
Auburn University (Cl)
Baylor University (Cl)
Case Western Reserve University (Cl)
George Washington University (Ph.D.) (Cl)
Georgia State University (Cl)
Illinois School of Professional Psychology–Chicago Campus (Cl)
Loyola University of Chicago (Cl)
Purdue University (Cl)
Rutgers University (Ph.D.) (Cl)
Rutgers University (Psy.D.) (Cl)
St. Louis University (Cl)
Southern Illinois University (Cl)
University of Georgia (Cl)
University of Montana (Cl)
University of North Dakota (Cl)
University of Pittsburgh (Cl)
University of Tennessee (Cl)
University of Texas at Austin (Cl)
University of Texas Southwestern Medical Center at Dallas (Cl)
University of Utah (Cl)
University of Washington (Cl)

Vanderbilt University–Department of Psychology (Cl)
Virginia Consortium Program in Clinical Psychology (Cl)
Wright Institute (Cl)

Posttraumatic Stress Disorder/Trauma

Alliant International University–San Diego (Psy.D.) (Cl)
Auburn University (Cl)
Duke University (Cl)
Florida Institute of Technology (Cl)
Pepperdine University (Cl)
University of Houston (Co)
University of Mississippi (Cl)
University of Nevada–Reno (Cl)
University of North Texas (Cl)
University of Pittsburgh (Cl)
Western Michigan University (Cl)

Prevention

Arizona State University (Cl)
Boston College (Co)
University of Missouri–Columbia (Cl)
University of Vermont (Cl)

Private Practice

Brigham Young University (Cl)
Iowa State University (Co)
James Madison University (Cm)

Psychiatric Emergency Care

University of Pittsburgh (Cl)
University of Texas Southwestern Medical Center at Dallas (Cl)

Psychoanalytic/Psychodynamic Therapy

American University (Cl)
Antioch/New England Graduate School (Cl)
Arizona State University (Cl)
Brigham Young University (Cl)
Catholic University of America (Cl)
Central Michigan University (Cl)
Columbia University, Teachers College (Cl)
Concordia University (Cl)
Fielding Graduate Institute (Cl)
Fuller Theological Seminary (Ph.D. & Psy.D.) (Cl)
George Mason University (Cl)
George Washington University (Ph.D.) (Cl)
Illinois School of Professional Psychology–Chicago Campus (Cl)
Kent State University (Cl)
New York University (Cl)
Nova Southeastern University (Ph.D. & Psy.D.) (Cl)
Rutgers University (Ph.D.) (Cl)
Rutgers University (Psy.D.) (Cl)
St. John's University (Cl)
St. Louis University (Cl)
University of Colorado (Cl)
University of Denver (Psy.D.) (Cl)
University of Louisville (Cl)
University of Massachusetts at Amherst (Cl)
University of Minnesota (Cl)

University of Montana (Cl)
University of North Carolina at Chapel Hill (Cl)
University of North Dakota (Cl)
University of Pennsylvania (Cl)
University of Rochester (Cl)
University of Utah (Cl)
University of Wisconsin–Madison (Cl)
Virginia Consortium Program in Clinical Psychology (Cl)
Widener University (Cl)
Wright Institute (Cl)
Yale University (Cl)
Yeshiva University (Cl)

Psychotherapy Integration

Adelphi University (Cl)
Brigham Young University (Cl)

Rational-Emotive Therapy

Rutgers University (Ph.D.) (Cl)
Rutgers University (Psy.D.) (Cl)
St. John's University (Cl)
University of North Dakota (Cl)
University of Utah (Cl)

Rehabilitation

Alliant International University–San Diego (Ph.D. & Psy.D.) (Cl)
Antioch/New England Graduate School (Cl)
Brigham Young University (Cl)
Florida State University (Cl)
Georgia School of Professional Psychology (Cl)
Georgia State University (Cl)
Illinois School of Professional Psychology–Chicago Campus (Psy.D. & Ph.D.) (Cl)
Illinois School of Professional Psychology–Chicago Northwest (Psy.D. & Ph.D.) (Cl)
Indiana University–Purdue University Indianapolis (Cl)
MCP Hahnemann University of the Health Sciences (Cl)
Ohio State University (Co)
Pepperdine University (Cl)
Queen's University (Cl)
Southern Illinois University (Cl)
Southern Illinois University (Co)
University at Albany/State University of New York (Co)
University of Hawaii at Manoa (Cl)
University of Missouri–Columbia (Cl)
University of Missouri–Columbia (Co)
University of Oklahoma (Co)
University of Texas Southwestern Medical Center at Dallas (Cl)
University of Victoria (Cl)
University of Western Ontario (Cl)
Virginia Commonwealth University (Co)
York University–Clinical-Developmental Area (Cl)

Religion/Spirituality

Biola University (Ph.D.) (Cl)
Biola University (Psy.D.) (Cl)
Forest Institute of Professional Psychology (Cl)
Illinois School of Professional Psychology–Chicago Campus (Cl)
Pepperdine University (Cl)

Rural Mental Health/Psychology

Antioch/New England Graduate School (Cl)
Baylor University (Cl)
Indiana State University (Cl)
New Mexico State University (Co)
Oklahoma State University (Co)
Southern Illinois University (Co)
Texas A&M University (Cl)
University of Kentucky (Co)
University of North Dakota (Cl)
University of South Dakota (Cl)
University of Wyoming (Cl)

Schizophrenia/Psychosis

Baylor University (Cl)
Binghamton University/State University of New York (Cl)
Boston University (Cl)
Case Western Reserve University (Cl)
Florida State University (Cl)
George Washington University (Ph.D. & Psy.D.) (Cl)
Howard University (Cl)
Indiana University (Cl)
Kent State University (Cl)
Louisiana State University (Cl)
Michigan State University (Cl)
Northeastern University (Cm)
Northwestern University (Cl)
Pepperdine University (Cl)
Rutgers University (Ph.D.) (Cl)
Rutgers University (Psy.D.) (Cl)
University of Houston (Cl)
University of Illinois at Urbana–Champaign (Cl)
University of Maryland–Baltimore County (Cl)
University of Minnesota (Cl)
University of Montana (Cl)
University of Pittsburgh (Cl)
University of Texas at Austin (Cl)
University of Virginia–Department of Psychology (Cl)
University of Wisconsin–Madison (Cl)
Vanderbilt University–Department of Psychology (Cl)
Virginia Consortium Program in Clinical Psychology (Cl)
Wayne State University (Cl)
Wright Institute (Cl)

School/Educational

Adler School of Professional Psychology (Cl)
Alliant International University–Fresno (Ph.D. & Psy.D.) (Cl)
Argosy University–Honolulu Campus (Cl)
Arizona State University (Cl)
Baylor University (Cl)
Binghamton University/State University of New York (Cl)
Biola University (Ph.D.) (Cl)
Biola University (Psy.D.) (Cl)
Boston College (Co)
Bowling Green State University (Cl)
Brigham Young University (Cl)
Central Michigan University (Cl)
Concordia University (Cl)

Duke University (Cl)
Florida State University (Cm)
Illinois School of Professional Psychology–Chicago Campus (Cl)
Illinois School of Professional Psychology–Chicago Northwest (Cl)
Indiana University (Cl)
Indiana University–Purdue University Indianapolis (Cl)
Louisiana State University (Cl)
James Madison University (Cm)
Miami University (Cl)
Our Lady of the Lake University (Co)
Queen's University (Cl)
Rutgers University (Ph.D.) (Cl)
Rutgers University (Psy.D.) (Cl)
San Diego State University/University of California–San Diego (Cl)
Syracuse University (Cl)
University of California–Santa Barbara (Cm)
University of Hawaii at Manoa (Cl)
University of Illinois at Urbana–Champaign (Cl)
University of Maine (Cl)
University of Memphis (Cl)
University of New Mexico (Cl)
University of North Carolina at Greensboro (Cl)
University of Virginia–Department of Human Services (Cl)
University of Waterloo (Cl)
Utah State University (Cm)
Vanderbilt University–Peabody College (Cl)
Virginia Commonwealth University (Cl)
West Virginia University (Cl)
Widener University (Cl)
Yeshiva University (Cl & Cm)
York University–Clinical-Developmental Area (Cl)

Sex Therapy/Deviation and Dysfunction

Alliant International University–Fresno (Ph.D. & Psy.D.) (Cl)
Argosy University–Twin Cities (Cl)
Carlos Albizu University (Cl)
Indiana University (Cl)
MCP Hahnemann University of the Health Sciences (Cl)
Ohio State University (Cl)
Rutgers University (Ph.D.) (Cl)
Rutgers University (Psy.D.) (Cl)
Southern Illinois University (Co)
University at Buffalo/State University of New York (Cl)
University of Georgia (Cl)
University of Houston (Cl)
University of Rhode Island (Cl)
University of South Florida (Cl)
University of Tennessee (Cl)
University of Utah (Cl)
Widener University (Cl)

Sleep Disorders

Southern Illinois University (Cl)
University of Arizona (Cl)
University of Memphis (Cl)
University of Texas Southwestern Medical Center at Dallas (Cl)
Virginia Consortium Program in Clinical Psychology (Cl)

Smoking Cessation

Indiana University (Cl)
University of Mississippi (Cl)
University of Pittsburgh (Cl)
University of Rochester (Cl)

Sports Psychology

Carlos Albizu University–San Juan (Cl)
Illinois Institute of Technology (Cl)
University of Manitoba (Cl)
University of Washington (Cl)

Stress

Indiana University of Pennsylvania (Cl)
Loyola College in Maryland (Cl)
Loyola University of Chicago (Cl)
Nova Southeastern University (Ph.D. & Psy.D.) (Cl)
Southern Illinois University (Co)
University of Connecticut (Cl)
University of Florida (Cl)
University of Georgia (Cl)
University of Wisconsin–Milwaukee (Cl)

Substance Abuse/Addiction

Adelphi University (Cl)
Antioch/New England Graduate School (Cl)
Argosy University–Honolulu Campus (Cl)
Auburn University (Co)
Baylor University (Cl)
Binghamton University/State University of New York (Cl)
Brigham Young University (Cl)
Fairleigh Dickinson University (Cl)
Florida Institute of Technology (Cl)
Duke University (Cl)
George Washington University (Ph.D. (Cl)
Georgia School of Professional Psychology (Cl)
Illinois School of Professional Psychology–Chicago Campus (Cl)
Illinois School of Professional Psychology–Chicago Northwest (Cl)
Long Island University (Cl)
Loyola University of Chicago (Cl)
New Mexico State University (Co)
Northern Illinois University (Cl)
Nova Southeastern University (Ph.D. & Psy.D.) (Cl)
Ohio University (Cl)
Pepperdine University ((Cl)
Rutgers University (Ph.D.) (Cl)
Rutgers University (Psy.D.) (Cl)
Southern Illinois University (Cl)
Southern Illinois University (Co)
University at Albany/State University of New York (Cl)
University at Albany/State University of New York (Co)
Syracuse University (Cl)
Texas A&M University (Cl)
Uniformed Services University of Health Sciences (Cl)
University of Cincinnati (Cl)
University of Colorado (Cl)
University of Florida (Co)
University of Georgia (Cl)
University of Houston (Co)

University of Manitoba (Cl)
University of Maryland–Baltimore County (Cl)
University of Memphis (Cl)
University of Memphis (Co)
University of Miami (Cl)
University of Minnesota (Cl)
University of Mississippi (Cl)
University of Montana (Cl)
University of Nebraska–Lincoln (Cl)
University of Nevada–Reno (Cl)
University of North Dakota (Cl)
University of Pittsburgh (Cl)
University of South Florida (Cl)
University of Texas at Austin (Cl)
University of Utah (Co)
University of Vermont (Cl)
University of Washington (Cl)
University of Wisconsin–Madison (Cl)
Virginia Commonwealth University (Cl & Co)
Virginia Consortium Program in Clinical Psychology (Cl)
Virginia Polytechnic Institute and State University (Cl)
Wright Institute (Cl)
York University–Adult Clinical Program (Cl)

Suicide Prevention

Baylor University (Cl)
University of Southern Mississippi (Cl)

Supervision

Antioch/New England Graduate School (Cl)
Binghamton University/State University of New York (Cl)
Fuller Theological Seminary (Ph.D. & Psy.D.) (Cl)
Georgia State University (Cl)
New York University (Cl)
University of California–Los Angeles (Cl)
University of Denver (Psy.D.) (Cl)
University of Georgia (Cl)
University of Manitoba (Cl)
University of Maryland (Co)
University of Massachusetts at Amherst (Cl)
University of Northern Colorado (Co)
University of Southern Mississippi (Co)
Wright State University (Cl)

Veterans Hospital/Medical Center

Argosy University–Honolulu Campus (Cl)
Brigham Young University (Cl)
Indiana State University (Co)
Iowa State University (Co)
New School for Social Research (Cl)
Ohio State University (Co)
Oklahoma State University (Co)
Southern Illinois University (Co)
Stony Brook University/State University of New York (Cl)
Texas A&M University (Co)
Uniformed Services University of Health Sciences (Cl)
University of Akron (Co)
University at Albany/State University of New York (Co)
University of Houston (Co)
University of Iowa (Co)
University of Kentucky (Co)
University of Missouri–Columbia (Cl)
University of Missouri–Columbia (Co)
University of Oklahoma (Co)
University of Oregon (Co)
University of Pittsburgh (Co)
University of Southern Mississippi (Co)
University of Texas at Austin (Co)
University of Utah (Co)
Virginia Commonwealth University (Co)
West Virginia University (Co)

Victim/Violence/Sexual Abuse

Alliant International University–Fresno (Ph.D. & Psy.D.) (Cl)
Alliant International University–San Diego (Psy.D.) (Cl)
Antioch/New England Graduate School (Cl)
Auburn University (Cl)
Baylor University (Cl)
Boston College (Co)
Boston University (Cl)
Bowling Green State University (Cl)
Carlos Albizu University–San Juan (Cl)
Clark University (Cl)
Duke University (Cl)
Florida Institute of Technology (Cl)
Fuller Theological Seminary (Ph.D. & Psy.D.) (Cl)
George Washington University (Ph.D.) (Cl)
Georgia State University (Cl)
Howard University (Cl)
Illinois Institute of Technology (Cl)
Illinois School of Professional Psychology–Chicago Campus (Cl)
Indiana State University (Cl)
Indiana University (Cl)
Loyola University of Chicago (Cl)
Michigan State University (Cl)
Northern Illinois University (Cl)
Oklahoma State University (Co)
Rutgers University (Ph.D.) (Cl)
Rutgers University (Psy.D.) (Cl)
St. Louis University (Cl)
Southern Illinois University (Cl)
University of Arkansas (Cl)
University of California–Santa Barbara (Cm)
University of Delaware (Cl)
University of Florida (Co)
University of Georgia (Cl)
University of Houston (Cl)
University of Illinois at Urbana–Champaign (Co)
University of Iowa (Cl)
University of Manitoba (Cl)
University of Memphis (Co)
University of Miami (Cl)
University of Missouri–St. Louis (Cl)
University of Montana (Cl)
University of Nebraska–Lincoln (Cl)
University of Nevada–Reno (Cl)
University of North Carolina at Chapel Hill (Cl)
University of North Dakota (Cl)
University of Oklahoma (Co)
University of Pennsylvania (Cm)
University of Pittsburgh (Cl & Co)
University of Rochester (Cl)
University of Southern Mississippi (Co)
University of Toledo (Cl)

University of Utah (Co)
University of Virginia–Department of Psychology (Cl)
Virginia Consortium Program in Clinical Psychology (Cl)
West Virginia University (Cl)
Wright State University (Cl)

Vocational/Career Development

Florida State University (Cm)
New Mexico State University (Co)
Southern Illinois University (Co)
Temple University (Co)
Uniformed Services University of Health Sciences (Cl)
University of Florida (Co)
University of Maryland (Co)
University of Missouri–Columbia (Co)
University of Nebraska–Lincoln (Co)
University of Texas Southwestern Medical Center at Dallas (Cl)
University of Western Ontario (Cl)
Virginia Commonwealth University (Co)
Virginia Consortium Program in Clinical Psychology (Cl)

Weight Management

Allegheny University of the Health Sciences (Cl)
Oklahoma State University (Cl)
University at Buffalo/State University of New York (Cl)
University of Florida (Cl)
University of Pittsburgh (Cl)

Women's Studies/Issues

Alliant International University–Alameda (Ph.D. & Psy.D.) (Cl)
Northeastern University (Cm)
Oklahoma State University (Co)
Texas A&M University (Co)
University of Illinois at Urbana–Champaign (Cl)
University of Iowa (Co)
University of Missouri–Columbia (Co)
University of Missouri–St. Louis (Cl)
University of Utah (Co)

Miscellaneous

adjustment reactions–University of Illinois at Chicago (Cl)
attachment disorder–University of Montana (Cl)
behavioral dentistry–West Virginia University (Cl)
cancer survivorship–University of Illinois at Urbana–Champaign (Cl)
child custody evaluation–Alliant International University–San Diego (Ph.D.) (Cl)
clinical outcome studies–George Washington University (Psy.D.) (Cl)
creative & expressive arts–Chicago School of Professional Psychology (Cl)
data management systems–Virginia Polytechnic Institute and State University (Cl)
day treatment–Nova Southeastern University (Ph.D. & Psy.D) (Cl); Argosy University–Honolulu Campus (Cl)
diabetes–University of Miami (Cl)
diversity–Biola University (Ph.D.) (Cl)
early intervention–Utah State University (Cm)
empirically supported psychotherapy–University of Wyoming (Cl)
epilepsy clinic–Argosy University–Twin Cities (Cl)
functional analytic therapy–University of Montana (Cl)
gambling–University of Memphis (Cl)
gender disorder clinic–York University–Clinical-Developmental Area (Cl)
homeless shelters–Long Island University (Cl)
interpersonal therapy–Yale University (Cl)
low income–New Mexico State University (Co)
media and psychology–University of Massachusetts at Boston (Cl); Alliant International University–San Diego (Psy.D.) (Cl)
medication management–Nova Southeastern University (Ph.D. & Psy.D.) (Cl)
military–George Fox University (Cl)
motivational interviewing–University of Montana (Cl)
needs assessment/program evaluation–Bowling Green State University (Cl)
neuroimaging–University of Connecticut (Cl)
neurology–Texas Tech University (Cl)
peer relationships–Dalhousie University (Cl)
personal injury–Brigham Young University (Cl)
primary/interdisciplinary care–University of Wyoming (Cl)
psychopharmacology–Forest Institute of Professional Psychology (Psy.D.) (Cl)
public sector impairment treatment–Duke University (Cl)
short-term psychotherapy–Adelphi University (Cl)
skills treatment and enhancement program (STEP)–Nova Southeastern University (Ph.D. & Psy.D.) (Cl)
social stereotypes–University of Massachusetts at Boston (Cl)
systems management–Virginia Polytechnic Institute and State University (Cl)
systems therapy–Clark University (Cl)
third world placements–Brigham Young University (Cl)
virtual reality intervention–Alliant International University–San Diego (Ph.D. & Psy.D.) (Cl)

REFERENCES

Actkinson, T. R. (2000). Masters and myth. *Eye on Psi Chi, 5*(4), 19–25.

American Psychological Association. (1986). *Careers in psychology*. Washington, DC: Author.

American Psychological Association. (2000). *Graduate study in psychology*. Washington, DC: Author.

American Psychological Association Research Office. (1997). *Demographic characteristics of Division 12 and Division 17 members: 1997*. Washington, DC: Author.

American Psychological Association Research Office. (2000). *1998–1999 Survey of Graduate Departments of Psychology*. Washington, DC: Author.

Anderson, N., & Shackleton, V. (1990). Decision making in the graduate selection interview: A field study. *Journal of Occupational Psychology, 63*, 63–76.

APA Practice Directorate. (1991). *Summary of psychology licensing or certification laws*. Washington, DC: Author.

APA Public Interest Directorate. (1992). *Financial aid resources for ethnic minorities pursuing undergraduate, graduate, and post-doctoral study in psychology*. Washington, DC: American Psychological Association.

Appleby, D., Keenan, J., & Mauer, B. (1999). Applicant characteristics valued by graduate programs in psychology. *Eye on Psi Chi, 3*(3), 39.

Association of State and Provincial Psychology Boards and National Register of Health Service Providers in Psychology. (1999). *Doctoral psychology programs meeting designation criteria*. Washington, DC: National Register.

Astin, A. W., Green, K. C., & Korn, W. S. (1987). *The American freshman: Twenty year trends 1966–85*. University of California, Cooperative Institutional Research Program, American Council on Education.

Ault, R. L. (1993). To waive or not to waive? Students' misconceptions about the confidentiality choice for letters of recommendation. *Teaching of Psychology, 20*, 44–45.

Barron, J. (1986). Search for survival and identity—and power. *The Clinical Psychologist, 39*, 61–63.

Bechtoldt, H., Norcross, J. C., Wyckoff, L. A., Pokrywa, M. L., & Campbell, L. F. (2001). Theoretical orientations and employment settings of clinical and counseling psychologists: A comparative study. *The Clinical Psychologist, 54*(1), 3–6.

Belar, C. D. (1998). Graduate education in clinical psychology: "We're not in Kansas anymore." *American Psychologist, 53*, 456–464.

Bernal, M. E., Sirolli, A. A., Weisser, S. K., Ruiz, J. A., Chamberlain, V. J., & Knight, G. P. (1999). Relevance of multicultural training to students' applications to clinical psychology programs. *Cultural Diversity and Ethnic Minority Psychology, 5*, 43–55.

Bernstein, B. L., & Kerr, B. (1993). Counseling psychology and the scientist–practitioner model: Implementation and implications. *The Counseling Psychologist, 21*, 136–151.

Bersoff, D. N., Goodman-Delahunty, J., Grisso, J. T., Hans, V. P., Poythress, N. G., & Roesch, R. G. (1997). Training in law and psychology: Models from the Villanova Conference. *American Psychologist, 52*, 1301–1310.

Boitano, J. J. (1999, August). *Graduate training in neuroscience*. Paper presented at the 107th annual convention of the American Psychological Association, Boston, MA.

Bonifzi, D. Z., Crespy, S. D., & Reiker, P. (1997). Value of a master's degree for gaining admission to doctoral programs in psychology. *Teaching of Psychology, 24*, 176–182.

Bottoms, B. L., & Nysse, K. L. (1999). Applying to graduate school: Writing a compelling personal statement. *Eye on Psi Chi, 19*(3), 20–22.

Boudreau, R. A., Killip, S. M., MacInnis, S. H., Milloy, D. G., & Rogers, T. B. (1983). An evaluation of Graduate Record Examinations as predictors of graduate success in a Canadian context. *Canadian Psychology, 24*, 191–199.

Brems, C., & Johnson, M. E. (1997). Comparison of recent graduates of clinical versus counseling psychology programs. *Journal of Psychology, 131*, 91–99.

Bullock, M. (1997, July/August). Federal funding is available for psychology graduate students. *Psychological Science Agenda*, p. 4.

Buskist, W., & Mixon, A. (1998). *Master's programs in psychology and counseling psychology*. Needham Heights, MA: Allyn & Bacon.

REFERENCES

Cashin, J. R., & Landrum, R. E. (1991). Undergraduate students' perceptions of graduate admissions in psychology. *Psychological Reports, 69,* 1107–1110.

Ceci, S. J., & Peters, D. (1984). Letters of reference: A naturalistic study of the effects of confidentiality. *American Psychologist, 39,* 29–31.

Chapman, C. P., & Lane, H. C. (1997). Perceptions about the use of letters of recommendation. *The Advisor, 17,* 31–36.

Chernyshenko, O. S., & Ones, D. S. (1999). How selective are psychology graduate programs? The effect of the selection ration on GRE score validity. *Educational and Psychological Measurement, 59,* 951–961.

Collins, L. H. (2001, Winter). Does research experience make a significant differene in graduate admissions? *Eye on Psi Chi,* pp. 26–28.

Conway, J. B. (1988). Differences among clinical psychologists: Scientists, practitioners, and scientist–practitioners. *Professional Psychology: Research and Practice, 19,* 642–655.

Corcoran, K. J., Michels, J. L., & Ahina, L. K. (1999, August). *Clinical surfing: Clinical psychology doctoral programs on the web.* Paper presented at the 107th annual convention of the American Psychological Association, Boston, MA.

Couch, J. V., & Benedict, J. O. (1983). Graduate school admission variables: An analysis of 1980–81 students. *Teaching of Psychology, 10,* 3–6.

Coyle, S. L., & Bae, Y. (1987). *Summary report 1986: Doctorate recipients from United States universities.* Washington, DC: National Academy Press.

Crowe, M. B., Grogan, J. M., Jacobs, R. R., Lindsay, C. A., & Mack, M. M. (1985). Delineation of the roles of clinical psychology: A survey of practice in psychology. *Professional Psychology: Research and Practice, 16,* 124–137.

Dattilio, F. (1992). Doctoral studies for master's level licensed psychologists. *The Pennsylvania Psychologist Quarterly, 52*(2), 7, 11.

Dollinger, S. J. (1989). Predictive validity of the Graduate Record Examination in a clinical psychology program. *Professional Psychology: Research and Practice, 20,* 56–58.

Drummond, F., Rodolfa, E., & Smith, D. (1981). A survey of APA- and non-APA-approved internship programs. *American Psychologist, 36,* 411–414.

Eddy, B., Lloyd, P. J., & Lubin, B. (1987). Enhancing the application to doctoral professional programs: Suggestions from a national survey. *Teaching of Psychology, 14,* 160–163.

Educational Testing Service. (1995). *Practicing to take the GRE Psychology Test* (3rd ed.). Princeton, NJ: Author.

Elam, C. L., et al. (1998). Letters of recommendation: Medical school admission committee members' recommendations. *The Advisor, 18,* 4–6.

Farry, J., Norcross, J. C., Mayne, T. J., & Sayette, M. A. (1995, August). *Acceptance rates and financial aid in clinical psychology: An update.* Poster presented at the 103rd annual convention of the American Psychological Association, New York, NY.

Ferrari, J. R., & Davis, S. F. (2001, Winter). Undergraduate student journals: Perceptions by faculty. *Eye on Psi Chi,* pp. 13–17.

Fitzgerald, L. F., & Osipow, S. H. (1986). An occupational analysis of counseling psychology. How special is the specialty? *American Psychologist, 41,* 535–544.

Fox, R. E., Barclay, A. G., & Rodgers, D. A. (1982). The foundations of professional psychology. *American Psychologist, 37,* 306–312.

Fretz, B. R. (1976). Finding careers with a bachelor's degree in psychology. *Psi Chi Newsletter, 2*(2), 5–9.

Fretz, B. R., & Stang, D. J. (1980). *Preparing for graduate study in psychology: Not for seniors only!* Washington, DC: American Psychological Association.

Gaddy, C. D., Charlot-Swilley, D., Nelson, P. D., & Reich, J. N. (1995). Selected outcomes of accredited programs. *Professional Psychology: Research and Practice, 26,* 507–513.

Gartner, J. D. (1986). Antireligious prejudice in admissions to doctoral programs in clinical psychology. *Professional Psychology: Research and Practice, 17,* 473–475.

Gehlman, S., Wicherski, M., & Kohout, J. (1995). *Characteristics of graduate departments of psychology: 1993–1994.* Washington, DC: American Psychological Association Research Office.

Goldberg, E. L., & Alliger, G. M. (1992). Assessing the validity of the GRE for students in psychology: A validity generalization approach. *Educational and Psychological Measurement, 52,* 1019–1027.

Golding, J. M., Lang, K., Eymard, L. A., & Shadish, W. R. (1988). The buck stops here: A survey of the financial status of Ph.D. graduate students in psychology, 1966–1987. *American Psychologist, 43,* 1089–1091.

Goliszek, A. (2000). *The complete medical school preparation and admissions guide.* New York: Healthnet Press.

Gordon, R. A. (1990). Research productivity in master's-level psychology programs. *Professional Psychology: Research and Practice, 21,* 33–36.

Graduate Record Examinations. (2001). *2001–2002 GRE information and registration bulletin.* Princeton, NJ: Educational Testing Service.

Halgin, R. P. (1986). Advising undergraduates who wish to become clinicians. *Teaching of Psychology, 13,* 7–12.

Hayes, S. C., & Hayes, L. J. (1989). Writing your vitae. *APS Observor, 2*(3), 15–17.

Heppner, P. P., & Downing, N. E. (1982). Job interviewing for new psychologists: Riding the emotional rollercoaster. *Professional Psychology, 13,* 334–341.

Hersh, J. B., & Poey, K. (1984). A proposed interviewing guide for intern applicants. *Professional Psychology, 15,* 3–5.

Hershey, J. M., Kopplin, D. A., & Cornell, J. E. (1991). Doctors of psychology: Their career experiences and attitudes toward degree and training. *Professional Psychology: Research and Practice, 22,* 351–356.

Hines, D. (1985). Admissions criteria for ranking master's-level applicants to clinical doctoral programs. *Teaching of Psychology, 13,* 64–66.

Holmes, C. B., & Beishline, M. J. (1996, August). *Doctoral admission rates for students with GRE scores below 1000.* Poster presented at the 104th annual meeting of the American Psychological Association, Toronto.

How do professional schools' graduates compare with traditional graduates? (1997). *APS Observer, 10,* 6–9.

Howard, A., Pion, G. M., Gottfredson, G. D., Flattau, P. E., Oskamp, S., Pfafflin, S. M., Bray, D. W., & Burstein, A. G. (1986). The changing face of American psychology: A report from the Committee on Employment and Human Resources. *American Psychologist, 41,* 1311–1327.

Howard, G. S., Cole, D. A., & Maxwell, S. E. (1987). Research productivity in psychology based on publication in the journals of the American Psychological Association. *American Psychologist, 42*, 975–986.

Ilardi, S. S., Rodriguez-Hanley, A., Roberts, M. G., & Seigel, J. (2000). On the origins of clinical psychology faculty: Who is training the trainers? *Clinical Psychology: Science and Practice, 7*, 346–354.

Ingram, R. E. (1983). The GRE in the graduate admissions process: Is how it is used justified by the evidence of its validity? *Professional Psychology: Research and Practice, 14*, 711–714.

Jacob, M. C. (1987). Managing the internship application experience: Advice from an exhausted but content survivor. *The Counseling Psychologist, 15*, 146–155.

Jalbert, N. L. (1996, Fall). Psi Chi should be more than one line on your resume. *Eye on Psi Chi*, p. 64.

Jay, M. (1999). *Cracking the GRE Psychology* (5th ed.). Princton: The Princeton Review.

Jensen, A. R. (1998). *The g factor: The science of mental ability*. Westport, CT: Praeger.

Kalat, J. W., & Matlin, M. W. (2000). The GRE Psychology Test: A useful but poorly understood test. *Teaching of Psychology, 27*, 24–27.

Keith-Spiegel, P. (1991). *The complete guide to graduate school admission*. Hillsdale, NJ: Lawrence Erlbaum.

Keith-Spiegel, P., Tabachnick, B. G., & Spiegel, G. B. (1994). When demand exceeds supply: Second-order criteria used by graduate school selection committees. *Teaching of Psychology, 21*, 79–81.

Keith-Spiegel, P., & Wiederman, M. W. (2000). *The complete guide to graduate school admission* (2nd ed.). Mahwah, NJ: Erlbaum.

Keller, J. W., Beam, K. J., Maier, K. A., & Pietrowski, C. (1995, April). *Research or clinical experience: What doctoral applicants need to know*. Paper presented at the annual meeting of the Southeastern Psychological Association, Savannah, GA.

Kellogg, R. T. (2000). *Best preparation for the GRE in psychology*. Piscataway, NJ: Research & Education Association.

King, D. W., Beehr, T. A., & King, L. A. (1986). Doctoral student selection in one professional psychology program. *Journal of Clinical Psychology, 42*, 399–407.

Kohout, J. L., & Wicherski, M. M. (1992). *1991 salaries in psychology*. Washington, DC: American Psychological Association.

Kohout, J., & Wicherski, M. (1993). *1991–1992 characteristics of graduate departments of psychology*. Washington, DC: American Psychological Association.

Kohout, J. & Wicherski, M. (1999). *1997 doctorate employment survey*. Washington, DC: American Psychological Association Research Office.

Kohout, J., Wicherski, M., & Pion, G. (1991). *Characteristics of graduate departments of psychology: 1988–89*. Washington, DC: American Psychological Association.

Kopala, M., Keitel, M. A., Suzuki, L. A., Alexander, C. M., Ponterotto, J. G., Reynolds, A. L., & Hennessy, J. J. (1995). Doctoral admissions in counseling psychology at Fordham University. *Teaching of Psychology, 22*, 133–135.

Korn, J. H. (1984). New odds on acceptance into Ph.D. programs in psychology. *American Psychologist, 39*, 179–180.

Kuncel, N. R., Hezlett, S. A., & Ones, D. S. (2001). A comprehensive meta-analysis of the predictive validity of the graduate record examinations: Implications for graduate student selection and performance. *Psychological Bulletin, 127*, 162–181.

Kupfersmid, J., & Fiola, M. (1991). Comparison of EPPP scores among graduates of varying psychology programs. *American Psychologist, 46*, 534–535.

Kyle, T. M. (2000, July/August). Investigating and choosing: The decision-making process among first-year graduate students. *APA Monitor*, p. 19.

Lovitts, B. E., & Nelson, C. (2000, November–December). Attrition from Ph.D. programs. *Academe*, pp. 44–50.

Lubin, B. (1993). Message of the president. *Psi Chi Newsletter, 19*(3), 1, 34.

Mayne, T. J., Norcross, J. C., & Sayette, M. A. (1994). Admission requirements, acceptance rates, and financial assistance in clinical psychology programs: Diversity across the practice–research continuum. *American Psychologist, 49*, 605–611.

McGaha, S., & Minder, C. (1993). Factors influencing performance on the Examination for Professional Practice in Psychology (EPPP). *Professional Psychology: Research and Practice, 24*, 107–109.

McWade, P. (1996). *Financing graduate school*. Princeton, NJ: Peterson's Guides.

Megargee, E. I. (1990). *A guide to obtaining a psychology internship*. Muncie, IN: Accelerated Development.

Minke, K. M., & Brown, D. T. (1996). Preparing psychologists to work with children: A comparison of curricula in child-clinical and school psychology programs. *Professional Psychology: Research and Practice, 27*, 631–634.

Mitchell, S. L. (1996). Getting a foot in the door: The written internship application. *Professional Psychology: Research and Practice, 27*, 90–92.

Morrison, T., & Morrison, M. (1995). A meta-analytic assessment of the predictive validity of the quantitative and verbal components of the Graduate Record Examination with graduate grade point average representing the criterion of graduate success. *Educational and Psychological Measurement, 55*, 309–316.

Munoz-Dunbar, R., & Stanton, A. L. (1999). Ethnic diversity in clinical psychology: Recruitment and admission practices among doctoral programs. *Teaching of Psychology, 26*, 259–263.

Murray, B. (1996). Psychology remains top college major. *APA Monitor, 27*, 1, 42.

Murray, T. M., & Williams, S. (1999). *Analyses of data from graduate study in psychology: 1997–98*. Washington, DC: American Psychological Association Research Office.

Nauta, M. M. (2000). Assessing the accuracy of psychology undergraduates' perceptions of graduate admissions criteria. *Teaching of Psychology, 27*, 277–280.

Nevid, J. S., & Gildea, T. J. (1984). The admissions process in clinical training: The role of the personal interview. *Professional Psychology: Research and Practice, 15*, 18–25.

Norcross, J. C., Alford, B. A., & DeMichele, J. T. (1992). The future of psychotherapy: Delphi data and concluding observations. *Psychotherapy, 29*, 150–158.

Norcross, J. C., Gallagher, K. M., & Prochaska, J. O. (1989). The Boulder and/or the Vail model: Training preferences of clinical psychologists. *Journal of Clinical Psychology, 45*, 822–828.

Norcross, J. C., & Goldfried, M. R. (Eds.). (1992). *Handbook of psychotherapy integration*. New York: Basic Books.

Norcross, J. C., Hanych, J. M., & Terranova, R. D. (1996). Graduate study in psychology: 1992–1993. *American Psychologist, 51*, 631–643.

Norcross, J. C., & Kaplan, K. J. (1995). Training in psychotherapy integration. Integrative/eclectic programs. *Journal of Psychotherapy Integration, 5*(3).

Norcross, J. C., Karg, R. S., & Prochaska, J. O. (1997a). Clinical psychologists in the 1990s: Part I. *The Clinical Psychologist, 50*(2), 4–9.

Norcross, J. C., Karg, R. S., & Prochaska, J. O. (1997b). Clinical psychologists in the 1990s: Part II. *The Clinical Psychologist, 50*(3), 4–11.

Norcross, J. C., Sayette, M. A., Mayne, T. J., Karg, R. S., & Turkson, M. A. (1998). Selecting a doctoral program in professional psychology: Some comparisons among Ph.D. counseling, Ph.D. clinical, and Psy.D. clinical psychology programs. *Professional Psychology: Research and Practice, 29*, 609–614.

O'Donohue, W., Plaud, J. J., Mowatt, A. M., & Fearon, J. R. (1989). Current status of curricula of doctoral training programs in clinical psychology. *Professional Psychology: Research and Practice, 20*, 196–197.

Osborne, R. E. (1996, Fall). The "personal" side of graduate school personal statements. *Eye on Psi Chi*, pp. 14–15.

Pendlebury, D. A. (1996). Which psychology papers, places, and people have made a mark? *APS Observer, 9*, 14–18.

Peterson, D. R. (1976). Need for the doctor of psychology degree in professional psychology. *American Psychologist, 31*, 792–798.

Peterson, D. R. (1982). Origins and development of the Doctor of Psychology concept. In G. R. Caddy, D. C. Rimm, H. Watson, & J. H. Johnson (Eds.), *Educating professional psychologists* (pp. 19–38). New Brunswick, NJ: Transaction Books.

Peterson, D. R., Eaton, M. M., Levine, A. R., & Snepp, F. P. (1982). Career experiences of doctors of psychology. *Professional Psychology, 13*, 268–277.

Peterson's grants for graduate and postdoctoral study (4th ed.). (1995). Princeton, NJ: Peterson's.

Piotrowski, C., & Keller, J. W. (1996). Research or clinical experience: What doctoral applicants need to know. *Journal of Instructional Psychology, 23*, 126–127.

Prevoznak, M. A., & Bubka, A. (1999, April). *Word-a-day method in preparation for the GRE*. Poster presented at the annual meeting of the Eastern Psychological Association, Providence, RI.

Psychological Corporation. (1994). *Miller Analogies Test: Technical manual*. San Antonio, TX: Author.

Purdy, J. E., Reinehr, R. C., & Swartz, J. D. (1989). Graduate admissions criteria of leading psychology departments. *American Psychologist, 44*, 960–961.

Raphael, S., & Halpert, L. H. (1999). *Graduate Record Examination—Psychology* (3rd ed.). New York: Prentice Hall.

Rem, R., Oren, E. M., & Childrey, G. (1987). Selection of graduate students in clinical psychology: Use of cutoff scores and interviews. *Professional Psychology: Research and Practice, 18*, 485–488.

Resnick, J. H. (1991). Finally, a definition of clinical psychology: A message from the President, Division 12. *The Clinical Psychologist, 44*(1), 3–4.

Rheingold, H. L. (1994). *The psychologist's guide to an academic career*. Washington, DC: American Psychological Association.

Robyak, J. E., & Goodyear, R. K. (1984). Graduate school origins of diplomates and fellows in professional psychology. *Professional Psychology: Research and Practice, 15*, 379–387.

Sachs, M. L., Burke, K. L., & Schrader, D. C. (2001). *Directory of graduate programs in applied sport psychology* (6th ed.). Morgantown, WV: Fitness Information Technology.

Salzinger, K. (Chair). (1998, August). *Combined professional–scientific psychology: Greater than the sum of its parts?* Symposium presented at the 106th annual convention of the American Psychological Association, San Francisco, CA.

Sayette, M. A., & Mayne, T. J. (1990). Survey of current clinical and research trends in clinical psychology. *American Psychologist, 45*, 1263–1267.

Sayette, M. A., Mayne, T. J., Norcross, J. C., & Giuffre, D. E. (1999, June). *Letting a hundred flowers bloom? Ph.D. clinical psychology training in the 1990s*. Paper presented at annual meeting of the Academy of Psychological Clinical Science, Denver, CO.

Schaefer, S. E. (1995). Stigmatization of psychology doctoral program applicants who have a history of psychological counseling. *Dissertation Abstracts, 57*(02B), 1427.

Schneider, L. M., & Briel, J. B. (1990). *Validity of the GRE: 1988–89 summary report*. Princeton, NJ: Educational Testing Service.

Scott, W. C., & Silka, L. D. (1974). Applying to graduate school in psychology: A perspective and guide. *Journal Supplement Abstract Service*, MS. 597.

Shaffer, D. R., & Tomarelli, M. (1981). Bias in the ivory tower: An unintended consequence of the Buckley Amendment for graduate admissions. *Journal of Applied Psychology, 66*, 7–11.

Smith, R. A. (1985). Advising beginning psychology majors for graduate school. *Teaching of Psychology, 12*, 194–198.

Snepp, F. P., & Peterson, D. R. (1988). Evaluative comparison of Psy.D. and Ph.D. students by clinical internship supervisors. *Professional Psychology: Research and Practice, 19*, 180–183.

Society for Industrial and Organizational Psychology. (1998). *Graduate training in industrial/organizational psychology and related fields*. Bowling Green, OH: Author.

Stapp, J., Tucker, A. M., & VandenBos, G. R. (1985). Census of psychological personnel: 1983. *American Psychologist, 40*, 1317–1351.

Steinpreis, R., Queen, L., & Tennen, H. (1992). The education of clinical psychologists: A survey of training directors. *The Clinical Psychologist, 45*, 87–94.

Sternberg, R. J. (Ed.). (1997). *Career paths in psychology: Where your degree can take you*. Washington, DC: American Psychological Association.

Sternberg, R. J., & Williams, W. M. (1997). Does the graduate record examination predict meaningful success in the graduate training of psychologists? *American Psychologist, 52*, 630–641.

Stewart, A. E., & Stewart, E. A. (1996). A decision-making technique for choosing a psychology internship. *Professional Psychology: Research and Practice, 27*, 521–526.

Stewart, D. W., & Spille, H. A. (1988). *Diploma mills: Degrees of fraud*. New York: Macmillan.

Stoup, C. M., & Benjamin, L. T. (1982). Graduate study in psychology. *American Psychologist, 37*, 1186–1202.

Strickland, B. R. (1985). Over the Boulder(s) and through the Vail. *The Clinical Psychologist, 38*, 52–56.

Terry, R. L. (1996, December). Characteristics of psychology departments at primarily undergraduate institutions. *Council on Undergraduate Research Quarterly,* pp. 86–90.

Tibbits-Kleber, A. L., & Howell, R. J. (1987). Doctoral training in clinical psychology: A students' perspective. *Professional Psychology: Research and Practice, 18*, 634–639.

Tipton, R. M. (1983). Clinical and counseling psychology: A study of roles and functions. *Professional Psychology: Research and Practice, 14*, 837–846.

Titus, J. B., & Buxman, N. J. (1999). Is Psi Chi meeting its mission statement? *Eye on Psi Chi, 3*(3), 16–18.

Todd, D. M., & Farinato, D. (1992). A local resource for advising applicants to clinical psychology graduate programs. *Teaching of Psychology, 19*, 52–54.

Toia, A., Herron, W. G., Primavera, L. H., & Javier, R. A. (1997). Ethnic diversification in clinical psychology training. *Cultural Diversity and Mental Health, 3,* 193–206.

Toma, J. D., & Cross, M. E. (1998). Intercollegiate athletics and student college choice: Exploring the impact of championship seasons on undergraduate applications. *Research in Higher Education, 39,* 633–661.

Tryon, G. S. (1985). What can our students learn from regional psychology conventions? *Teaching of Psychology, 12*, 227–228.

Tryon, G. S. (2000). Doctoral training issues in school and clinical child psychology. *Professional Psychology: Research and Practice, 31,* 85–87.

Turkington, C. (1986). Practitioner training. *APA Monitor, 17*(1), 14, 17.

Turkson, M. A., & Norcross, J. C. (1996, March). *Doctoral training in counseling psychology: Admission statistics, student characteristics, and financial assistance.* Paper presented at the annual conference of the Eastern Psychological Association, Philadelphia, PA.

VandeCreek, L., & Fleisher, M. (1984). The role of practicum in the undergraduate psychology curriculum. *Teaching of Psychology, 11*, 9–14.

VandenBos, G. E., Stapp, J., & Kilburg, R. R. (1981). Health service providers in psychology. *American Psychologist, 36*, 1395–1418.

Walfish, S., Stenmark, D. E., Shealy, J. S., & Shealy, S. E. (1989). Reasons why applicants select clinical psychology graduate programs. *Professional Psychology: Research and Practice, 20*, 350–354.

Walfish, S., & Sumprer, G. F. (1984). Employment opportunities for graduates of APA-approved and non-APA-approved training programs. *American Psychologist, 39*, 1199–1200.

Waters, J., Drew, B., & Ayers, J. (1988). Integrating conflicting needs in curriculum planning: Advice to faculty. In P. J. Woods (Ed.), *Is psychology for them?* Washington, DC: American Psychological Association.

Watkins, C. E., Lopez, F. G., Campbell, V. L., & Himmell, C. D. (1986a). Contemporary counseling psychology: Results of a national survey. *Journal of Counseling Psychology, 33*, 301–309.

Watkins, C. E., Lopez, F. G., Campbell, V. L., & Himmell, C. D. (1986b). Counseling psychology and clinical psychology: Some preliminary comparative data. *American Psychologist, 41*, 581–582.

Whitbourne, S. K. (1999, April). *A guide to personal statements.* Paper presented at the 70th annual meeting of the Eastern Psychological Association, Boston, MA.

Wicherski, M., & Kohout, J. (1992). *Characteristics of graduate departments of psychology: 1990–1991.* Washington, DC: American Psychological Association.

Young, K. S., & VandeCreek, L. (1996, March). *Ethnic minority selection procedures in clinical training graduate admissions.* Paper presented at the 67th annual meeting of the Eastern Psychological Association, Philadelphia, PA.

Yu, L. M., Rinaldi, S. A., Templer, D. I., Colbert, L. A., Siscoe, K., & Van Patten, K. (1997). Scores on the Examination for Professional practice in Psychology as a function of attributes of clinical psychology graduate programs. *Psychological Science, 8*(5), 340–350.

Zebala, J. A., Jones, D. B., & Jones, S. B. (1999). *Medical school admissions: The insider's guide.* New Haven, CT: Mustang.